YOWAMUS
PEDAL
WATARU WATANABE

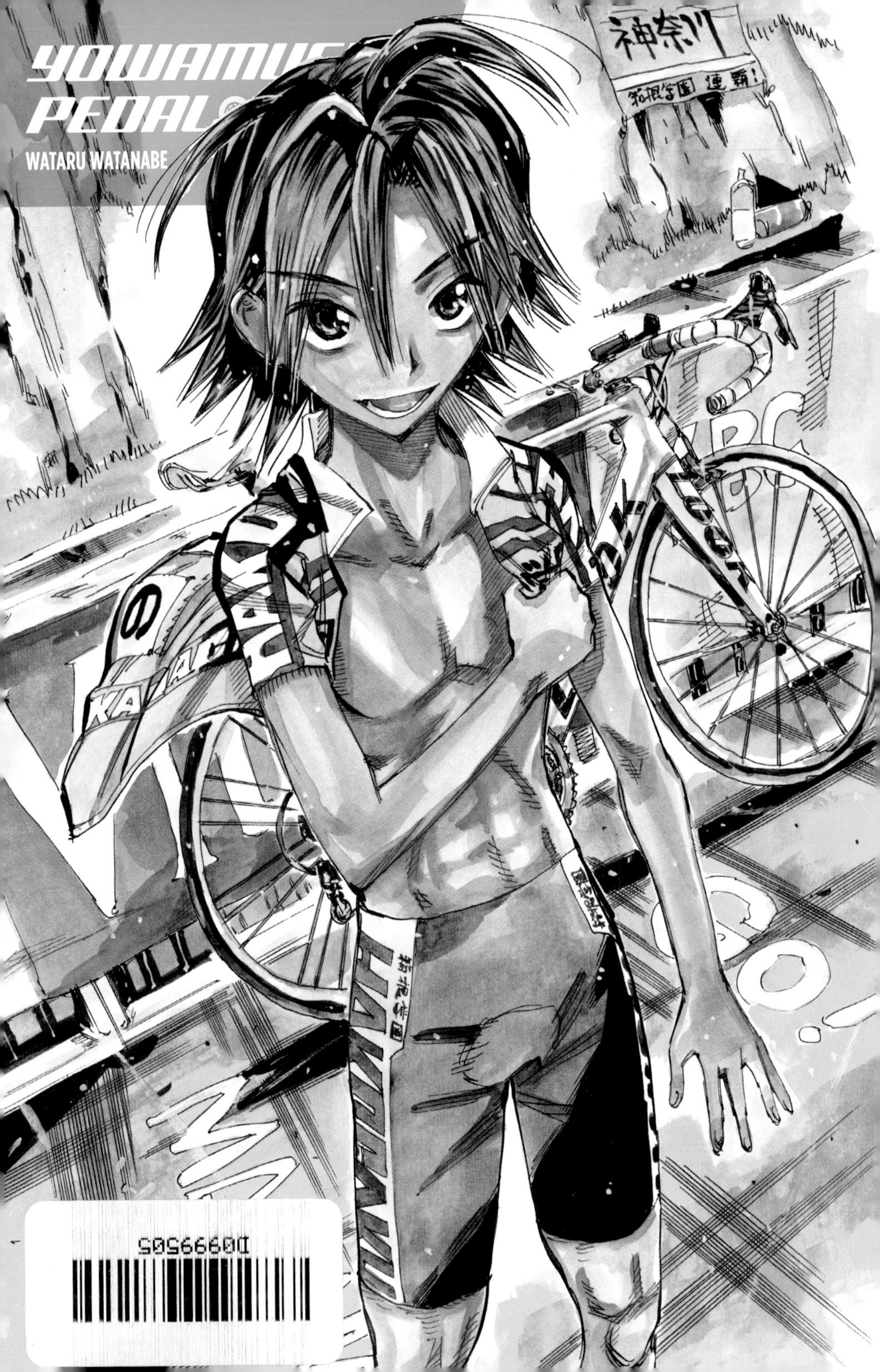
神奈川
箱根学園 連覇!

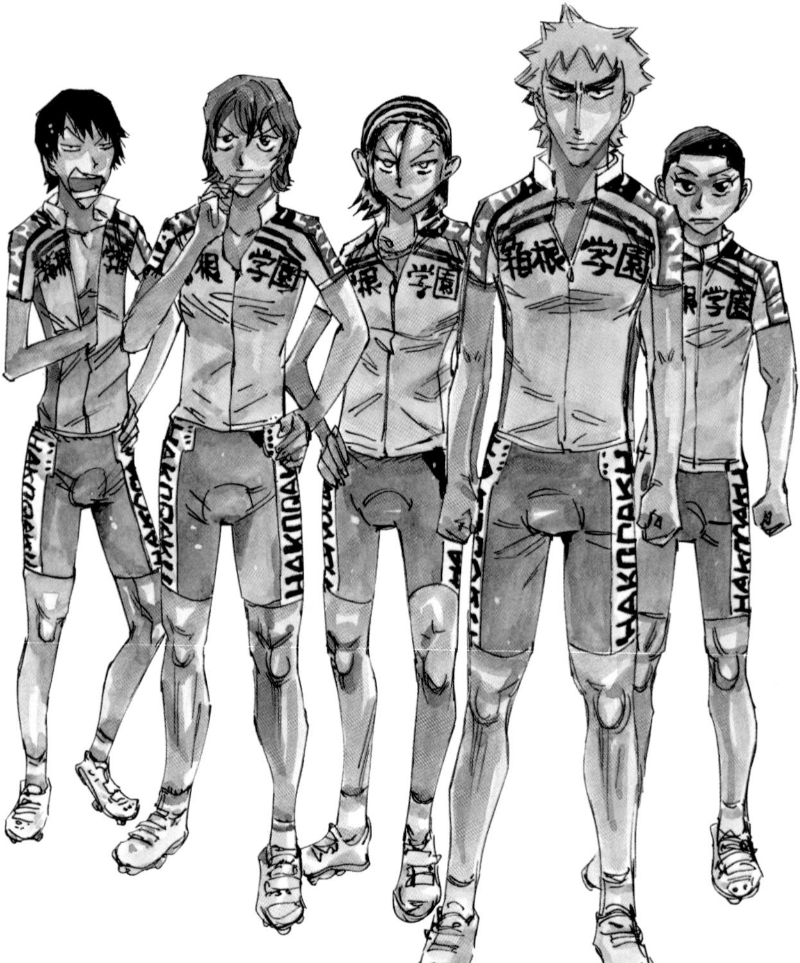
箱根学園
HAKOGAKU

YOWAMUSHI PEDAL

WATARU WATANABE

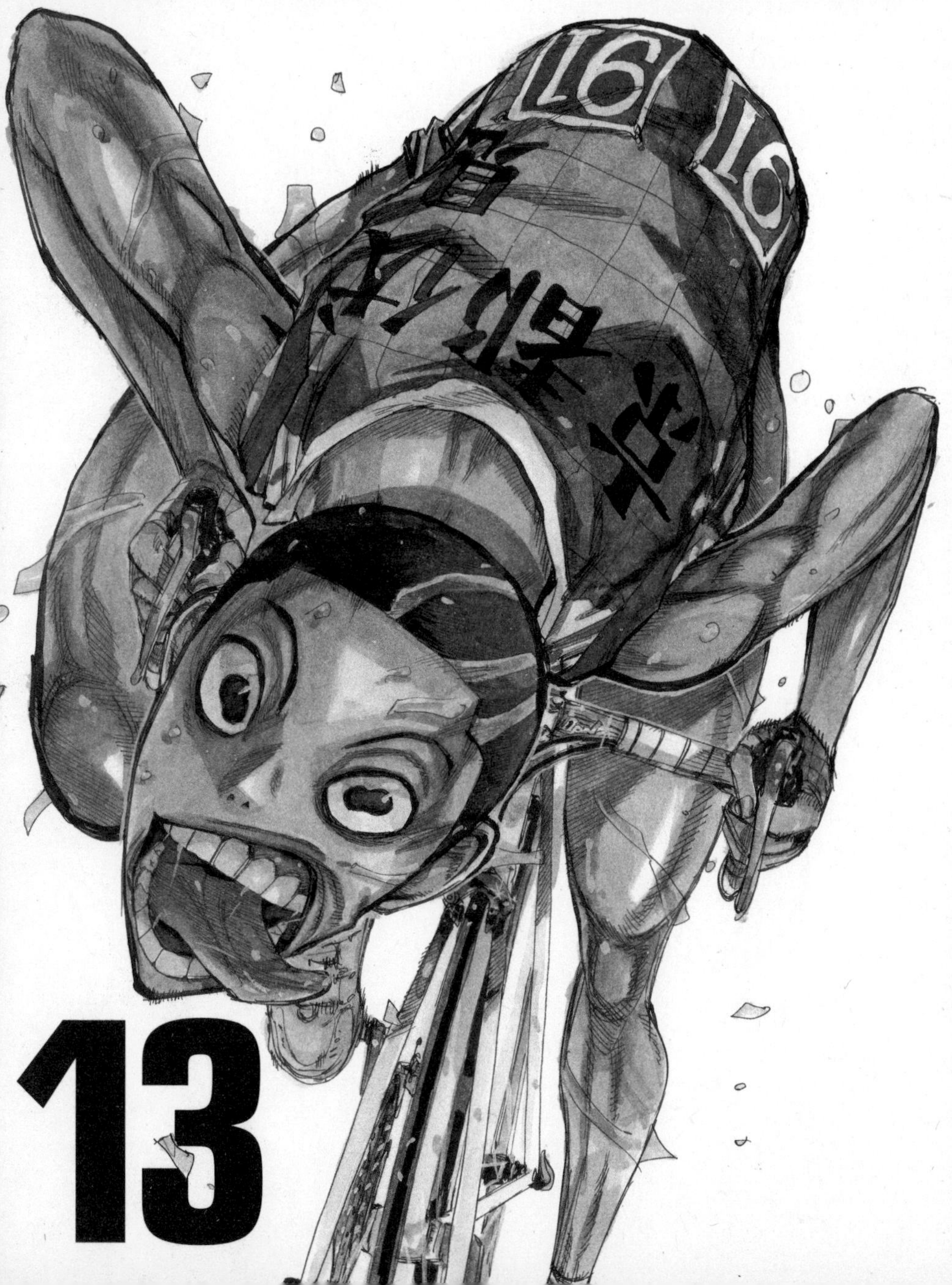

13

YOWAMUSHI PEDAL

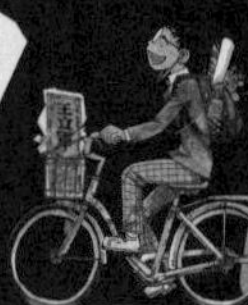

STORY & CHARACTER INTRODUCTION

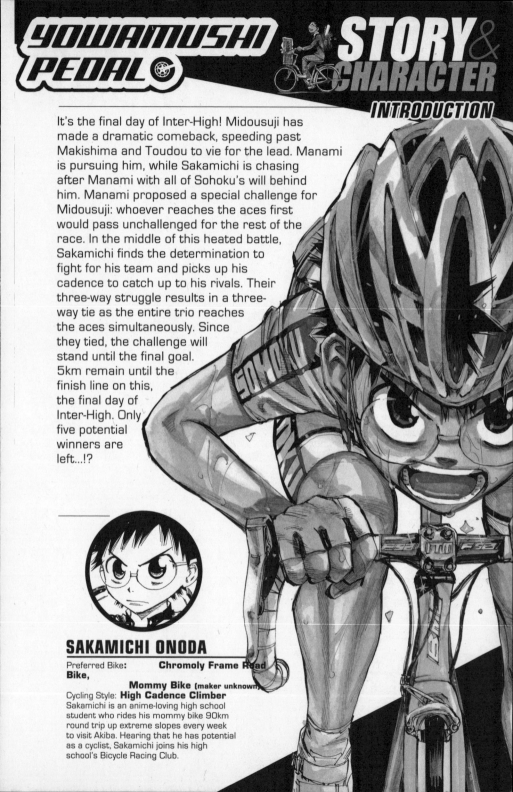

It's the final day of Inter-High! Midousuji has made a dramatic comeback, speeding past Makishima and Toudou to vie for the lead. Manami is pursuing him, while Sakamichi is chasing after Manami with all of Sohoku's will behind him. Manami proposed a special challenge for Midousuji: whoever reaches the aces first would pass unchallenged for the rest of the race. In the middle of this heated battle, Sakamichi finds the determination to fight for his team and picks up his cadence to catch up to his rivals. Their three-way struggle results in a three-way tie as the entire trio reaches the aces simultaneously. Since they tied, the challenge will stand until the final goal. 5km remain until the finish line on this, the final day of Inter-High. Only five potential winners are left...!?

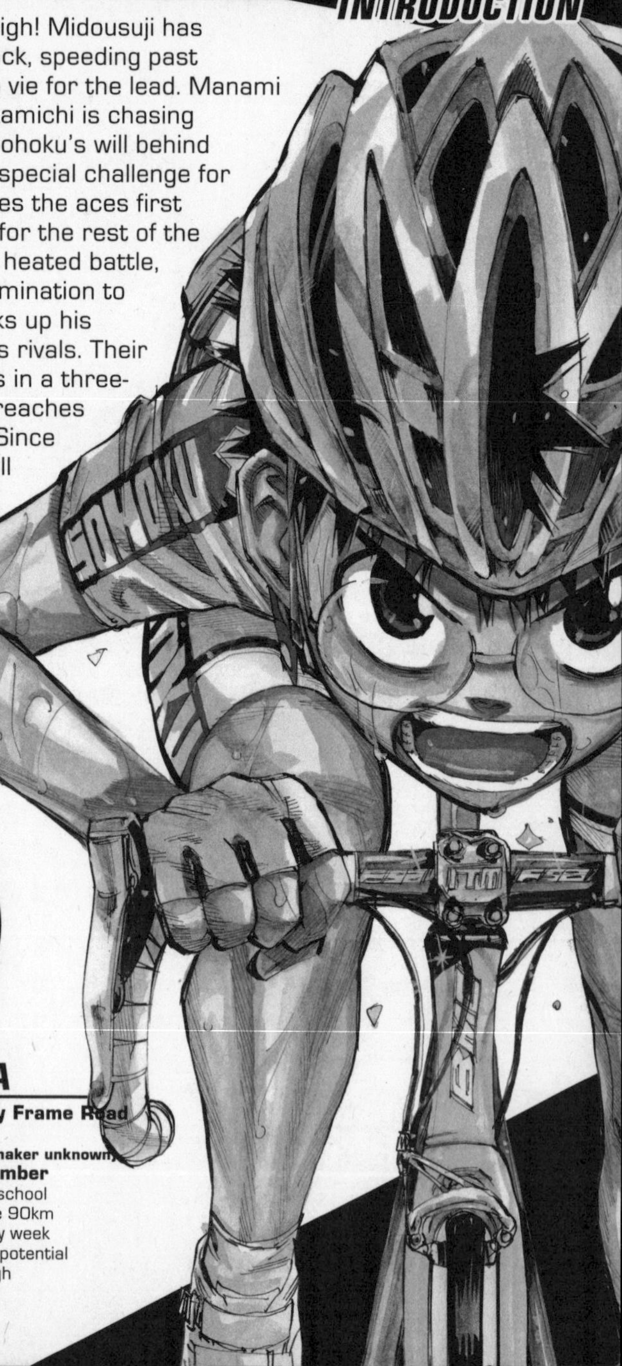
SOHOKU

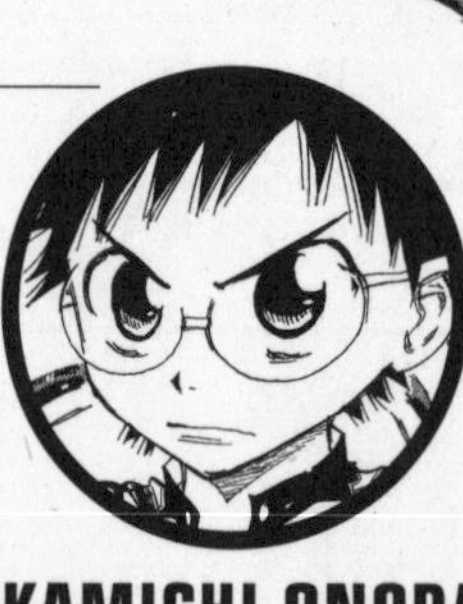

SAKAMICHI ONODA

Preferred Bike: **Chromoly Frame Road Bike,**
Mommy Bike (maker unknown)
Cycling Style: **High Cadence Climber**
Sakamichi is an anime-loving high school student who rides his mommy bike 90km round trip up extreme slopes every week to visit Akiba. Hearing that he has potential as a cyclist, Sakamichi joins his high school's Bicycle Racing Club.

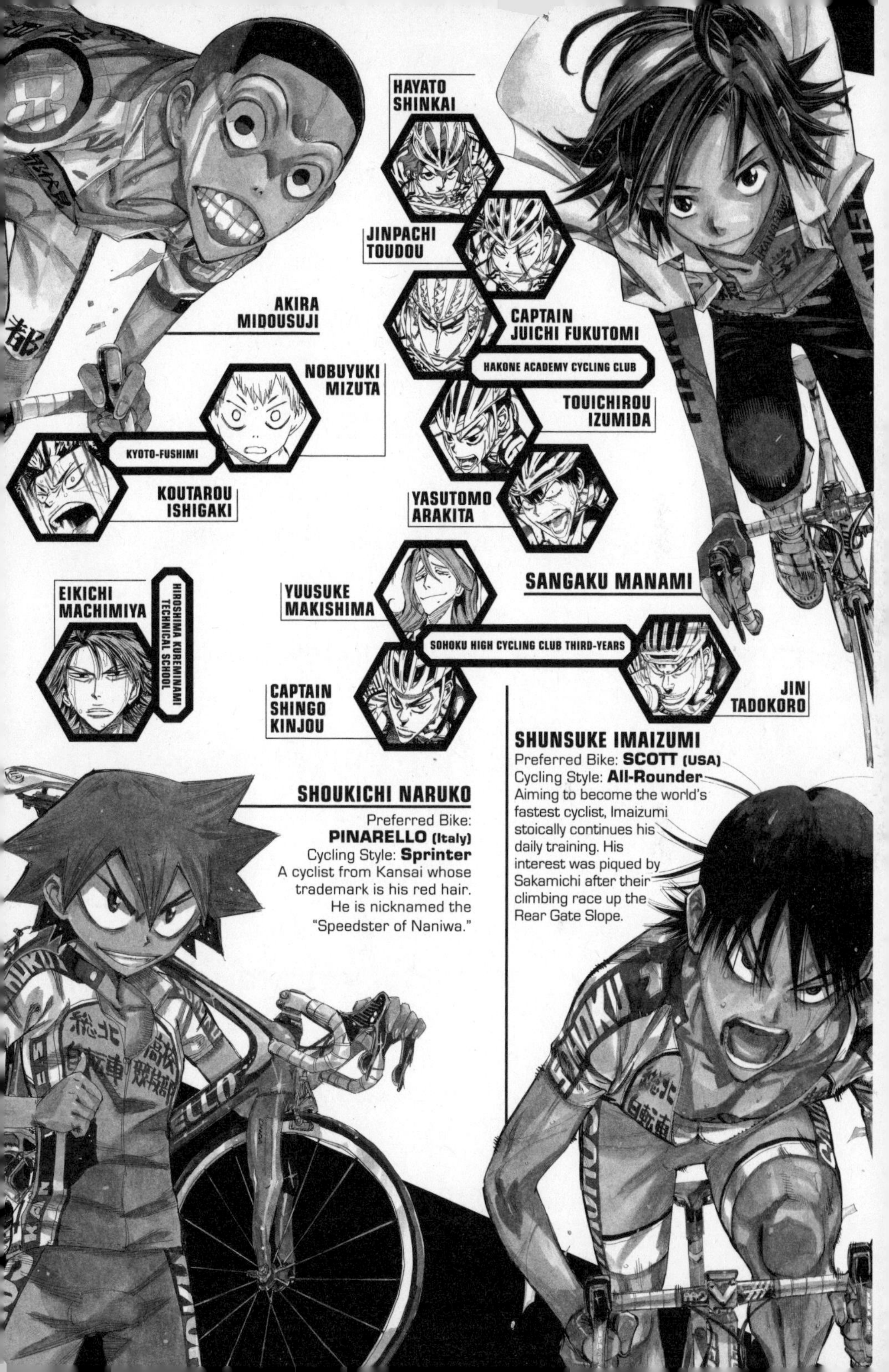

HAYATO SHINKAI
JINPACHI TOUDOU
CAPTAIN JUICHI FUKUTOMI
HAKONE ACADEMY CYCLING CLUB
TOUICHIROU IZUMIDA
YASUTOMO ARAKITA
SANGAKU MANAMI
AKIRA MIDOUSUJI
NOBUYUKI MIZUTA
KYOTO-FUSHIMI
KOUTAROU ISHIGAKI
HIROSHIMA KUREMINAMI TECHNICAL SCHOOL
EIKICHI MACHIMIYA
YUUSUKE MAKISHIMA
SOHOKU HIGH CYCLING CLUB THIRD-YEARS
JIN TADOKORO
CAPTAIN SHINGO KINJOU
SHUNSUKE IMAIZUMI
Preferred Bike: SCOTT (USA)
Cycling Style: All-Rounder
Aiming to become the world's fastest cyclist, Imaizumi stoically continues his daily training. His interest was piqued by Sakamichi after their climbing race up the Rear Gate Slope.
SHOUKICHI NARUKO
Preferred Bike: PINARELLO (Italy)
Cycling Style: Sprinter
A cyclist from Kansai whose trademark is his red hair. He is nicknamed the "Speedster of Naniwa."

VOL.13

YOWAMUSHI PEDAL CONTENTS

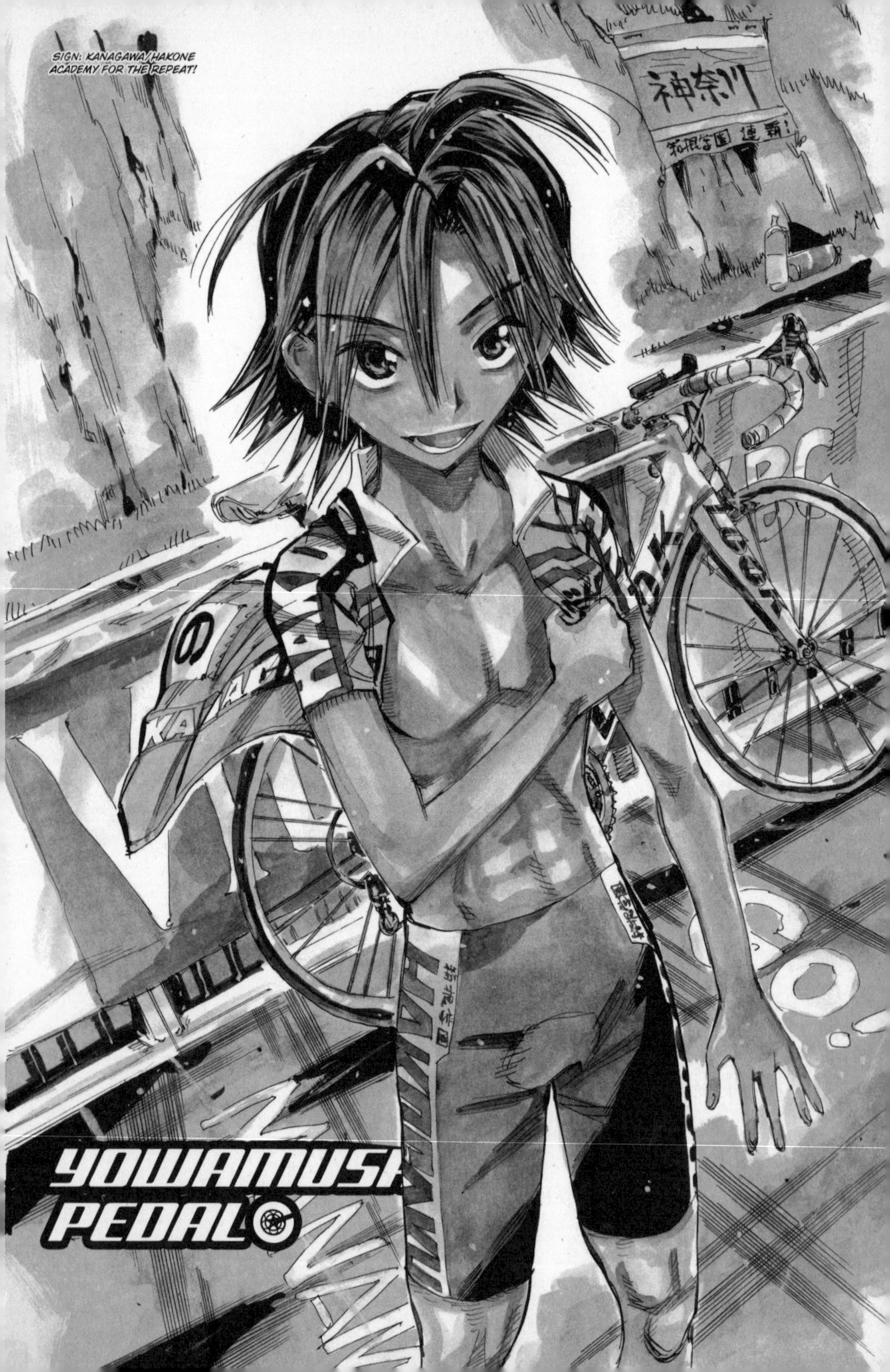
SIGN: KANAGAWA/HAKONE ACADEMY FOR THE REPEAT!
神奈川
箱根学園 連覇!
YOWAMUSHI PEDAL

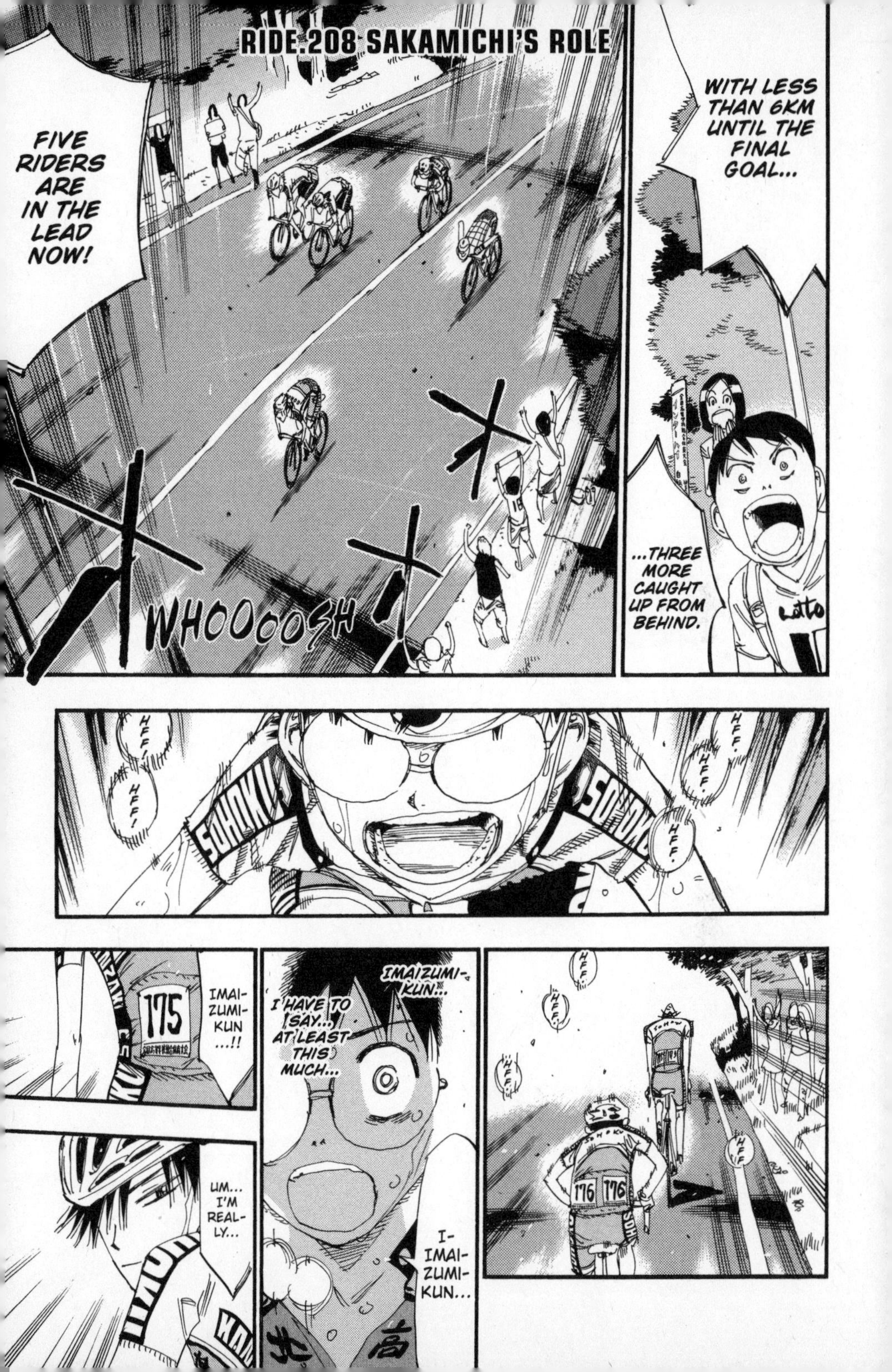
RIDE.208 SAKAMICHI'S ROLE
WITH LESS THAN 6KM UNTIL THE FINAL GOAL...
...THREE MORE CAUGHT UP FROM BEHIND.
FIVE RIDERS ARE IN THE LEAD NOW!
WHOOOOOSH
HFF! HFF!
HFF. HFF.
HFF.
HFF.
HFF.
HFF.
HFF
IMAIZUMI-KUN...
I HAVE TO SAY... AT LEAST THIS MUCH...
I-IMAIZUMI-KUN...
IMAI-ZUMI-KUN...!!
UM... I'M REAL-LY...

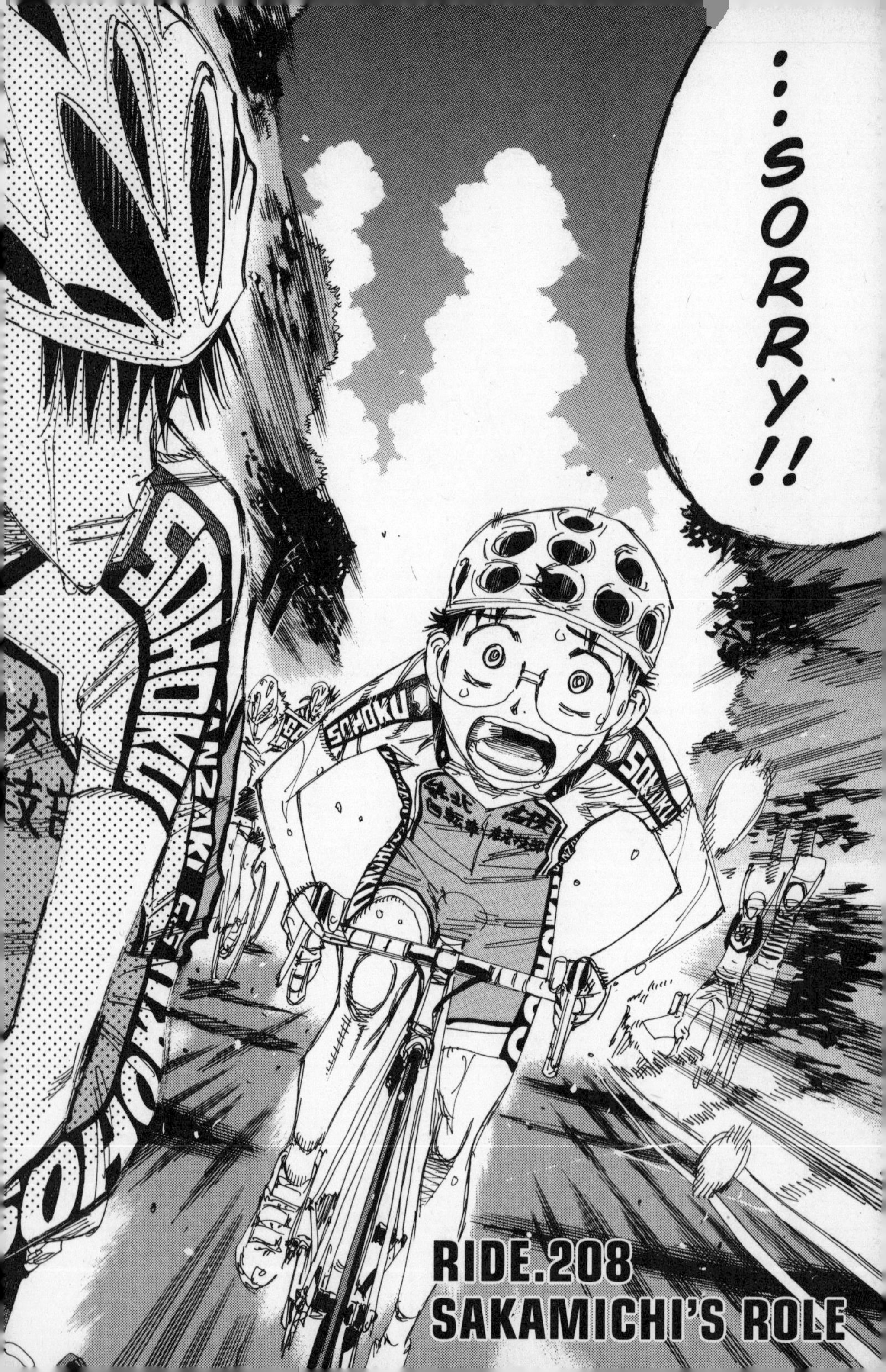
...SORRY!!

RIDE.208
SAKAMICHI'S ROLE

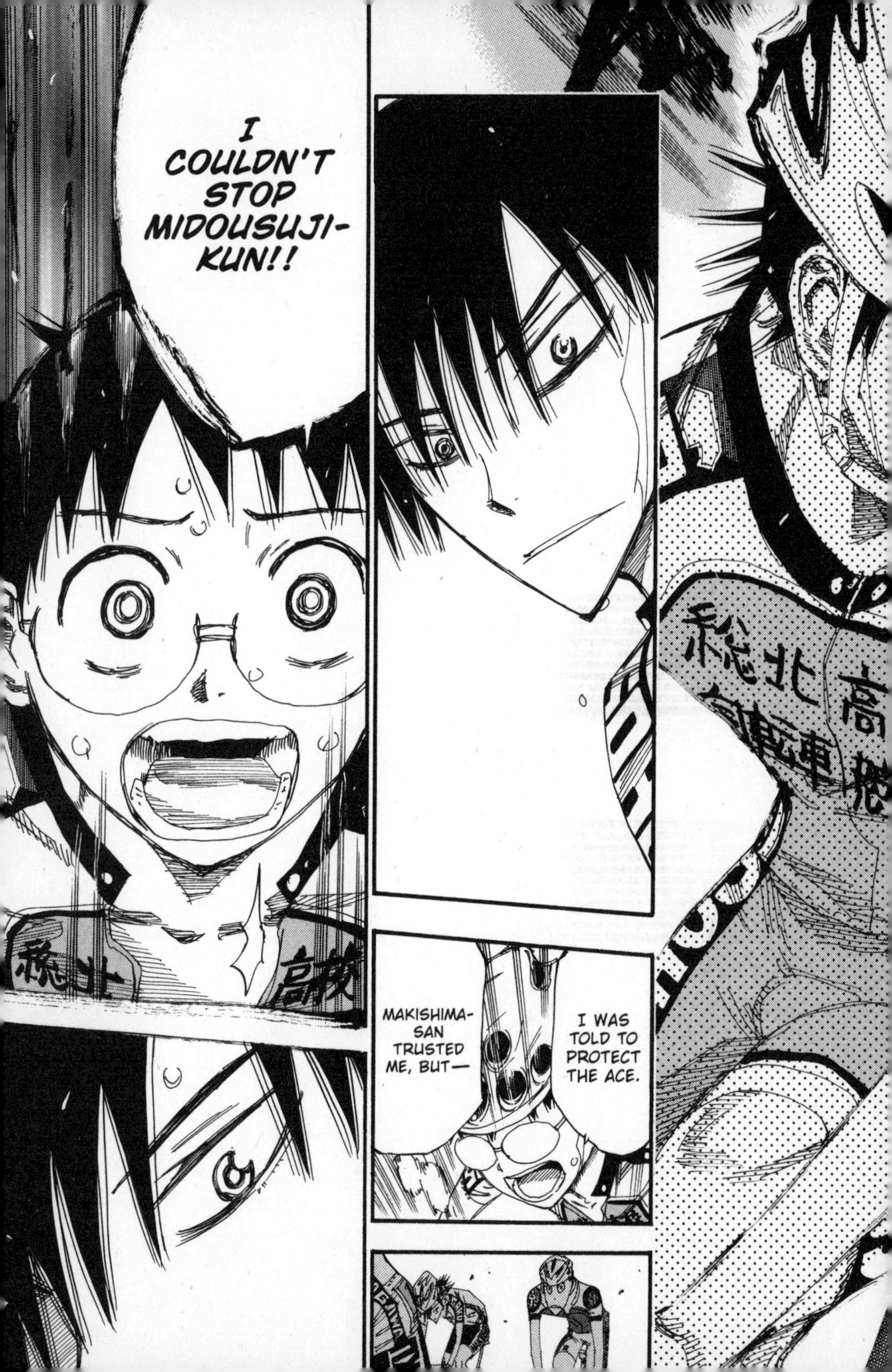

I WAS TOLD TO PROTECT THE ACE.
MAKISHIMA-SAN TRUSTED ME, BUT—
I COULDN'T STOP MIDOUSUJI-KUN!!

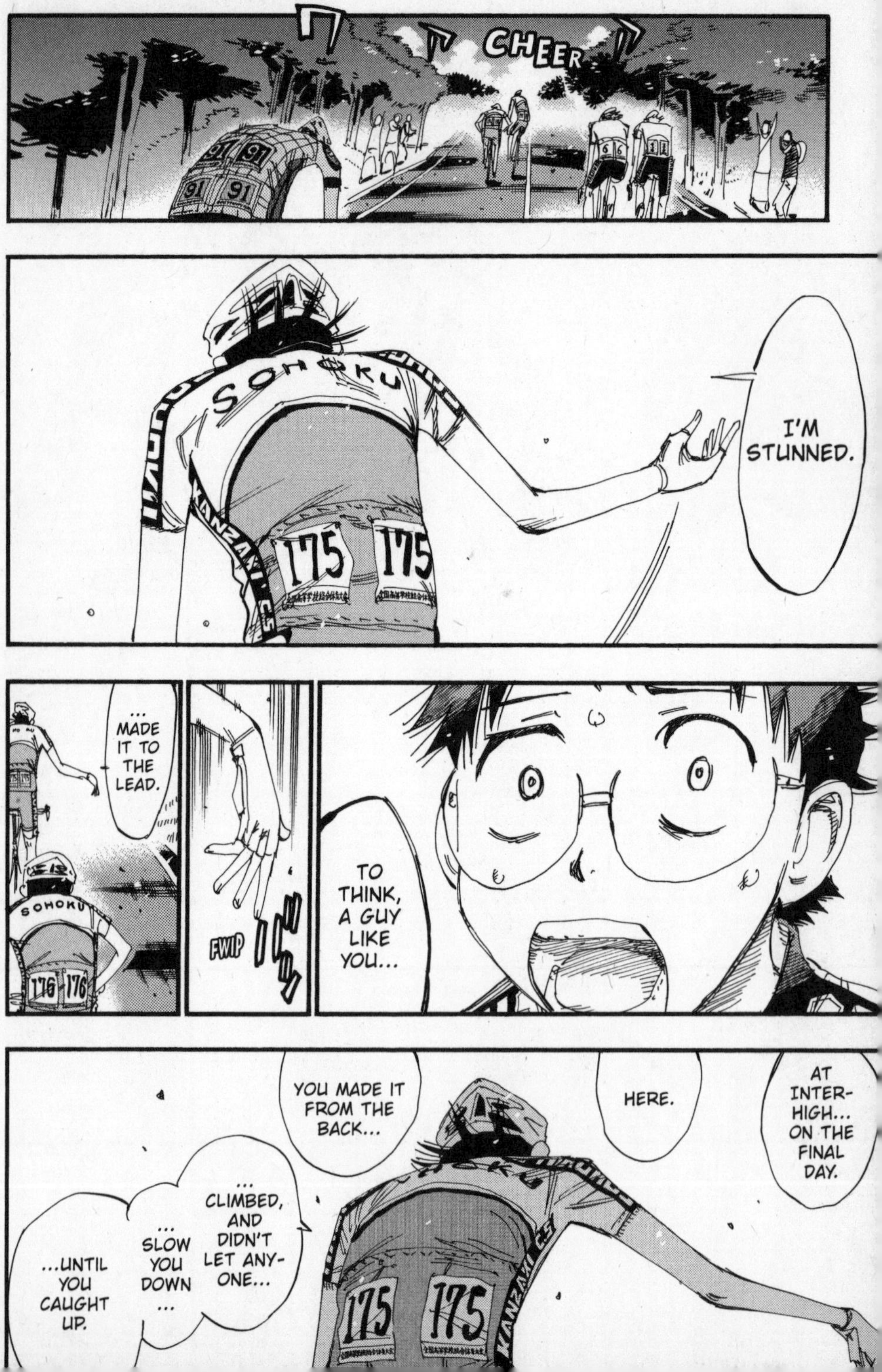
CHEER
I'M STUNNED.
TO THINK, A GUY LIKE YOU...
FWIP
...MADE IT TO THE LEAD.
AT INTER-HIGH... ON THE FINAL DAY.
HERE.
YOU MADE IT FROM THE BACK...
...CLIMBED, AND DIDN'T LET ANY-ONE...
...SLOW YOU DOWN...
...UNTIL YOU CAUGHT UP.

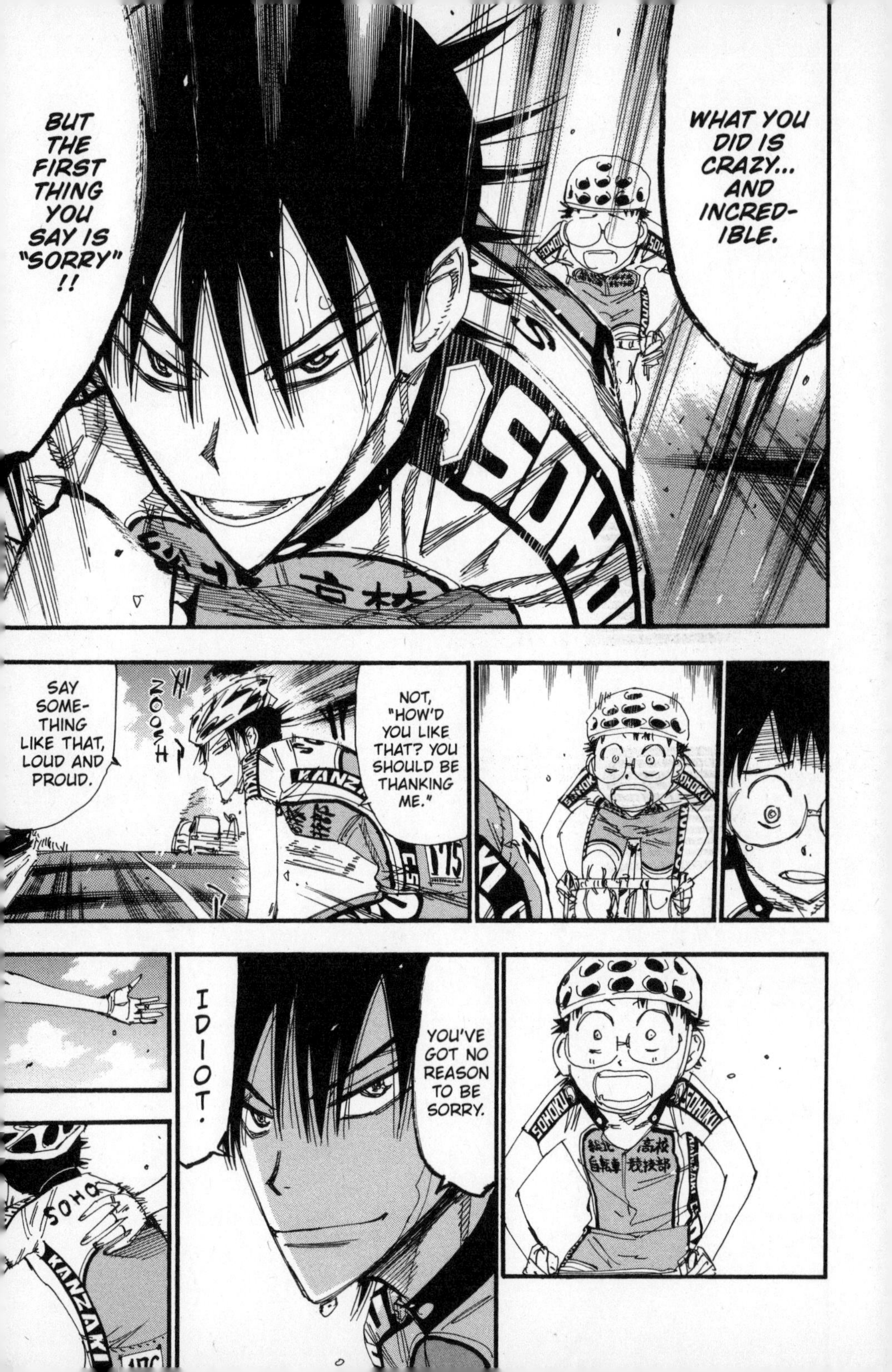
WHAT YOU DID IS CRAZY... AND INCREDIBLE.
BUT THE FIRST THING YOU SAY IS "SORRY"!!
NOT, "HOW'D YOU LIKE THAT? YOU SHOULD BE THANKING ME."
ZOOSH
SAY SOMETHING LIKE THAT, LOUD AND PROUD.
YOU'VE GOT NO REASON TO BE SORRY.
IDIOT.

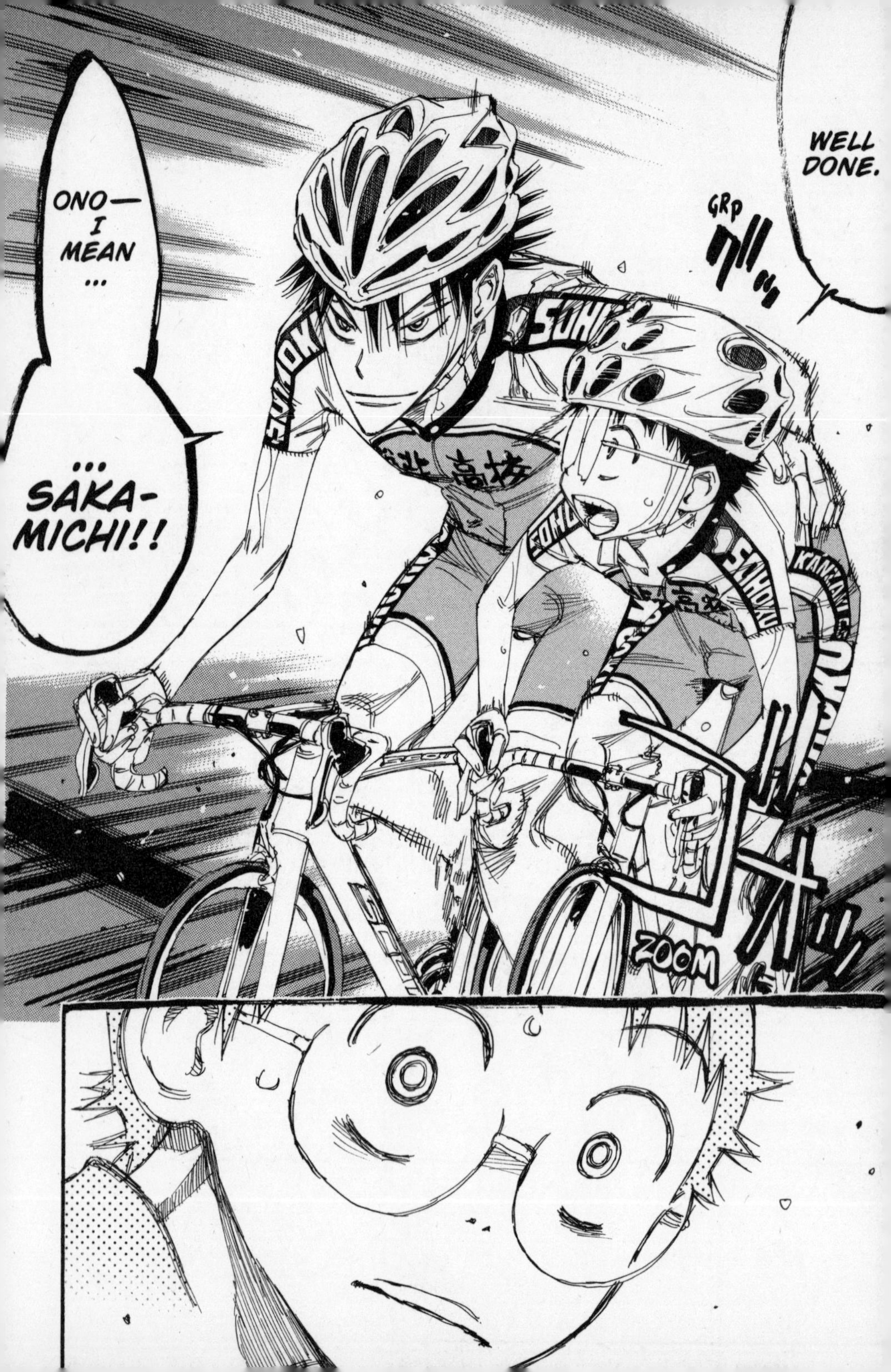
WELL DONE.
GRP
ONO— I MEAN ...
... SÄKA-MICHI!!
ZOOM

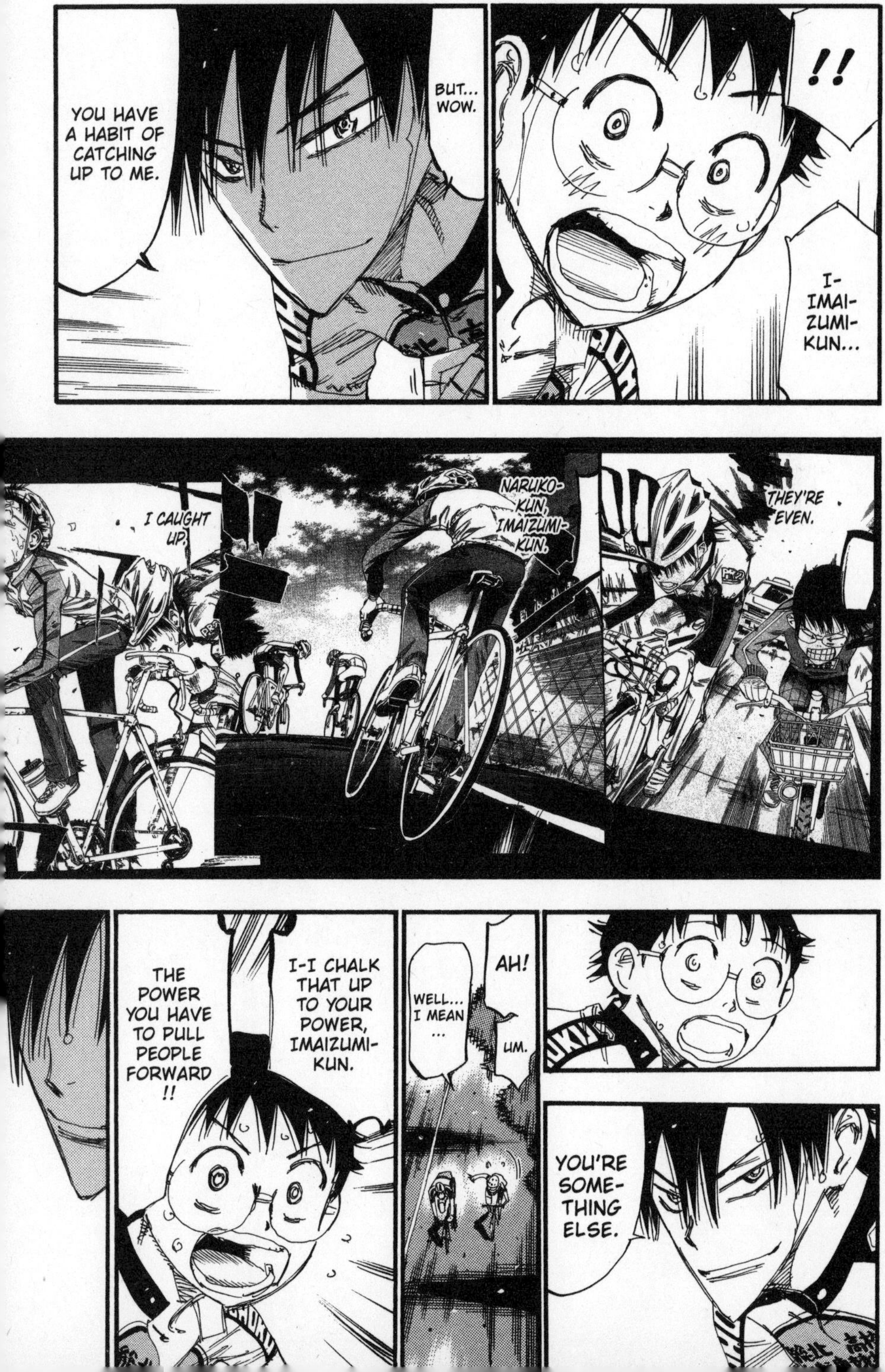
!!
I- IMAI- ZUMI- KUN...
BUT... WOW.
YOU HAVE A HABIT OF CATCHING UP TO ME.
THEY'RE EVEN.
NARUKO- KUN, IMAIZUMI- KUN.
I CAUGHT UP.
YOU'RE SOME- THING ELSE.
AH!
WELL... I MEAN ...
UM.
I-I CHALK THAT UP TO YOUR POWER, IMAIZUMI- KUN.
THE POWER YOU HAVE TO PULL PEOPLE FORWARD !!

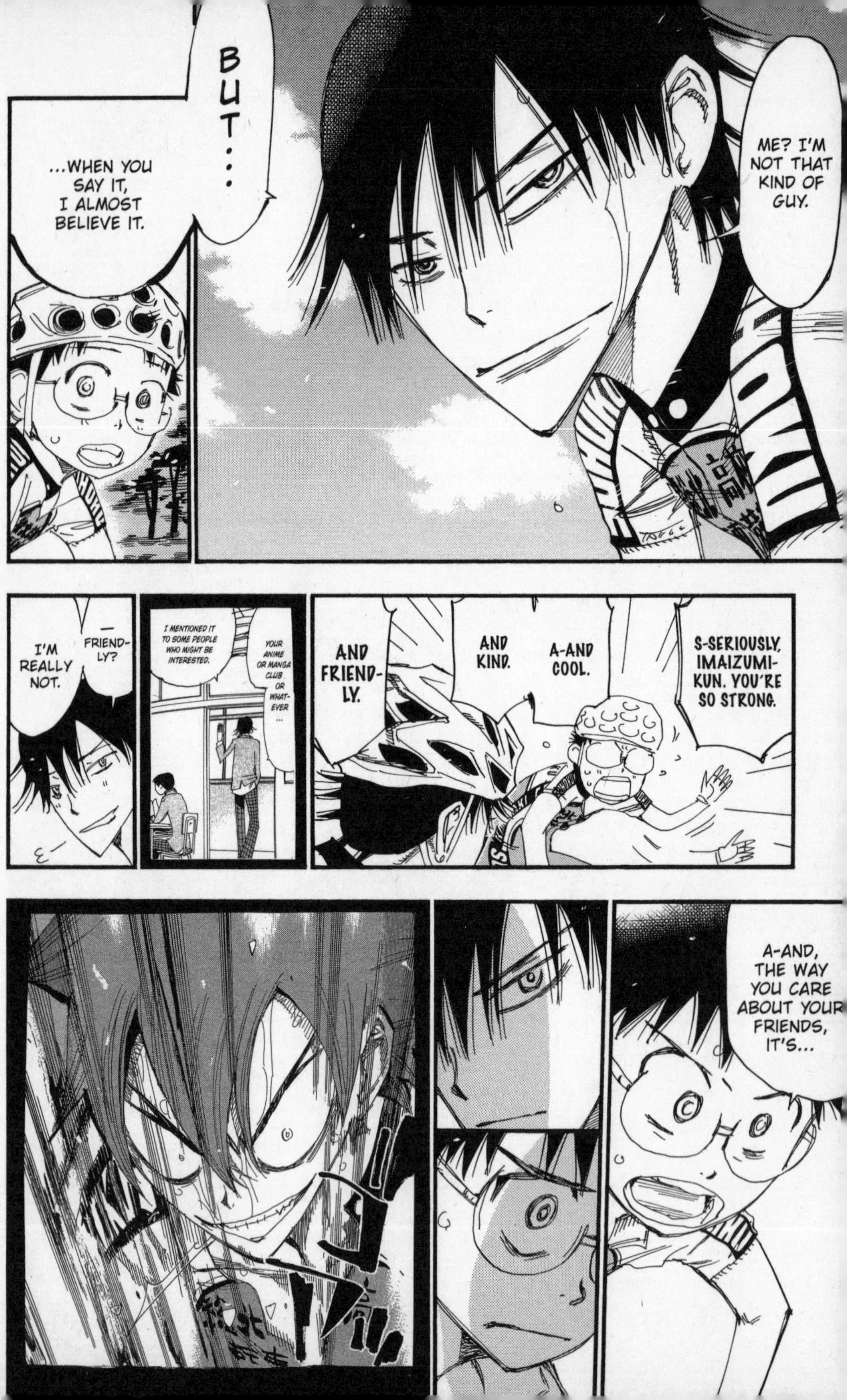
ME? I'M NOT THAT KIND OF GUY.
BUT...
...WHEN YOU SAY IT, I ALMOST BELIEVE IT.
S-SERIOUSLY, IMAIZUMI-KUN. YOU'RE SO STRONG.
A-AND COOL.
AND KIND.
AND FRIENDLY.
YOUR ANIME OR MANGA CLUB OR WHATEVER...
I MENTIONED IT TO SOME PEOPLE WHO MIGHT BE INTERESTED.
—FRIENDLY?
I'M REALLY NOT.
A-AND, THE WAY YOU CARE ABOUT YOUR FRIENDS, IT'S...

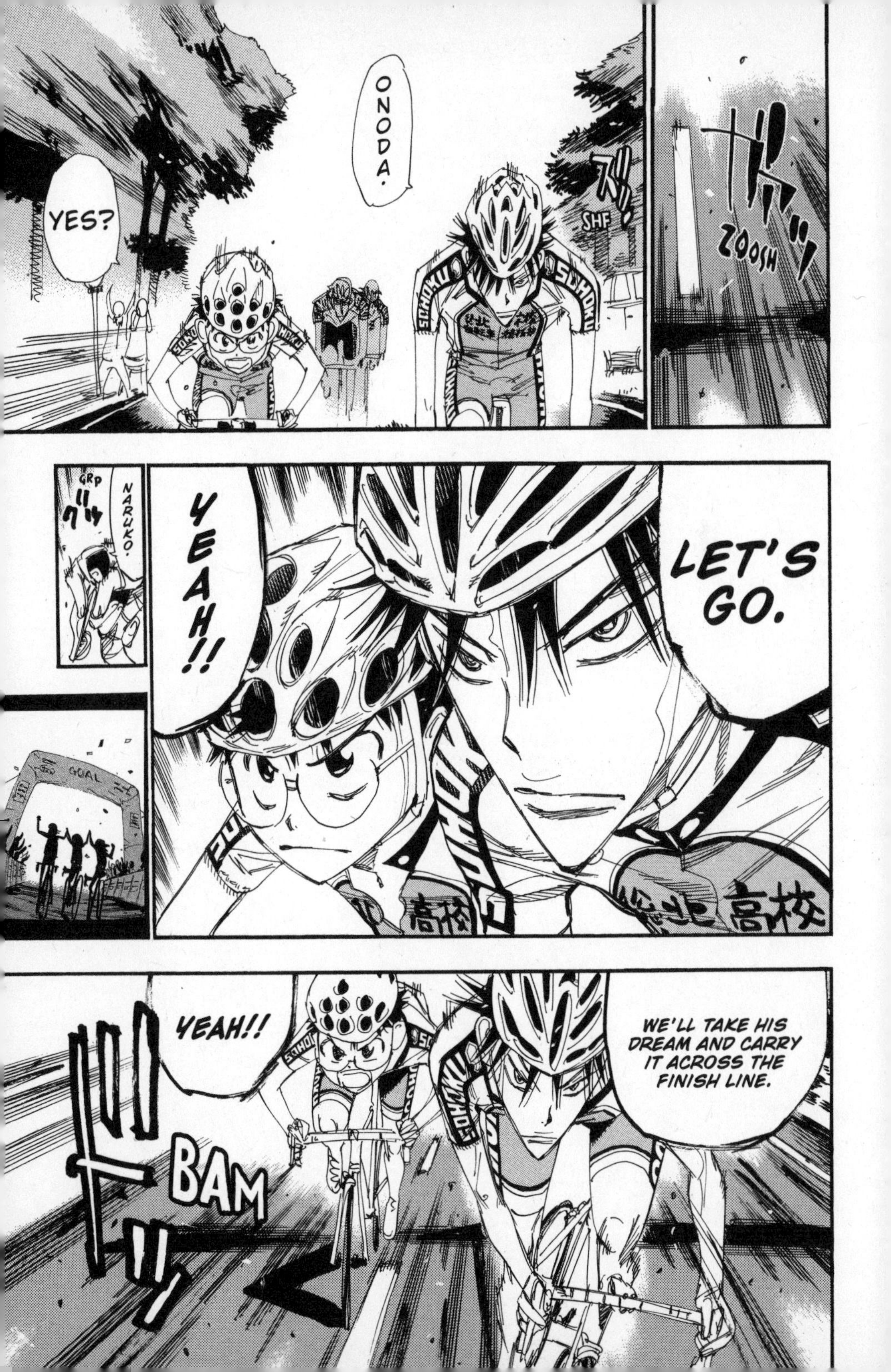
ZOOSH
ONODA.
SHF
YES?
LET'S GO.
YEAH!!
NARUKO.
GRP
GOAL
WE'LL TAKE HIS DREAM AND CARRY IT ACROSS THE FINISH LINE.
YEAH!!
BAM

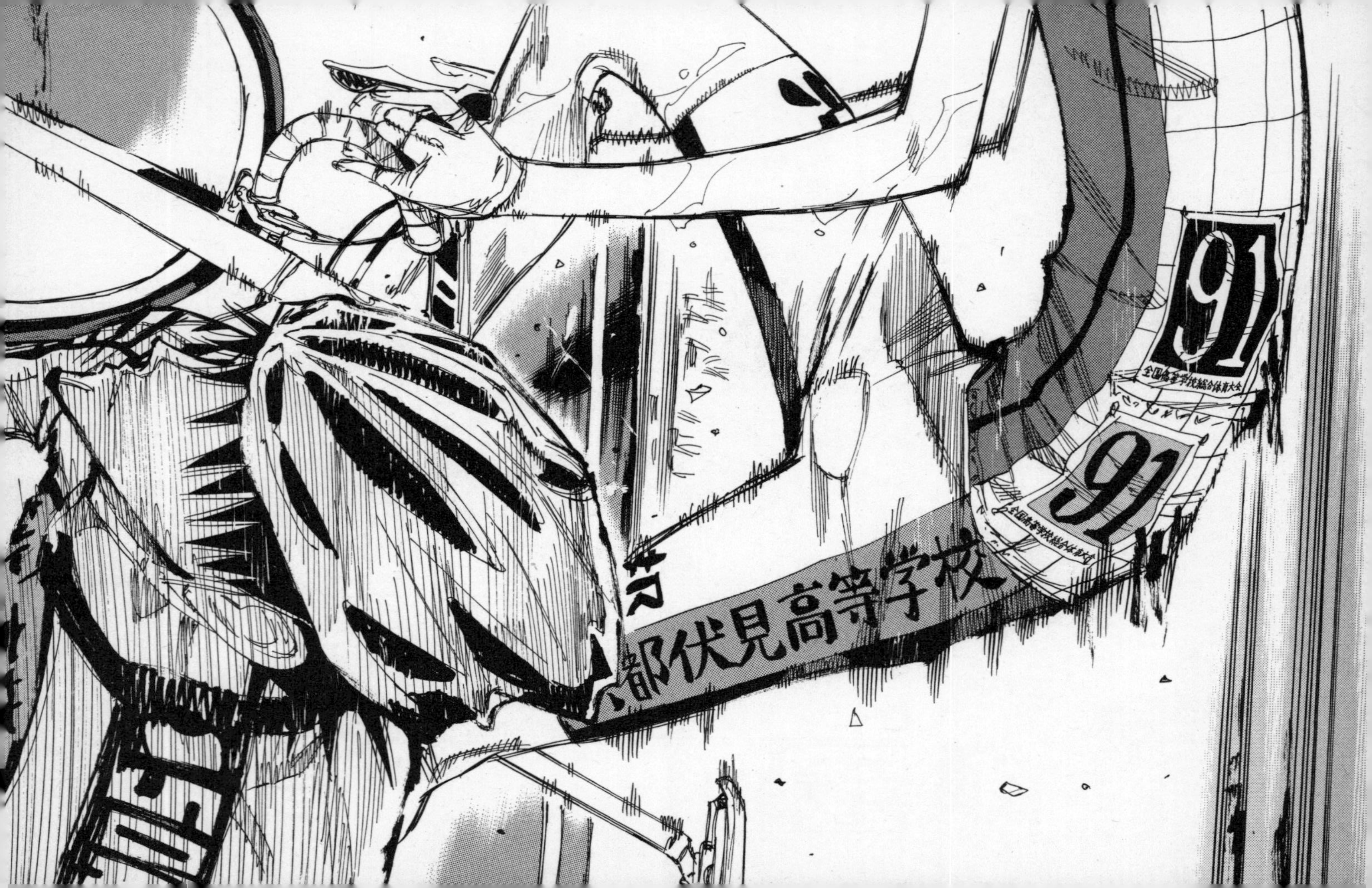
91
91
都伏見高等学校

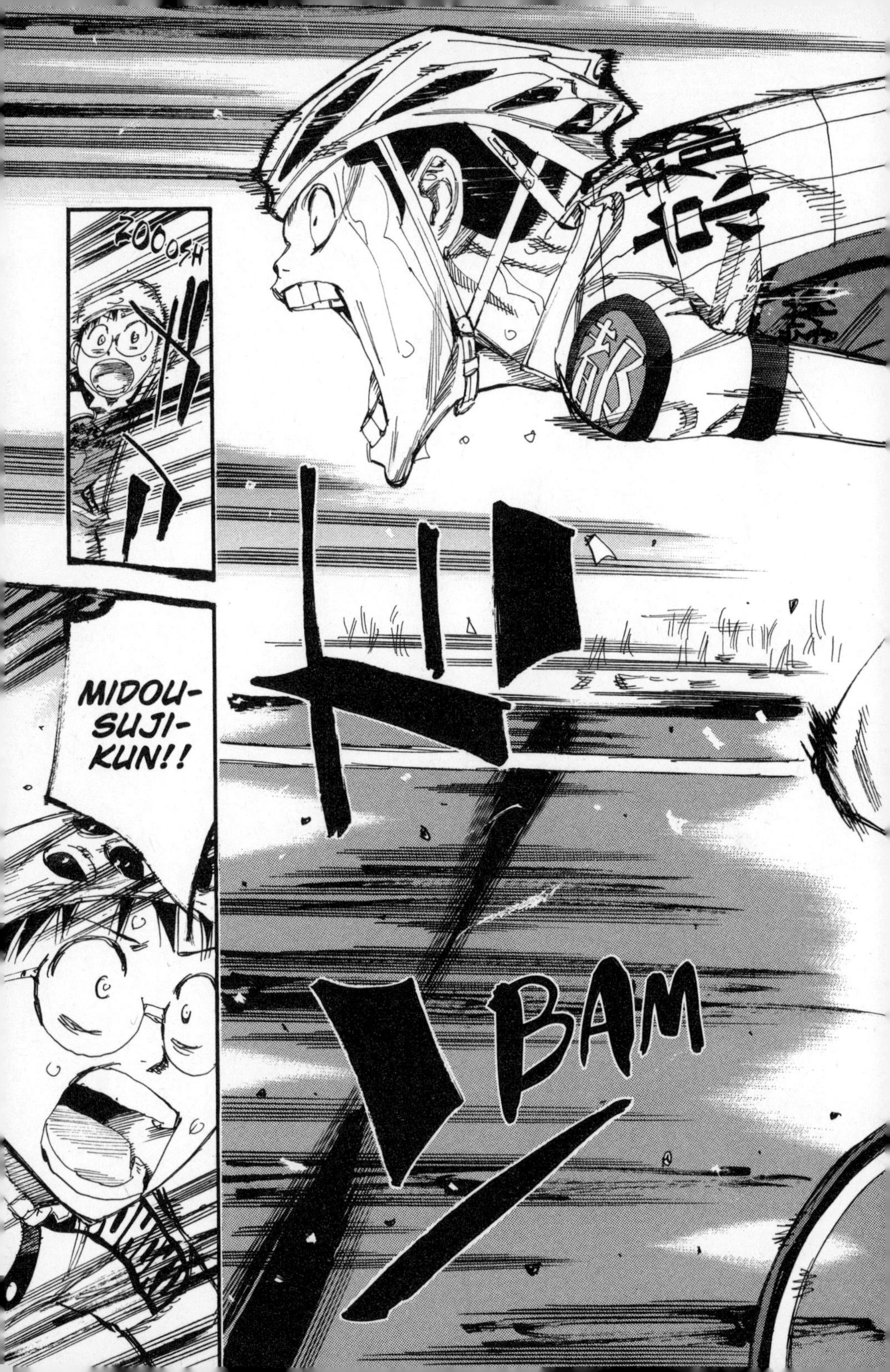
BAM
ZOOOSH
MIDOU-SUJI-KUN!!

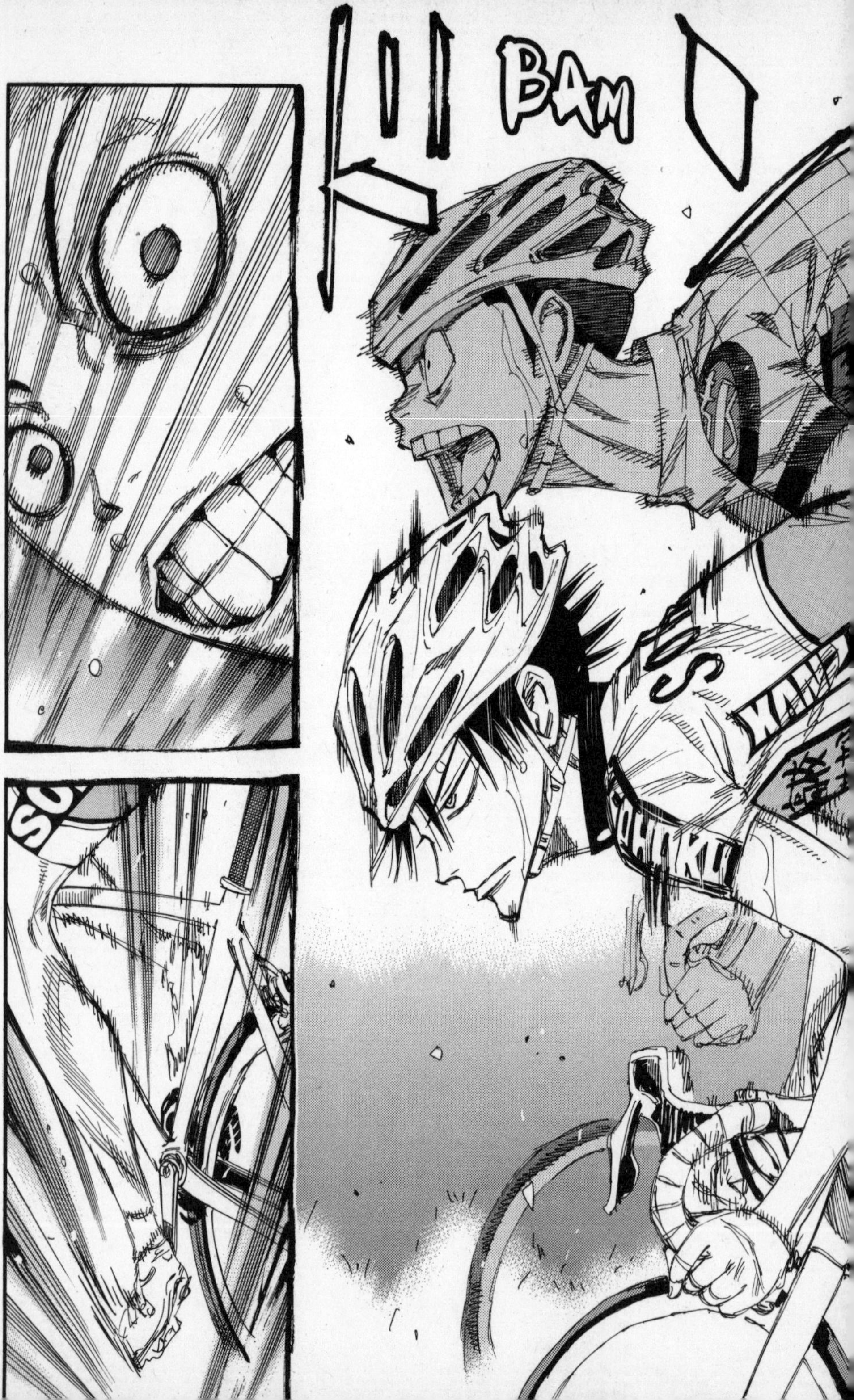
BAM

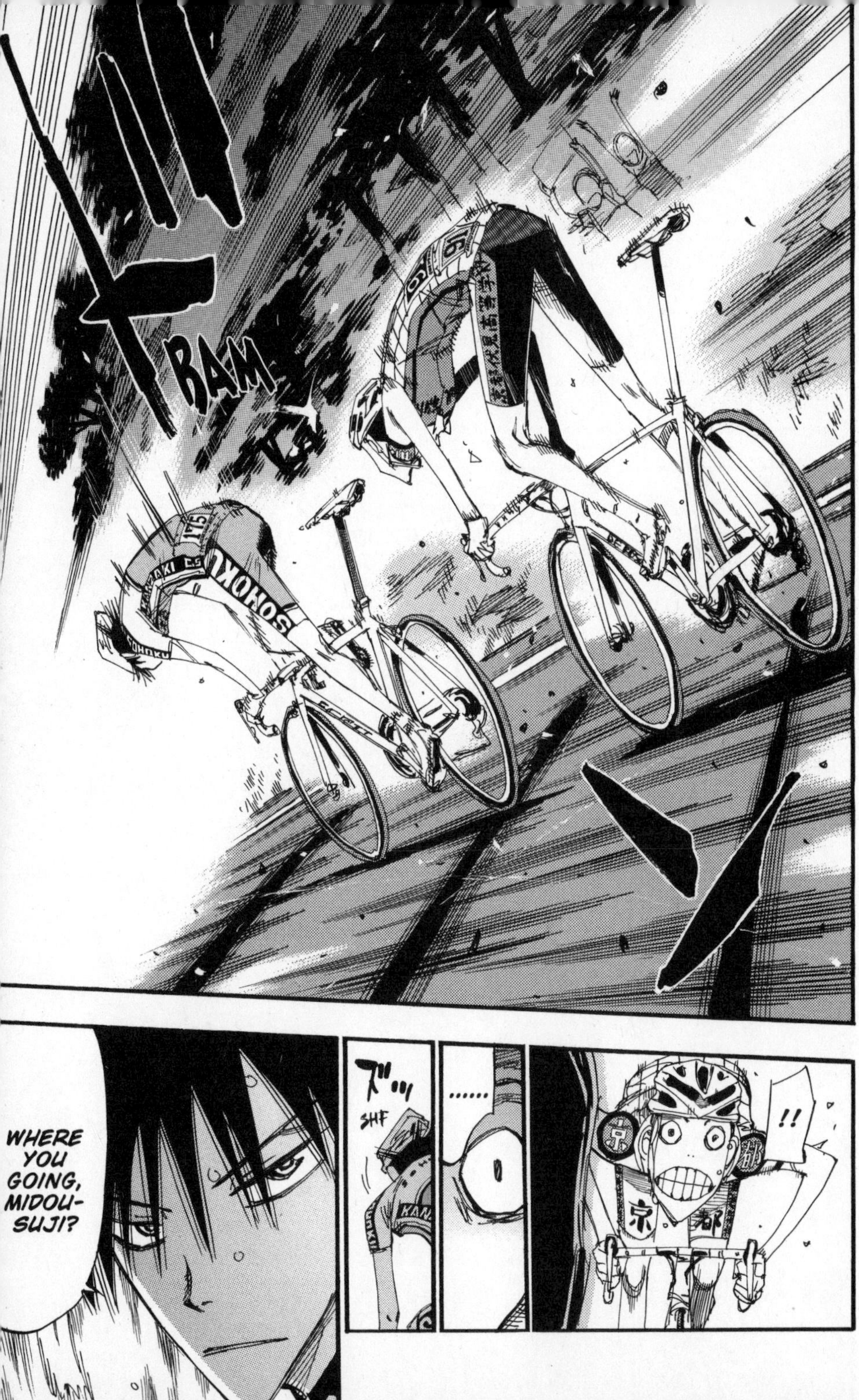
BAM
!!
......
SHF
WHERE YOU GOING, MIDOUSUJI?

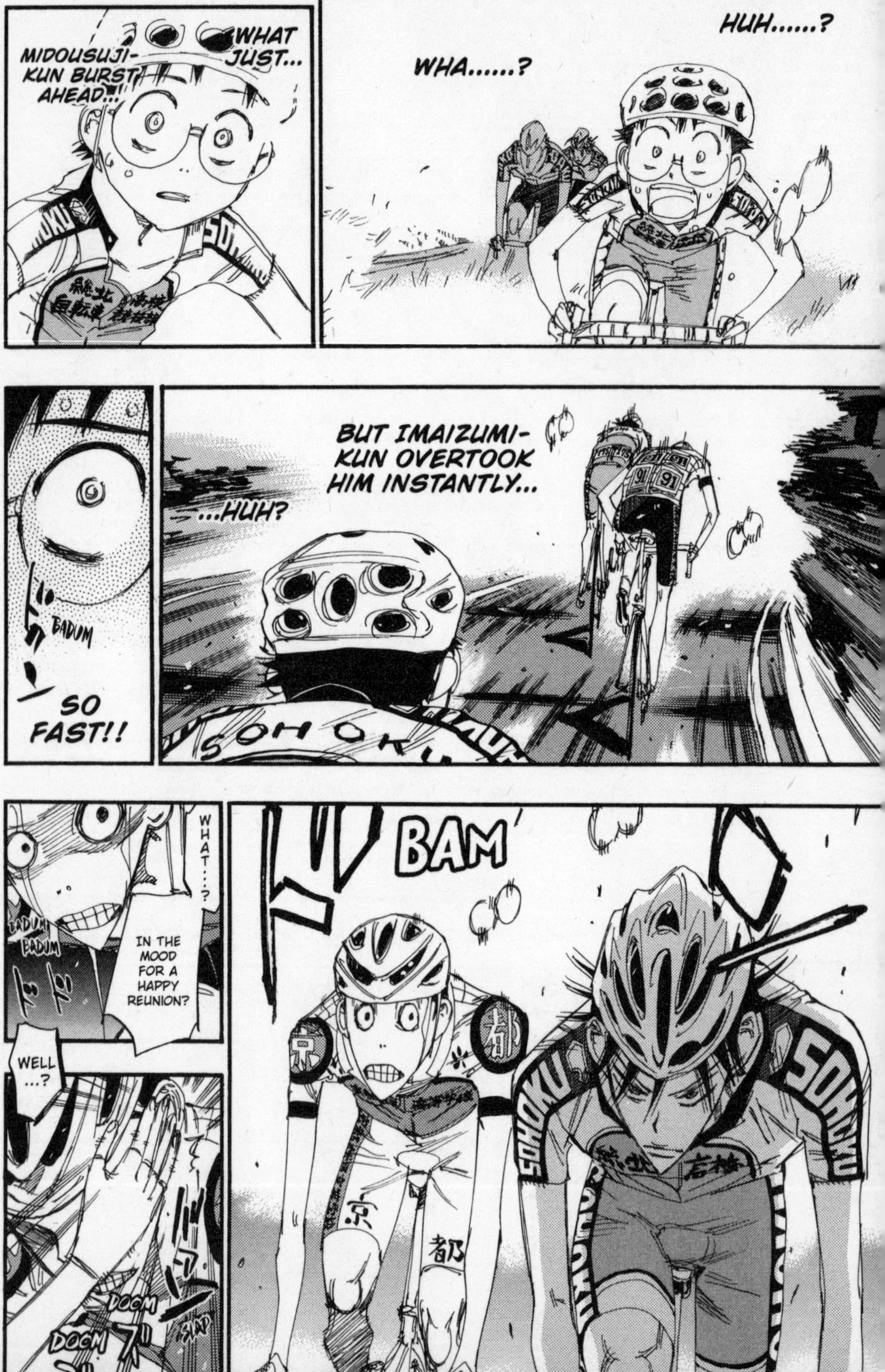
HUH......?
WHA......?
WHAT JUST...
MIDOUSUJI-KUN BURST AHEAD...
BUT IMAIZUMI-KUN OVERTOOK HIM INSTANTLY...
...HUH?
BADUM
SO FAST!!
BAM
WHAT...?
IN THE MOOD FOR A HAPPY REUNION?
BADUM BADUM
WELL...?
DOOM
SLAP
DOOM

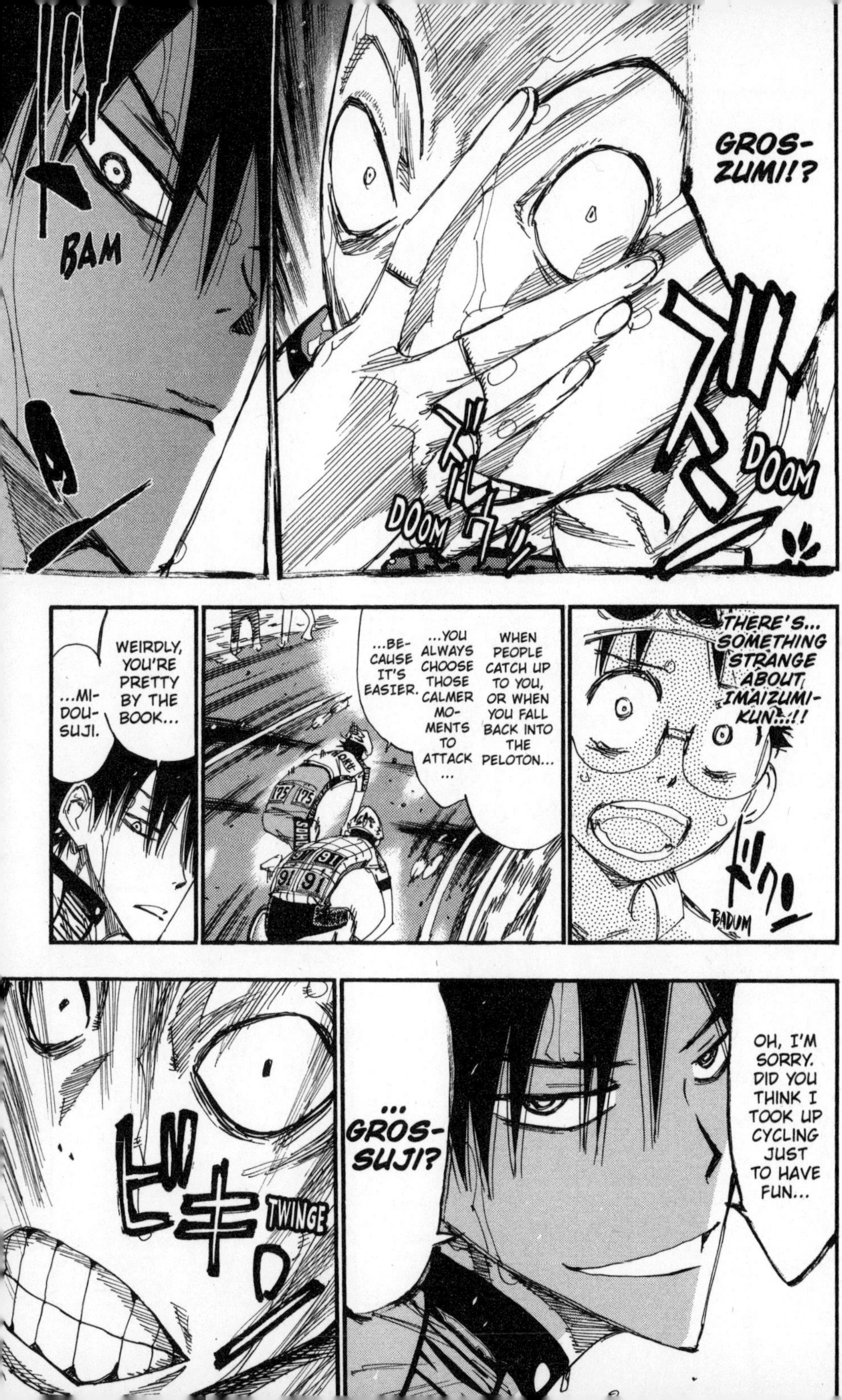
GROS-ZUMI!?
DOOM
DOOM
BAM
THERE'S... SOMETHING STRANGE ABOUT IMAIZUMI-KUN...!!
BADUM
WHEN PEOPLE CATCH UP TO YOU, OR WHEN YOU FALL BACK INTO THE PELOTON...
...YOU ALWAYS CHOOSE THOSE CALMER MOMENTS TO ATTACK...
...BECAUSE IT'S EASIER.
WEIRDLY, YOU'RE PRETTY BY THE BOOK...
...MIDOUSUJI.
OH, I'M SORRY. DID YOU THINK I TOOK UP CYCLING JUST TO HAVE FUN...
...GROS-SUJI?
TWINGE

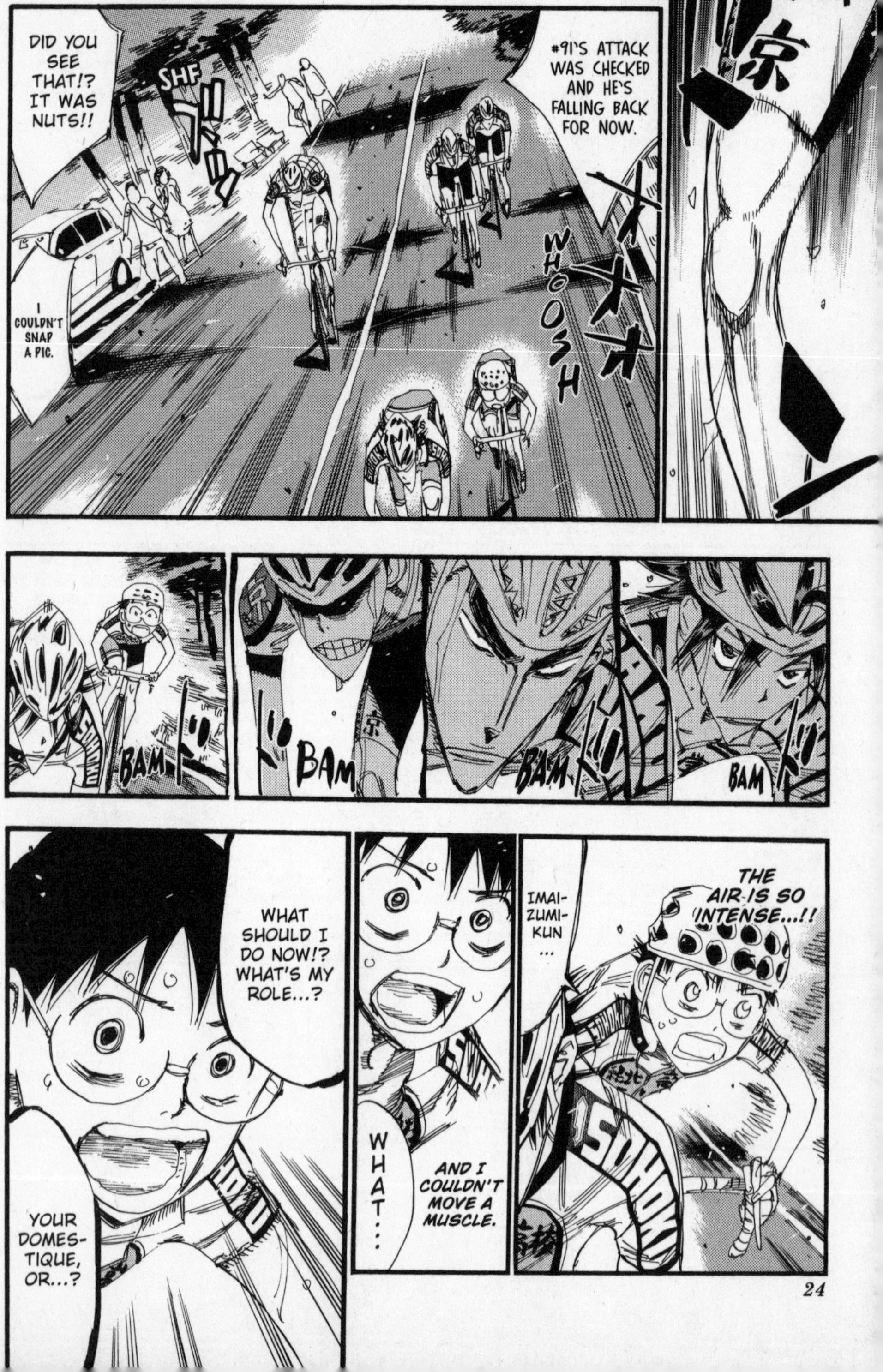
BAM
#91'S ATTACK WAS CHECKED AND HE'S FALLING BACK FOR NOW.
WHOOSH
SHF
DID YOU SEE THAT!? IT WAS NUTS!!
I COULDN'T SNAP A PIC.
BAM
BAM
BAM
BAM
THE AIR IS SO INTENSE...!!
IMAIZUMI-KUN...
AND I COULDN'T MOVE A MUSCLE.
WHAT...
WHAT SHOULD I DO NOW!? WHAT'S MY ROLE...?
YOUR DOMESTIQUE, OR...?

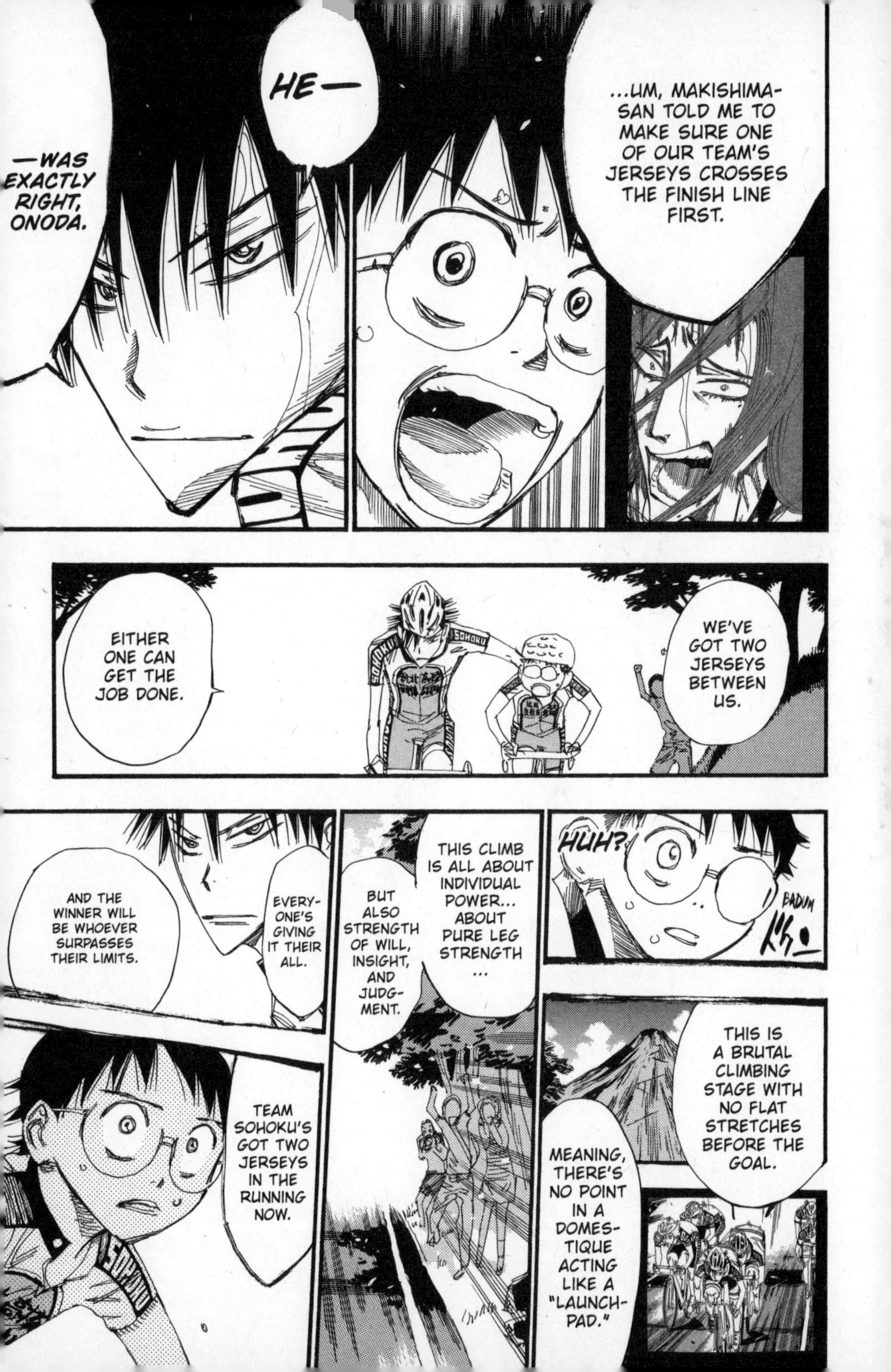
...UM, MAKISHIMA-SAN TOLD ME TO MAKE SURE ONE OF OUR TEAM'S JERSEYS CROSSES THE FINISH LINE FIRST.
HE—
—WAS EXACTLY RIGHT, ONODA.
WE'VE GOT TWO JERSEYS BETWEEN US.
EITHER ONE CAN GET THE JOB DONE.
HUH?
BADUM
THIS CLIMB IS ALL ABOUT INDIVIDUAL POWER... ABOUT PURE LEG STRENGTH...
BUT ALSO STRENGTH OF WILL, INSIGHT, AND JUDGMENT.
EVERYONE'S GIVING IT THEIR ALL.
AND THE WINNER WILL BE WHOEVER SURPASSES THEIR LIMITS.
THIS IS A BRUTAL CLIMBING STAGE WITH NO FLAT STRETCHES BEFORE THE GOAL.
MEANING, THERE'S NO POINT IN A DOMESTIQUE ACTING LIKE A "LAUNCHPAD."
TEAM SOHOKU'S GOT TWO JERSEYS IN THE RUNNING NOW.

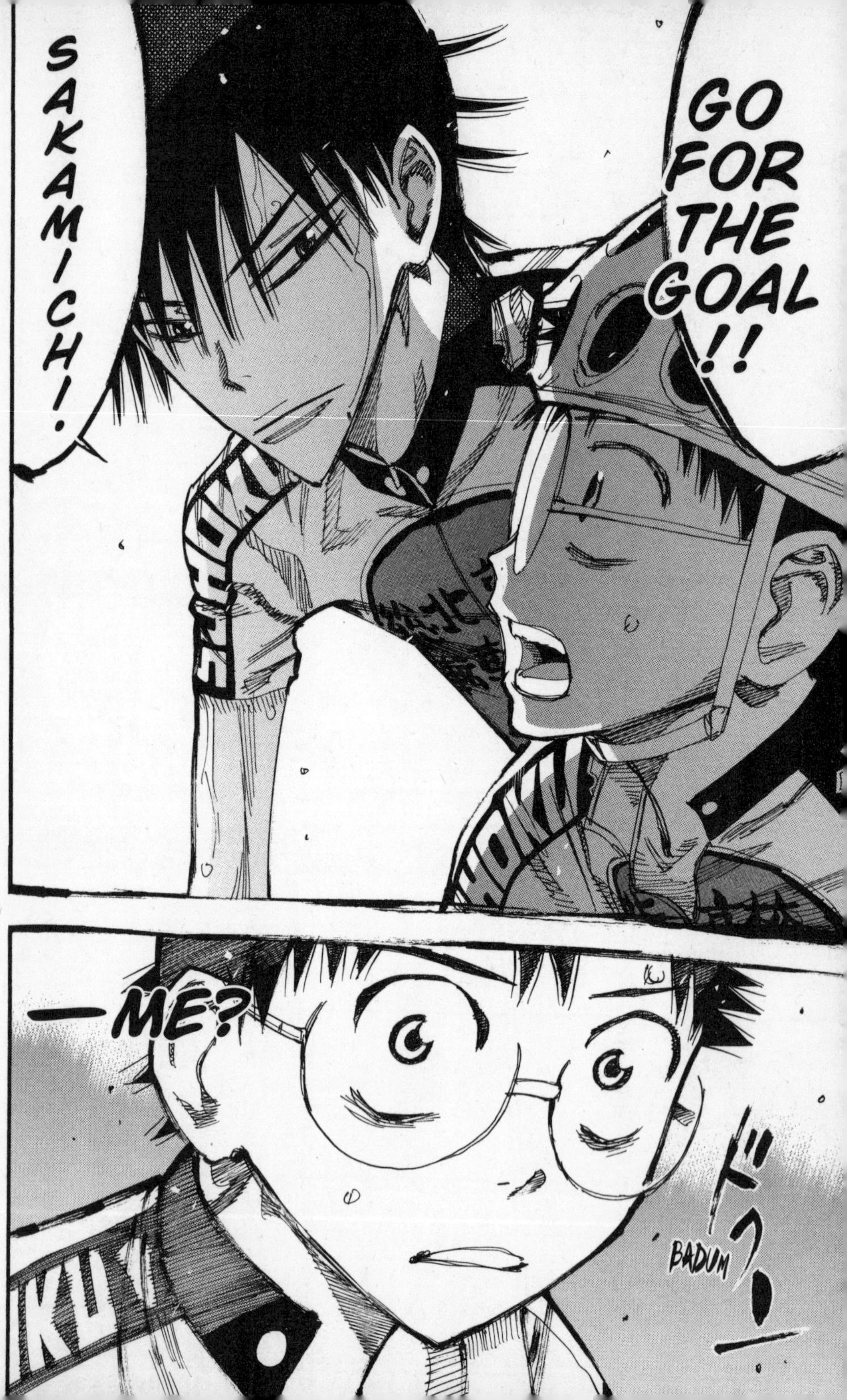
GO FOR THE GOAL!!
SAKAMICHI!
—ME?
BADUM

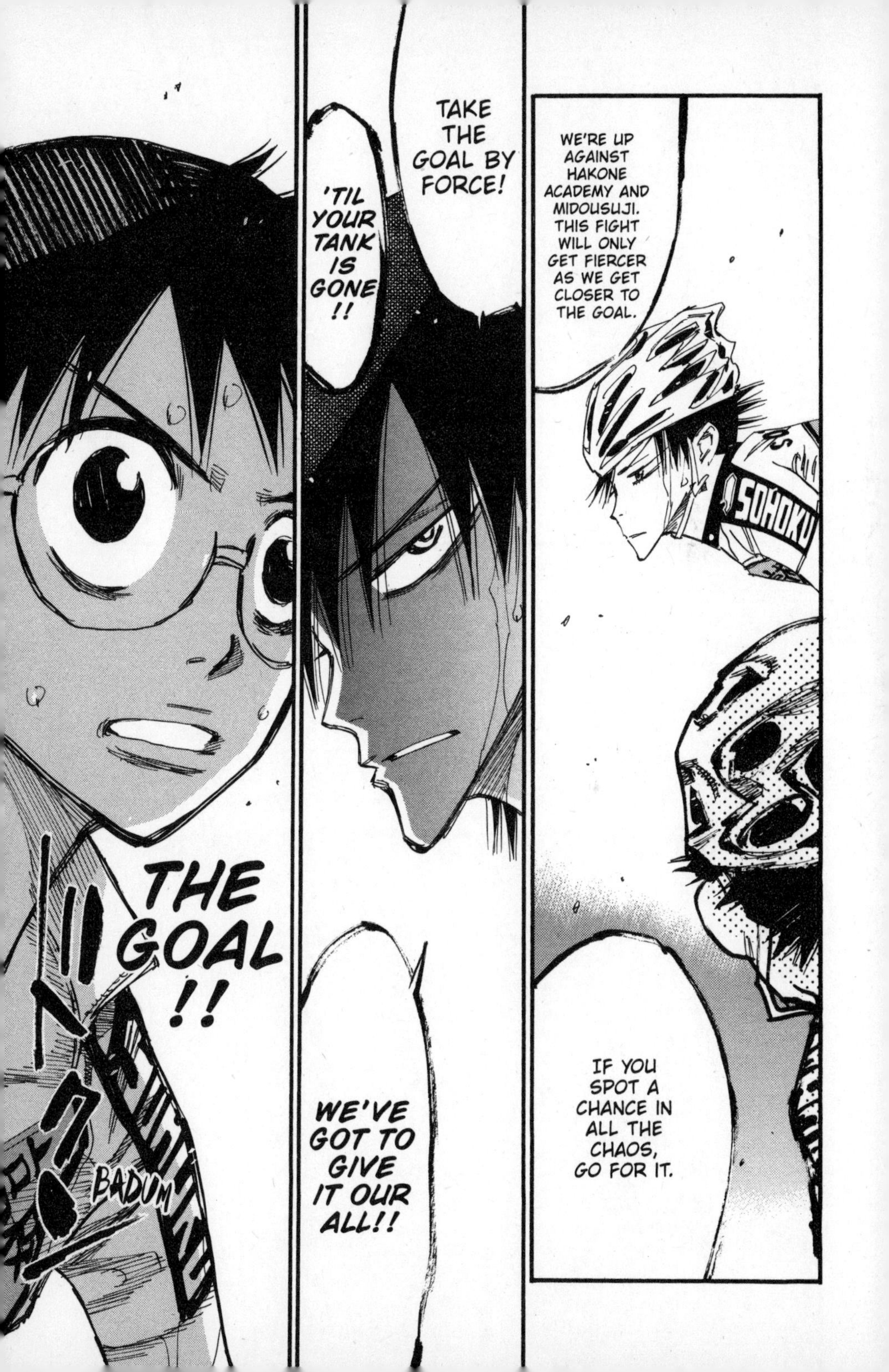
WE'RE UP AGAINST HAKONE ACADEMY AND MIDOUSUJI. THIS FIGHT WILL ONLY GET FIERCER AS WE GET CLOSER TO THE GOAL.
SOHOKU
IF YOU SPOT A CHANCE IN ALL THE CHAOS, GO FOR IT.
TAKE THE GOAL BY FORCE!
'TIL YOUR TANK IS GONE!!
WE'VE GOT TO GIVE IT OUR ALL!!
THE GOAL!!
BADUM

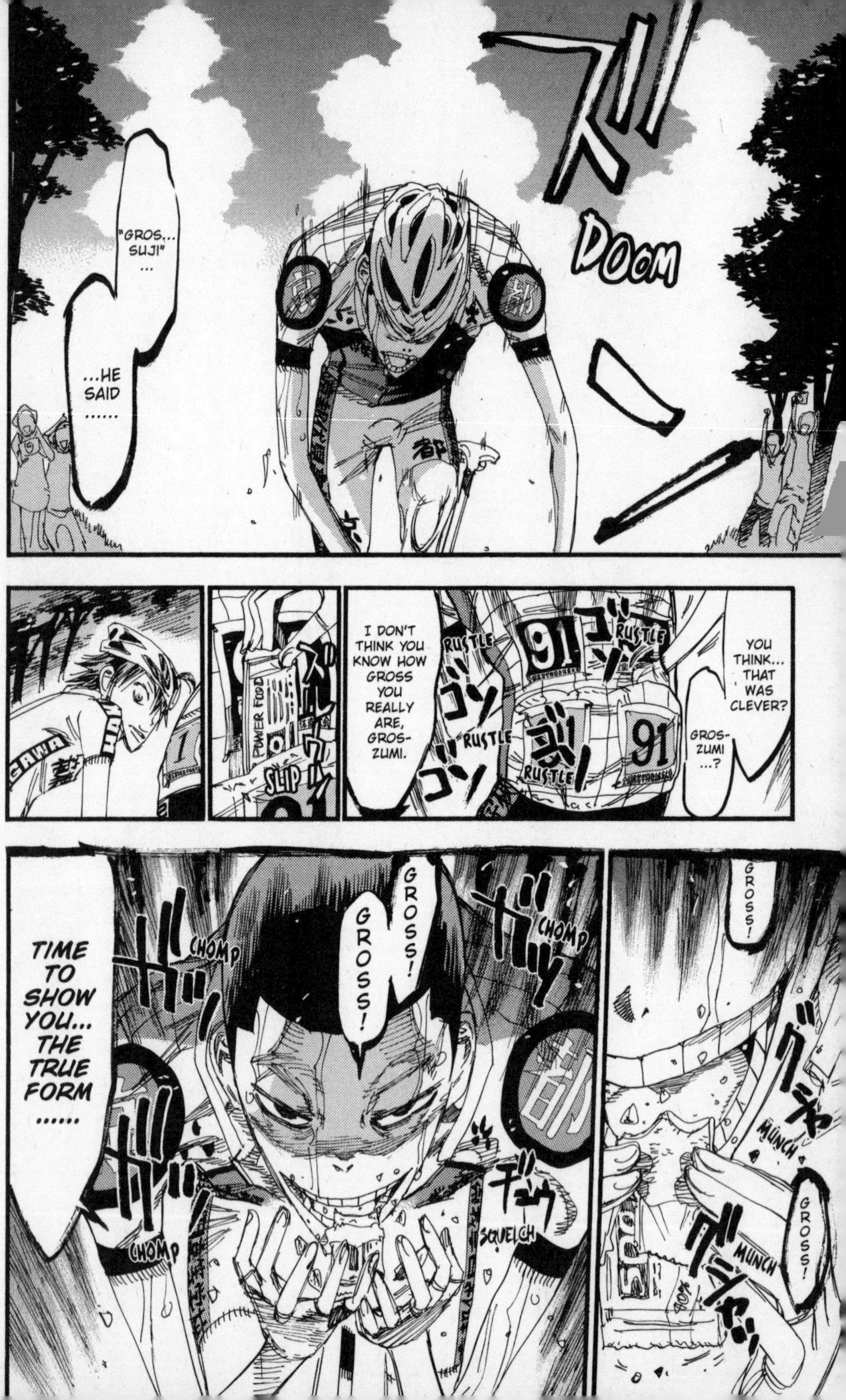
"GROS... SUJI" ...
...HE SAID ......
DOOM
YOU THINK... THAT WAS CLEVER?
GROS-ZUMI ...?
RUSTLE
RUSTLE
RUSTLE
RUSTLE
I DON'T THINK YOU KNOW HOW GROSS YOU REALLY ARE, GROS-ZUMI.
POWER FOOD
SLIP
GROSS!
MUNCH
MUNCH
GROSS!
GROSS!
GROSS!
CHOMP
TIME TO SHOW YOU... THE TRUE FORM ......
CHOMP
SQUELCH
CHOMP

RIDE.209 EROSION

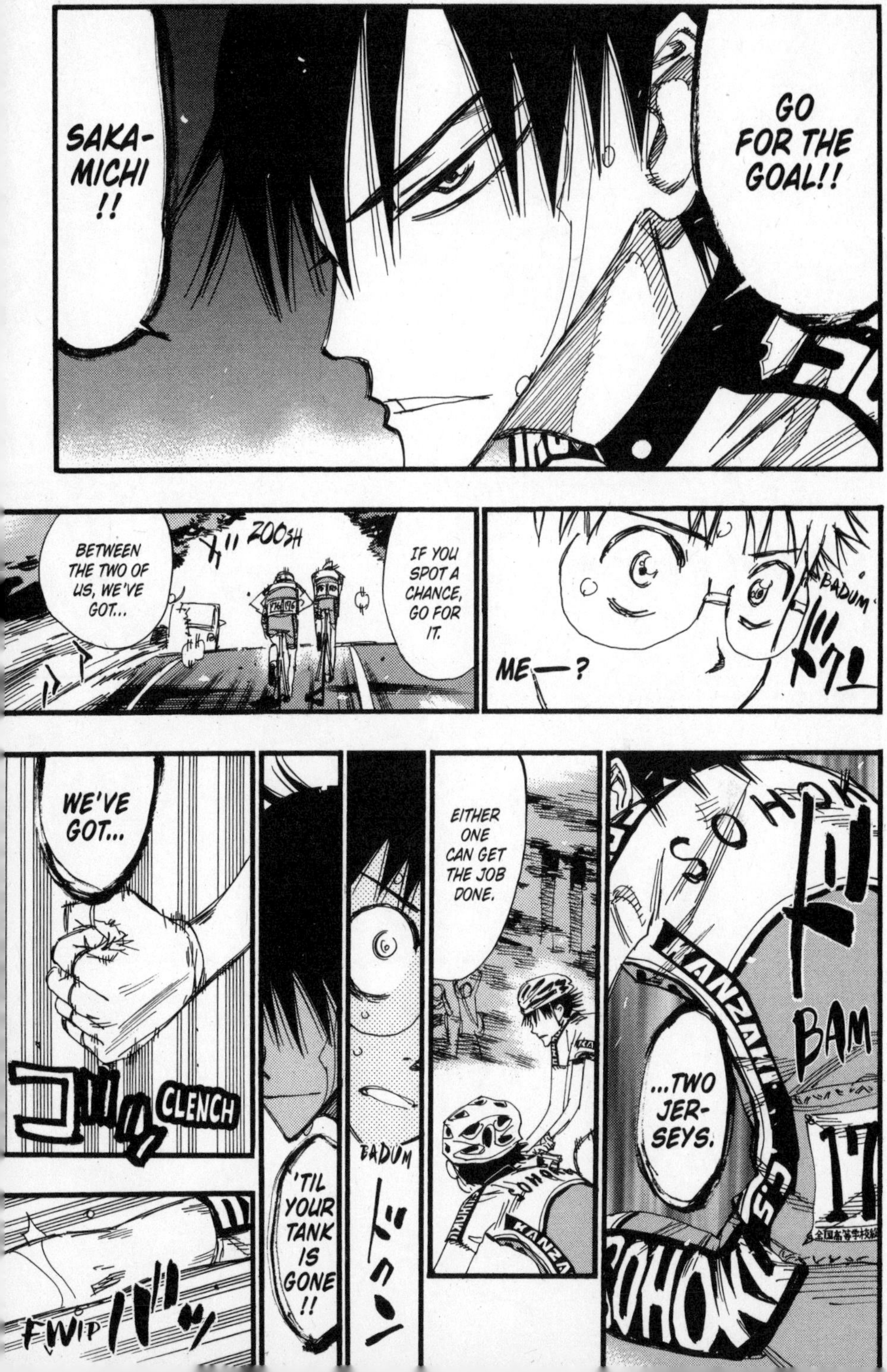
GO FOR THE GOAL!!
SAKA-MICHI!!
BADUM
ME—?
IF YOU SPOT A CHANCE, GO FOR IT.
ZOOSH
BETWEEN THE TWO OF US, WE'VE GOT...
BAM
...TWO JER-SEYS.
EITHER ONE CAN GET THE JOB DONE.
BADUM
'TIL YOUR TANK IS GONE!!
WE'VE GOT...
CLENCH
FWIP

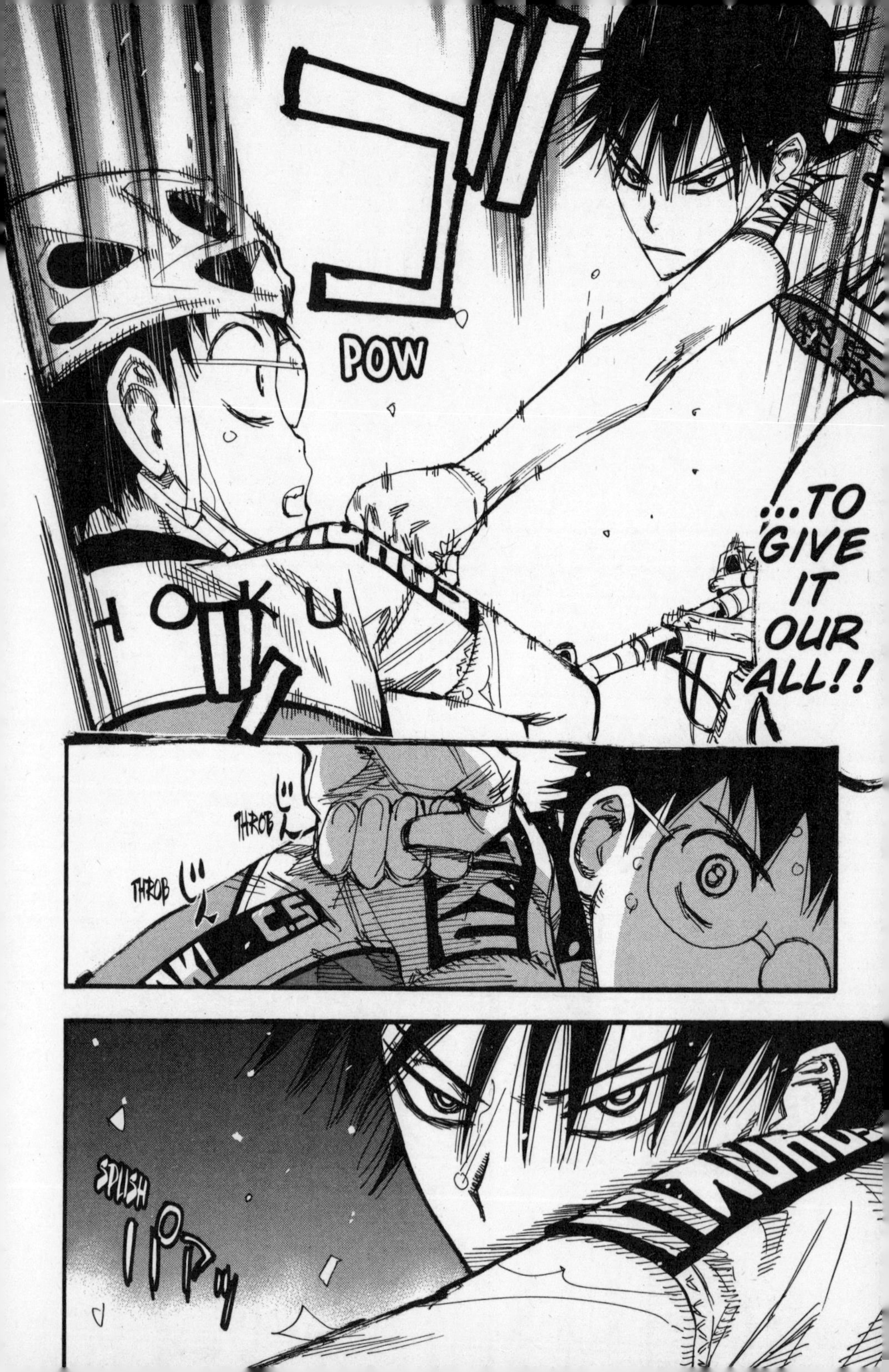
...TO GIVE IT OUR ALL!!
ゴッ
POW
THROB じん
THROB じん
SPLISH

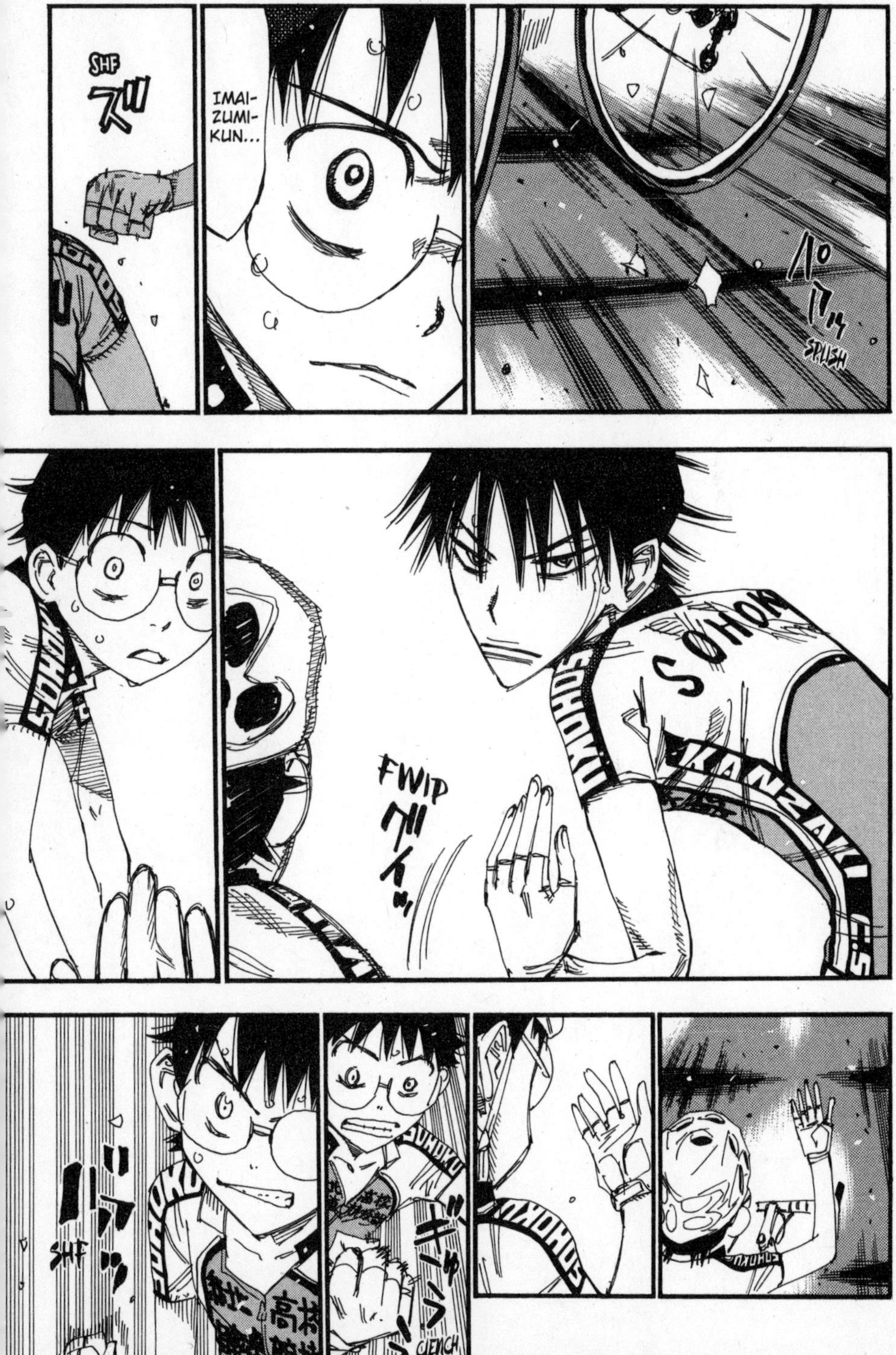
SPLISH
IMAI-
ZUMI-
KUN...
SHF
FWIP
CLENCH
SHF

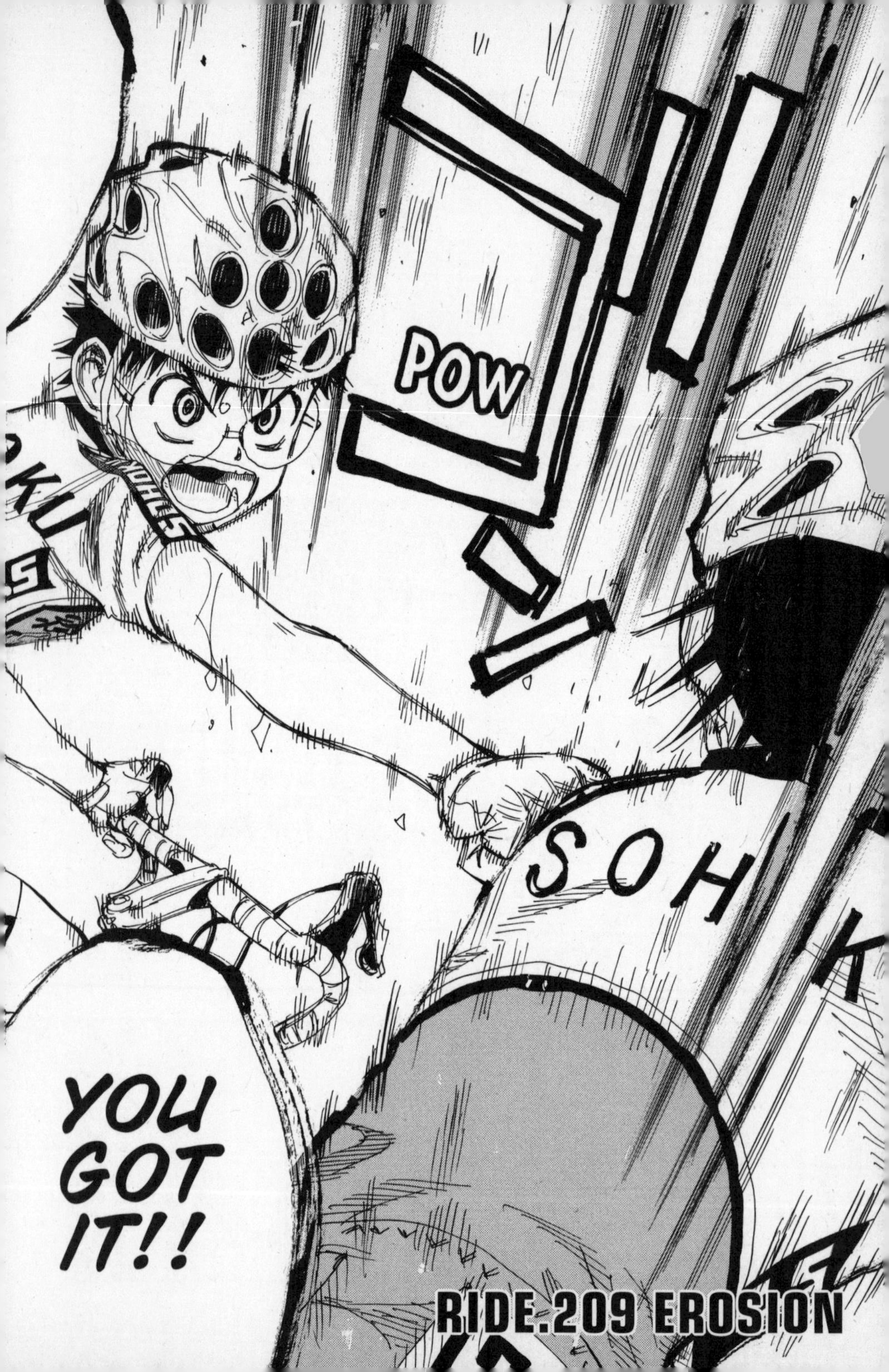
POW
SOHK
YOU GOT IT!!
RIDE.209 EROSION

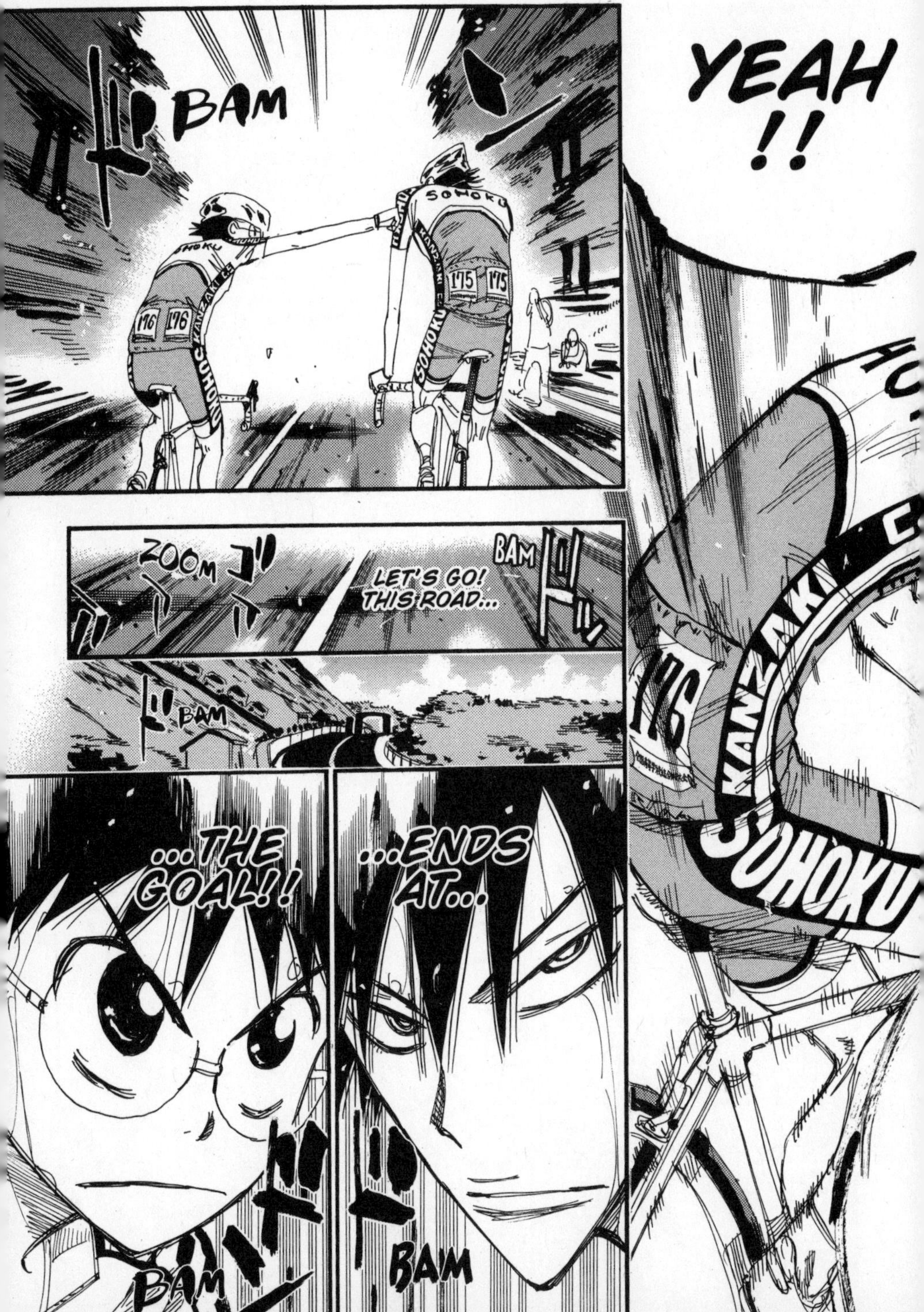
YEAH !!
BAM
BAM
LET'S GO! THIS ROAD...
ZOOM
BAM
...ENDS AT...
BAM
...THE GOAL!!
BAM

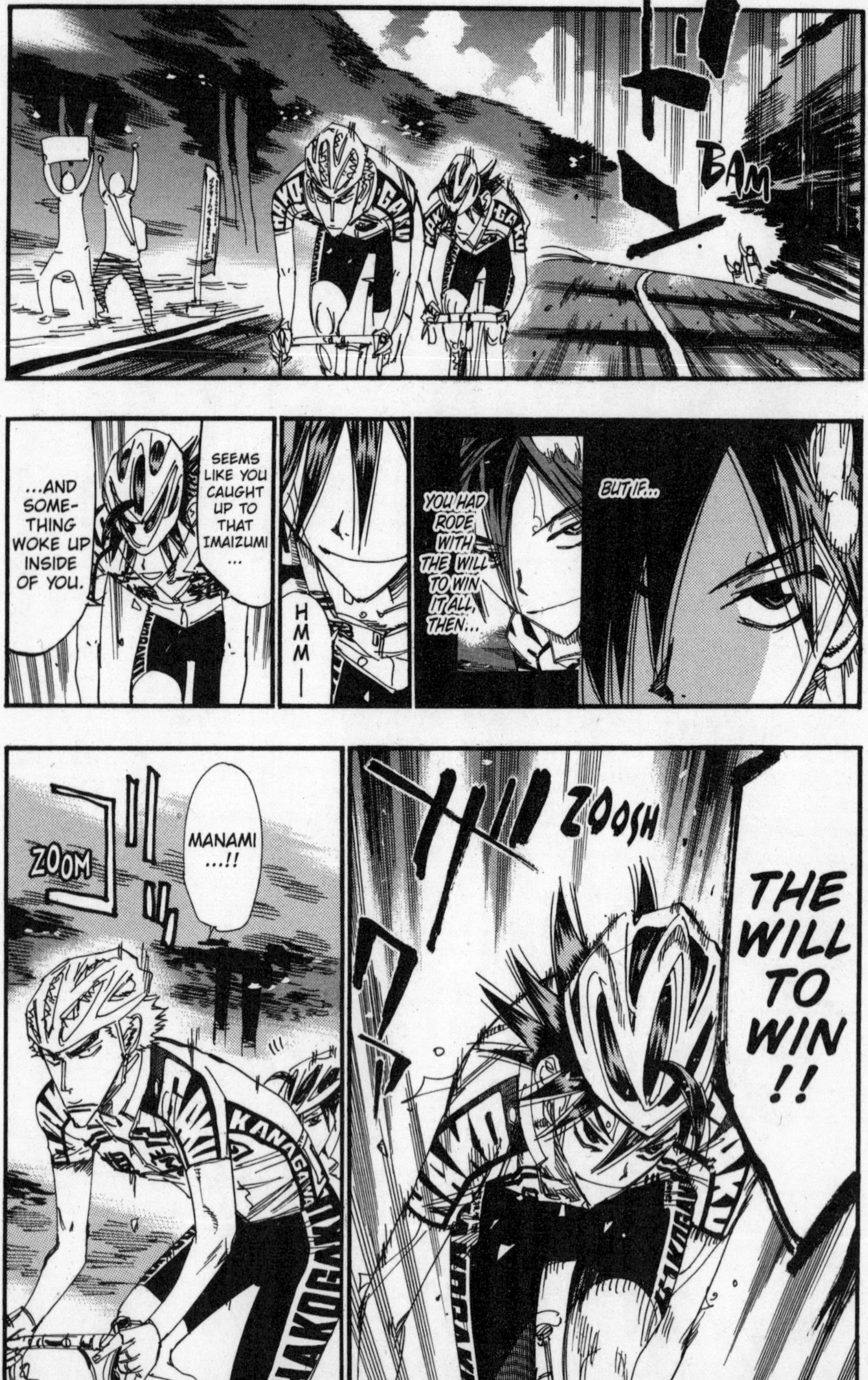
BAM
BUT IF...
YOU HAD RODE WITH THE WILL TO WIN IT ALL, THEN...
HMM!
SEEMS LIKE YOU CAUGHT UP TO THAT IMAIZUMI...
...AND SOMETHING WOKE UP INSIDE OF YOU.
ZOOSH
THE WILL TO WIN!!
MANAMI...!!
ZOOM

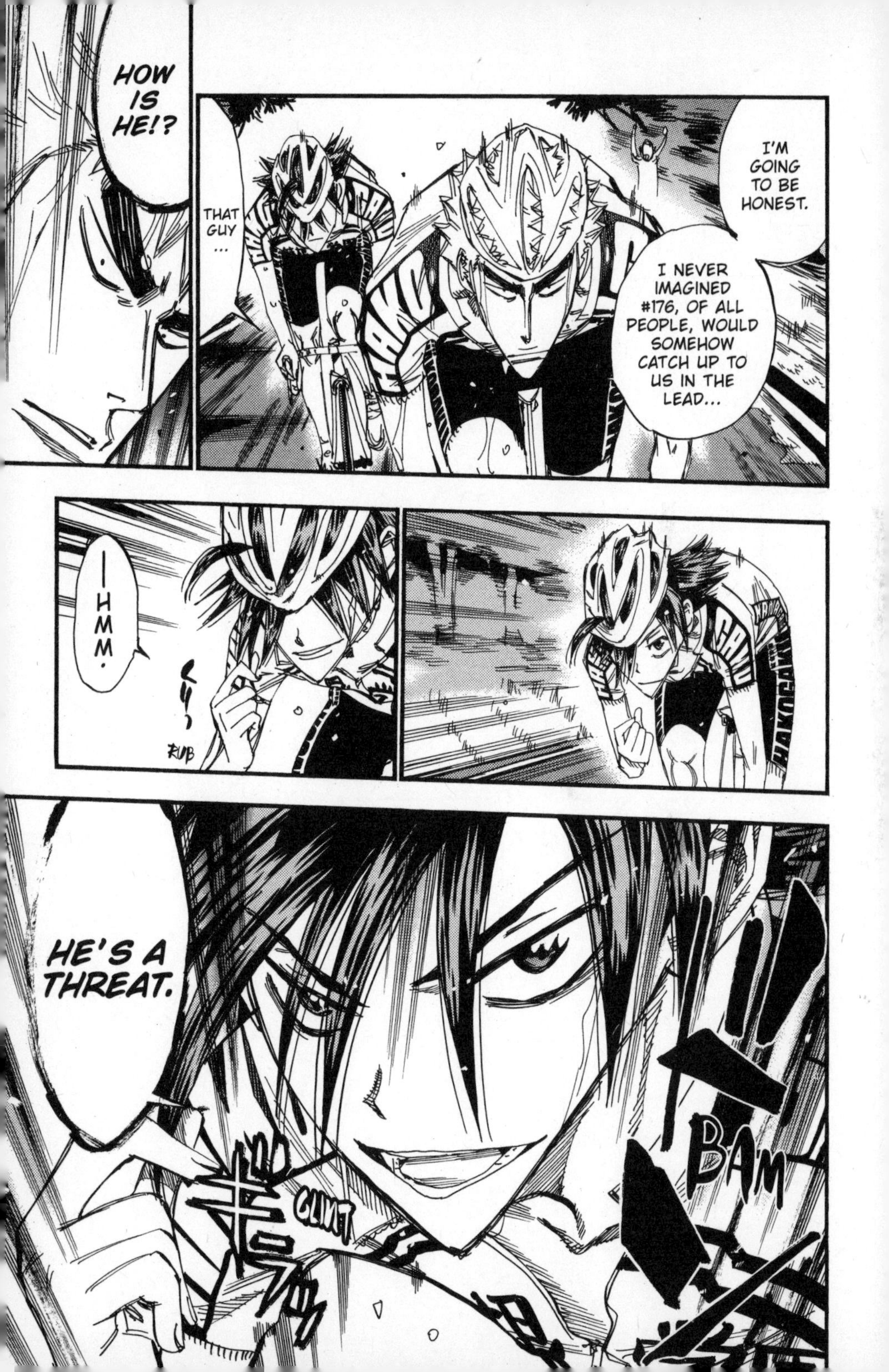

I'M GOING TO BE HONEST.
I NEVER IMAGINED #176, OF ALL PEOPLE, WOULD SOMEHOW CATCH UP TO US IN THE LEAD...
THAT GUY ...
HOW IS HE!?
—HMM.
RUB
HE'S A THREAT.
BAM
CLINK

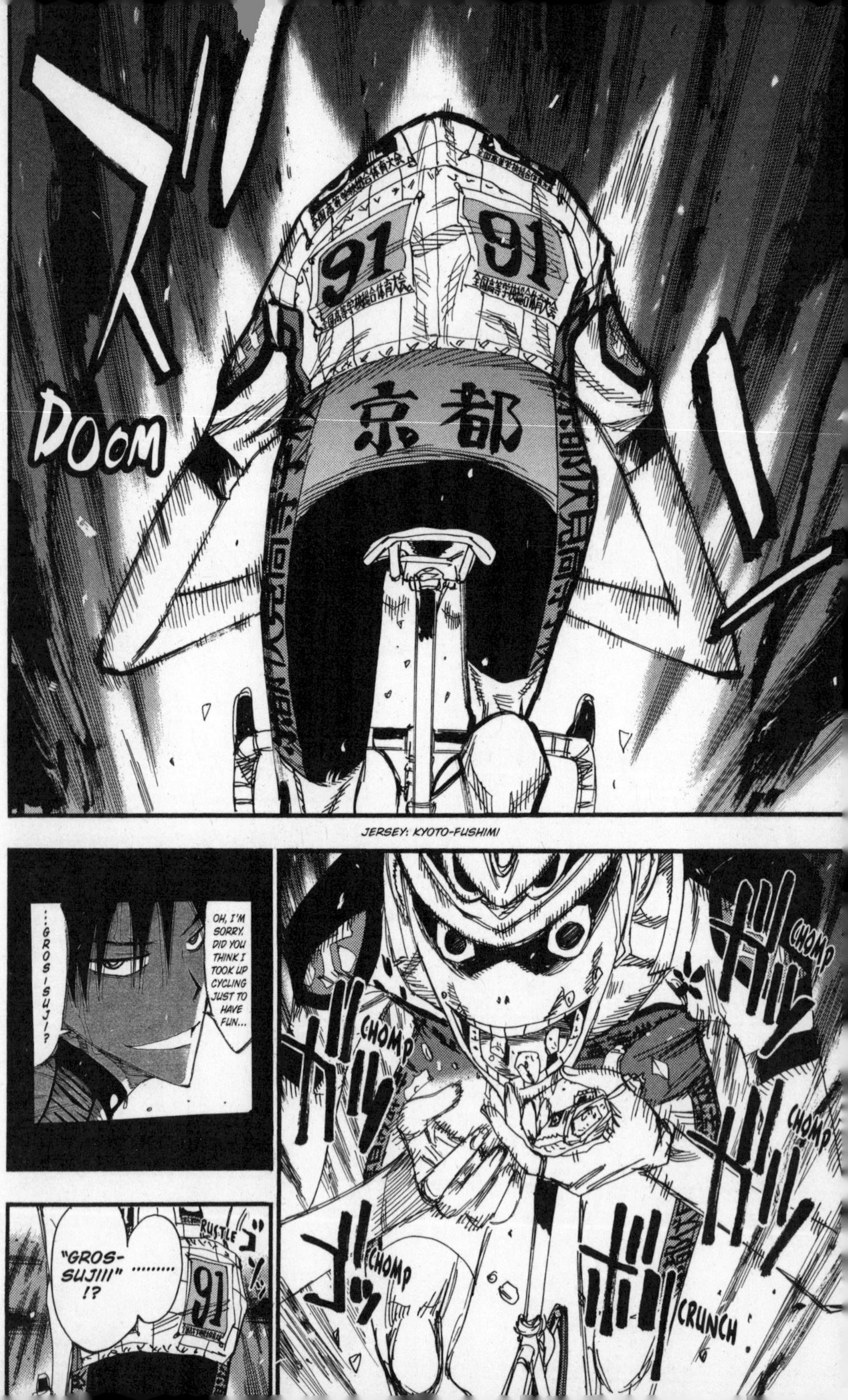
DOOM
JERSEY: KYOTO-FUSHIMI
CHOMP
CHOMP
CHOMP
CHOMP
CRUNCH
OH, I'M SORRY. DID YOU THINK I TOOK UP CYCLING JUST TO HAVE FUN...
...GROSISUJI?
RUSTLE
"GROS-SUJIII" !?
....

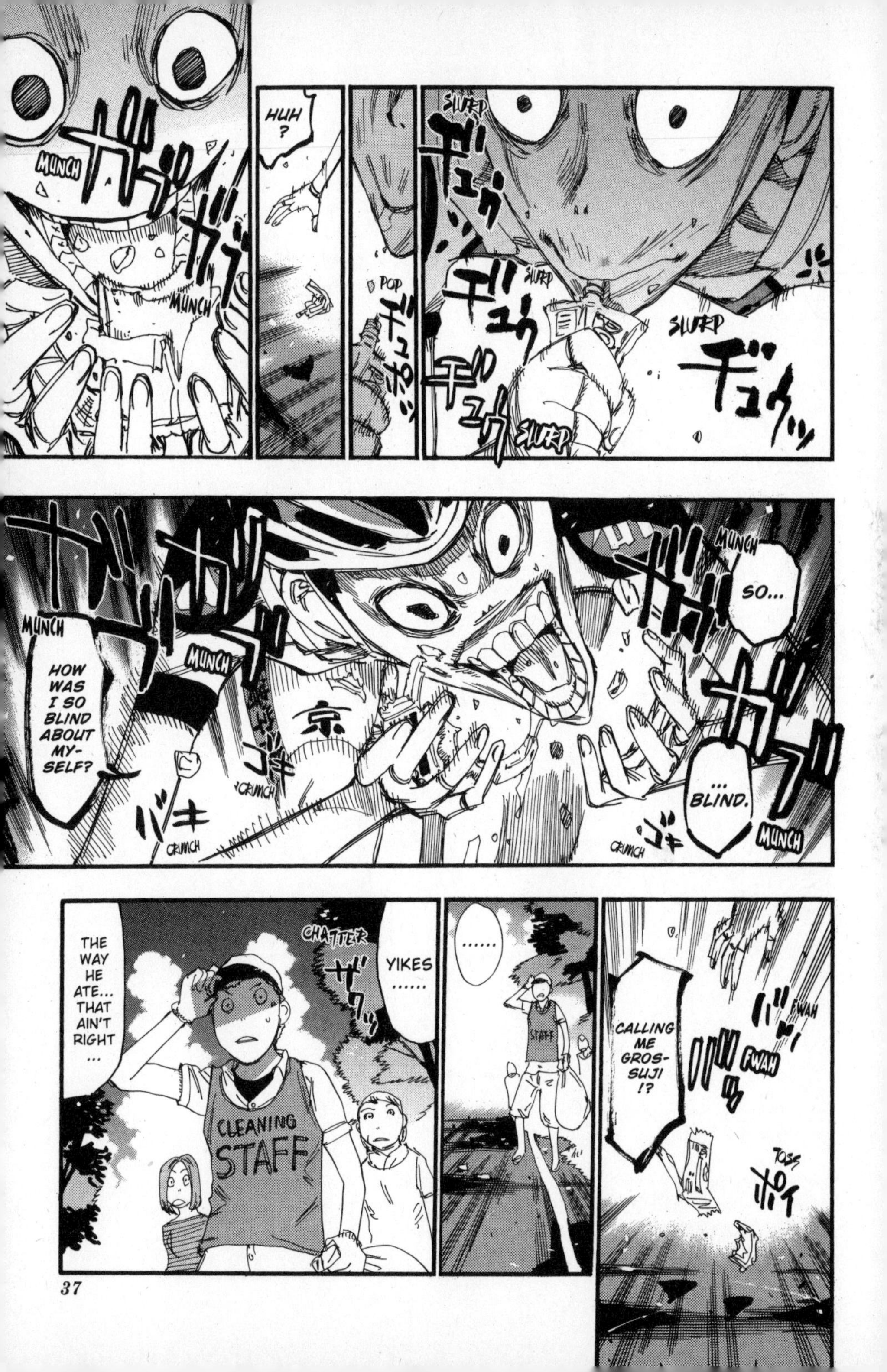
SLURP
SLURP
SLURP
SLURP
POP
HUH?
MUNCH
MUNCH
MUNCH
SO...
...BLIND.
MUNCH
CRUNCH
CRUNCH
MUNCH
HOW WAS I SO BLIND ABOUT MY-SELF?
CRUNCH
MUNCH
CALLING ME GROS-SUJI!?
FWAH
FWAH
TOSS
......
STAFF
YIKES......
CHATTER
THE WAY HE ATE... THAT AIN'T RIGHT...
CLEANING STAFF

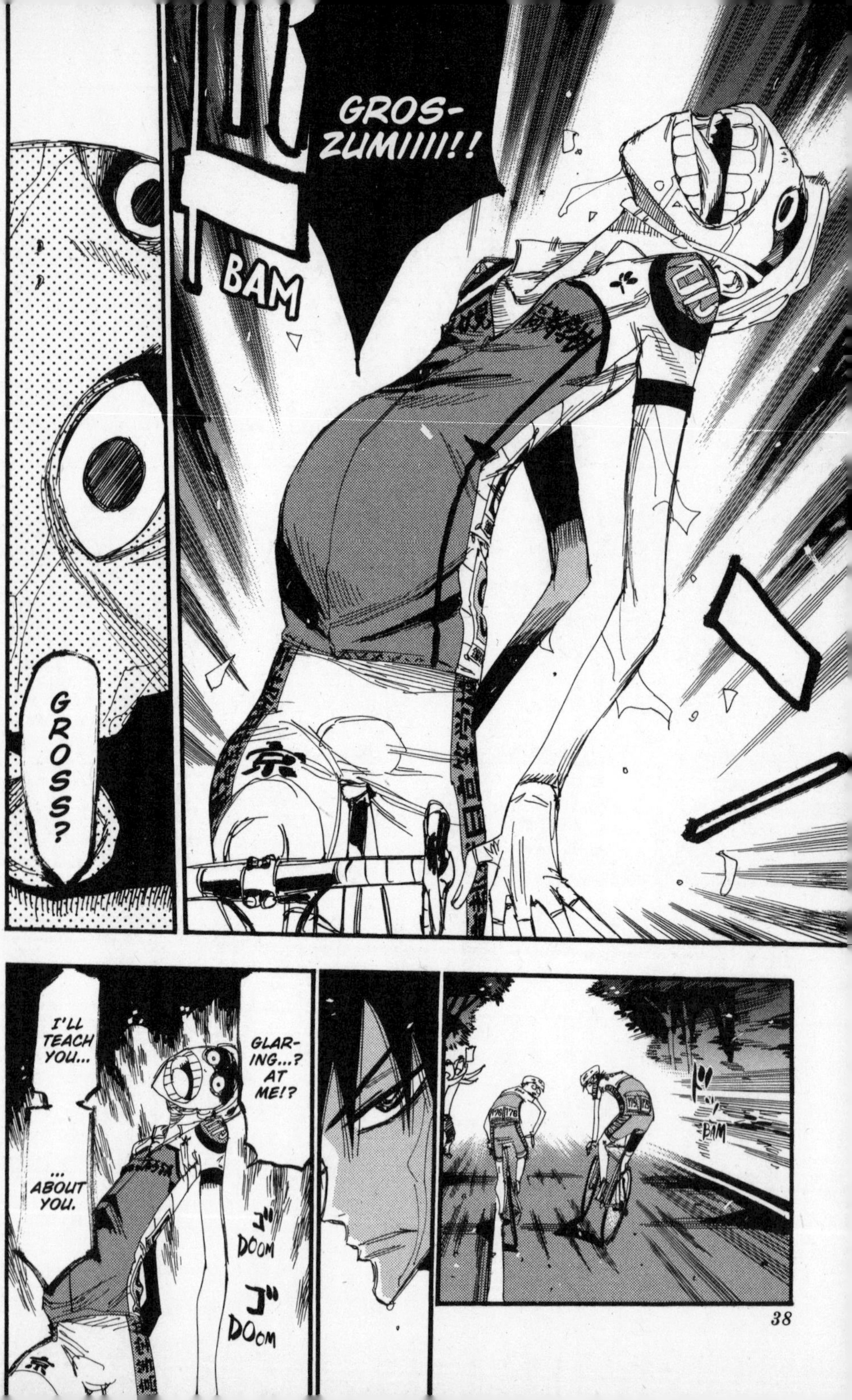
GROS-
ZUMI!!!!!!
BAM
GROSS?
ド
BAM
GLAR-
ING...?
AT
ME!?
ゴ
DOOM
ゴ
DOOM
I'LL
TEACH
YOU...
...
ABOUT
YOU.

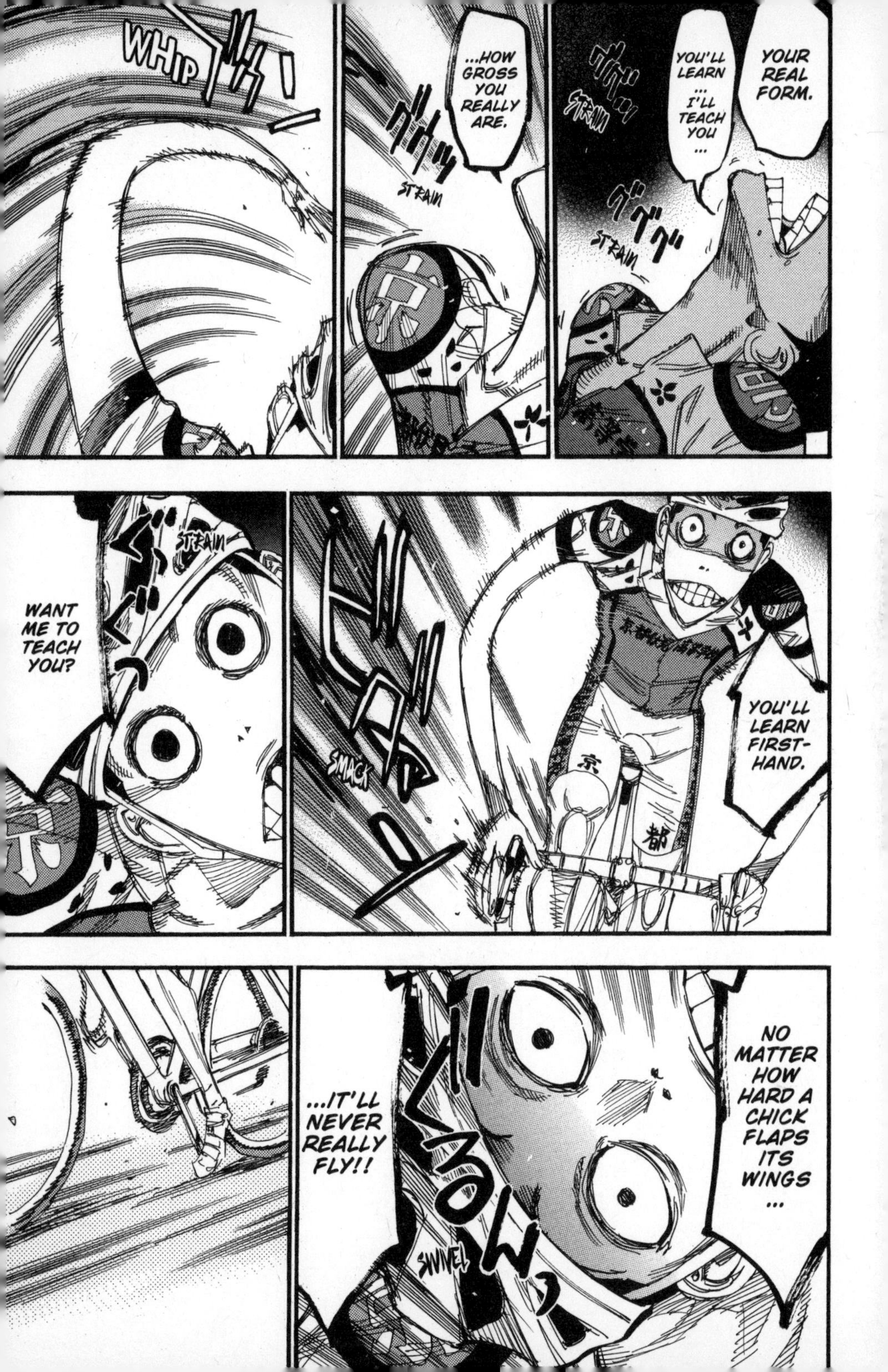
YOUR REAL FORM.
YOU'LL LEARN ... I'LL TEACH YOU ...
STRAIN
STRAIN
...HOW GROSS YOU REALLY ARE.
STRAIN
WHIP
YOU'LL LEARN FIRST-HAND.
SMACK
WANT ME TO TEACH YOU?
STRAIN
NO MATTER HOW HARD A CHICK FLAPS ITS WINGS ...
...IT'LL NEVER REALLY FLY!!
SWIVEL

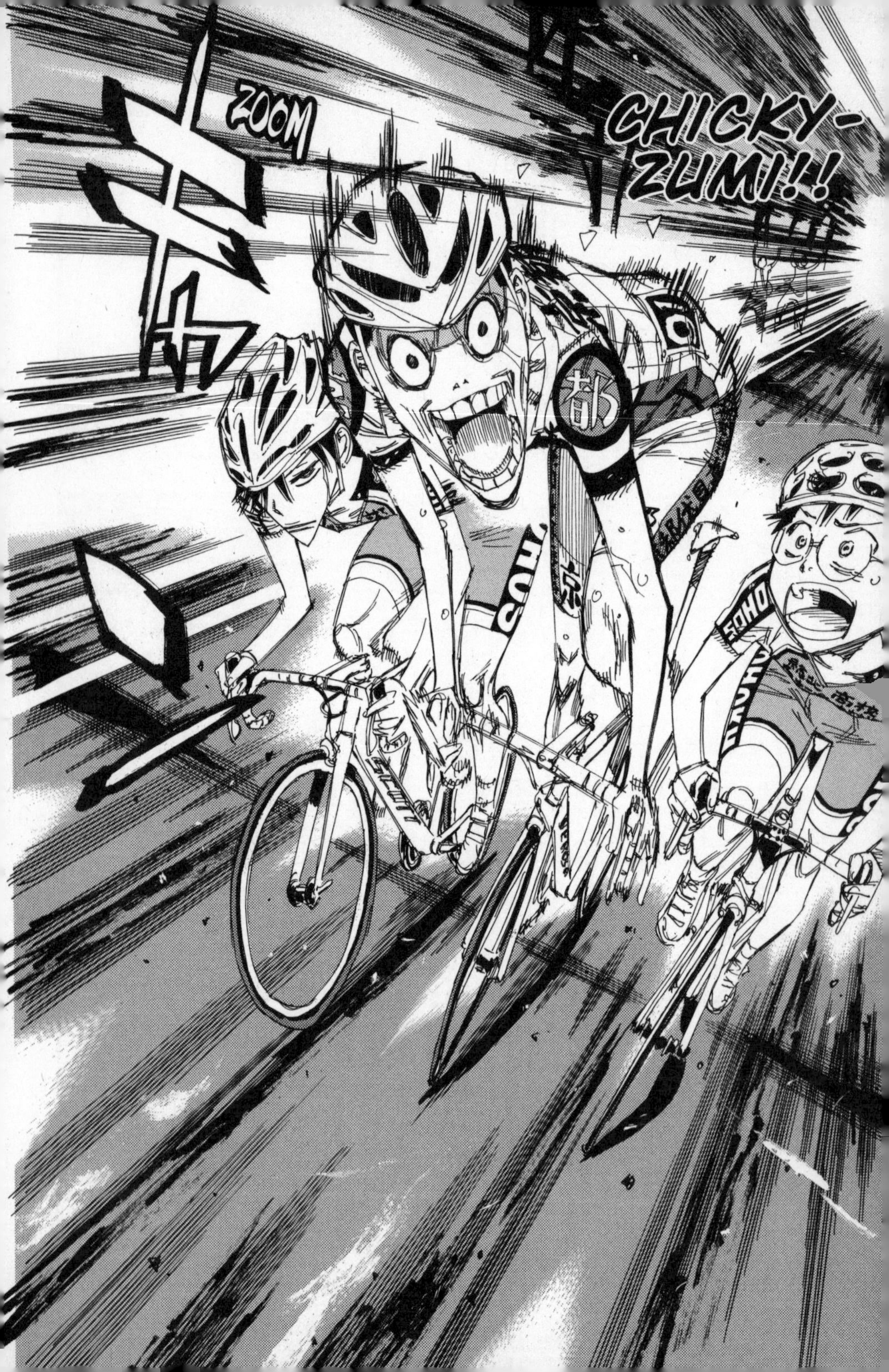
CHICKY-ZUMI!!
ZOOM

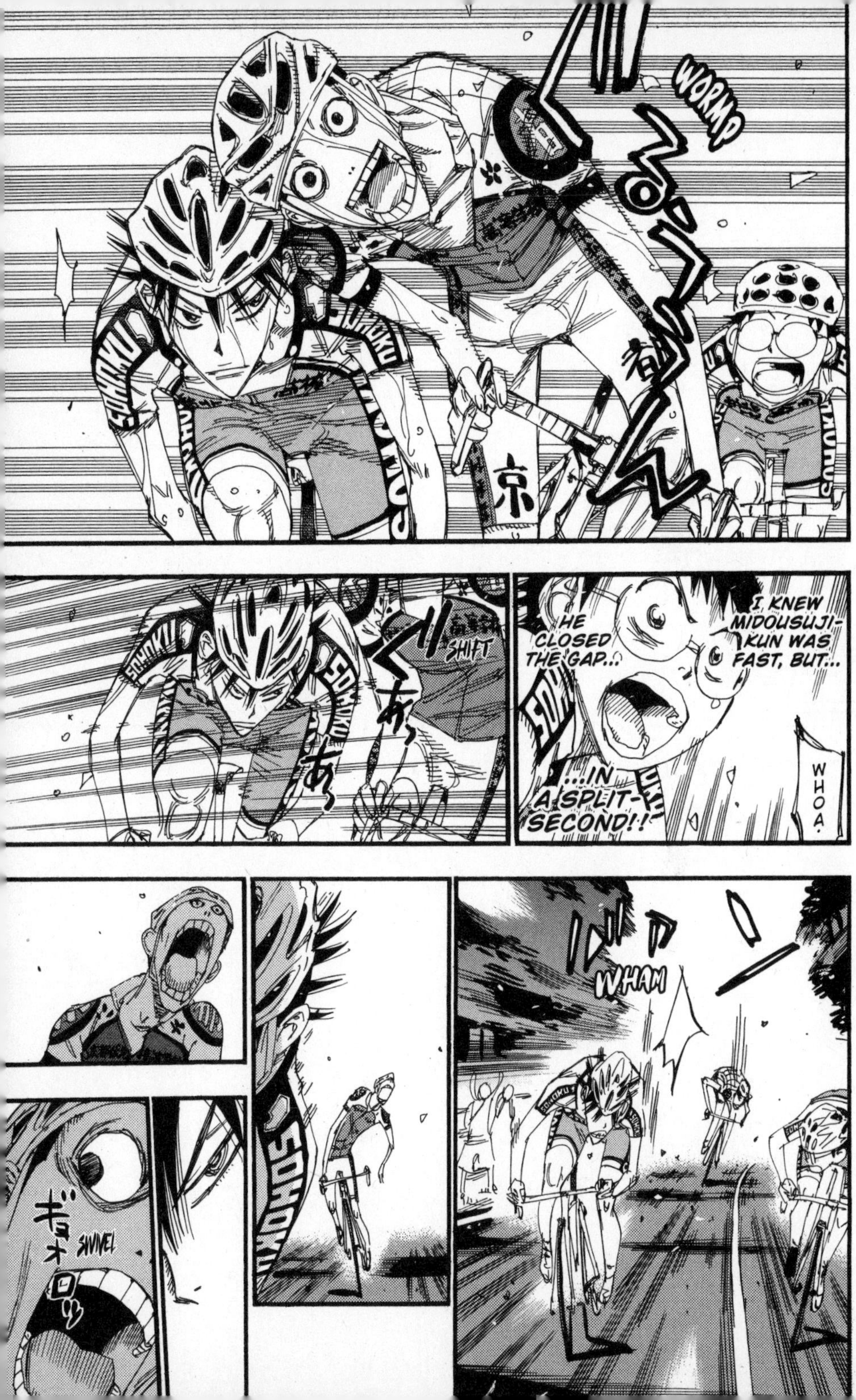

WORMP
SHIFT
I KNEW MIDOUSUJI-KUN WAS FAST, BUT...
HE CLOSED THE GAP...
WHOA.
...IN A SPLIT-SECOND!!
WHAM
SWIVEL

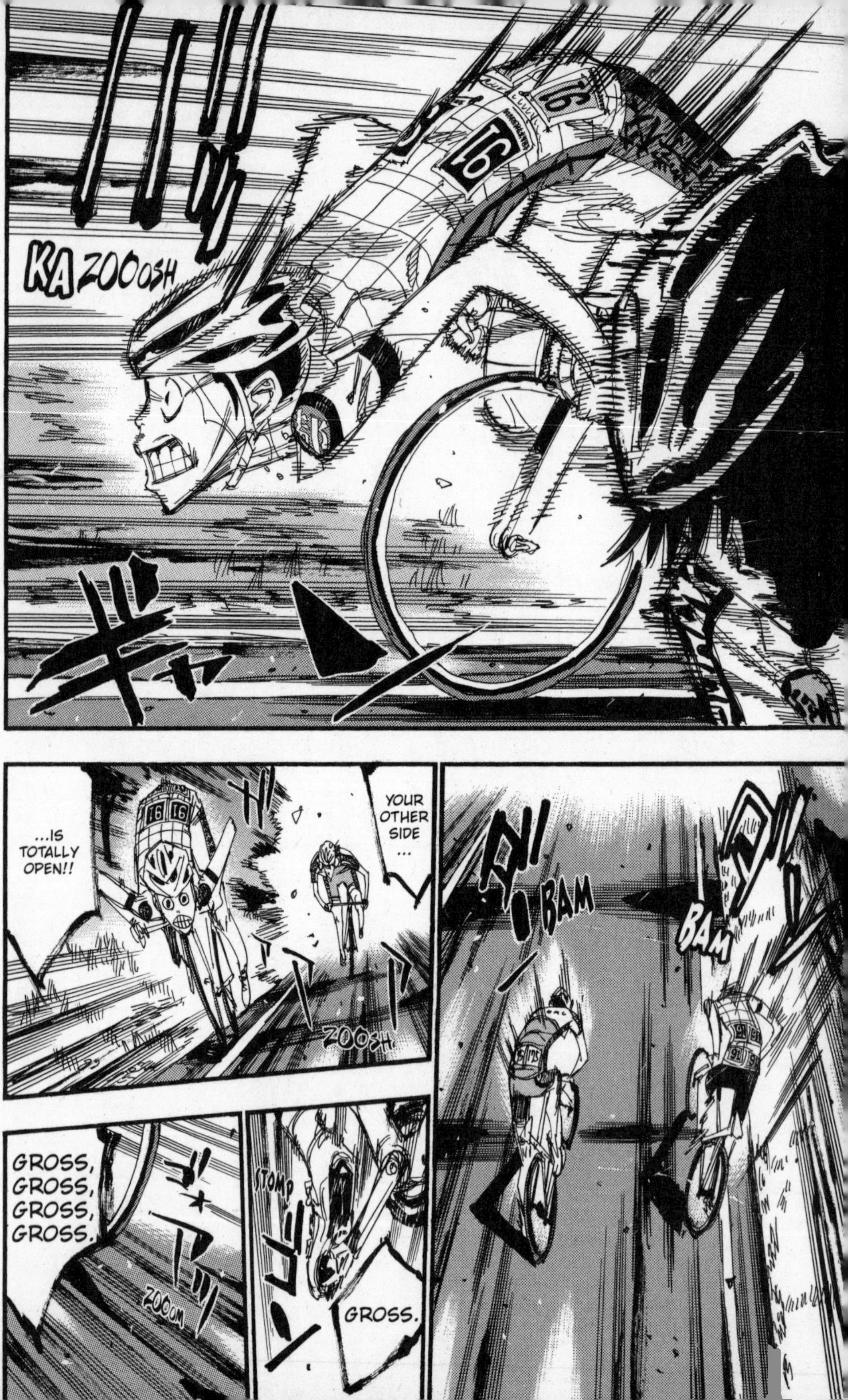
KAZOOOSH
BAM
BAM
YOUR OTHER SIDE ...
...IS TOTALLY OPEN!!
ZOOSH
STOMP
GROSS.
GROSS, GROSS, GROSS, GROSS.
ZOOM

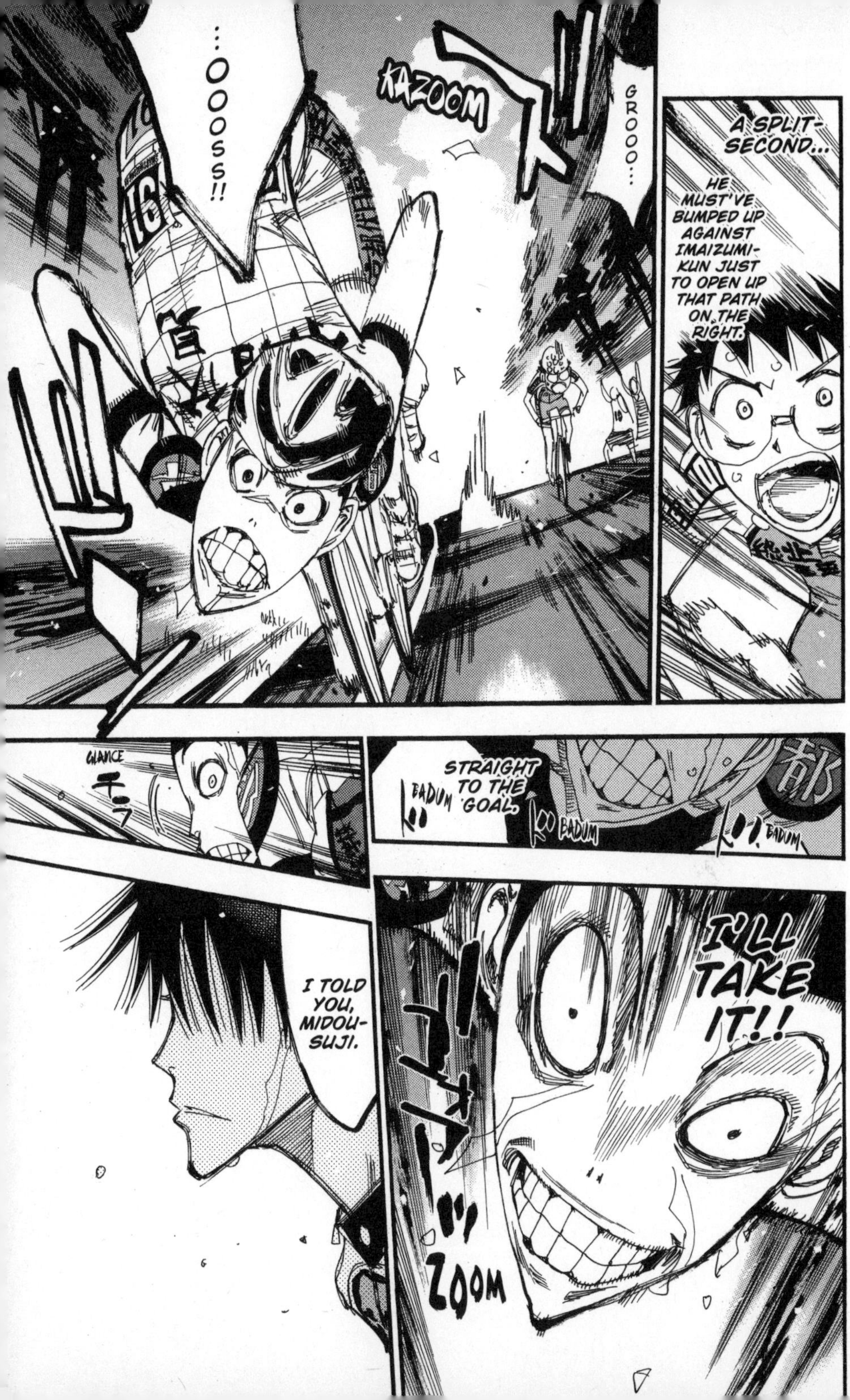
A SPLIT-SECOND...
HE MUST'VE BUMPED UP AGAINST IMAIZUMI-KUN JUST TO OPEN UP THAT PATH ON THE RIGHT.
GROOO...
KAZOOM
...OOOSS!!
BADUM
BADUM
STRAIGHT TO THE GOAL.
BADUM
GLANCE
I'LL TAKE IT!!
ZOOM
I TOLD YOU, MIDOU-SUJI.

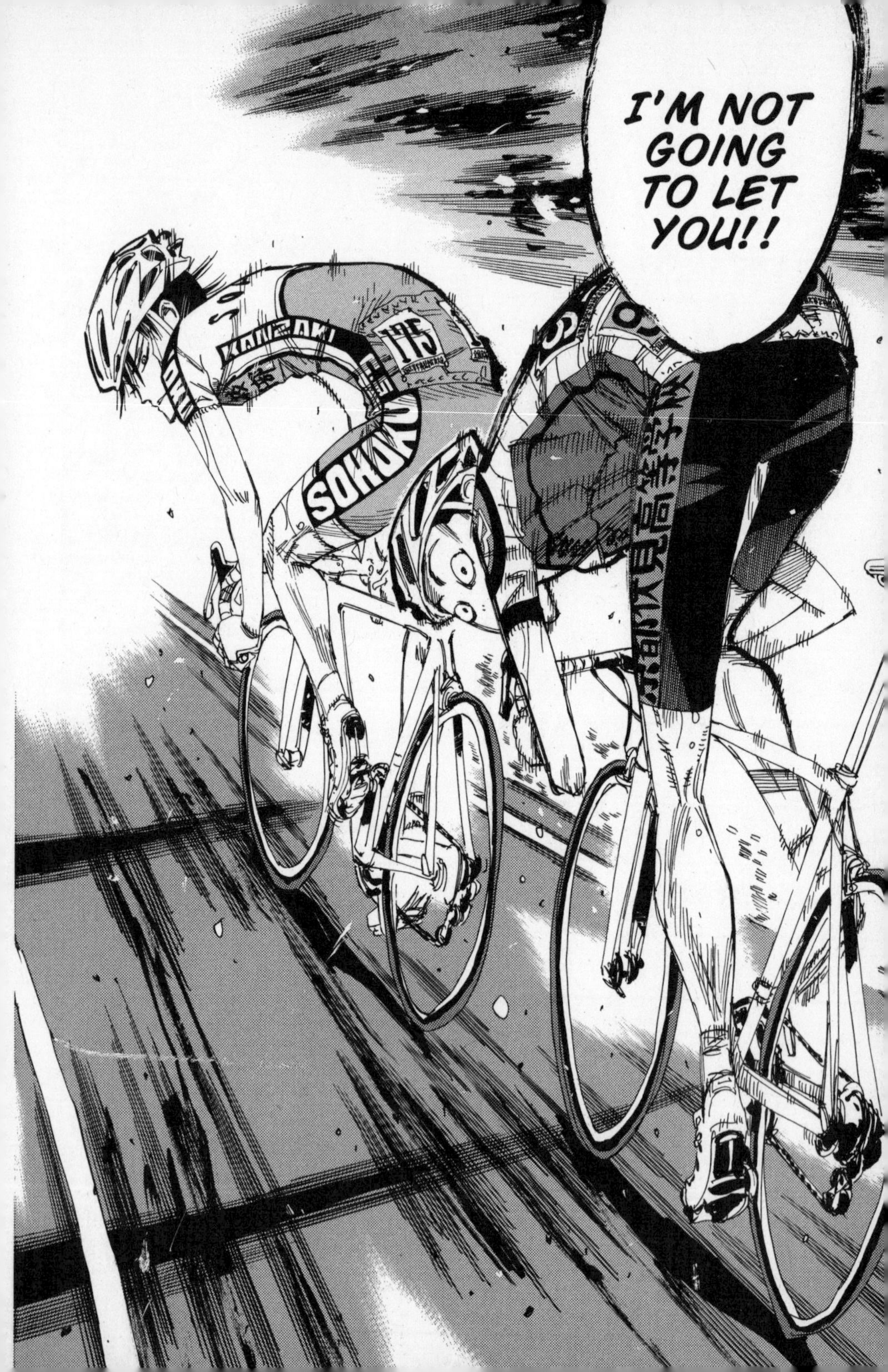
I'M NOT GOING TO LET YOU!!

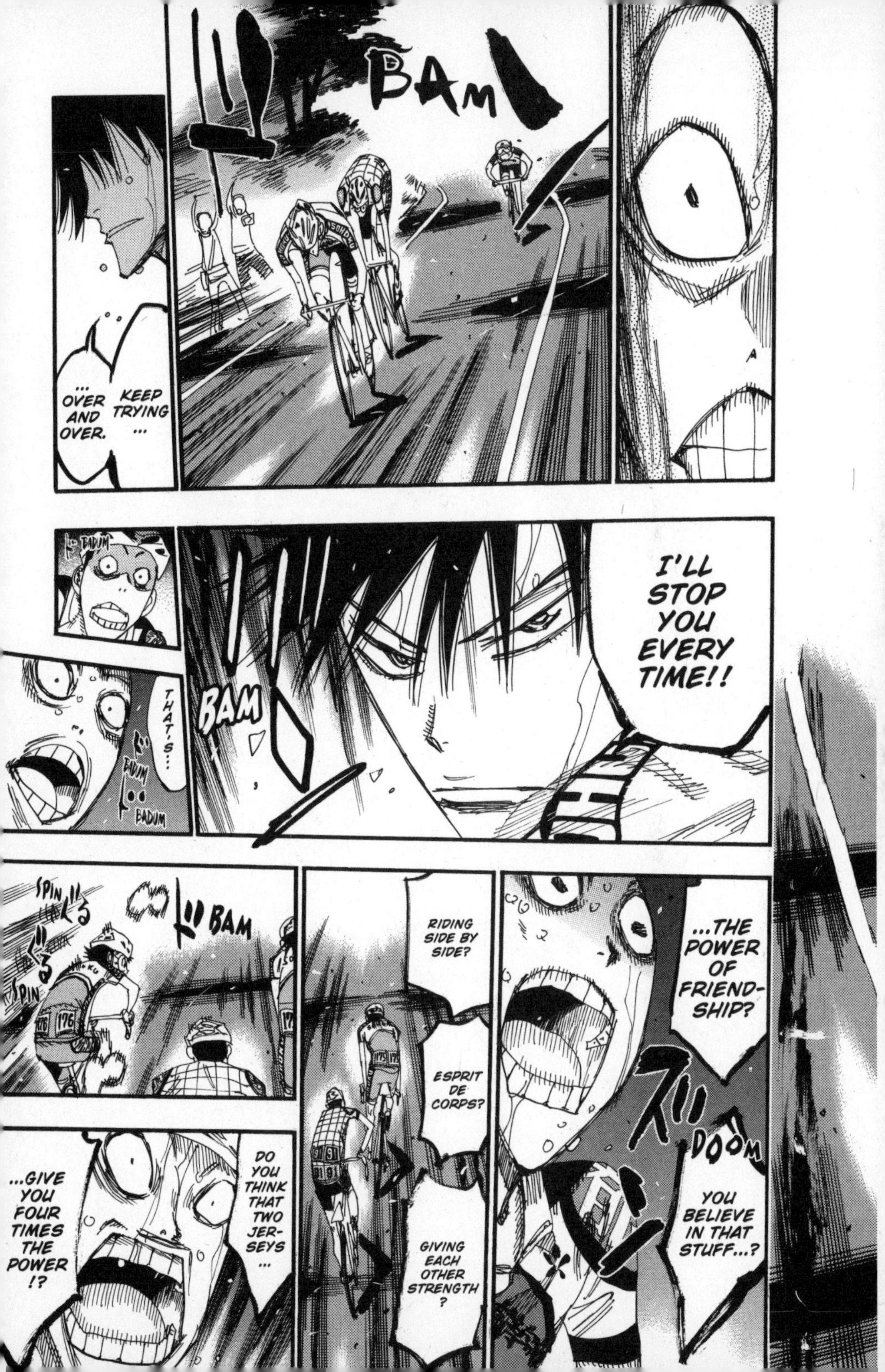
BAM
KEEP TRYING...
...OVER AND OVER.
I'LL STOP YOU EVERY TIME!!
BAM
BADUM
THAT'S...
BADUM
BADUM
...THE POWER OF FRIEND-SHIP?
DOOM
YOU BELIEVE IN THAT STUFF...?
RIDING SIDE BY SIDE?
ESPRIT DE CORPS?
GIVING EACH OTHER STRENGTH?
SPIN
SPIN
BAM
DO YOU THINK THAT TWO JER-SEYS...
...GIVE YOU FOUR TIMES THE POWER!?

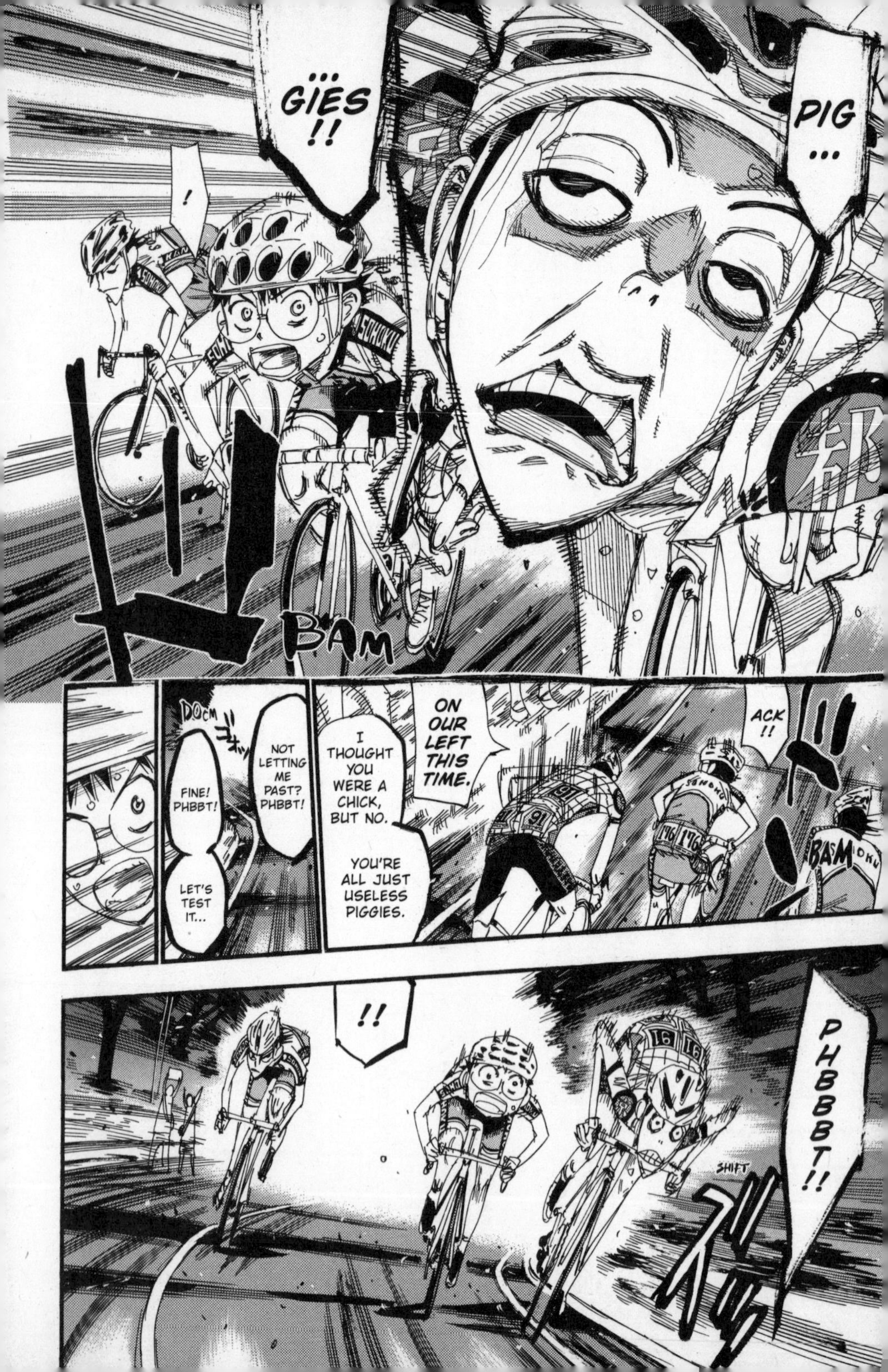
PIG...
...GIES!!
!
BAM
ACK!!
BAM
ON OUR LEFT THIS TIME.
I THOUGHT YOU WERE A CHICK, BUT NO.
YOU'RE ALL JUST USELESS PIGGIES.
DOOM
NOT LETTING ME PAST? PHBBT!
FINE! PHBBT!
LET'S TEST IT...
PHBBBT!!
SHIFT
!!

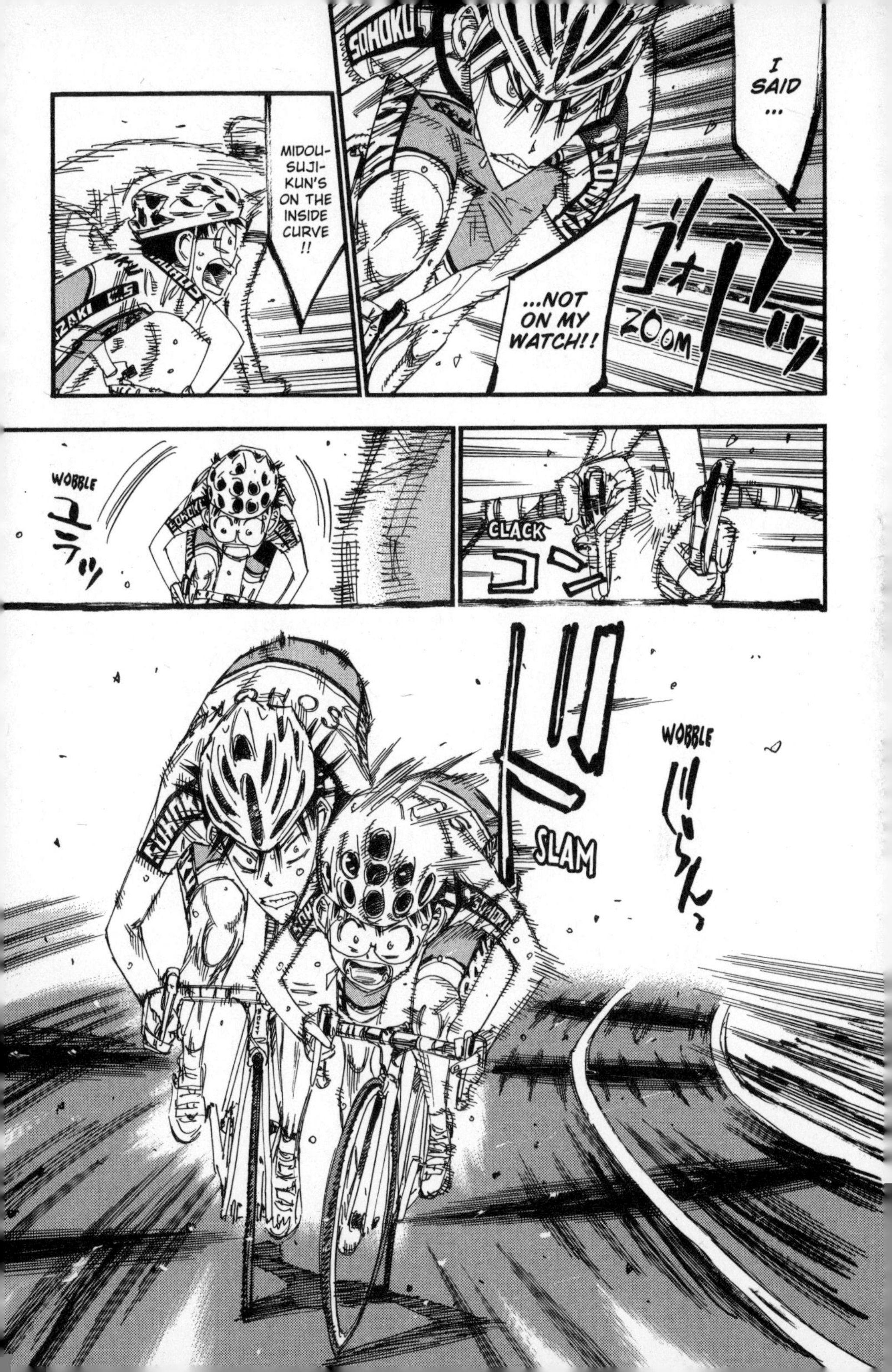
I SAID ...
...NOT ON MY WATCH!!
ZOOM
MIDOU-SUJI-KUN'S ON THE INSIDE CURVE !!
CLACK
WOBBLE
SLAM
WOBBLE

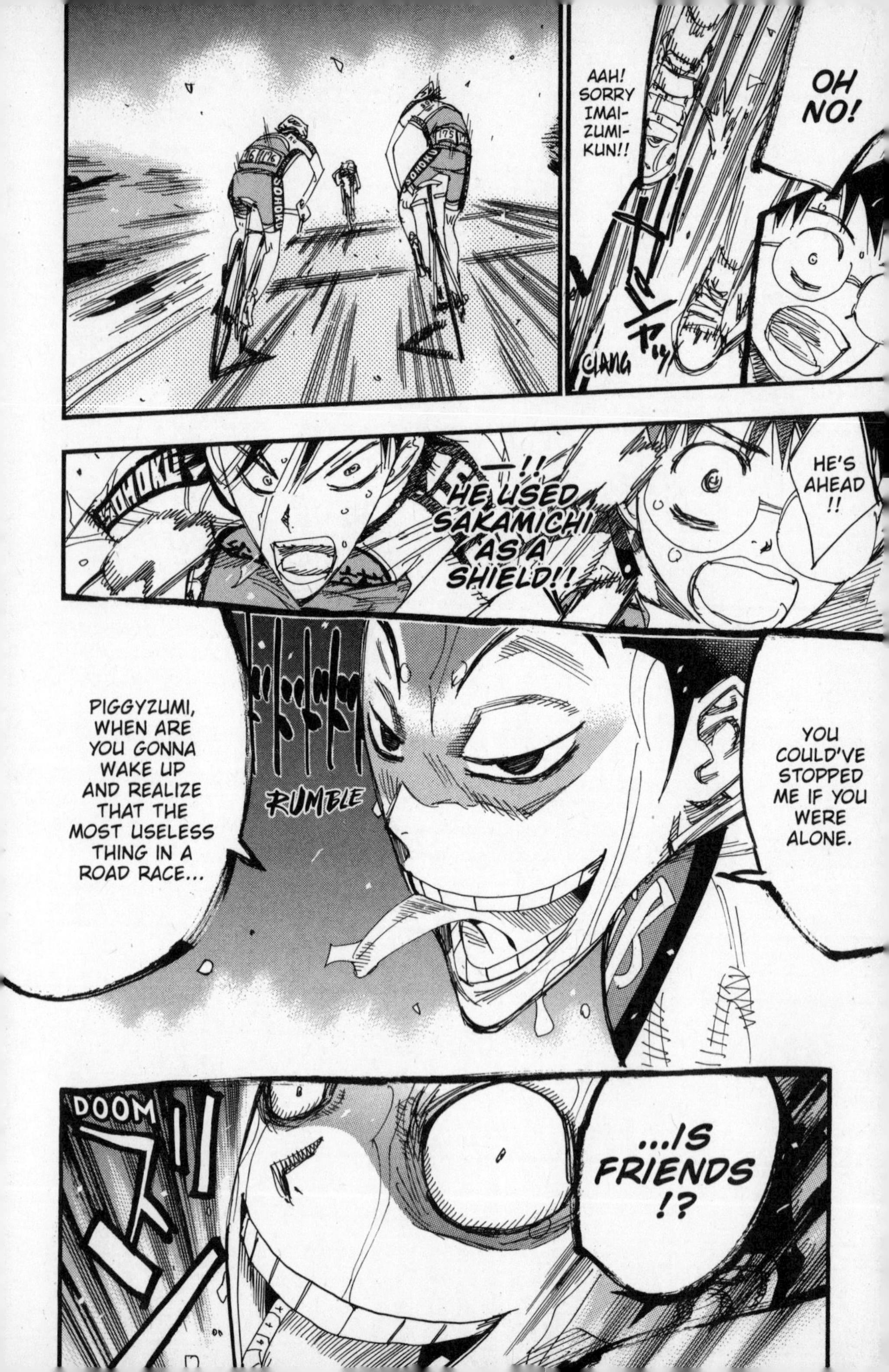
OH NO!
AAH! SORRY IMAIZUMI-KUN!!
CLANG
HE'S AHEAD!!
—!! HE USED SAKAMICHI AS A SHIELD!!
YOU COULD'VE STOPPED ME IF YOU WERE ALONE.
PIGGYZUMI, WHEN ARE YOU GONNA WAKE UP AND REALIZE THAT THE MOST USELESS THING IN A ROAD RACE...
RUMBLE
...IS FRIENDS!?
DOOM

RIDE.210 THE TIES THEY SHARE

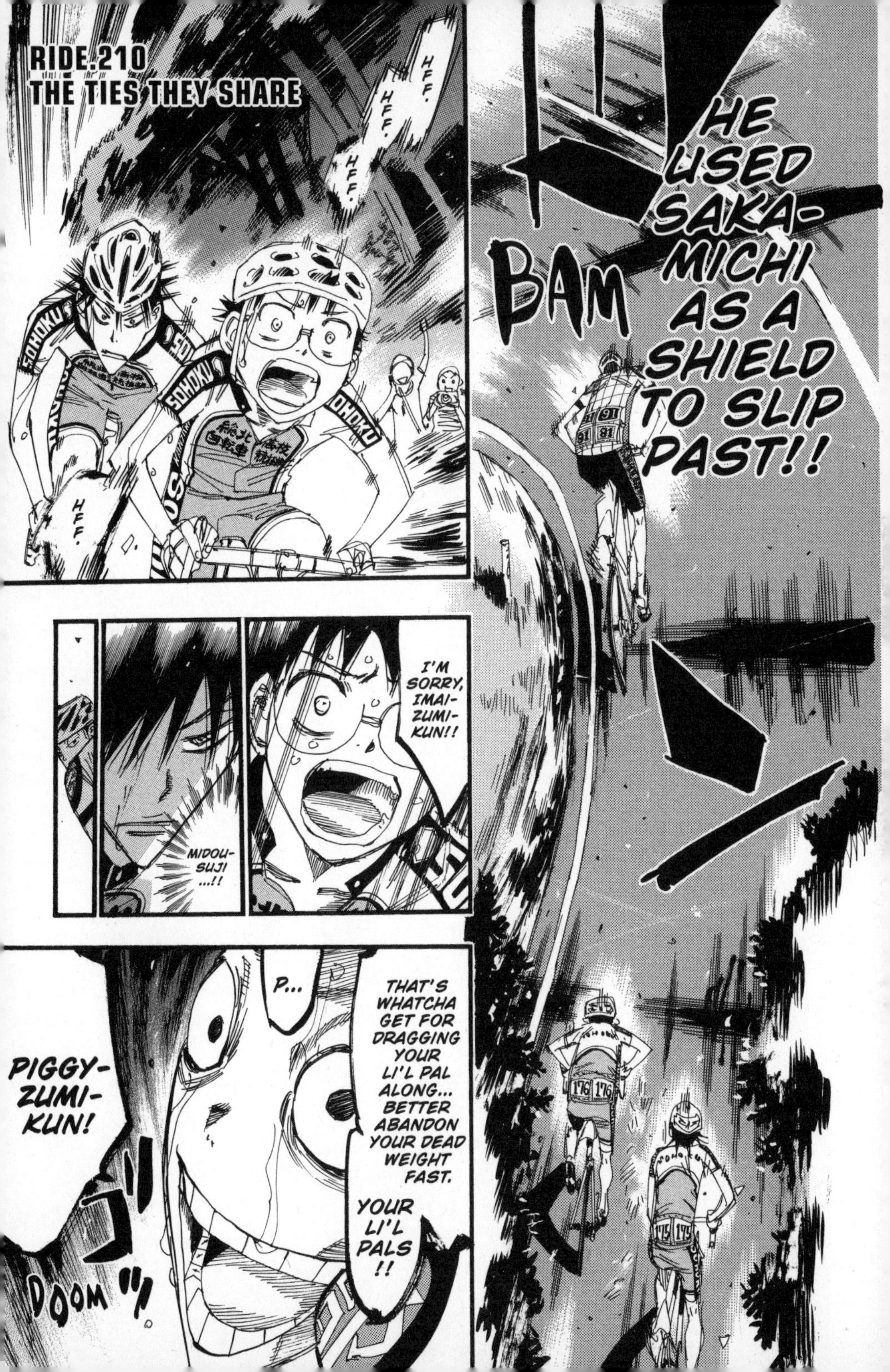
HE USED SAKA-MICHI AS A SHIELD TO SLIP PAST!!
BAM
HFF.
HFF.
HFF.
HFF.
HFF.
I'M SORRY, IMAI-ZUMI-KUN!!
MIDOU-SUJI ...!!
THAT'S WHATCHA GET FOR DRAGGING YOUR LI'L PAL ALONG... BETTER ABANDON YOUR DEAD WEIGHT FAST.
YOUR LI'L PALS !!
P...
PIGGY-ZUMI-KUN!
DOOM

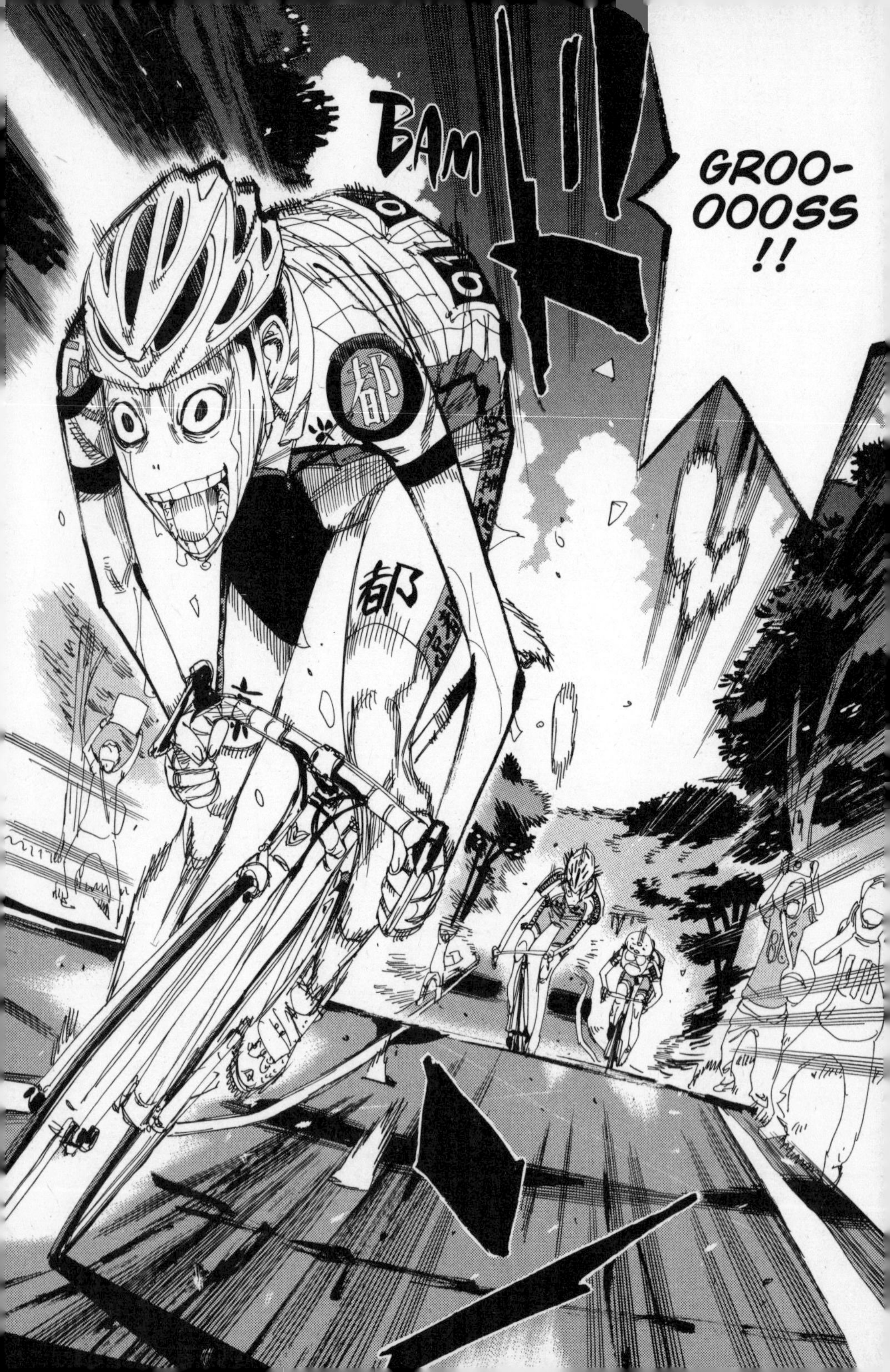
BAM
GROO-
OOOSS
!!

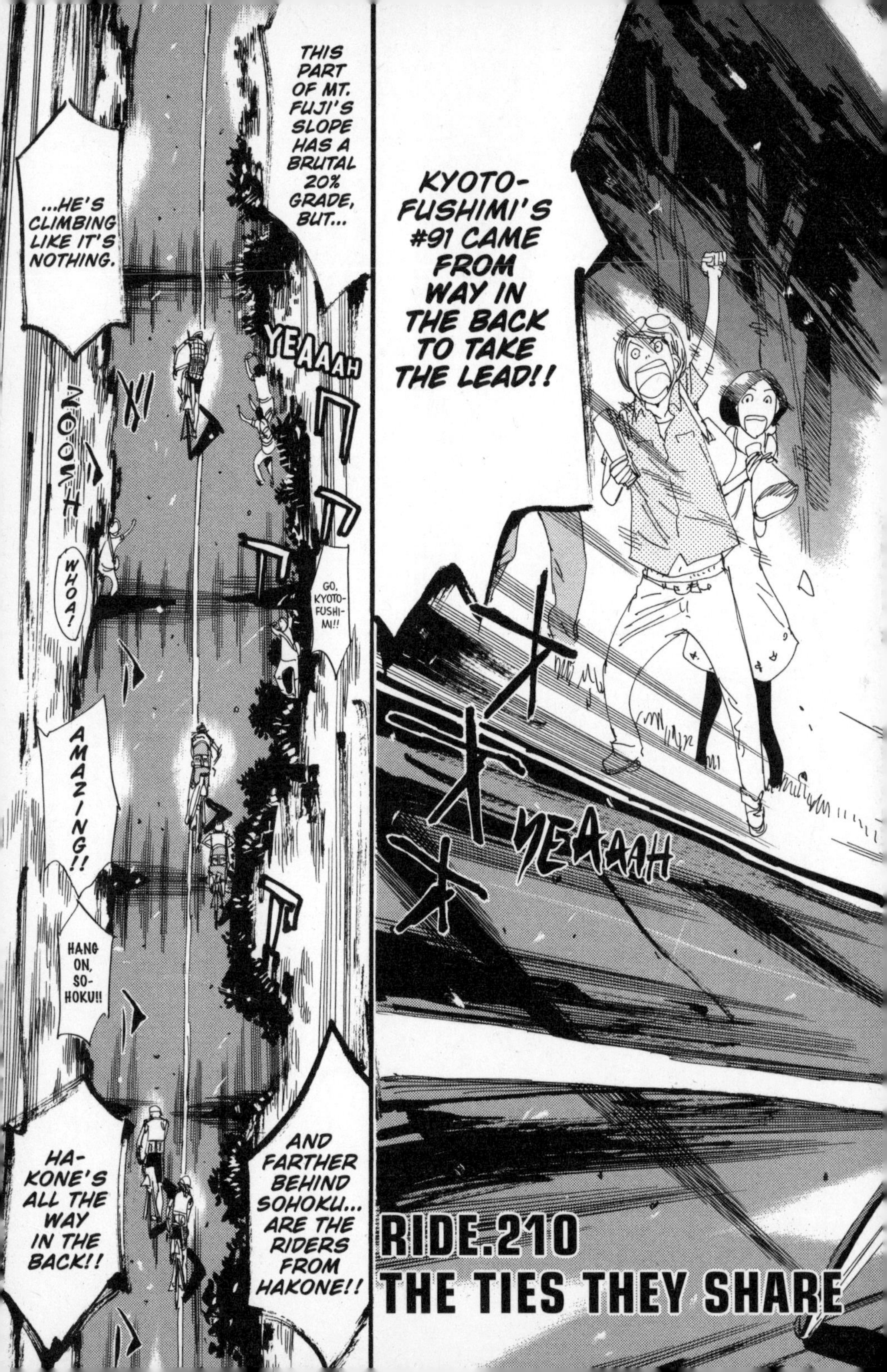
KYOTO-FUSHIMI'S #91 CAME FROM WAY IN THE BACK TO TAKE THE LEAD!!
YEAAAH
RIDE.210
THE TIES THEY SHARE
THIS PART OF MT. FUJI'S SLOPE HAS A BRUTAL 20% GRADE, BUT...
...HE'S CLIMBING LIKE IT'S NOTHING.
YEAAAH
ZOOSH
WHOA!
GO, KYOTO-FUSHIMI!!
AMAZING!!
HANG ON, SO-HOKU!!
AND FARTHER BEHIND SOHOKU... ARE THE RIDERS FROM HAKONE!!
HA-KONE'S ALL THE WAY IN THE BACK!!

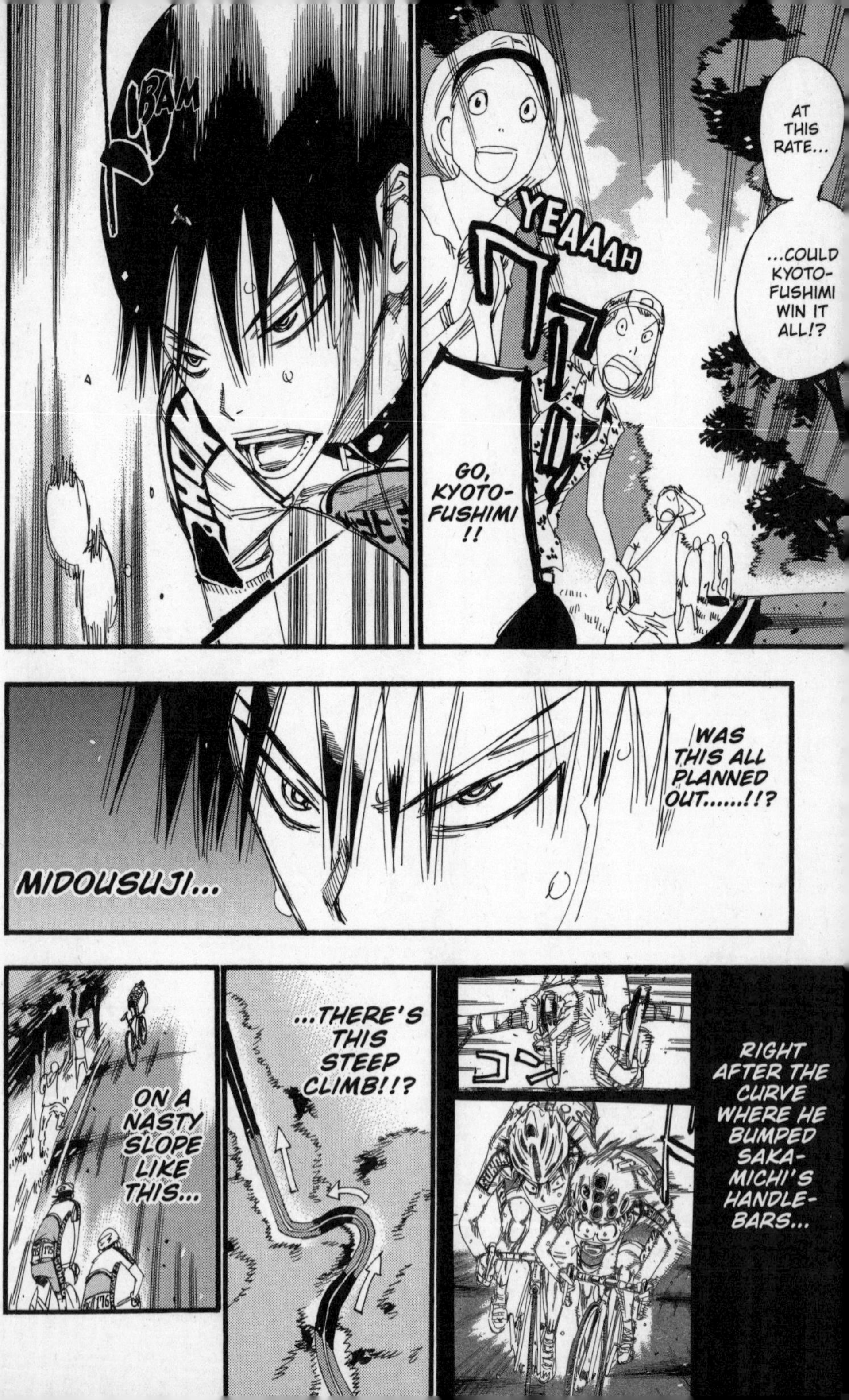
AT THIS RATE...
...COULD KYOTO-FUSHIMI WIN IT ALL!?
YEAAAAH
GO, KYOTO-FUSHIMI!!
BAM
WAS THIS ALL PLANNED OUT......!!?
MIDOUSUJI...
RIGHT AFTER THE CURVE WHERE HE BUMPED SAKAMICHI'S HANDLEBARS...
...THERE'S THIS STEEP CLIMB!!?
ON A NASTY SLOPE LIKE THIS...

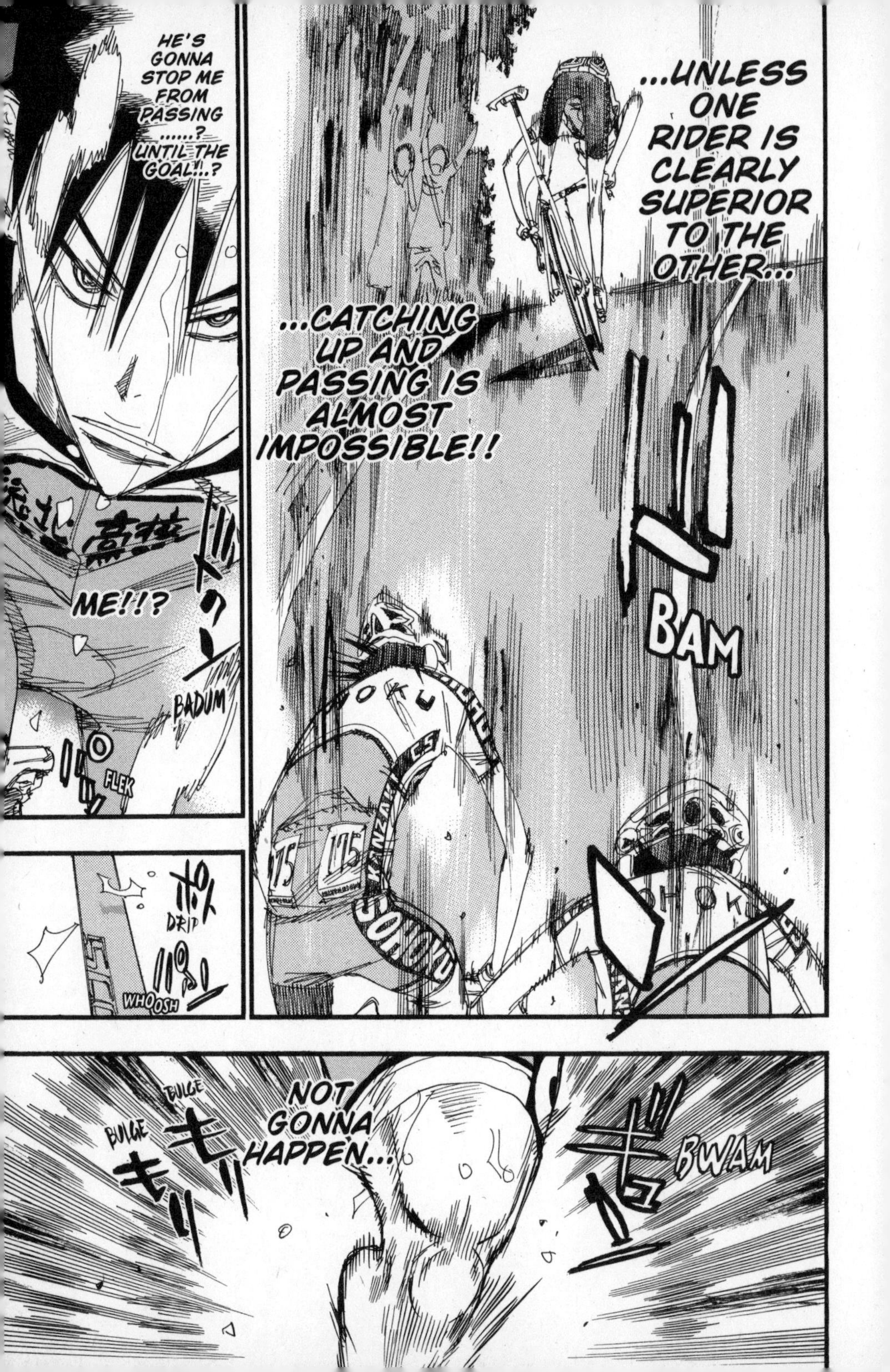
...UNLESS ONE RIDER IS CLEARLY SUPERIOR TO THE OTHER...
...CATCHING UP AND PASSING IS ALMOST IMPOSSIBLE!!
BAM
HE'S GONNA STOP ME FROM PASSING ......? UNTIL THE GOAL...?
ME!!?
BADUM
FLEK
DRIP
WHOOSH
BWAM
NOT GONNA HAPPEN...
BULGE
BULGE

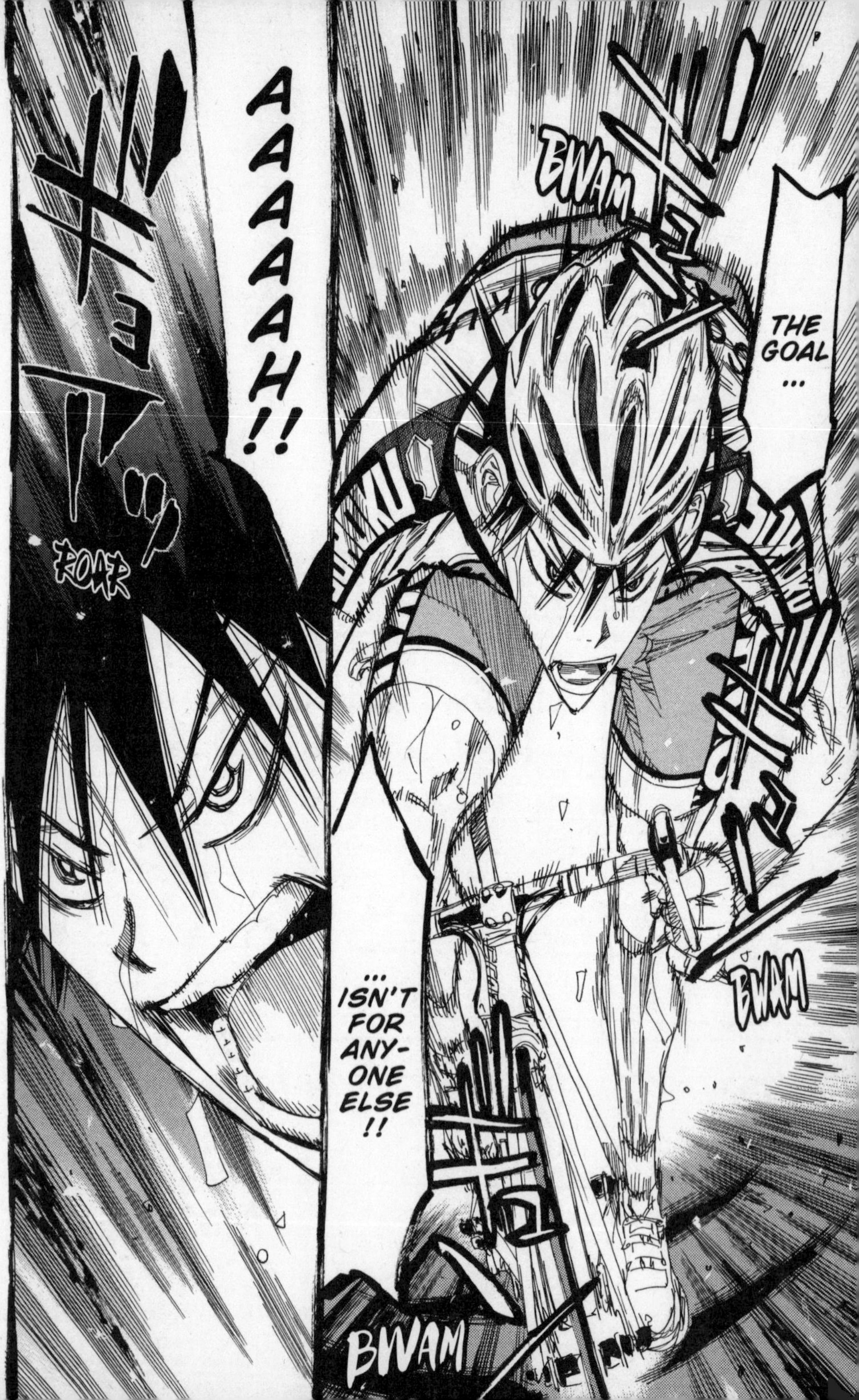
BWAM
THE GOAL ...
BWAM
... ISN'T FOR ANY-ONE ELSE !!
BWAM
AAAAAAH!!
ROAR

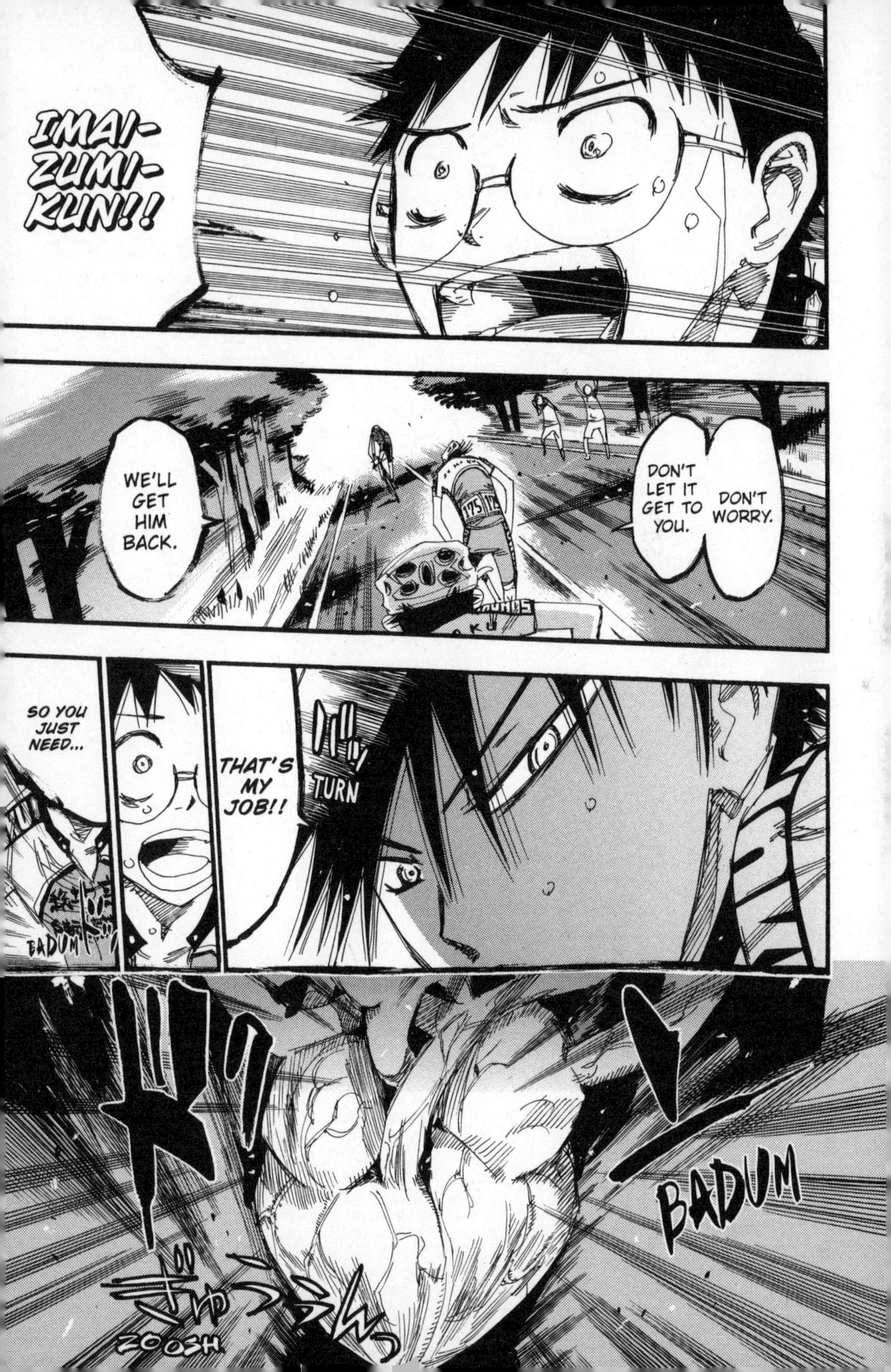
IMAI-ZUMI-KUN!!
DON'T WORRY.
DON'T LET IT GET TO YOU.
WE'LL GET HIM BACK.
TURN
THAT'S MY JOB!!
SO YOU JUST NEED...
BADUM
BADUM
ZOOSH

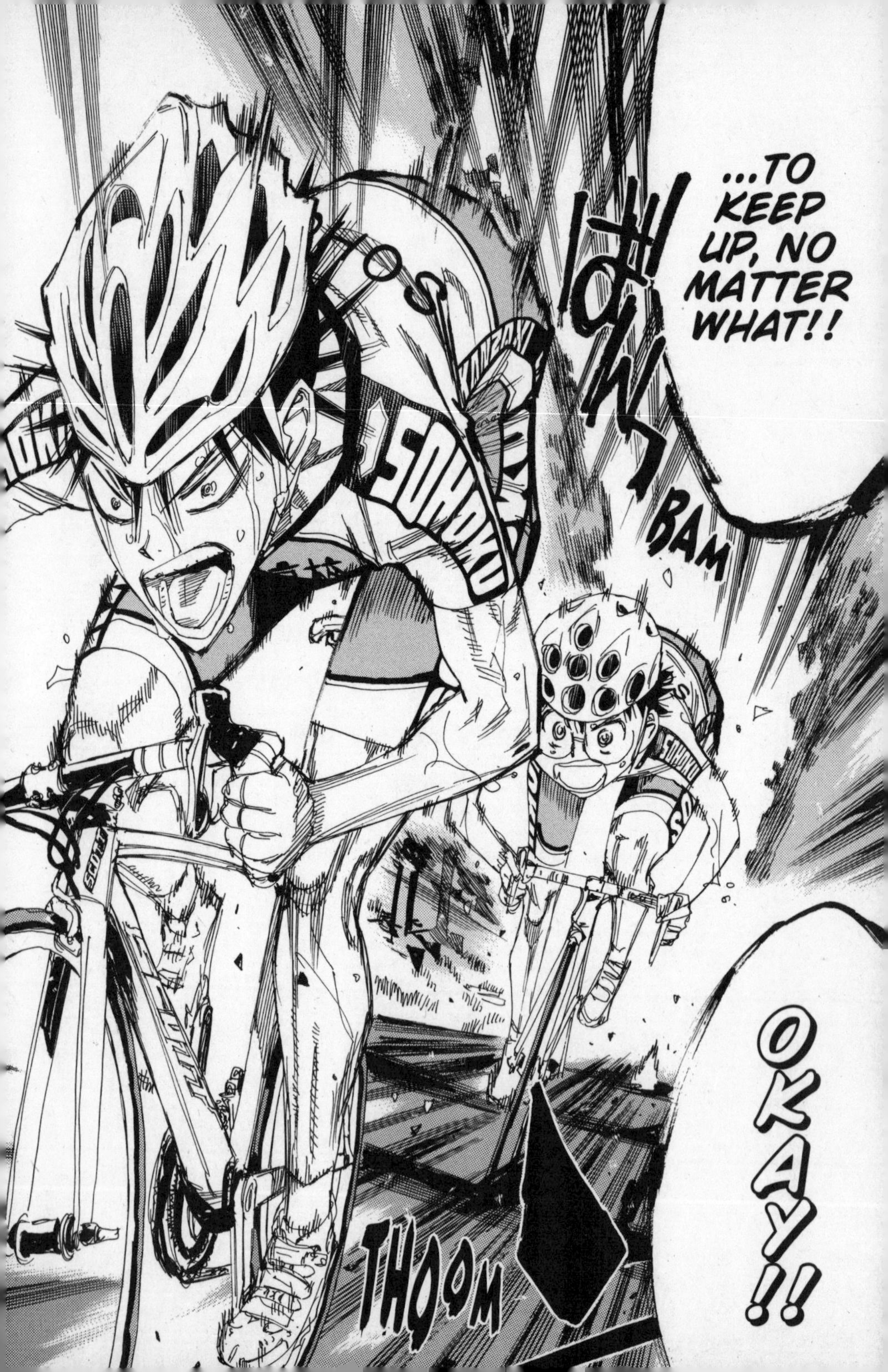
...TO KEEP UP, NO MATTER WHAT!!
BAM
OKAY!!
THOOM

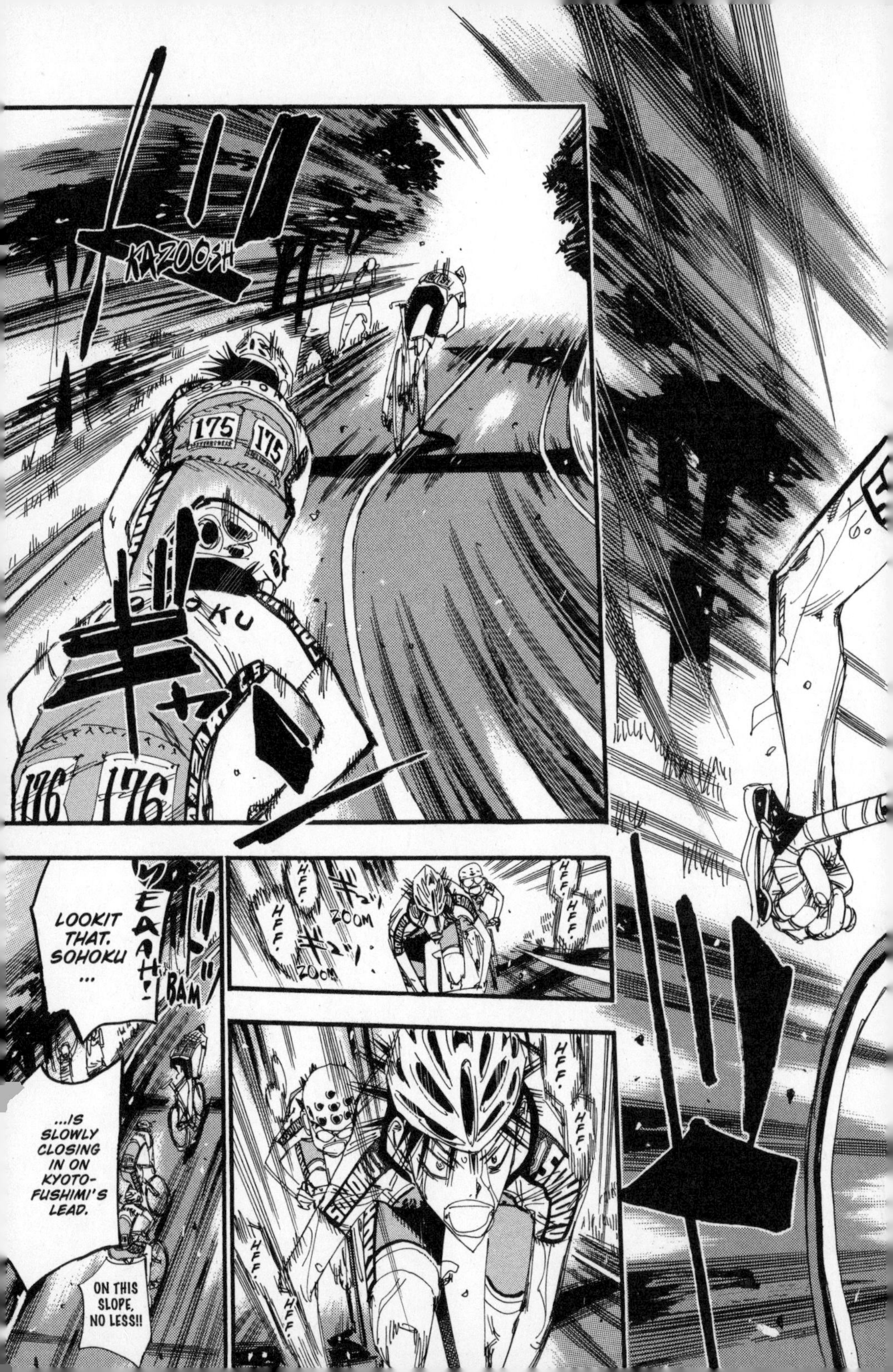
KAZOOSH
HFF. HFF.
HFF. HFF.
ZOOM
ZOOM
HFF. HFF.
HFF. HFF.
YEAAAH!!
BAM
LOOKIT THAT. SOHOKU ...
...IS SLOWLY CLOSING IN ON KYOTO-FUSHIMI'S LEAD.
ON THIS SLOPE, NO LESS!!

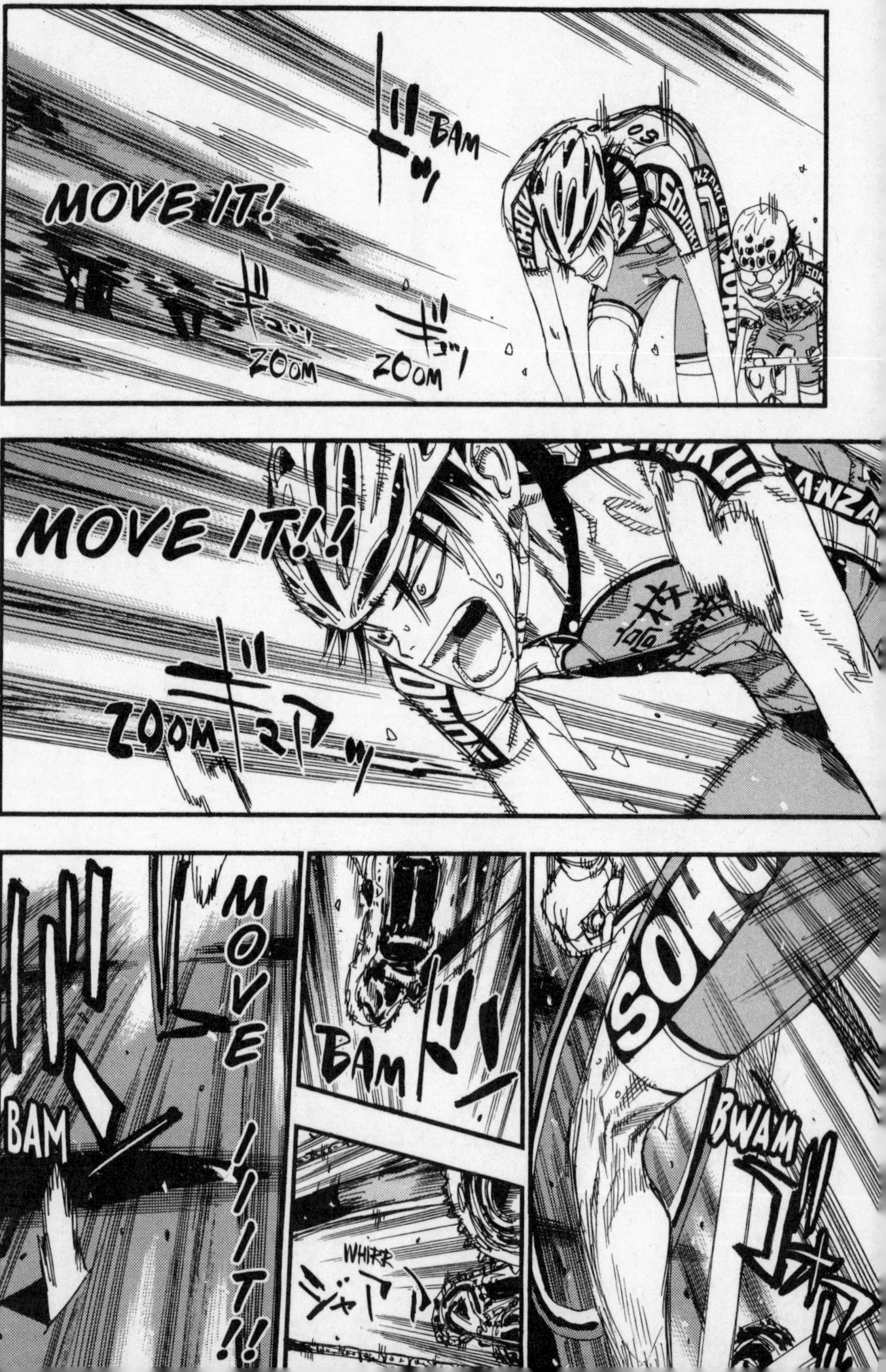
BAM
MOVE IT!
ZOOM
ZOOM
MOVE IT!!
ZOOM
BWAM
BAM
WHIRR
MOVE IT!!
BAM

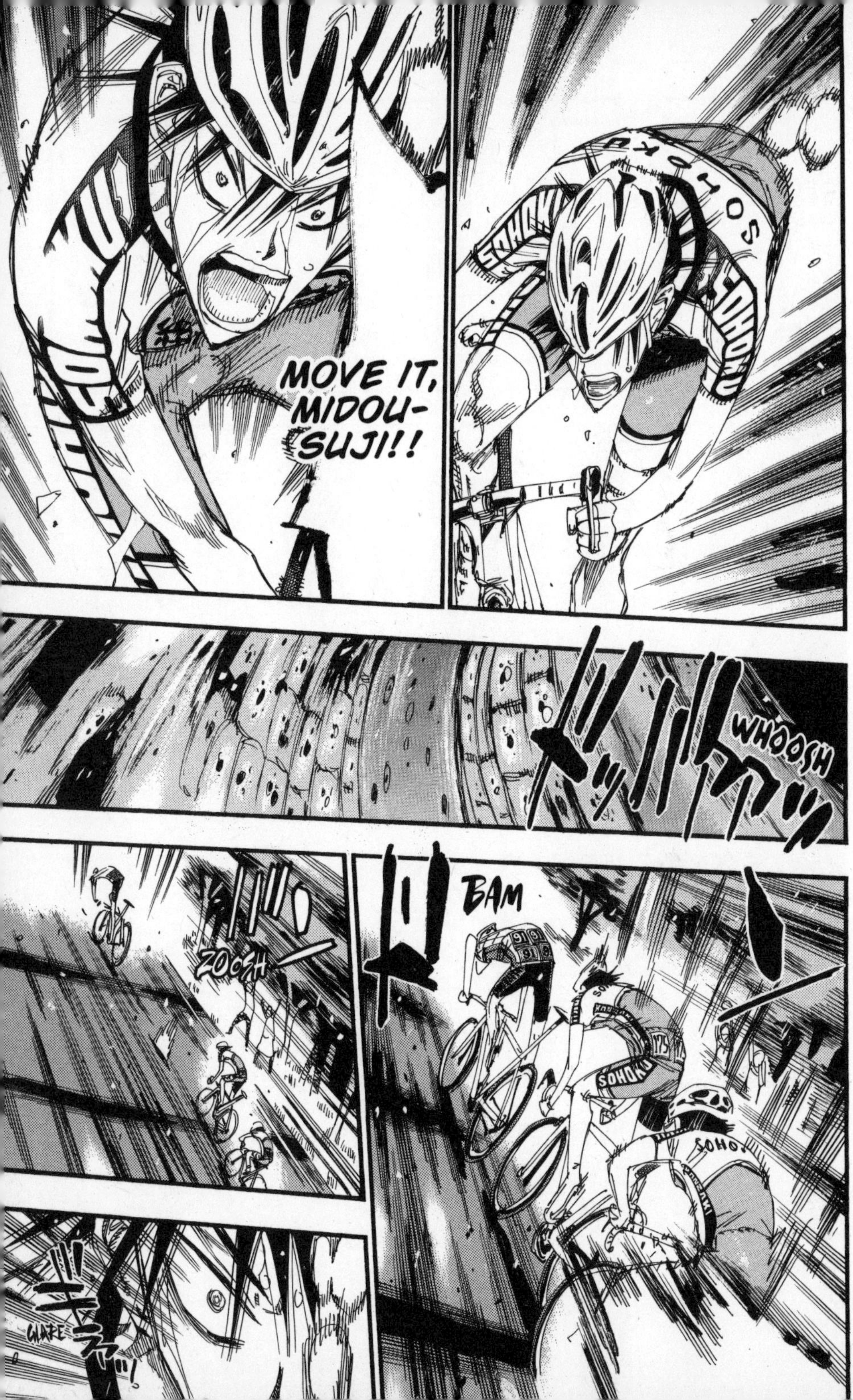
MOVE IT, MIDOU-SUJI!!
WHOOSH
BAM
ZOOSH
GLARE

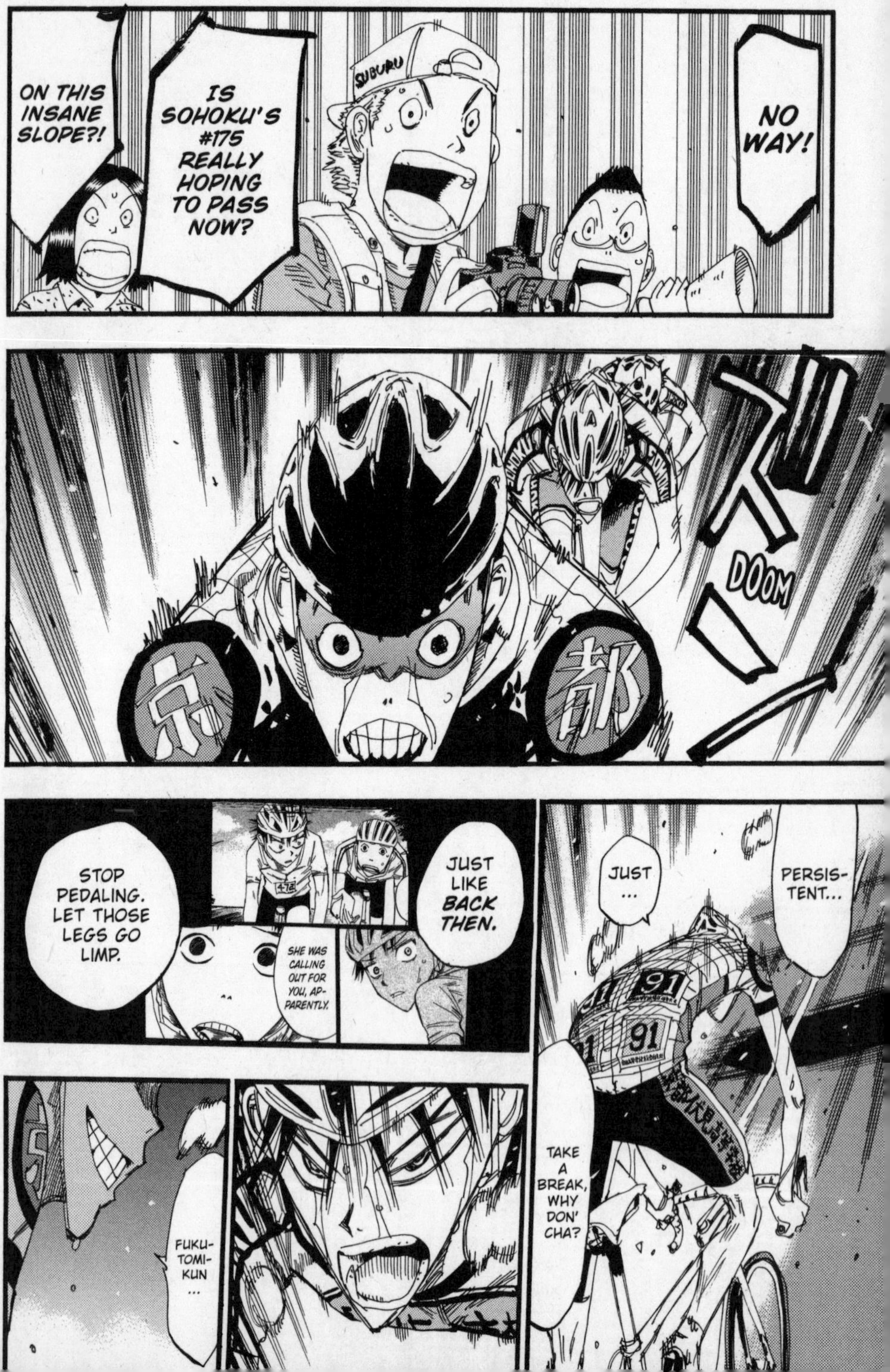
NO WAY!
IS SOHOKU'S #175 REALLY HOPING TO PASS NOW?
ON THIS INSANE SLOPE?!
DOOM
PERSIS-TENT...
JUST ...
TAKE A BREAK, WHY DON'CHA?
JUST LIKE BACK THEN.
SHE WAS CALLING OUT FOR YOU, AP-PARENTLY.
STOP PEDALING. LET THOSE LEGS GO LIMP.
FUKU-TOMI-KUN ...

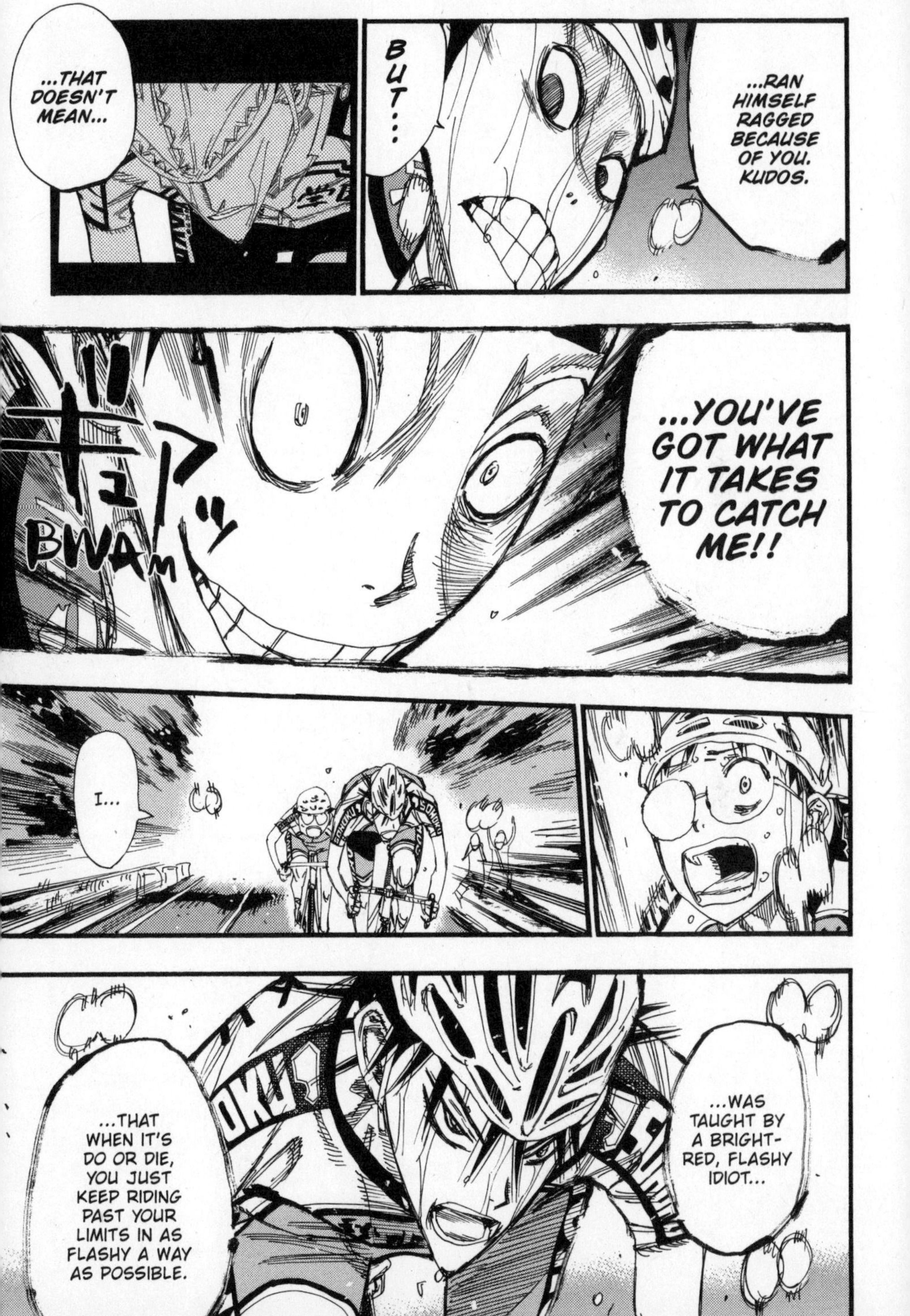
...RAN HIMSELF RAGGED BECAUSE OF YOU. KUDOS.
BUT...
...THAT DOESN'T MEAN...
...YOU'VE GOT WHAT IT TAKES TO CATCH ME!!
ギュアッ
BWAM
I...
...WAS TAUGHT BY A BRIGHT-RED, FLASHY IDIOT...
...THAT WHEN IT'S DO OR DIE, YOU JUST KEEP RIDING PAST YOUR LIMITS IN AS FLASHY A WAY AS POSSIBLE.

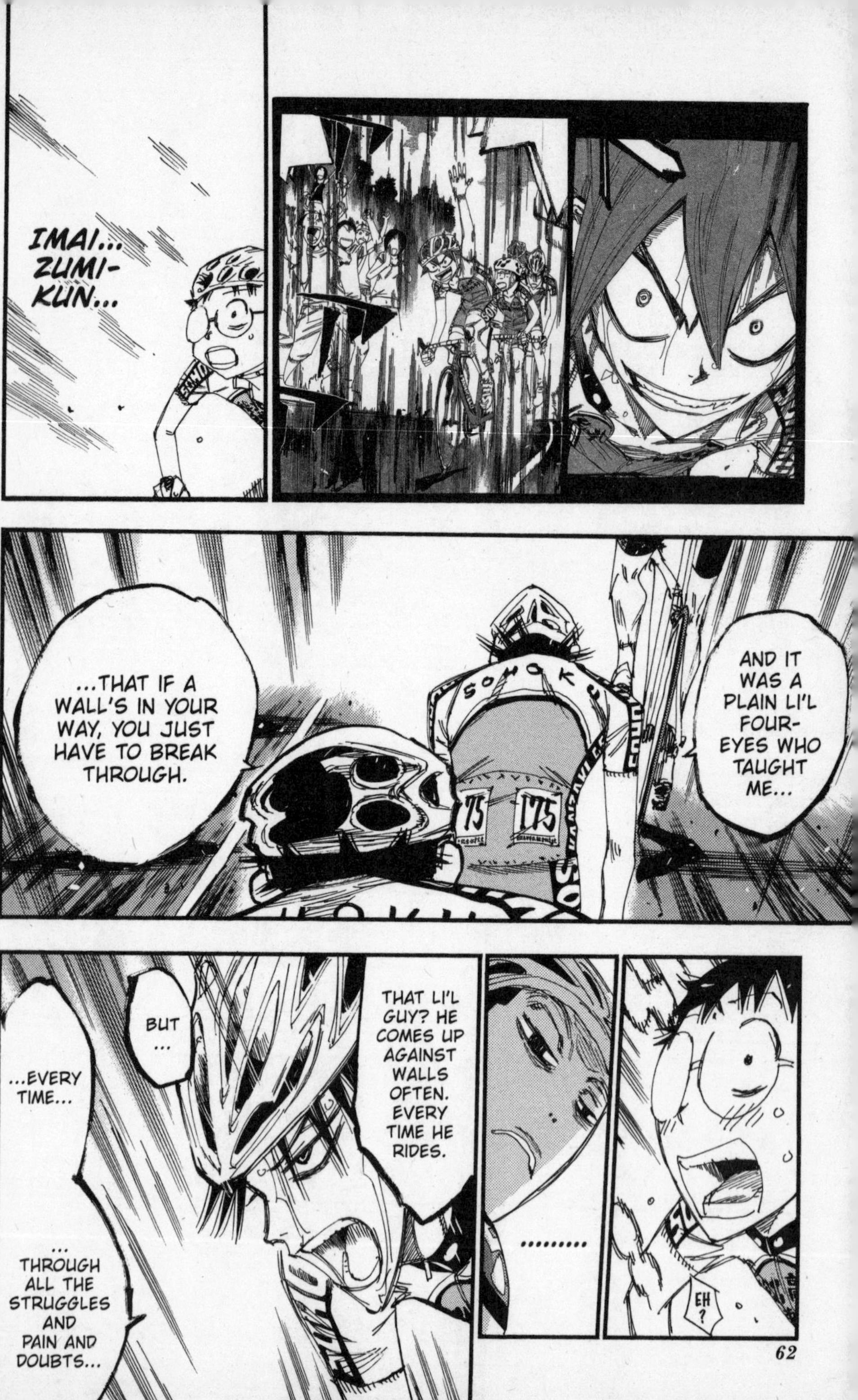
IMAI... ZUMI-KUN...
AND IT WAS A PLAIN LI'L FOUR-EYES WHO TAUGHT ME...
...THAT IF A WALL'S IN YOUR WAY, YOU JUST HAVE TO BREAK THROUGH.
EH?
....
THAT LI'L GUY? HE COMES UP AGAINST WALLS OFTEN. EVERY TIME HE RIDES.
BUT ...
...EVERY TIME...
... THROUGH ALL THE STRUGGLES AND PAIN AND DOUBTS...

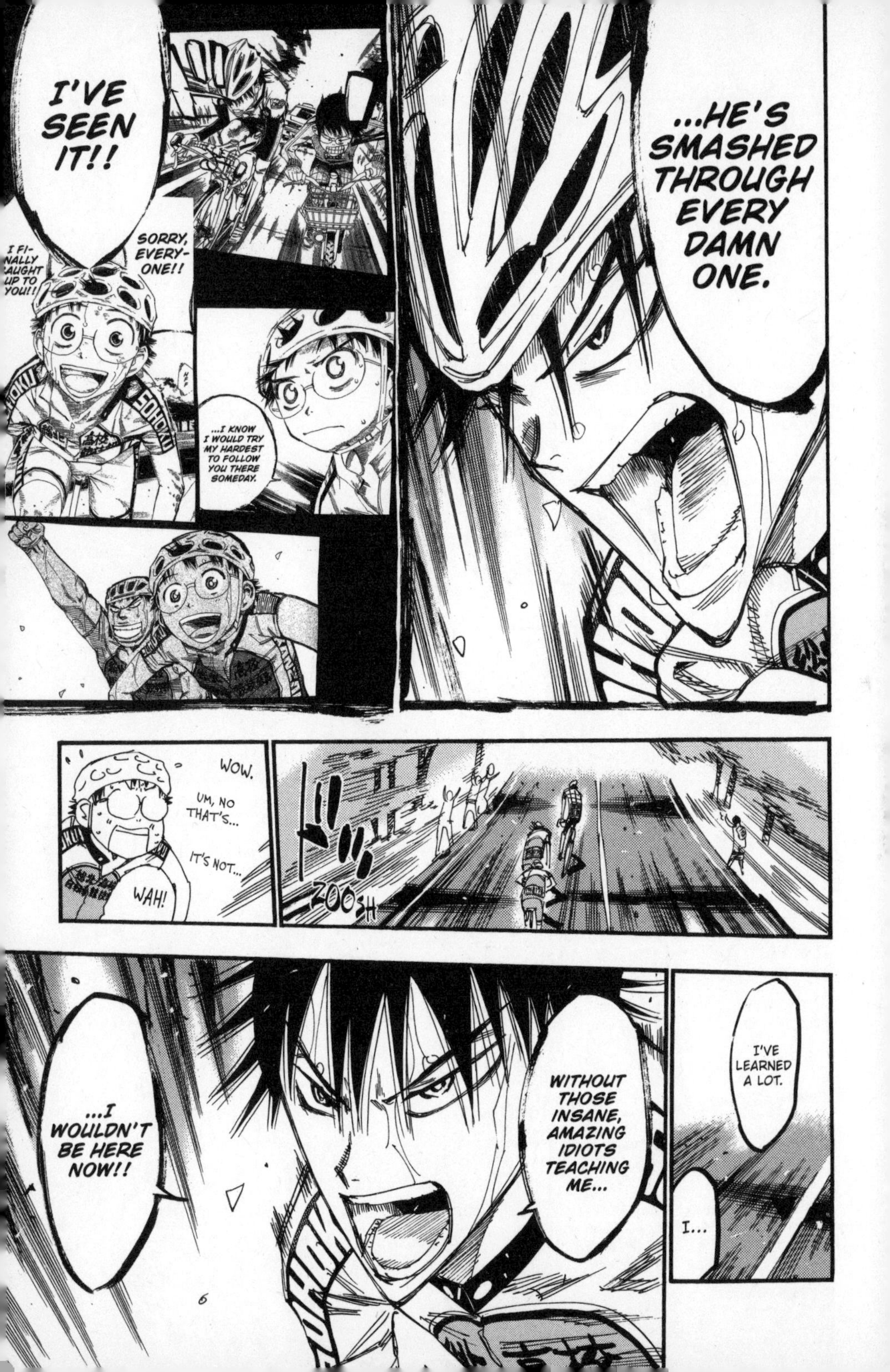
...HE'S SMASHED THROUGH EVERY DAMN ONE.
I'VE SEEN IT!!
...I KNOW I WOULD TRY MY HARDEST TO FOLLOW YOU THERE SOMEDAY.
SORRY, EVERY-ONE!!
I FI-NALLY CAUGHT UP TO YOU!!
ZOOSH
WOW.
UM, NO THAT'S...
IT'S NOT...
WAH!
I'VE LEARNED A LOT.
I...
WITHOUT THOSE INSANE, AMAZING IDIOTS TEACHING ME...
...I WOULDN'T BE HERE NOW!!

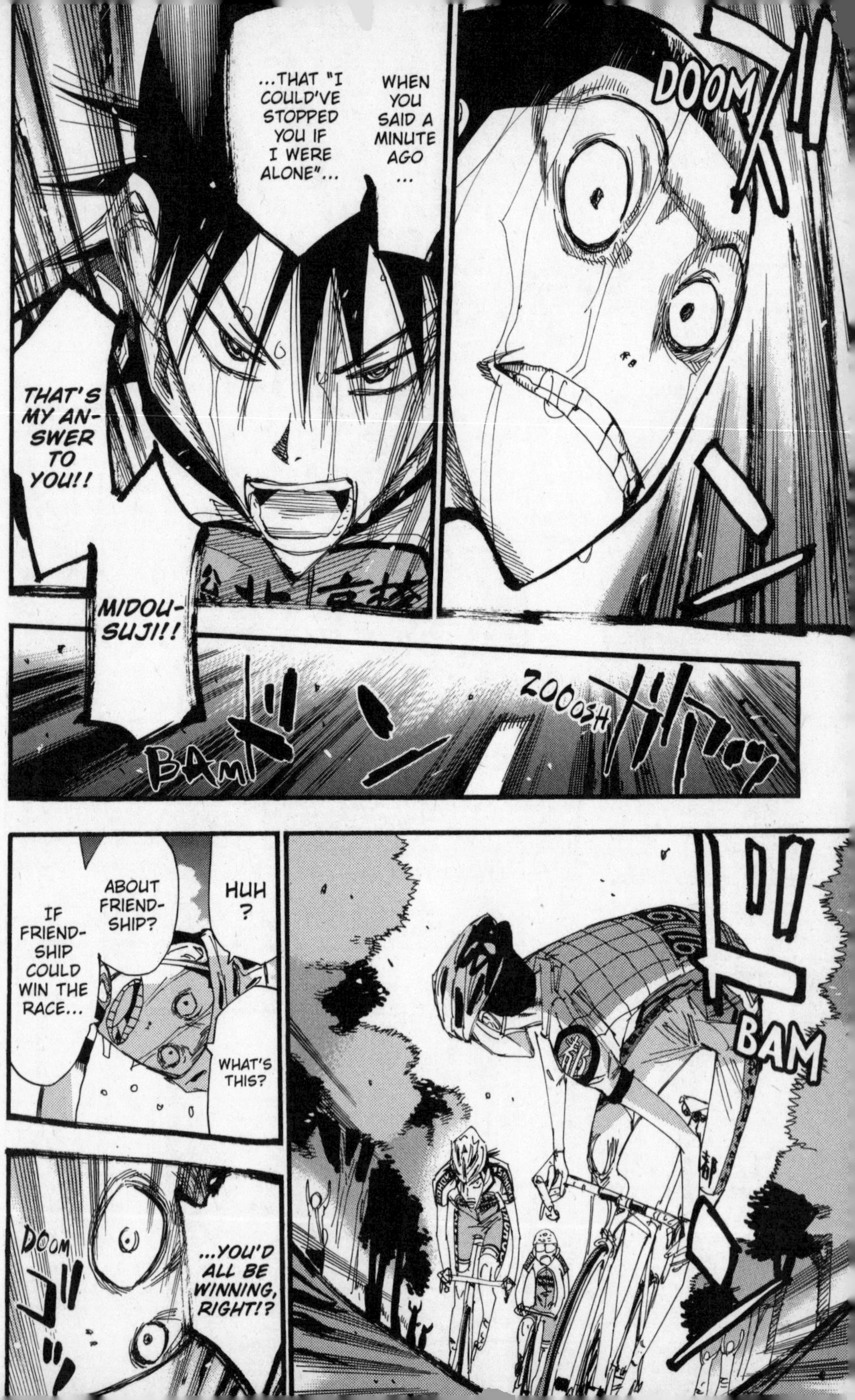
DOOM
WHEN YOU SAID A MINUTE AGO...
...THAT "I COULD'VE STOPPED YOU IF I WERE ALONE"...
THAT'S MY AN-SWER TO YOU!!
MIDOU-SUJI!!
ZOOOSH
BAM
BAM
HUH?
ABOUT FRIEND-SHIP?
IF FRIEND-SHIP COULD WIN THE RACE...
WHAT'S THIS?
DOOM
...YOU'D ALL BE WINNING, RIGHT!?

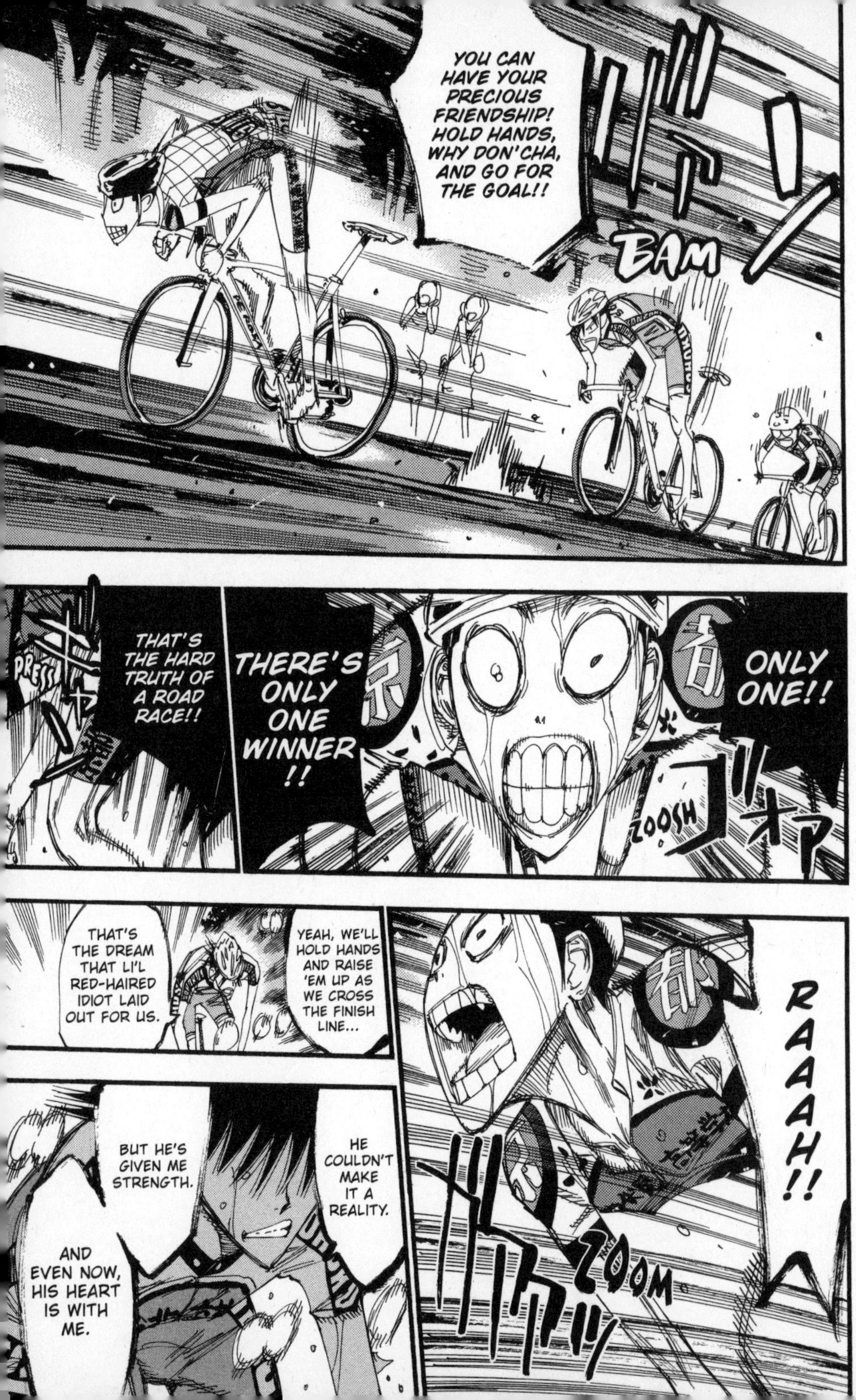
YOU CAN HAVE YOUR PRECIOUS FRIENDSHIP! HOLD HANDS, WHY DON'CHA, AND GO FOR THE GOAL!!
BAM
ONLY ONE!!
THERE'S ONLY ONE WINNER!!
ZOOSH
THAT'S THE HARD TRUTH OF A ROAD RACE!!
PRESS
RAAAAH!!
ZOOM
YEAH, WE'LL HOLD HANDS AND RAISE 'EM UP AS WE CROSS THE FINISH LINE...
THAT'S THE DREAM THAT LI'L RED-HAIRED IDIOT LAID OUT FOR US.
HE COULDN'T MAKE IT A REALITY.
BUT HE'S GIVEN ME STRENGTH.
AND EVEN NOW, HIS HEART IS WITH ME.

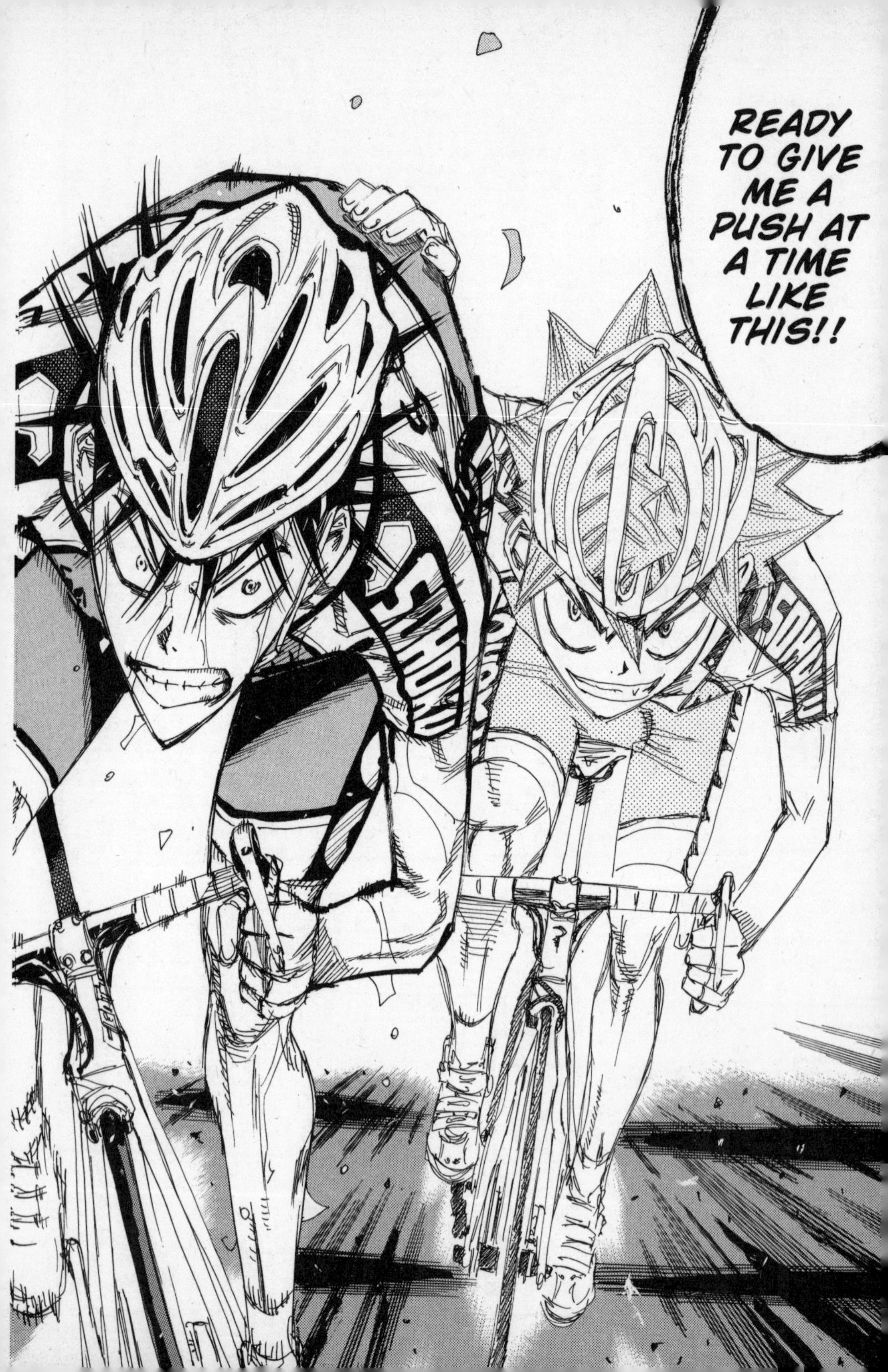
READY TO GIVE ME A PUSH AT A TIME LIKE THIS!!

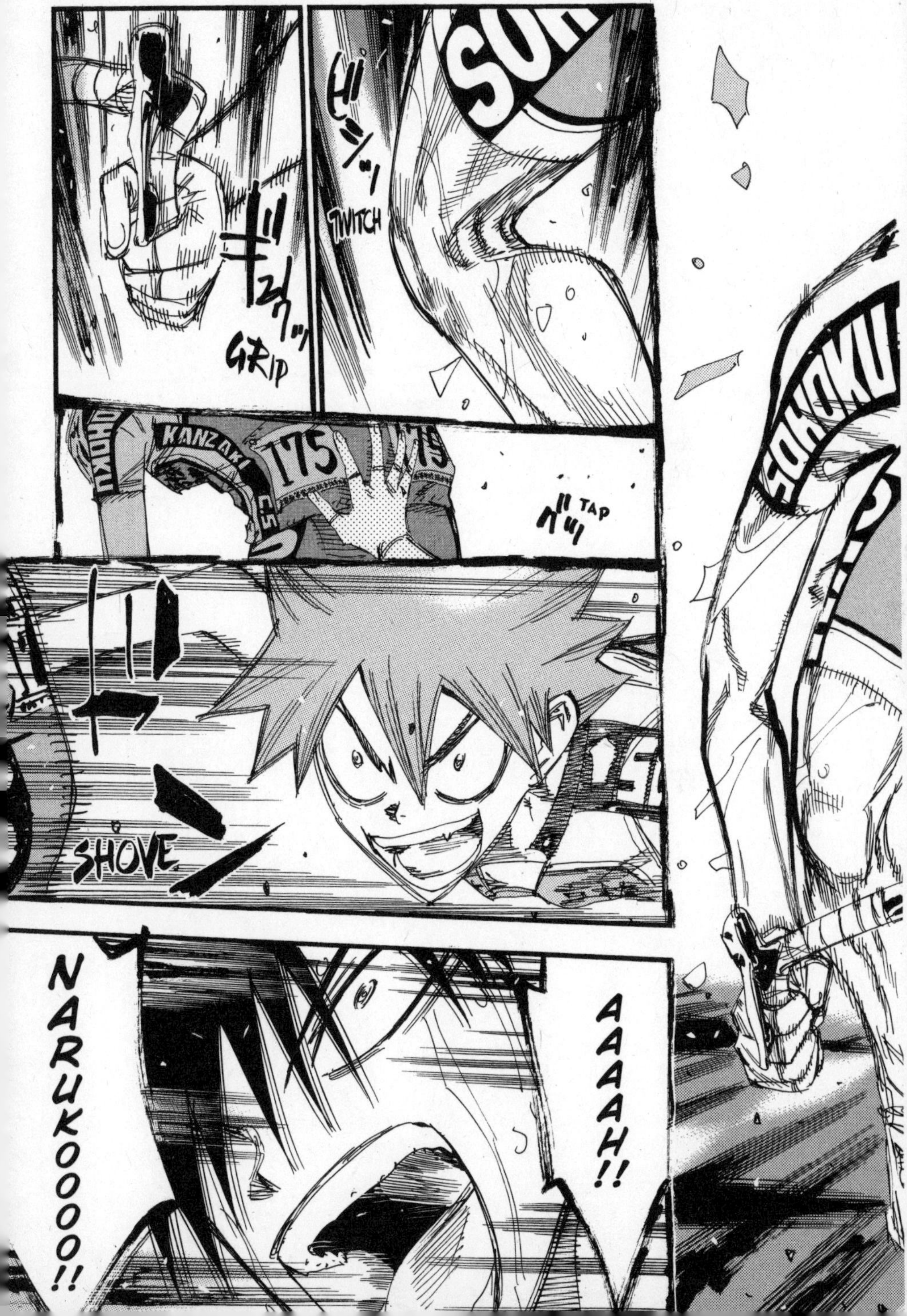
SOHOKU
TWITCH
GRIP
KANZAKI
175
TAP
SHOVE
AAAAAH!!
NARUKOOOOO!!

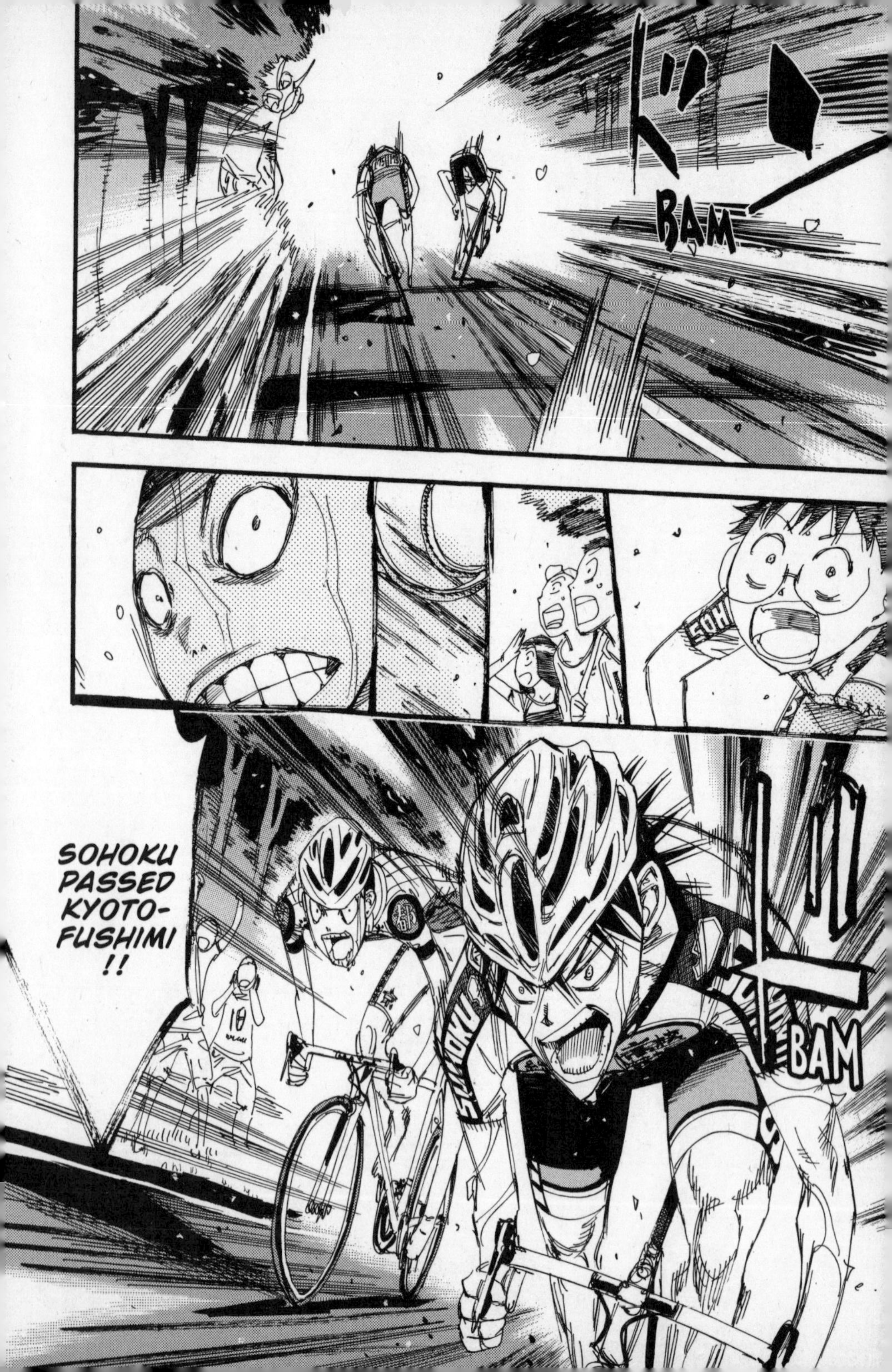
ドッ
BAM
SOHOKU PASSED KYOTO-FUSHIMI !!
BAM

RIDE.211 IMAIZUMI VS. MIDOUSUJI

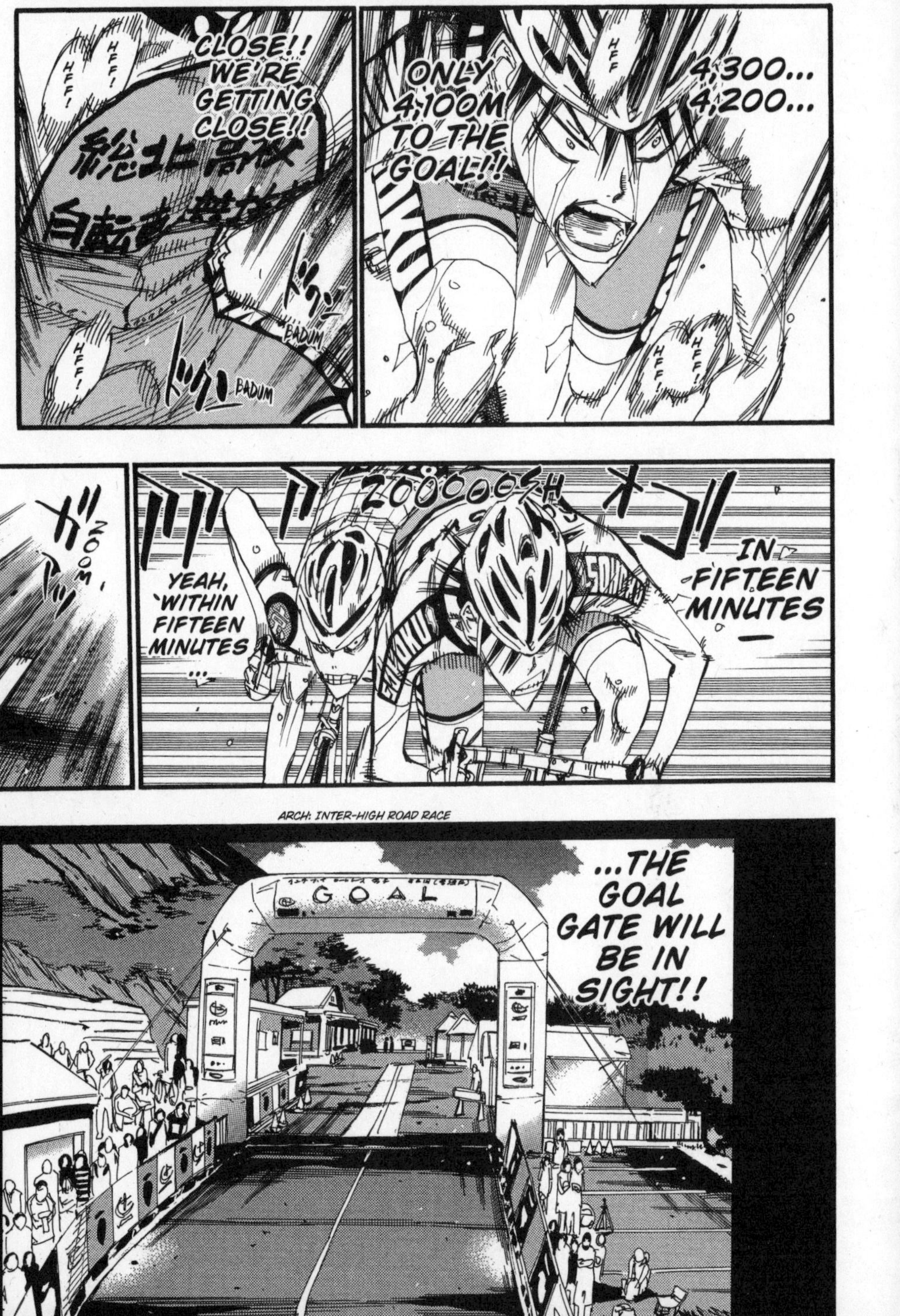
HFF
4,300...
4,200...
ONLY 4,100M TO THE GOAL!!
HFF! HFF!
HFF! HFF!
CLOSE!! WE'RE GETTING CLOSE!!
BADUM
HFF!
BADUM
IN FIFTEEN MINUTES—
ZOOOOOOSH
YEAH, WITHIN FIFTEEN MINUTES...
ZOOM!
ARCH: INTER-HIGH ROAD RACE
...THE GOAL GATE WILL BE IN SIGHT!!
GOAL

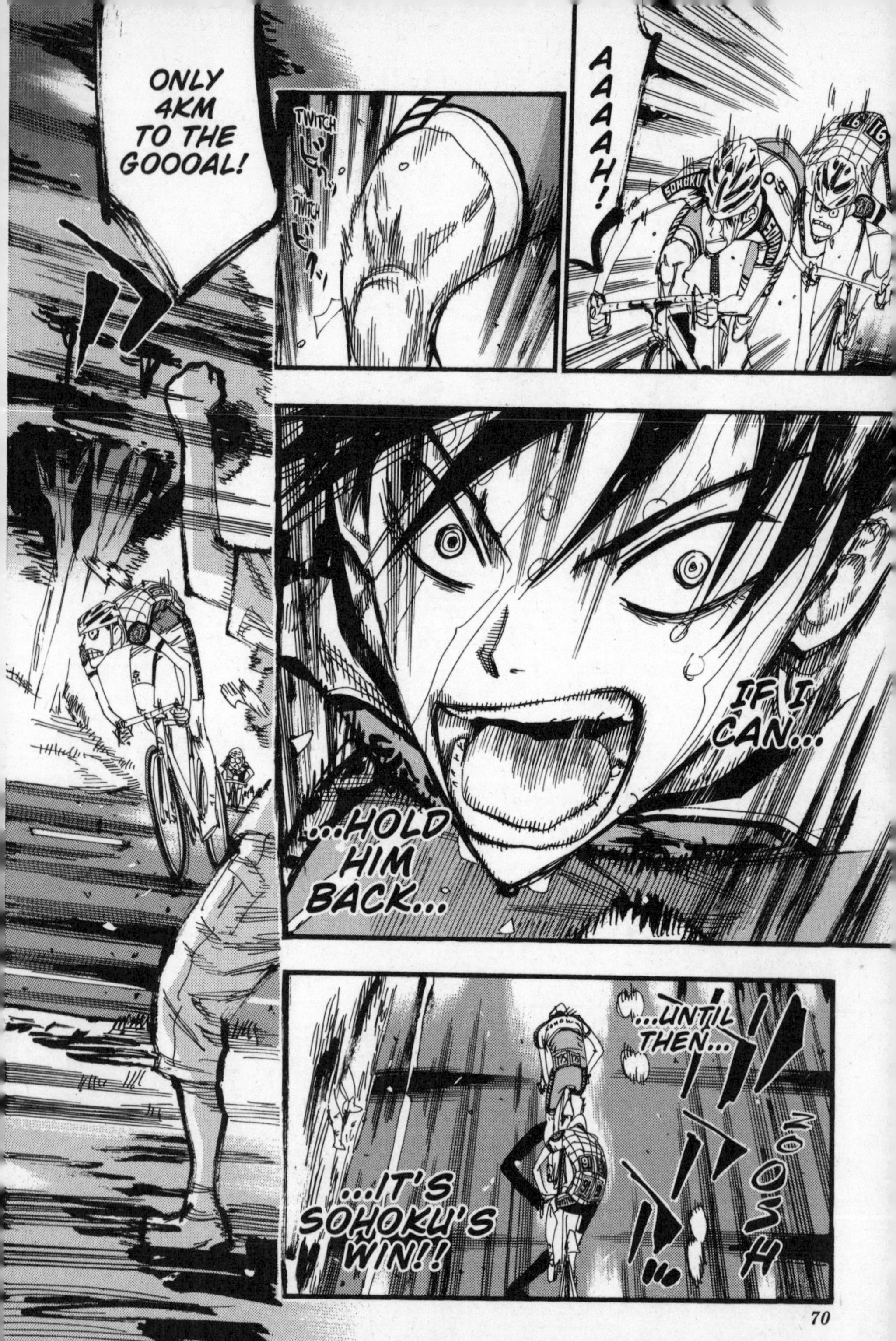
AAAAAH!
TWITCH
TWITCH
IF I CAN...
...HOLD HIM BACK...
...UNTIL THEN...
...IT'S SOHOKU'S WIN!!
ZOOSH
ONLY 4KM TO THE GOOOAL!

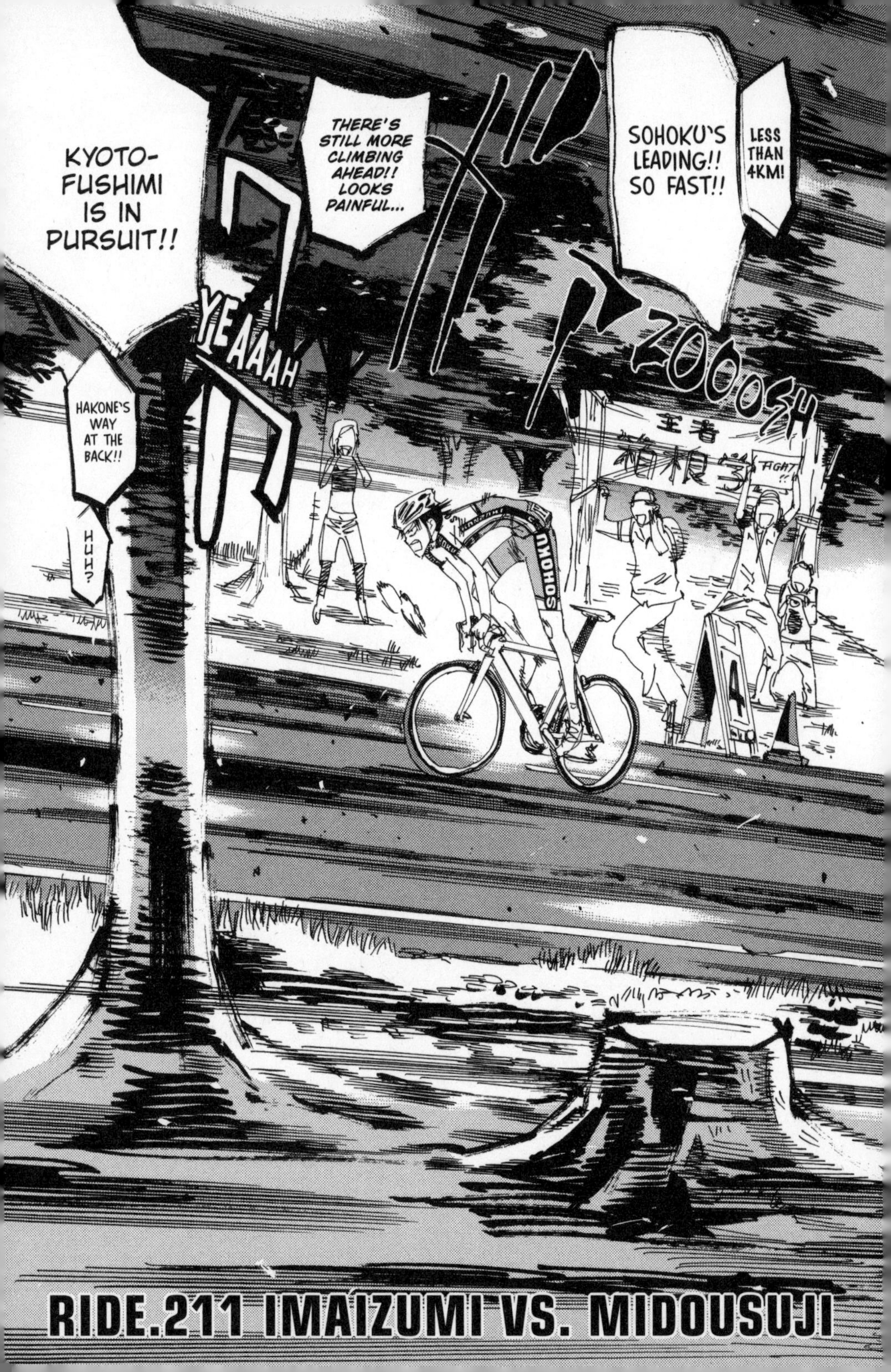

LESS THAN 4KM!
SOHOKU'S LEADING!! SO FAST!!
ZOOOOSH
THERE'S STILL MORE CLIMBING AHEAD!! LOOKS PAINFUL...
KYOTO-FUSHIMI IS IN PURSUIT!!
YEAAAH
FIGHT!!
HAKONE'S WAY AT THE BACK!!
HUH?

RIDE.211 IMAIZUMI VS. MIDOUSUJI

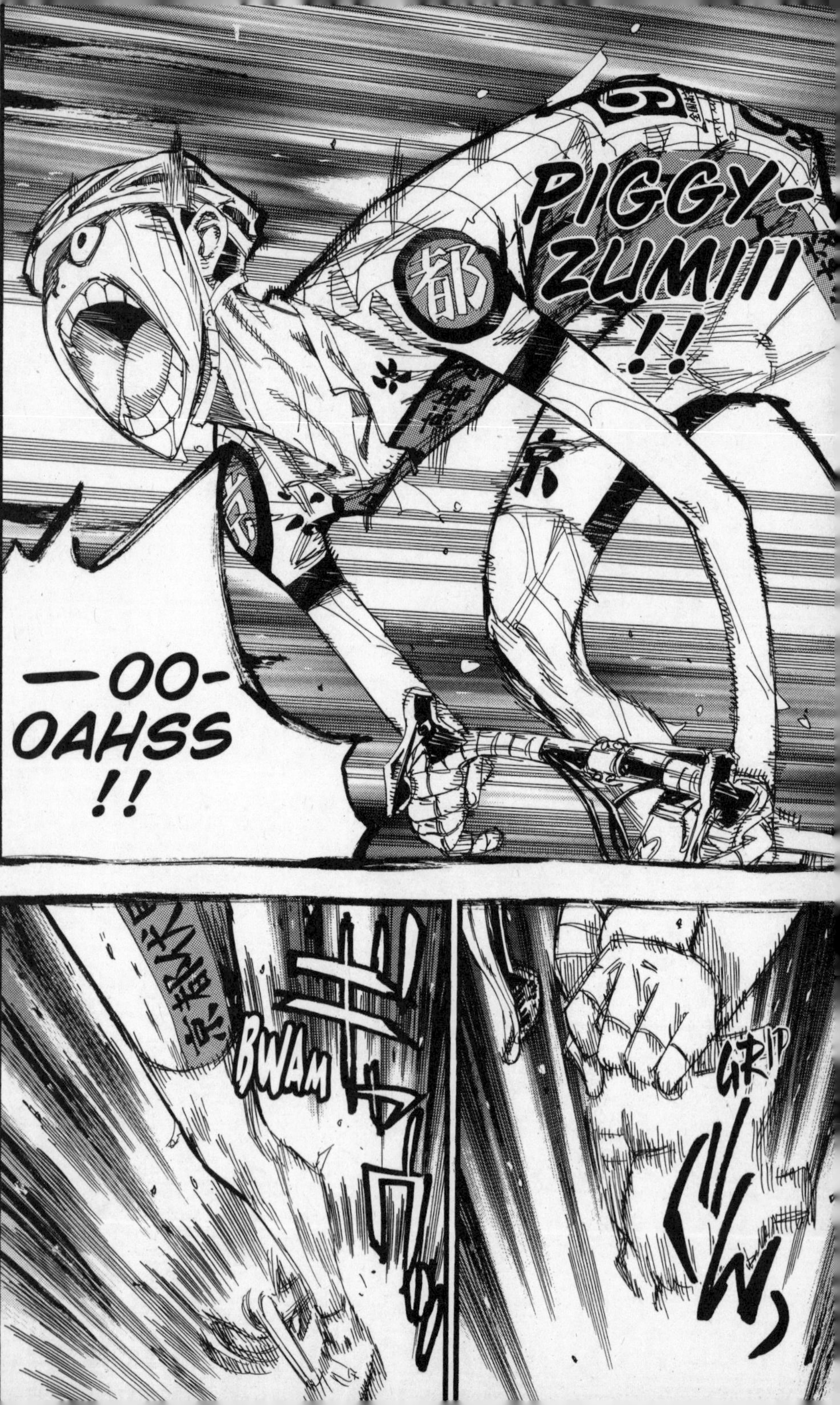
PIGGY-ZUMIII!!
—OO-OAHSS!!
GRIP
BWAM

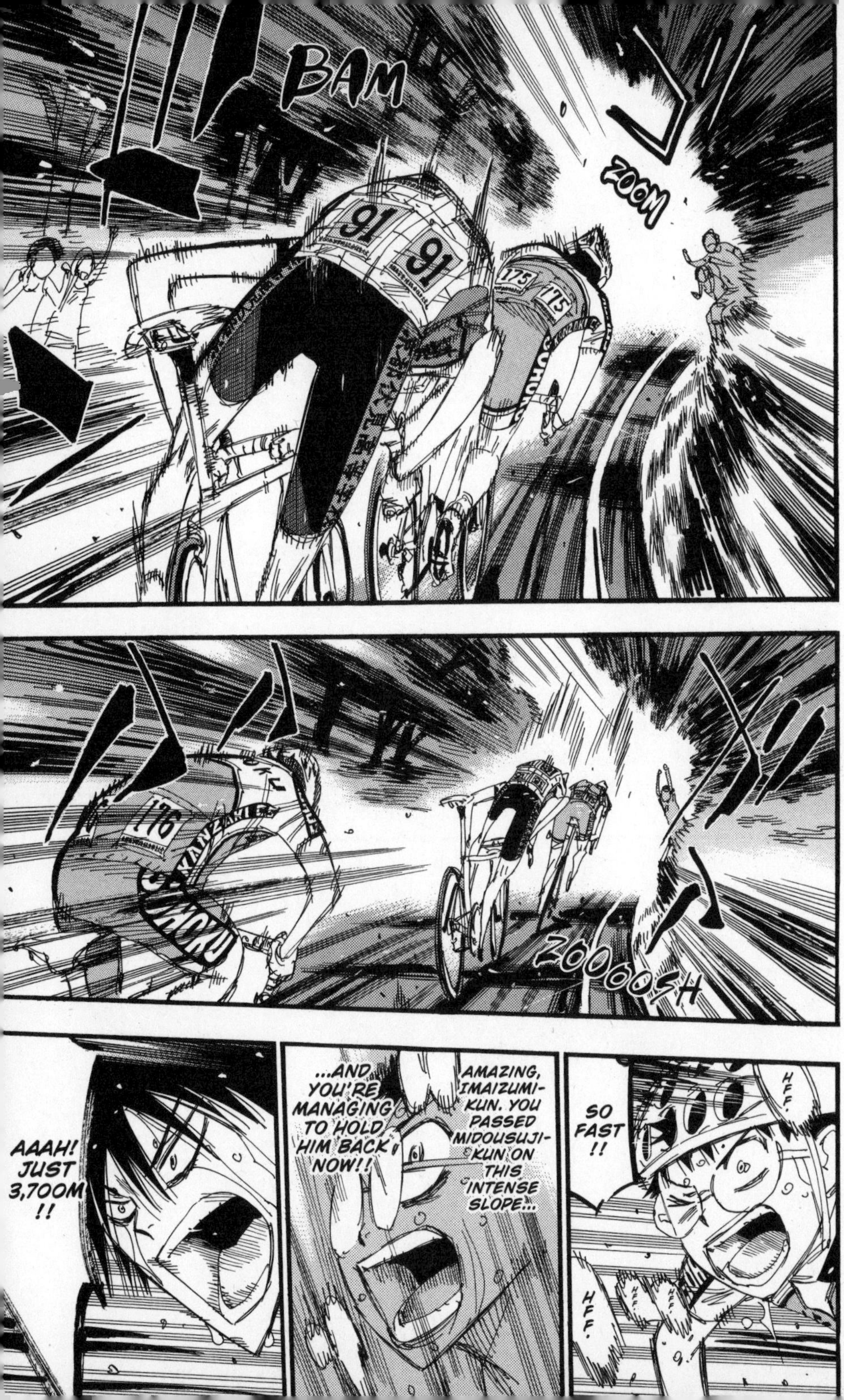
ZOOM
BAM
ZOOOOSH
HFF.
SO FAST!!
HFF.
HFF.
HFF.
AMAZING, IMAIZUMI-KUN. YOU PASSED MIDOUSUJI-KUN ON THIS INTENSE SLOPE...
...AND YOU'RE MANAGING TO HOLD HIM BACK NOW!!
AAAH! JUST 3,700M!!

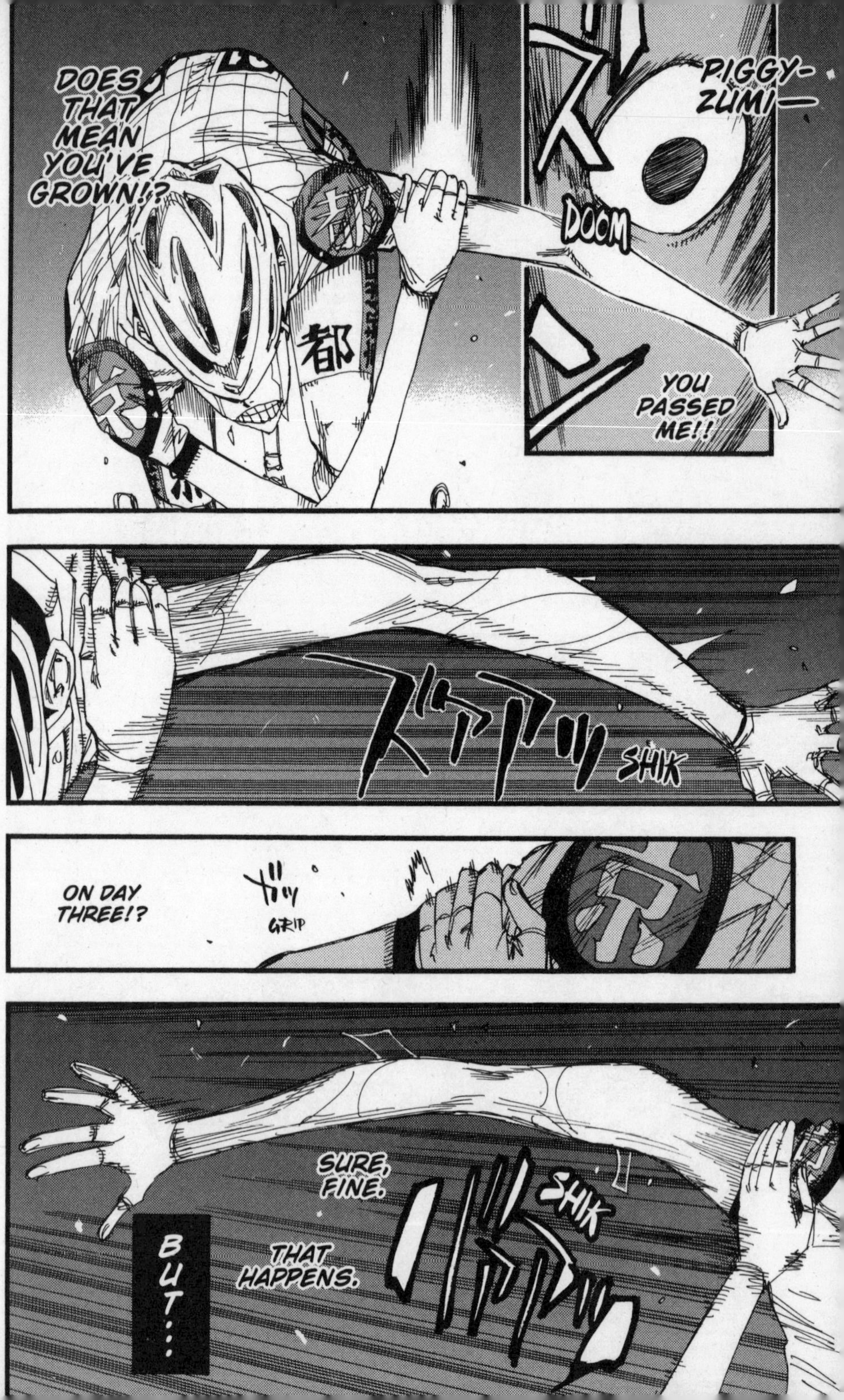
PIGGY-ZUMI—
DOOM
YOU PASSED ME!!
DOES THAT MEAN YOU'VE GROWN!?
SHIK
GRIP
ON DAY THREE!?
SURE, FINE.
SHIK
THAT HAPPENS.
BUT...

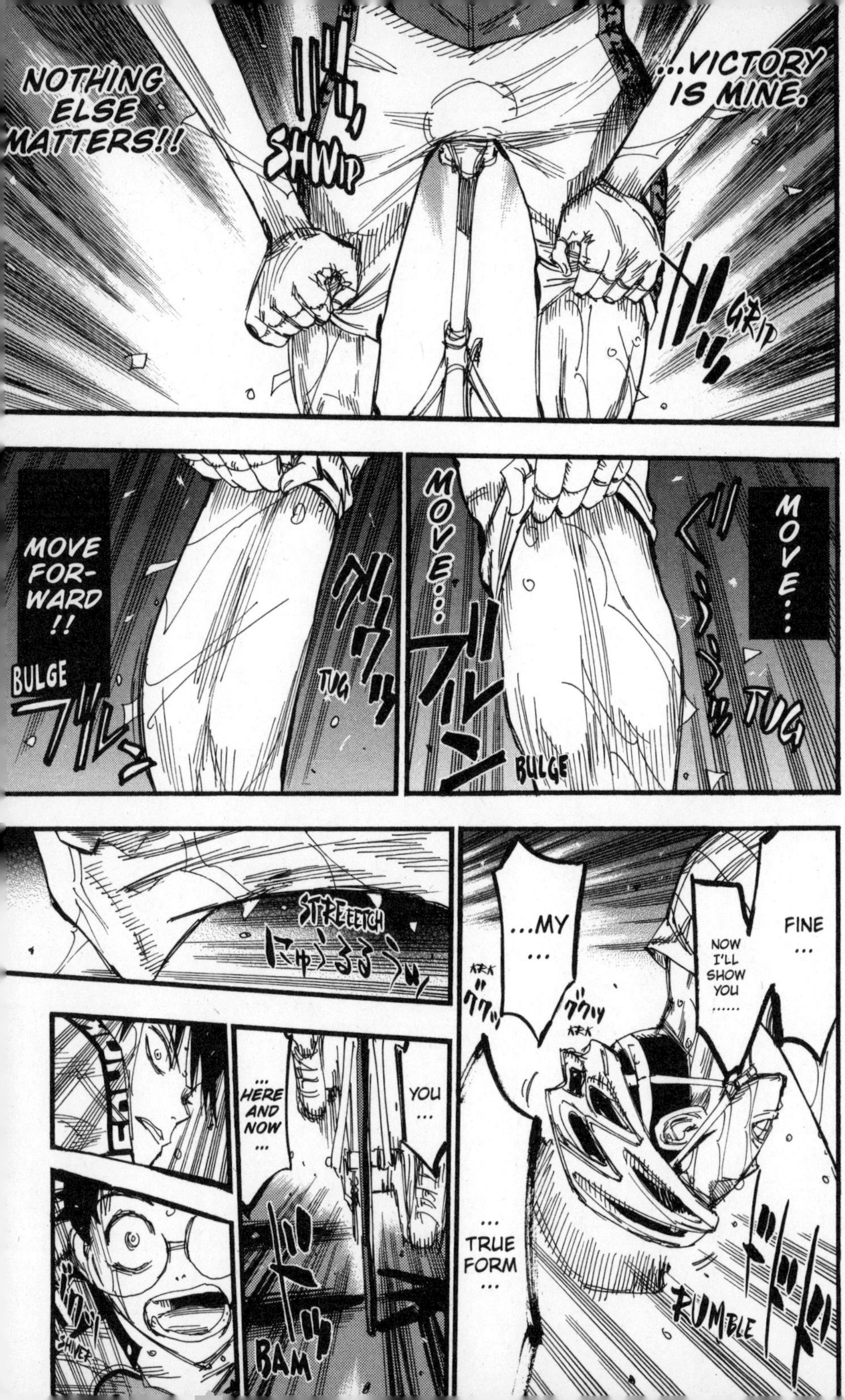
...VICTORY IS MINE.
NOTHING ELSE MATTERS!!
SHWIP
GRIP
MOVE...
TUG
MOVE...
BULGE
MOVE FOR-WARD!!
TUG
BULGE
FINE...
NOW I'LL SHOW YOU......
...MY...
KRK
KRK
...TRUE FORM...
RUMBLE
STREEETCH
YOU...
...HERE AND NOW...
BAM
SHIVER

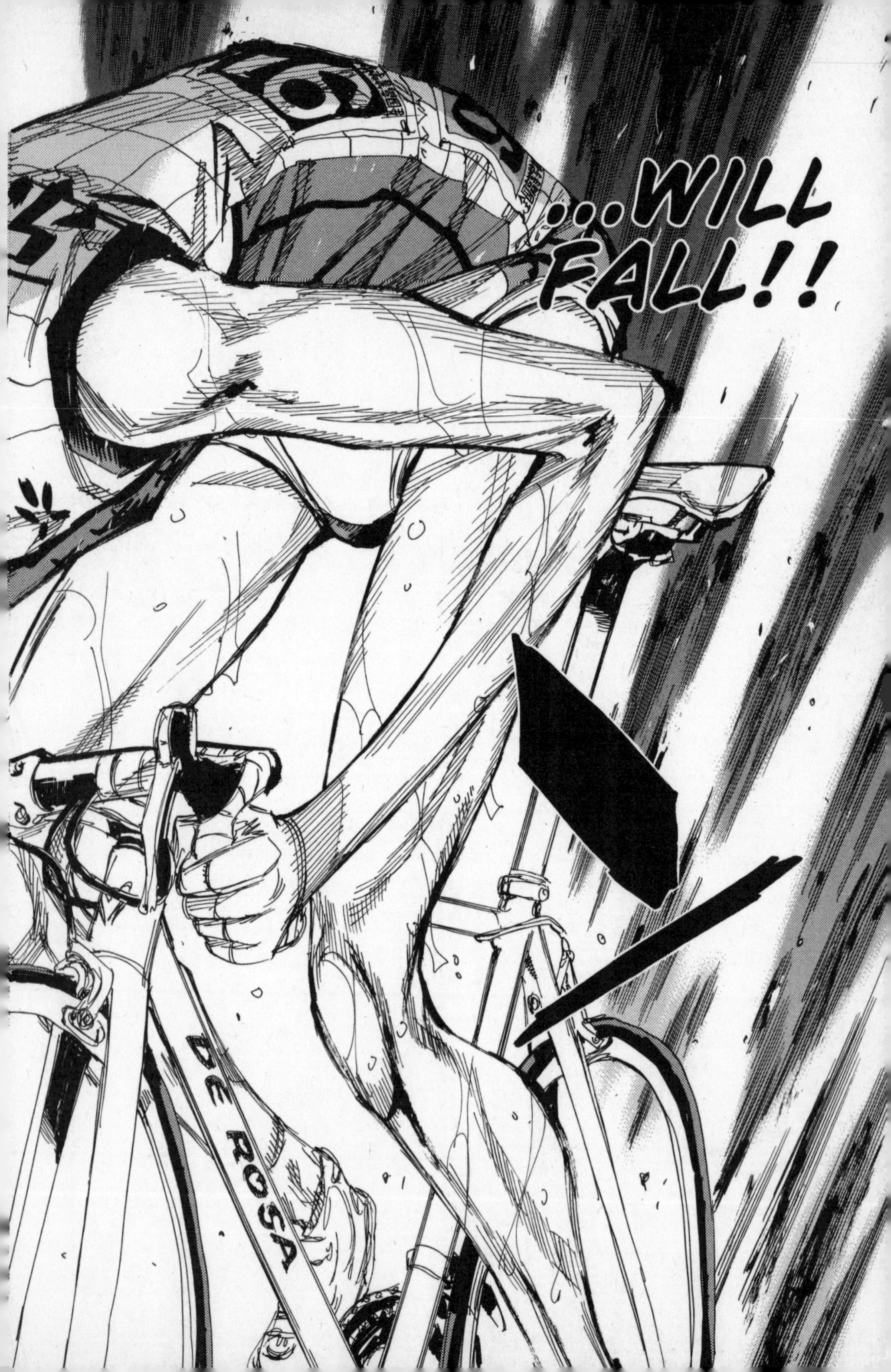
...WILL FALL!!
DE ROSA

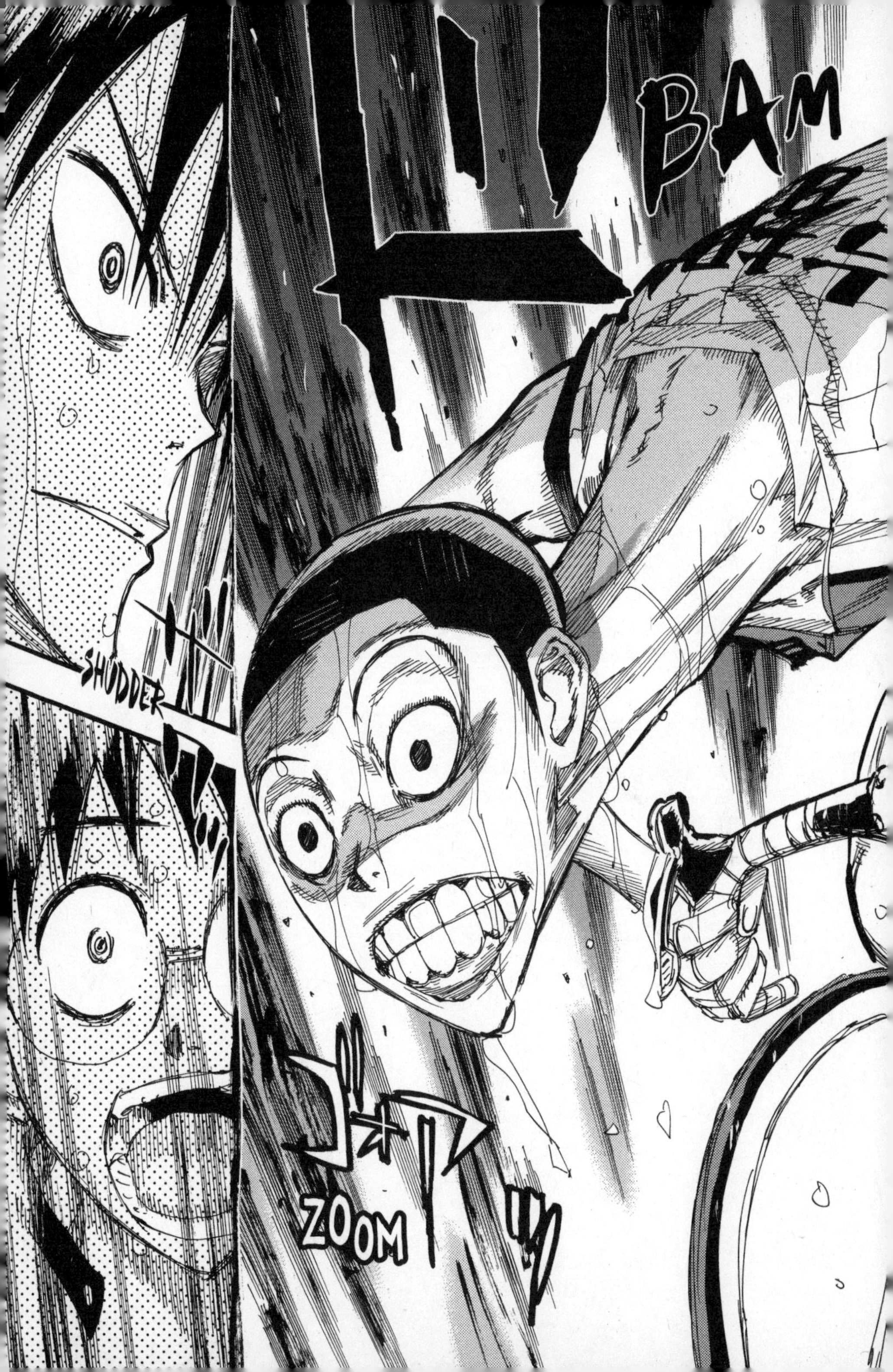
BAM
SHUDDER
ZOOM

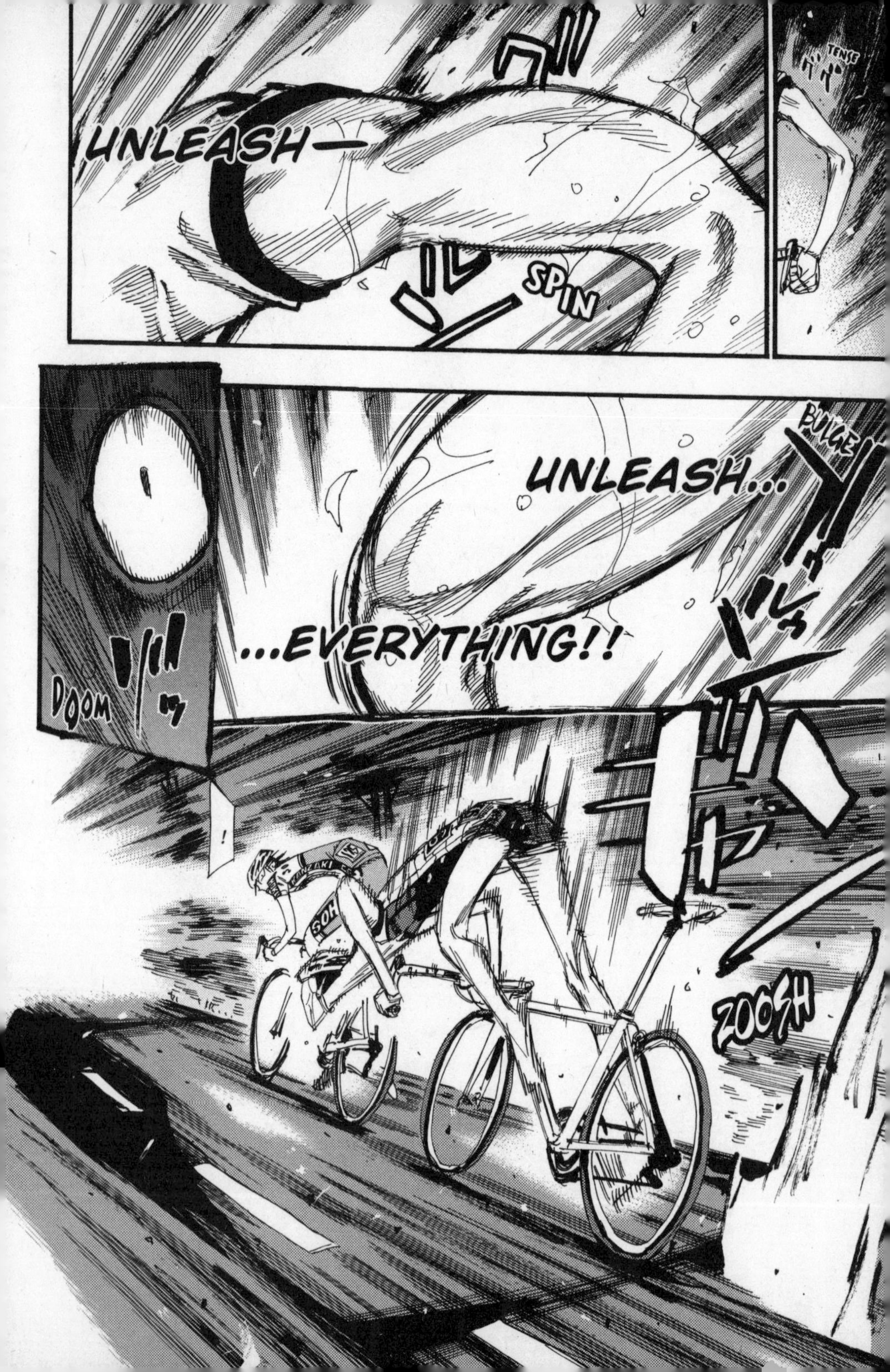
TENSE
UNLEASH—
SPIN
BULGE
UNLEASH...
...EVERYTHING!!
DOOM
ZOOSH
!

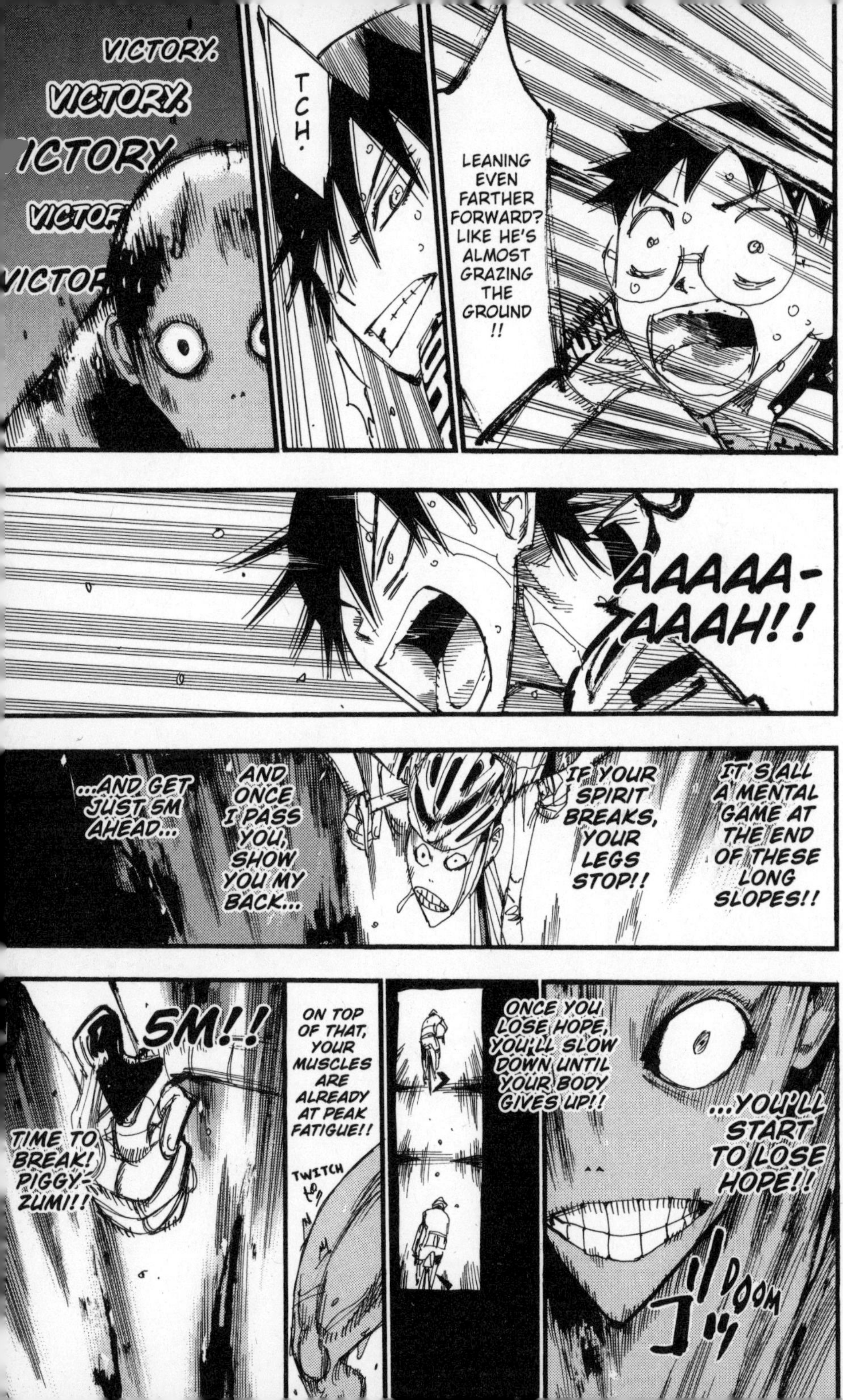
LEANING EVEN FARTHER FORWARD? LIKE HE'S ALMOST GRAZING THE GROUND!!
TCH.
VICTORY.
VICTORY.
VICTORY.
VICTOR
VICTOR
AAAAA-AAAAH!!
IT'S ALL A MENTAL GAME AT THE END OF THESE LONG SLOPES!!
IF YOUR SPIRIT BREAKS, YOUR LEGS STOP!!
AND ONCE I PASS YOU, SHOW YOU MY BACK...
...AND GET JUST 5M AHEAD...
...YOU'LL START TO LOSE HOPE!!
DOOM
ONCE YOU LOSE HOPE, YOU'LL SLOW DOWN UNTIL YOUR BODY GIVES UP!!
ON TOP OF THAT, YOUR MUSCLES ARE ALREADY AT PEAK FATIGUE!!
TWITCH
5M!!
TIME TO BREAK! PIGGY-ZUMI!!

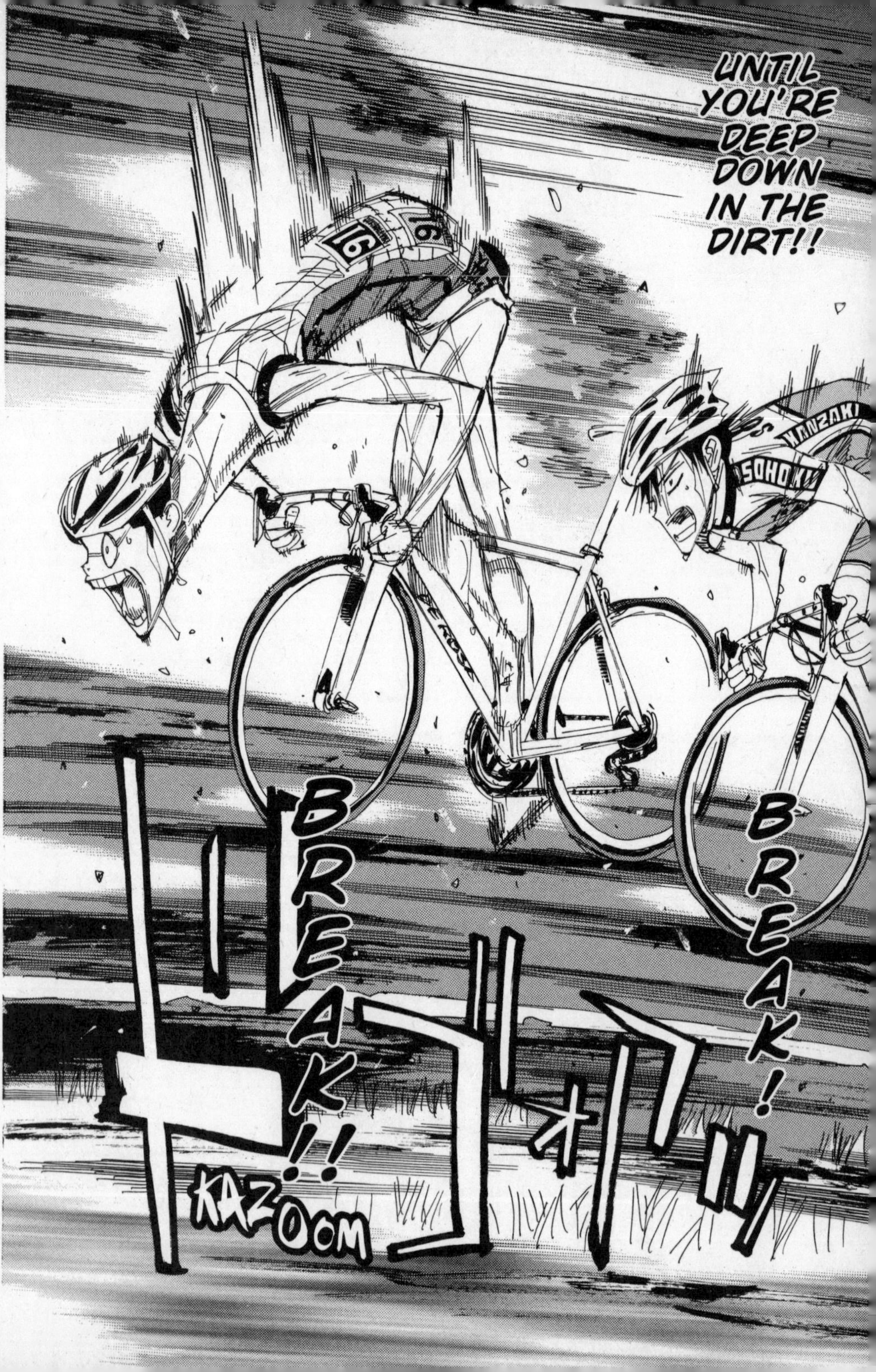
UNTIL YOU'RE DEEP DOWN IN THE DIRT!!
BREAK!
BREAK!!
KAZOOM

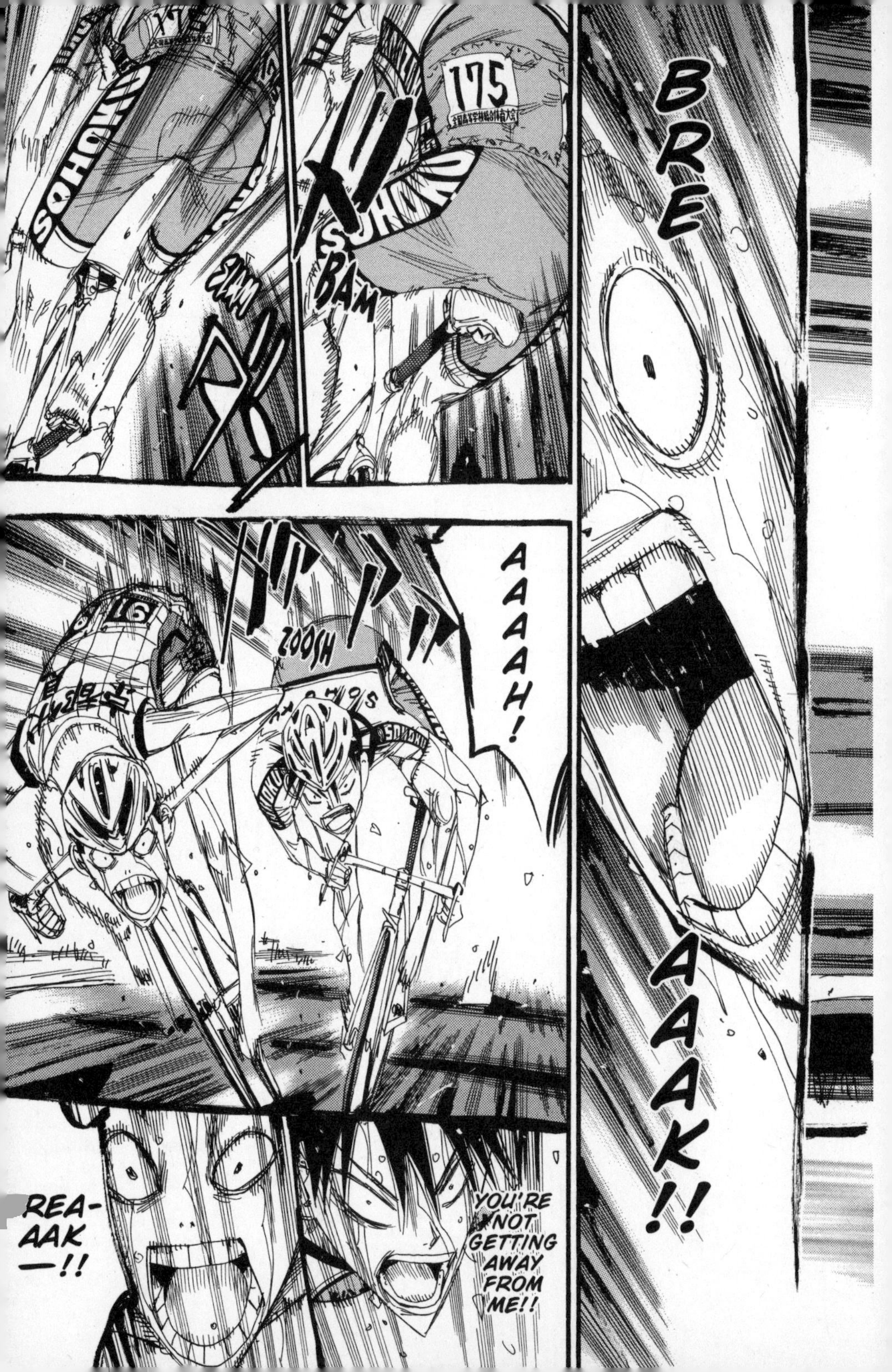
BREAAAAK!!
BAM
AAAAAH!
ZOOSH
YOU'RE NOT GETTING AWAY FROM ME!!
REA-AAK—!!

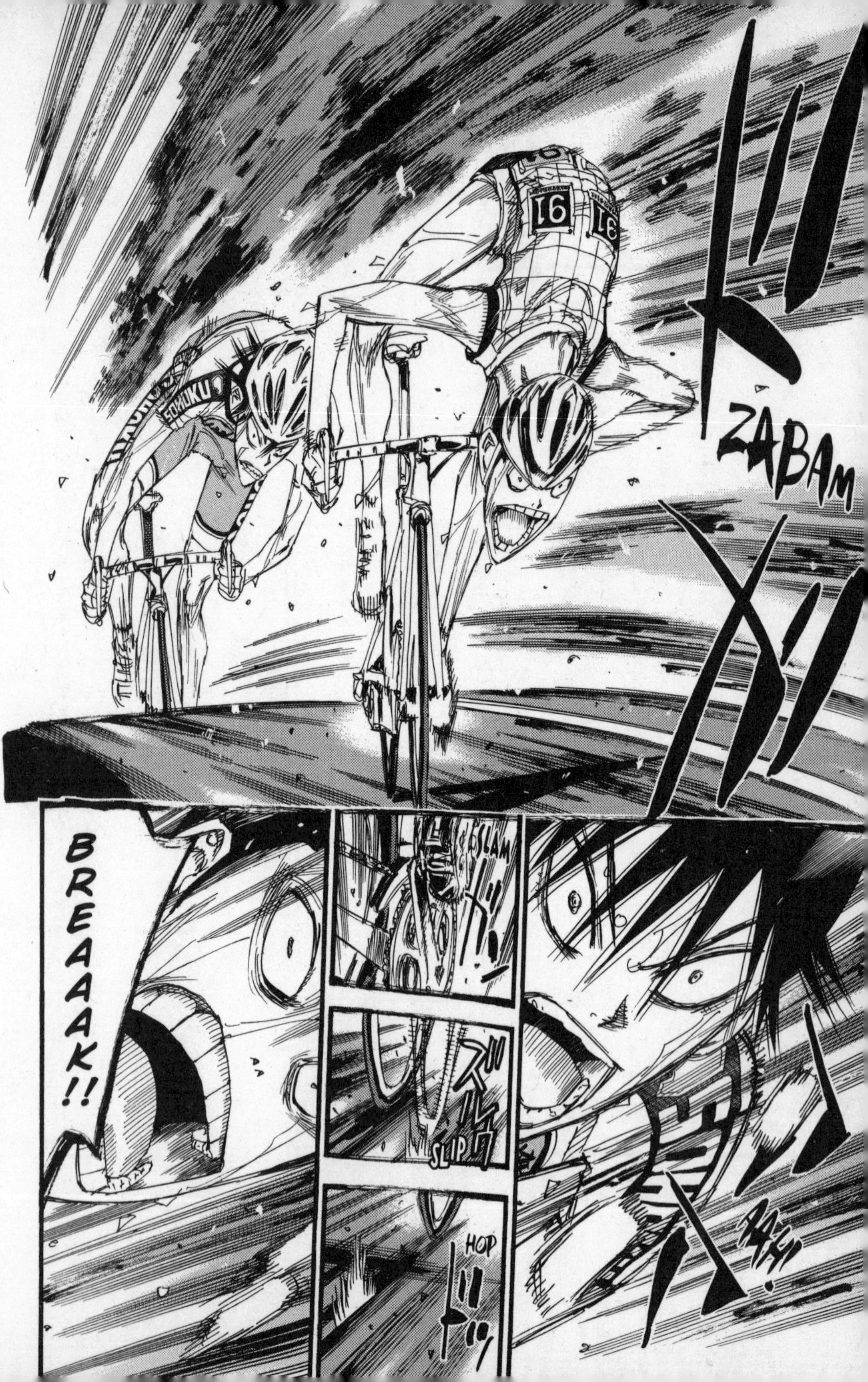
ZABAM
SLAM
SLIP
HOP
BREAAAAK!!

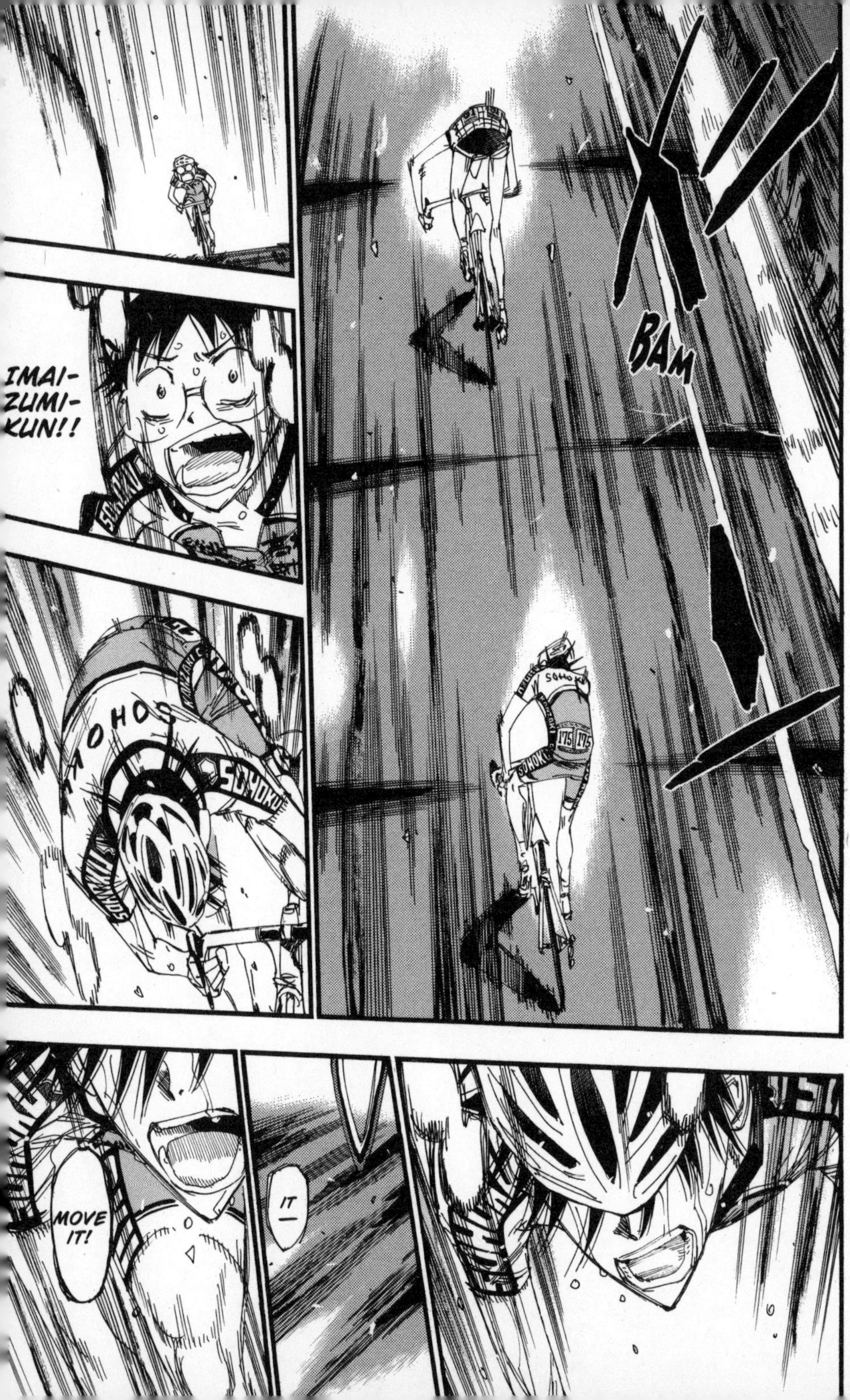
BAM
IMAI-ZUMI-KUN!!
IT—
MOVE IT!

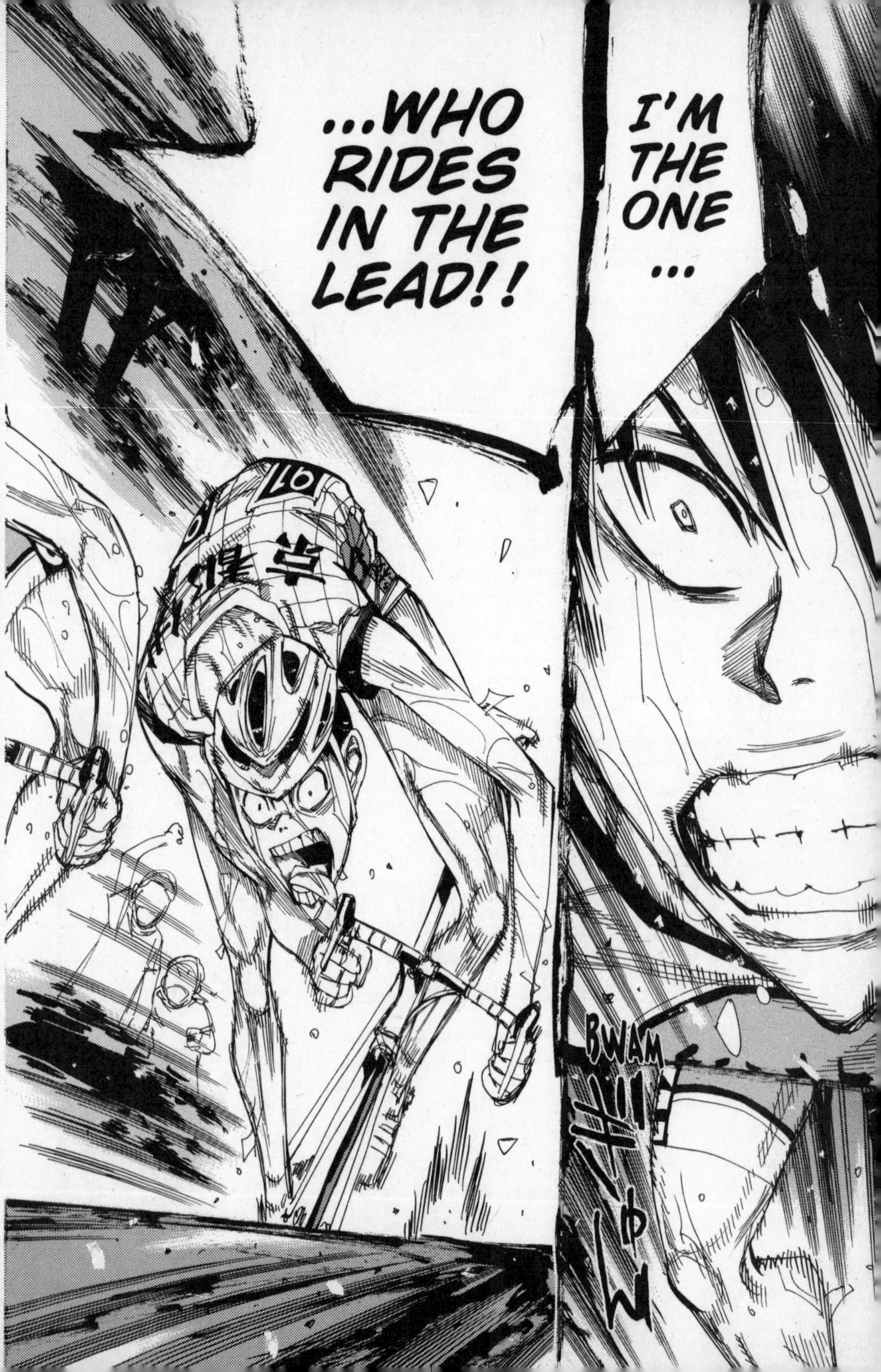
I'M THE ONE ...
...WHO RIDES IN THE LEAD!!
BWAM

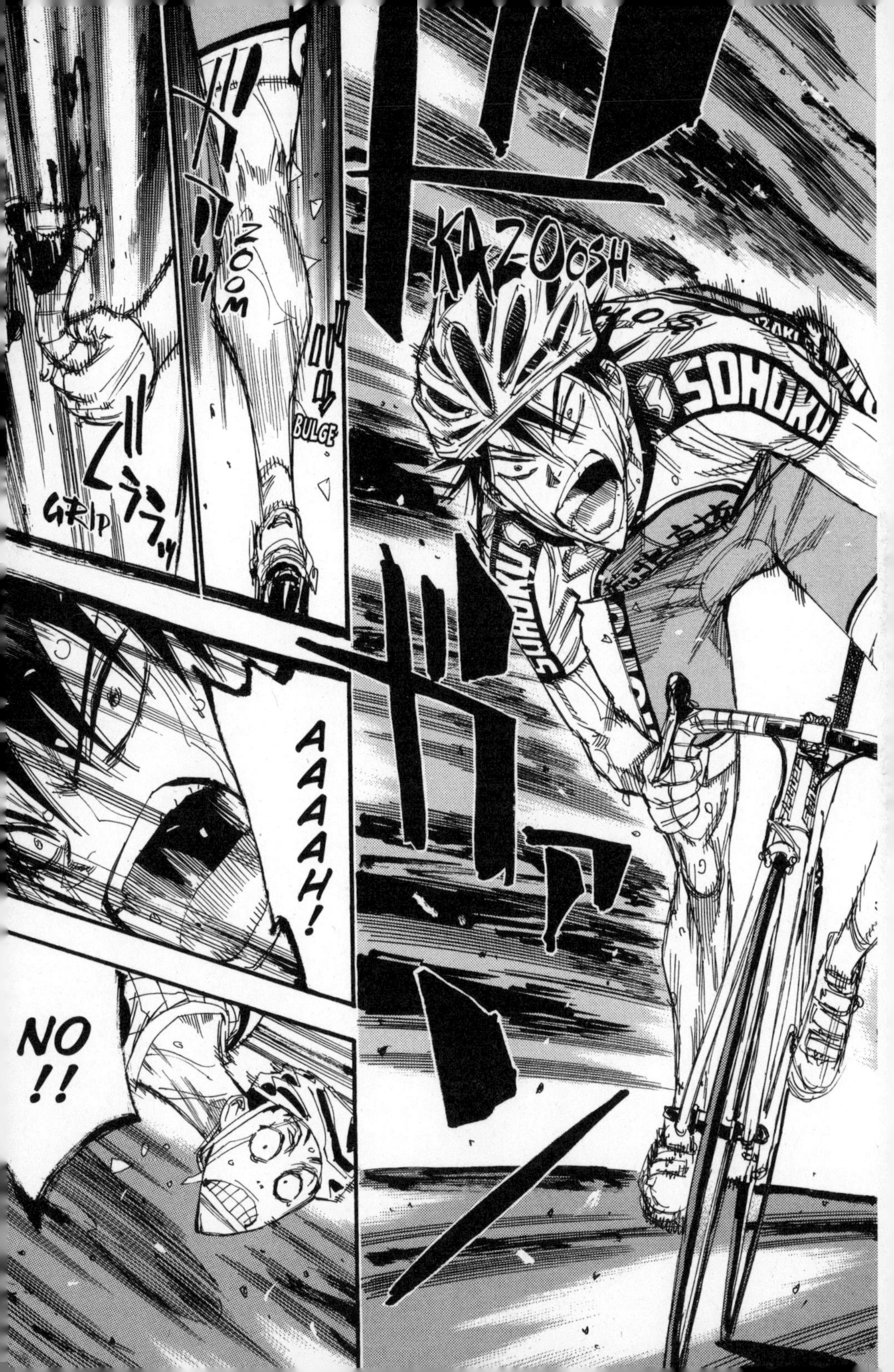
KAZOOSH
ZOOM
BULGE
GRIP
AAAAAH!
NO!!

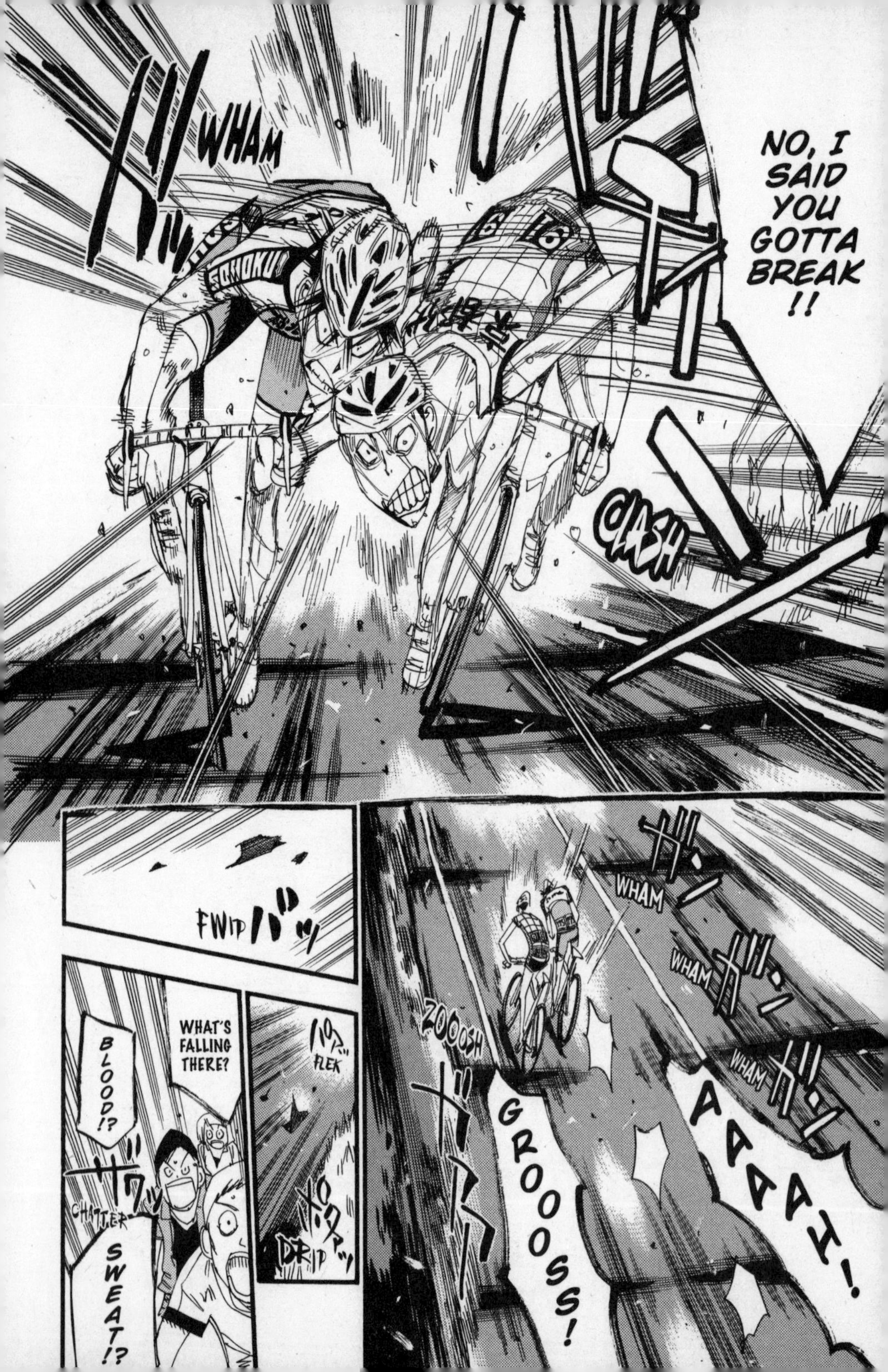
WHAM
NO, I SAID YOU GOTTA BREAK!!
CLASH
WHAM
WHAM
WHAM
AAAAH!
ZOOOSH
GROOOSS!
FWIP
FLEK
DRIP
WHAT'S FALLING THERE?
BLOOD!?
CHATTER
SWEAT!?

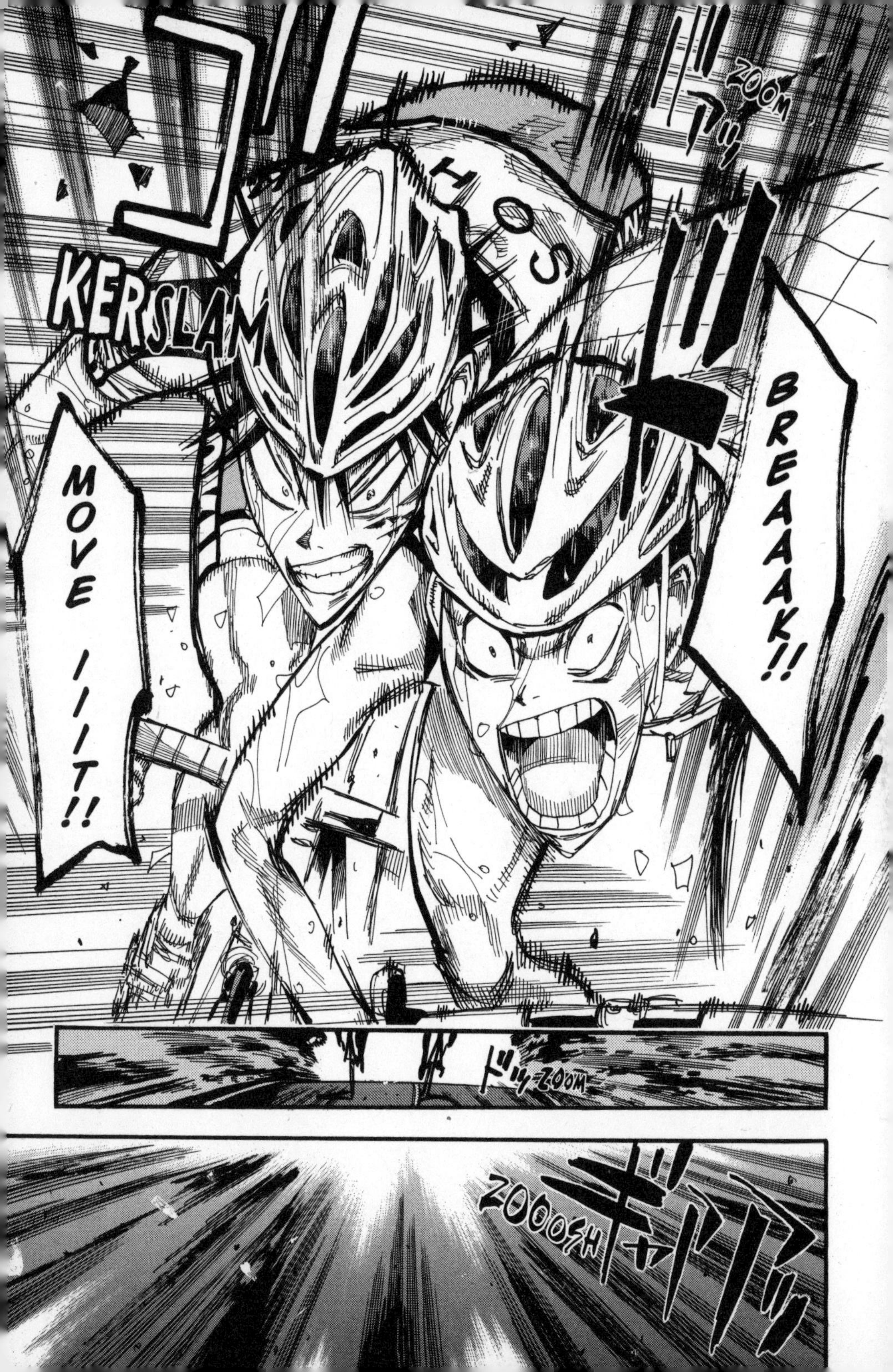
ZOOM
BREAAAK!!
KERSLAM
MOVE IIIIT!!
ZOOM
ZOOOSH

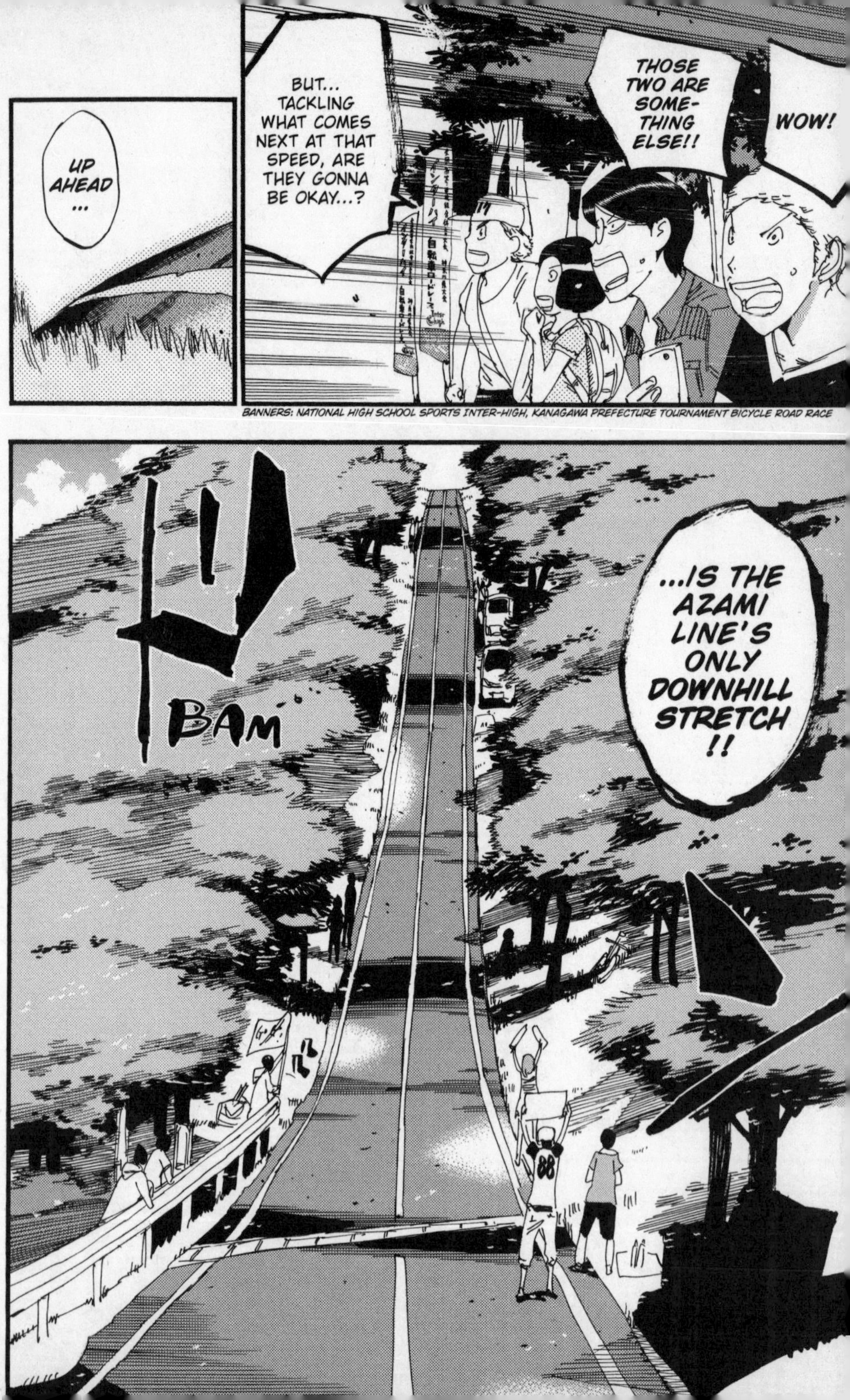

WOW!
THOSE TWO ARE SOME-THING ELSE!!
BUT... TACKLING WHAT COMES NEXT AT THAT SPEED, ARE THEY GONNA BE OKAY...?
BANNERS: NATIONAL HIGH SCHOOL SPORTS INTER-HIGH, KANAGAWA PREFECTURE TOURNAMENT BICYCLE ROAD RACE
UP AHEAD...
...IS THE AZAMI LINE'S ONLY DOWNHILL STRETCH!!
BAM

RIDE.212 BATTLE ON THE BRINK

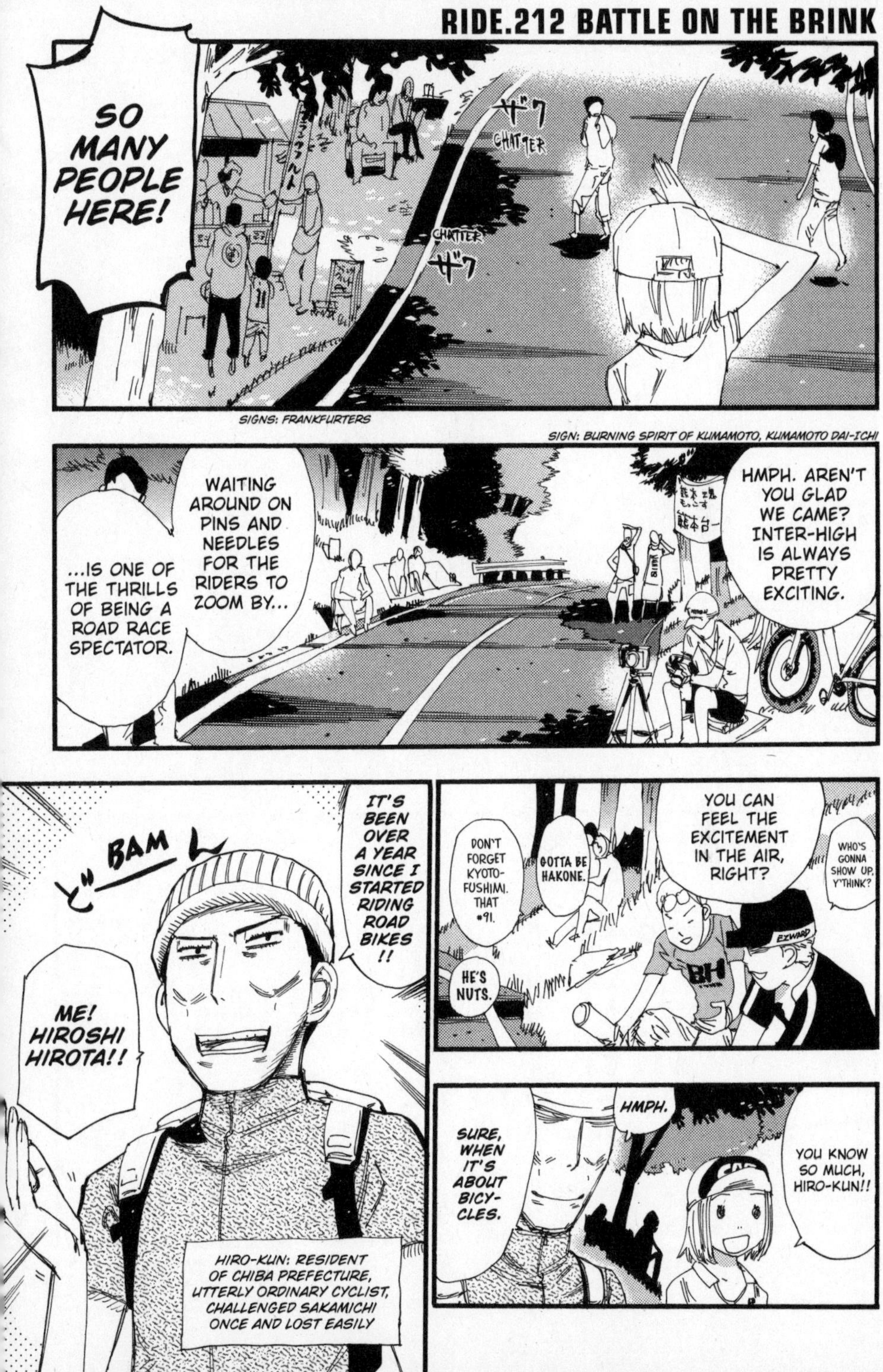
SO MANY PEOPLE HERE!
ザク CHATTER
ザク CHATTER
SIGNS: FRANKFURTERS
SIGN: BURNING SPIRIT OF KUMAMOTO, KUMAMOTO DAI-ICHI
HMPH. AREN'T YOU GLAD WE CAME? INTER-HIGH IS ALWAYS PRETTY EXCITING.
WAITING AROUND ON PINS AND NEEDLES FOR THE RIDERS TO ZOOM BY...
...IS ONE OF THE THRILLS OF BEING A ROAD RACE SPECTATOR.
WHO'S GONNA SHOW UP, Y'THINK?
YOU CAN FEEL THE EXCITEMENT IN THE AIR, RIGHT?
GOTTA BE HAKONE.
DON'T FORGET KYOTO-FUSHIMI. THAT #91.
HE'S NUTS.
YOU KNOW SO MUCH, HIRO-KUN!!
HMPH.
SURE, WHEN IT'S ABOUT BICYCLES.
IT'S BEEN OVER A YEAR SINCE I STARTED RIDING ROAD BIKES!!
BAM
ME! HIROSHI HIROTA!!
HIRO-KUN: RESIDENT OF CHIBA PREFECTURE, UTTERLY ORDINARY CYCLIST, CHALLENGED SAKAMICHI ONCE AND LOST EASILY

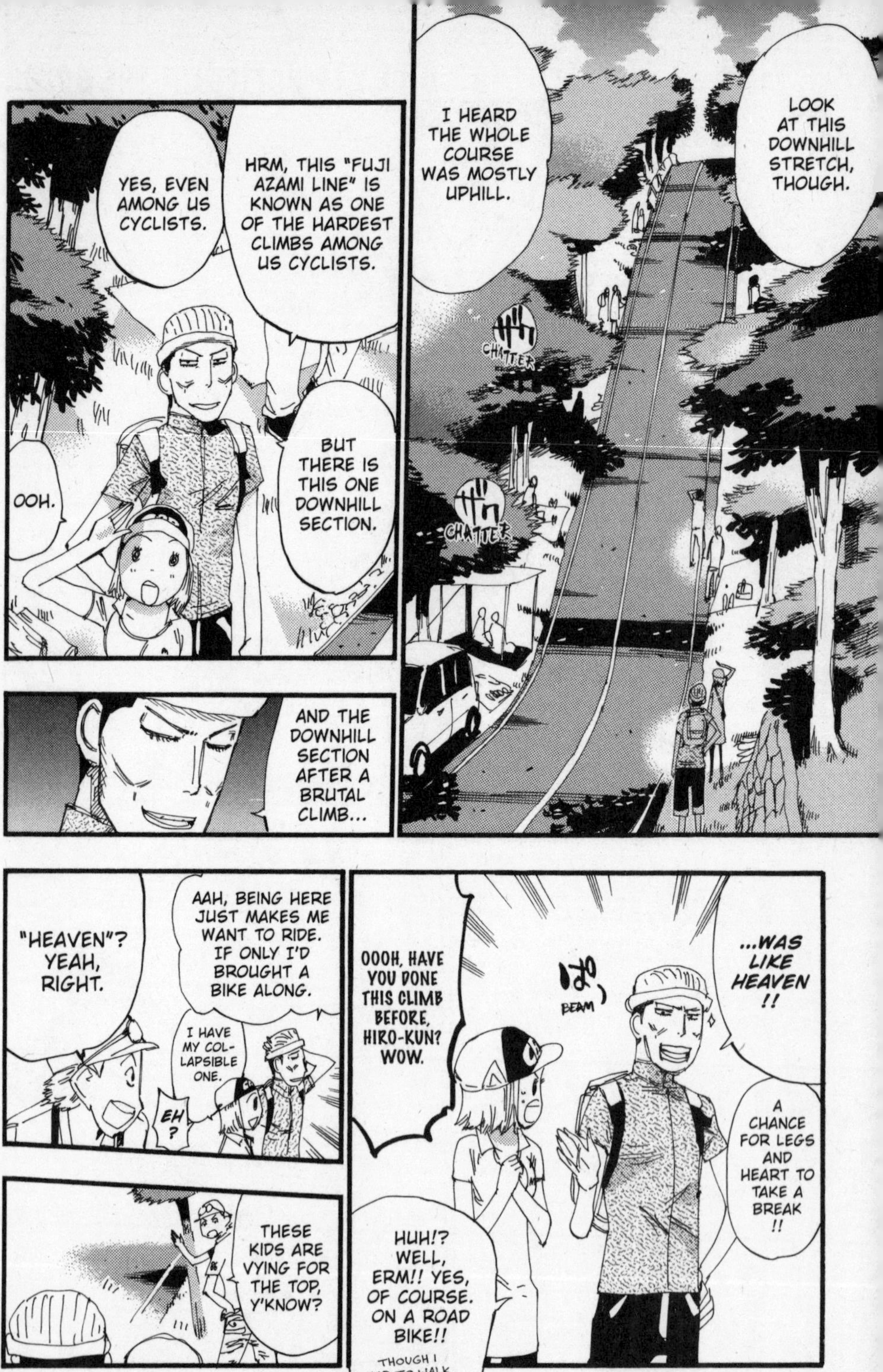
LOOK AT THIS DOWNHILL STRETCH, THOUGH.
I HEARD THE WHOLE COURSE WAS MOSTLY UPHILL.
CHATTER
CHATTER
HRM, THIS "FUJI AZAMI LINE" IS KNOWN AS ONE OF THE HARDEST CLIMBS AMONG US CYCLISTS.
YES, EVEN AMONG US CYCLISTS.
BUT THERE IS THIS ONE DOWNHILL SECTION.
OOH.
AND THE DOWNHILL SECTION AFTER A BRUTAL CLIMB...
...WAS LIKE HEAVEN!!
BEAM
A CHANCE FOR LEGS AND HEART TO TAKE A BREAK!!
OOOH, HAVE YOU DONE THIS CLIMB BEFORE, HIRO-KUN? WOW.
HUH!? WELL, ERM!! YES, OF COURSE. ON A ROAD BIKE!!
THOUGH I HAD TO WALK IT PART OF THE WAY.
AAH, BEING HERE JUST MAKES ME WANT TO RIDE. IF ONLY I'D BROUGHT A BIKE ALONG.
"HEAVEN"? YEAH, RIGHT.
I HAVE MY COL-LAPSIBLE ONE.
EH?
THESE KIDS ARE VYING FOR THE TOP, Y'KNOW?

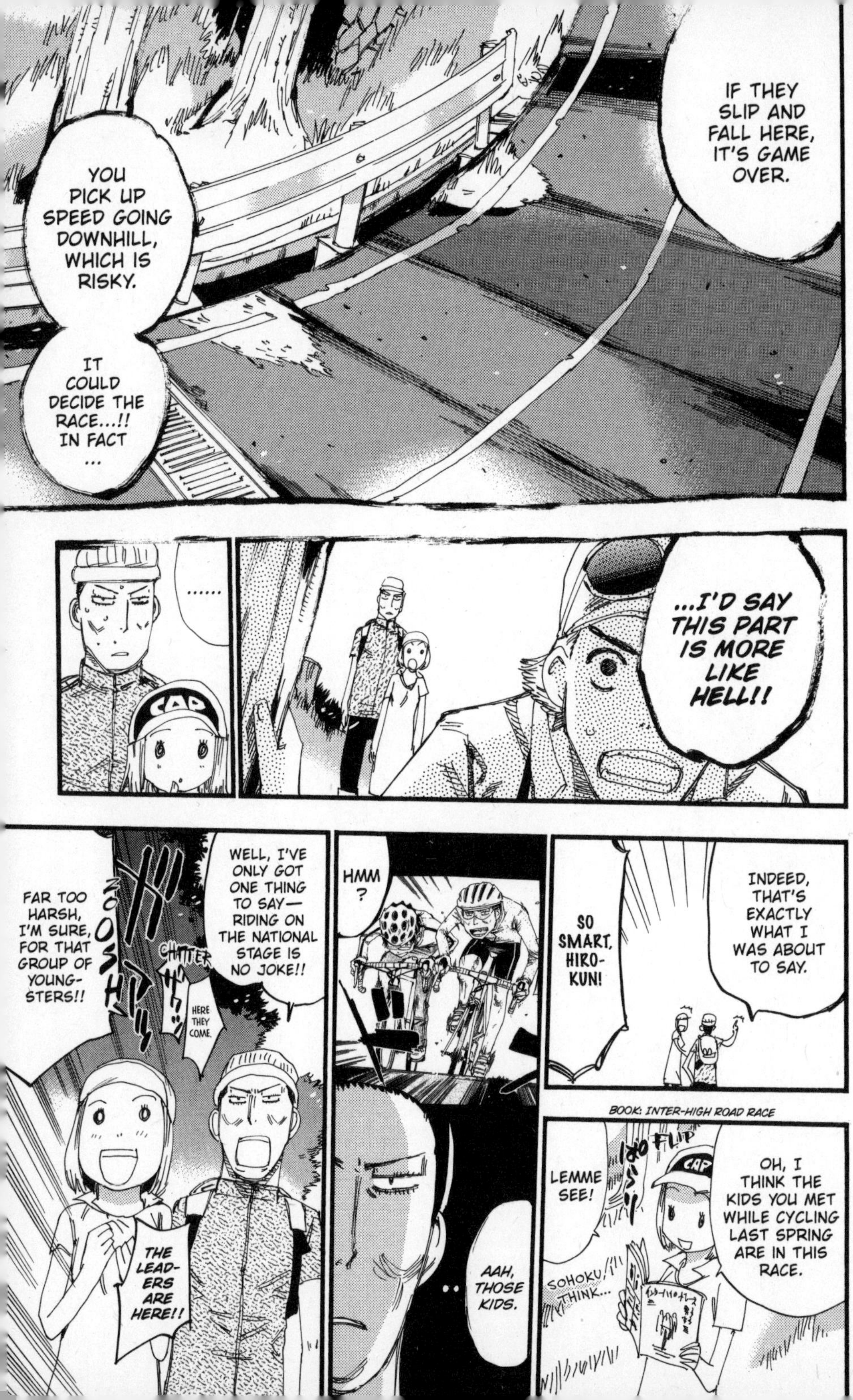
IF THEY SLIP AND FALL HERE, IT'S GAME OVER.
YOU PICK UP SPEED GOING DOWNHILL, WHICH IS RISKY.
IT COULD DECIDE THE RACE...!! IN FACT ...
...I'D SAY THIS PART IS MORE LIKE HELL!!
......
INDEED, THAT'S EXACTLY WHAT I WAS ABOUT TO SAY.
SO SMART, HIRO-KUN!
BOOK: INTER-HIGH ROAD RACE
OH, I THINK THE KIDS YOU MET WHILE CYCLING LAST SPRING ARE IN THIS RACE.
FLIP
LEMME SEE!
SOHOKU, THINK...
HMM?
AAH, THOSE KIDS.
WELL, I'VE ONLY GOT ONE THING TO SAY—RIDING ON THE NATIONAL STAGE IS NO JOKE!!
FAR TOO HARSH, I'M SURE, FOR THAT GROUP OF YOUNG-STERS!!
ZOOSH
CHATTER
HERE THEY COME.
THE LEADERS ARE HERE!!

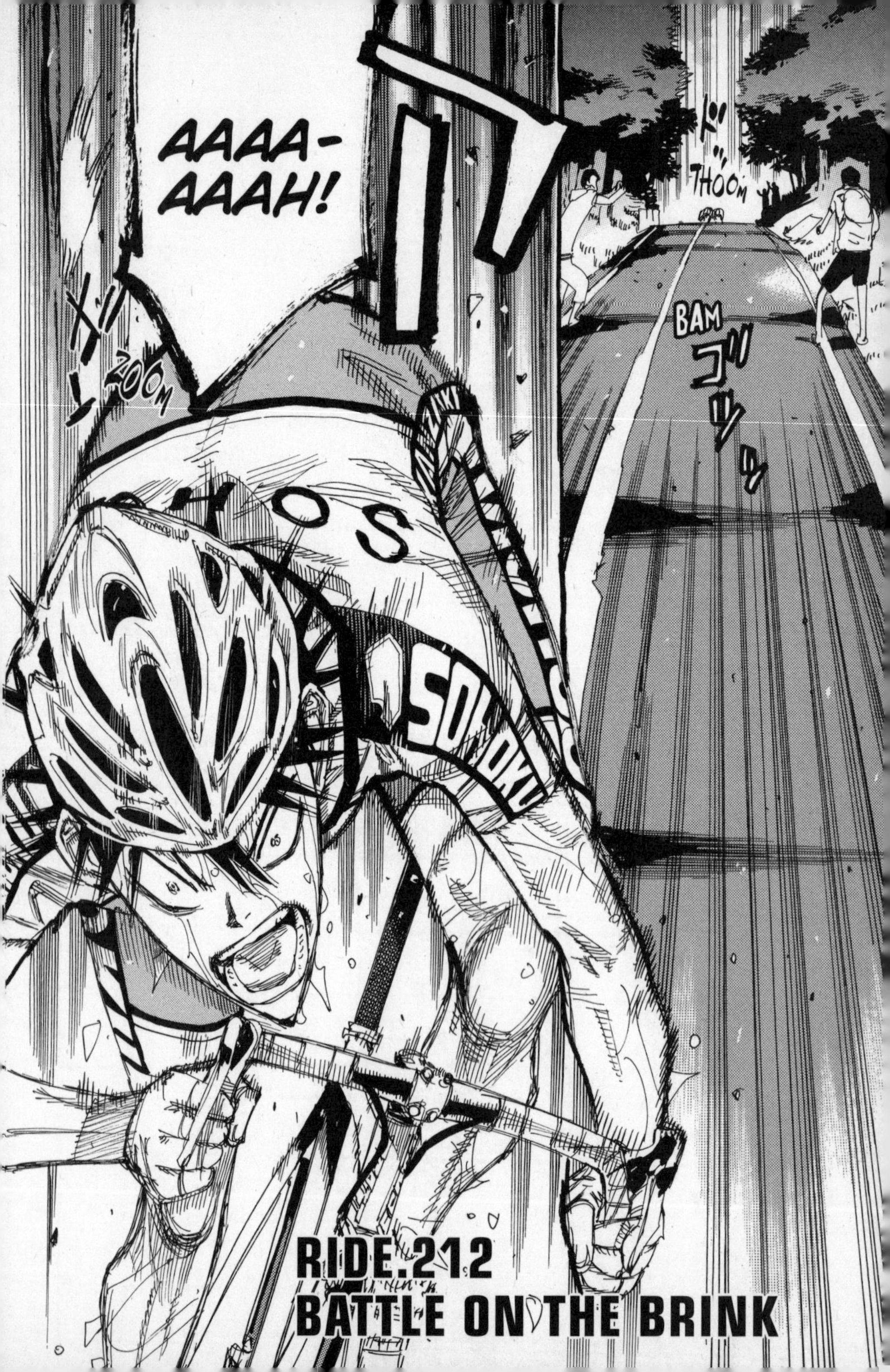
THOOM
BAM
AAAA-AAAAH!
ZOOM
RIDE.212
BATTLE ON THE BRINK

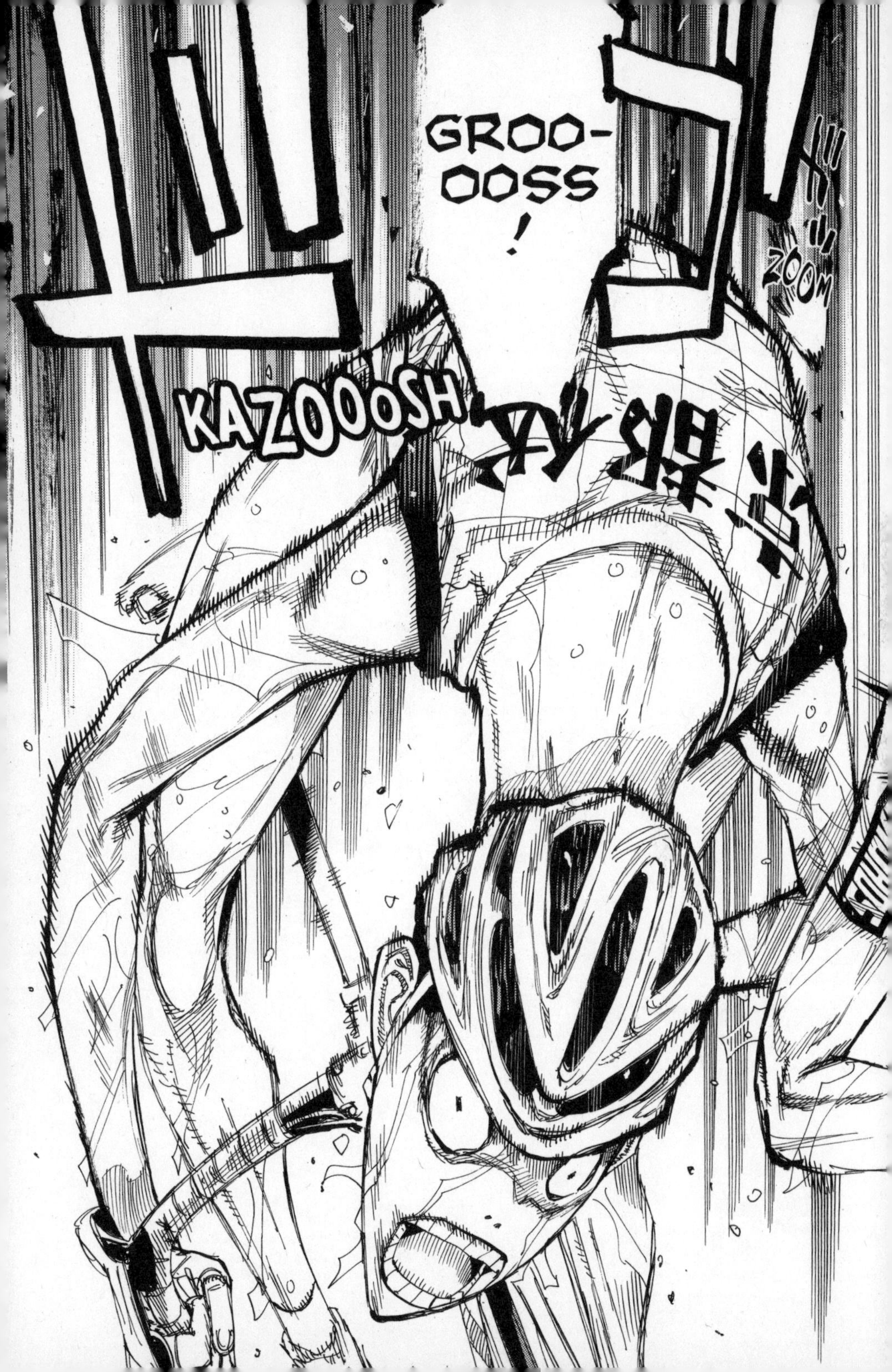
GROO-
OOSS
!
ZOOM
KAZOOOSH

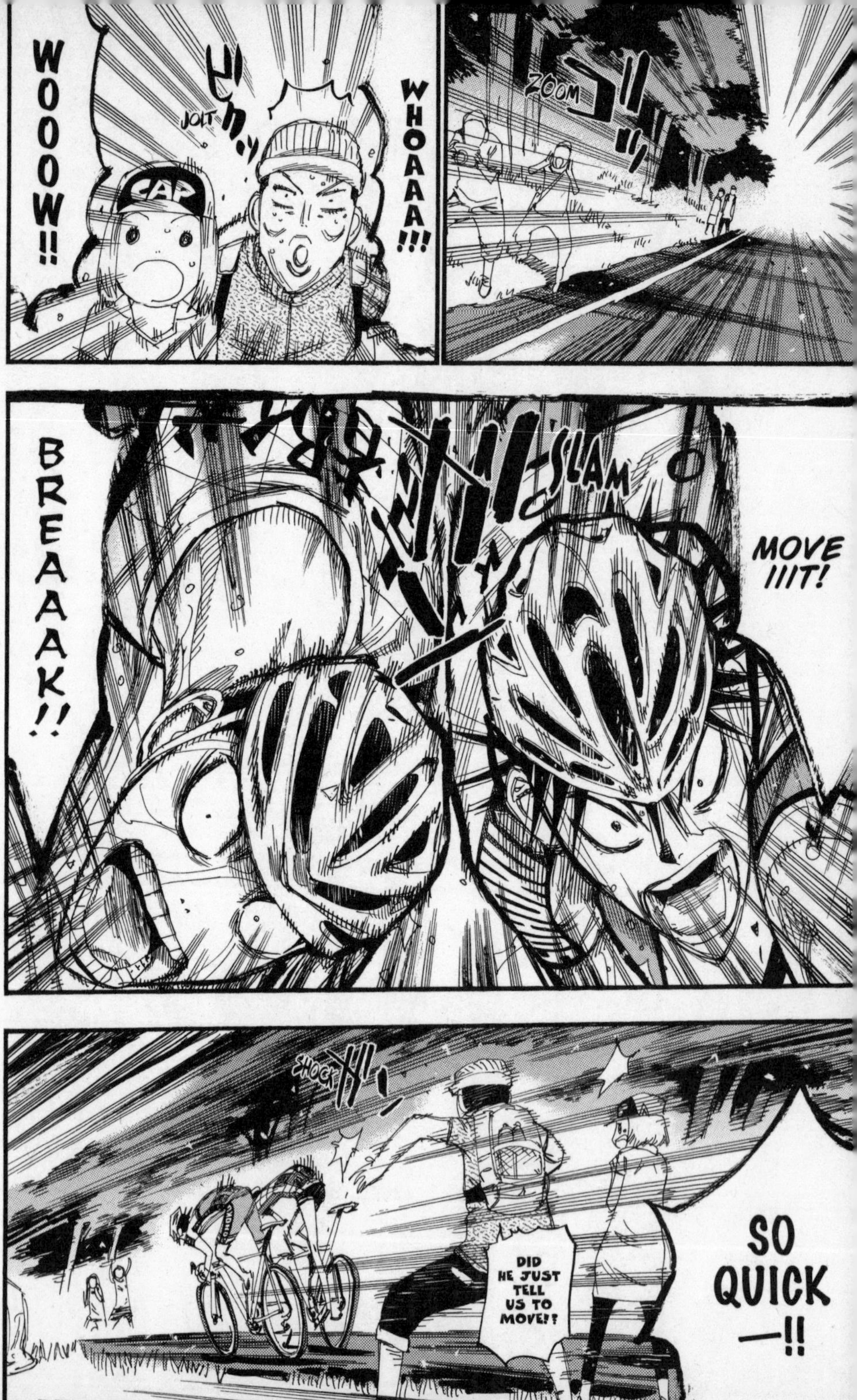

ZOOM
WHOAAAA!!!
JOLT
CAP
WOOOOW!!
MOVE IIIT!
SLAM
BREAAAK!!
SO QUICK—!!
DID HE JUST TELL US TO MOVE!?
SHOCK

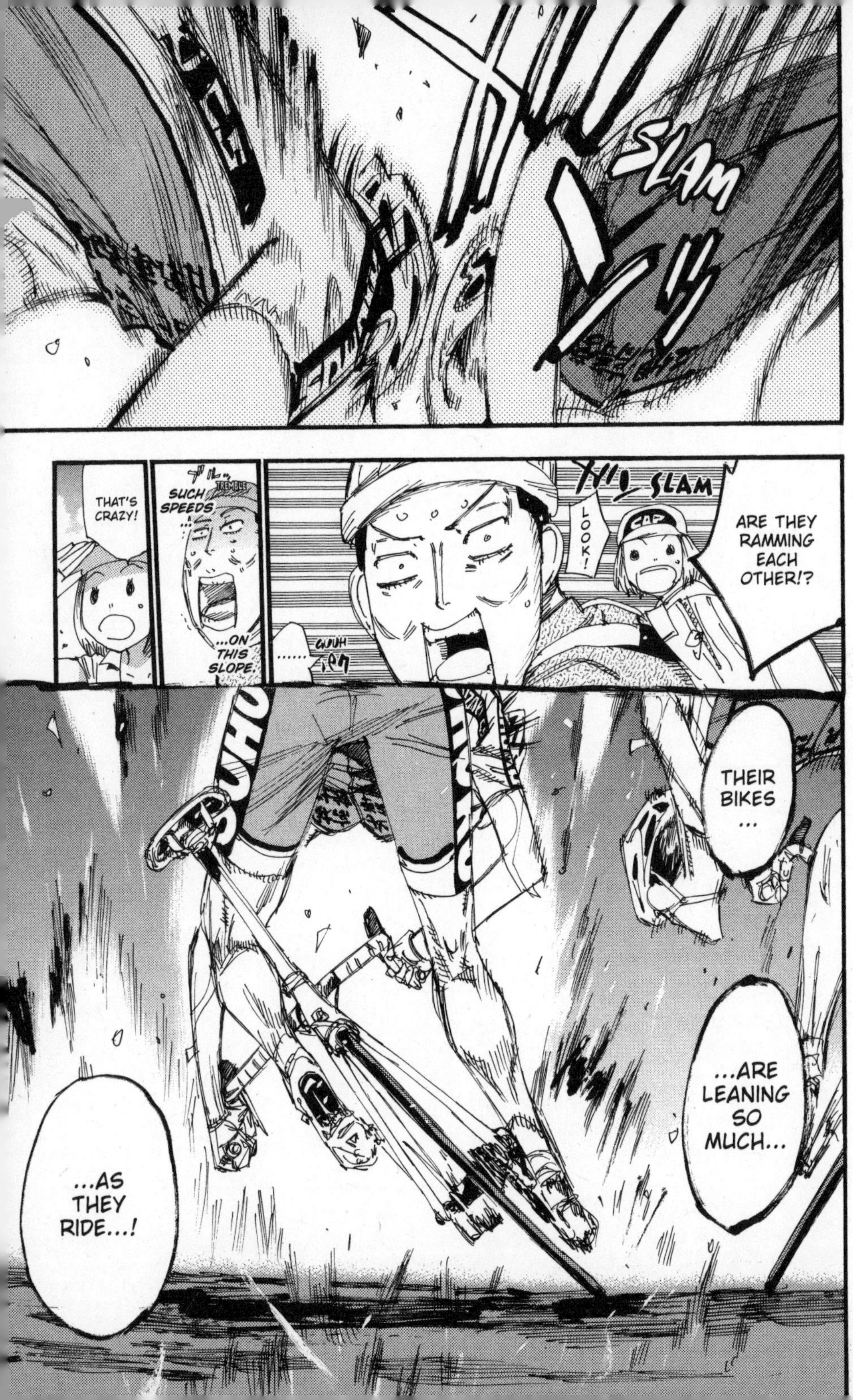
SLAM
SLAM
ARE THEY RAMMING EACH OTHER!?
LOOK!
GUUH
......
TREMBLE
SUCH SPEEDS...
...ON THIS SLOPE.
THAT'S CRAZY!
THEIR BIKES...
...ARE LEANING SO MUCH...
...AS THEY RIDE...!

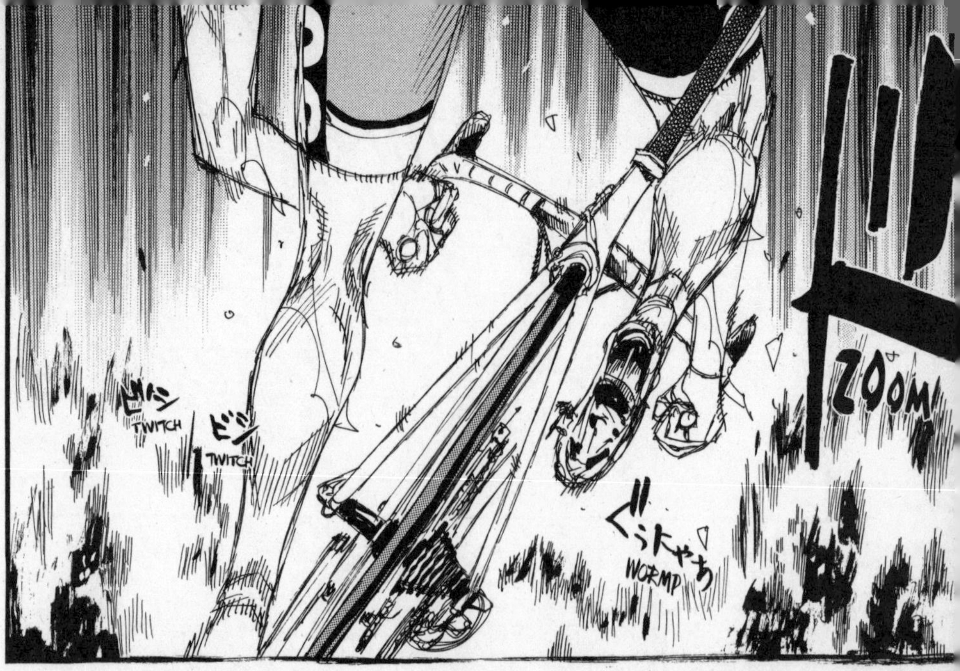
ZOOM
WORMP
TWITCH
TWITCH
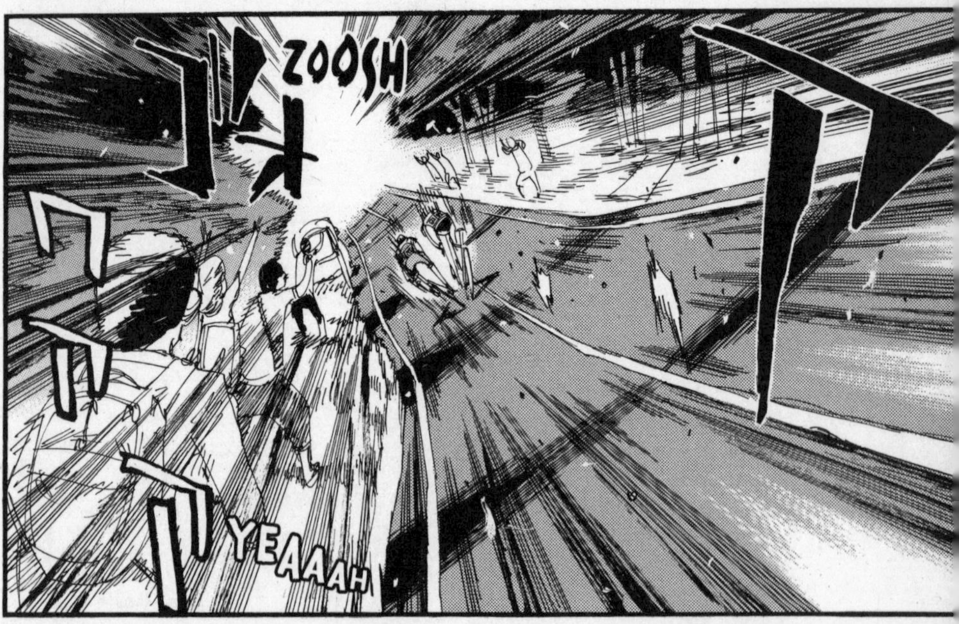
ZOOSH
YEAAAAH
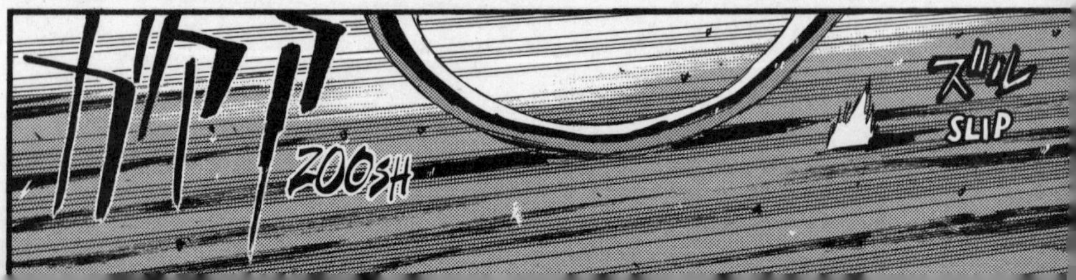
SLIP
ZOOSH

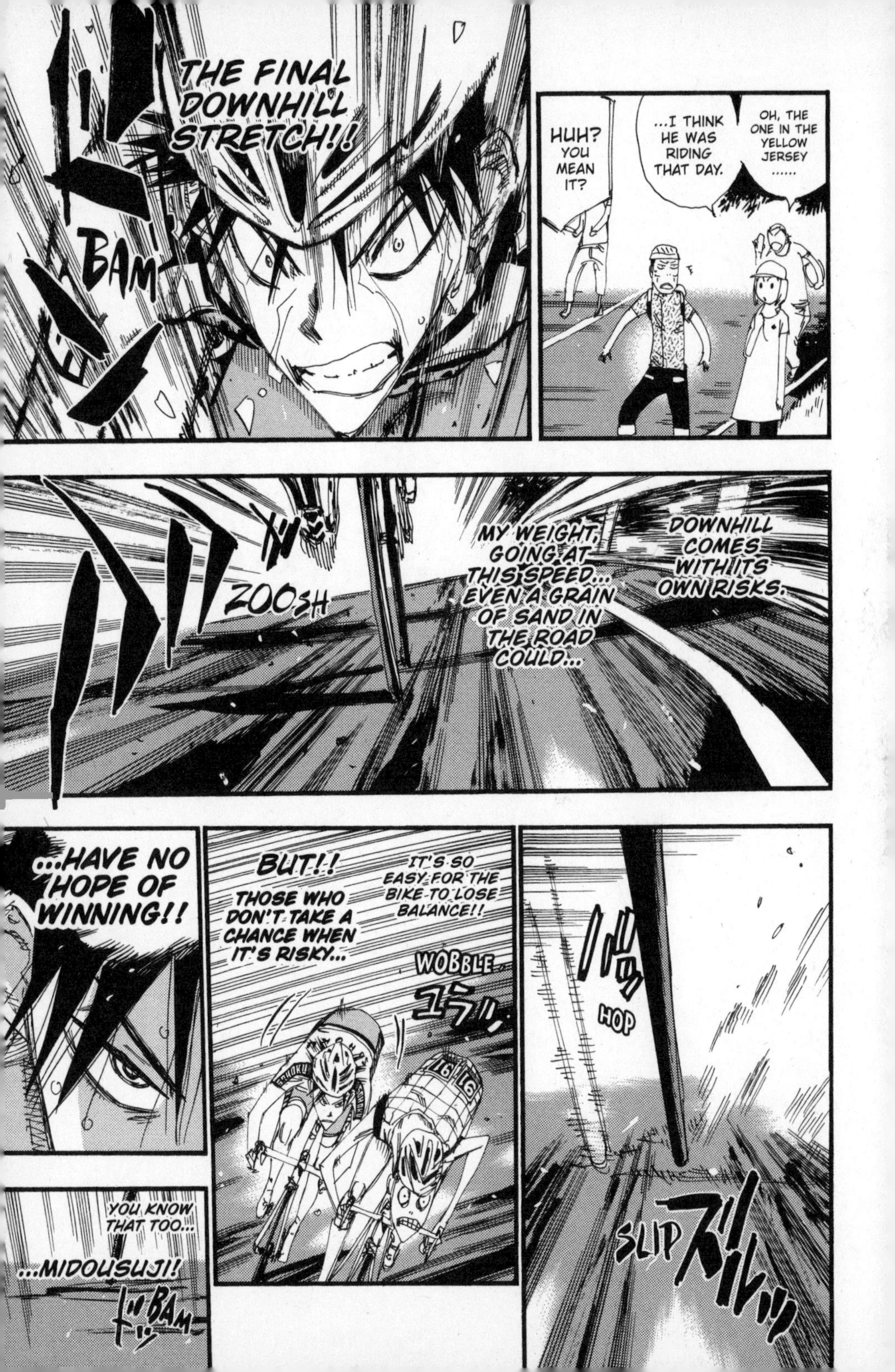
OH, THE ONE IN THE YELLOW JERSEY......
...I THINK HE WAS RIDING THAT DAY.
HUH? YOU MEAN IT?
THE FINAL DOWNHILL STRETCH!!
BAM
DOWNHILL COMES WITH ITS OWN RISKS.
MY WEIGHT, GOING AT THIS SPEED... EVEN A GRAIN OF SAND IN THE ROAD COULD...
ZOOSH
HOP
SLIP
IT'S SO EASY FOR THE BIKE TO LOSE BALANCE!!
BUT!!
THOSE WHO DON'T TAKE A CHANCE WHEN IT'S RISKY...
WOBBLE
...HAVE NO HOPE OF WINNING!!
YOU KNOW THAT TOO...
...MIDOUSUJI!
BAM

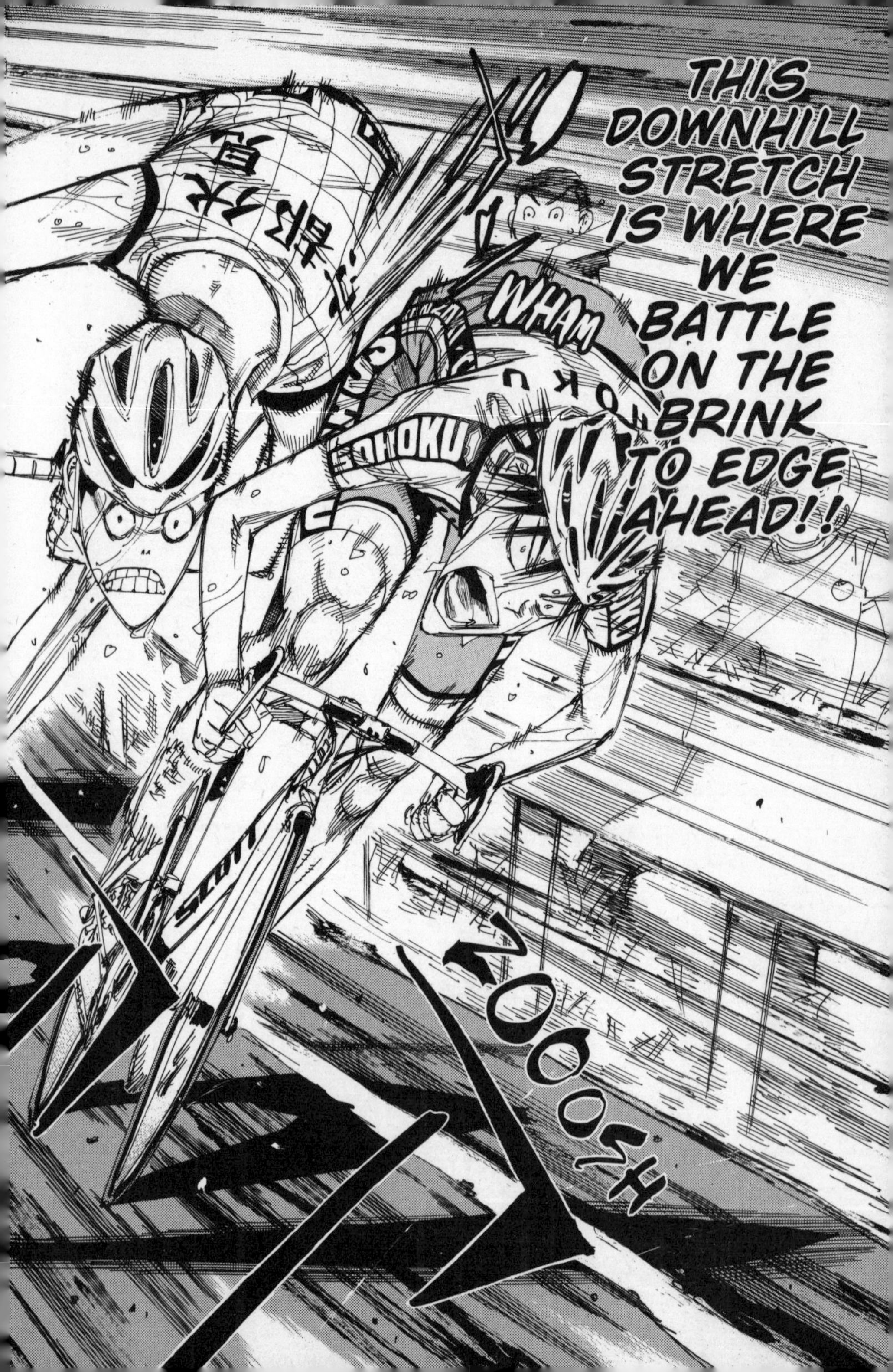

THIS DOWNHILL STRETCH IS WHERE WE BATTLE ON THE BRINK TO EDGE AHEAD!!
WHAM
SOHOKU
ZOOOSH

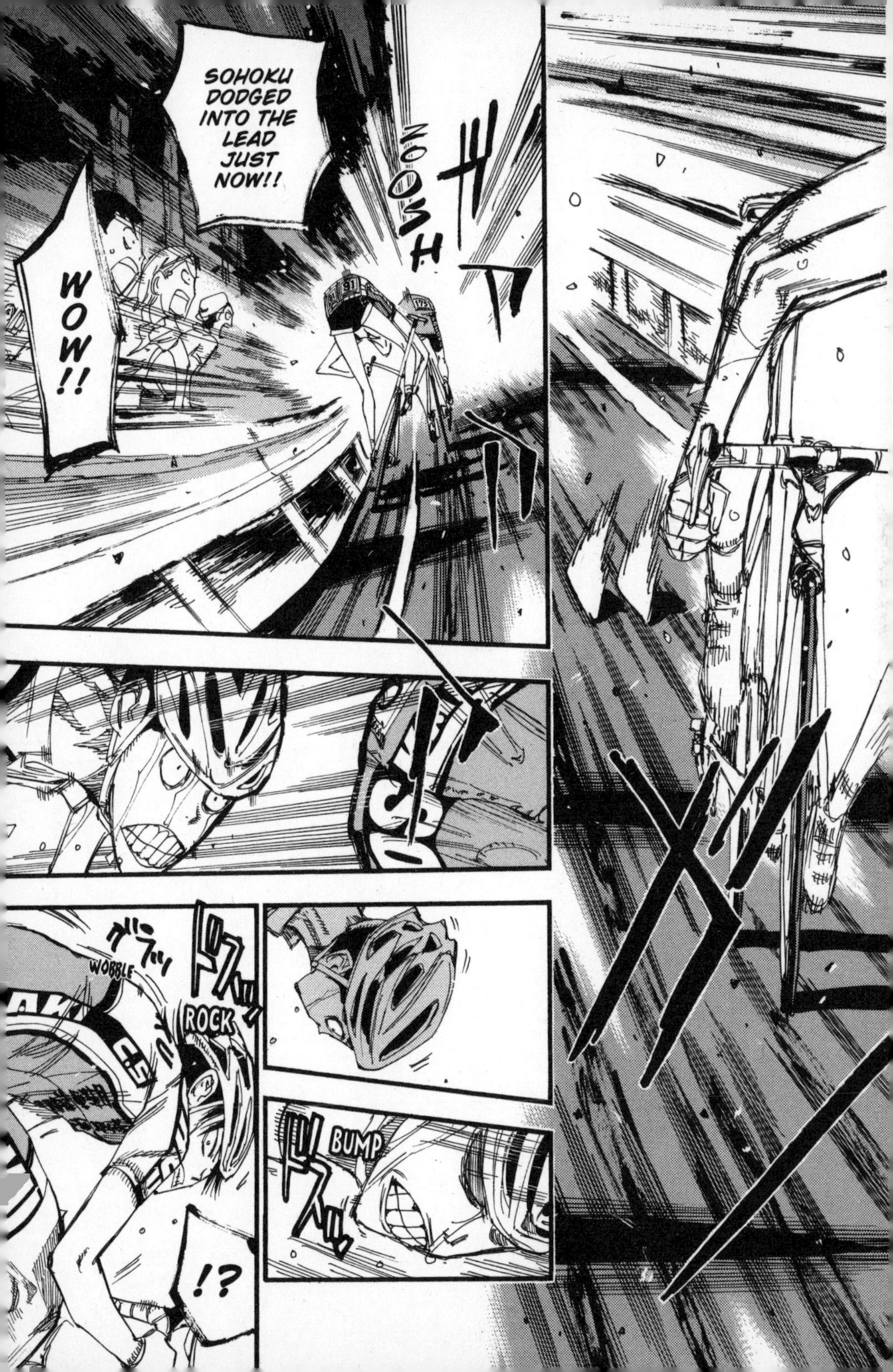

SOHOKU DODGED INTO THE LEAD JUST NOW!!
WHOOSH
WOW!!
BUMP
WOBBLE
ROCK
!?

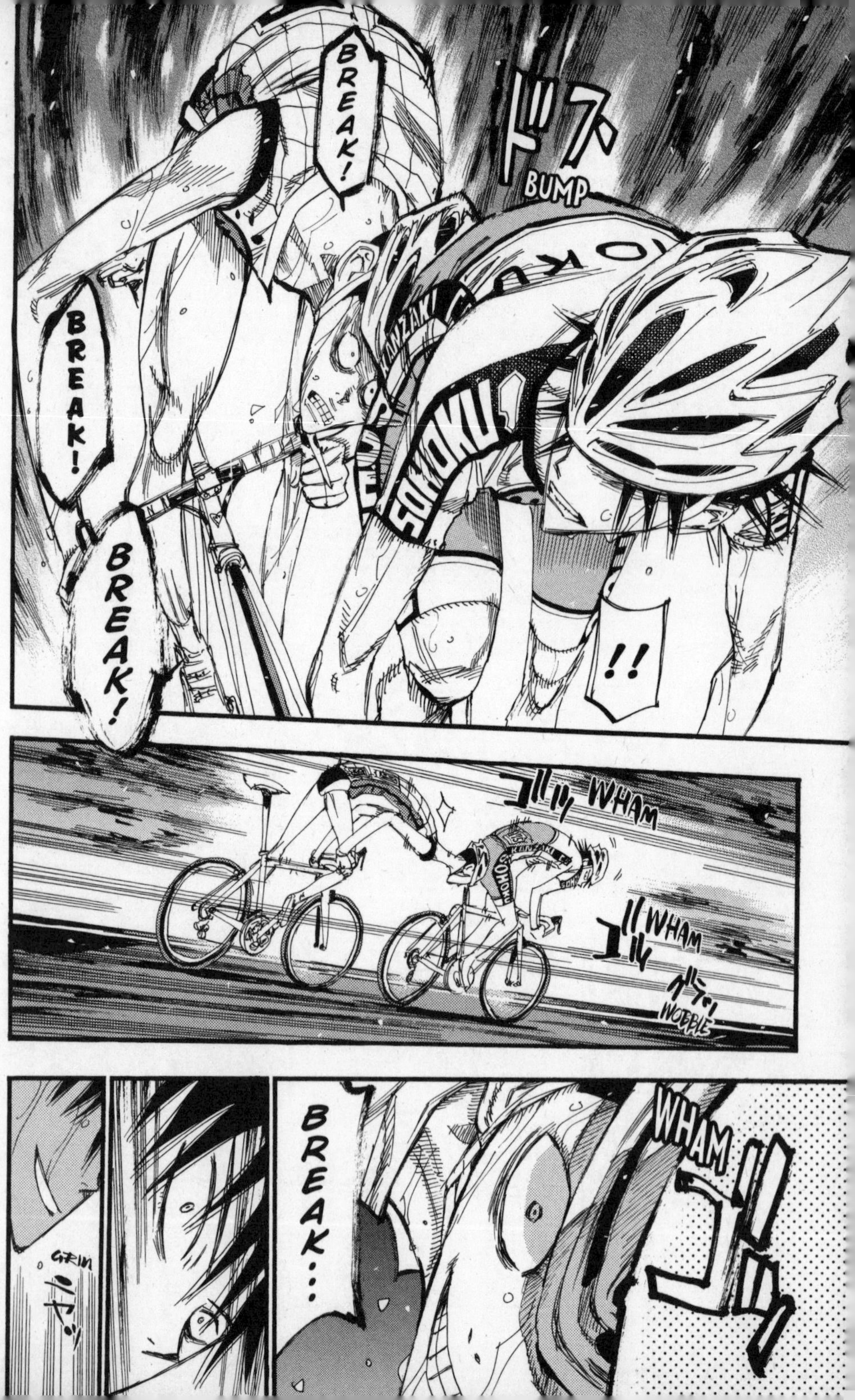
BUMP
BREAK!
BREAK!
BREAK!
!!
WHAM
WHAM
WOBBLE
WHAM!!
BREAK...
GRIN

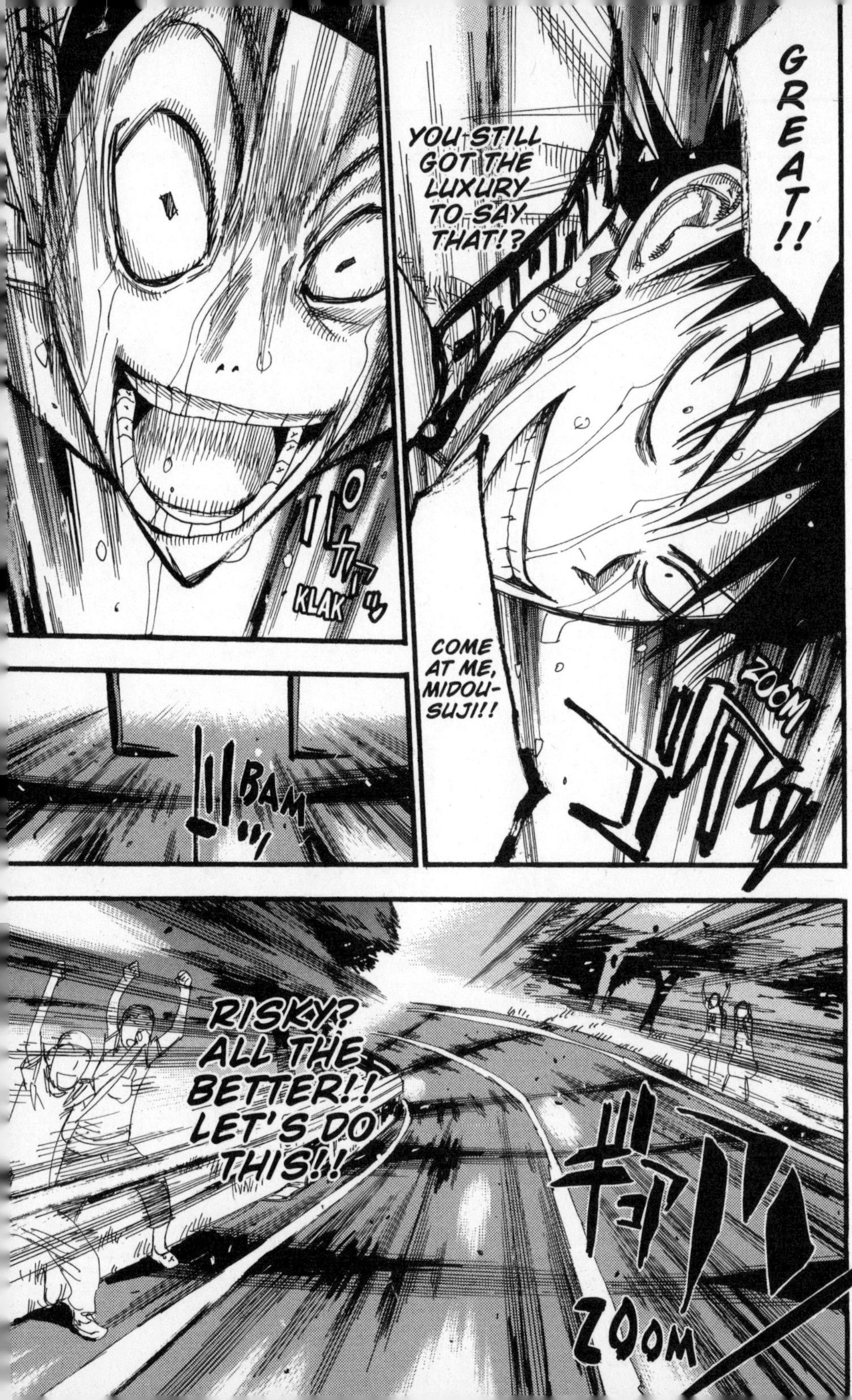
GREAT!!
YOU STILL GOT THE LUXURY TO SAY THAT!?
COME AT ME, MIDOUSUJI!!
ZOOM
KLAK
BAM
RISKY? ALL THE BETTER!! LET'S DO THIS!!
ZOOM

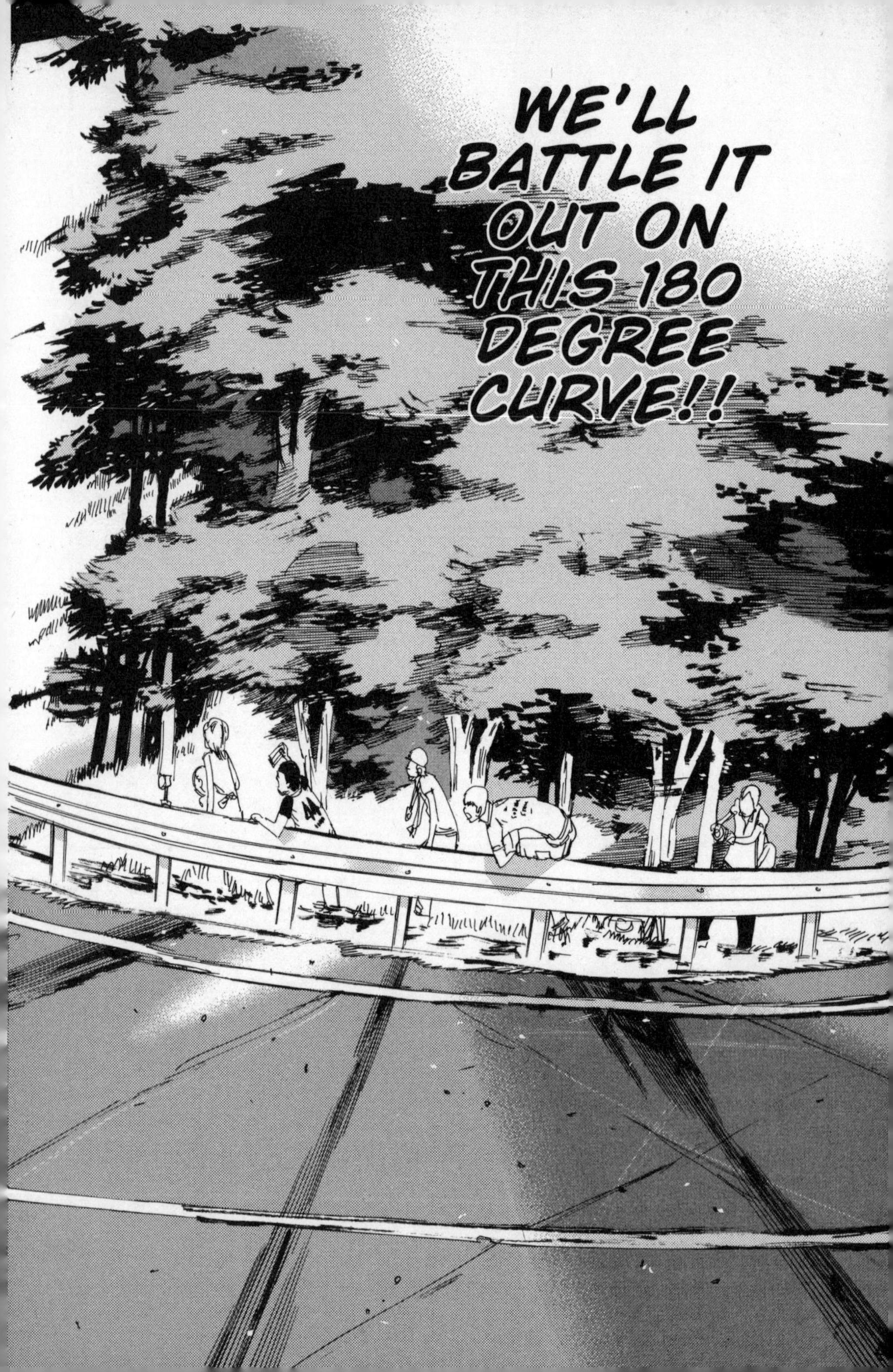
WE'LL BATTLE IT OUT ON THIS 180 DEGREE CURVE!!

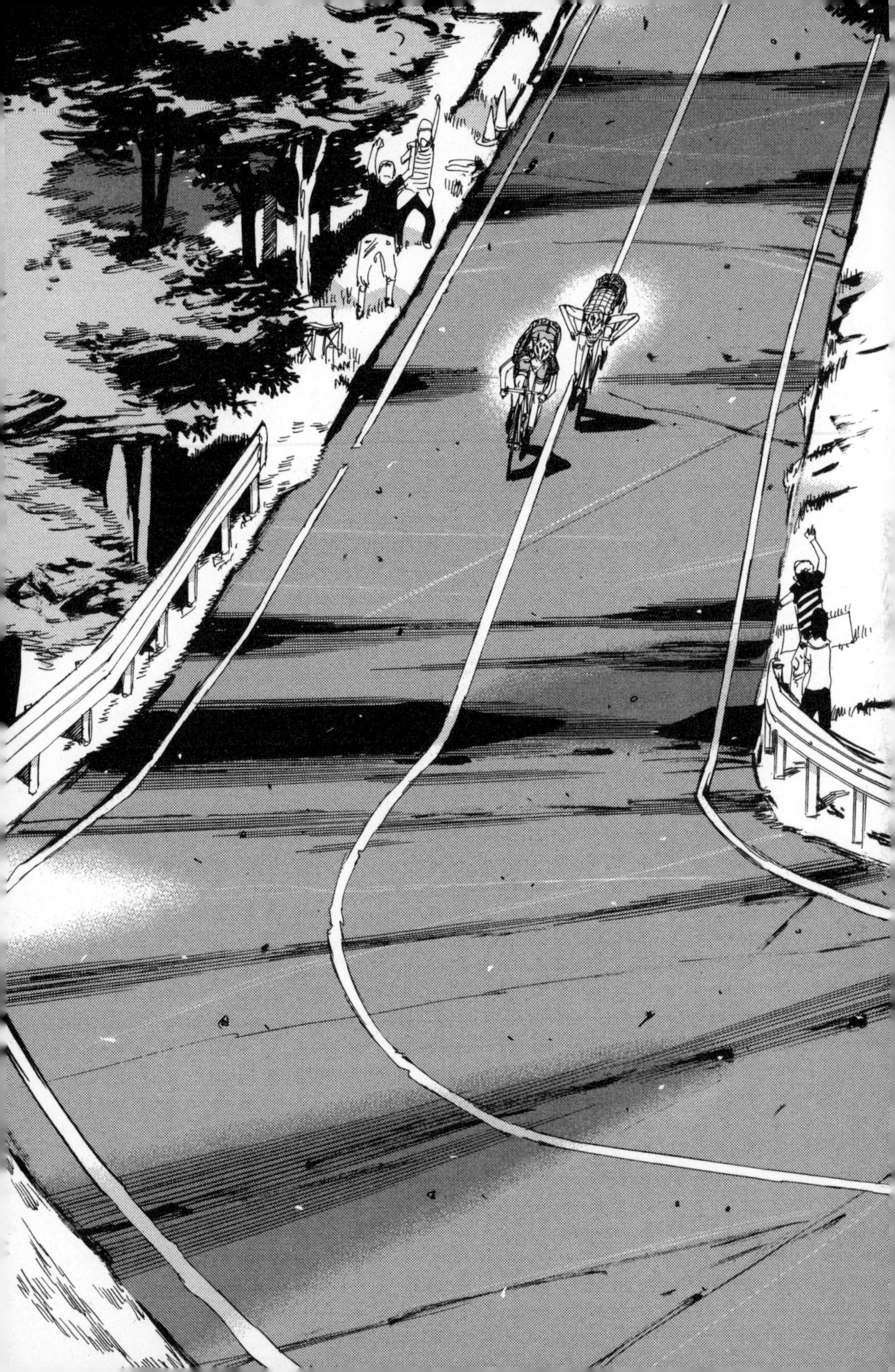

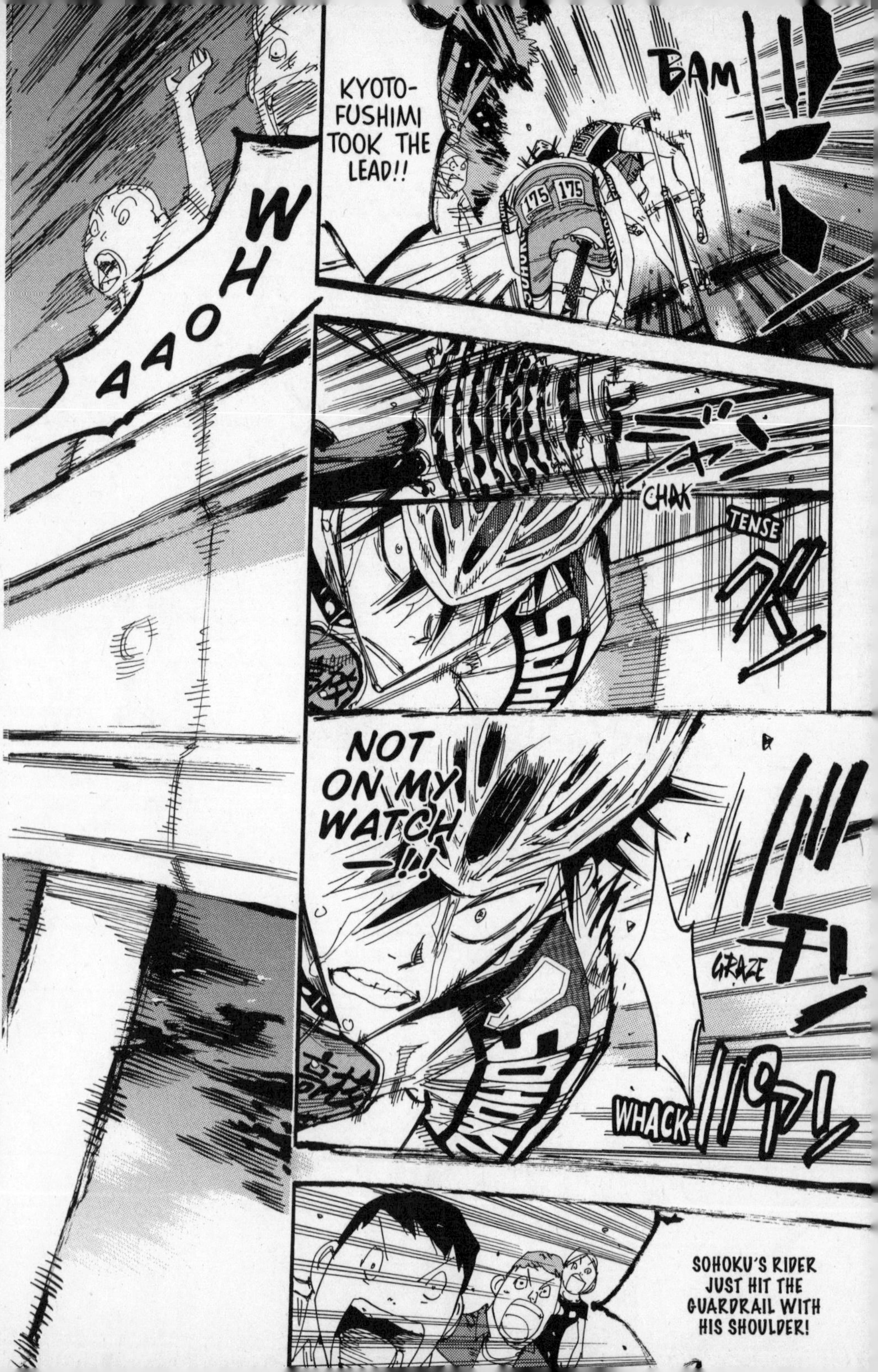
BAM
KYOTO-FUSHIMI TOOK THE LEAD!!
CHAK
TENSE
NOT ON MY WATCH—!!!
GRAZE
WHACK
SOHOKU'S RIDER JUST HIT THE GUARDRAIL WITH HIS SHOULDER!
WHOAAA

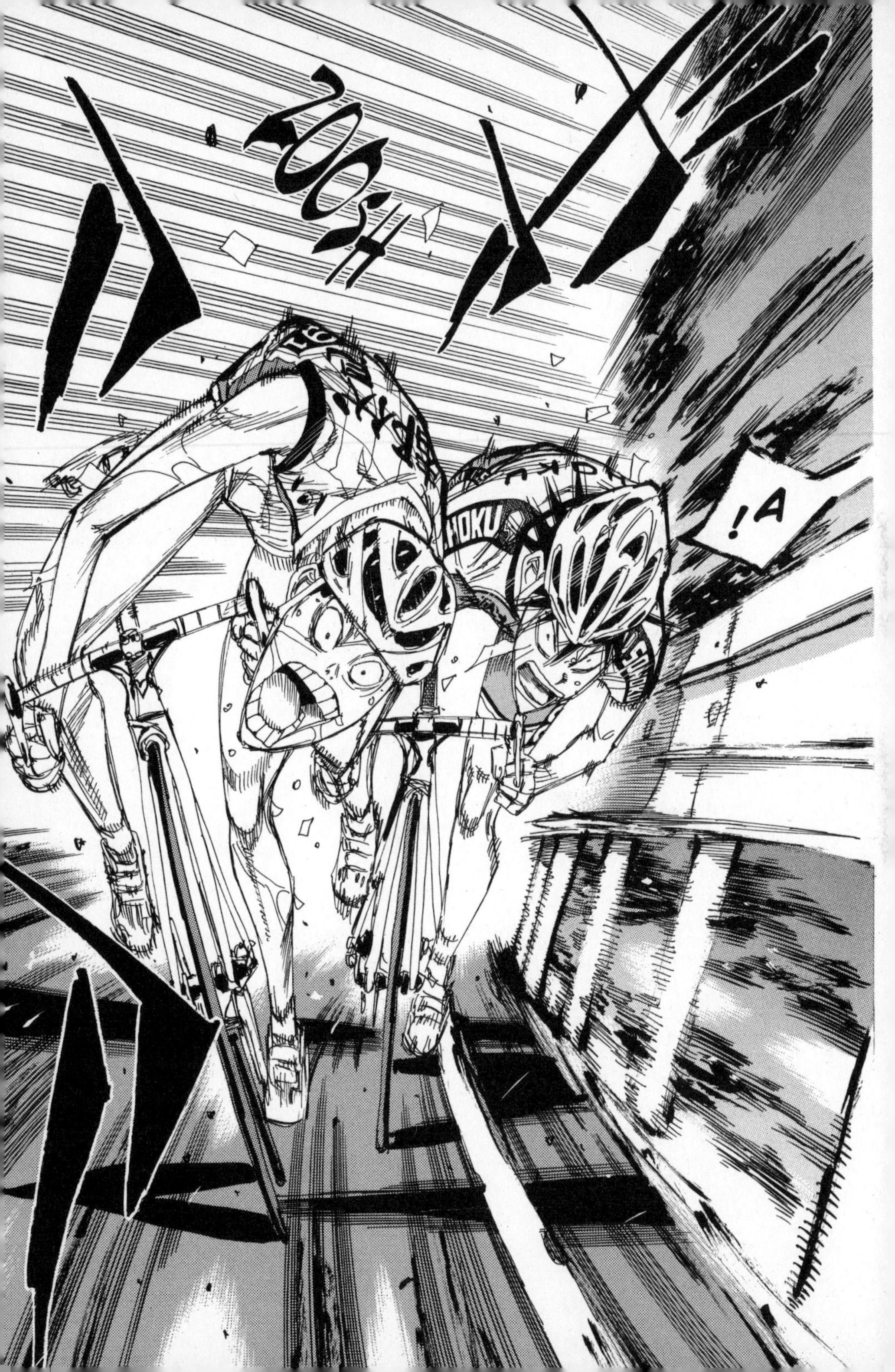
!A

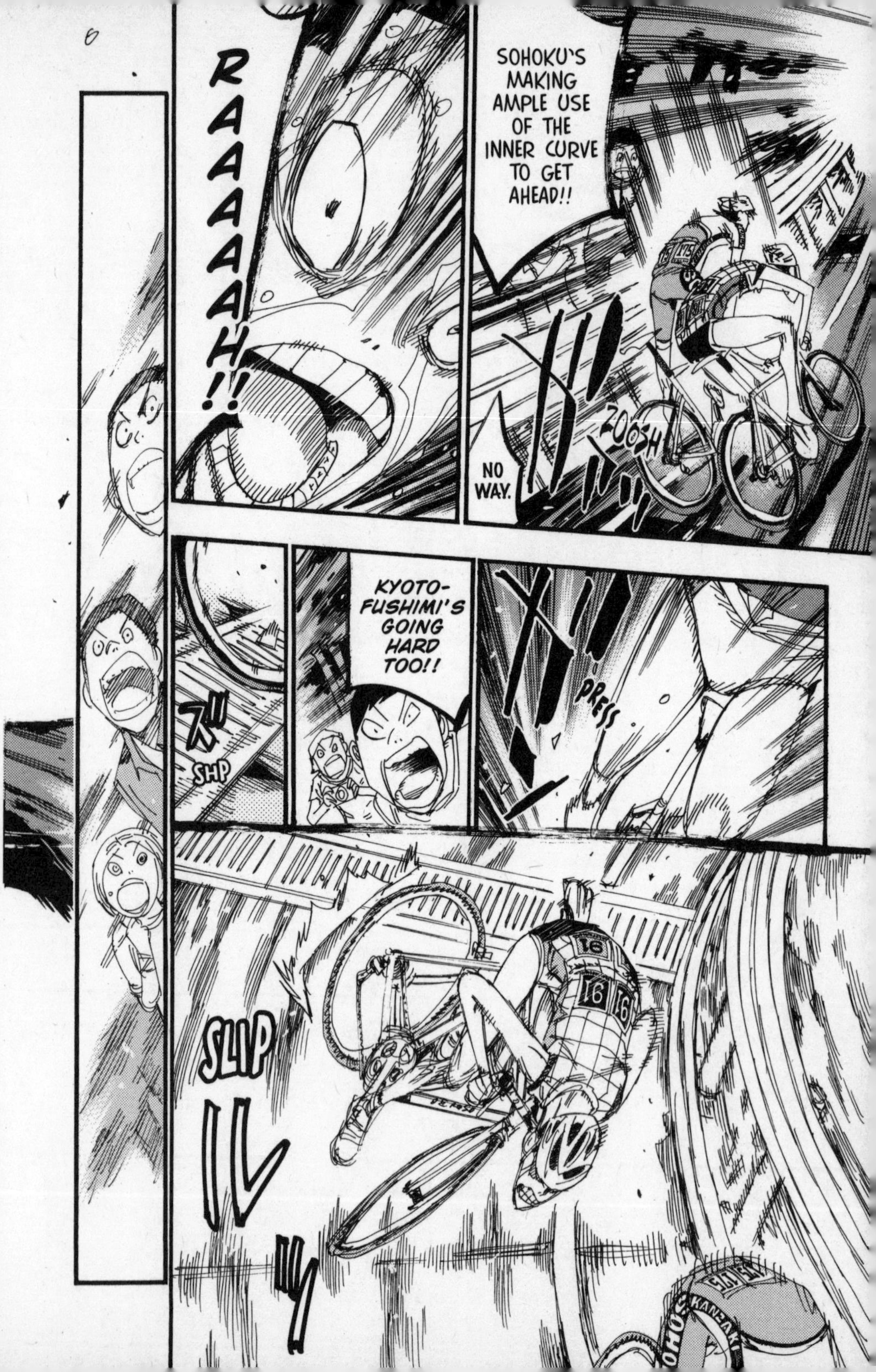
SOHOKU'S MAKING AMPLE USE OF THE INNER CURVE TO GET AHEAD!!
NO WAY.
ZOOSH
RAAAAAAH!!
PRESS
KYOTO-FUSHIMI'S GOING HARD TOO!!
SHP
SLIP

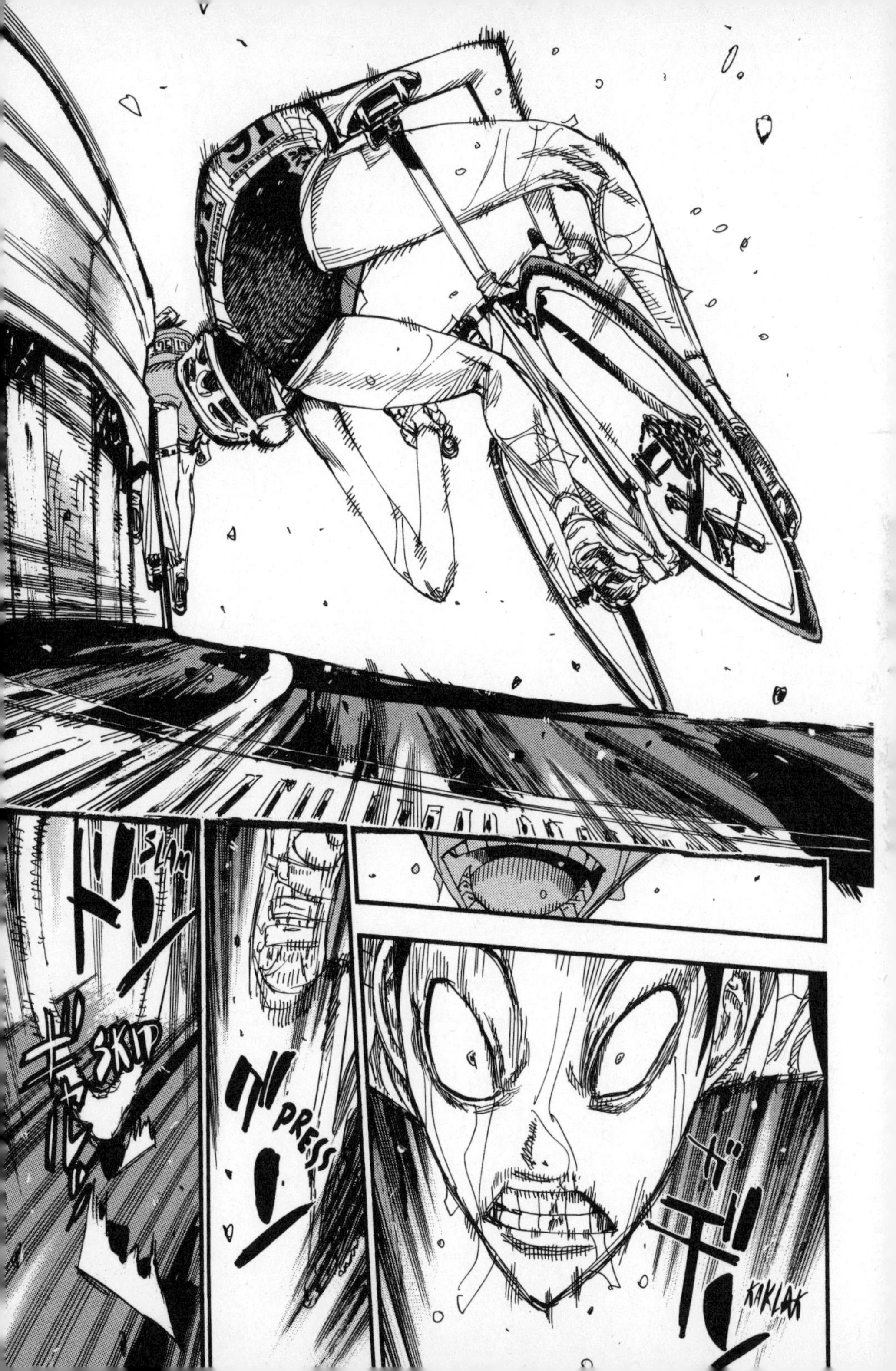
SLAM
SKID
PRESS
KAKLAK

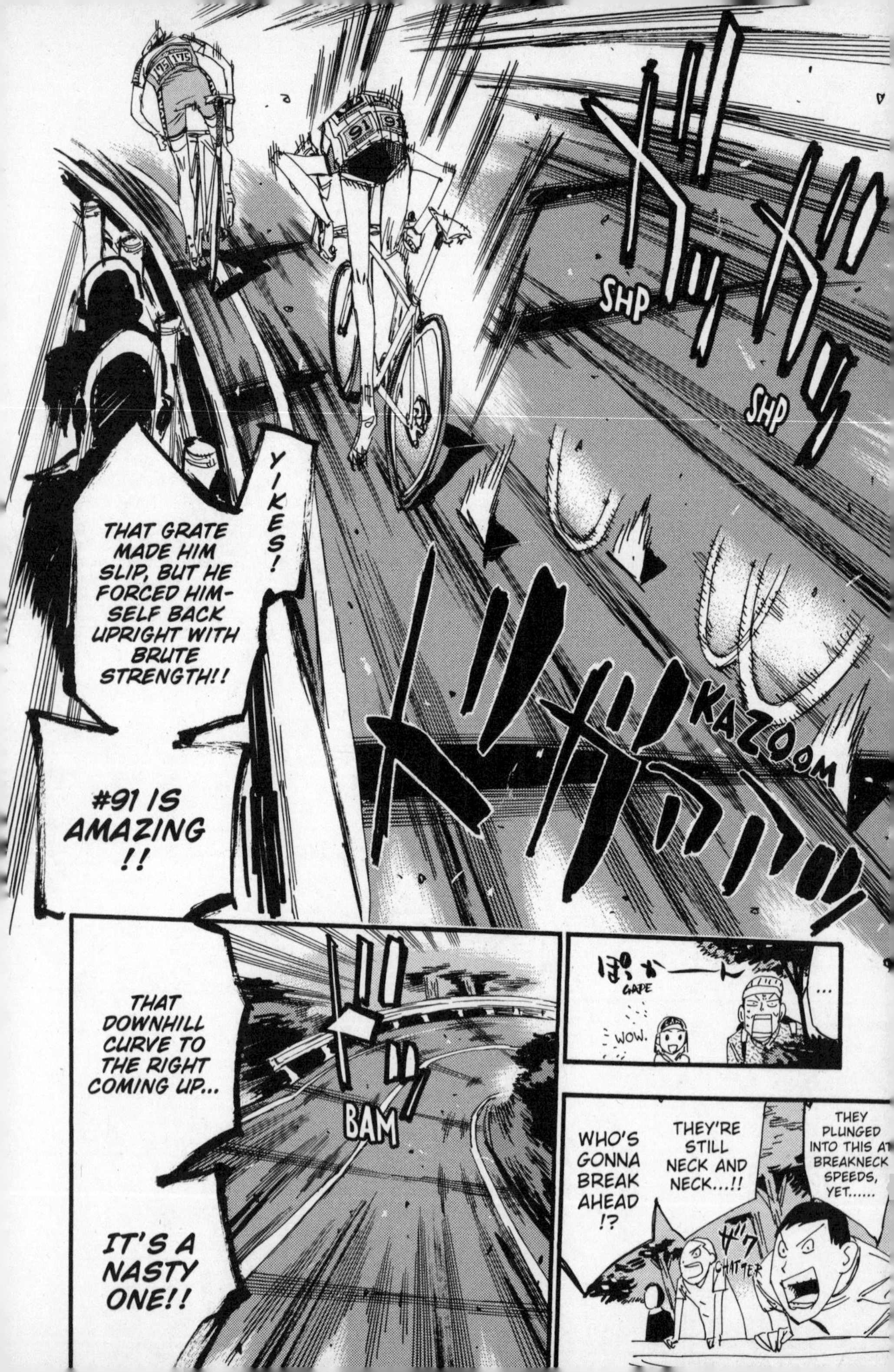
SHP
SHP
KAZOOM
YIKES!
THAT GRATE MADE HIM SLIP, BUT HE FORCED HIM-SELF BACK UPRIGHT WITH BRUTE STRENGTH!!
#91 IS AMAZING!!
ぽかーーん
GAPE
...
WOW.
THEY PLUNGED INTO THIS AT BREAKNECK SPEEDS, YET......
THEY'RE STILL NECK AND NECK...!!
WHO'S GONNA BREAK AHEAD!?
ザク
CHATTER
BAM
THAT DOWNHILL CURVE TO THE RIGHT COMING UP...
IT'S A NASTY ONE!!

RIDE.213 WHAT LIES BEYOND THE FIGHT

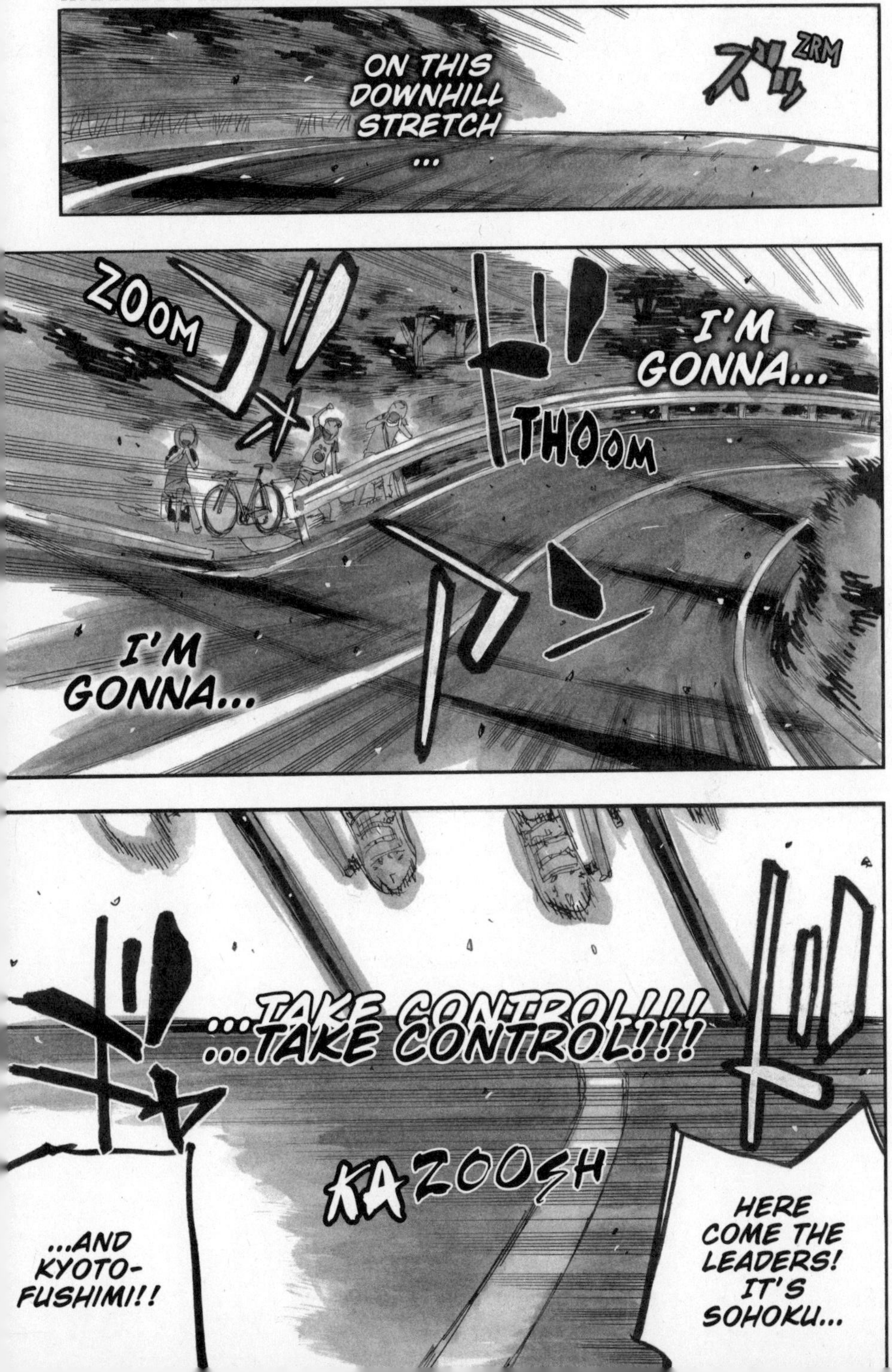
ZRM
ON THIS DOWNHILL STRETCH ...
I'M GONNA...
ZOOM
THOOM
I'M GONNA...
...TAKE CONTROL!!!
...TAKE CONTROL!!!
HERE COME THE LEADERS! IT'S SOHOKU...
KAZOOSH
...AND KYOTO-FUSHIMI!!

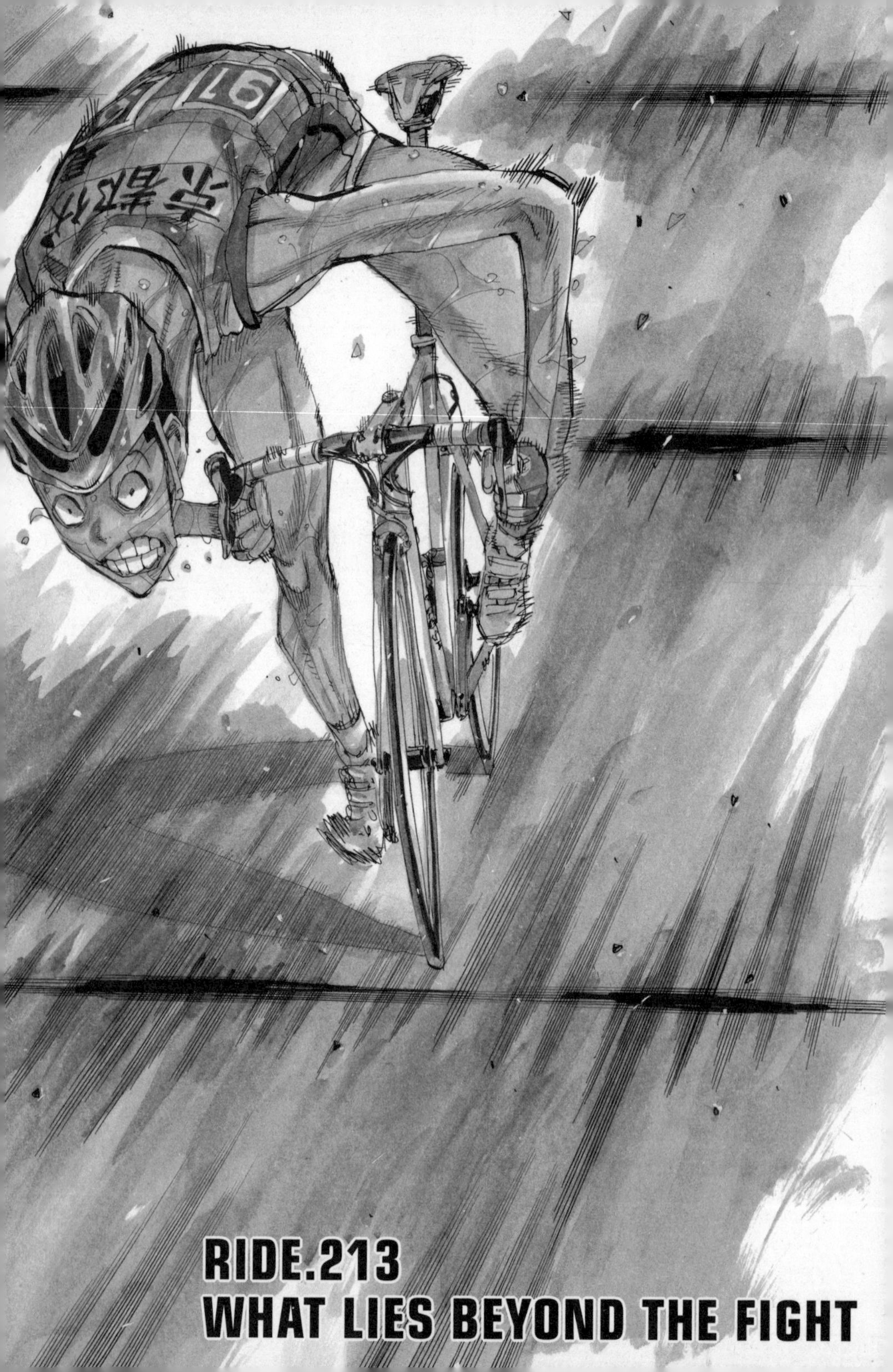

RIDE.213
WHAT LIES BEYOND THE FIGHT

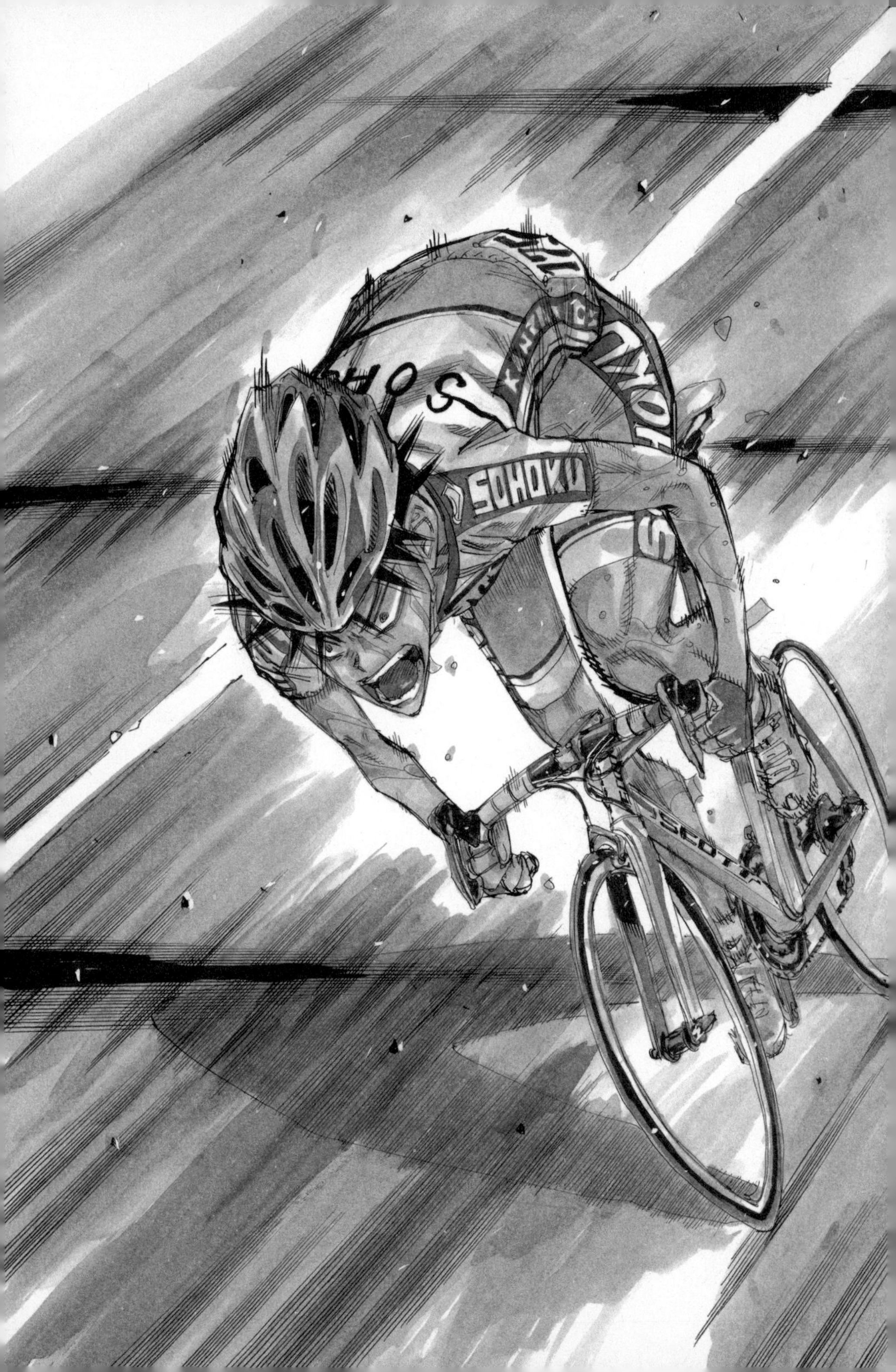
SOHOKU

FATAL BATTLE
HOKU

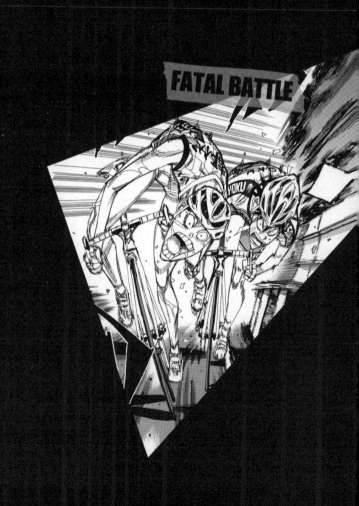

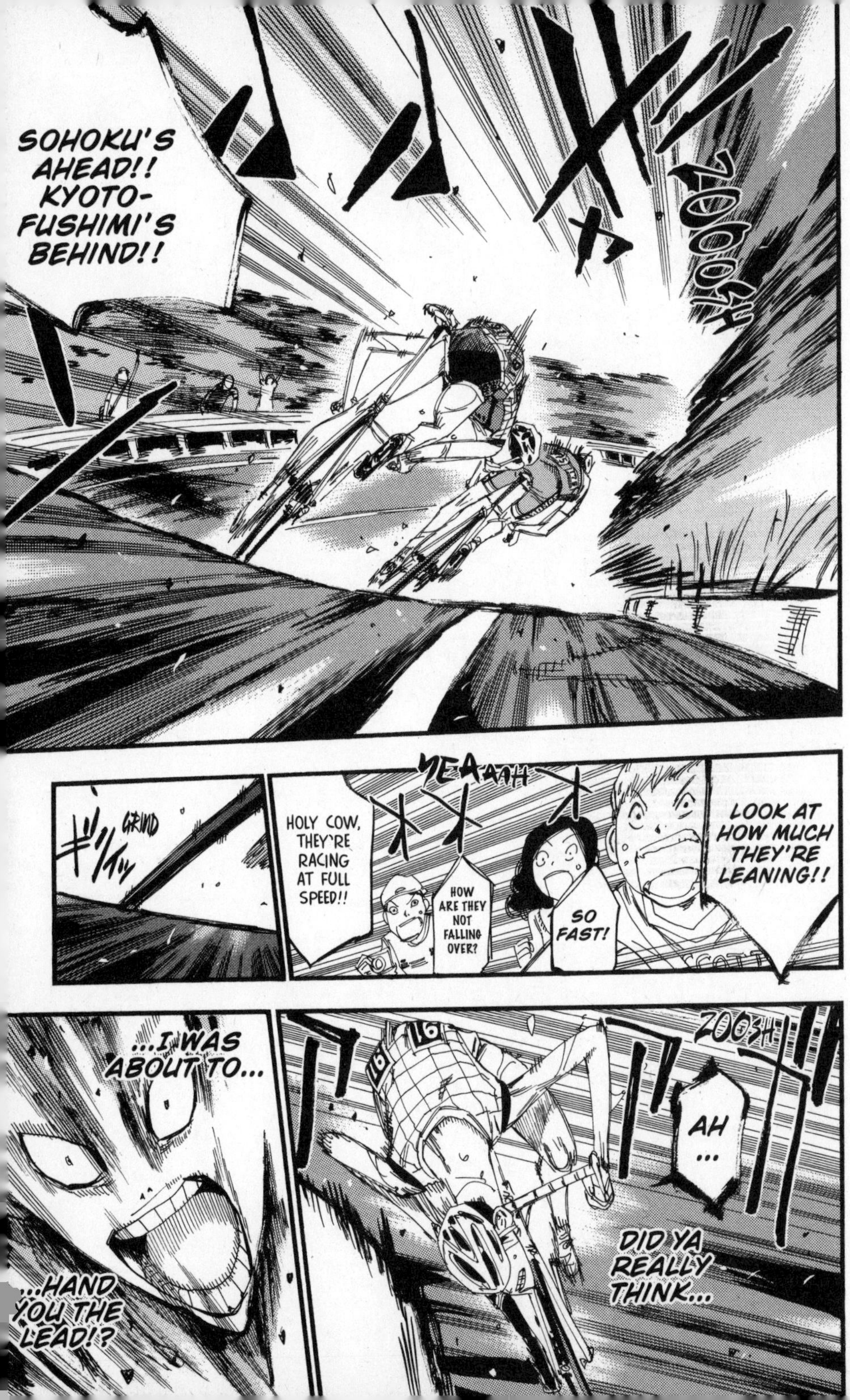
ZOOOSH
SOHOKU'S AHEAD!! KYOTO-FUSHIMI'S BEHIND!!
YEAAAH
LOOK AT HOW MUCH THEY'RE LEANING!!
SO FAST!
HOW ARE THEY NOT FALLING OVER?
HOLY COW, THEY'RE RACING AT FULL SPEED!!
GRIND
ZOOSH
AH ...
DID YA REALLY THINK...
...I WAS ABOUT TO...
...HAND YOU THE LEAD!?

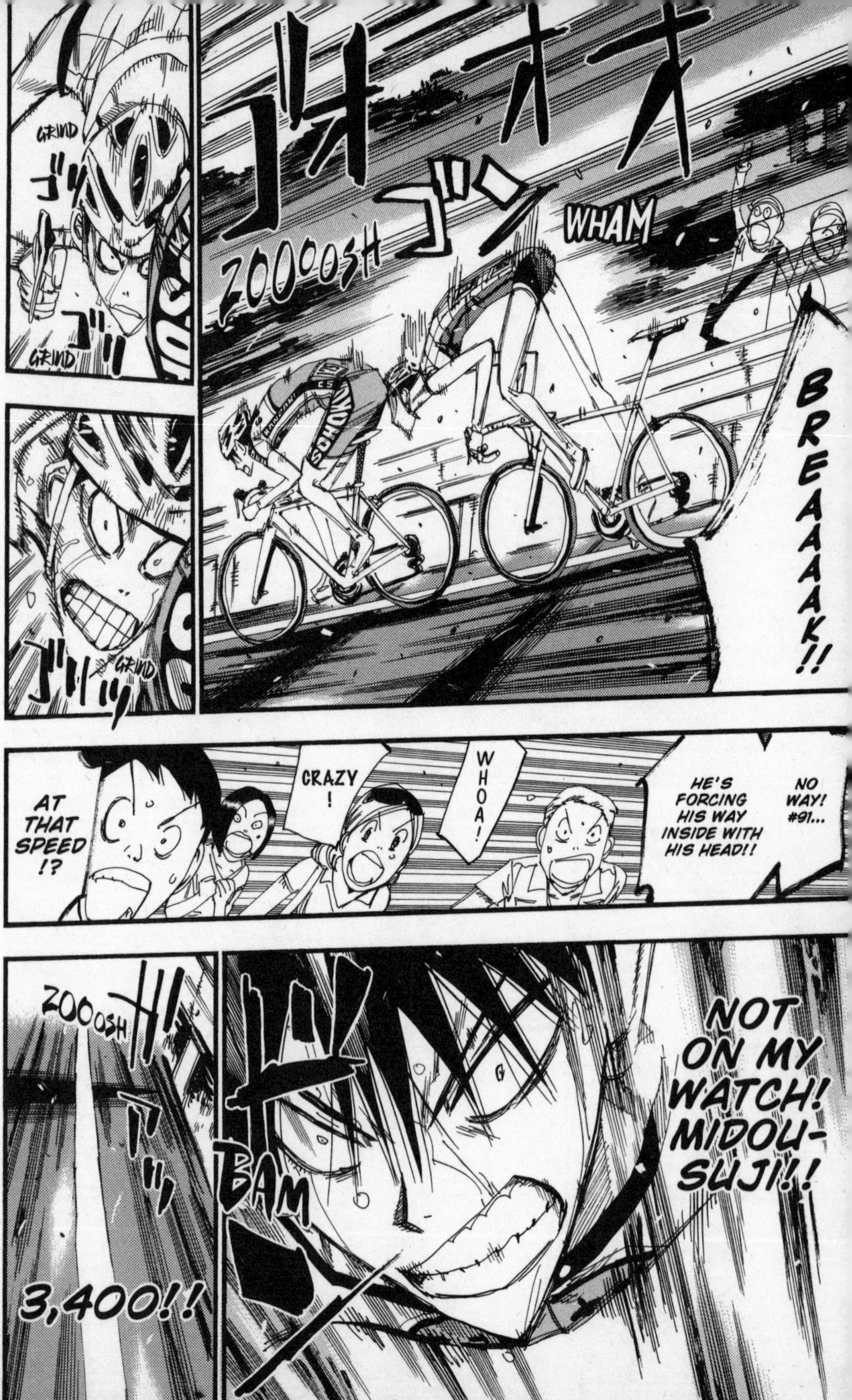
ZOOOOSH
WHAM
BREAAAAAK!!
GRIND
GRIND
GRIND
NO WAY! #91...
HE'S FORCING HIS WAY INSIDE WITH HIS HEAD!!
WHOA!
CRAZY!
AT THAT SPEED!?
NOT ON MY WATCH! MIDOU-SUJI!!
BAM
ZOOOSH
3,400!!

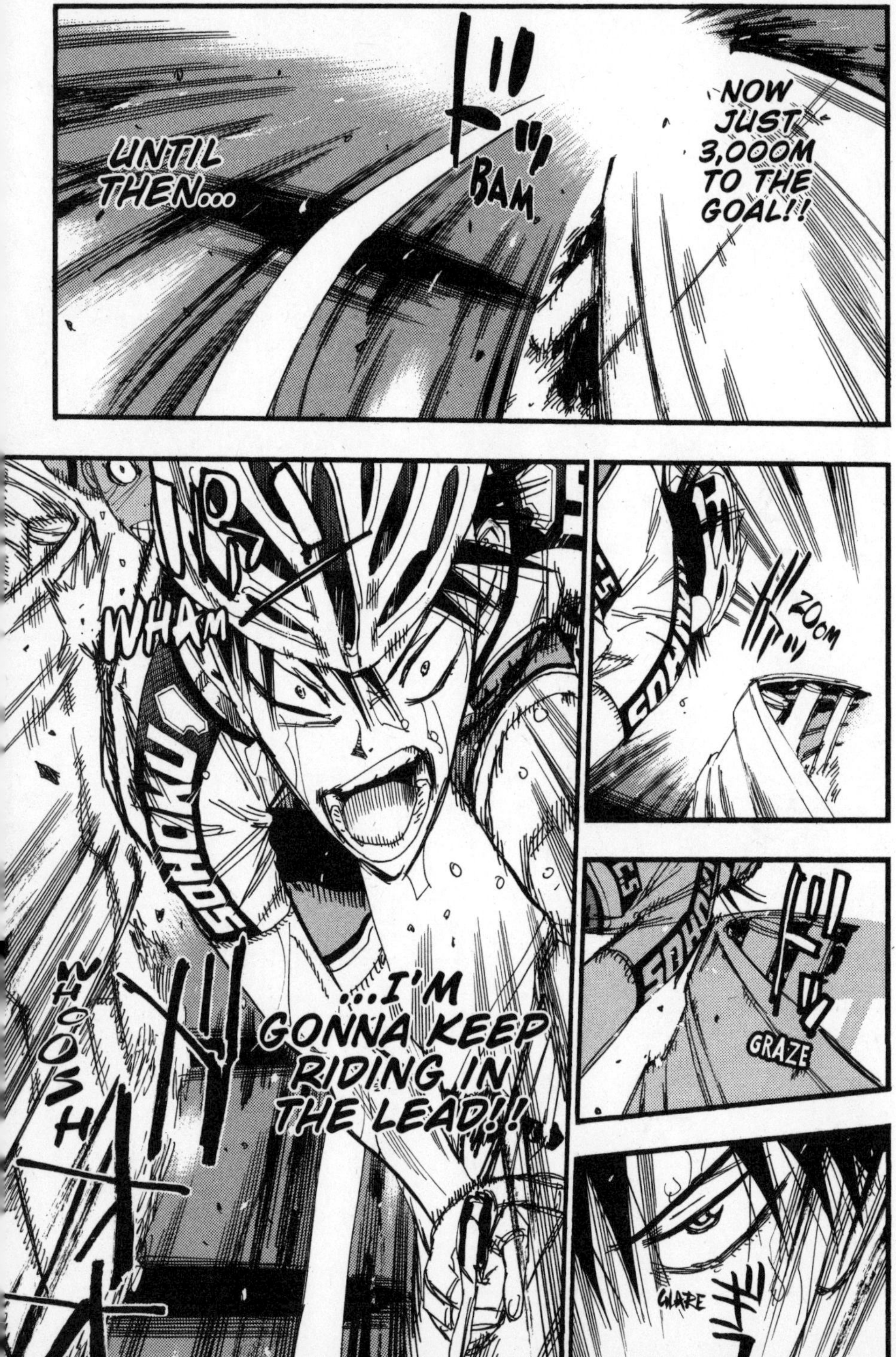
NOW JUST 3,000M TO THE GOAL!!
BAM
UNTIL THEN...
ZOOM
GRAZE
GLARE
WHAM
...I'M GONNA KEEP RIDING IN THE LEAD!!
WHOOSH

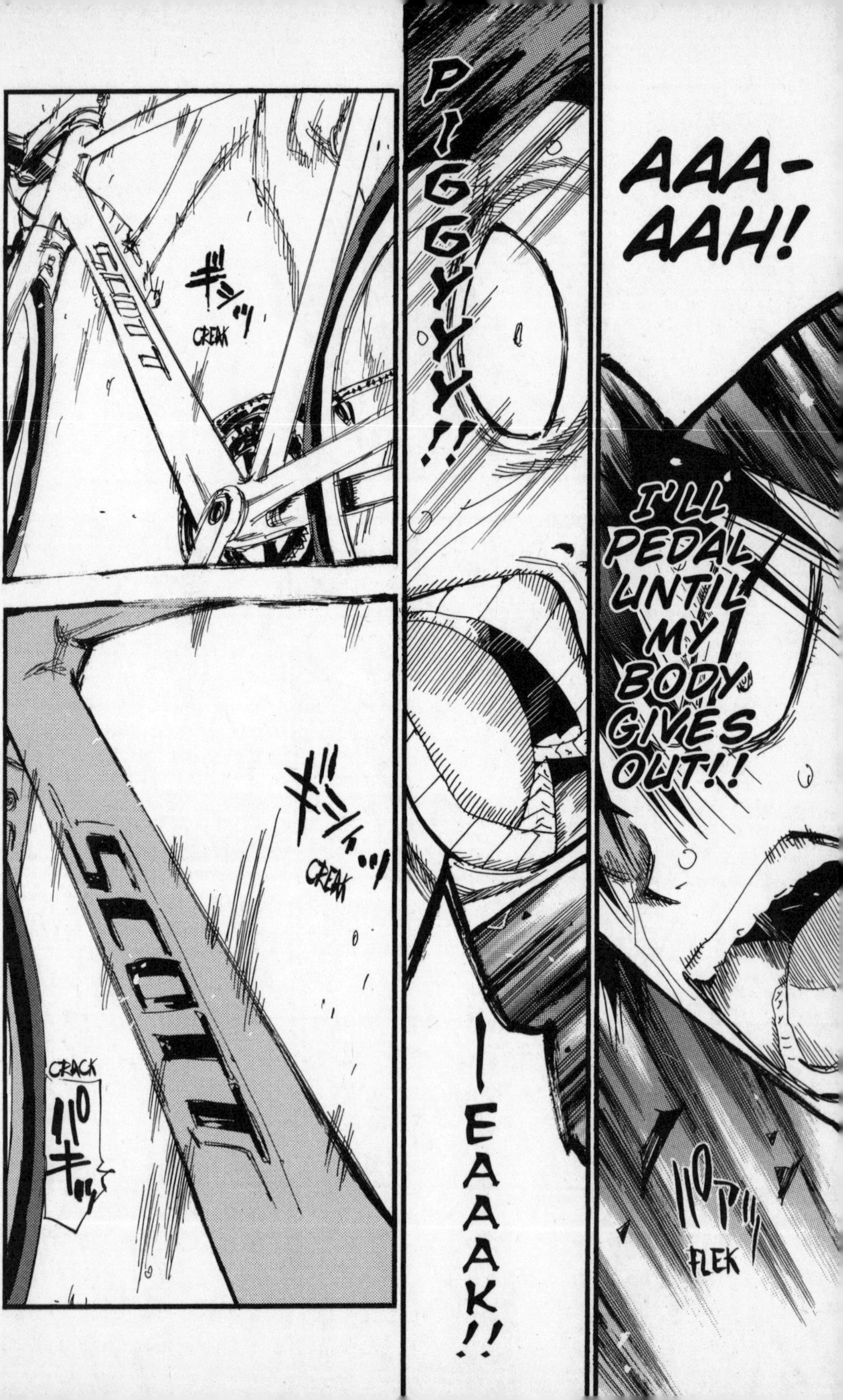
AAA-AAH!
I'LL PEDAL UNTIL MY BODY GIVES OUT!!
FLEK
PIGGYYY!!
EAAAAK!!
CREAK
CREAK
CRACK

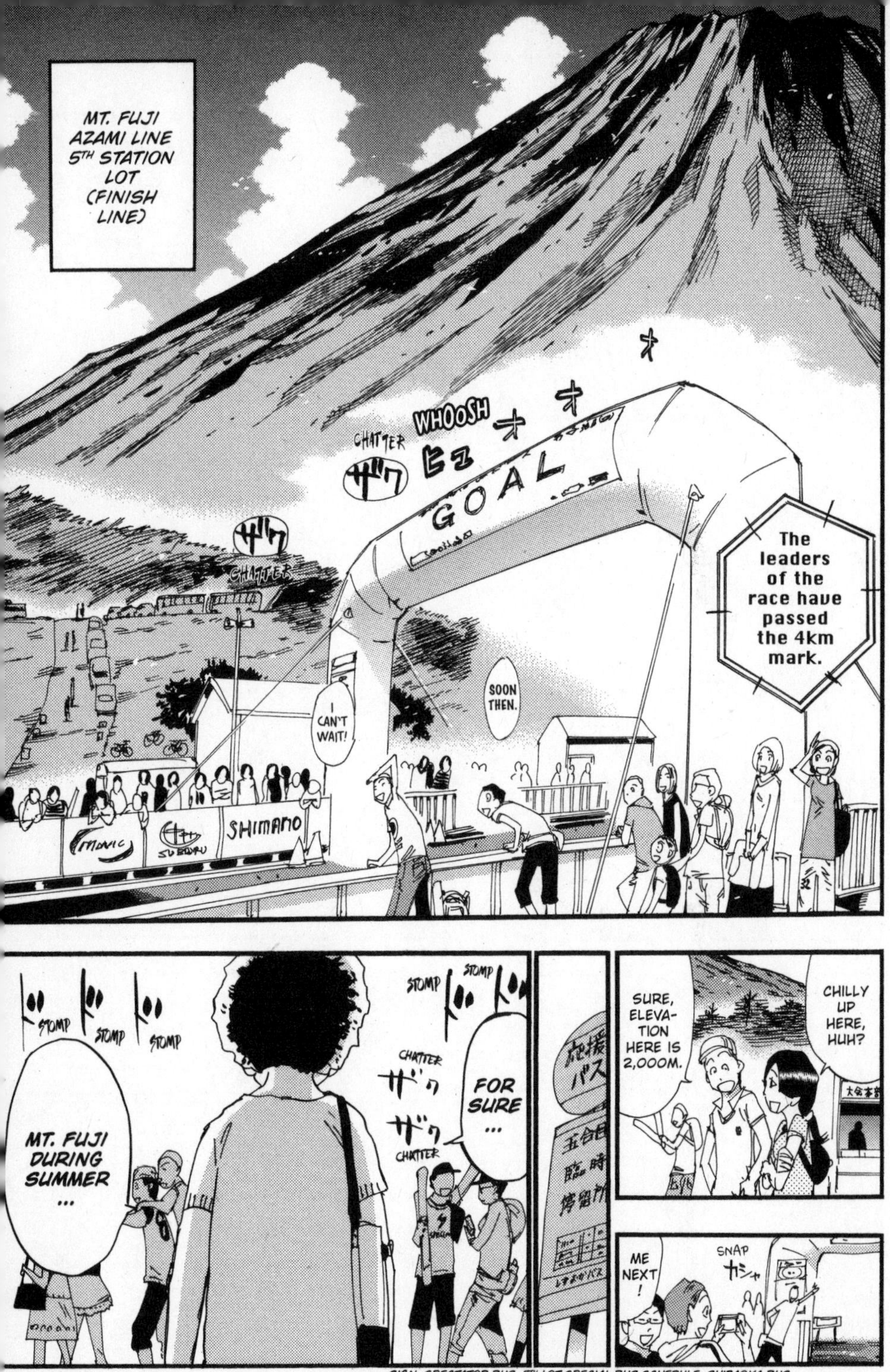
MT. FUJI AZAMI LINE 5TH STATION LOT (FINISH LINE)
WHOOSH
CHATTER
CHATTER
GOAL
The leaders of the race have passed the 4km mark.
SOON THEN.
I CAN'T WAIT!
SHIMANO
CHILLY UP HERE, HUH?
SURE, ELEVATION HERE IS 2,000M.
SNAP
ME NEXT!
STOMP
STOMP
CHATTER
CHATTER
FOR SURE ...
STOMP
STOMP
STOMP
MT. FUJI DURING SUMMER ...

SIGN: SPECTATOR BUS, 5TH LOT SPECIAL BUS SCHEDULE, SHIZAOKA BUS

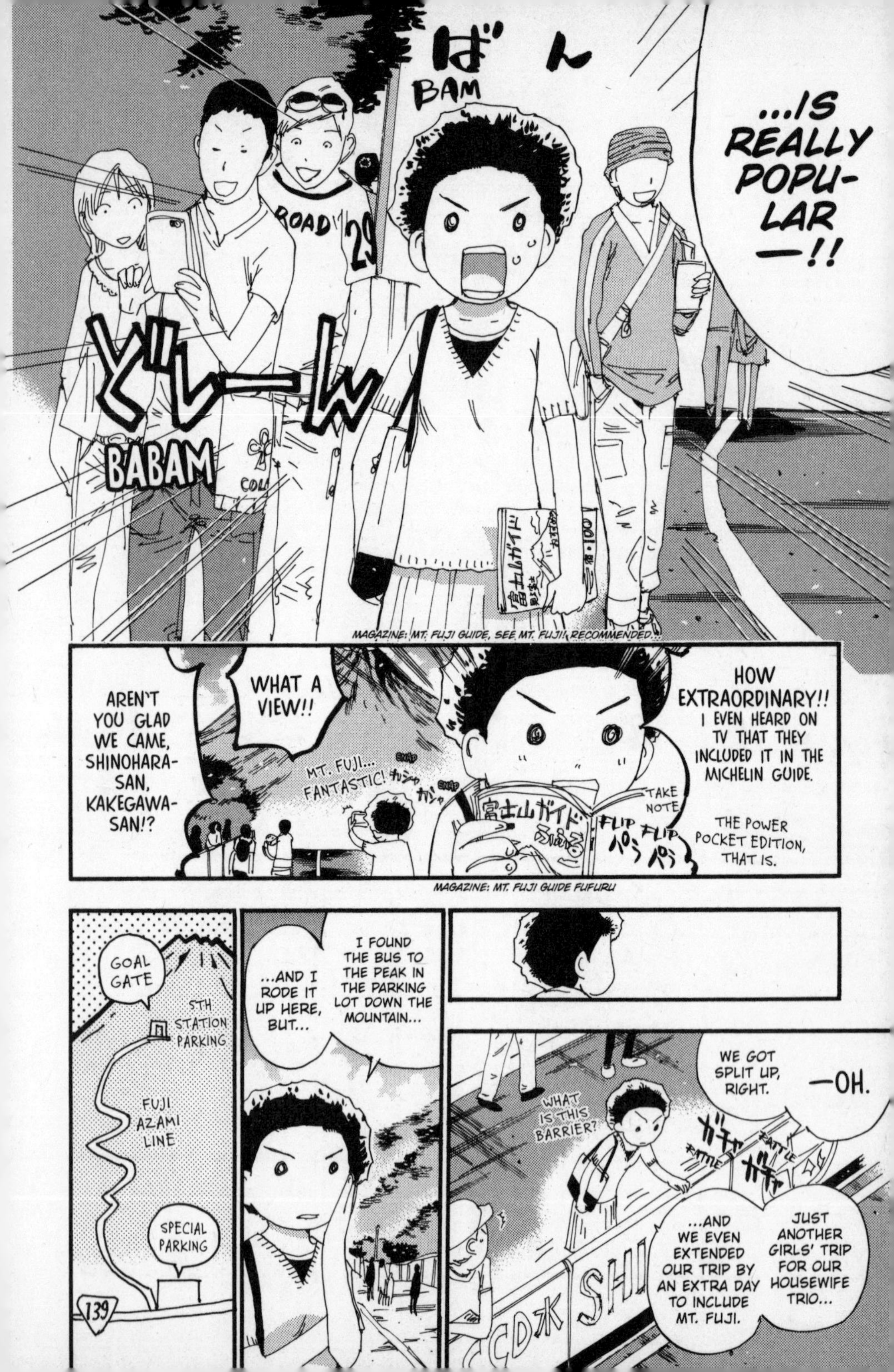
...IS REALLY POPU-LAR—!!
ばん
BAM
どーん
BABAM
MAGAZINE: MT. FUJI GUIDE, SEE MT. FUJI!! RECOMMENDED...
HOW EXTRAORDINARY!! I EVEN HEARD ON TV THAT THEY INCLUDED IT IN THE MICHELIN GUIDE.
TAKE NOTE
FLIP FLIP
THE POWER POCKET EDITION, THAT IS.
WHAT A VIEW!!
MT. FUJI... FANTASTIC!
SNAP SNAP
AREN'T YOU GLAD WE CAME, SHINOHARA-SAN, KAKEGAWA-SAN!?
MAGAZINE: MT. FUJI GUIDE FUFURU
—OH.
WE GOT SPLIT UP, RIGHT.
JUST ANOTHER GIRLS' TRIP FOR OUR HOUSEWIFE TRIO...
...AND WE EVEN EXTENDED OUR TRIP BY AN EXTRA DAY TO INCLUDE MT. FUJI.
RATTLE RATTLE
WHAT IS THIS BARRIER?
I FOUND THE BUS TO THE PEAK IN THE PARKING LOT DOWN THE MOUNTAIN...
...AND I RODE IT UP HERE, BUT...
GOAL GATE
5TH STATION PARKING
FUJI AZAMI LINE
SPECIAL PARKING
139

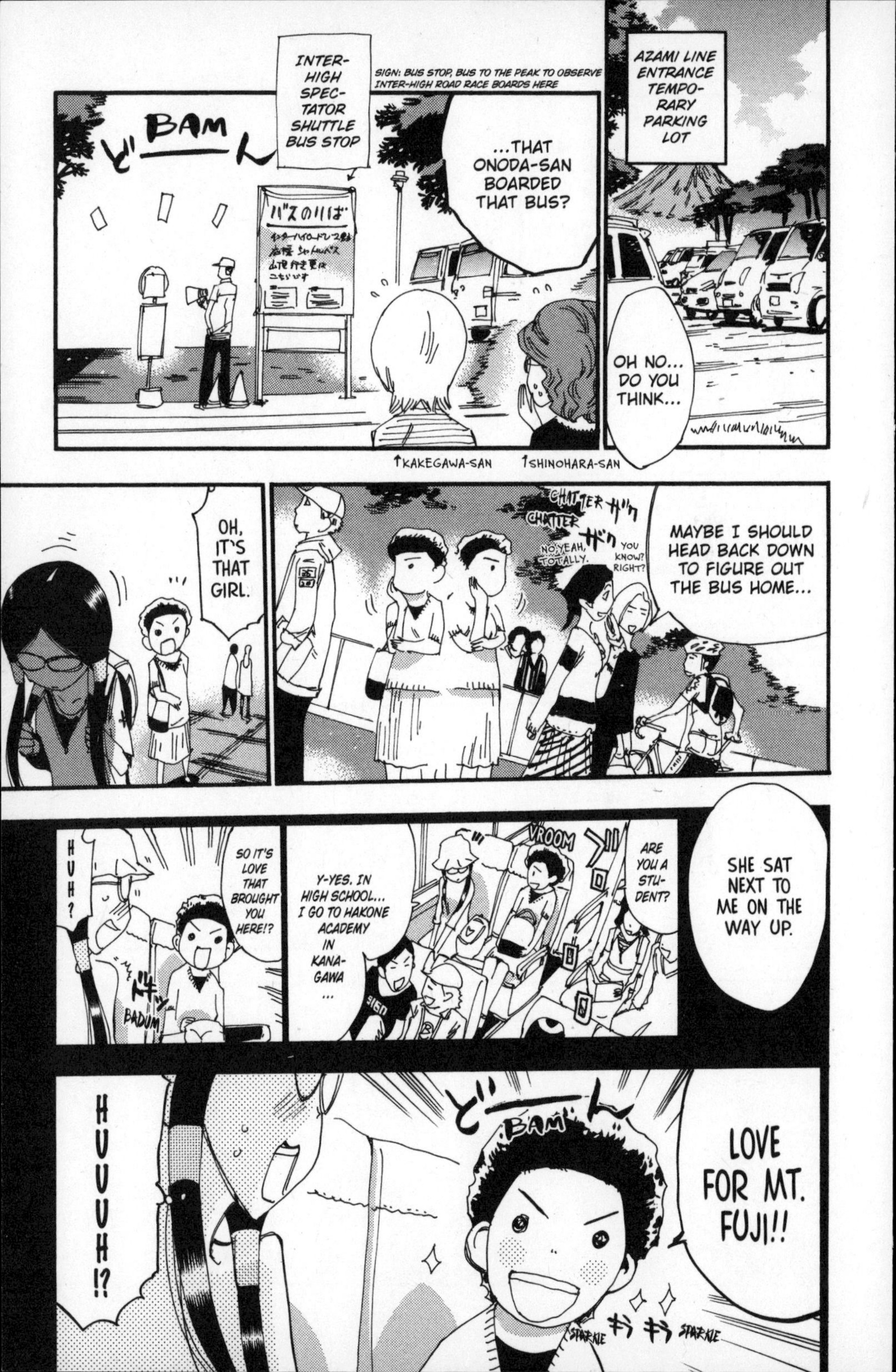

AZAMI LINE ENTRANCE TEMPORARY PARKING LOT
OH NO... DO YOU THINK...
INTER-HIGH SPECTATOR SHUTTLE BUS STOP
SIGN: BUS STOP, BUS TO THE PEAK TO OBSERVE INTER-HIGH ROAD RACE BOARDS HERE
...THAT ONODA-SAN BOARDED THAT BUS?
BAM
バスのりば
↑KAKEGAWA-SAN
↑SHINOHARA-SAN
MAYBE I SHOULD HEAD BACK DOWN TO FIGURE OUT THE BUS HOME...
CHATTER
CHATTER
YOU KNOW? RIGHT?
NO, YEAH, TOTALLY.
OH, IT'S THAT GIRL.
SHE SAT NEXT TO ME ON THE WAY UP.
ARE YOU A STUDENT?
VROOM
Y-YES. IN HIGH SCHOOL... I GO TO HAKONE ACADEMY IN KANAGAWA...
SO IT'S LOVE THAT BROUGHT YOU HERE!?
HUH?
BADUM
LOVE FOR MT. FUJI!!
BAM
HUUUUH!?
SPARKLE
SPARKLE

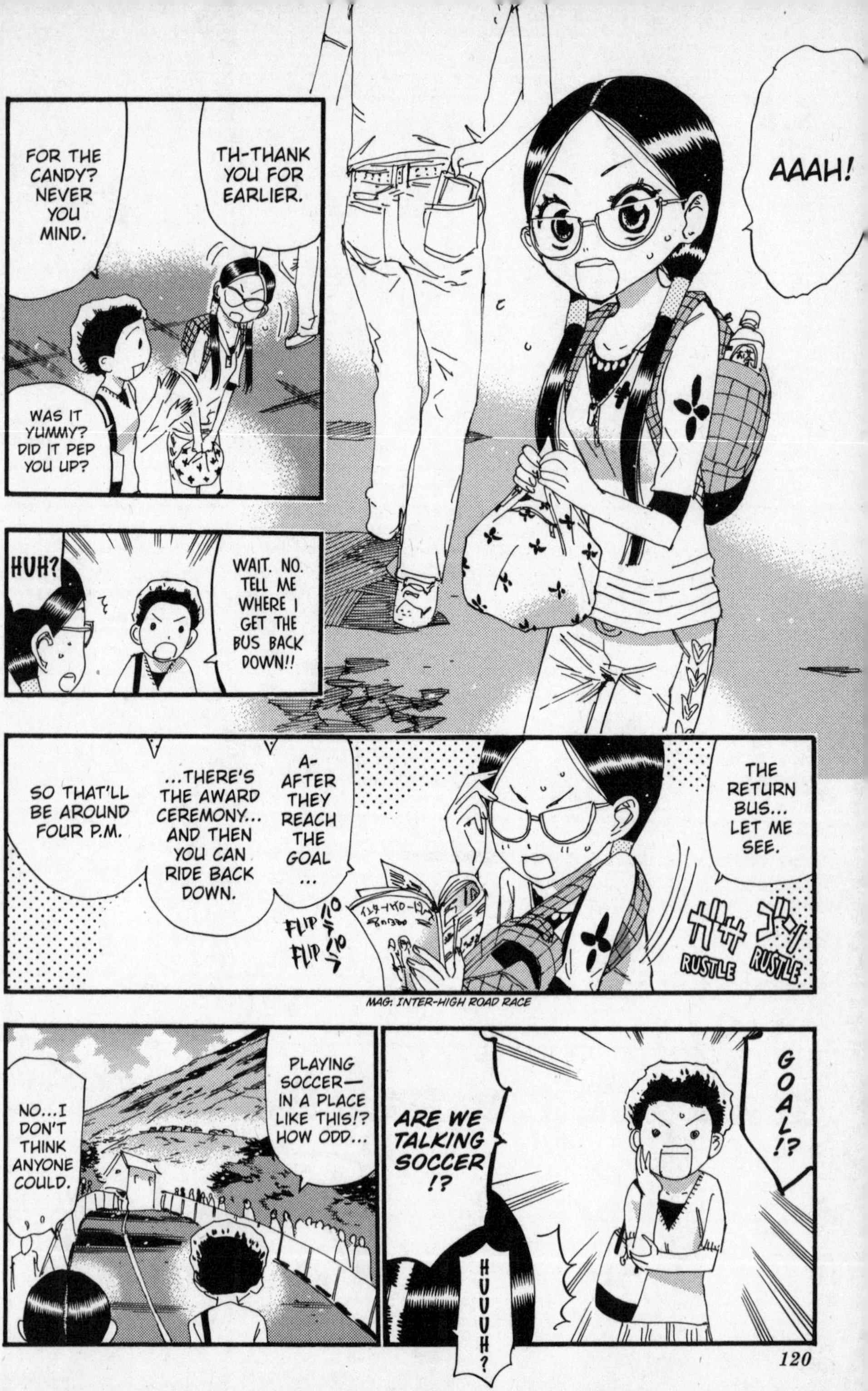
AAAH!
TH-THANK YOU FOR EARLIER.
FOR THE CANDY? NEVER YOU MIND.
WAS IT YUMMY? DID IT PEP YOU UP?
WAIT. NO. TELL ME WHERE I GET THE BUS BACK DOWN!!
HUH?
THE RETURN BUS... LET ME SEE.
RUSTLE RUSTLE
A-AFTER THEY REACH THE GOAL...
FLIP FLIP
...THERE'S THE AWARD CEREMONY... AND THEN YOU CAN RIDE BACK DOWN.
SO THAT'LL BE AROUND FOUR P.M.
MAG: INTER-HIGH ROAD RACE
GOAL!?
ARE WE TALKING SOCCER!?
HUUUH?
PLAYING SOCCER— IN A PLACE LIKE THIS!? HOW ODD...
NO...I DON'T THINK ANYONE COULD.

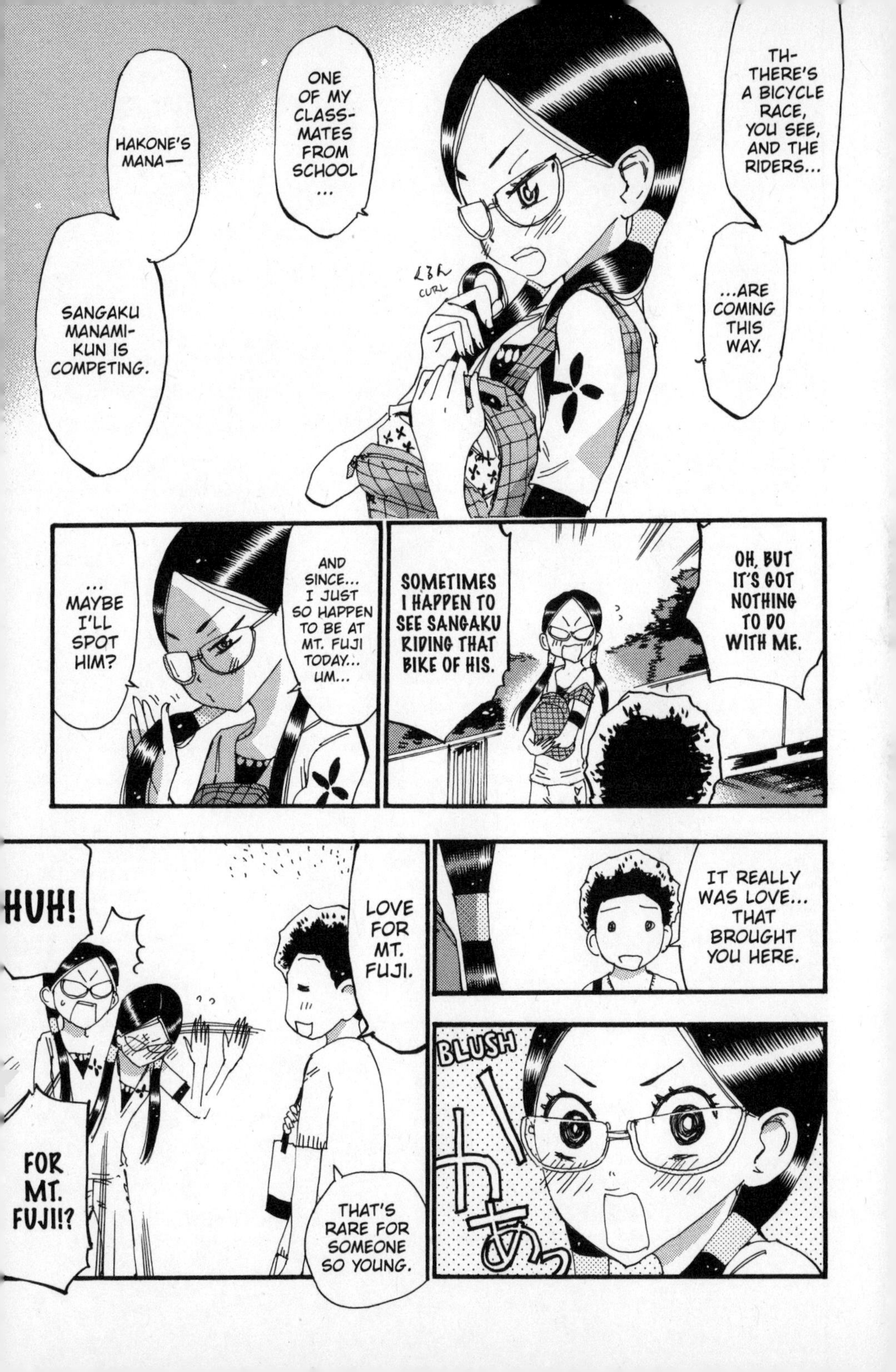
TH-THERE'S A BICYCLE RACE, YOU SEE, AND THE RIDERS...
...ARE COMING THIS WAY.
くるん CURL
ONE OF MY CLASSMATES FROM SCHOOL ...
HAKONE'S MANA—
SANGAKU MANAMI-KUN IS COMPETING.
OH, BUT IT'S GOT NOTHING TO DO WITH ME.
SOMETIMES I HAPPEN TO SEE SANGAKU RIDING THAT BIKE OF HIS.
AND SINCE... I JUST SO HAPPEN TO BE AT MT. FUJI TODAY... UM...
... MAYBE I'LL SPOT HIM?
IT REALLY WAS LOVE... THAT BROUGHT YOU HERE.
BLUSH
わぁっ
LOVE FOR MT. FUJI.
THAT'S RARE FOR SOMEONE SO YOUNG.
HUH!
FOR MT. FUJI!!?

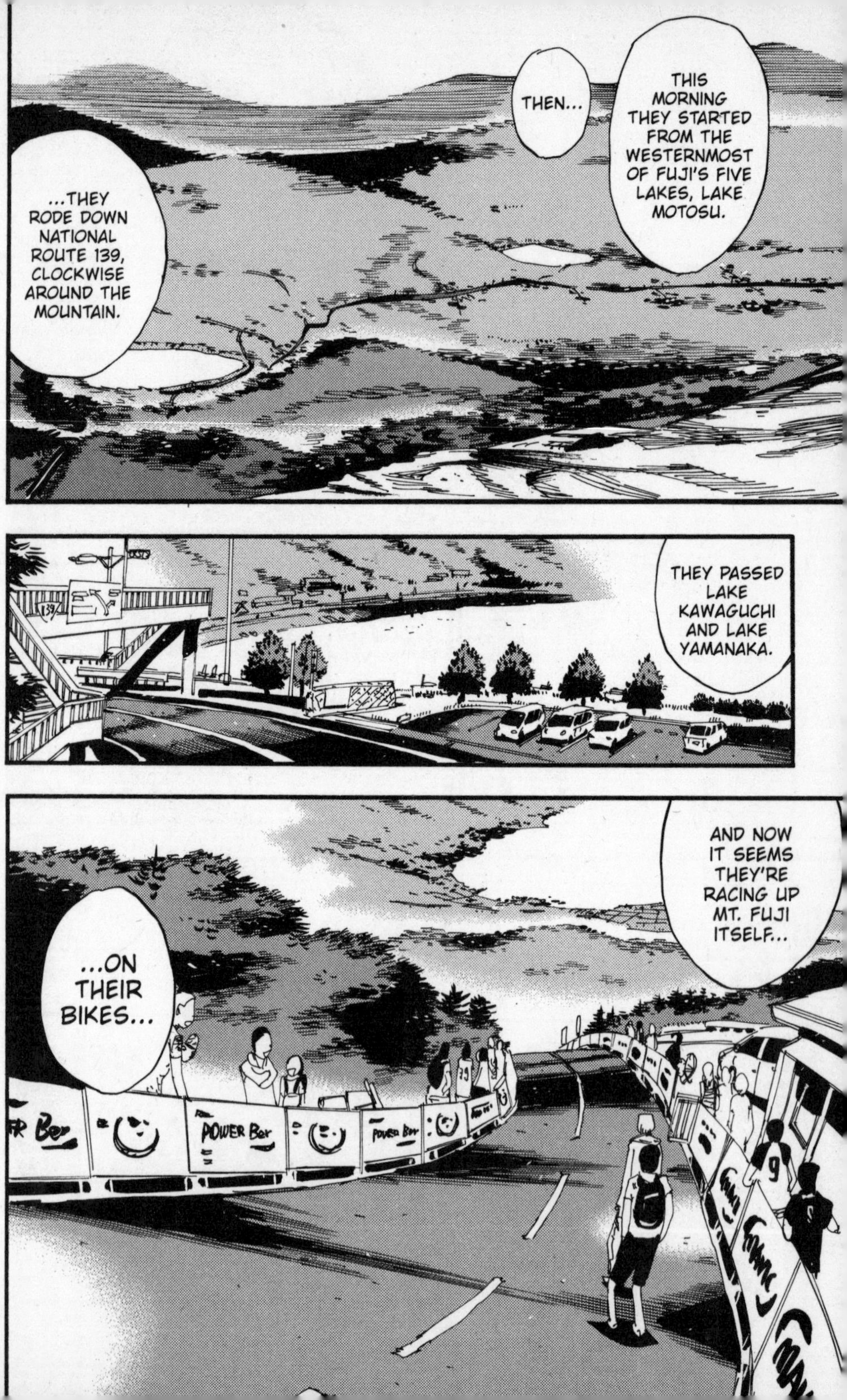
THIS MORNING THEY STARTED FROM THE WESTERNMOST OF FUJI'S FIVE LAKES, LAKE MOTOSU.
THEN...
...THEY RODE DOWN NATIONAL ROUTE 139, CLOCKWISE AROUND THE MOUNTAIN.
THEY PASSED LAKE KAWAGUCHI AND LAKE YAMANAKA.
AND NOW IT SEEMS THEY'RE RACING UP MT. FUJI ITSELF...
...ON THEIR BIKES...

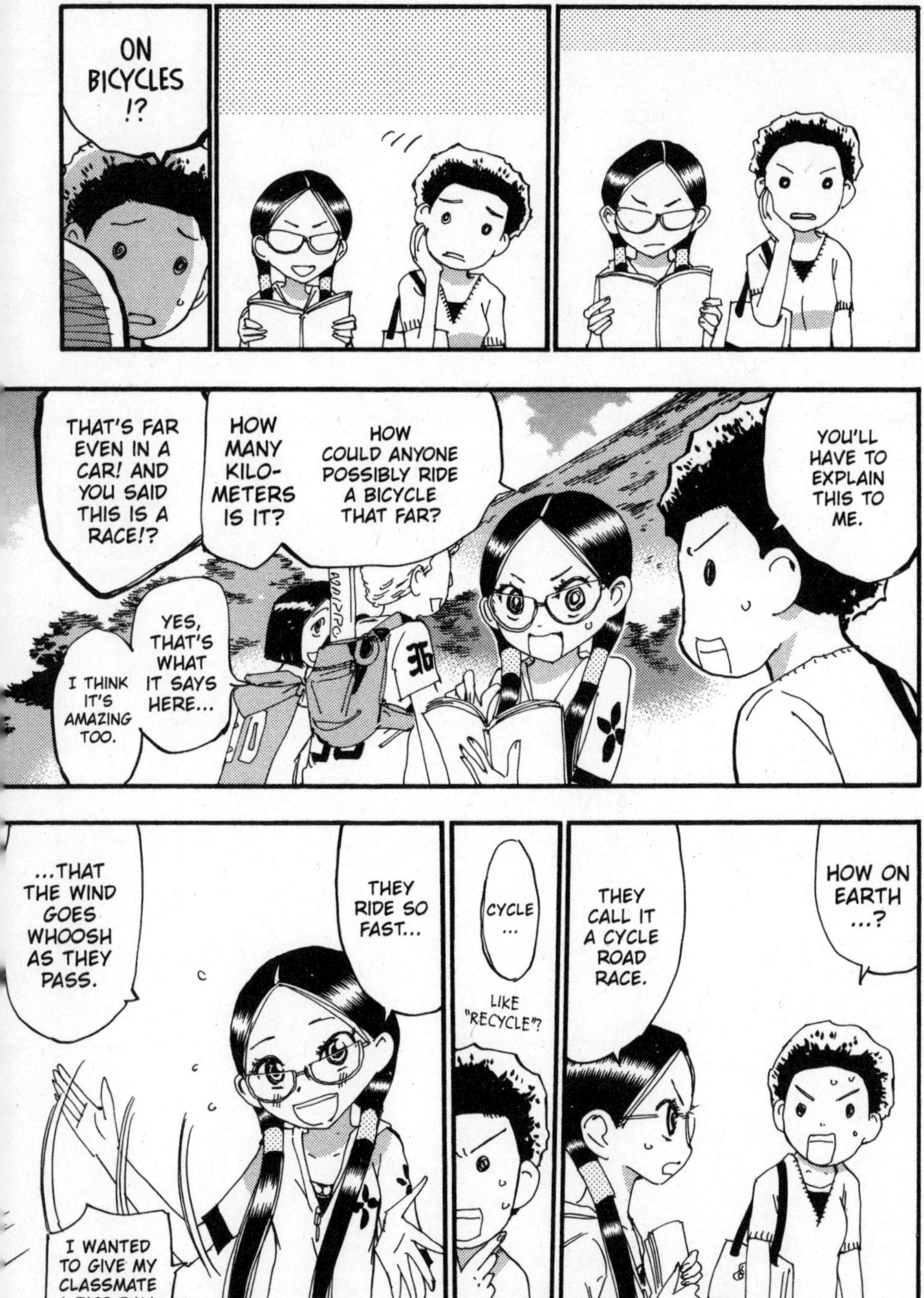
ON BICYCLES !?
YOU'LL HAVE TO EXPLAIN THIS TO ME.
HOW COULD ANYONE POSSIBLY RIDE A BICYCLE THAT FAR?
HOW MANY KILO-METERS IS IT?
THAT'S FAR EVEN IN A CAR! AND YOU SAID THIS IS A RACE!?
YES, THAT'S WHAT IT SAYS HERE...
I THINK IT'S AMAZING TOO.
HOW ON EARTH ...?
THEY CALL IT A CYCLE ROAD RACE.
CYCLE ...
LIKE "RECYCLE"?
THEY RIDE SO FAST...
...THAT THE WIND GOES WHOOSH AS THEY PASS.
I WANTED TO GIVE MY CLASSMATE A RICE BALL YESTERDAY, BUT...

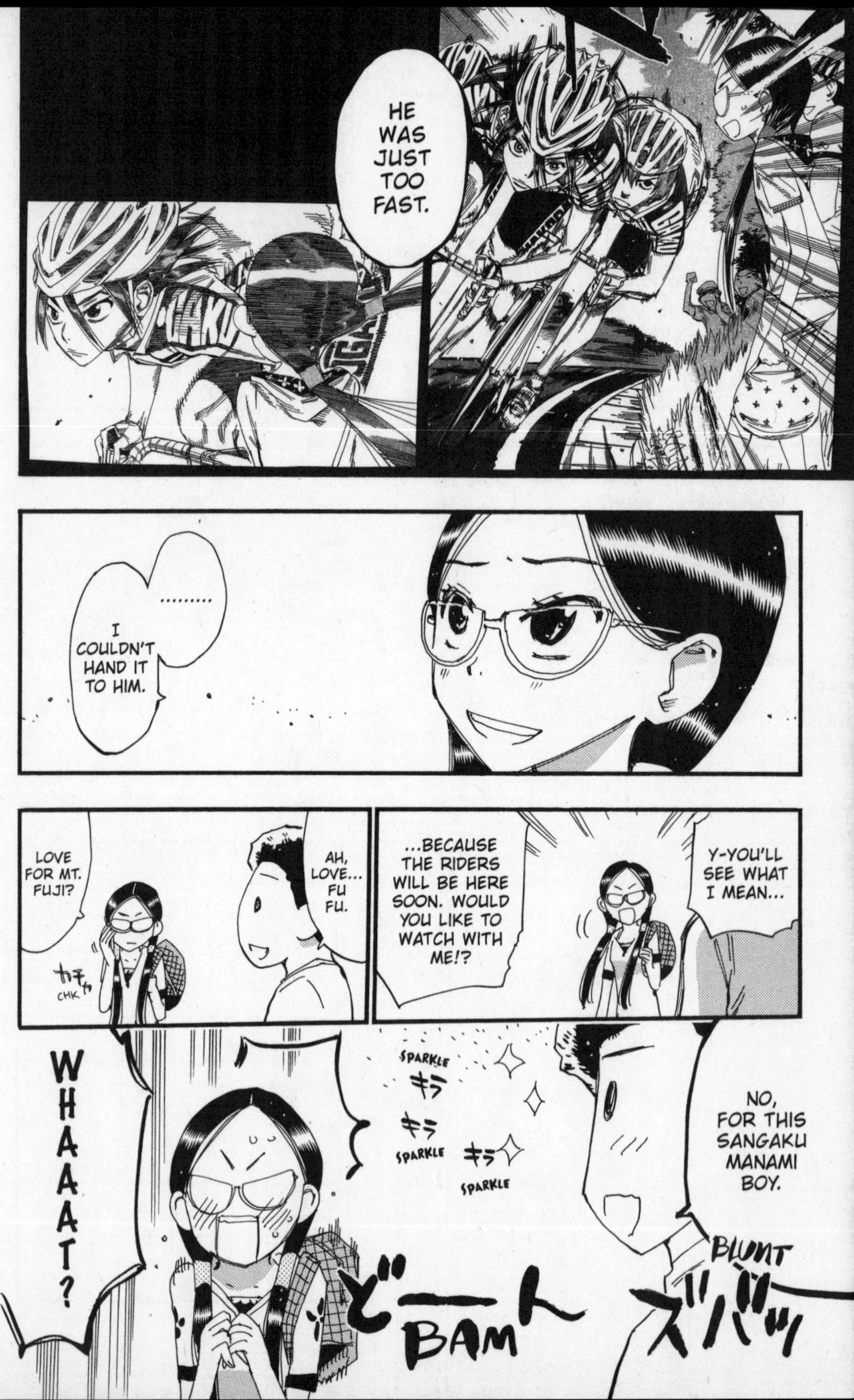
HE WAS JUST TOO FAST.
....
I COULDN'T HAND IT TO HIM.
Y-YOU'LL SEE WHAT I MEAN...
...BECAUSE THE RIDERS WILL BE HERE SOON. WOULD YOU LIKE TO WATCH WITH ME!?
AH, LOVE... FU FU.
LOVE FOR MT. FUJI?
CHK
NO, FOR THIS SANGAKU MANAMI BOY.
BLUNT
SPARKLE
SPARKLE
SPARKLE
BAM
WHAAAT?

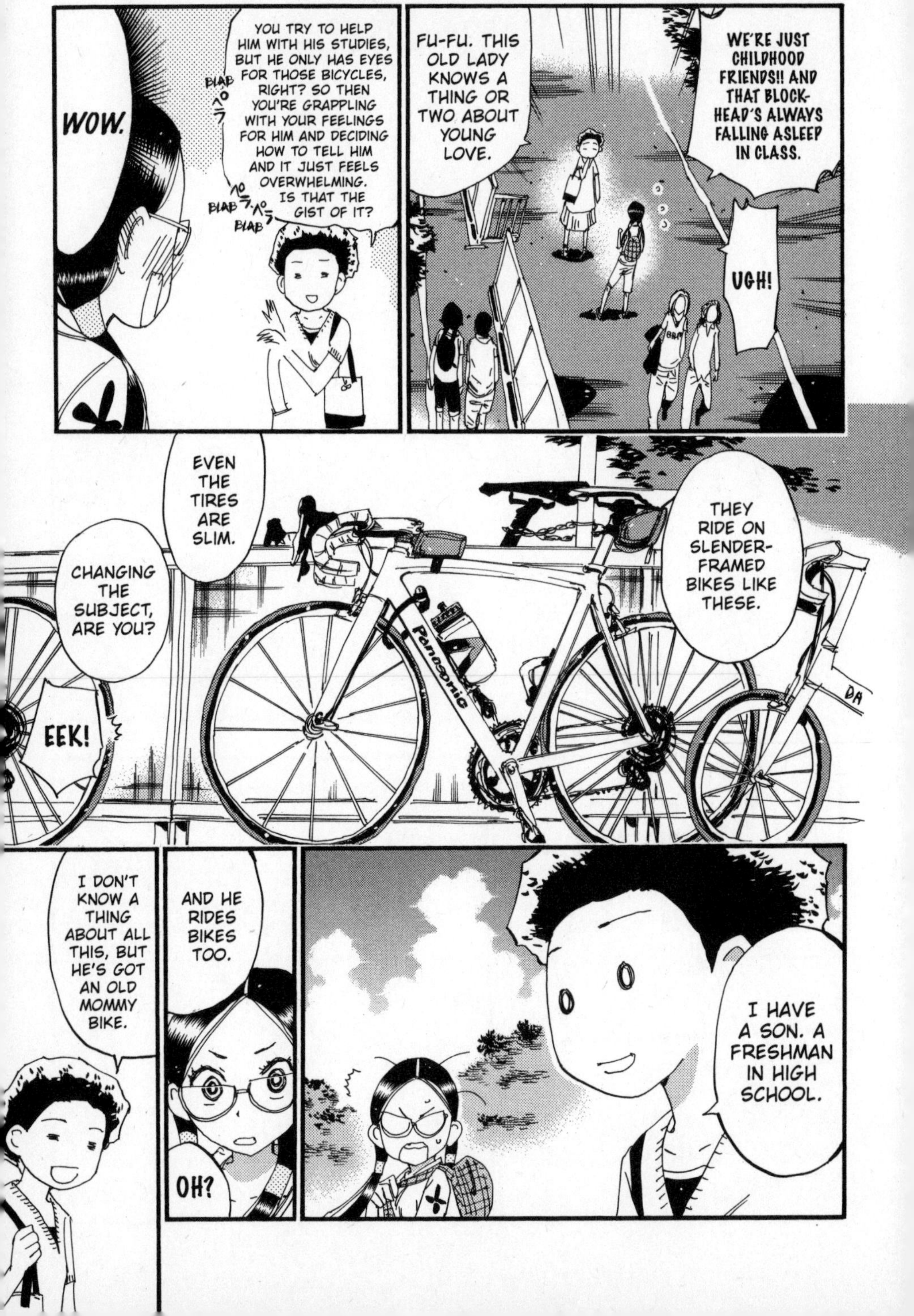
WE'RE JUST CHILDHOOD FRIENDS!! AND THAT BLOCKHEAD'S ALWAYS FALLING ASLEEP IN CLASS.
FU-FU. THIS OLD LADY KNOWS A THING OR TWO ABOUT YOUNG LOVE.
UGH!
YOU TRY TO HELP HIM WITH HIS STUDIES, BUT HE ONLY HAS EYES FOR THOSE BICYCLES, RIGHT? SO THEN YOU'RE GRAPPLING WITH YOUR FEELINGS FOR HIM AND DECIDING HOW TO TELL HIM AND IT JUST FEELS OVERWHELMING. IS THAT THE GIST OF IT?
BLAB
BLAB
BLAB
WOW.
THEY RIDE ON SLENDER-FRAMED BIKES LIKE THESE.
EVEN THE TIRES ARE SLIM.
CHANGING THE SUBJECT, ARE YOU?
EEK!
I HAVE A SON. A FRESHMAN IN HIGH SCHOOL.
AND HE RIDES BIKES TOO.
OH?
I DON'T KNOW A THING ABOUT ALL THIS, BUT HE'S GOT AN OLD MOMMY BIKE.

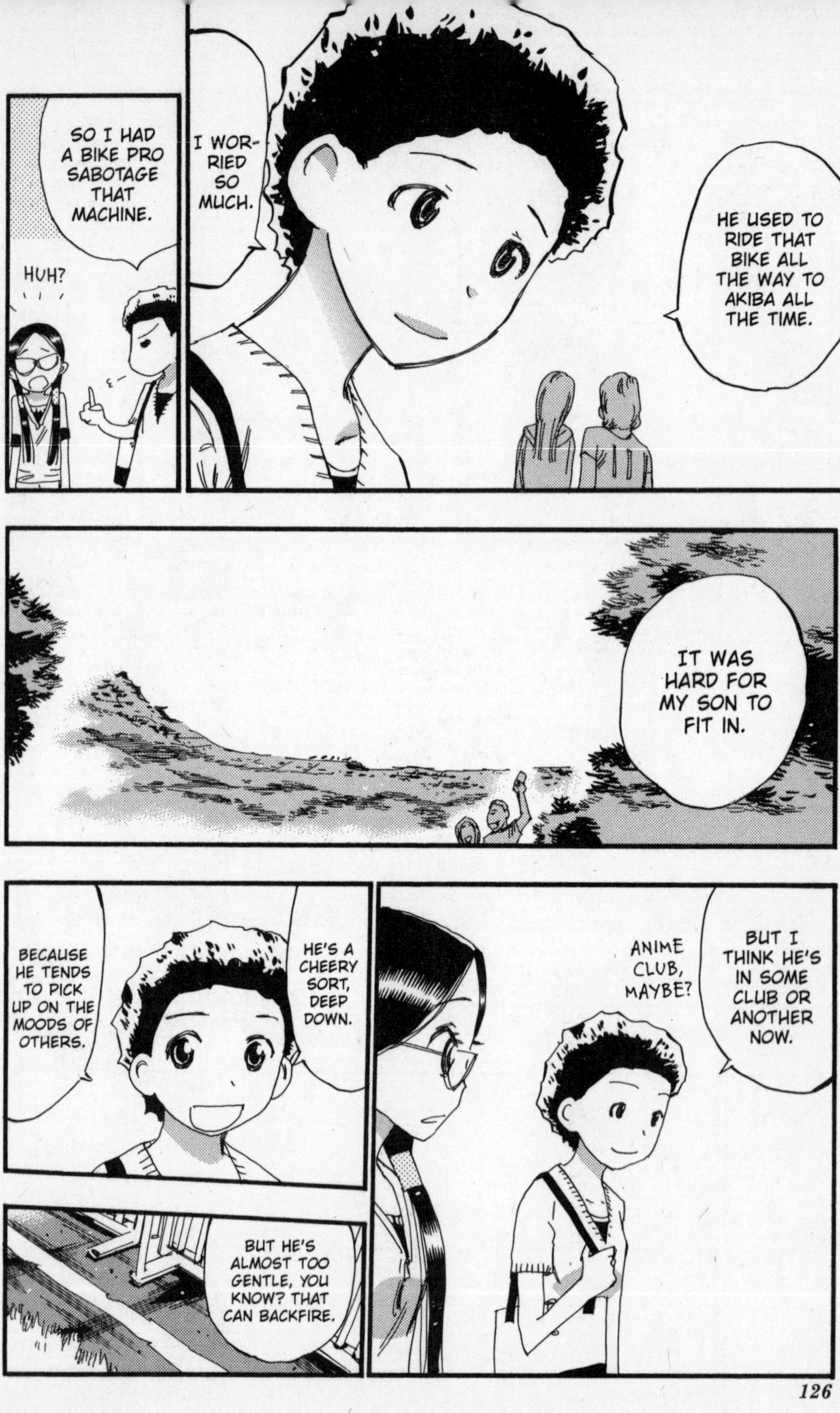
HE USED TO RIDE THAT BIKE ALL THE WAY TO AKIBA ALL THE TIME.
I WOR-RIED SO MUCH.
SO I HAD A BIKE PRO SABOTAGE THAT MACHINE.
HUH?
IT WAS HARD FOR MY SON TO FIT IN.
BUT I THINK HE'S IN SOME CLUB OR ANOTHER NOW.
ANIME CLUB, MAYBE?
HE'S A CHEERY SORT, DEEP DOWN.
BECAUSE HE TENDS TO PICK UP ON THE MOODS OF OTHERS.
BUT HE'S ALMOST TOO GENTLE, YOU KNOW? THAT CAN BACKFIRE.

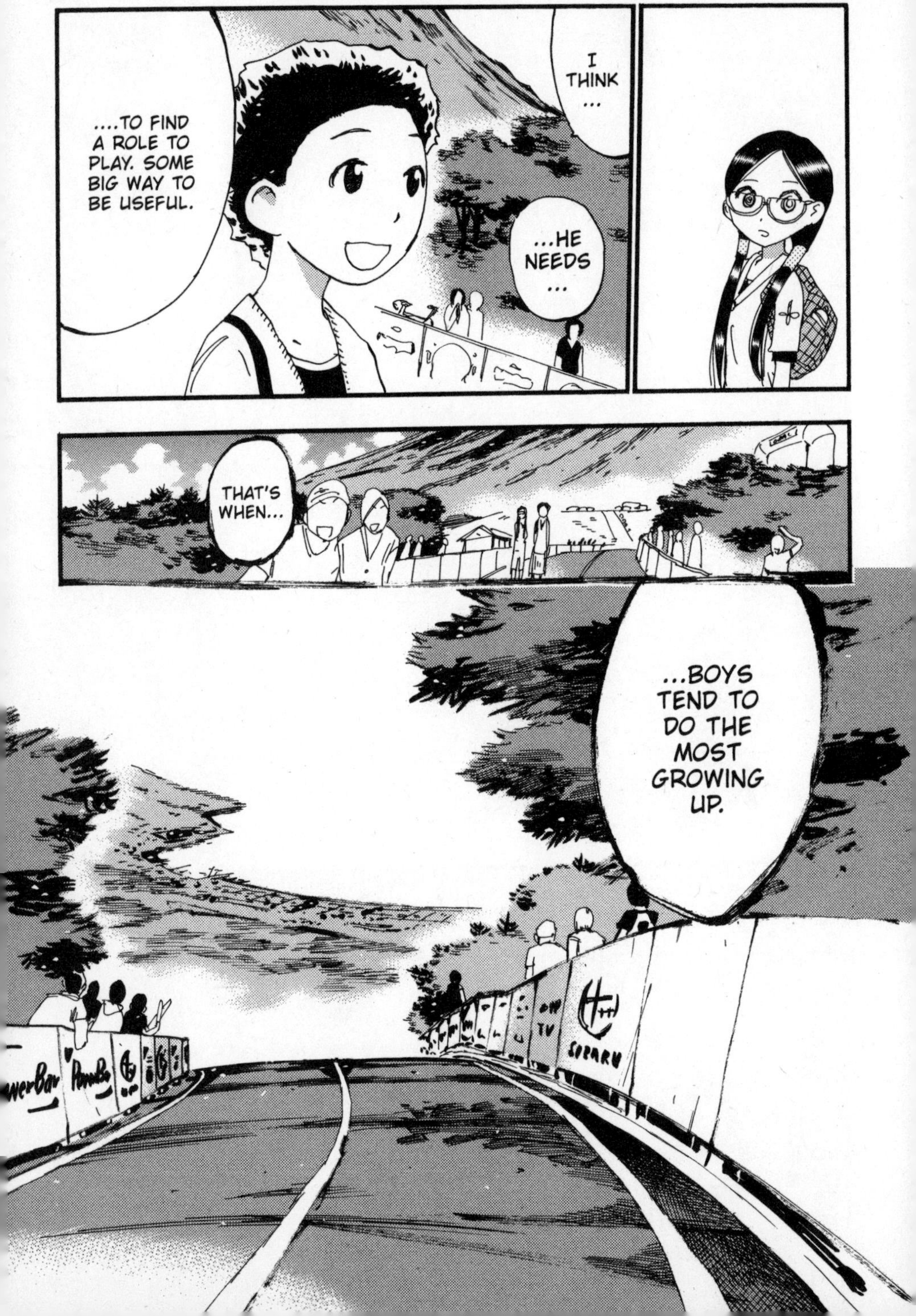
I THINK ...
...HE NEEDS ...
....TO FIND A ROLE TO PLAY. SOME BIG WAY TO BE USEFUL.
THAT'S WHEN...
...BOYS TEND TO DO THE MOST GROWING UP.

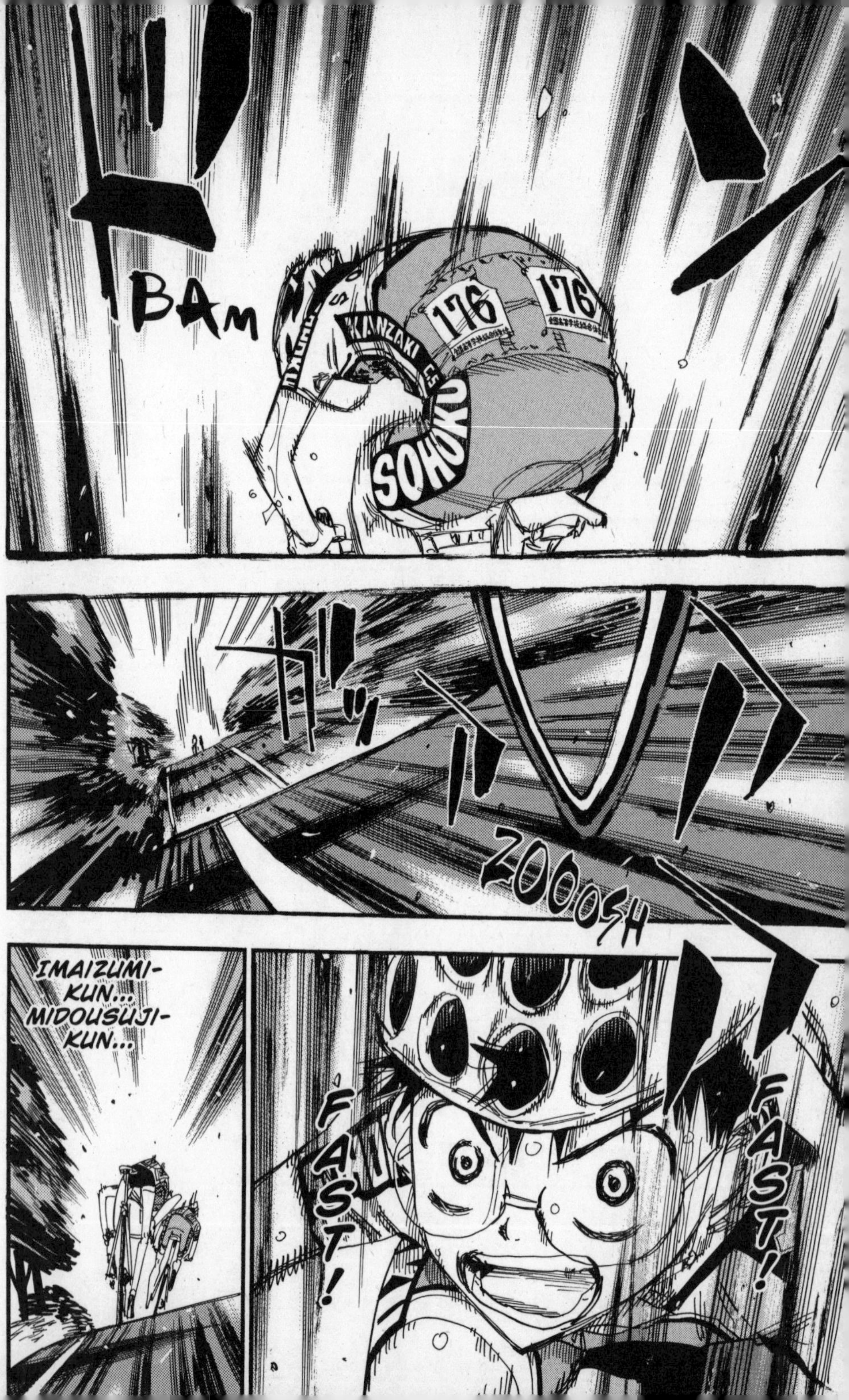
176
176
KANZAKI CS
SOHOKU
BAM
ZOOOOSH
FAST!
FAST!
IMAIZUMI-KUN... MIDOUSUJI-KUN...

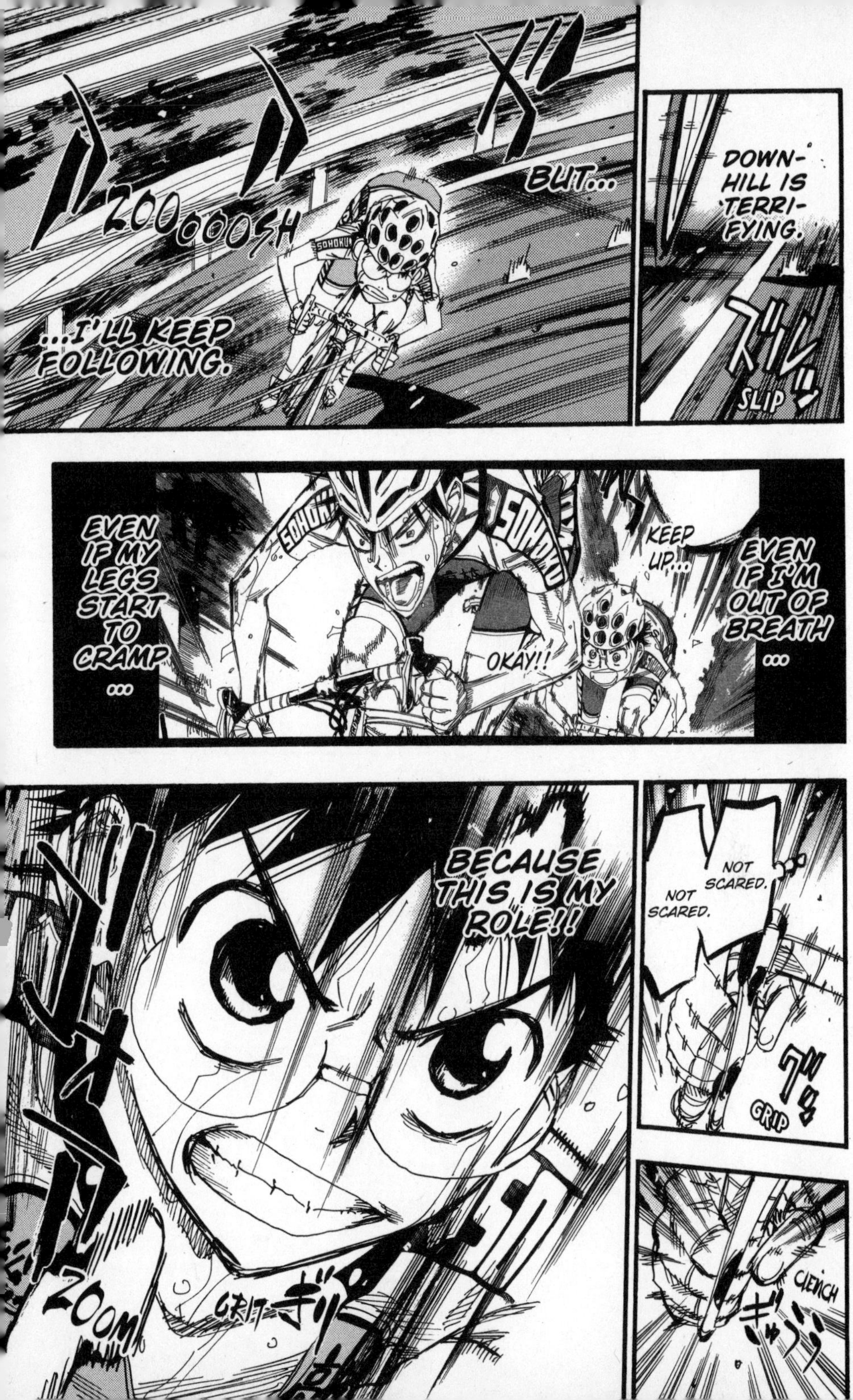

DOWN-HILL IS TERRI-FYING.
SLIP
BUT...
ZOOOOOOSH
...I'LL KEEP FOLLOWING.
EVEN IF I'M OUT OF BREATH...
KEEP UP...
OKAY!!
EVEN IF MY LEGS START TO CRAMP...
NOT SCARED.
NOT SCARED.
GRIP
CLENCH
BECAUSE THIS IS MY ROLE!!
GRIT
ZOOM

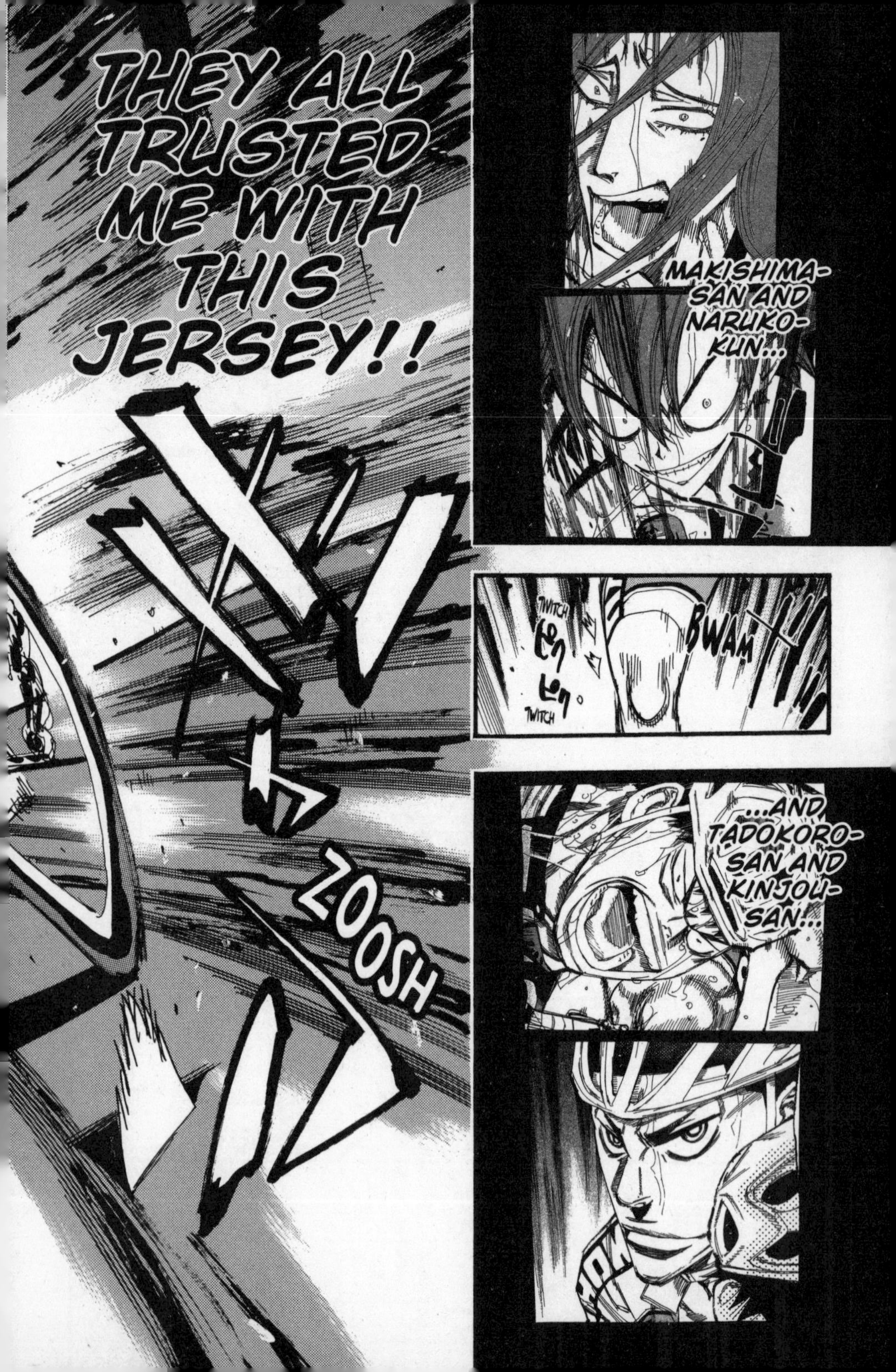
MAKISHIMA-SAN AND NARUKO-KUN...
TWITCH
ピク
ピク
TWITCH
BWAM
...AND TADOKORO-SAN AND KINJOU-SAN...
THEY ALL TRUSTED ME WITH THIS JERSEY!!
ZOOSH

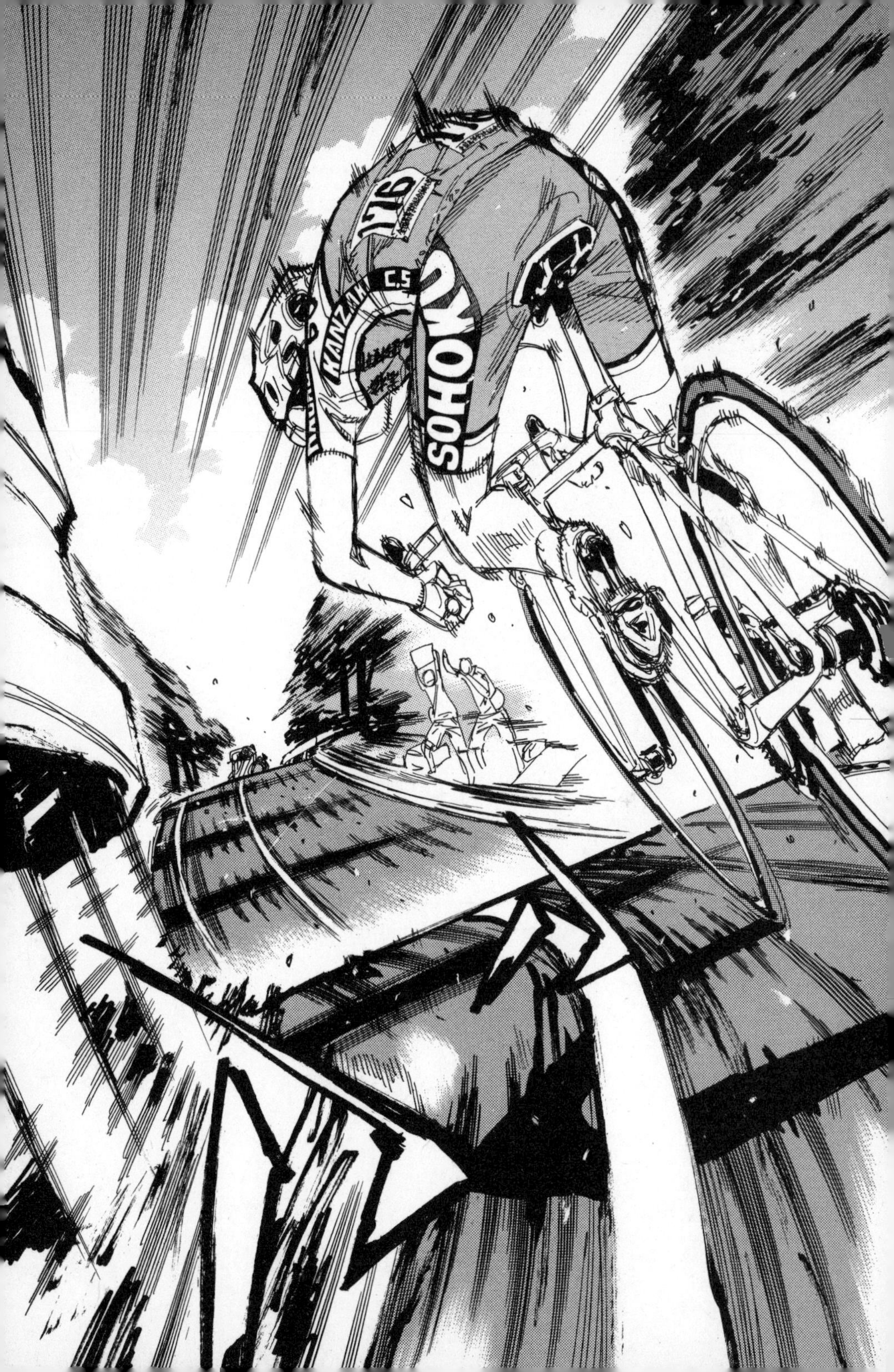
176
C.S

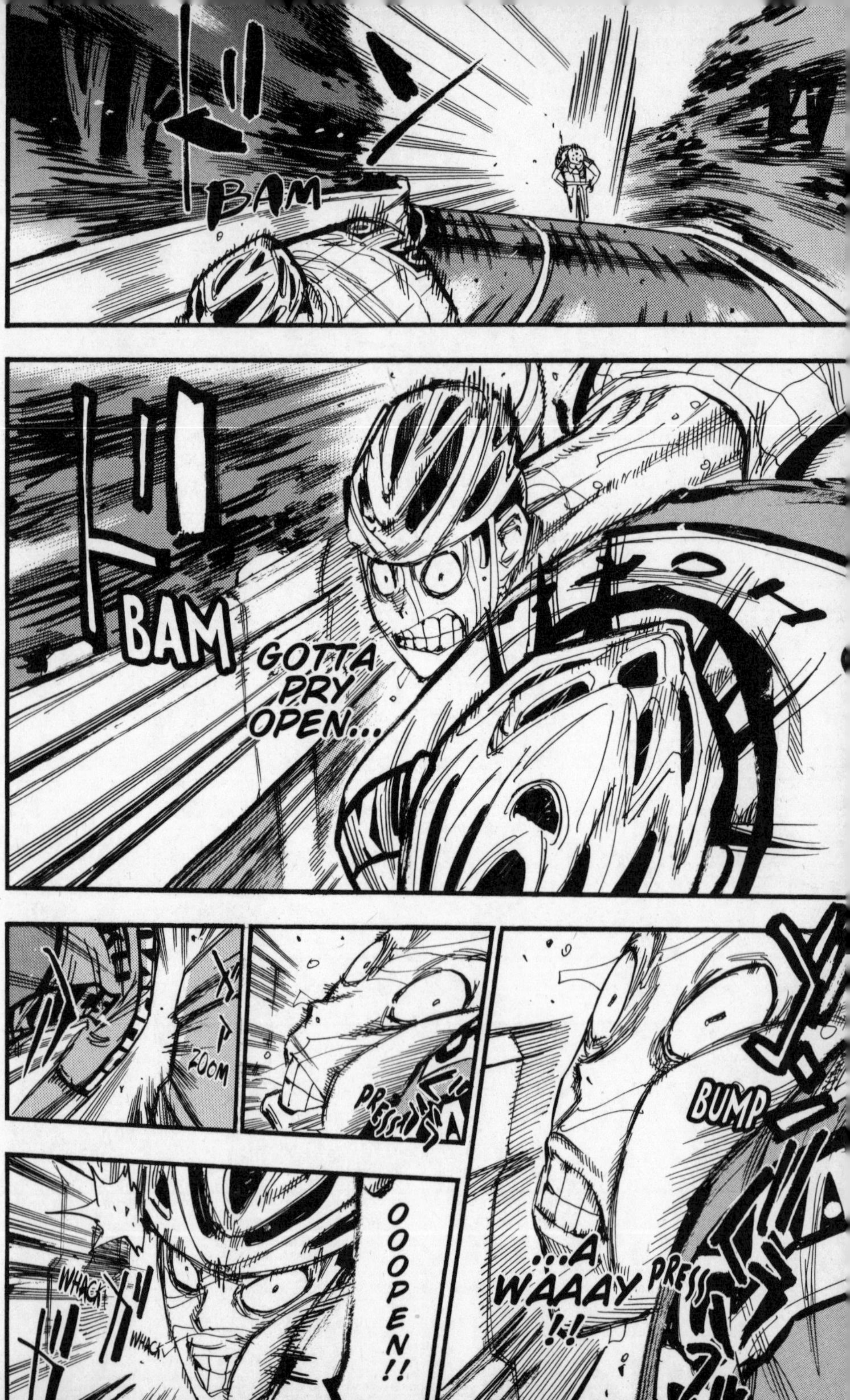
BAM
BAM
GOTTA PRY OPEN...
BUMP
...A WAAAY PRESS!!
PRESS
ZOOM
OOOPEN!!
WHACK
WHACK

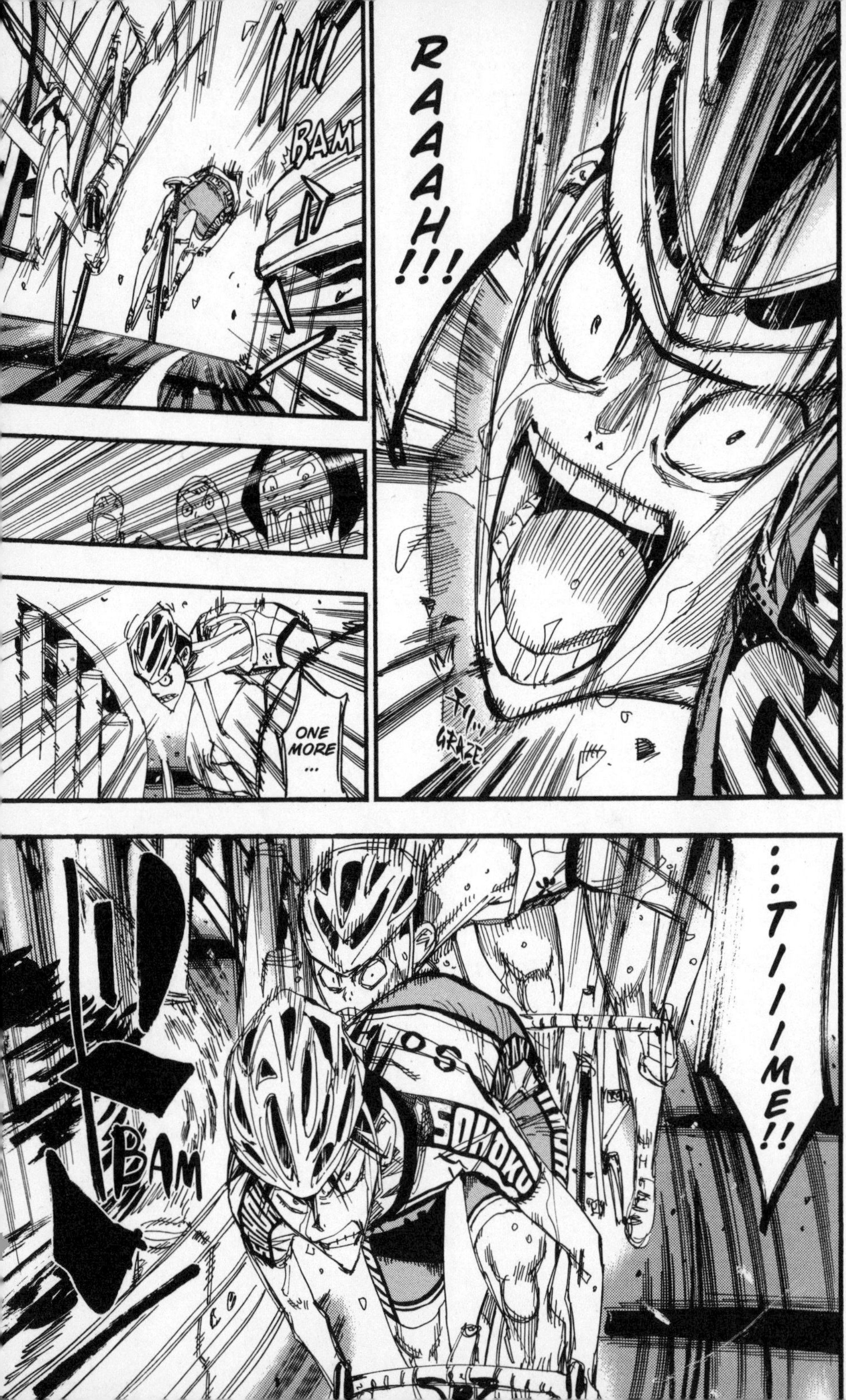
RAAAAH!!!
GRAZE
BAM
ONE MORE ...
...TIIIIME!!
BAM

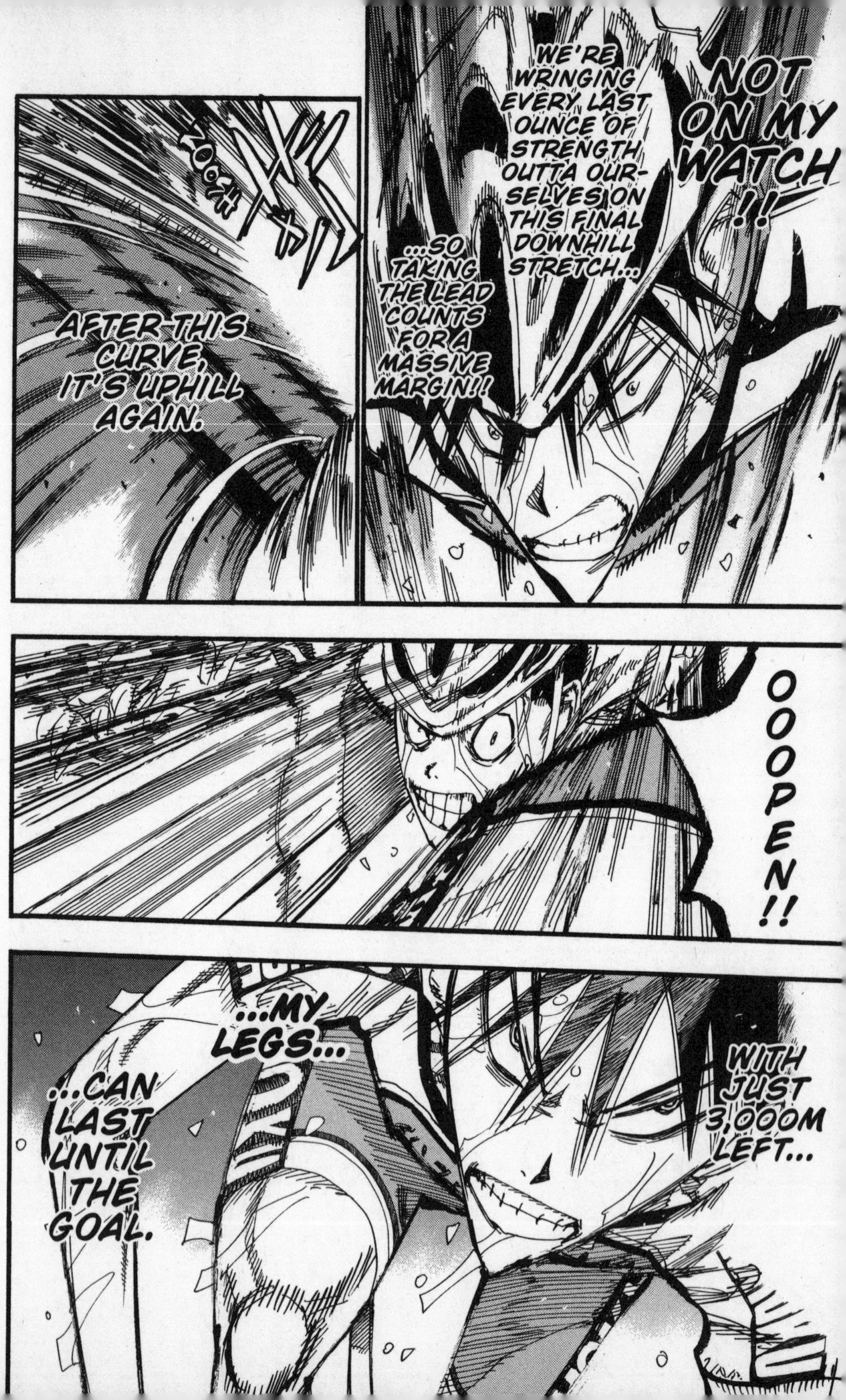
NOT ON MY WATCH!!
WE'RE WRINGING EVERY LAST OUNCE OF STRENGTH OUTTA OURSELVES ON THIS FINAL DOWNHILL STRETCH...
...SO TAKING THE LEAD COUNTS FOR A MASSIVE MARGIN!!
ZOOM!!
AFTER THIS CURVE, IT'S UPHILL AGAIN.
OOOOPEN!!
WITH JUST 3,000M LEFT...
...MY LEGS...
...CAN LAST UNTIL THE GOAL.

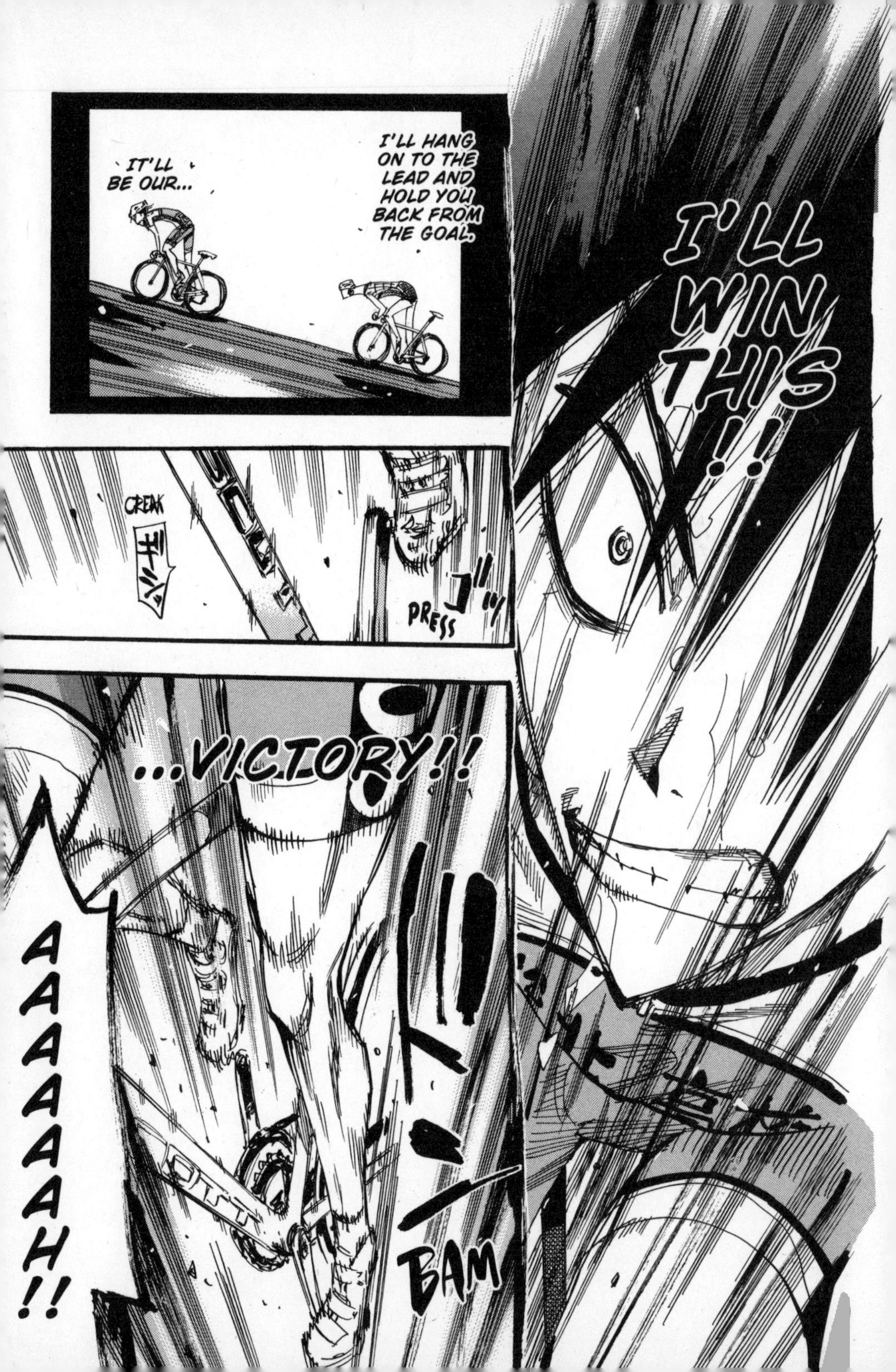
I'LL WIN THIS!!
I'LL HANG ON TO THE LEAD AND HOLD YOU BACK FROM THE GOAL.
IT'LL BE OUR...
PRESS
ギシッ
CREAK
...VICTORY!!
BAM
AAAAAAAAH!!

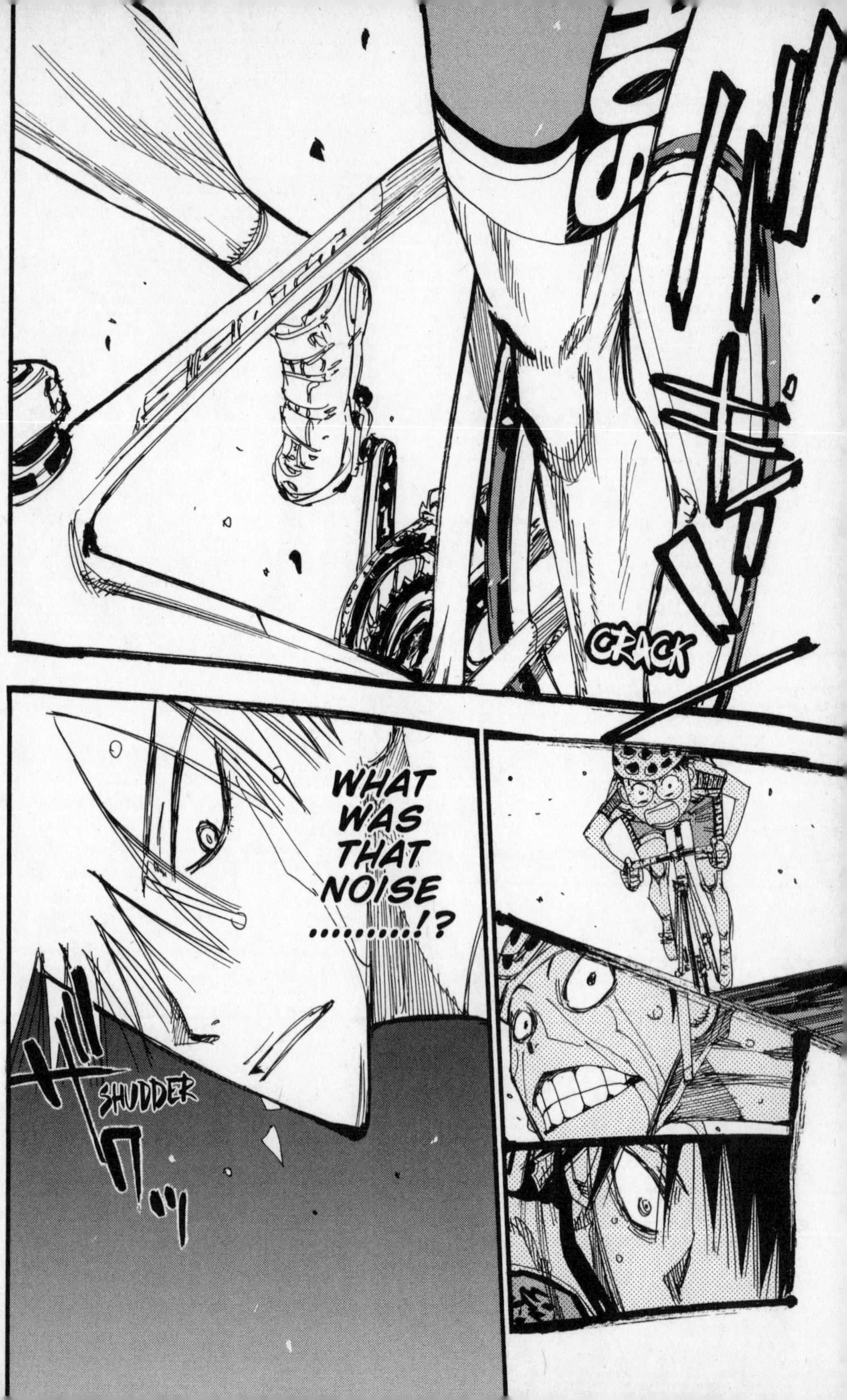
CRACK
WHAT WAS THAT NOISE ....!?
SHUDDER

RIDE.214 FULL SPEED AHEAD

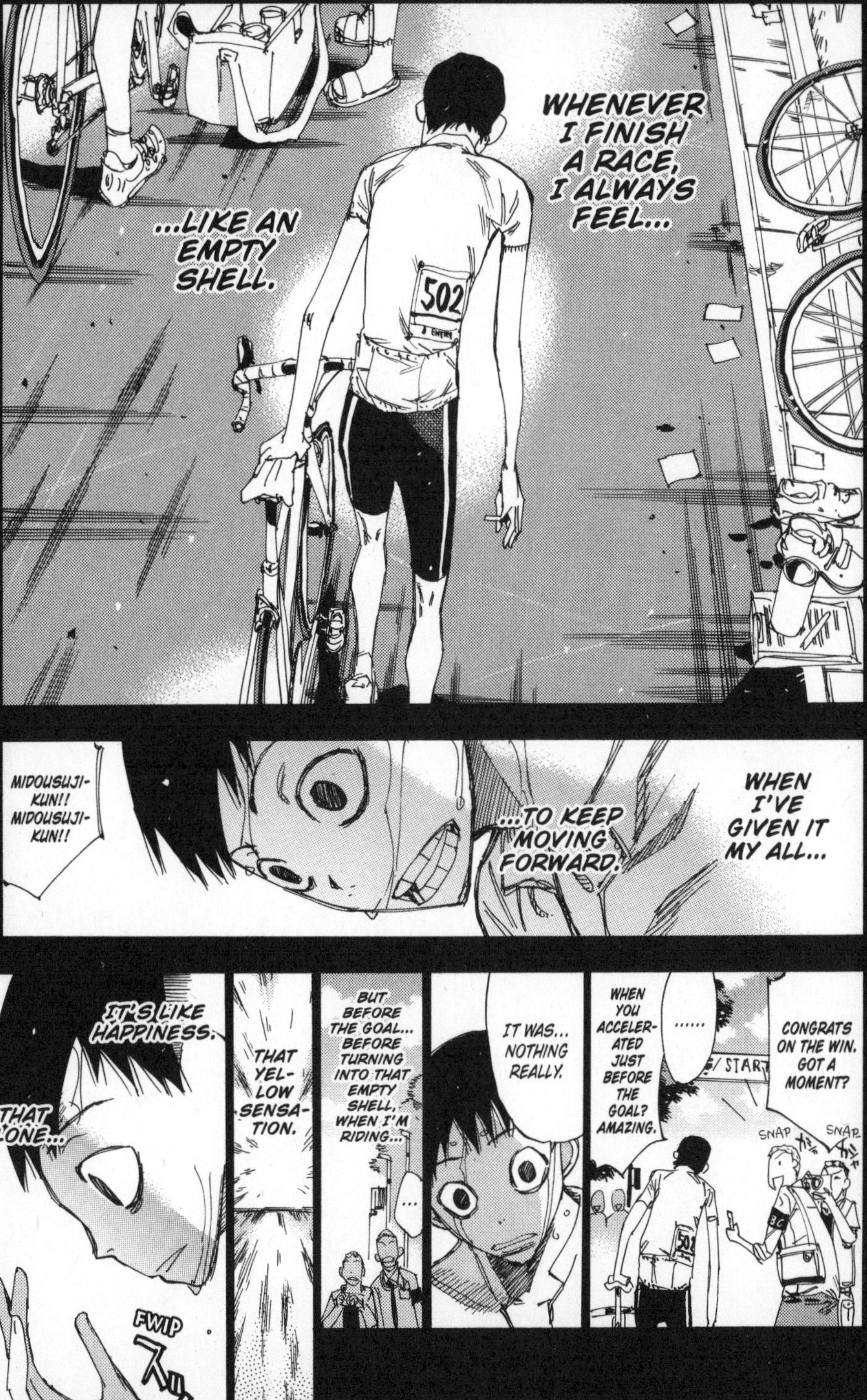
WHENEVER I FINISH A RACE, I ALWAYS FEEL...
...LIKE AN EMPTY SHELL.
502
WHEN I'VE GIVEN IT MY ALL...
...TO KEEP MOVING FORWARD.
MIDOUSUJI-KUN!! MIDOUSUJI-KUN!!
CONGRATS ON THE WIN. GOT A MOMENT?
SNAP
SNAP
......
WHEN YOU ACCELERATED JUST BEFORE THE GOAL? AMAZING.
IT WAS... NOTHING REALLY.
BUT BEFORE THE GOAL... BEFORE TURNING INTO THAT EMPTY SHELL, WHEN I'M RIDING...
...
THAT YELLOW SENSATION.
IT'S LIKE HAPPINESS.
THAT ALONE...
FWIP

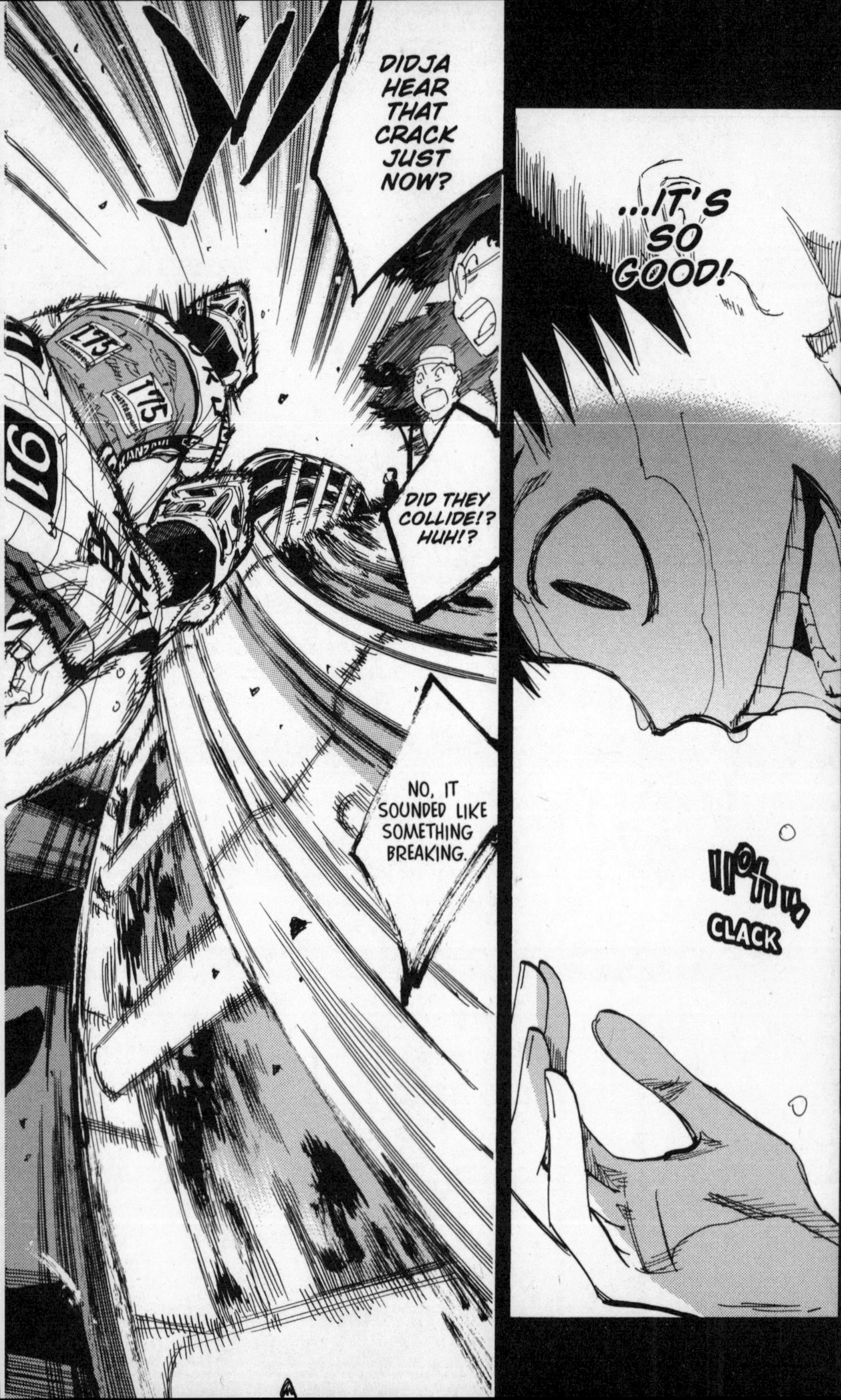
...IT'S SO GOOD!
CLACK
DIDJA HEAR THAT CRACK JUST NOW?
DID THEY COLLIDE!? HUH!?
NO, IT SOUNDED LIKE SOMETHING BREAKING.

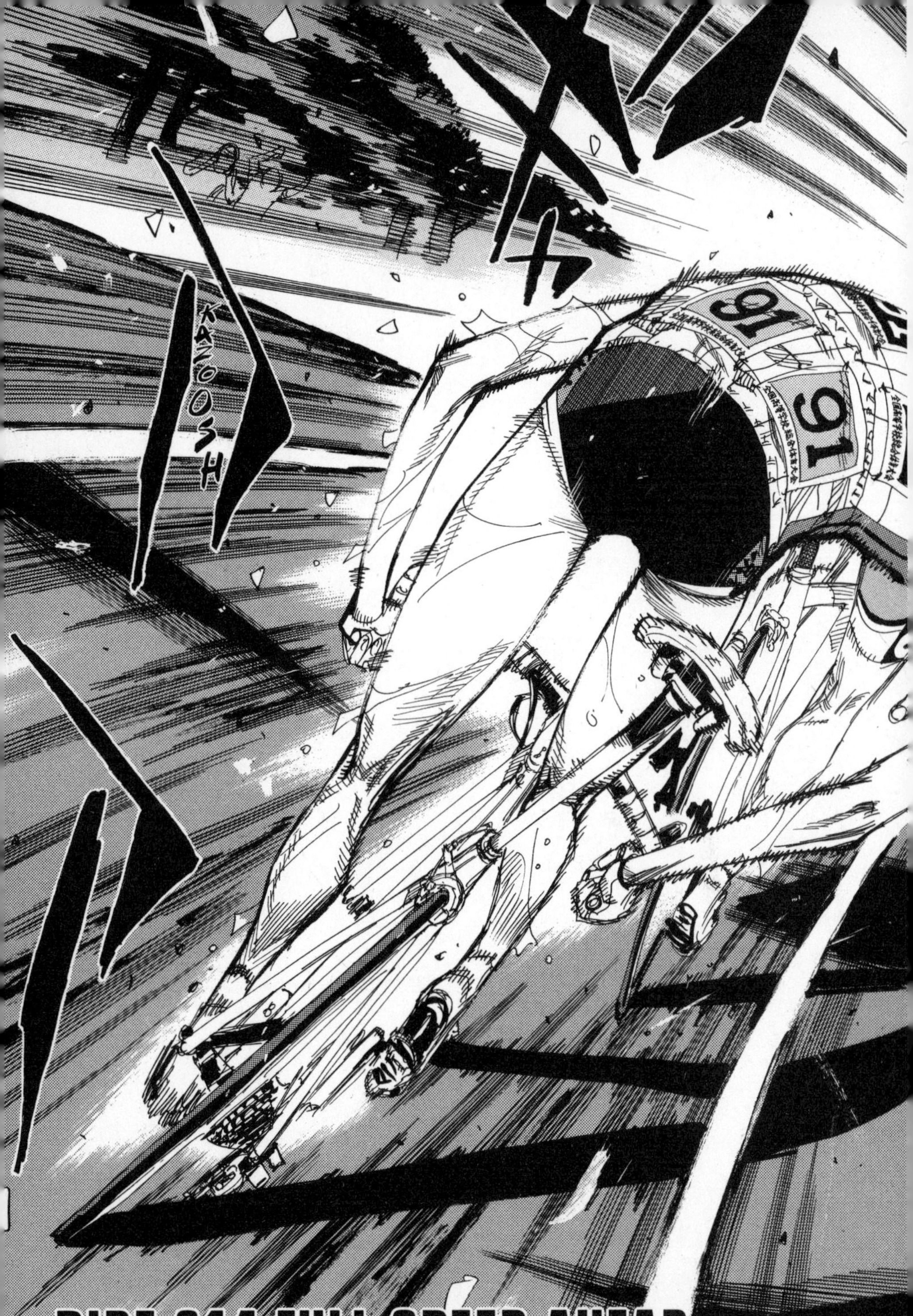
KAZOOSH

RIDE.214 FULL SPEED AHEAD

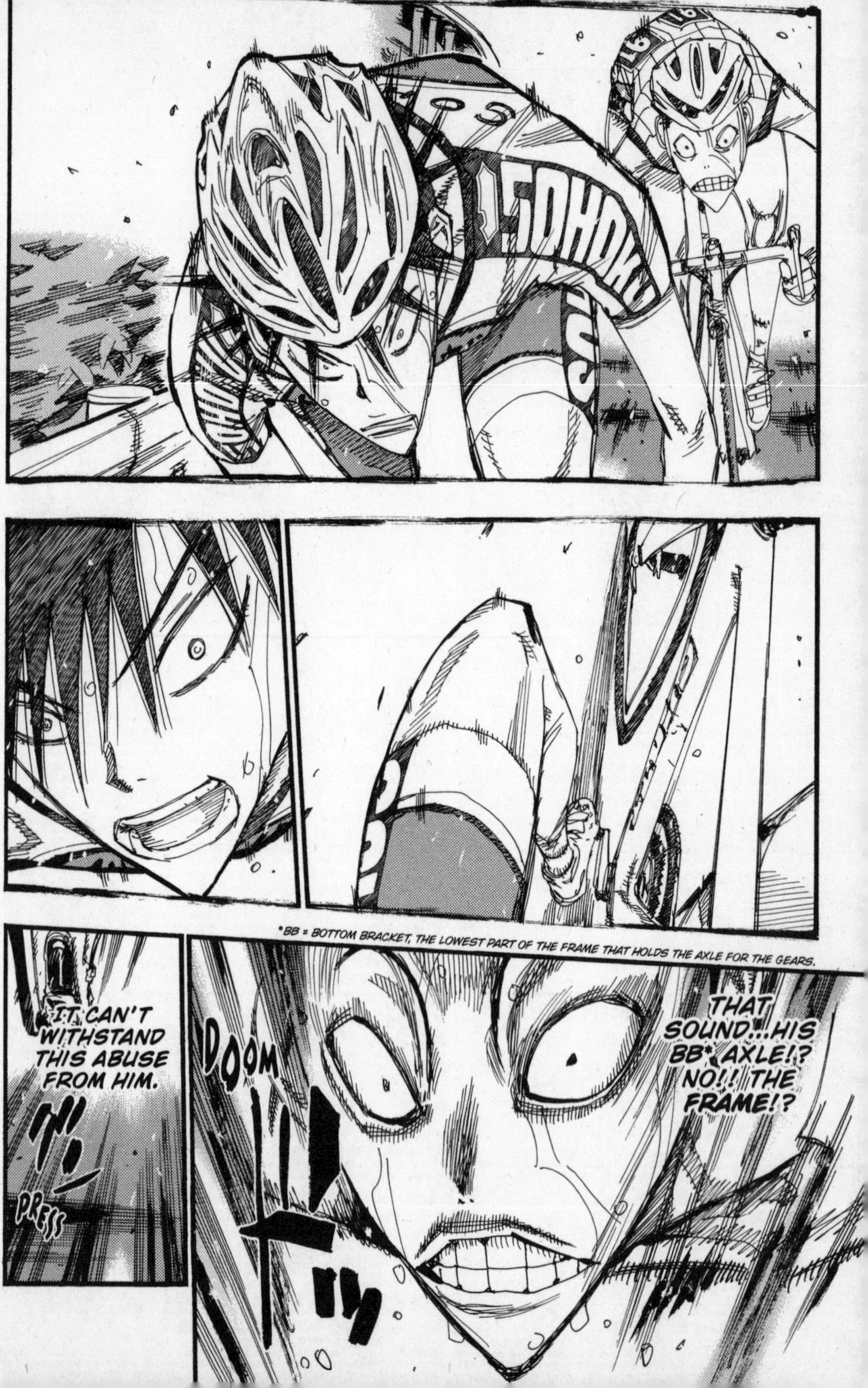
THAT SOUND...HIS BB* AXLE!? NO!! THE FRAME!?
DOOM
IT CAN'T WITHSTAND THIS ABUSE FROM HIM.
PRESS
*BB = BOTTOM BRACKET, THE LOWEST PART OF THE FRAME THAT HOLDS THE AXLE FOR THE GEARS.

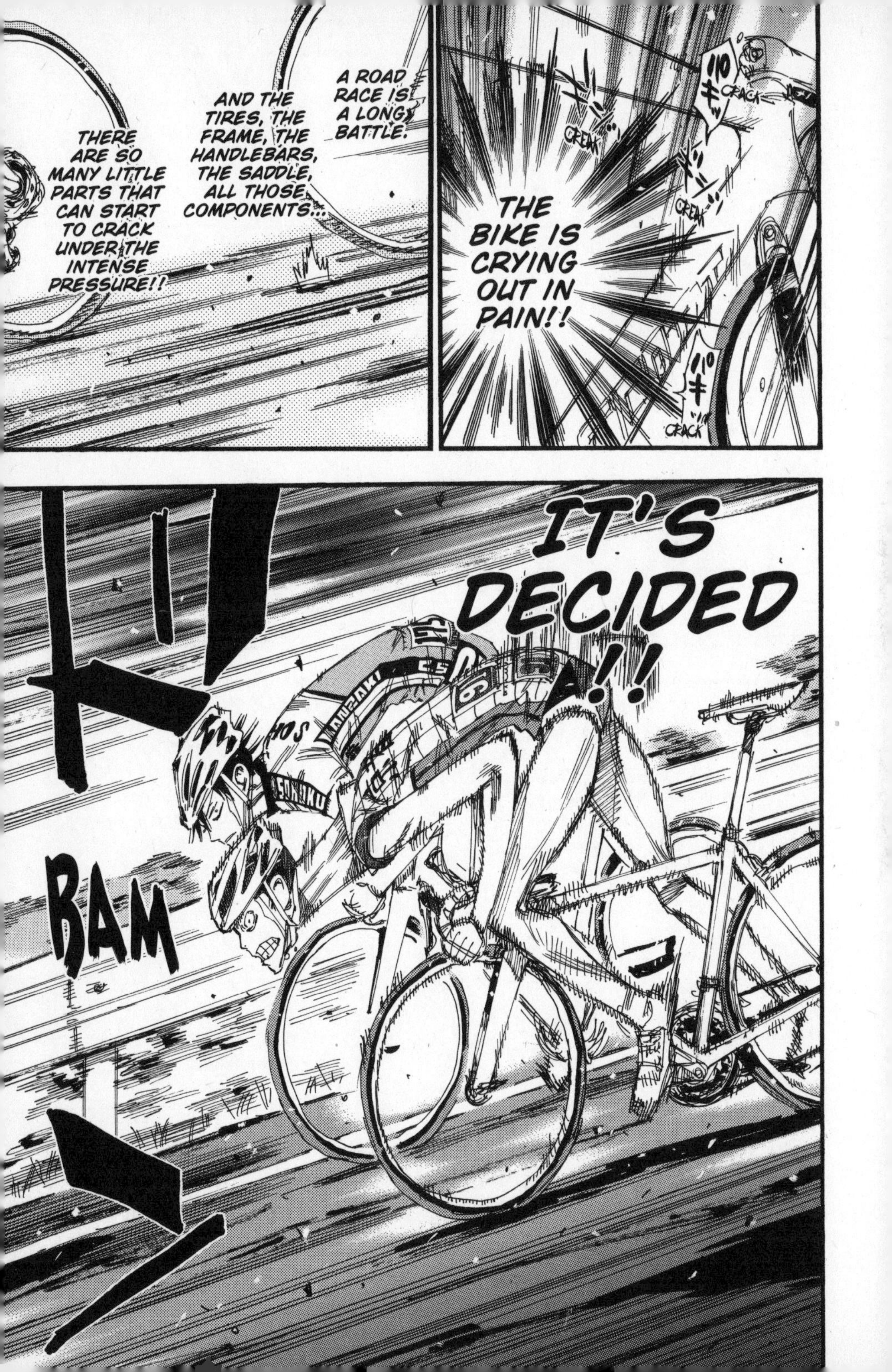
CRACK
CREAK
CREAK
THE BIKE IS CRYING OUT IN PAIN!!
CRACK
A ROAD RACE IS A LONG BATTLE.
AND THE TIRES, THE FRAME, THE HANDLEBARS, THE SADDLE, ALL THOSE COMPONENTS...
THERE ARE SO MANY LITTLE PARTS THAT CAN START TO CRACK UNDER THE INTENSE PRESSURE!!
IT'S DECIDED!!!
BAM

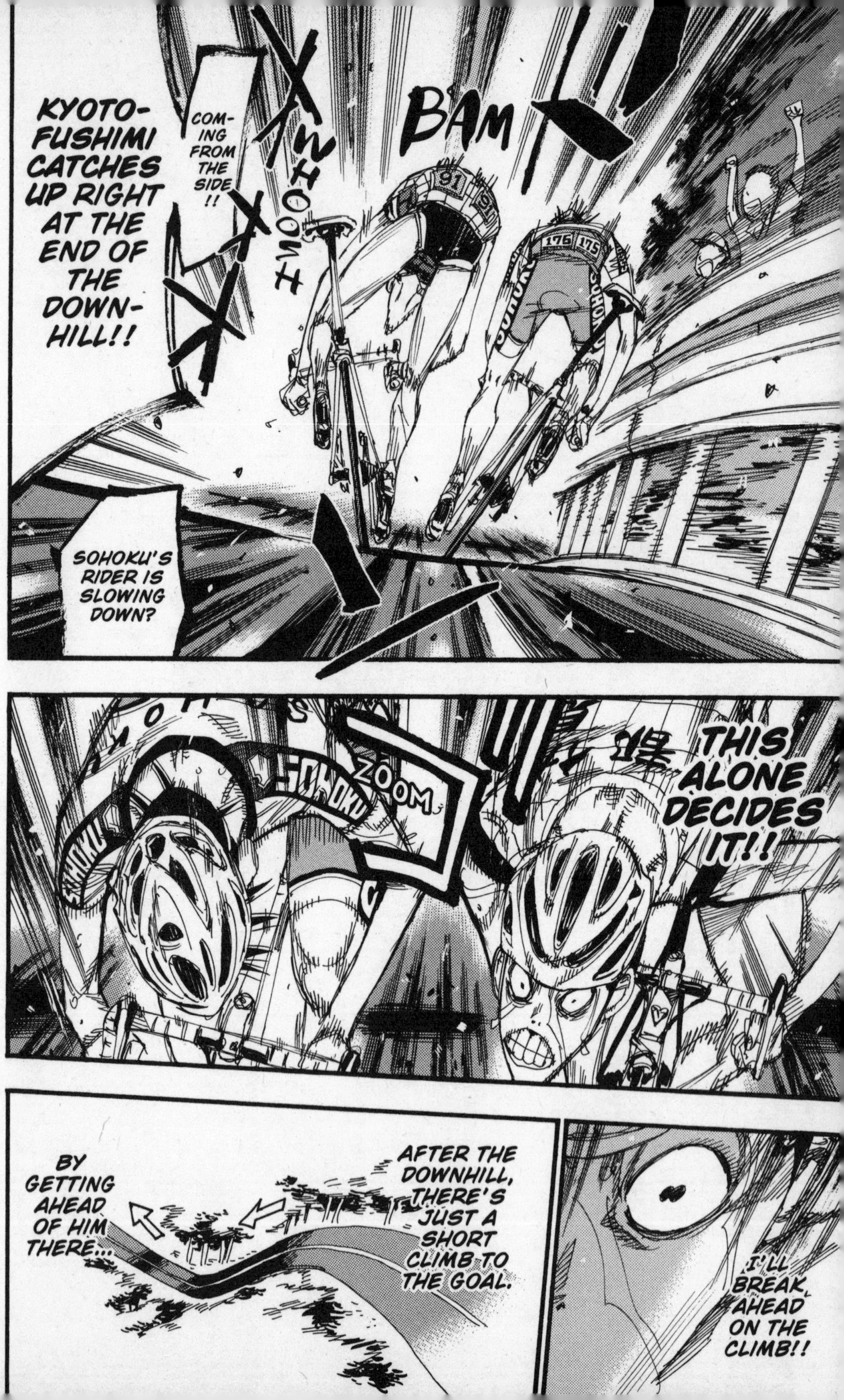

BAM
WHOOSH
COMING FROM THE SIDE!!
KYOTO-FUSHIMI CATCHES UP RIGHT AT THE END OF THE DOWNHILL!!
SOHOKU'S RIDER IS SLOWING DOWN?
THIS ALONE DECIDES IT!!
ZOOM
I'LL BREAK AHEAD ON THE CLIMB!!
AFTER THE DOWNHILL, THERE'S JUST A SHORT CLIMB TO THE GOAL.
BY GETTING AHEAD OF HIM THERE...

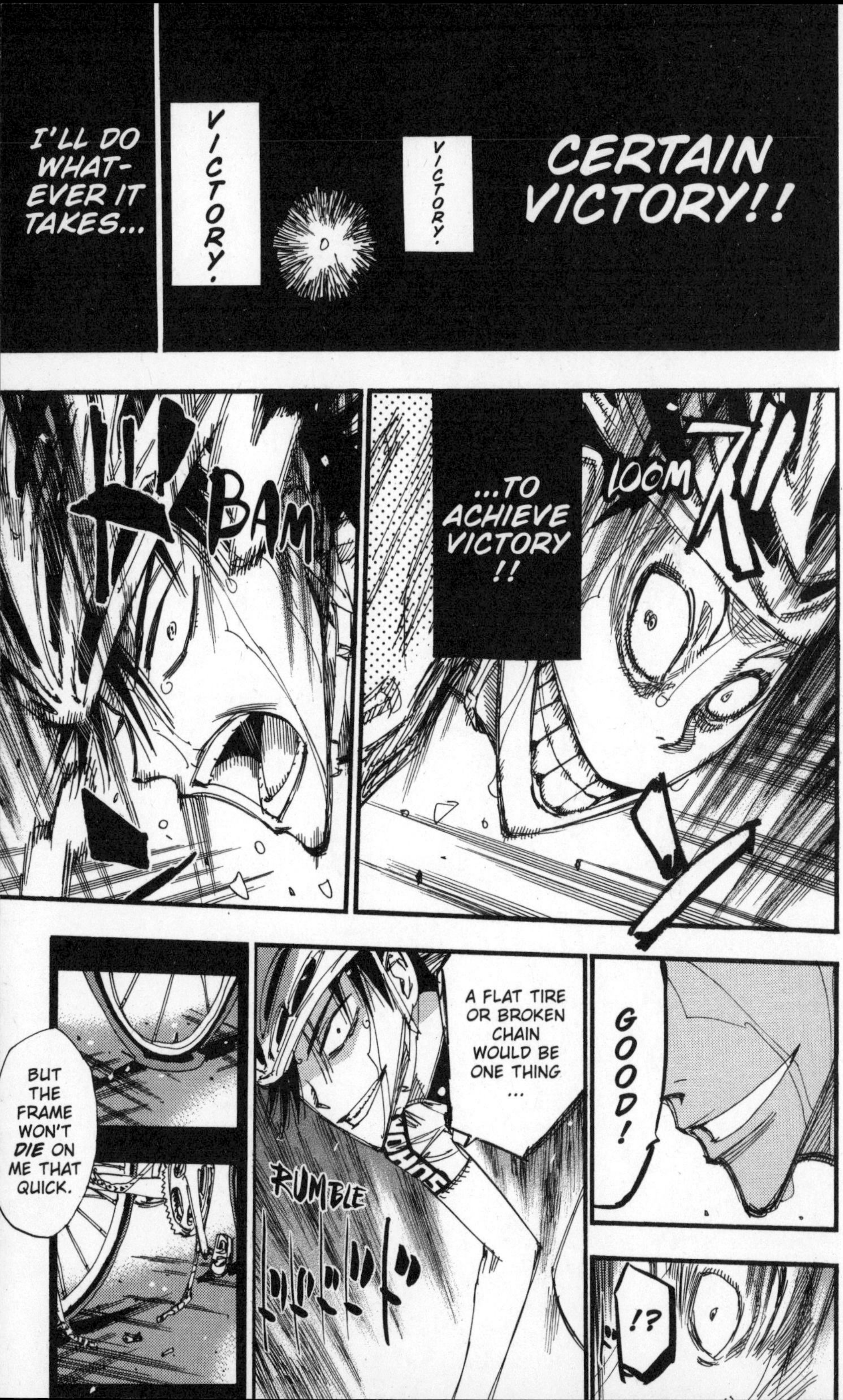
CERTAIN VICTORY!!
VICTORY.
VICTORY.
I'LL DO WHATEVER IT TAKES...
...TO ACHIEVE VICTORY!!
LOOM
BAM
GOOD!
!?
A FLAT TIRE OR BROKEN CHAIN WOULD BE ONE THING ...
RUMBLE
BUT THE FRAME WON'T *DIE* ON ME THAT QUICK.

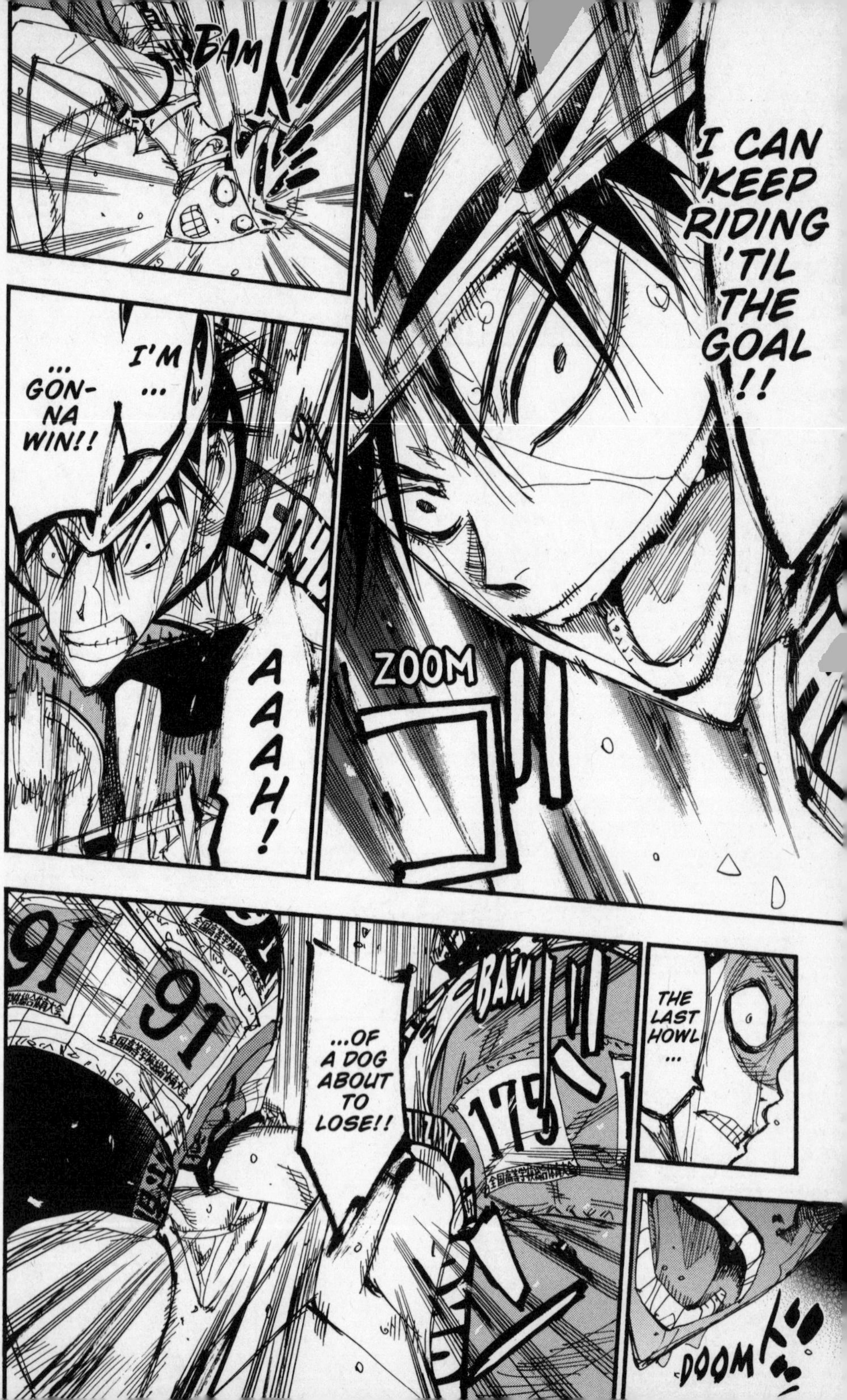
I CAN KEEP RIDING 'TIL THE GOAL!!
ZOOM
BAM
I'M...
...GON-NA WIN!!
AAAAH!
THE LAST HOWL...
DOOM
...OF A DOG ABOUT TO LOSE!!
BAM

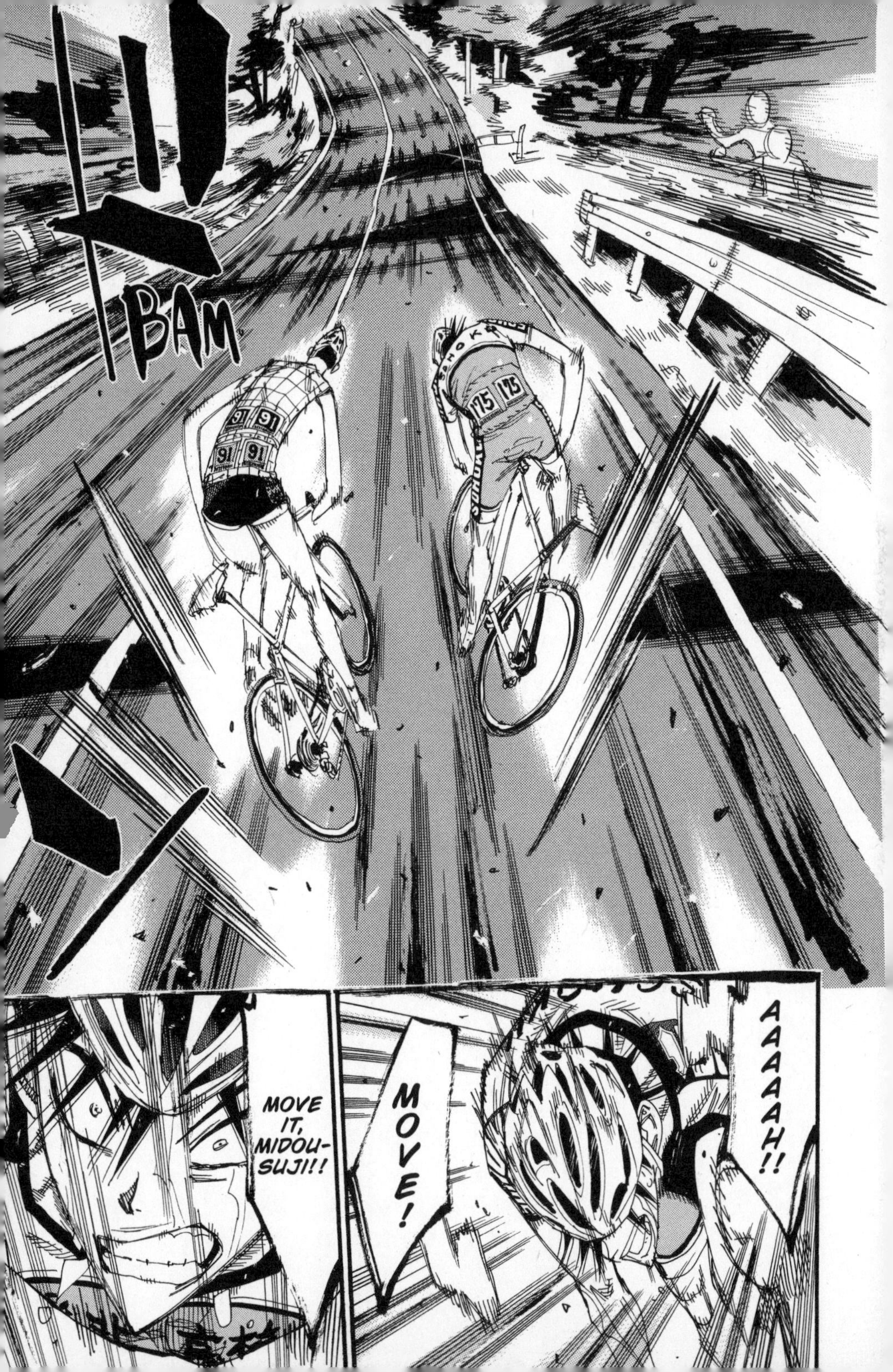

BAM
AAAAAAH!!
MOVE!
MOVE IT, MIDOU-SUJI!!

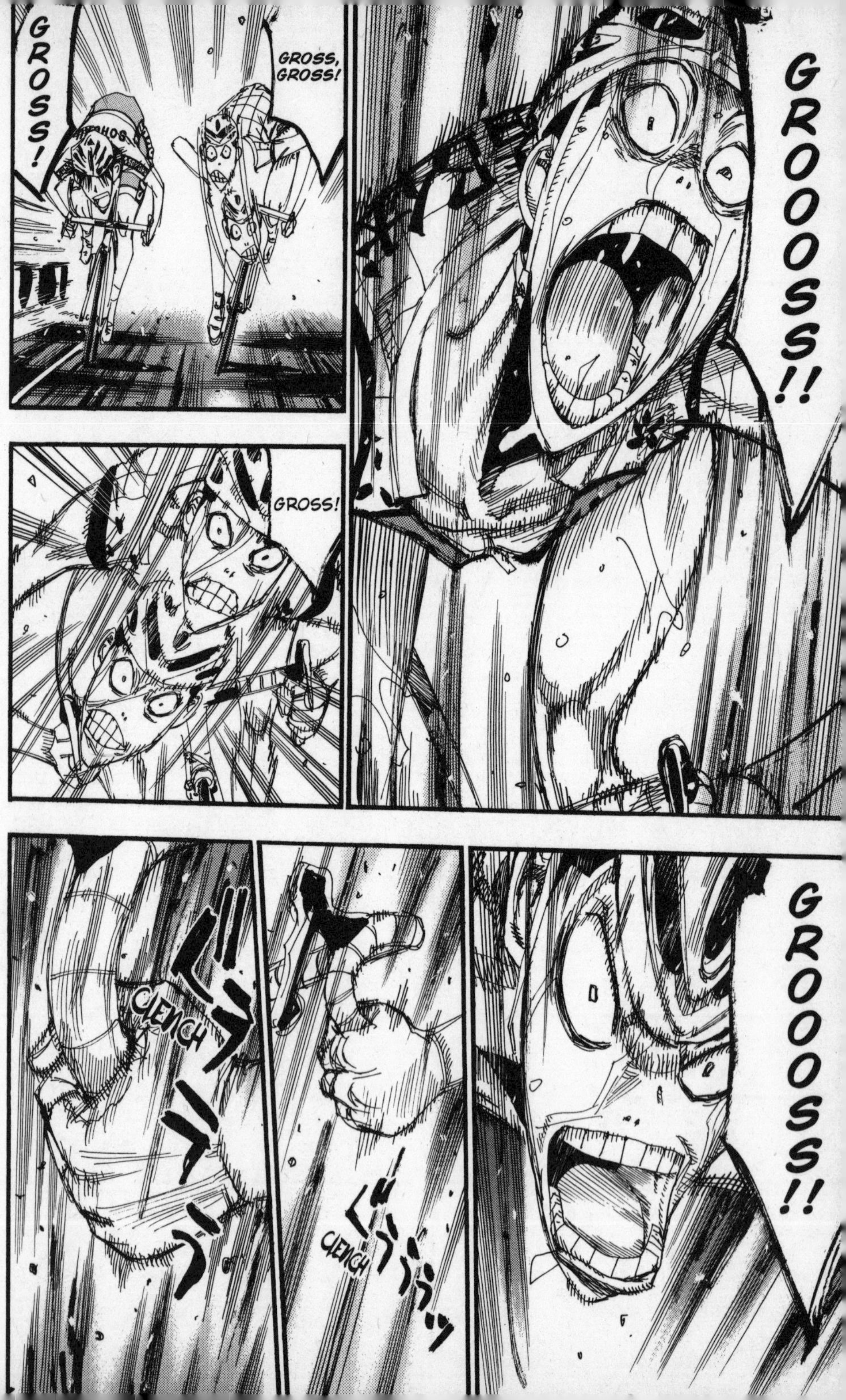
GROOOOSS!!
GROSS, GROSS!
GROSS!
GROSS!
GROOOOSS!!
CLENCH
CLENCH

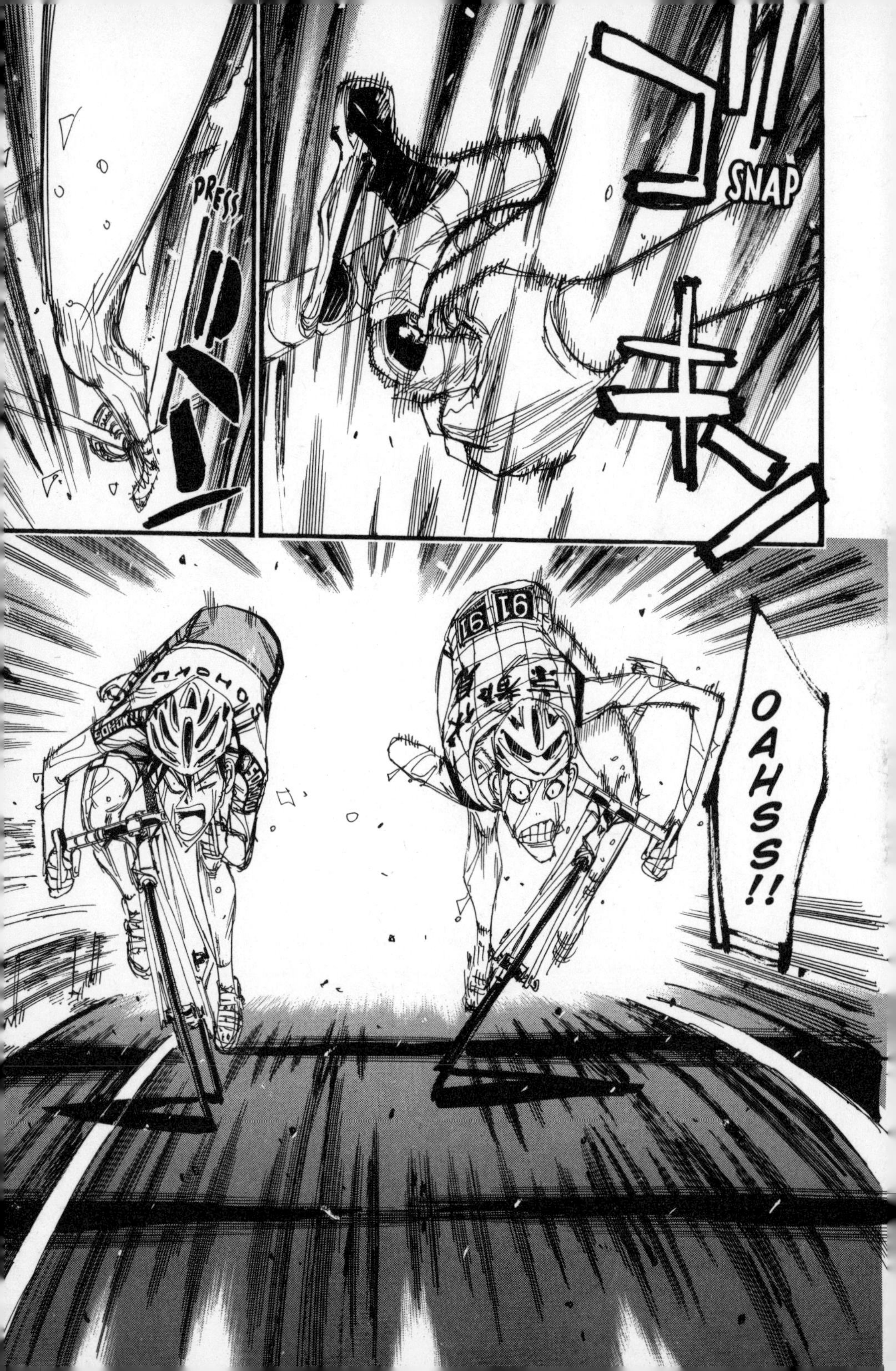

SNAP
PRESS
OAHSS!!

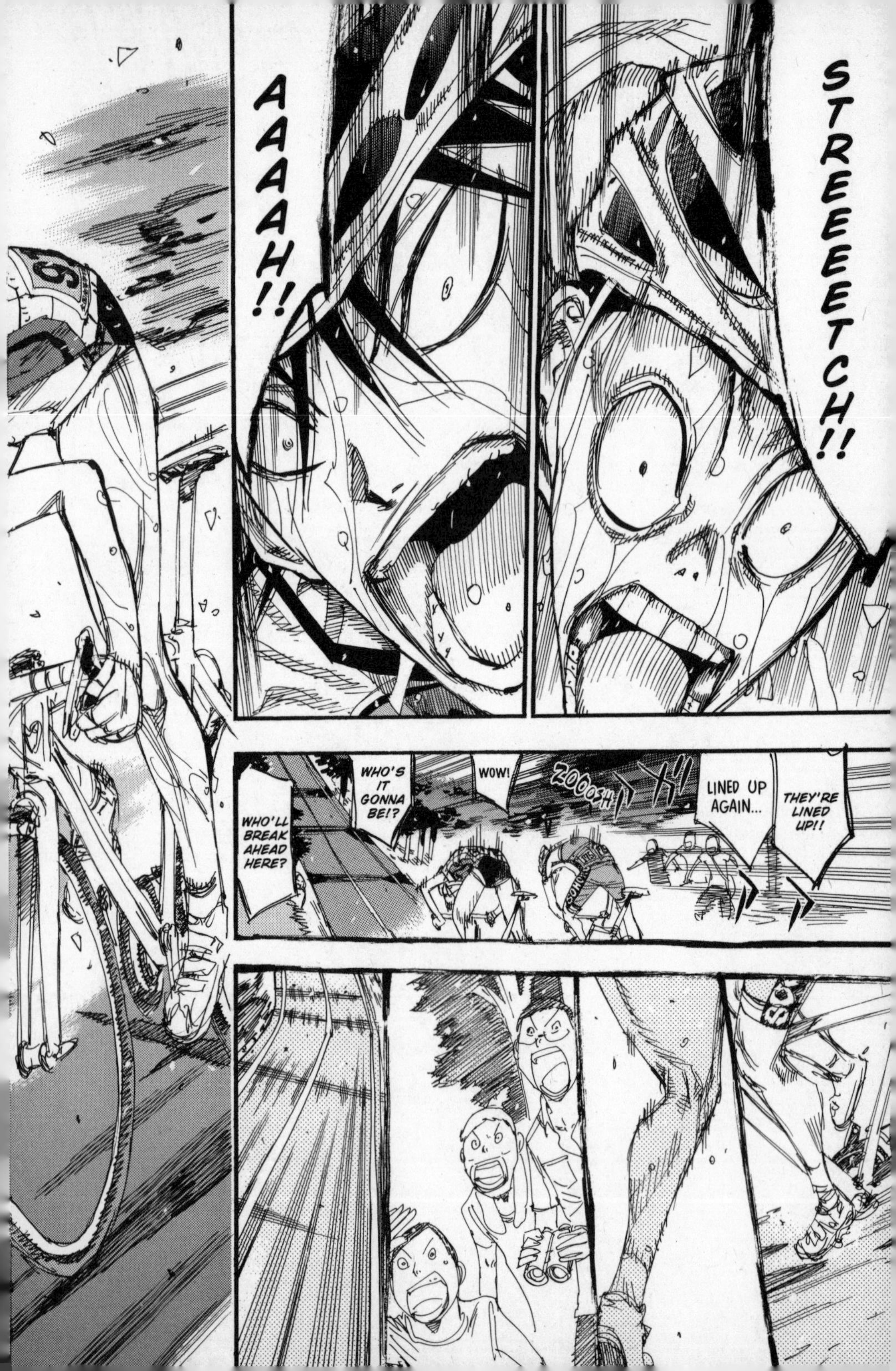
STREEEEETCH!!
AAAAAH!!
THEY'RE LINED UP!!
LINED UP AGAIN...
ZOOOSH
WOW!
WHO'S IT GONNA BE!?
WHO'LL BREAK AHEAD HERE?

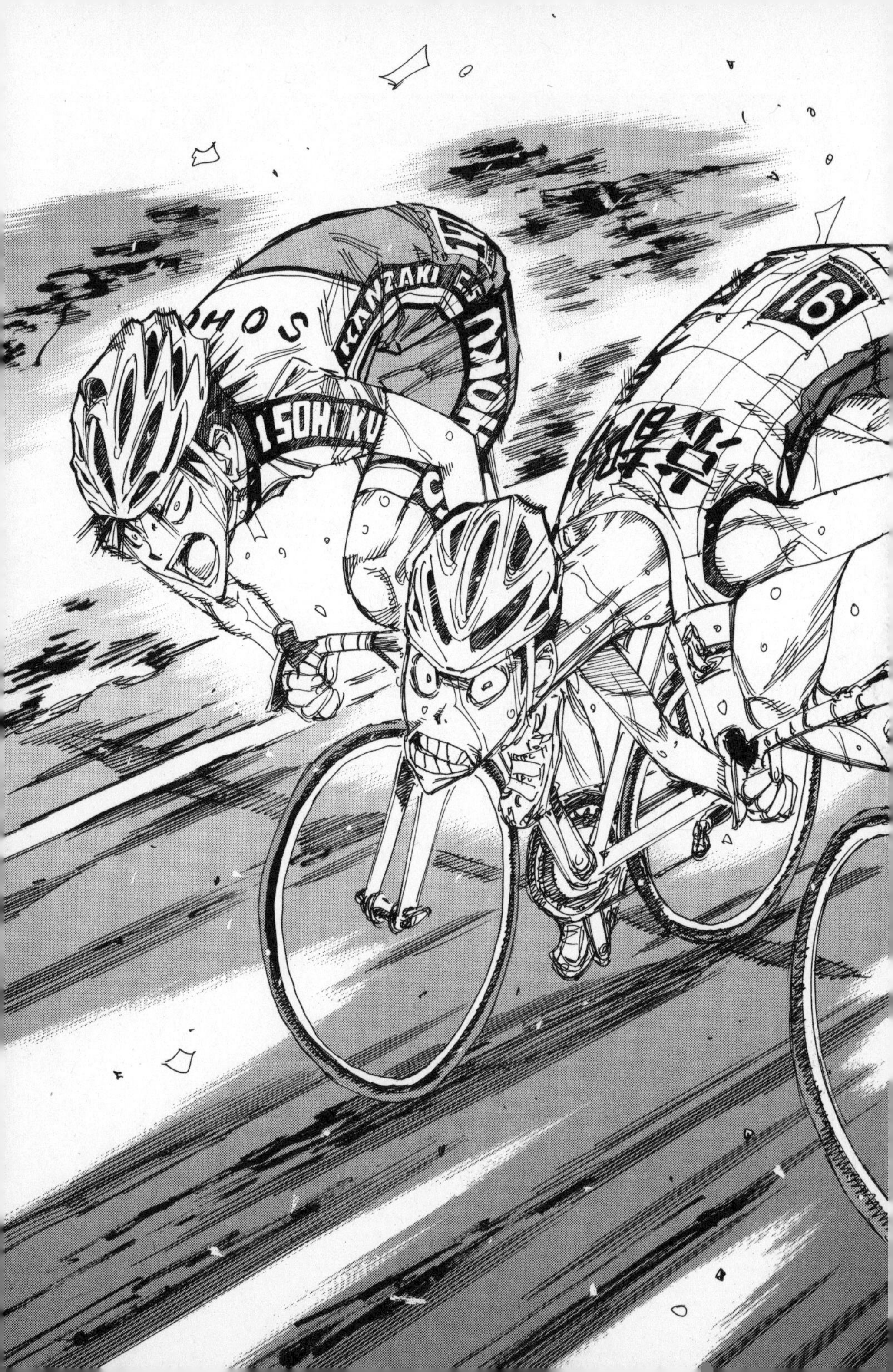
KANZAKI C.S
16

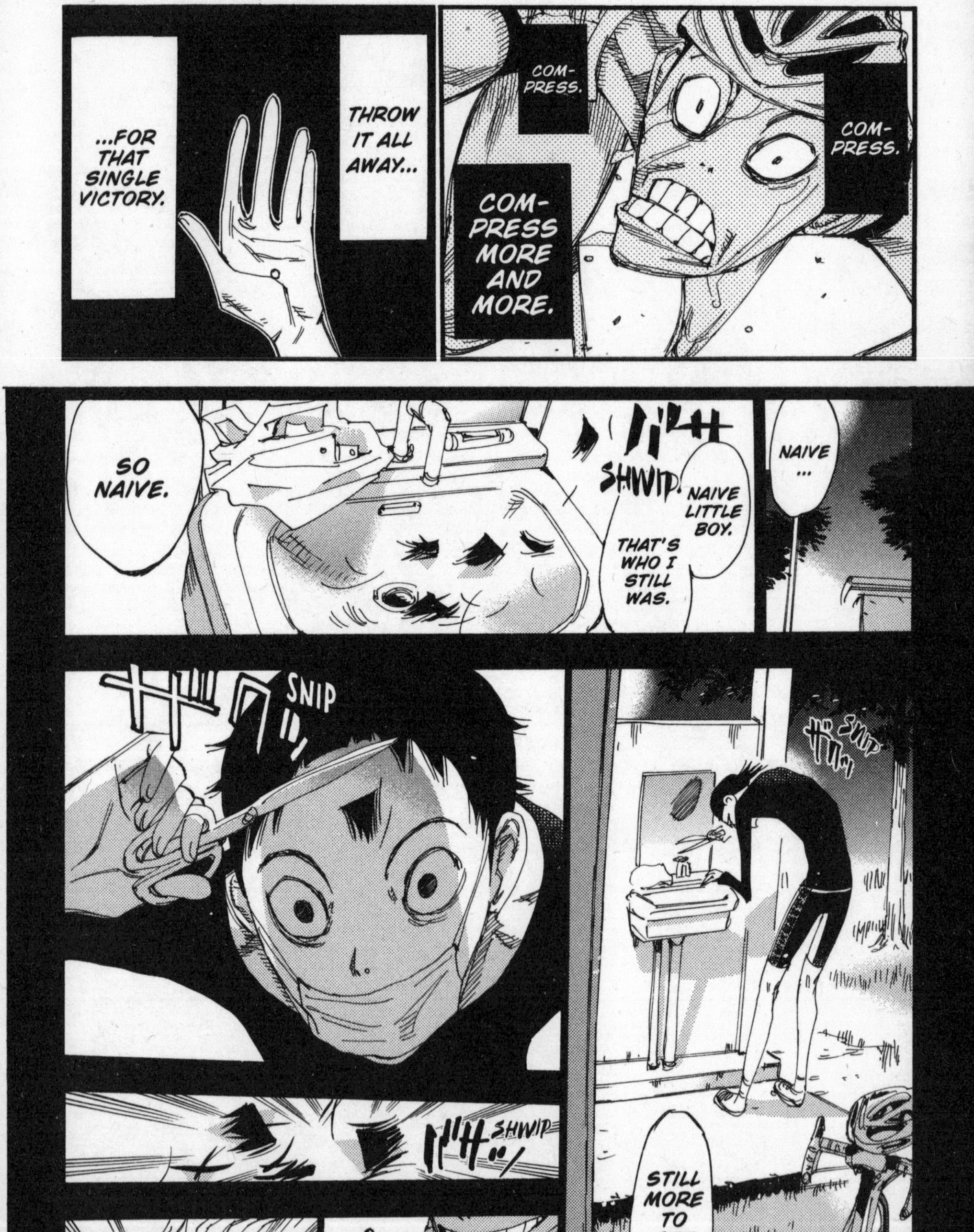
COM-PRESS.
COM-PRESS.
COM-PRESS MORE AND MORE.
THROW IT ALL AWAY...
...FOR THAT SINGLE VICTORY.
NAIVE ...
SHWIP
NAIVE LITTLE BOY.
THAT'S WHO I STILL WAS.
SO NAIVE.
SNIP
STILL MORE TO GET RID OF...
SNIP
SHWIP
CLACK
BAM

TUBE: ARON FALPHA GLUE

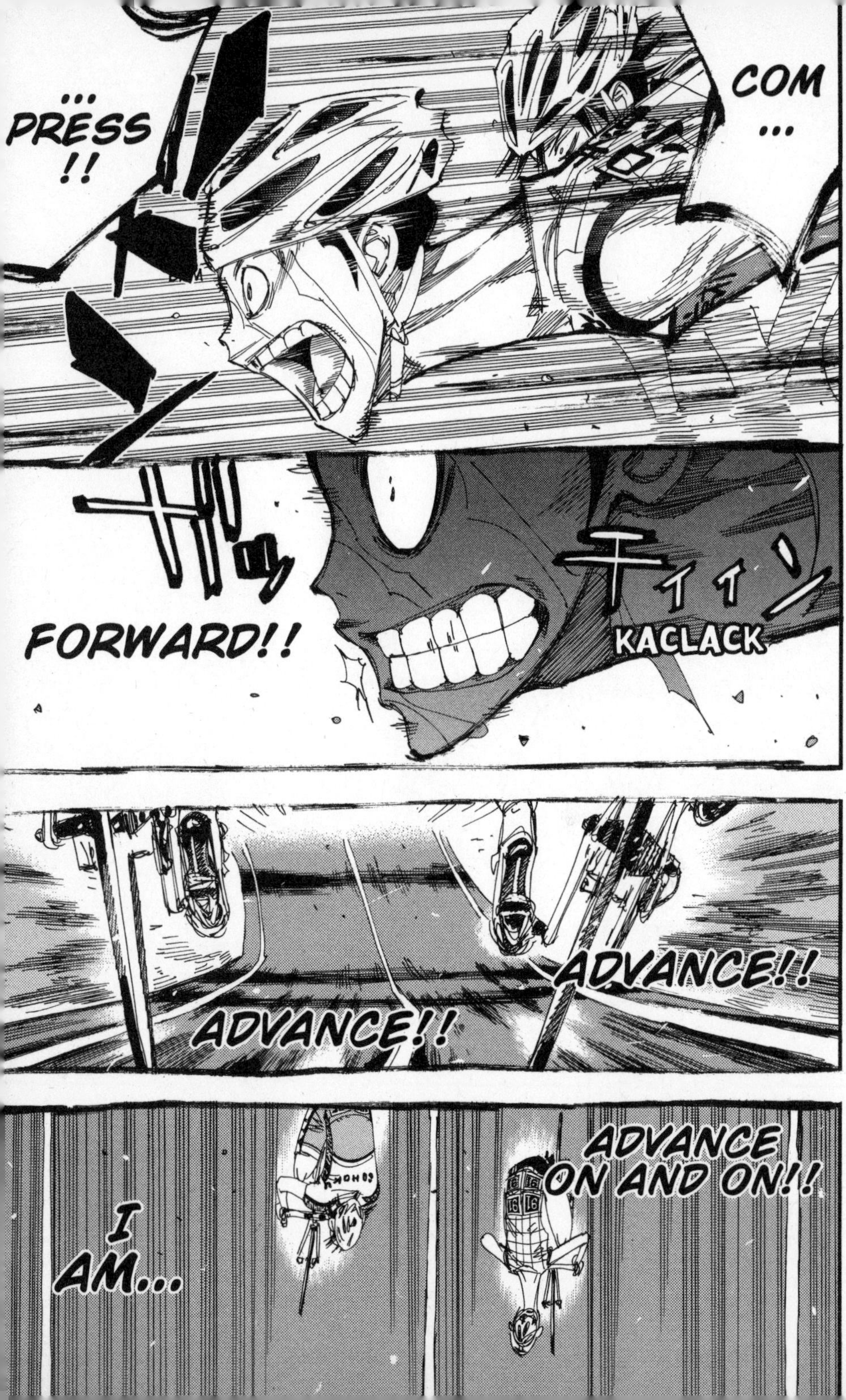
COM ...
... PRESS !!
KACLACK
FORWARD!!
ADVANCE!!
ADVANCE!!
ADVANCE ON AND ON!!
I AM...

...THE ONE WHO WILL CRUSH EVERYTHING IN THIS WORLD...

...WHO WILL FLY THROUGH THIS WORLD ON SPREAD WINGS...

...AKIRA MIDOUSUJI-KUN.

NO MATTER WHAT HAPPENS, KEEP MOVING AHEAD.

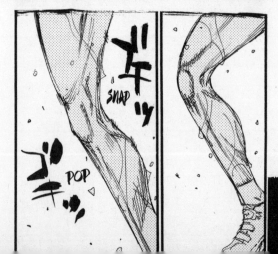

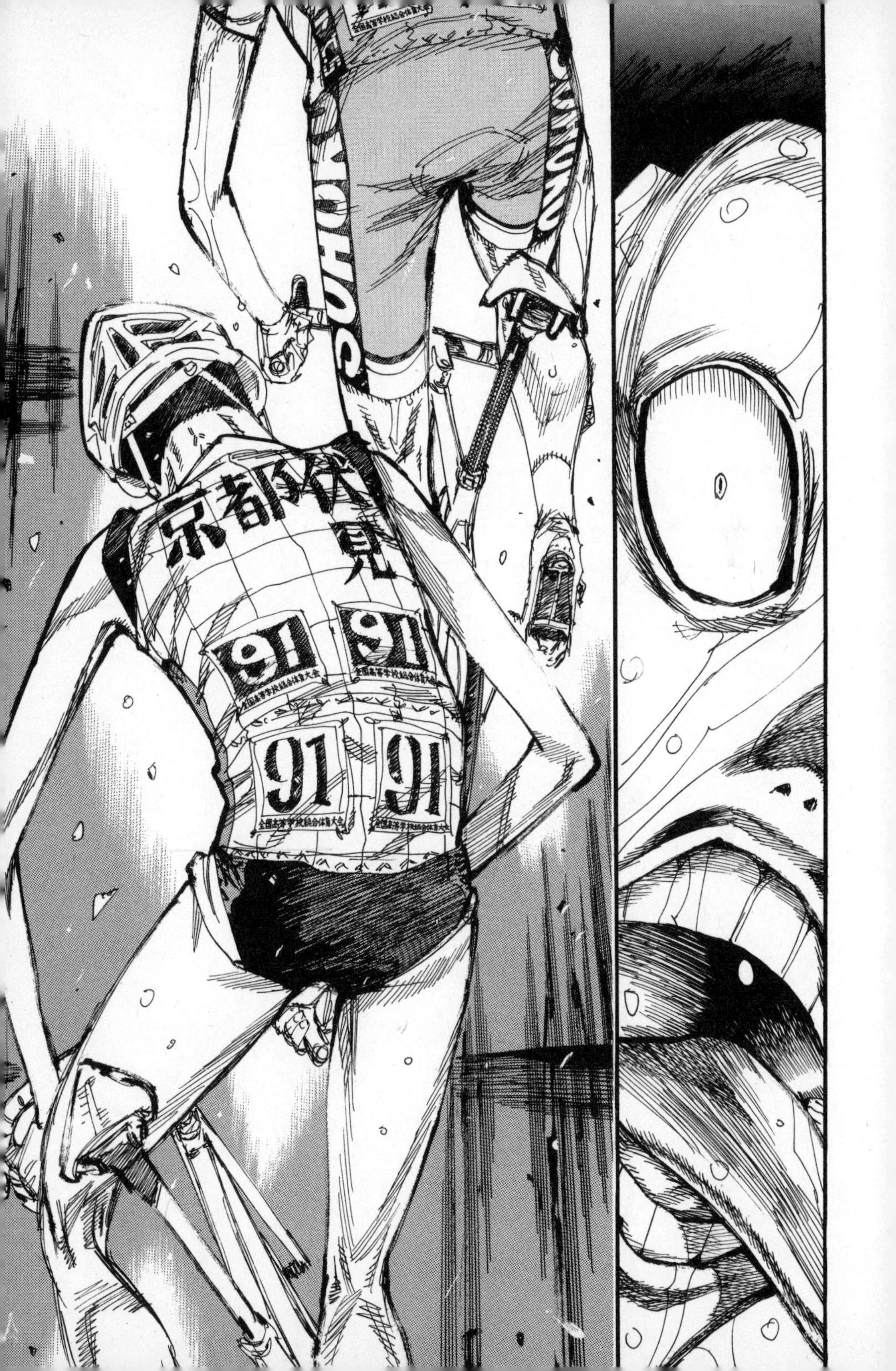
京都伏見
91

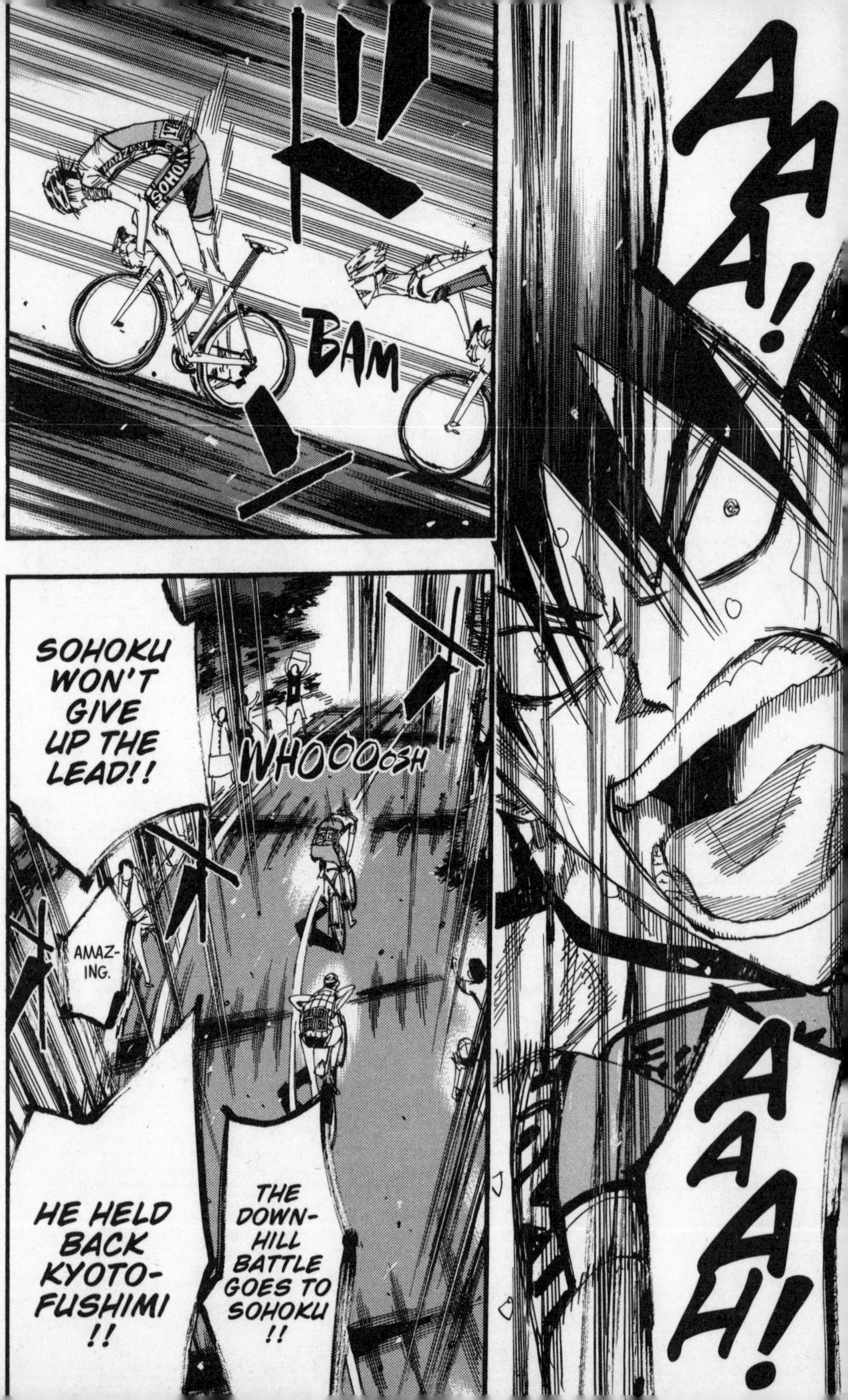
AAA!
AAAH!
BAM
WHOOOOSH
SOHOKU WON'T GIVE UP THE LEAD!!
AMAZING.
THE DOWNHILL BATTLE GOES TO SOHOKU!!
HE HELD BACK KYOTO-FUSHIMI!!

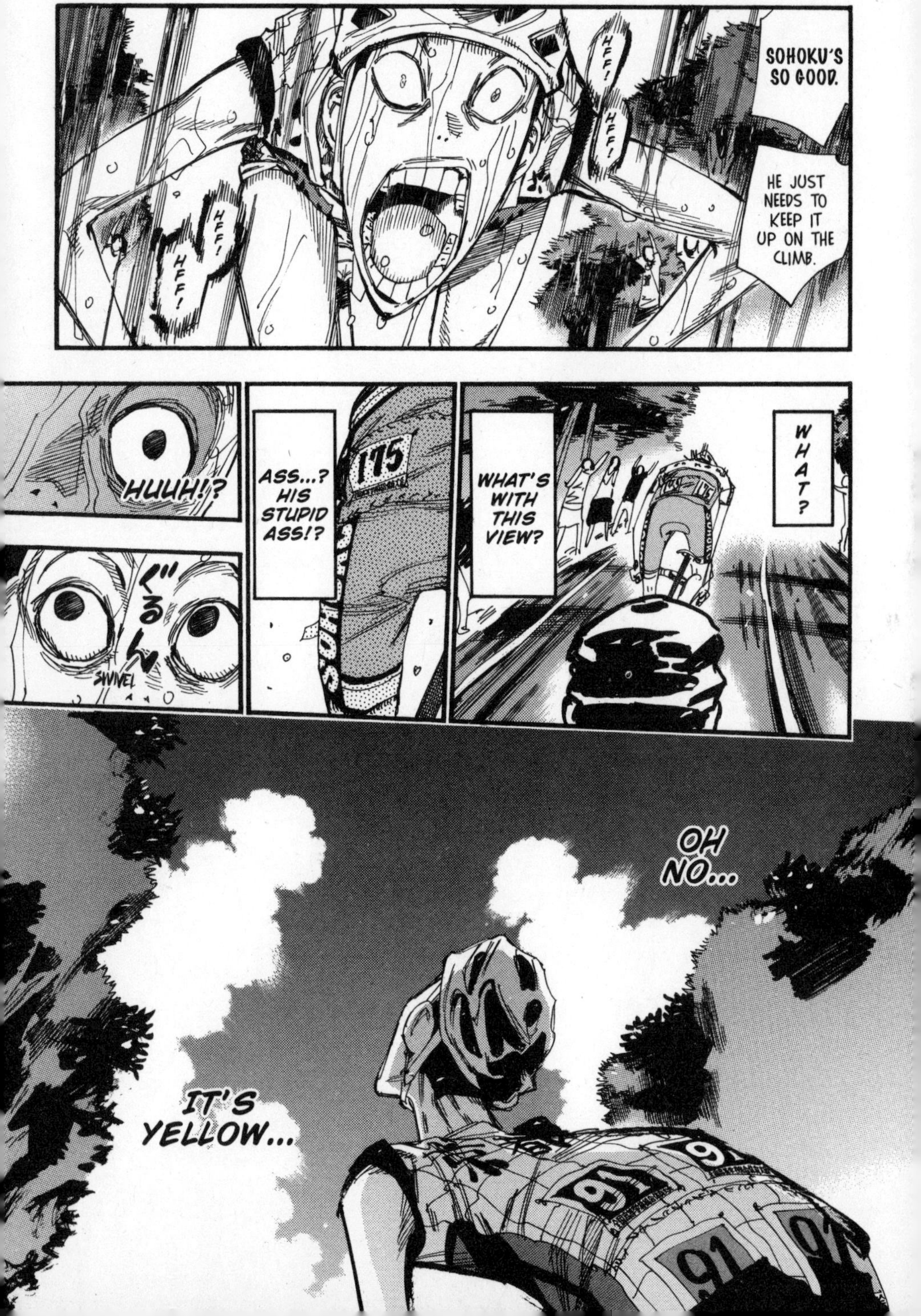
SOHOKU'S SO GOOD.
HE JUST NEEDS TO KEEP IT UP ON THE CLIMB.
HFF! HFF!
HFF! HFF!
WHAT?
WHAT'S WITH THIS VIEW?
ASS...? HIS STUPID ASS!?
HUUH!?
ぐるん
SWIVEL
OH NO...
IT'S YELLOW...

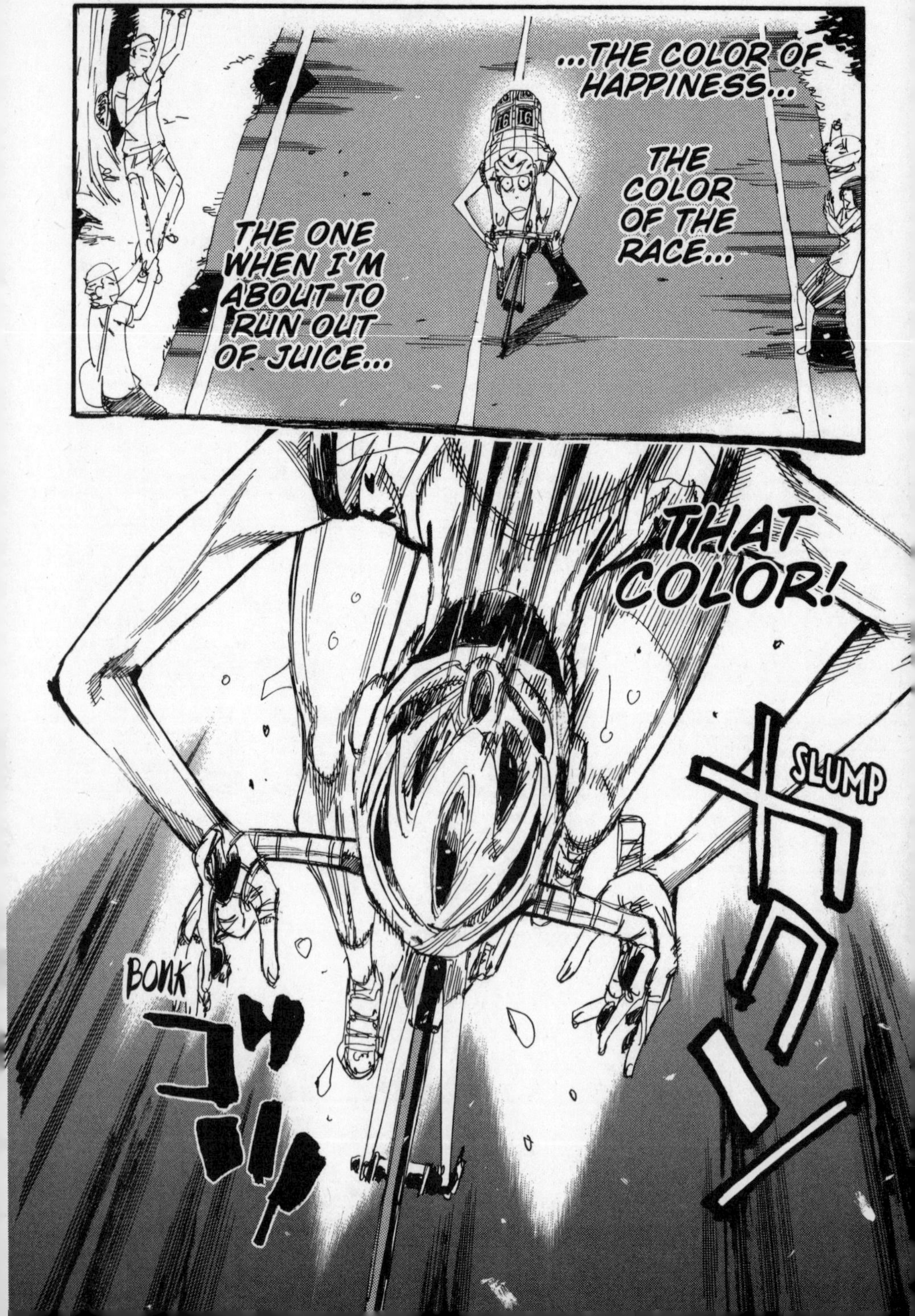

...THE COLOR OF HAPPINESS...
THE COLOR OF THE RACE...
THE ONE WHEN I'M ABOUT TO RUN OUT OF JUICE...
THAT COLOR!
SLUMP
BONK

RIDE.215 #91

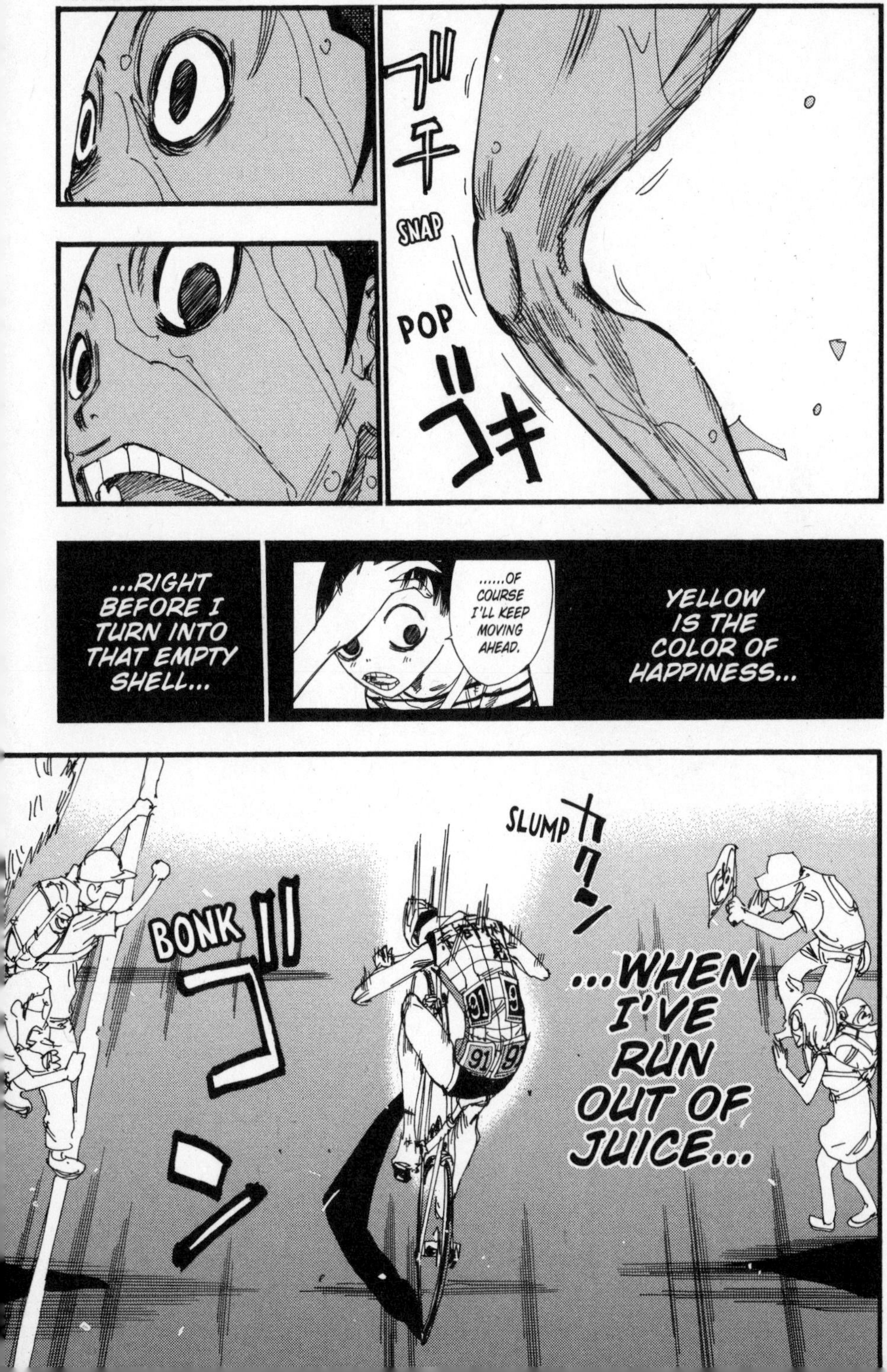
ブチ
SNAP
POP
ゴキ
YELLOW IS THE COLOR OF HAPPINESS...
......OF COURSE I'LL KEEP MOVING AHEAD.
...RIGHT BEFORE I TURN INTO THAT EMPTY SHELL...
SLUMP
カクン
...WHEN I'VE RUN OUT OF JUICE...
BONK
ゴン

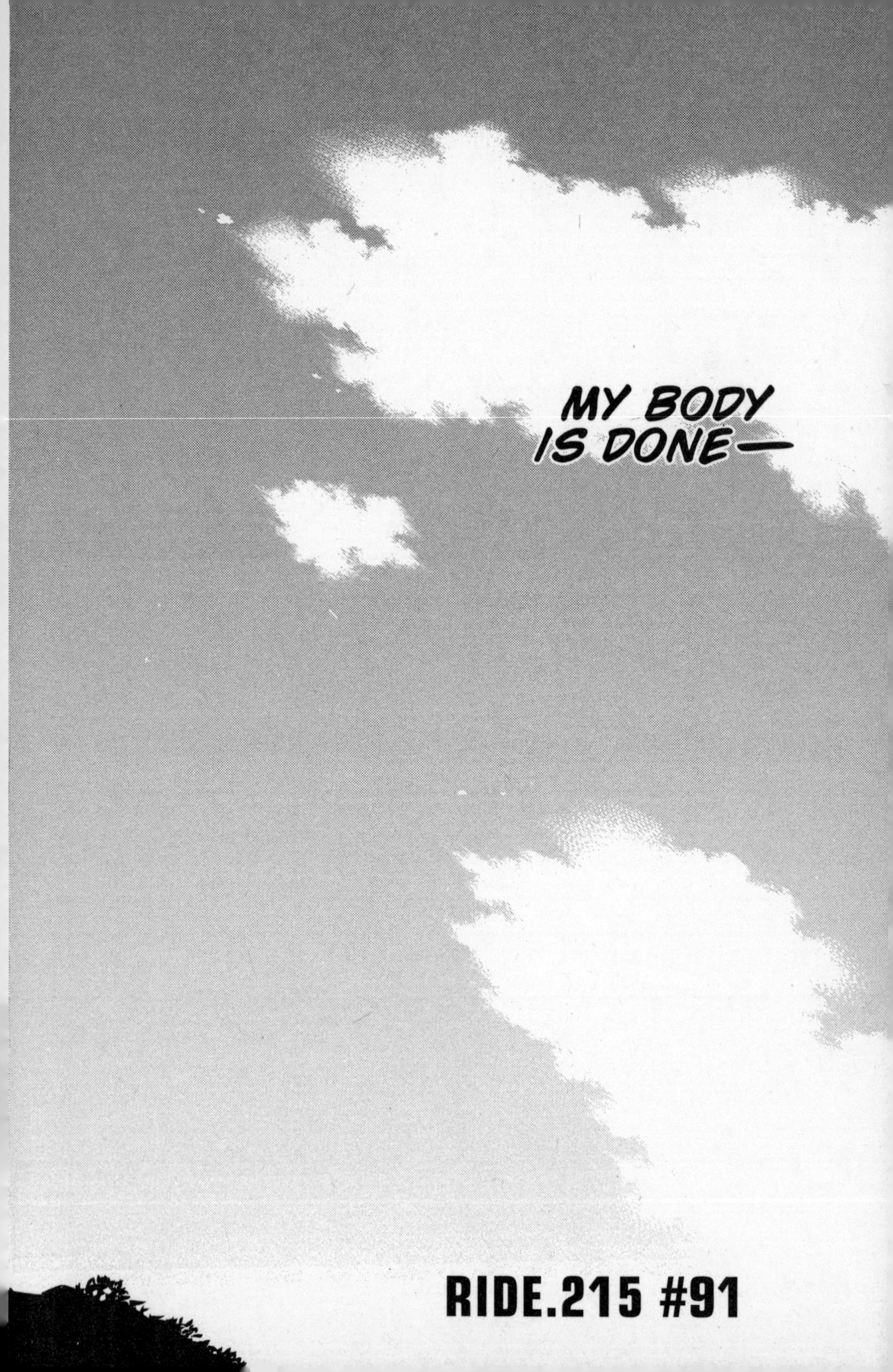
MY BODY IS DONE—

RIDE.215 #91

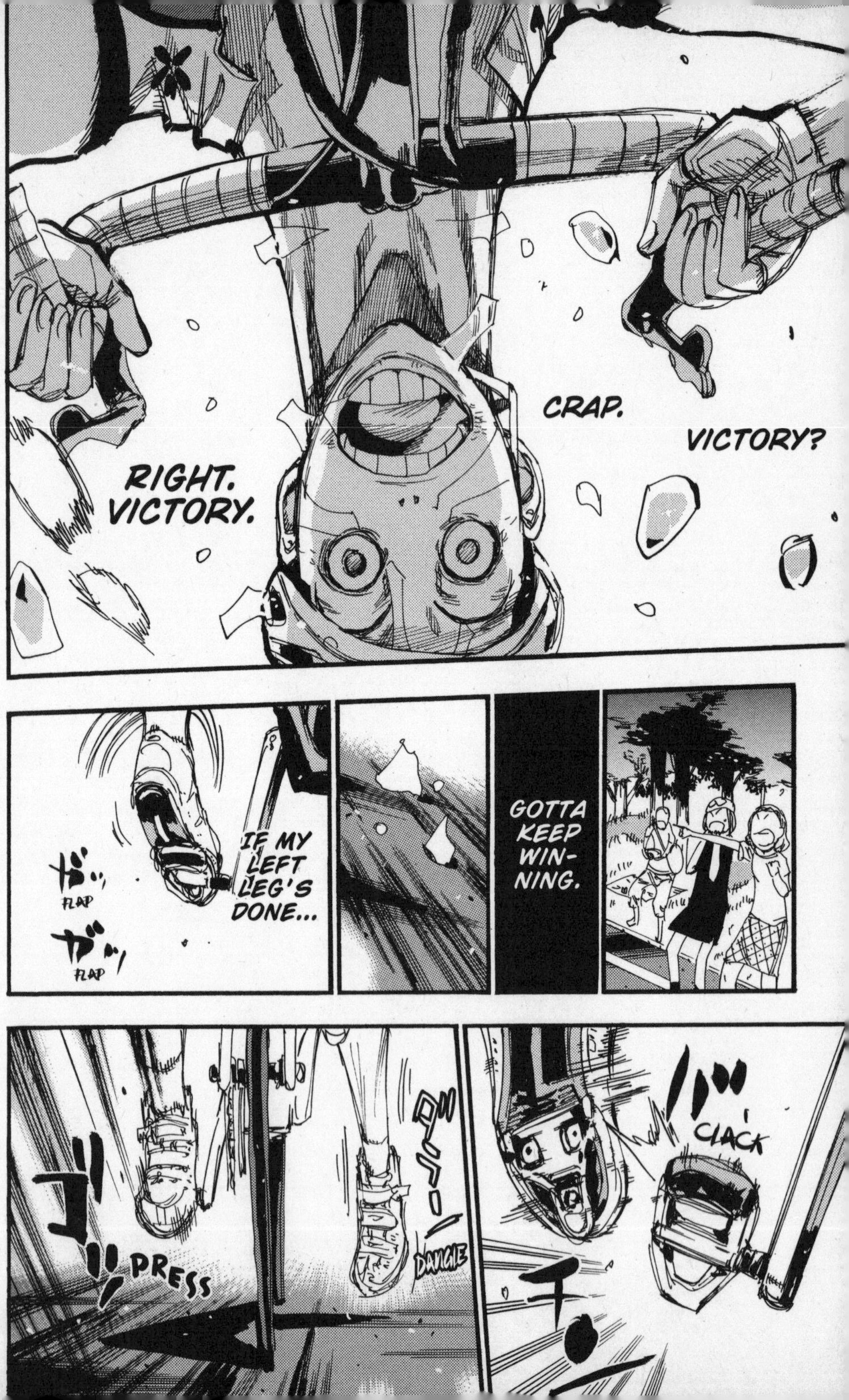
CRAP.
VICTORY?
RIGHT. VICTORY.
GOTTA KEEP WIN-NING.
IF MY LEFT LEG'S DONE...
FLAP
FLAP
CLACK
DANGLE
PRESS

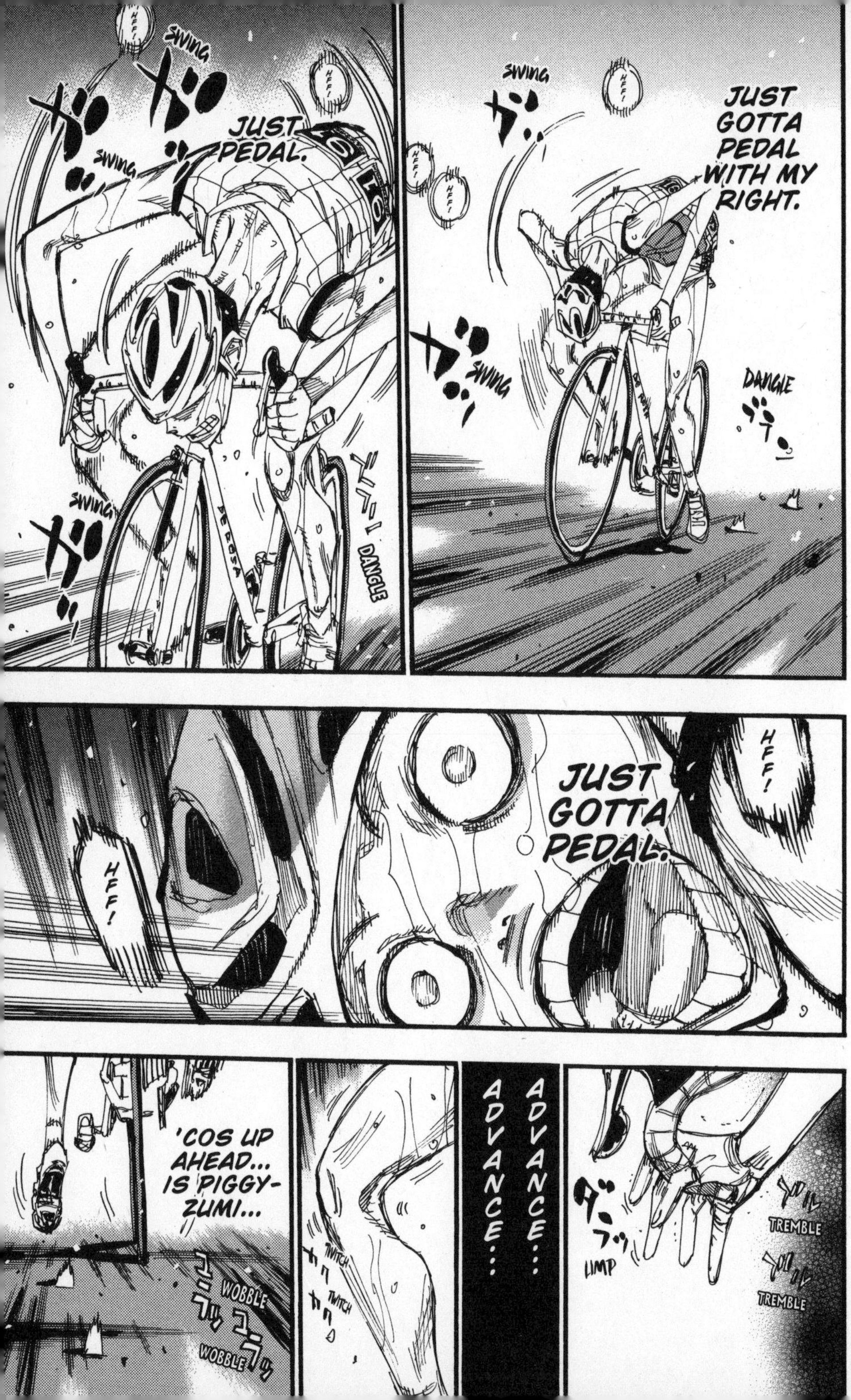
HFF!
HFF!
HFF!
SWING
JUST GOTTA PEDAL WITH MY RIGHT.
SWING
DANGLE
HFF!
HFF!
SWING
JUST PEDAL.
SWING
SWING
DANGLE
HFF!
JUST GOTTA PEDAL.
HFF!
TREMBLE
TREMBLE
LIMP
ADVANCE...
ADVANCE...
TWITCH
TWITCH
'COS UP AHEAD... IS PIGGY-ZUMI...
WOBBLE
WOBBLE

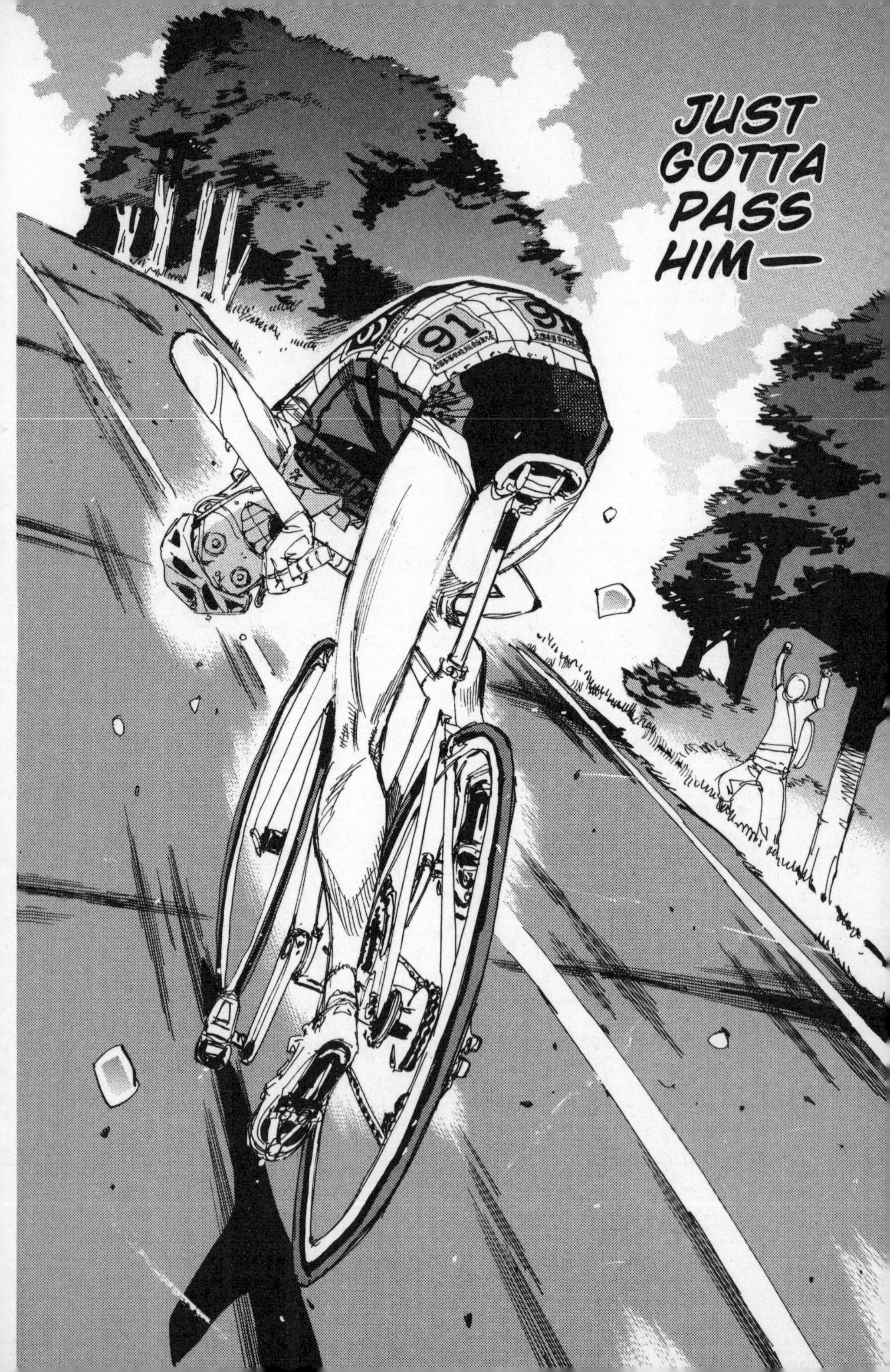
JUST GOTTA PASS HIM—

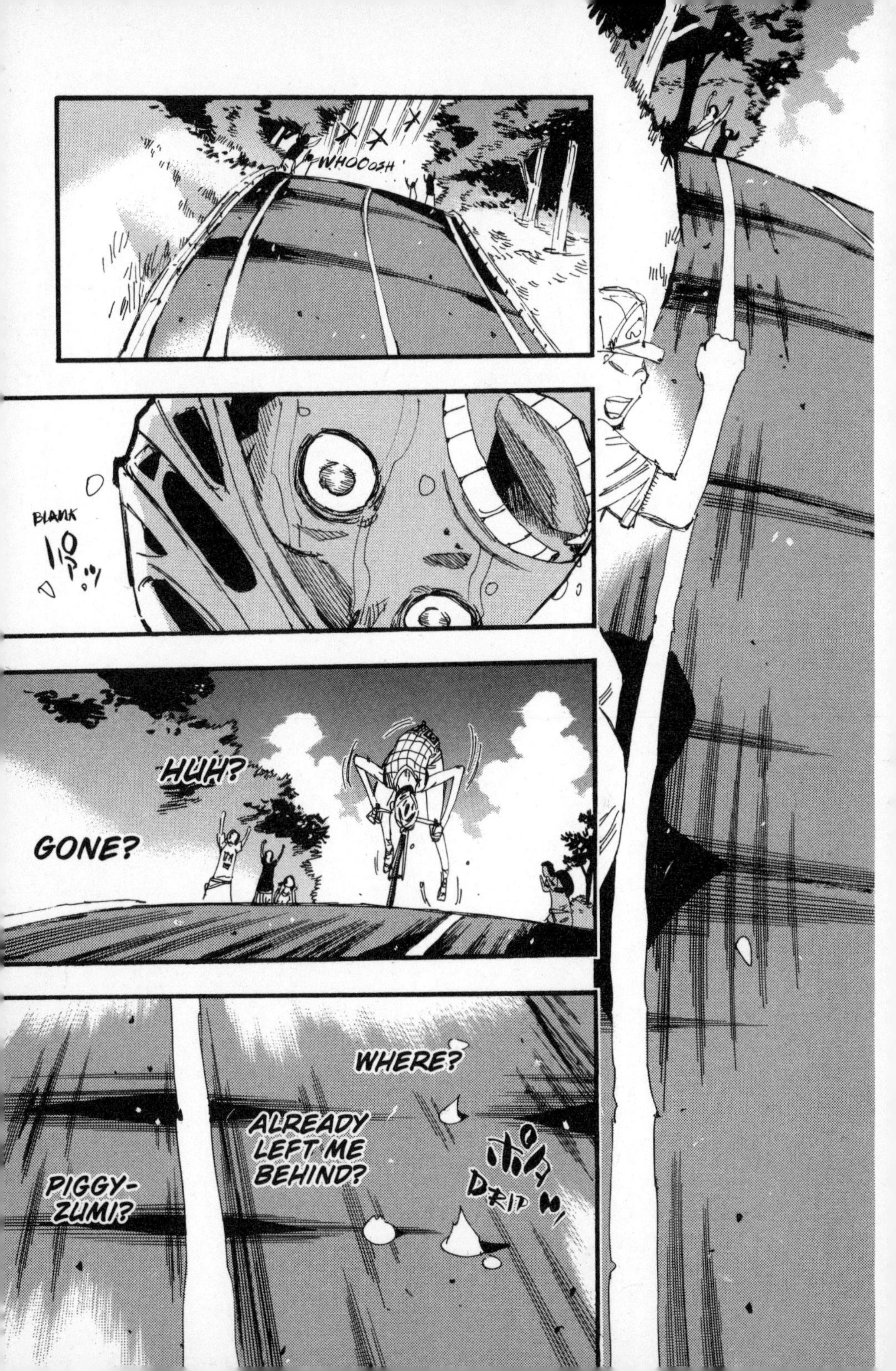
WHOOOSH
BLANK
HUH?
GONE?
WHERE?
DRIP
ALREADY LEFT ME BEHIND?
PIGGY-ZUMI?

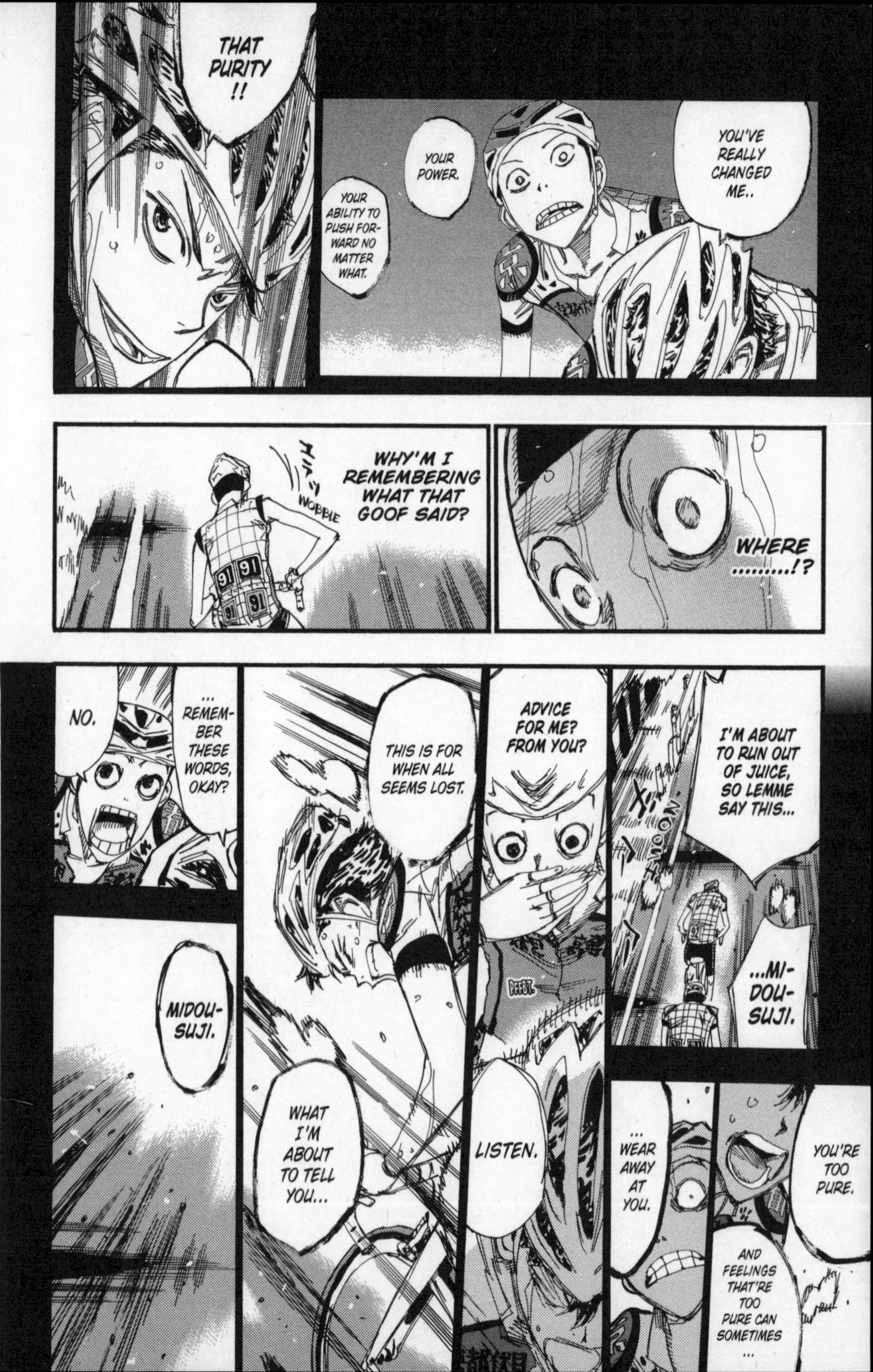
YOU'VE REALLY CHANGED ME..
YOUR POWER.
YOUR ABILITY TO PUSH FORWARD NO MATTER WHAT.
THAT PURITY !!
WHERE ....!?
WHY'M I REMEMBERING WHAT THAT GOOF SAID?
WOBBLE
I'M ABOUT TO RUN OUT OF JUICE, SO LEMME SAY THIS...
...MI-DOU-SUJI.
YOU'RE TOO PURE.
AND FEELINGS THAT'RE TOO PURE CAN SOMETIMES ...
... WEAR AWAY AT YOU.
ADVICE FOR ME? FROM YOU?
PFFBT.
LISTEN.
THIS IS FOR WHEN ALL SEEMS LOST.
WHAT I'M ABOUT TO TELL YOU...
... REMEMBER THESE WORDS, OKAY?
NO.
MIDOU-SUJI.

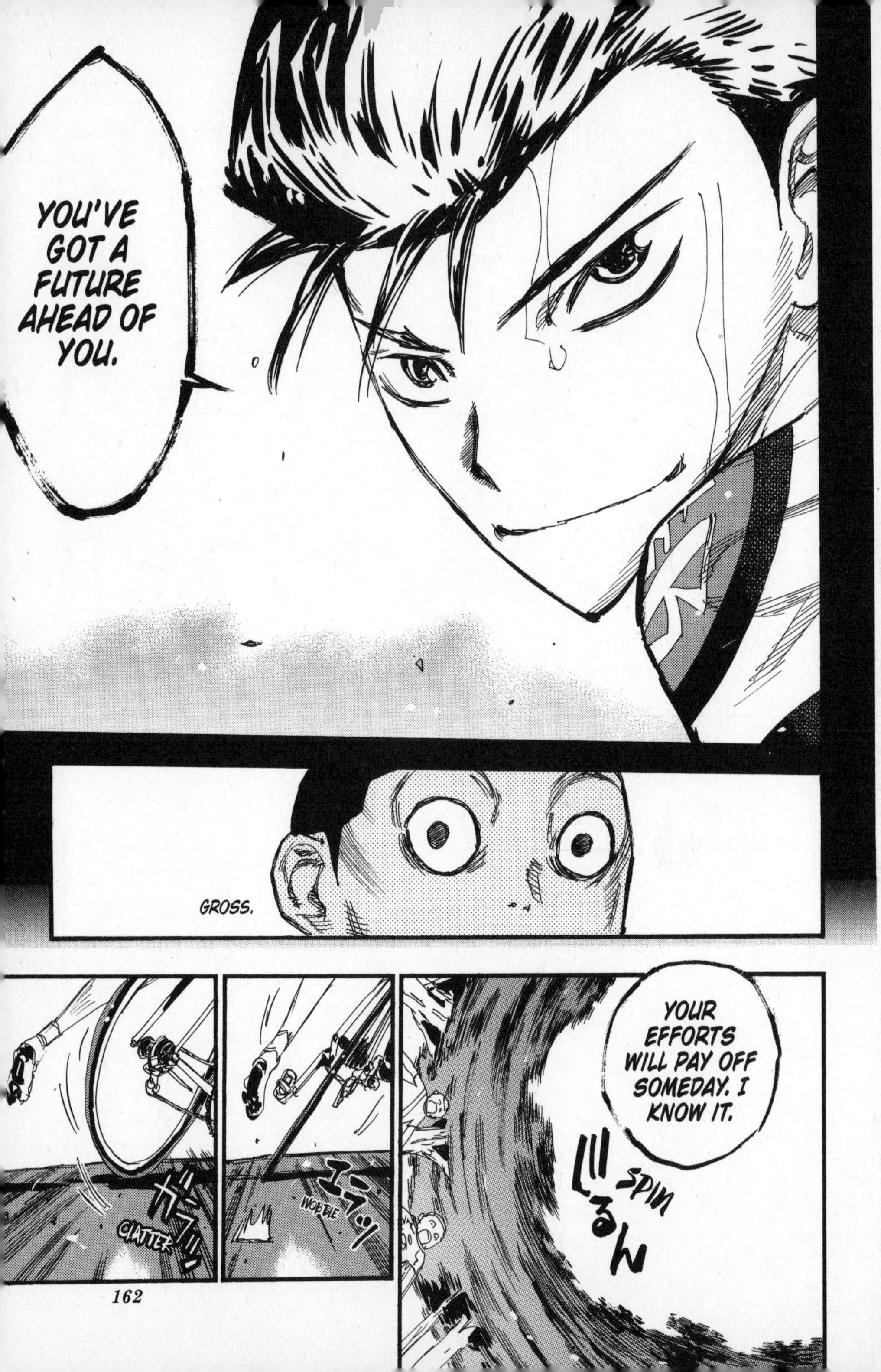
YOU'VE GOT A FUTURE AHEAD OF YOU.
GROSS.
YOUR EFFORTS WILL PAY OFF SOMEDAY. I KNOW IT.
SPIN
WOBBLE
CLATTER

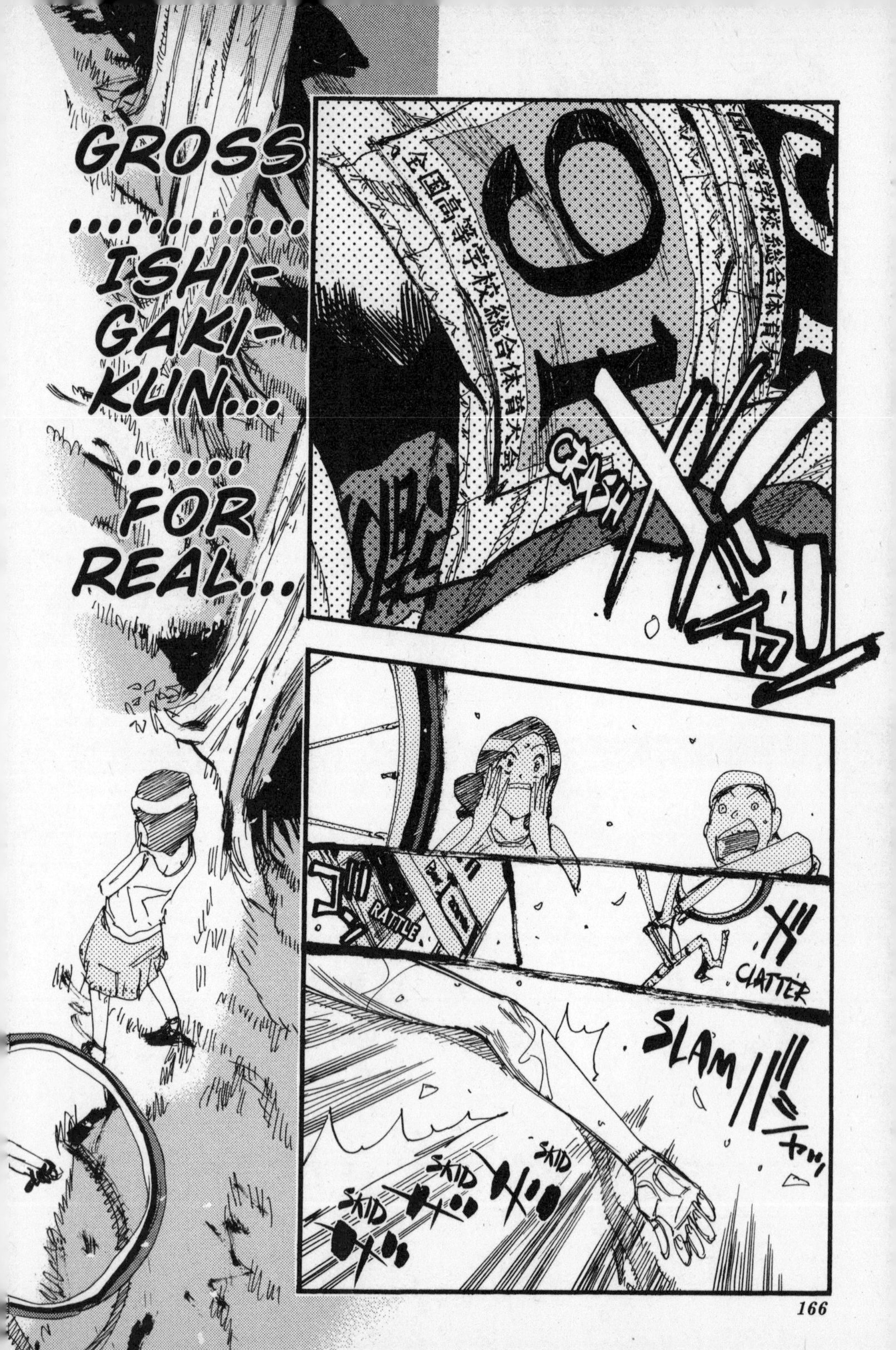
全国高等学校総合体育大会
CRASH
RATTLE
CLATTER
SLAM
SKID
SKID
SKID
GROSS
....
ISHI-GAKI-KUN...
.....
FOR REAL...

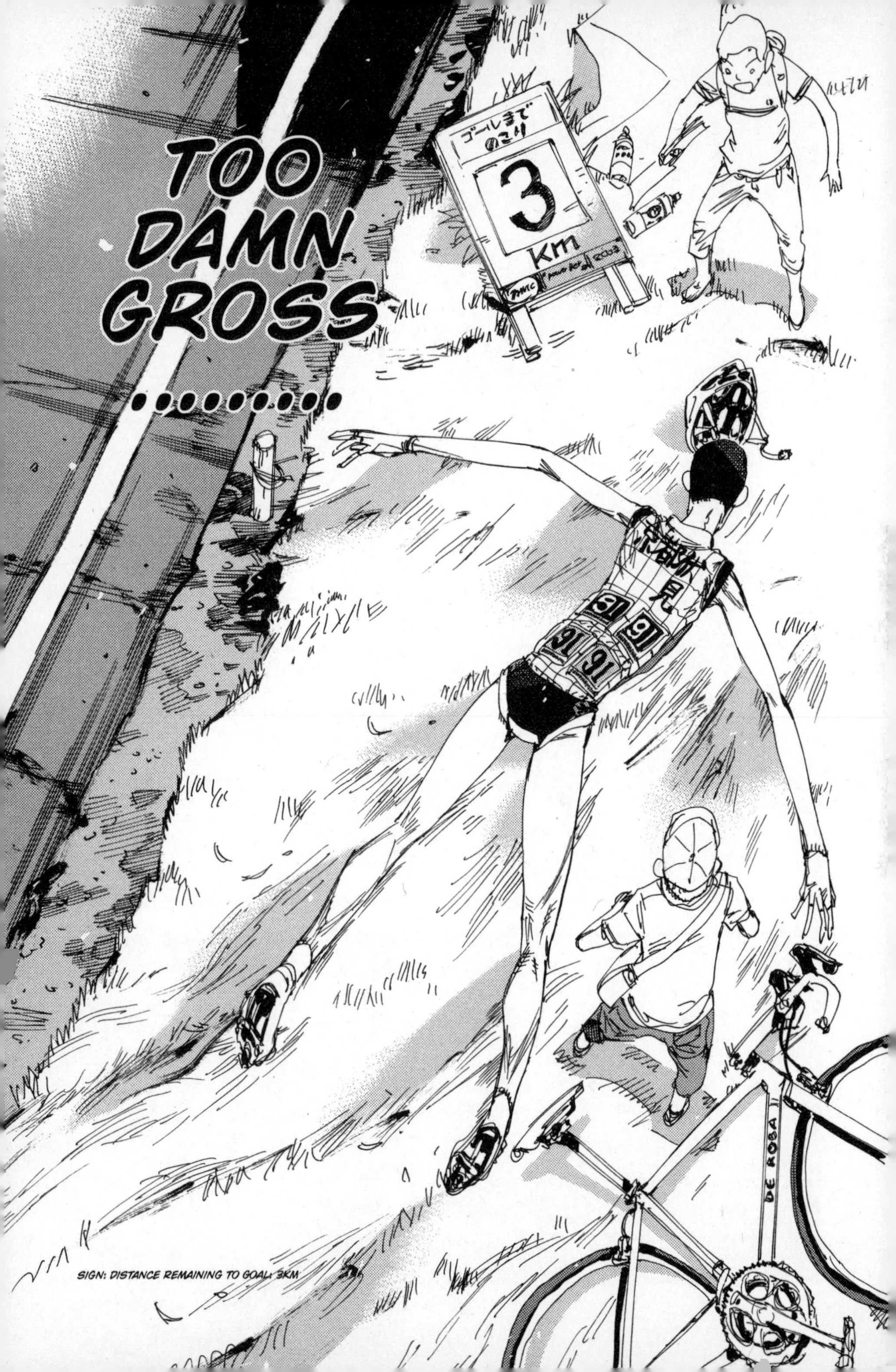
TOO DAMN GROSS ....
ゴールまでのこり
3
Km
SIGN: DISTANCE REMAINING TO GOAL: 3KM

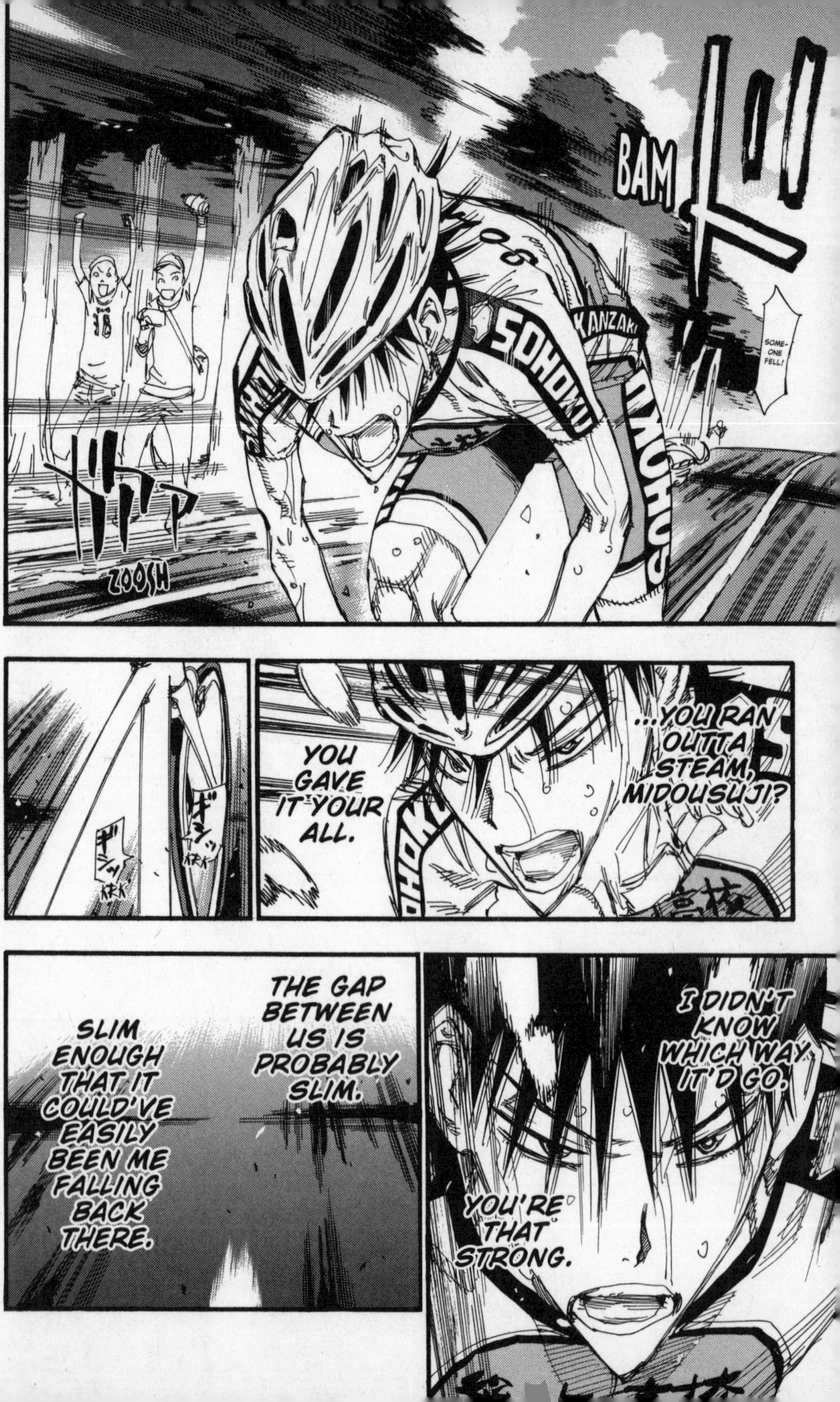
BAM
SOME-ONE FELL!
ZOOSH
...YOU RAN OUTTA STEAM, MIDOUSUJI?
YOU GAVE IT YOUR ALL.
KRK
KRK
I DIDN'T KNOW WHICH WAY IT'D GO.
YOU'RE THAT STRONG.
THE GAP BETWEEN US IS PROBABLY SLIM.
SLIM ENOUGH THAT IT COULD'VE EASILY BEEN ME FALLING BACK THERE.

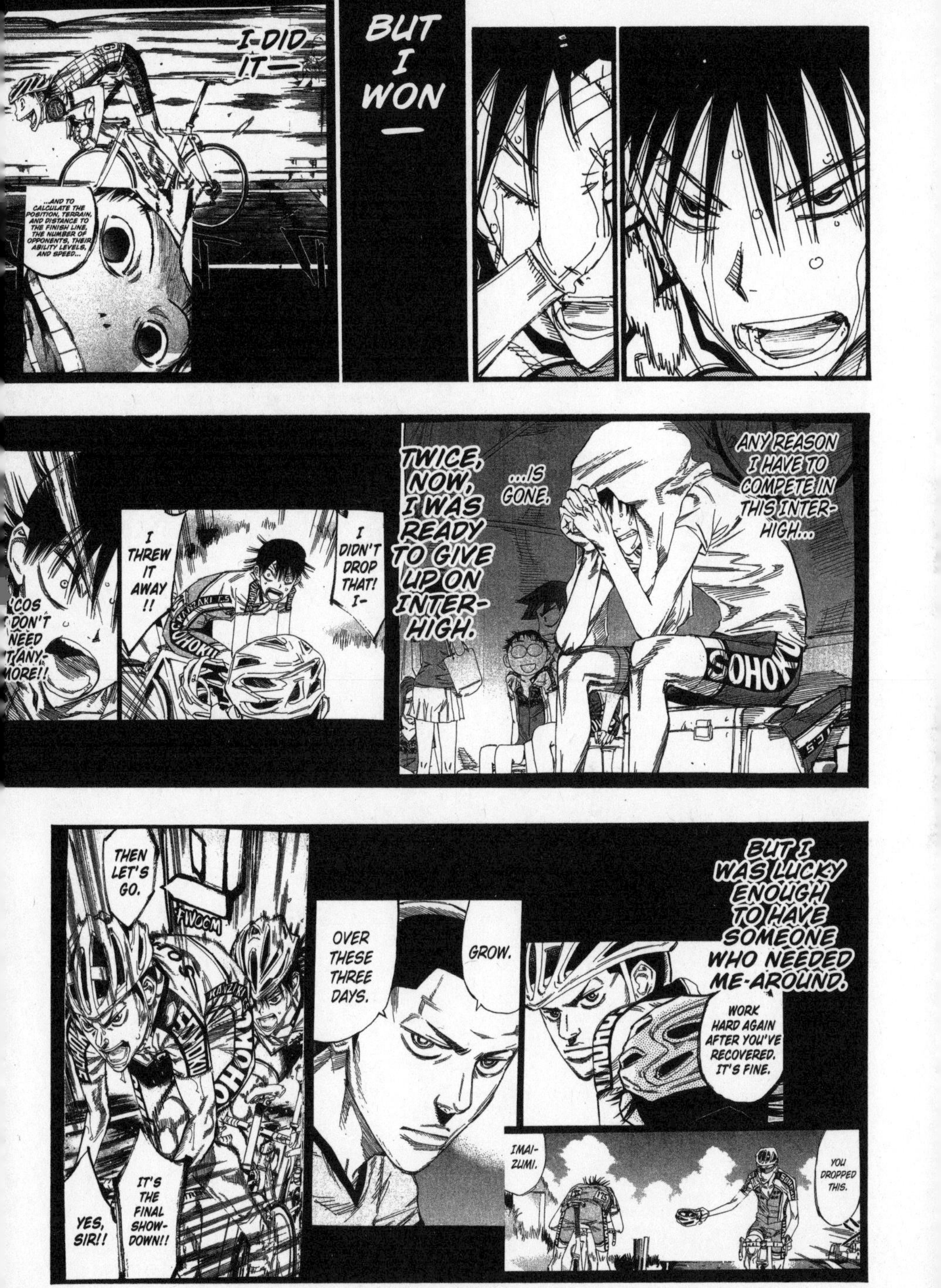

BUT I WON —
I-DID IT—
...AND TO CALCULATE THE POSITION, TERRAIN, AND DISTANCE TO THE FINISH LINE, THE NUMBER OF OPPONENTS, THEIR ABILITY LEVELS, AND SPEED...
ANY REASON I HAVE TO COMPETE IN THIS INTER-HIGH...
...IS GONE.
TWICE, NOW, I WAS READY TO GIVE UP ON INTER-HIGH.
I DIDN'T DROP THAT! I-
I THREW IT AWAY!!
'COS DON'T NEED T ANY-MORE!!
BUT I WAS LUCKY ENOUGH TO HAVE SOMEONE WHO NEEDED ME-AROUND.
WORK HARD AGAIN AFTER YOU'VE RECOVERED. IT'S FINE.
YOU DROPPED THIS.
IMAI-ZUMI.
GROW.
OVER THESE THREE DAYS.
THEN LET'S GO.
FWOOM
IT'S THE FINAL SHOW-DOWN!!
YES, SIR!!

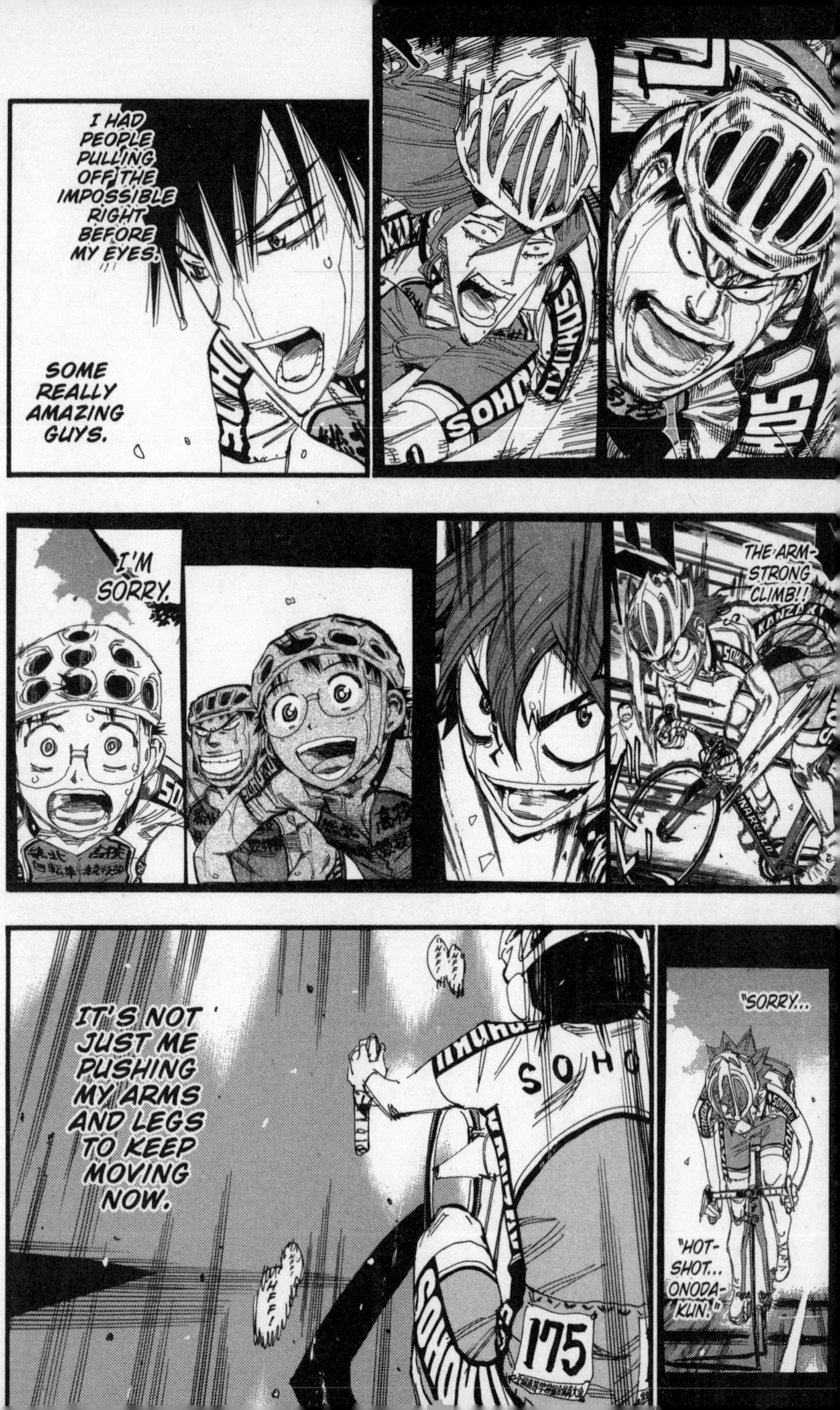
I HAD PEOPLE PULLING OFF THE IMPOSSIBLE RIGHT BEFORE MY EYES.
SOME REALLY AMAZING GUYS.
THE ARM-STRONG CLIMB!!
I'M SORRY.
"SORRY...
"HOT-SHOT... ONODA-KUN."
HFF! HFF!
IT'S NOT JUST ME PUSHING MY ARMS AND LEGS TO KEEP MOVING NOW.
HFF! HFF!
175

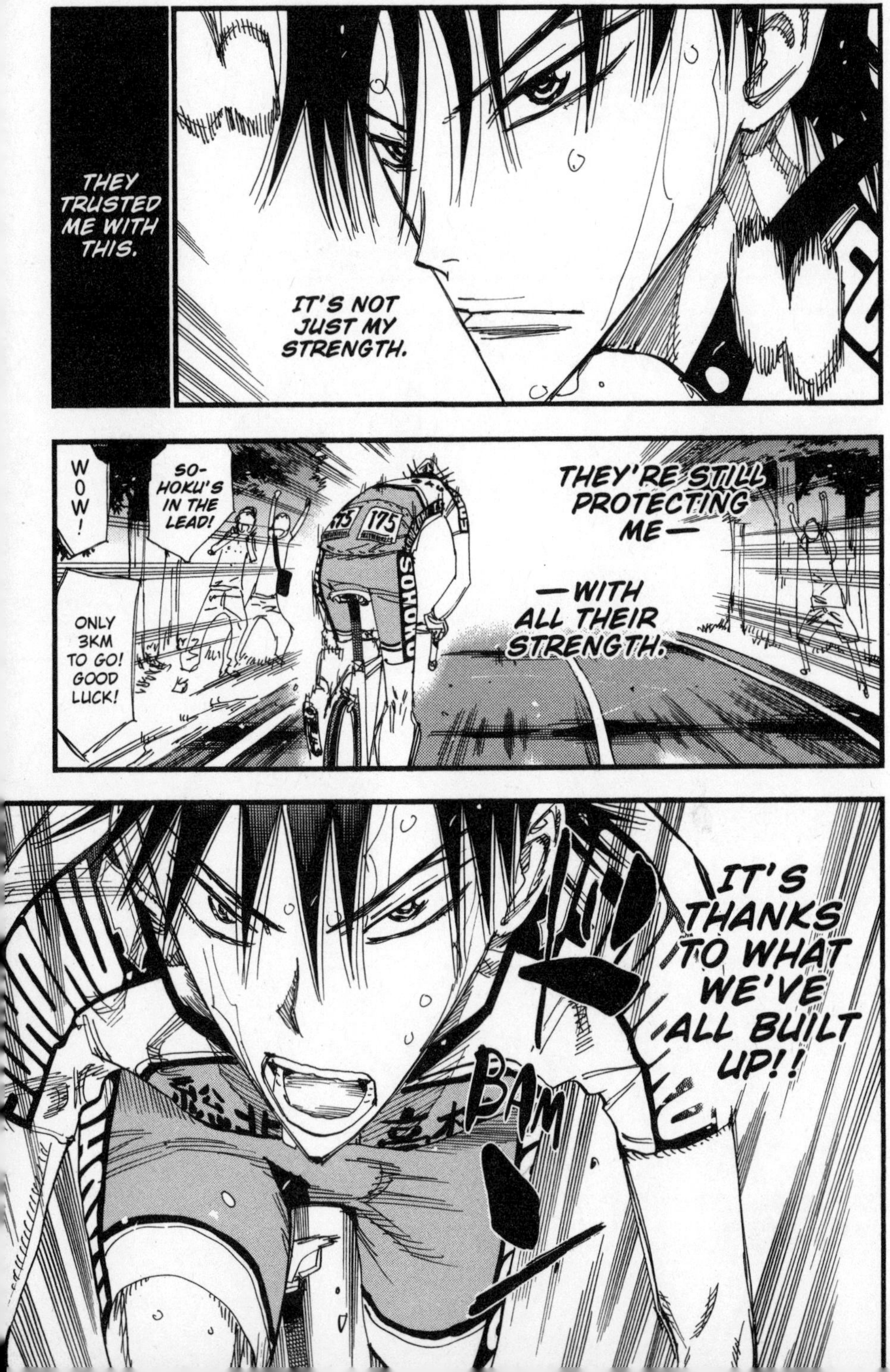
IT'S NOT JUST MY STRENGTH.
THEY TRUSTED ME WITH THIS.
THEY'RE STILL PROTECTING ME—
—WITH ALL THEIR STRENGTH.
SO-HOKU'S IN THE LEAD!
WOW!
ONLY 3KM TO GO! GOOD LUCK!
IT'S THANKS TO WHAT WE'VE ALL BUILT UP!!
BAM

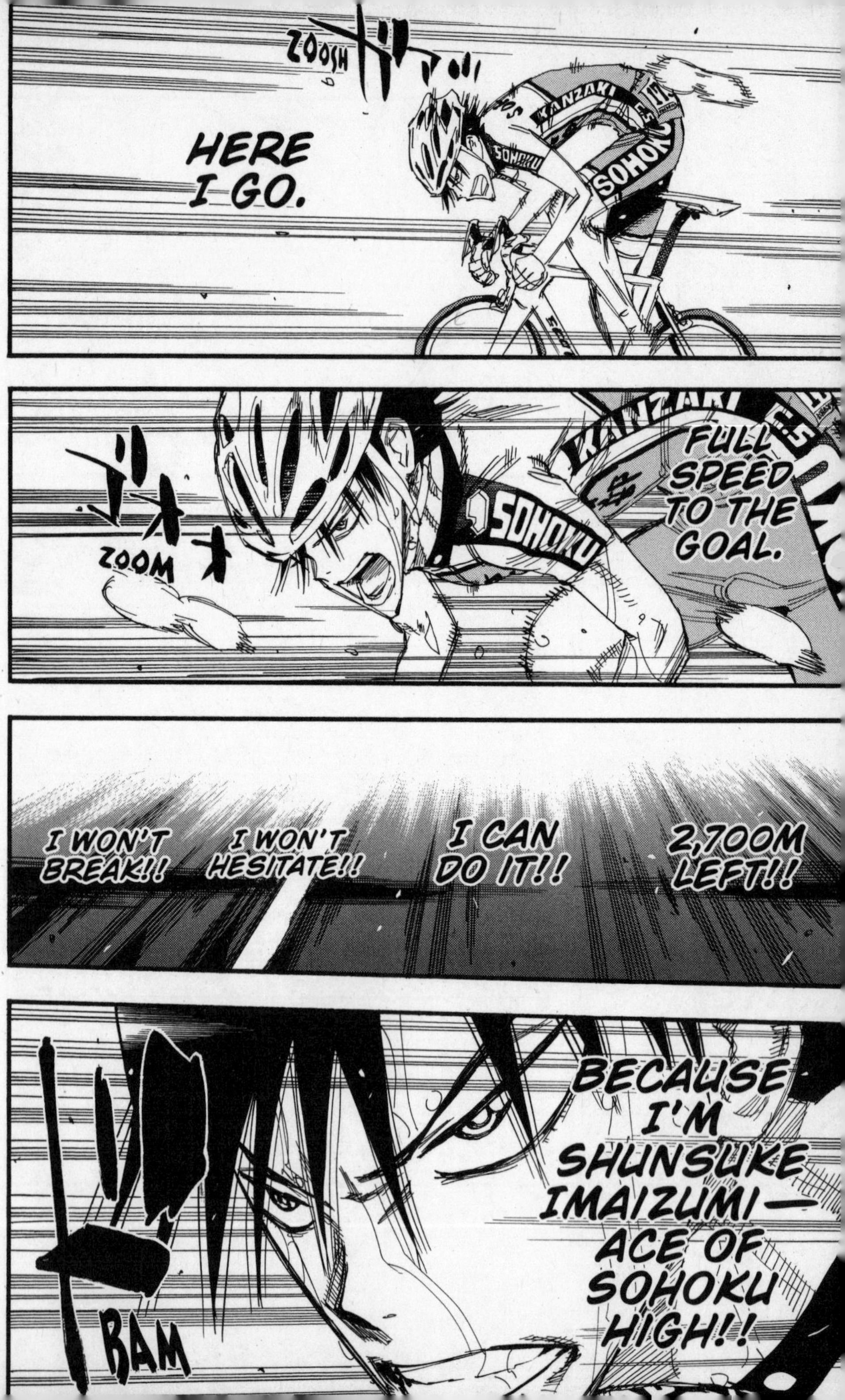
ZOOSH
HERE I GO.
FULL SPEED TO THE GOAL.
ZOOM
2,700M LEFT!!
I CAN DO IT!!
I WON'T HESITATE!!
I WON'T BREAK!!
BECAUSE I'M SHUNSUKE IMAIZUMI—ACE OF SOHOKU HIGH!!
BAM

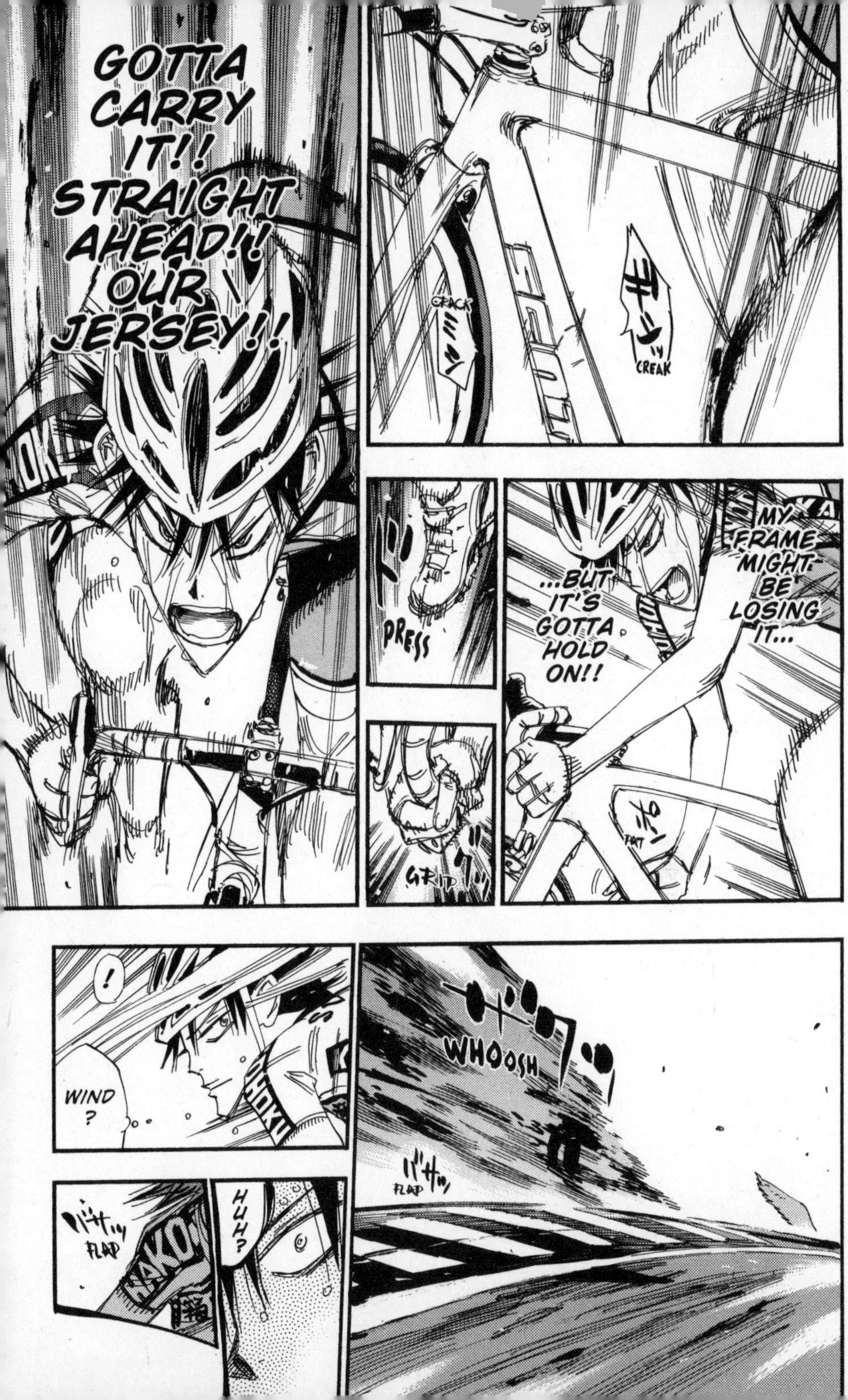
CREAK
CRACK
MY FRAME MIGHT BE LOSING IT...
...BUT IT'S GOTTA HOLD ON!!
PAT
PRESS
GRIP
GOTTA CARRY IT!! STRAIGHT AHEAD!! OUR JERSEY!!
WHOOSH
FLAP
!
WIND?
HUH?
FLAP

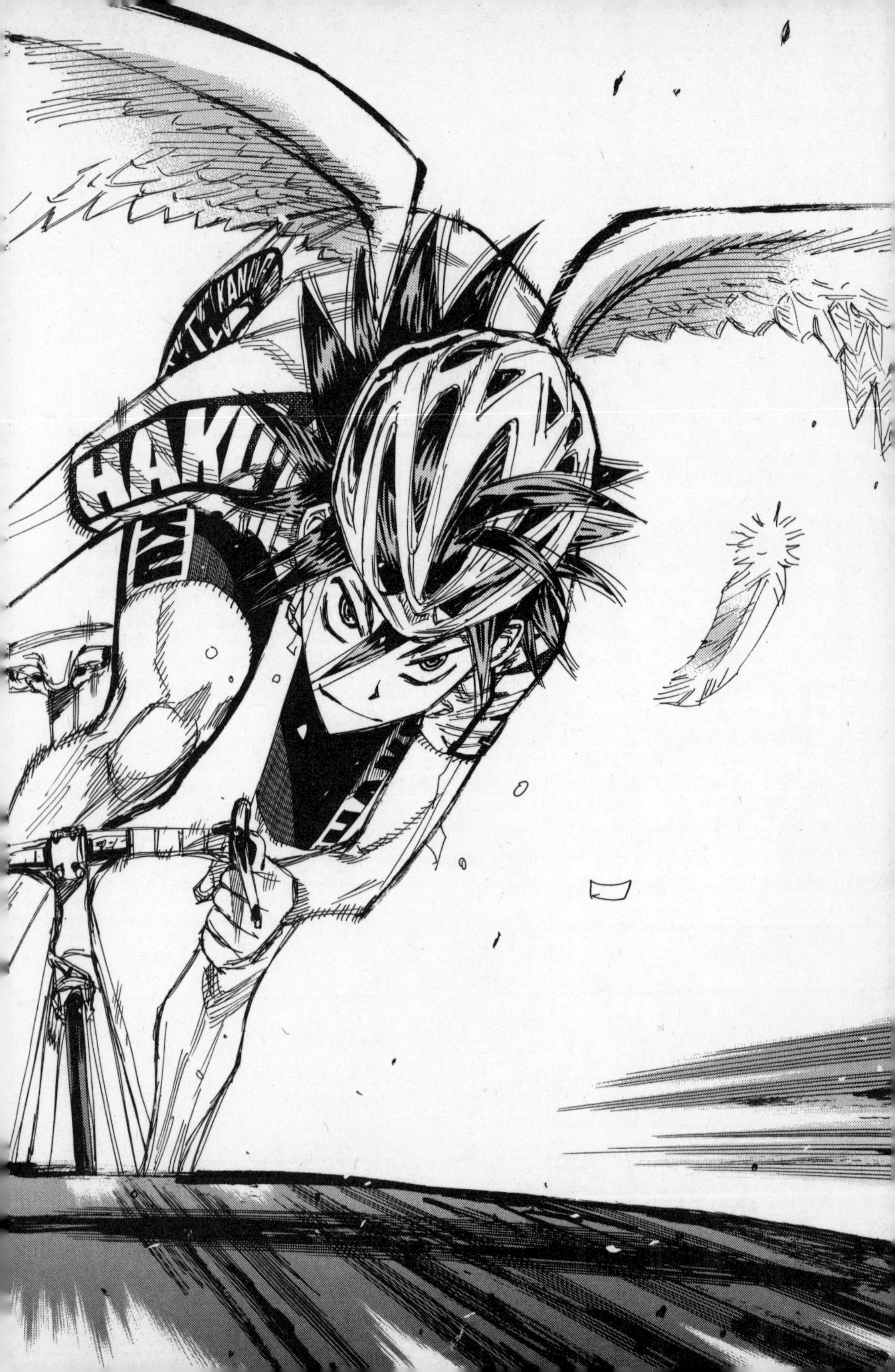

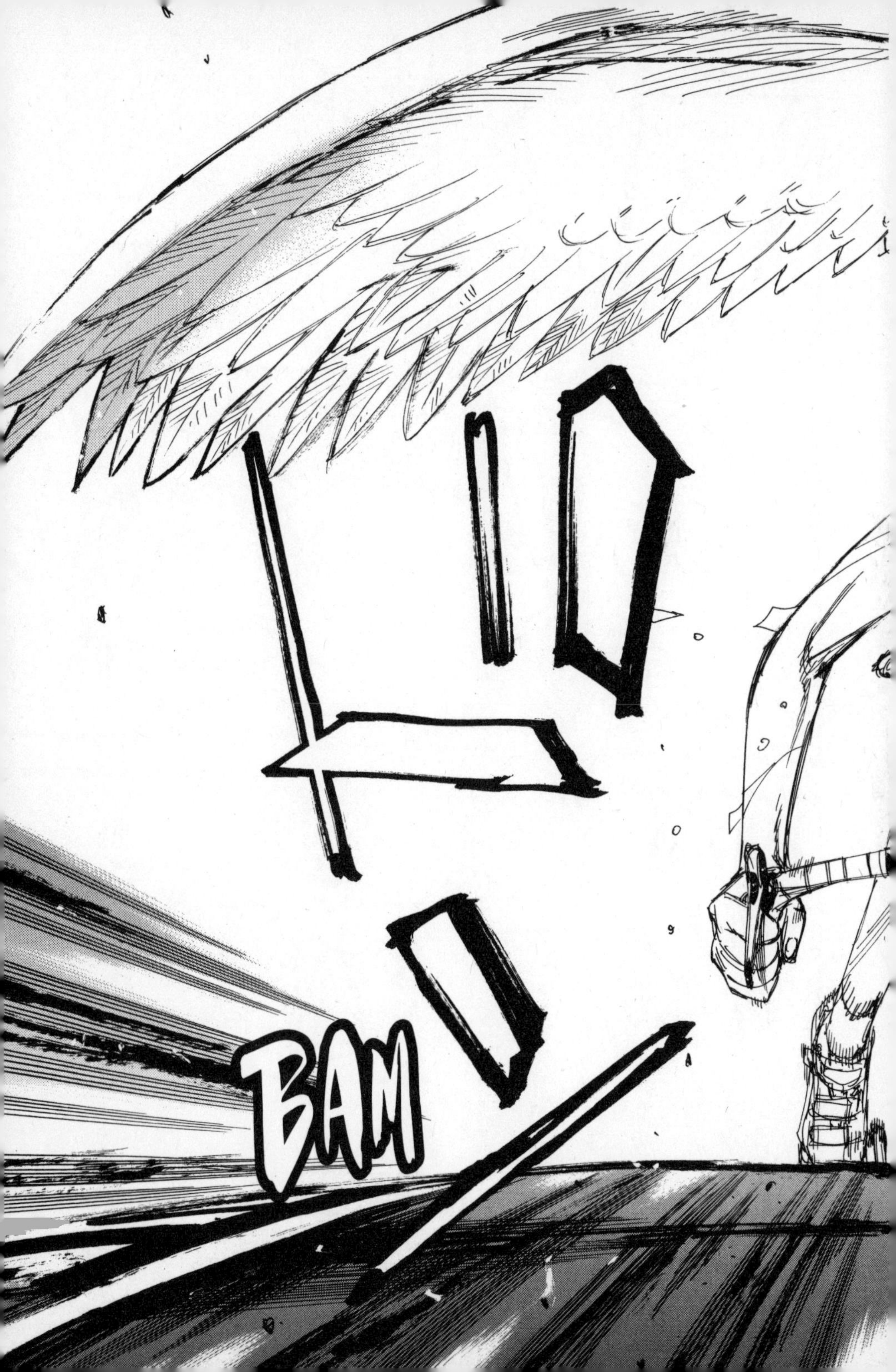
BAM

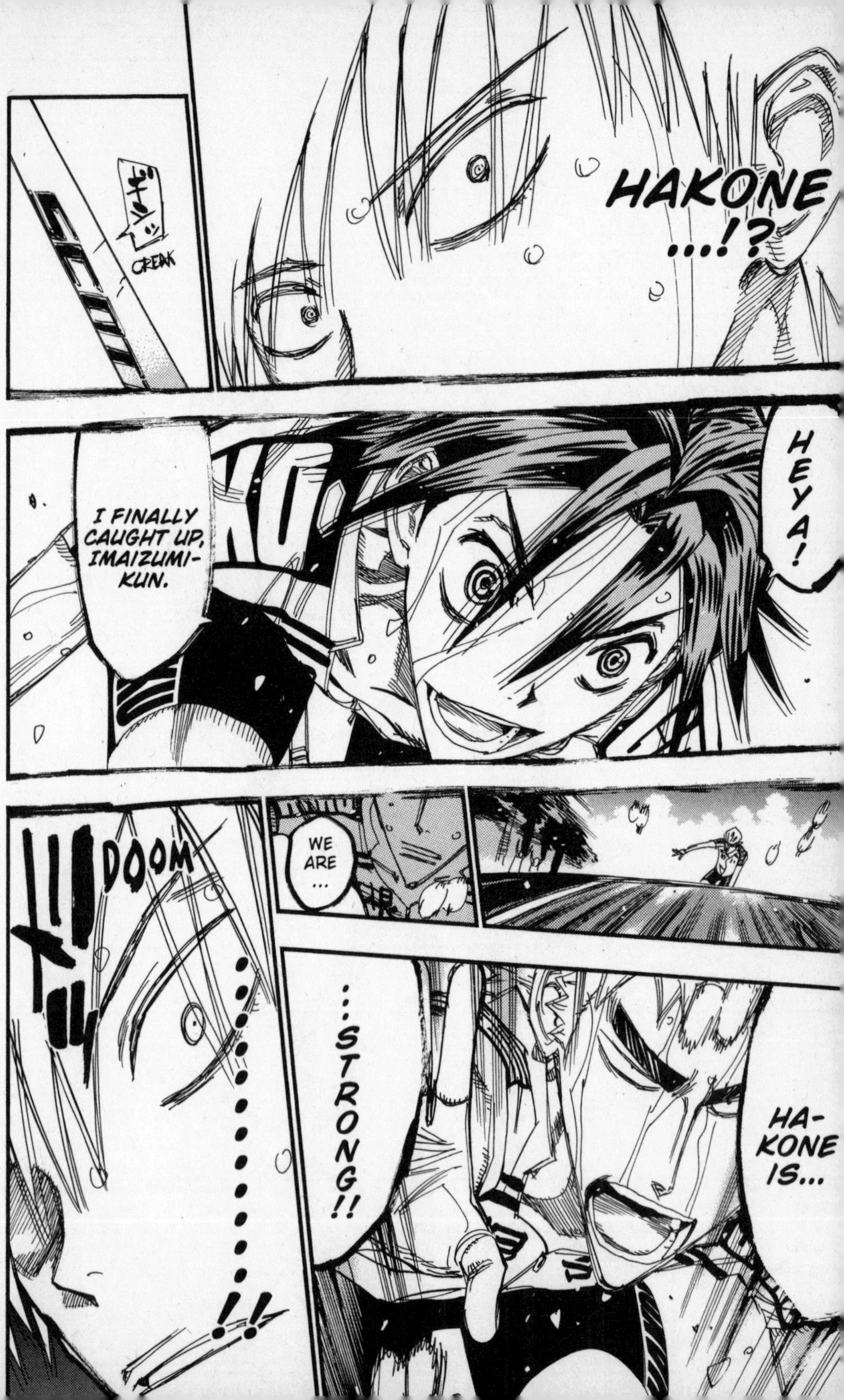

HAKONE ...!?
ギシッ
CREAK
HEYA!
I FINALLY CAUGHT UP, IMAIZUMI-KUN.
WE ARE ...
HAKONE IS...
...STRONG!!
DOOM
......!!

RIDE.216
THE SIXTH MAN

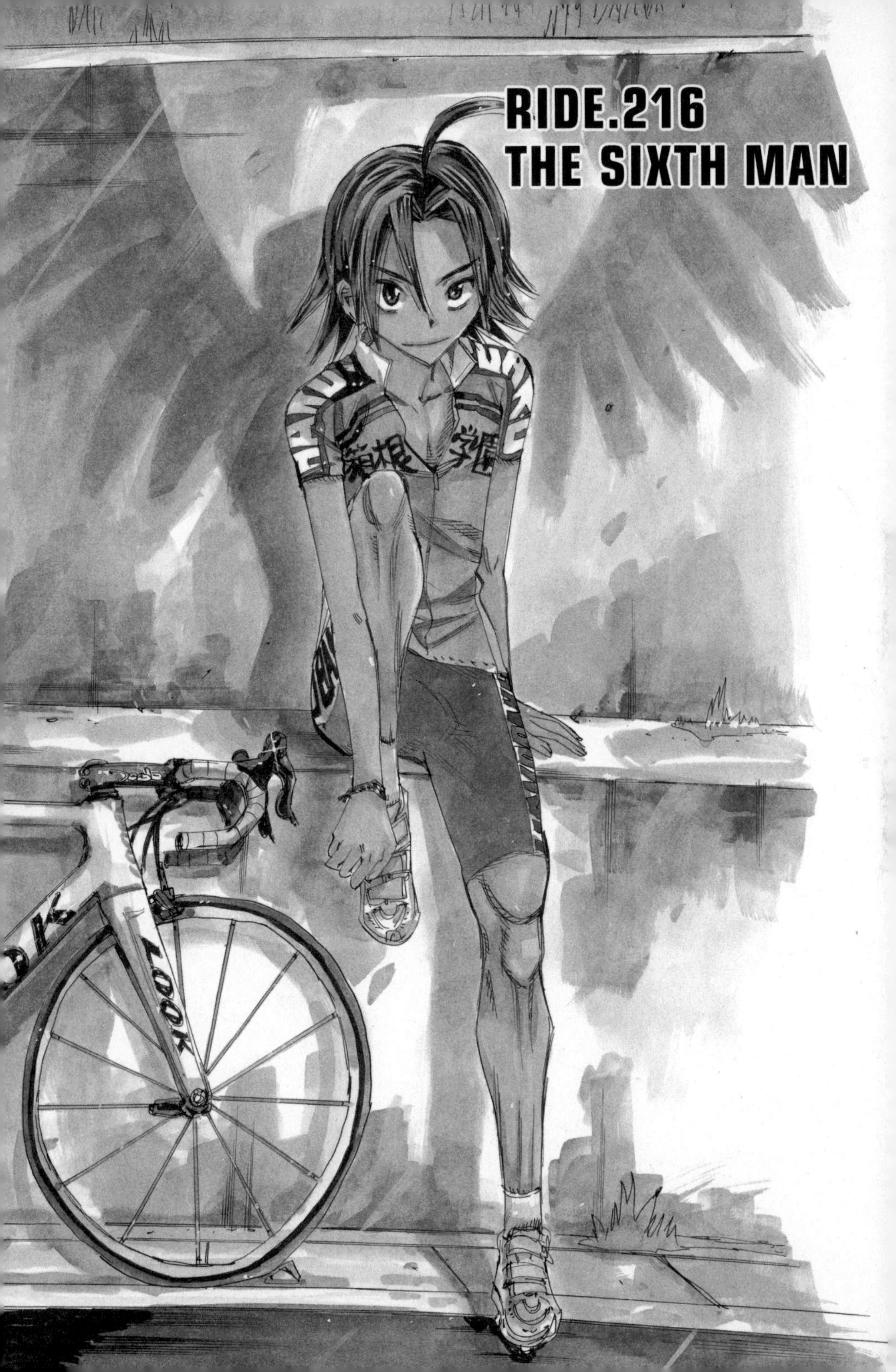
箱根学園
LOOK

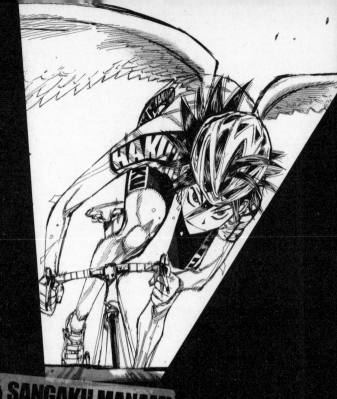

SANGAKU MANAMI

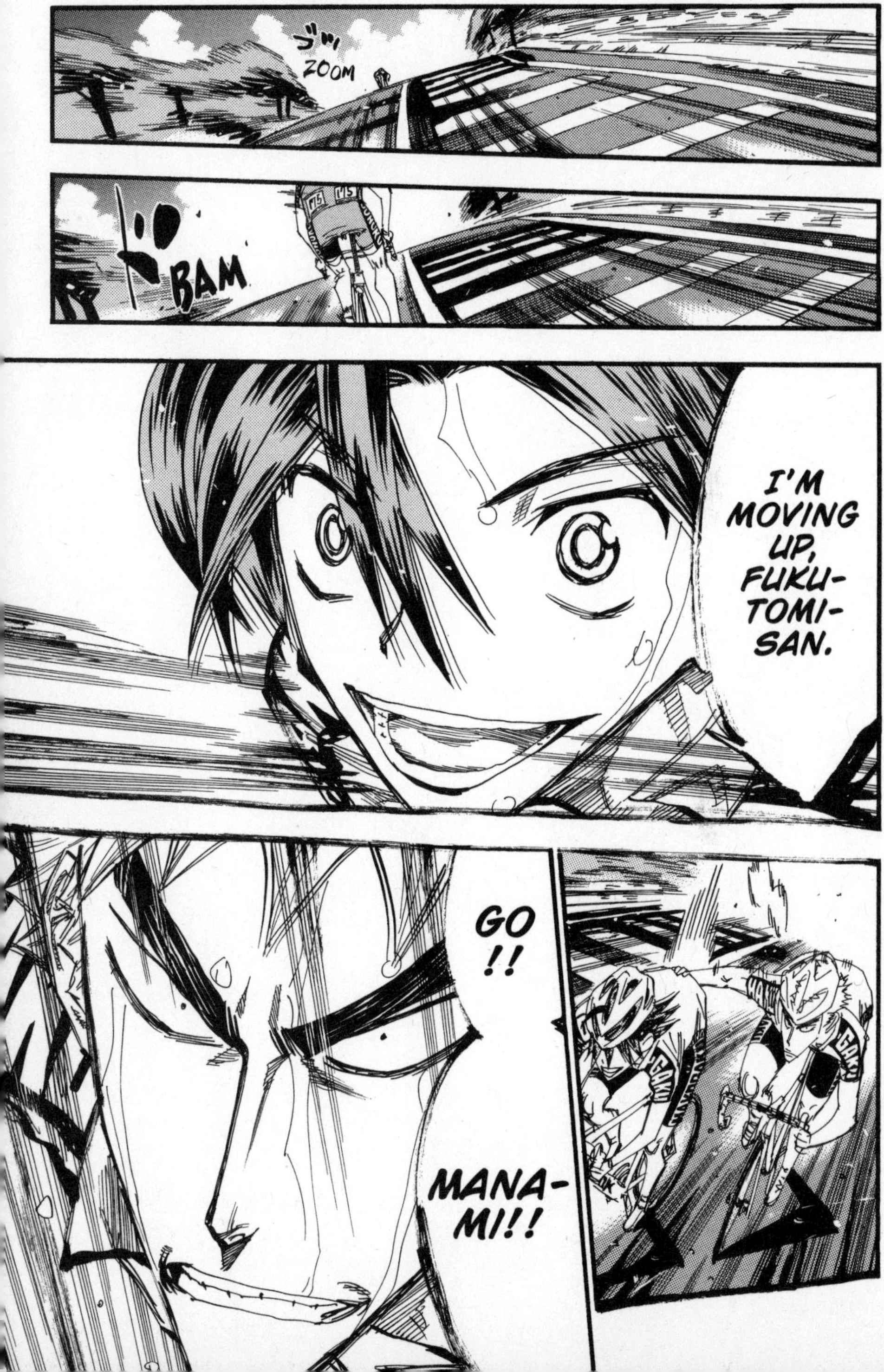
ゴッ
ZOOM
BAM
I'M MOVING UP, FUKU-TOMI-SAN.
GO!!
MANA-MI!!

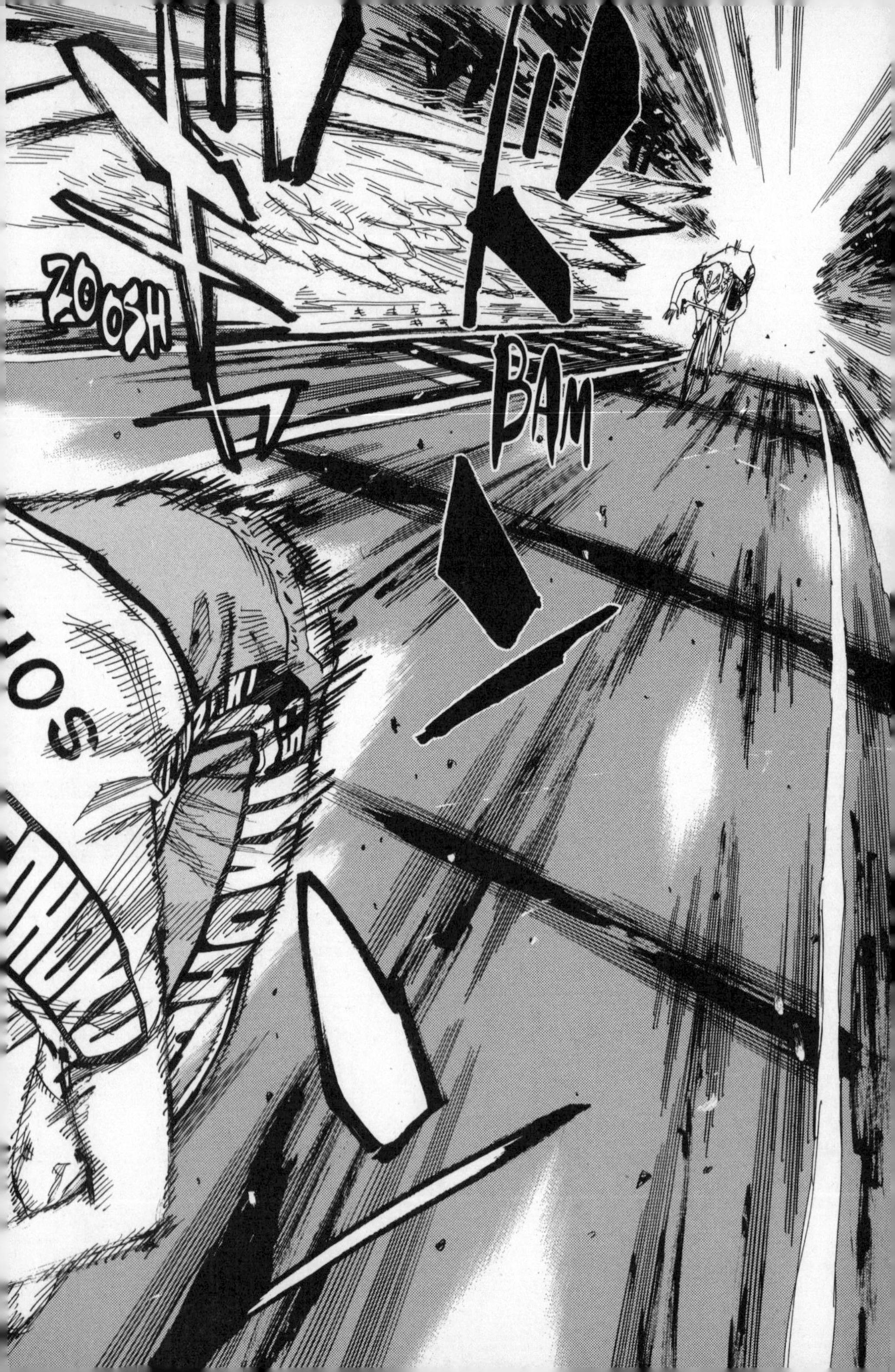
ZOOSH
BAM

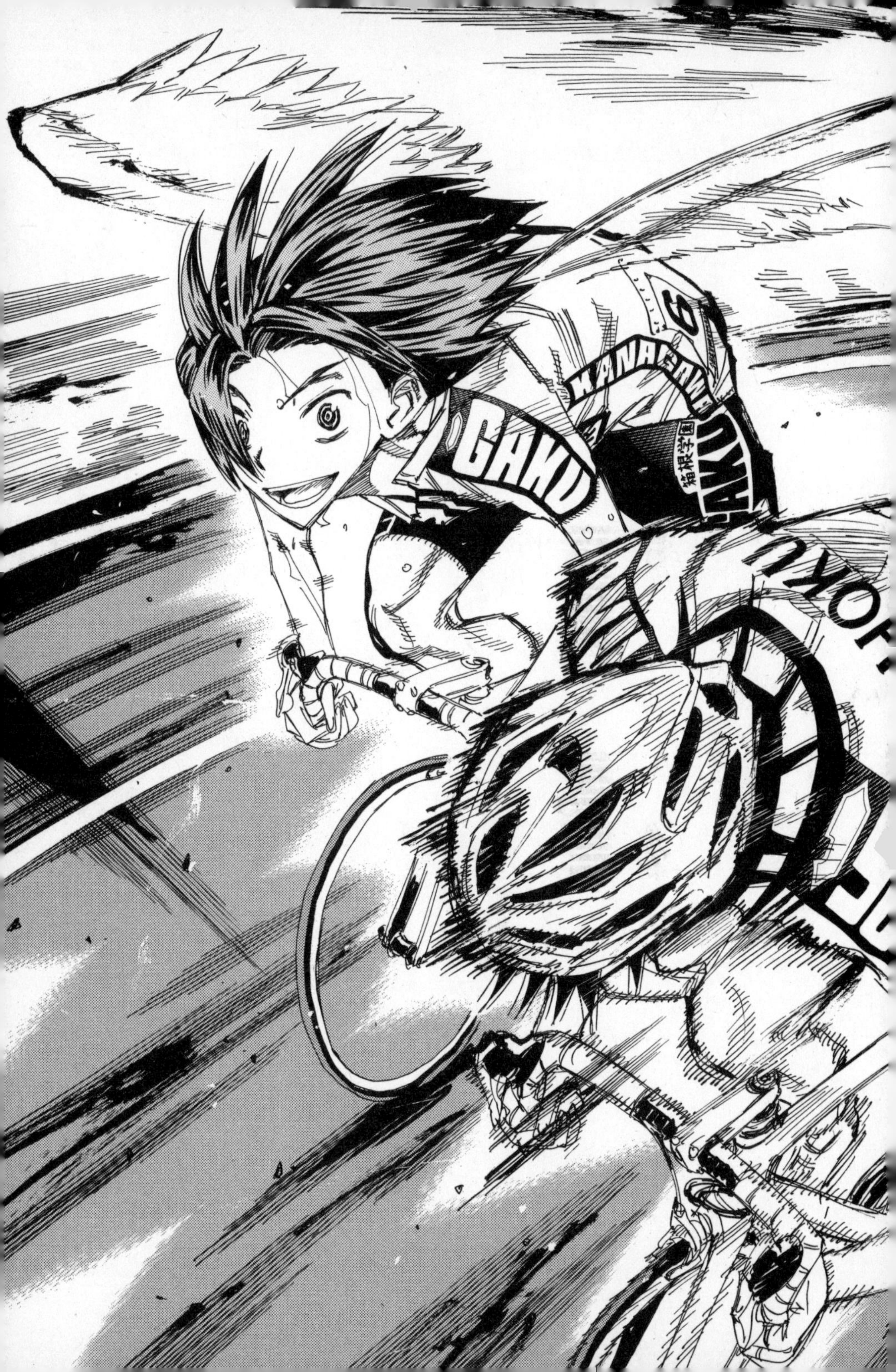
GAKU
箱根学園

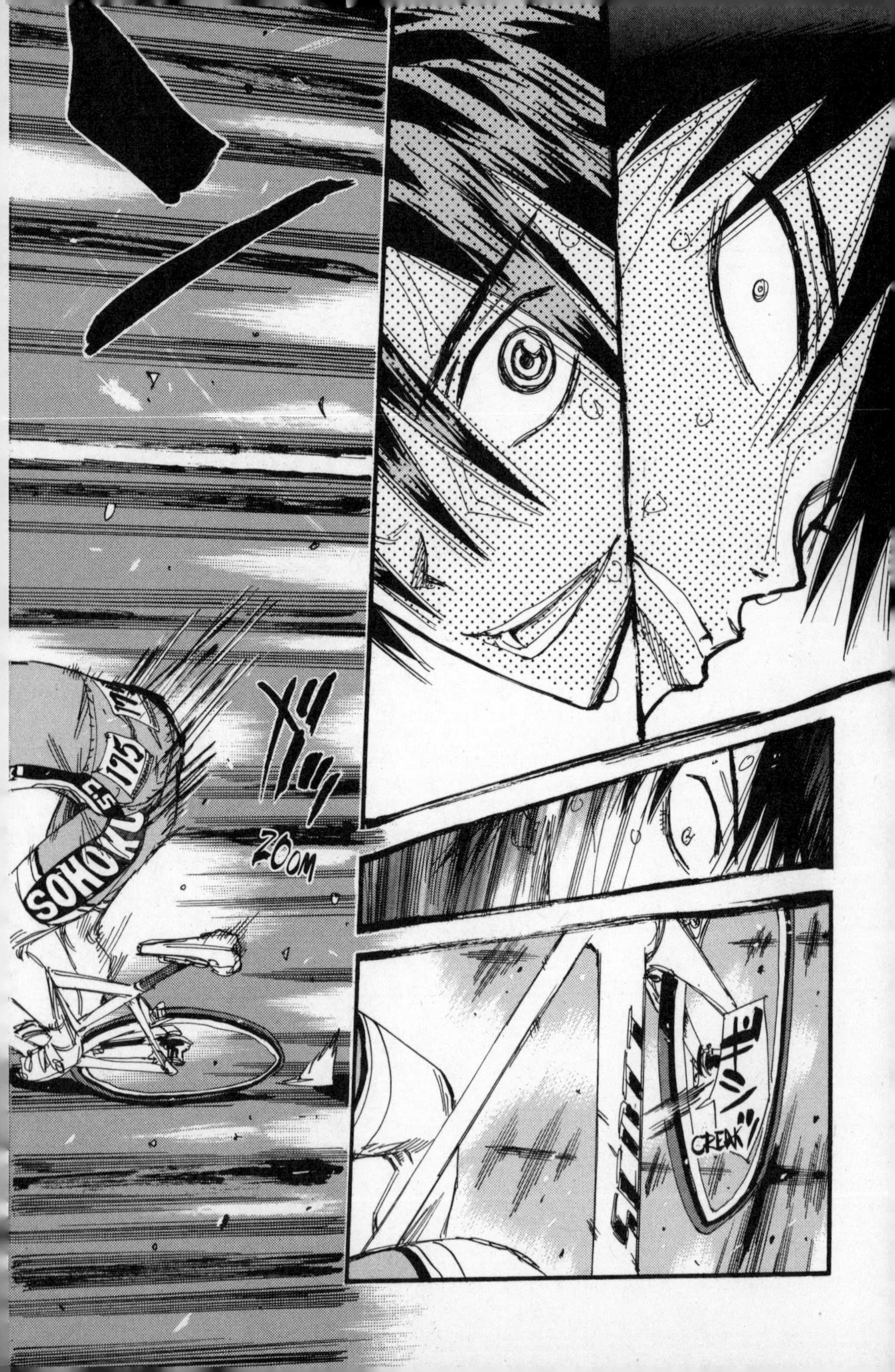
CREAK
ZOOM
SOHOKU
175

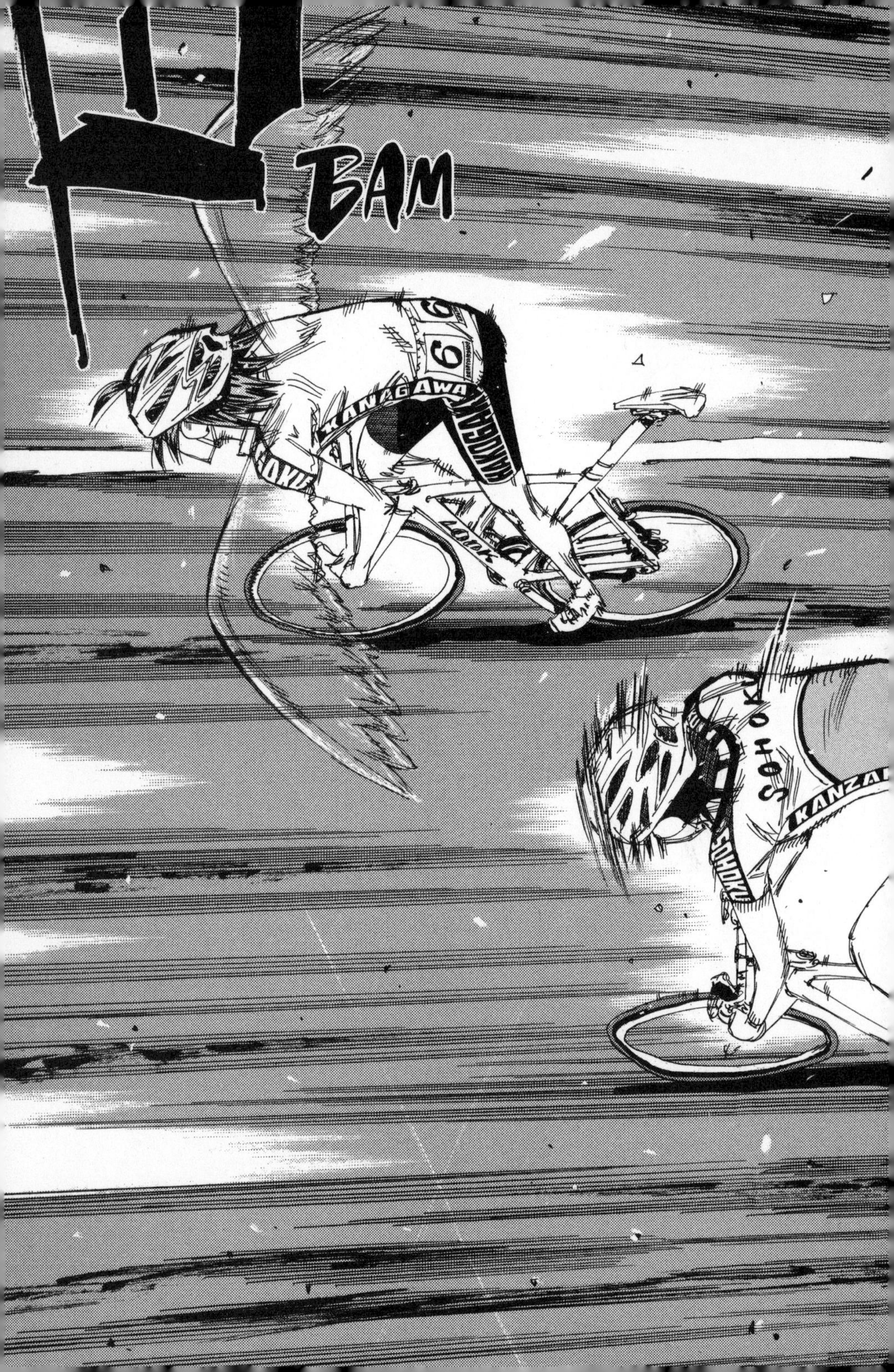
BAM
KANAGAWA
SOHOKU

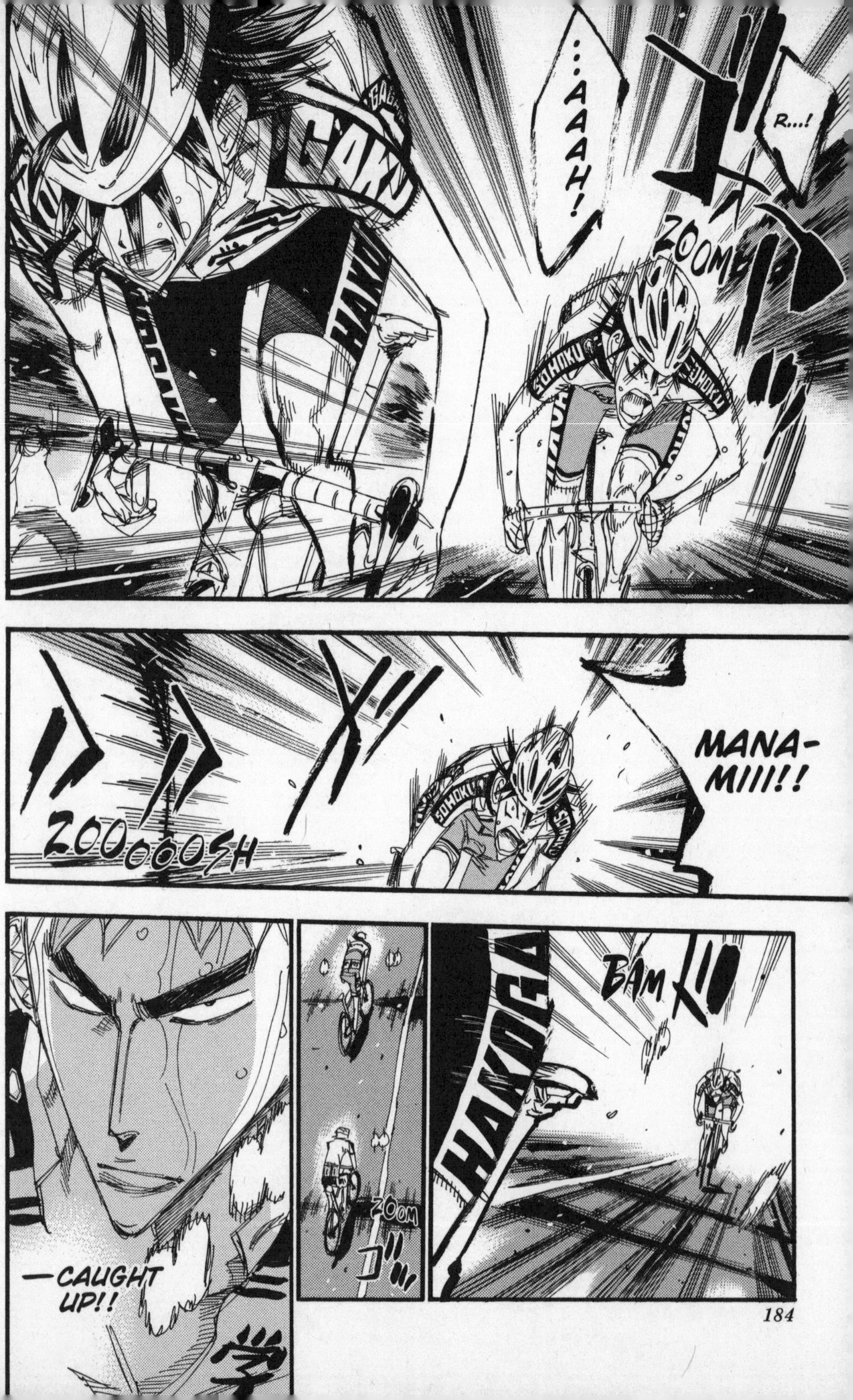
R...!
...AAAAH!
ZOOM
MANA-
MIII!!
ZOOOOOOSH
BAM
ZOOM
—CAUGHT
UP!!

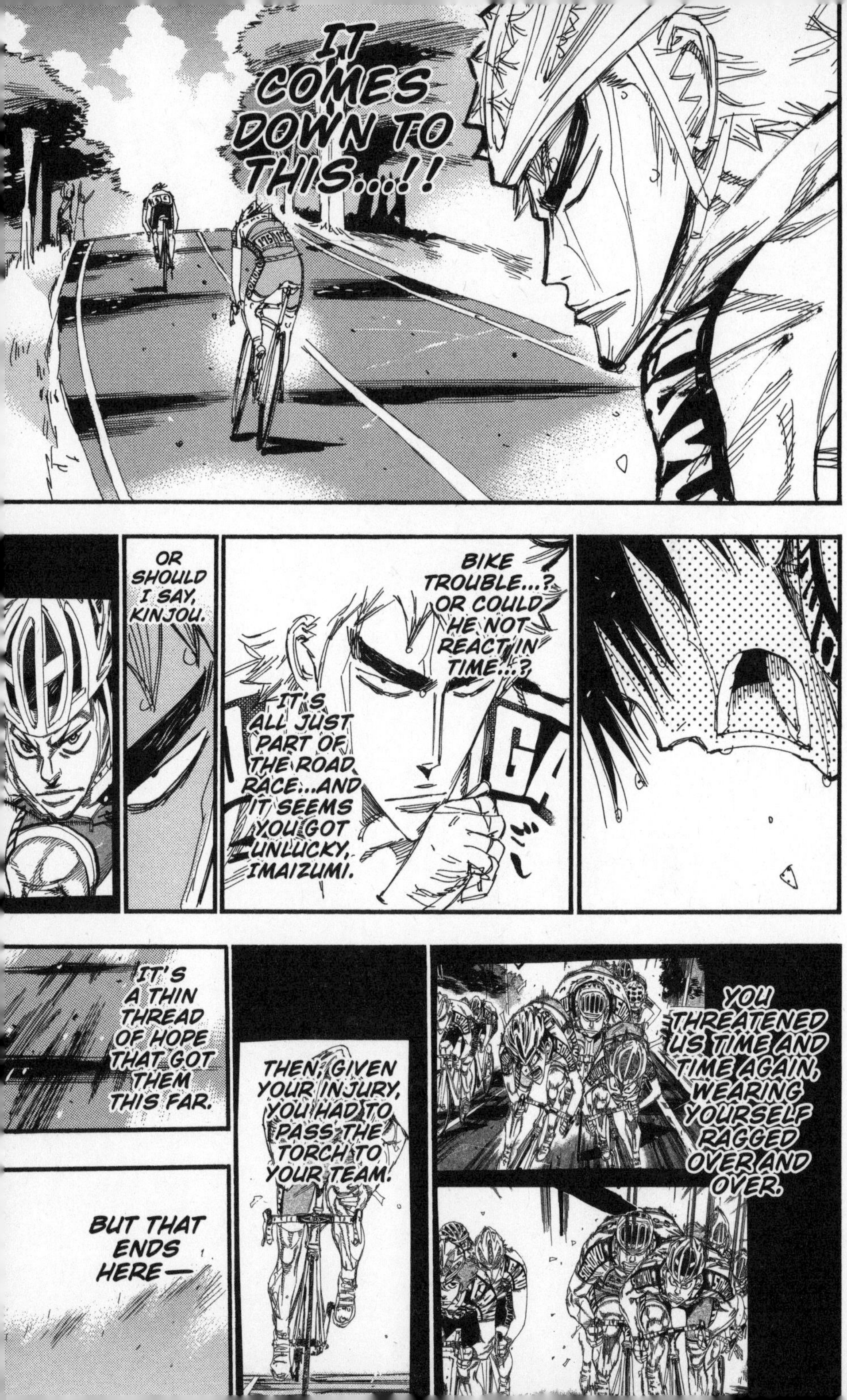
IT COMES DOWN TO THIS...!!
BIKE TROUBLE...? OR COULD HE NOT REACT IN TIME...?
IT'S ALL JUST PART OF THE ROAD RACE...AND IT SEEMS YOU GOT UNLUCKY, IMAIZUMI.
OR SHOULD I SAY, KINJOU.
YOU THREATENED US TIME AND TIME AGAIN, WEARING YOURSELF RAGGED OVER AND OVER.
THEN, GIVEN YOUR INJURY, YOU HAD TO PASS THE TORCH TO YOUR TEAM.
IT'S A THIN THREAD OF HOPE THAT GOT THEM THIS FAR.
BUT THAT ENDS HERE—

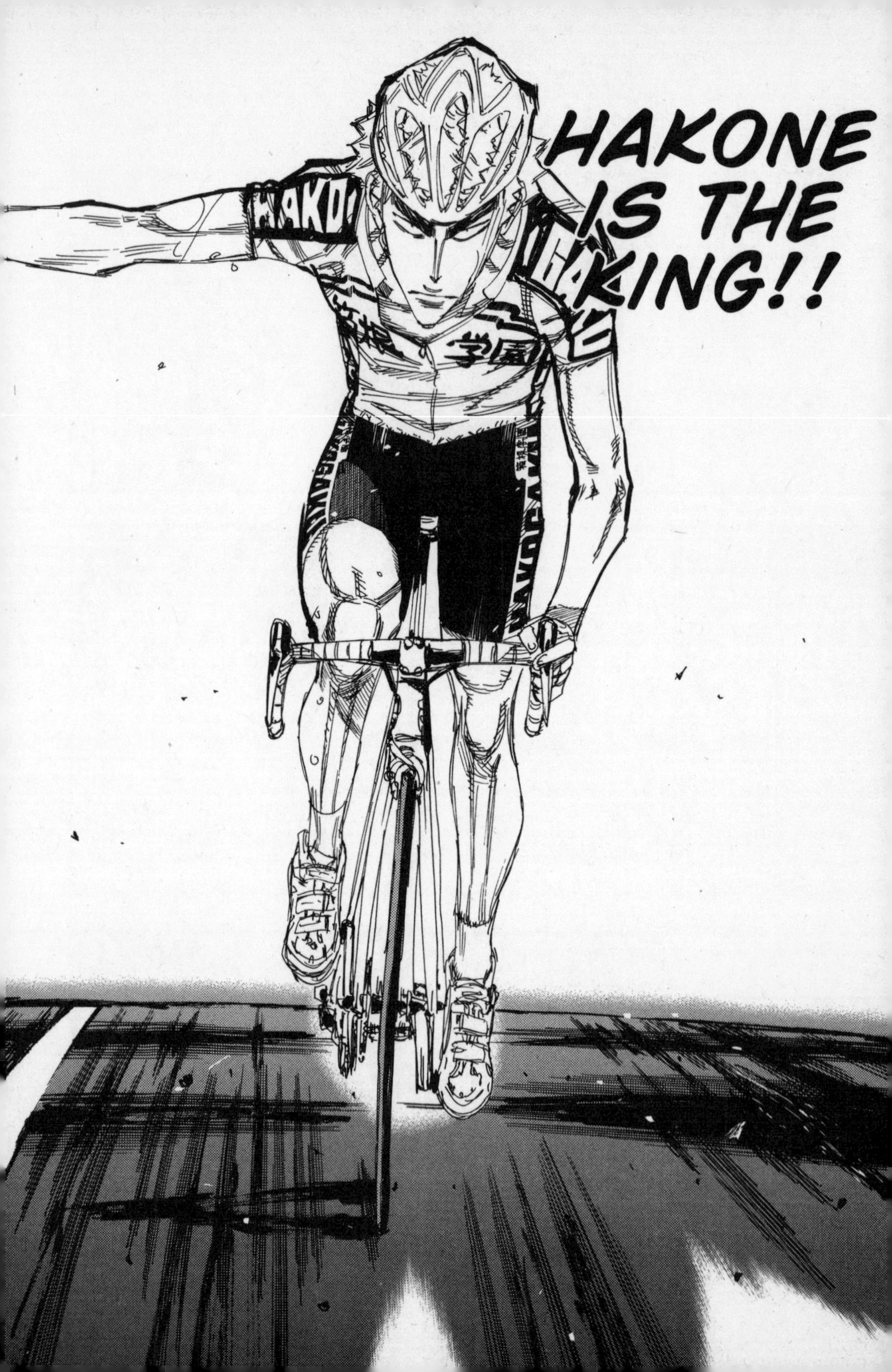
HAKONE IS THE KING!!

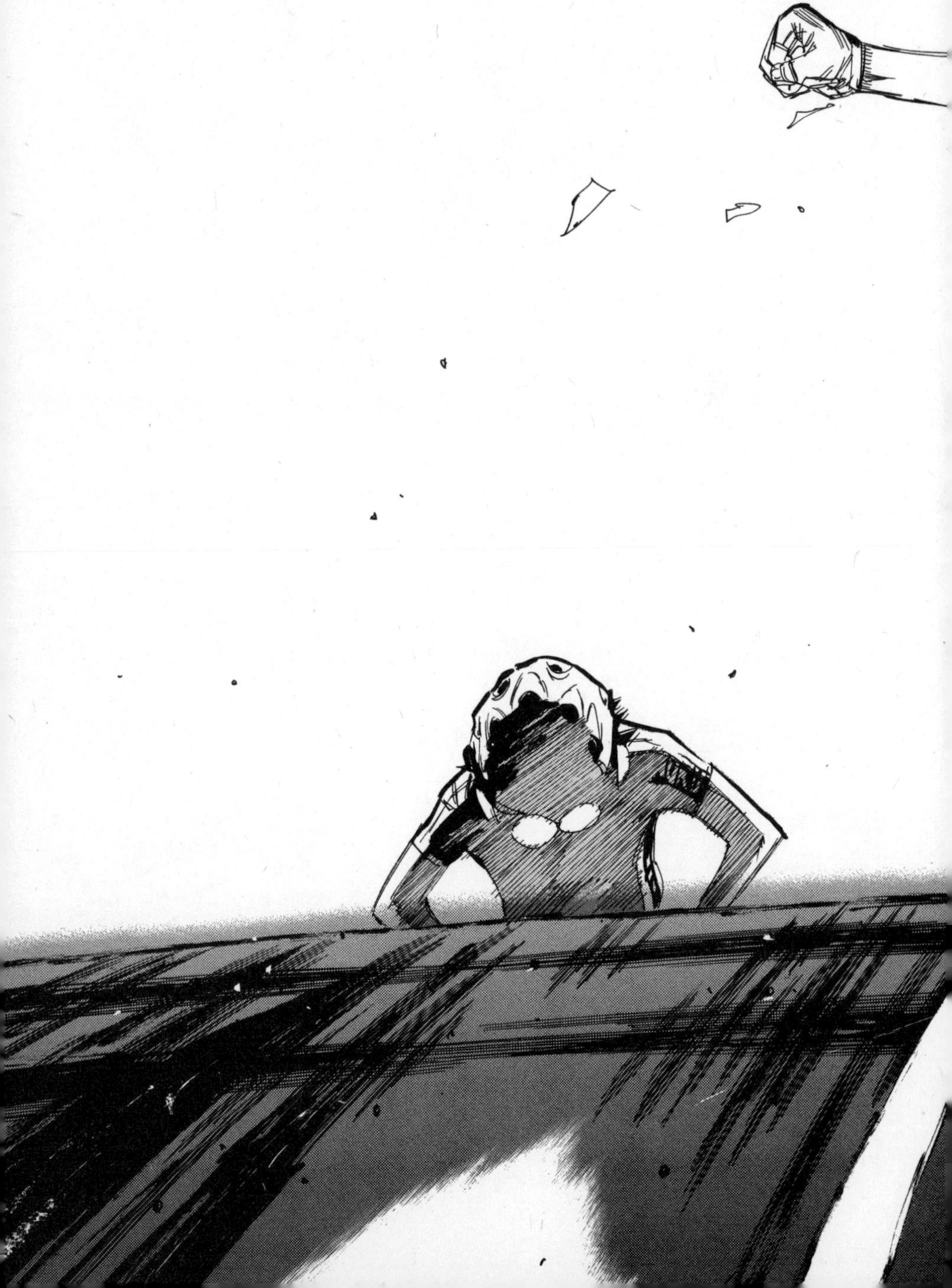

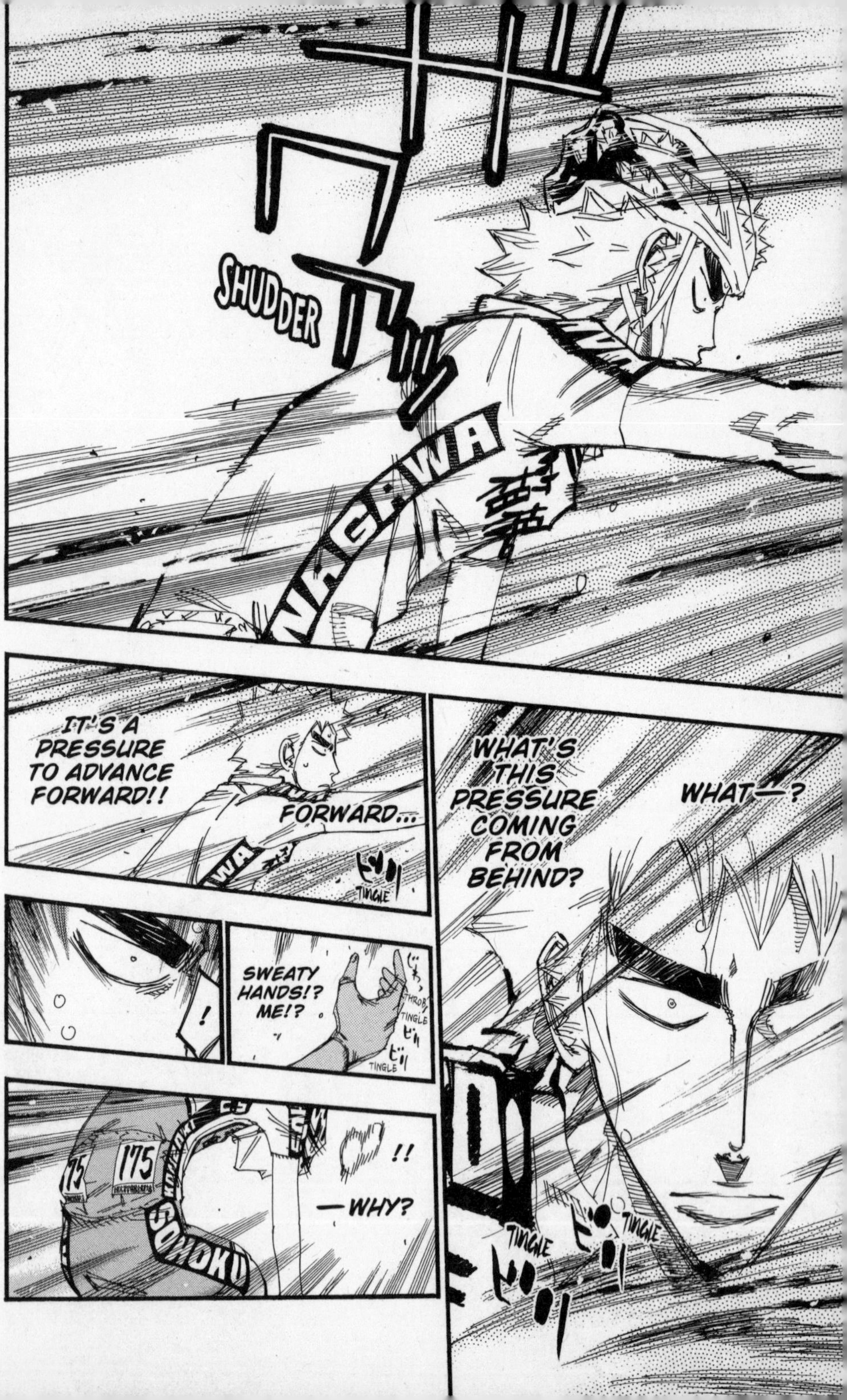
SHUDDER
WHAT—?
WHAT'S THIS PRESSURE COMING FROM BEHIND?
TINGLE
TINGLE
IT'S A PRESSURE TO ADVANCE FORWARD!!
FORWARD...
TINGLE
SWEATY HANDS!? ME!?
THROB
TINGLE
TINGLE
!
!!
—WHY?
175
SOHOKU

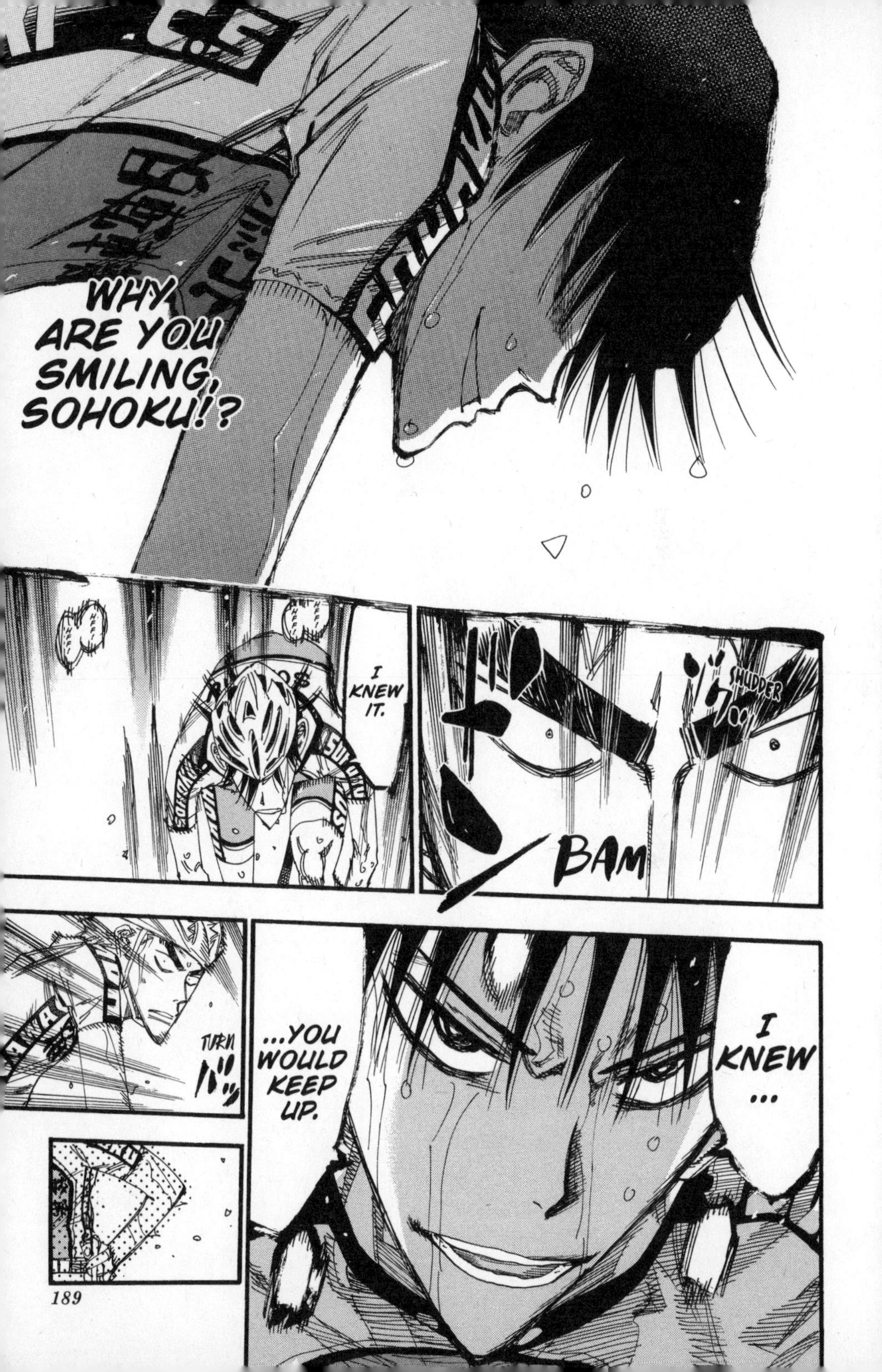
WHY ARE YOU SMILING, SOHOKU!?
SHUDDER
BAM
HEFF HEFF
HEFF HEFF
I KNEW IT.
I KNEW...
...YOU WOULD KEEP UP.
TURN

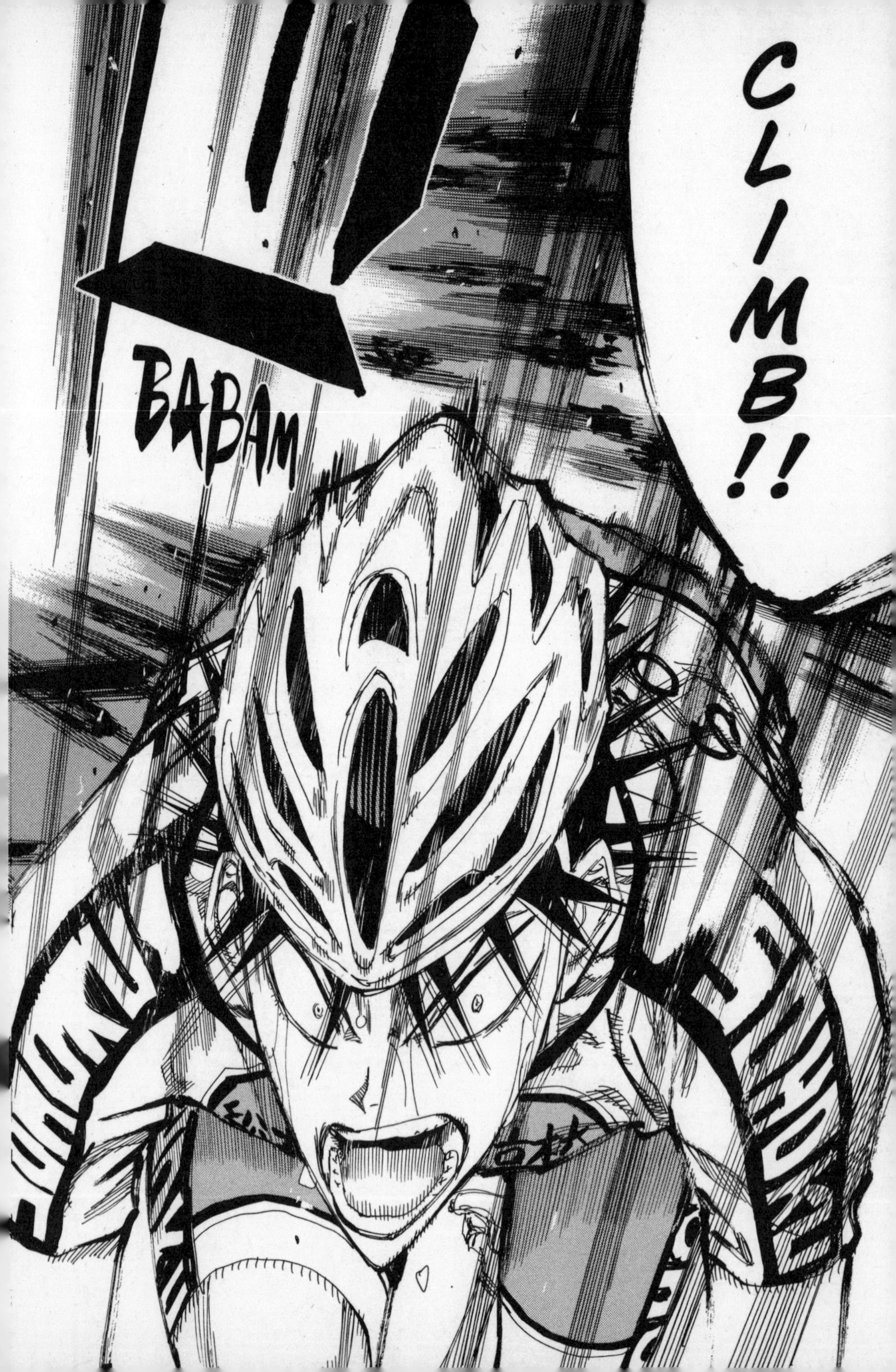

CLIMB!!
BABAM

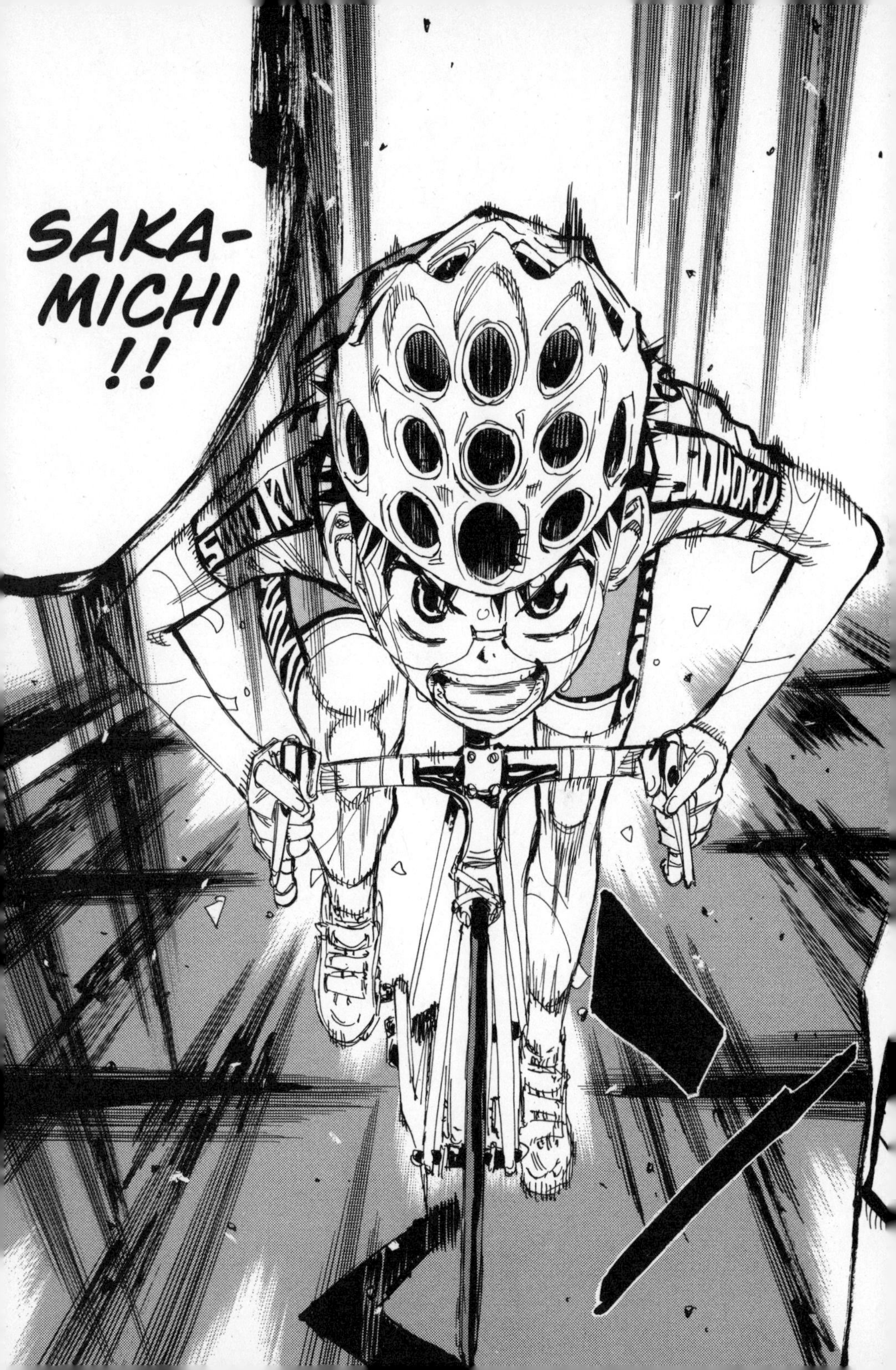
SAKA-
MICHI
!!

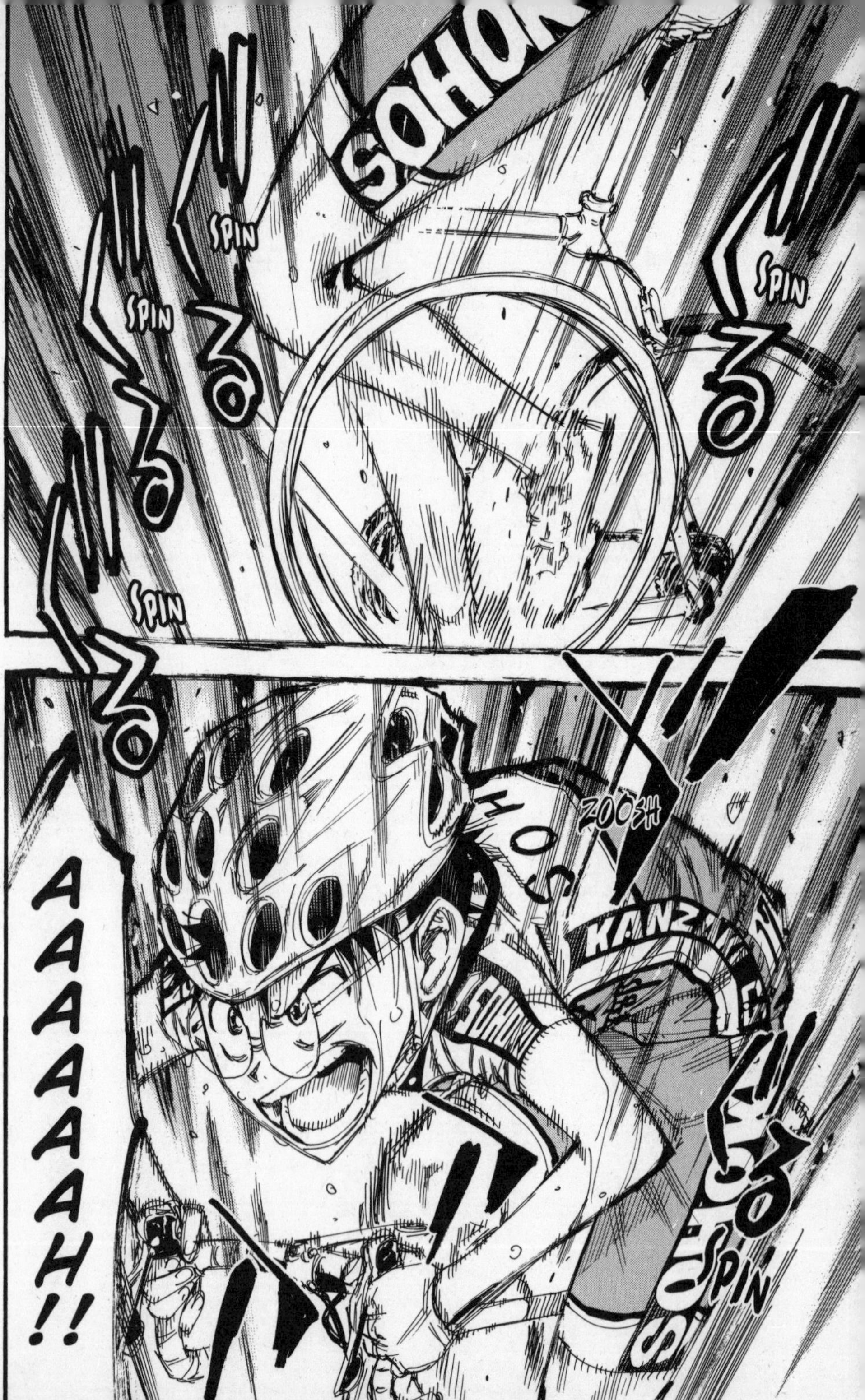
SPIN
SPIN
SPIN
SPIN
ZOOSH
AAAAAAH!!
SPIN

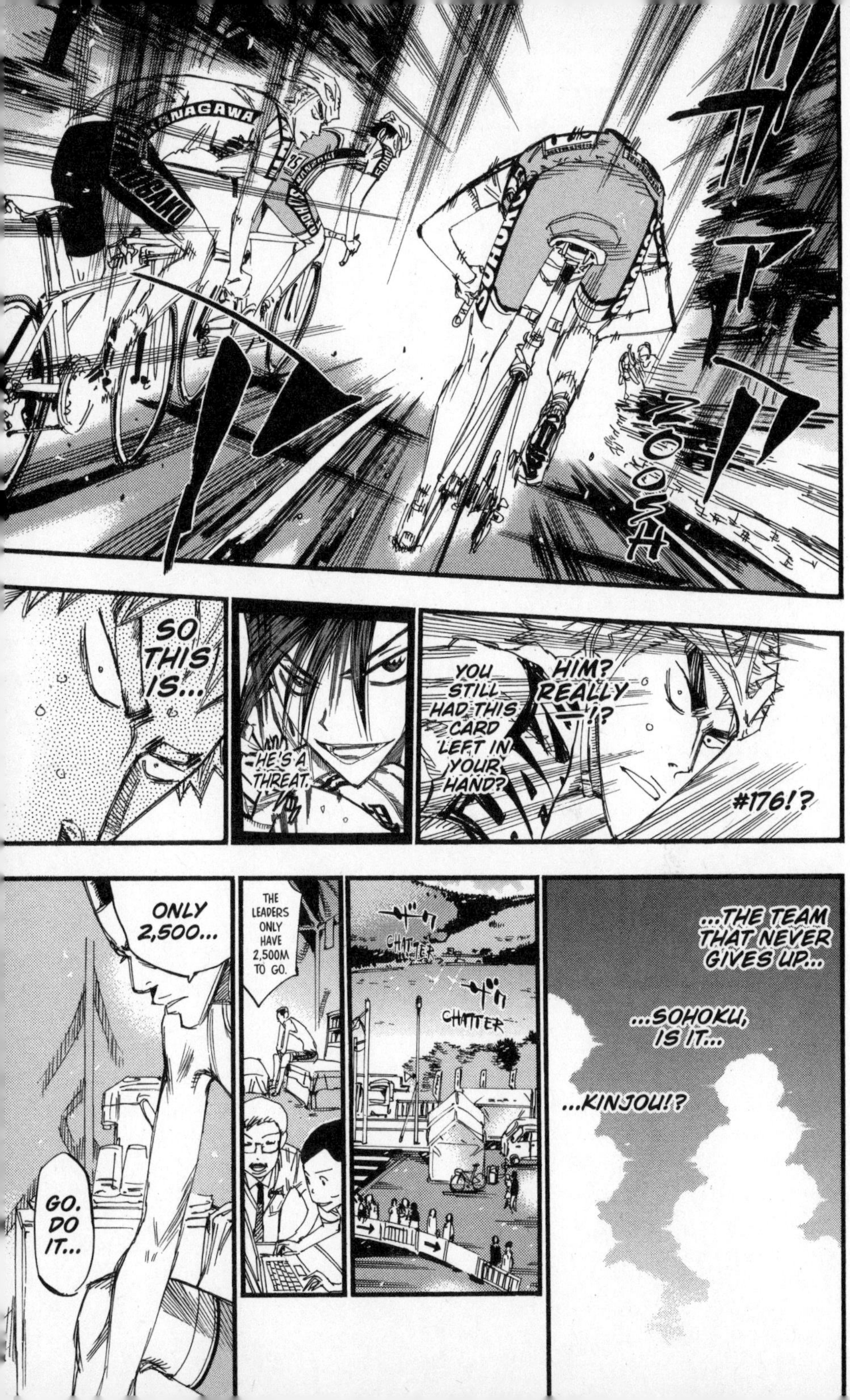
ZOOOSH
#176!?
HIM? REALLY!?
YOU STILL HAD THIS CARD LEFT IN YOUR HAND?
HE'S A THREAT.
SO THIS IS...
...THE TEAM THAT NEVER GIVES UP...
...SOHOKU, IS IT...
...KINJOU!?
CHATTER
CHATTER
THE LEADERS ONLY HAVE 2,500M TO GO.
ONLY 2,500...
GO. DO IT...

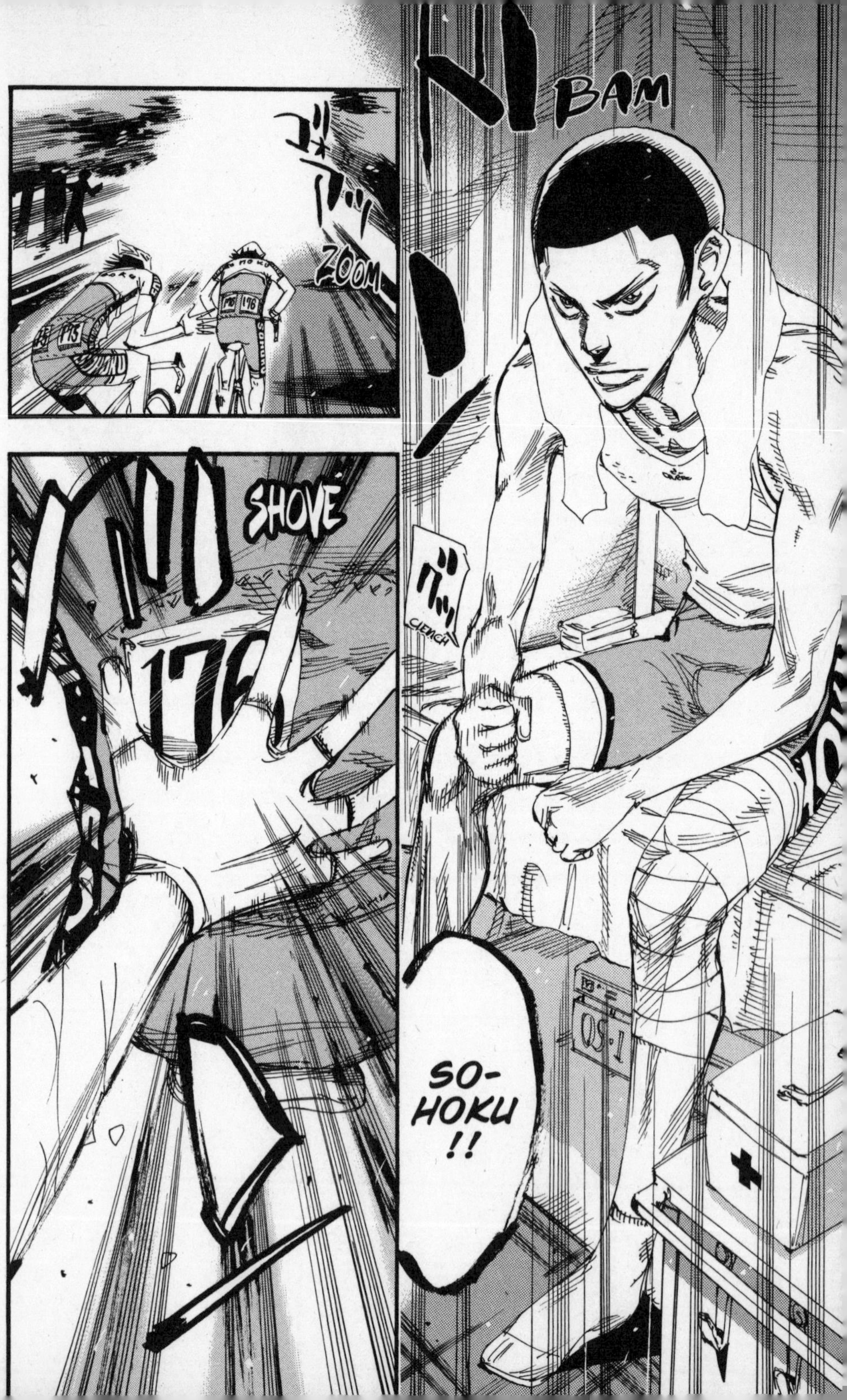

BAM
グッ
CLENCH
SO-HOKU!!
ZOOM
SHOVE

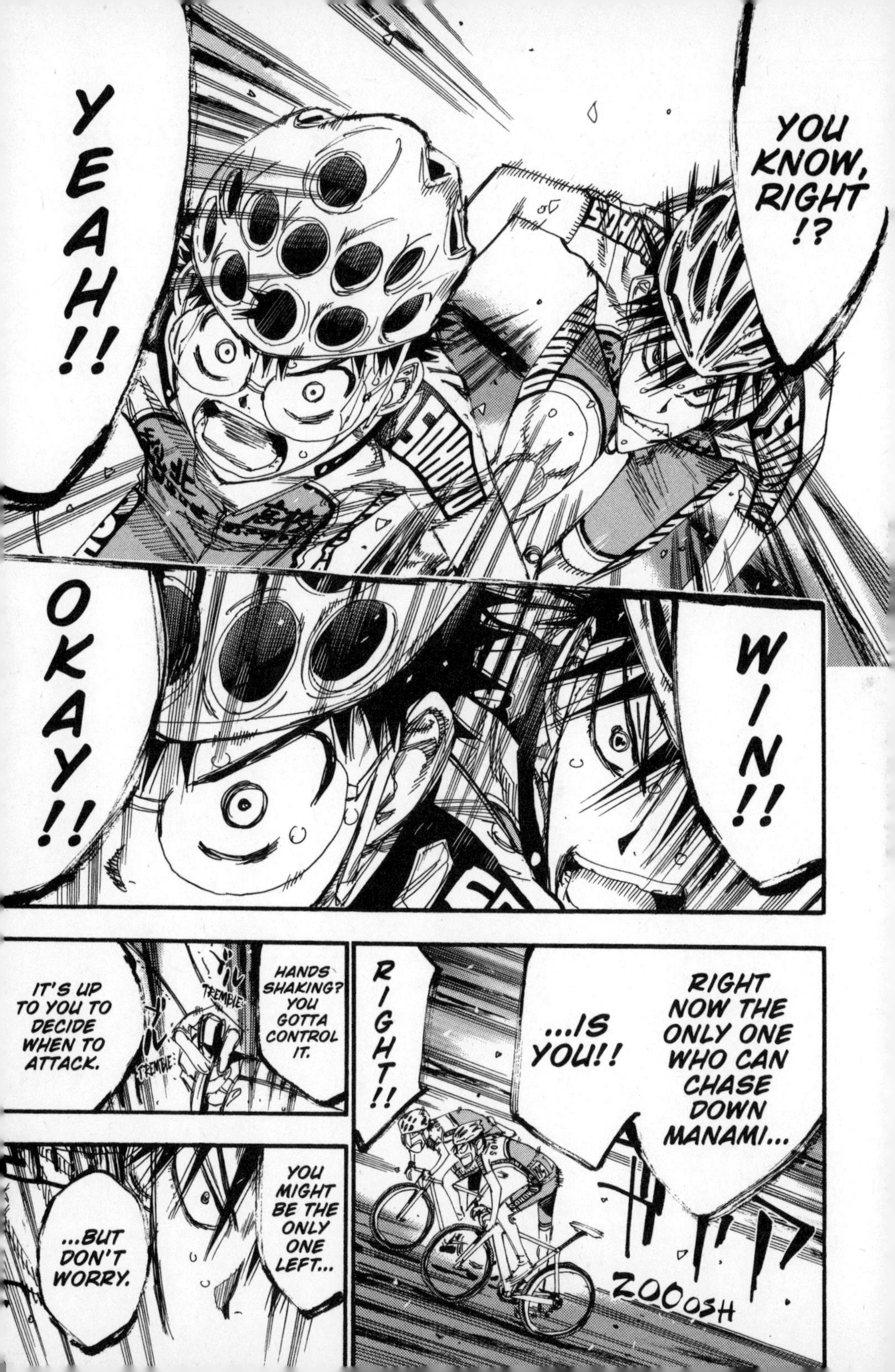
YOU KNOW, RIGHT!?
YEAH!!
WIN!!
OKAY!!
RIGHT NOW THE ONLY ONE WHO CAN CHASE DOWN MANAMI...
...IS YOU!!
RIGHT!!
ZOOOSH
HANDS SHAKING? YOU GOTTA CONTROL IT.
TREMBLE
TREMBLE
IT'S UP TO YOU TO DECIDE WHEN TO ATTACK.
YOU MIGHT BE THE ONLY ONE LEFT...
...BUT DON'T WORRY.

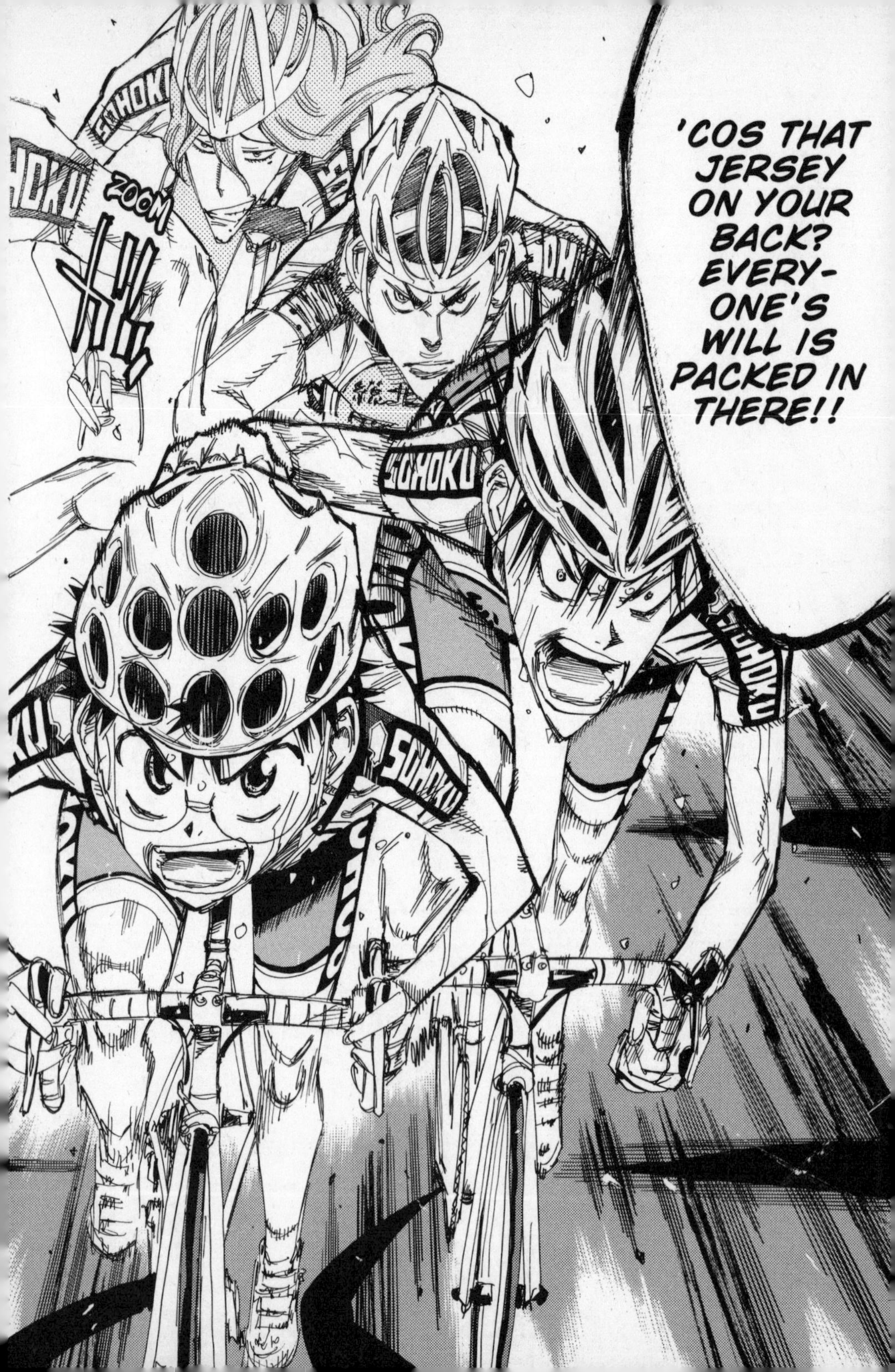
'COS THAT JERSEY ON YOUR BACK? EVERY-ONE'S WILL IS PACKED IN THERE!!
ZOOM

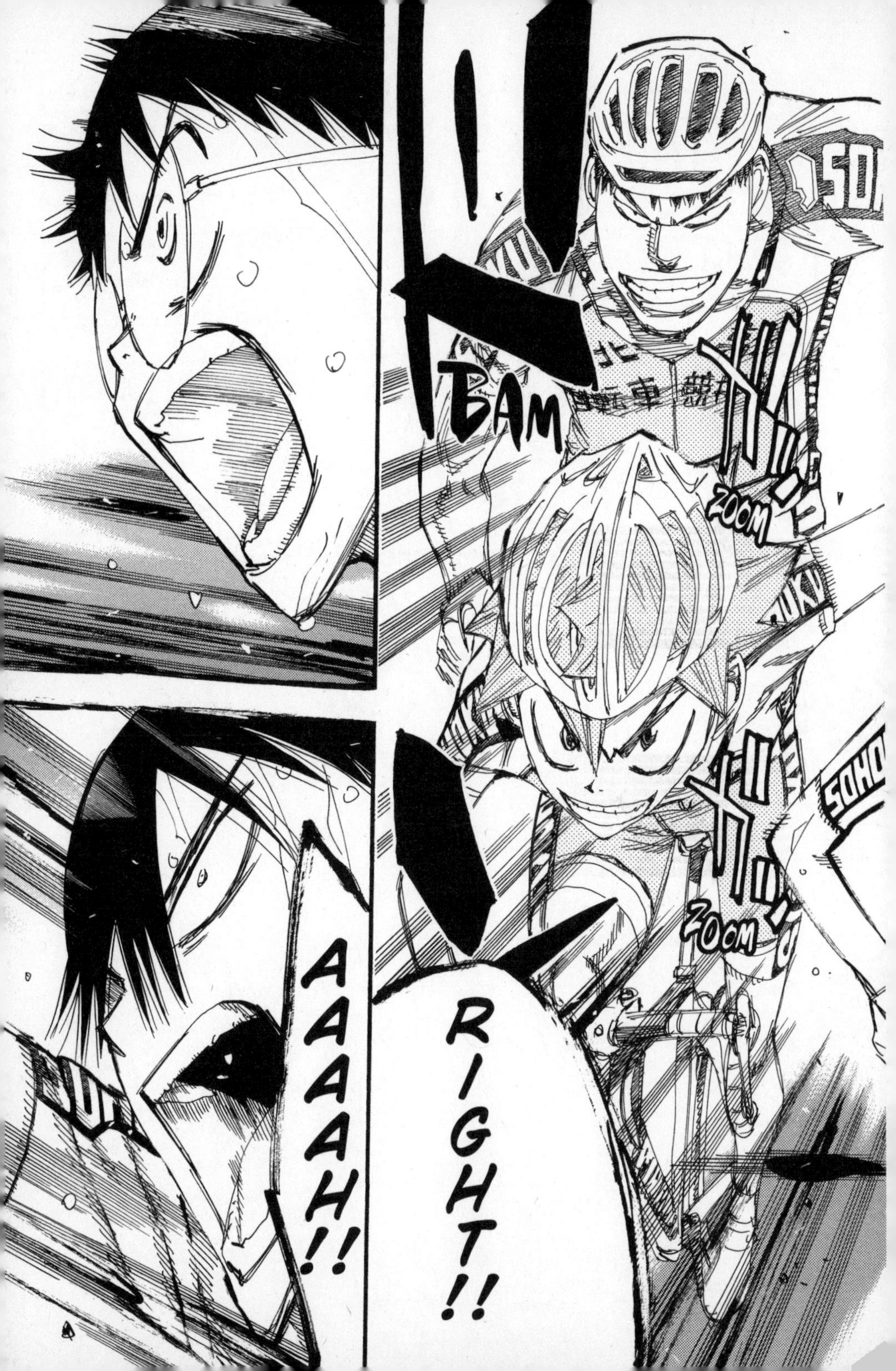
BAM
ZOOM
ZOOM
RIGHT!!
AAAAH!!

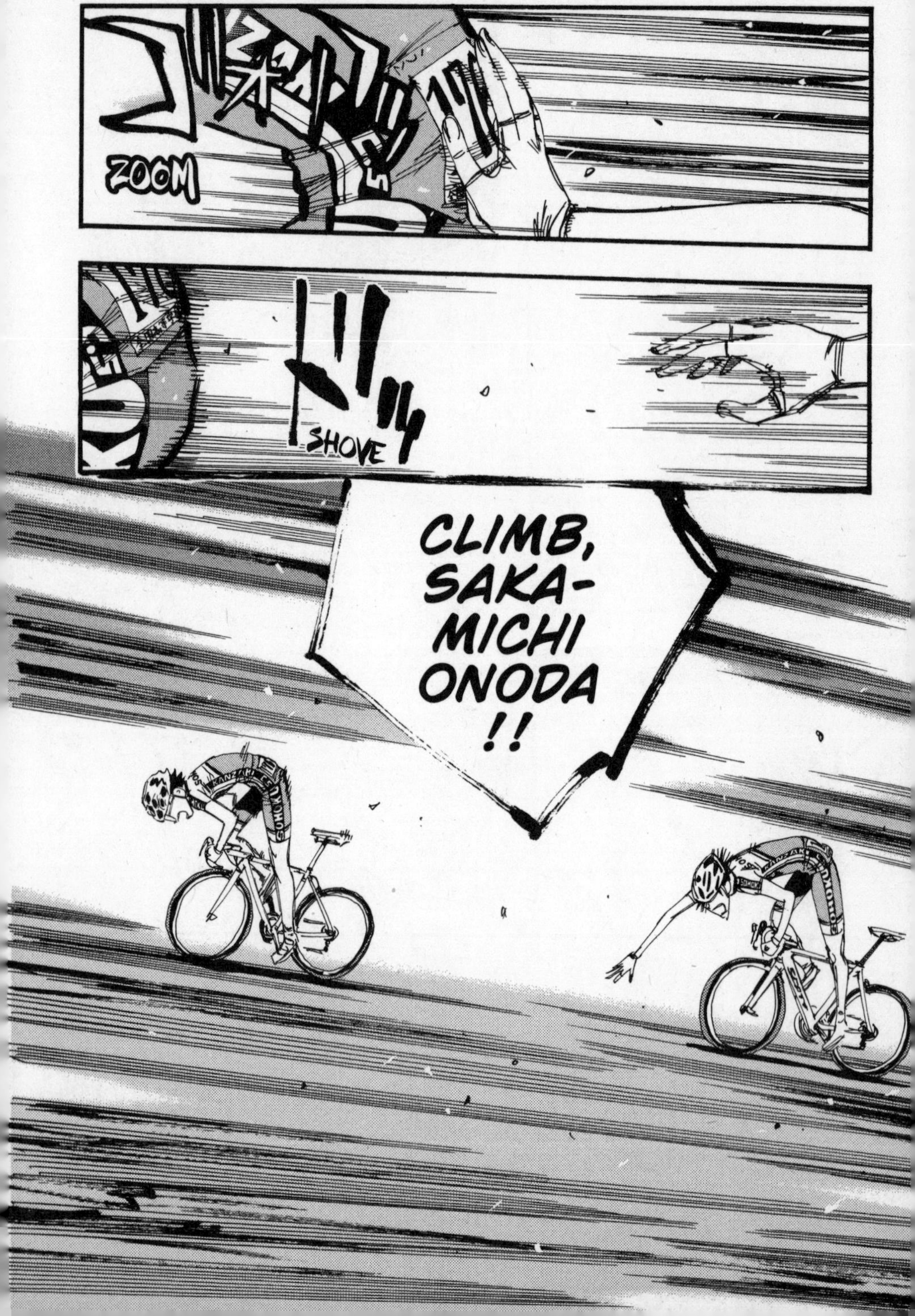
ZOOM
SHOVE
CLIMB, SAKA-MICHI ONODA!!

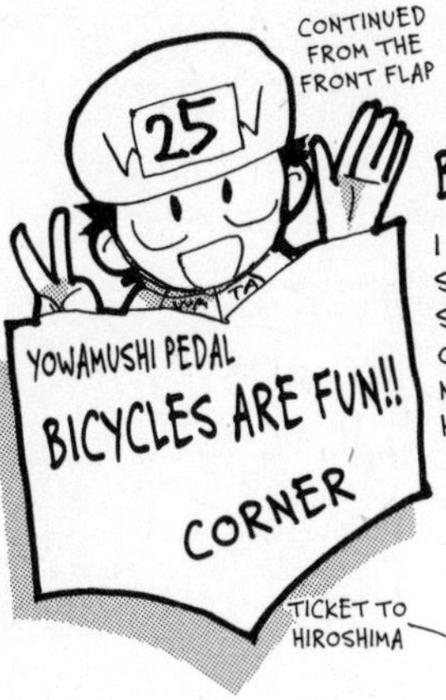

CONTINUED FROM THE FRONT FLAP
25
YOWAMUSHI PEDAL
BICYCLES ARE FUN!!
CORNER

AUGUST 6TH-9TH, 2012

HEIGHT OF SUMMER!! TOTAL DISTANCE OF 500KM!! OVER 4 DAYS!!

BIKE TRIP FROM HIROSHIMA TO NAGASAKI!!

I TAKE A BIKE TRIP EVERY SUMMER, AND THIS PAST ONE, I CHOSE TO START FROM HIROSHIMA. FROM HIROSHIMA, ALONG THE SHIMANAMI SEA ROUTE, CUTTING RIGHT THROUGH SHIKOKU AND EHIME, AND THEN ONTO KYUSHU VIA SHIP. THIS WAS MY FIRST FOUR-DAY-LONG TRIP. DID I MAKE IT TO MY HOMETOWN OF NAGASAKI IN ONE PIECE!? HERE'S THE FULL STORY.

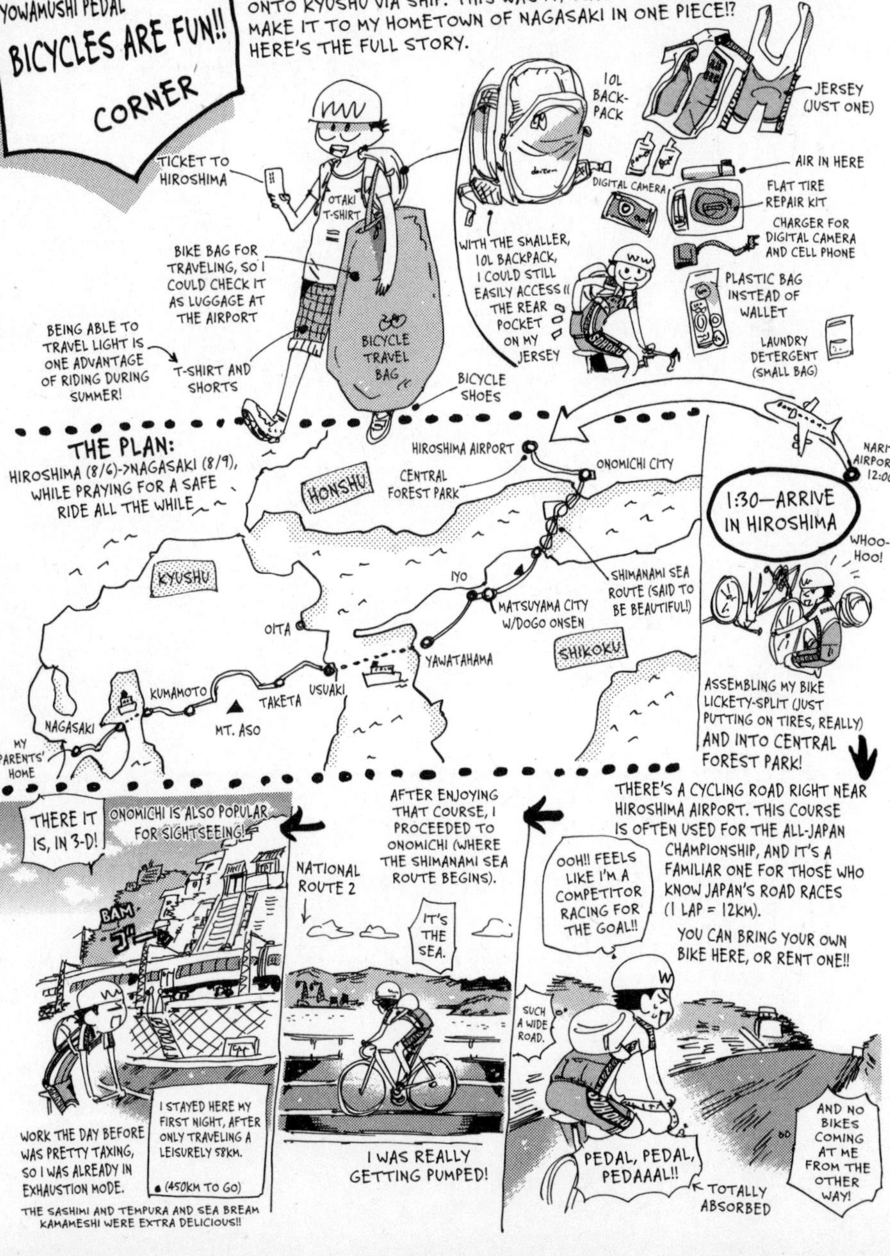

JERSEY (JUST ONE)
10L BACK-PACK
AIR IN HERE
FLAT TIRE REPAIR KIT
DIGITAL CAMERA
CHARGER FOR DIGITAL CAMERA AND CELL PHONE
PLASTIC BAG INSTEAD OF WALLET
LAUNDRY DETERGENT (SMALL BAG)
WITH THE SMALLER, 10L BACKPACK, I COULD STILL EASILY ACCESS THE REAR POCKET ON MY JERSEY
TICKET TO HIROSHIMA
OTAKI T-SHIRT
BIKE BAG FOR TRAVELING, SO I COULD CHECK IT AS LUGGAGE AT THE AIRPORT
BICYCLE TRAVEL BAG
BEING ABLE TO TRAVEL LIGHT IS ONE ADVANTAGE OF RIDING DURING SUMMER!
T-SHIRT AND SHORTS
BICYCLE SHOES
NARITA AIRPORT—12:00
1:30—ARRIVE IN HIROSHIMA
WHOO-HOO!
ASSEMBLING MY BIKE LICKETY-SPLIT (JUST PUTTING ON TIRES, REALLY) AND INTO CENTRAL FOREST PARK!
THE PLAN:
HIROSHIMA (8/6)->NAGASAKI (8/9), WHILE PRAYING FOR A SAFE RIDE ALL THE WHILE
HIROSHIMA AIRPORT
ONOMICHI CITY
CENTRAL FOREST PARK
HONSHU
SHIMANAMI SEA ROUTE (SAID TO BE BEAUTIFUL!)
IYO
MATSUYAMA CITY W/DOGO ONSEN
YAWATAHAMA
SHIKOKU
KYUSHU
OITA
USUKI
TAKETA
KUMAMOTO
MT. ASO
NAGASAKI
MY PARENTS' HOME
THERE'S A CYCLING ROAD RIGHT NEAR HIROSHIMA AIRPORT. THIS COURSE IS OFTEN USED FOR THE ALL-JAPAN CHAMPIONSHIP, AND IT'S A FAMILIAR ONE FOR THOSE WHO KNOW JAPAN'S ROAD RACES (1 LAP = 12KM).
YOU CAN BRING YOUR OWN BIKE HERE, OR RENT ONE!!
OOH!! FEELS LIKE I'M A COMPETITOR RACING FOR THE GOAL!!
SUCH A WIDE ROAD.
AND NO BIKES COMING AT ME FROM THE OTHER WAY!
PEDAL, PEDAL, PEDAAAL!!
TOTALLY ABSORBED
AFTER ENJOYING THAT COURSE, I PROCEEDED TO ONOMICHI (WHERE THE SHIMANAMI SEA ROUTE BEGINS).
NATIONAL ROUTE 2
IT'S THE SEA.
I WAS REALLY GETTING PUMPED!
THERE IT IS, IN 3-D!
ONOMICHI IS ALSO POPULAR FOR SIGHTSEEING!
BAM
I STAYED HERE MY FIRST NIGHT, AFTER ONLY TRAVELING A LEISURELY 58KM.
(450KM TO GO)
WORK THE DAY BEFORE WAS PRETTY TAXING, SO I WAS ALREADY IN EXHAUSTION MODE.
THE SASHIMI AND TEMPURA AND SEA BREAM KAMAMESHI WERE EXTRA DELICIOUS!!

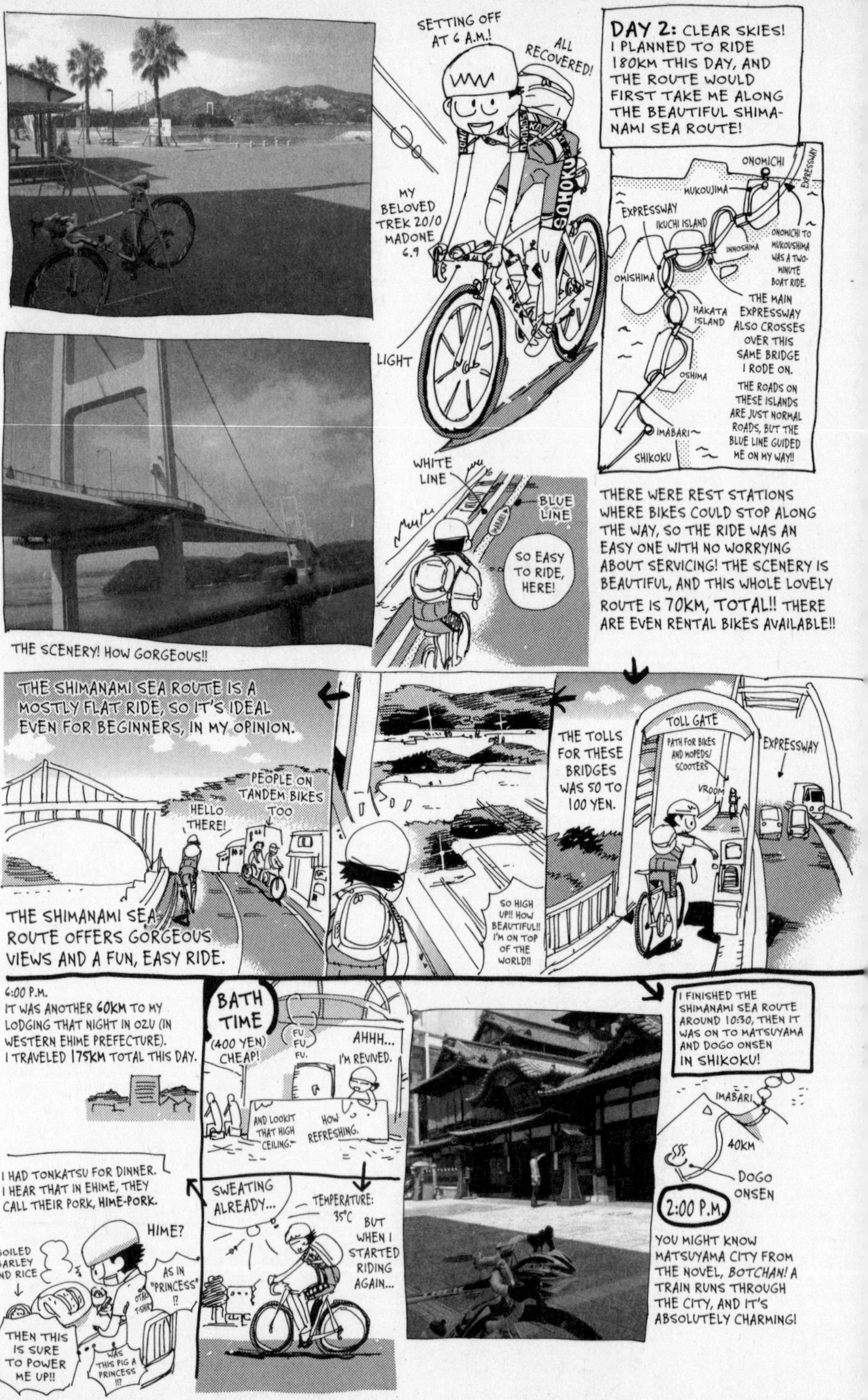
DAY 2: CLEAR SKIES! I PLANNED TO RIDE 180KM THIS DAY, AND THE ROUTE WOULD FIRST TAKE ME ALONG THE BEAUTIFUL SHIMANAMI SEA ROUTE!
ONOMICHI
EXPRESSWAY
MUKOUJIMA
EXPRESSWAY
IKUCHI ISLAND
INNOSHIMA
ONOMICHI TO MUKOUSHIMA WAS A TWO-MINUTE BOAT RIDE.
OMISHIMA
HAKATA ISLAND
THE MAIN EXPRESSWAY ALSO CROSSES OVER THIS SAME BRIDGE I RODE ON.
OSHIMA
THE ROADS ON THESE ISLANDS ARE JUST NORMAL ROADS, BUT THE BLUE LINE GUIDED ME ON MY WAY!!
IMABARI
SHIKOKU
SETTING OFF AT 6 A.M.!
ALL RECOVERED!
MY BELOVED TREK 20/0 MADONE 6.9
LIGHT
SOHOKU
THERE WERE REST STATIONS WHERE BIKES COULD STOP ALONG THE WAY, SO THE RIDE WAS AN EASY ONE WITH NO WORRYING ABOUT SERVICING! THE SCENERY IS BEAUTIFUL, AND THIS WHOLE LOVELY ROUTE IS 70KM, TOTAL!! THERE ARE EVEN RENTAL BIKES AVAILABLE!!
WHITE LINE
BLUE LINE
SO EASY TO RIDE, HERE!
THE SCENERY! HOW GORGEOUS!!
TOLL GATE
PATH FOR BIKES AND MOPEDS/SCOOTERS
EXPRESSWAY
THE TOLLS FOR THESE BRIDGES WAS 50 TO 100 YEN.
VROOM
SO HIGH UP!! HOW BEAUTIFUL!! I'M ON TOP OF THE WORLD!!
THE SHIMANAMI SEA ROUTE IS A MOSTLY FLAT RIDE, SO IT'S IDEAL EVEN FOR BEGINNERS, IN MY OPINION.
PEOPLE ON TANDEM BIKES TOO
HELLO THERE!
THE SHIMANAMI SEA ROUTE OFFERS GORGEOUS VIEWS AND A FUN, EASY RIDE.
I FINISHED THE SHIMANAMI SEA ROUTE AROUND 10:30, THEN IT WAS ON TO MATSUYAMA AND DOGO ONSEN IN SHIKOKU!
IMABARI
40KM
DOGO ONSEN
2:00 P.M.
YOU MIGHT KNOW MATSUYAMA CITY FROM THE NOVEL, BOTCHAN! A TRAIN RUNS THROUGH THE CITY, AND IT'S ABSOLUTELY CHARMING!
BATH TIME
(400 YEN) CHEAP!
FU FU FU.
AHHH... I'M REVIVED.
AND LOOKIT THAT HIGH CEILING.
HOW REFRESHING.
6:00 P.M. IT WAS ANOTHER 60KM TO MY LODGING THAT NIGHT IN OZU (IN WESTERN EHIME PREFECTURE). I TRAVELED 175KM TOTAL THIS DAY.
SWEATING ALREADY...
TEMPERATURE: 35°C
BUT WHEN I STARTED RIDING AGAIN...
I HAD TONKATSU FOR DINNER. I HEAR THAT IN EHIME, THEY CALL THEIR PORK, HIME-PORK.
HIME?
AS IN "PRINCESS" !?
BOILED BARLEY AND RICE
THEN THIS IS SURE TO POWER ME UP!!
WAS THIS PIG A PRINCESS !!?

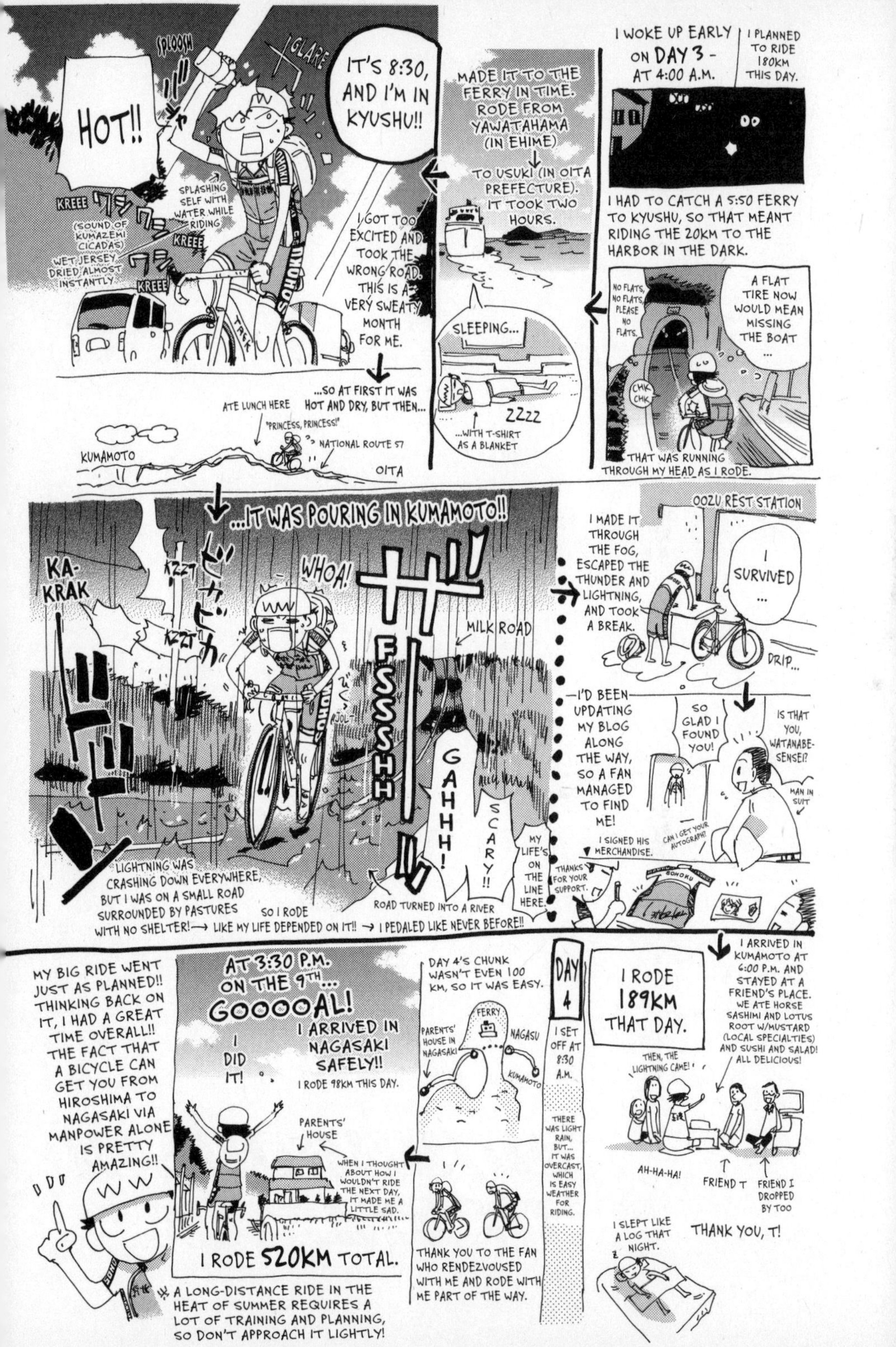

I WOKE UP EARLY ON DAY 3 - AT 4:00 A.M.
I PLANNED TO RIDE 180KM THIS DAY.
I HAD TO CATCH A 5:50 FERRY TO KYUSHU, SO THAT MEANT RIDING THE 20KM TO THE HARBOR IN THE DARK.
A FLAT TIRE NOW WOULD MEAN MISSING THE BOAT...
NO FLATS, NO FLATS, PLEASE NO FLATS.
CHK CHK
THAT WAS RUNNING THROUGH MY HEAD AS I RODE.
MADE IT TO THE FERRY IN TIME. RODE FROM YAWATAHAMA (IN EHIME) ↓ TO USUKI (IN OITA PREFECTURE). IT TOOK TWO HOURS.
SLEEPING...
ZZZZ
...WITH T-SHIRT AS A BLANKET
IT'S 8:30, AND I'M IN KYUSHU!!
GLARE
SPLOOSH
HOT!!
SPLASHING SELF WITH WATER WHILE RIDING
KREEE
(SOUND OF KUMAZEMI CICADAS)
KREEE
WET JERSEY DRIED ALMOST INSTANTLY.
KREEE
I GOT TOO EXCITED AND TOOK THE WRONG ROAD. THIS IS A VERY SWEATY MONTH FOR ME.
...SO AT FIRST IT WAS HOT AND DRY, BUT THEN...
ATE LUNCH HERE
"PRINCESS, PRINCESS!"
NATIONAL ROUTE 57
KUMAMOTO
OITA
...IT WAS POURING IN KUMAMOTO!!
KA-KRAK
KZZT
KZZT
WHOA!
MILK ROAD
FSSSHH
JOLT
GAHHH!
SCARY!!
MY LIFE'S ON THE LINE HERE.
LIGHTNING WAS CRASHING DOWN EVERYWHERE, BUT I WAS ON A SMALL ROAD SURROUNDED BY PASTURES WITH NO SHELTER! → SO I RODE LIKE MY LIFE DEPENDED ON IT!! → I PEDALED LIKE NEVER BEFORE!!
ROAD TURNED INTO A RIVER
OOZU REST STATION
I MADE IT THROUGH THE FOG, ESCAPED THE THUNDER AND LIGHTNING, AND TOOK A BREAK.
I SURVIVED...
DRIP...
I'D BEEN UPDATING MY BLOG ALONG THE WAY, SO A FAN MANAGED TO FIND ME!
IS THAT YOU, WATANABE-SENSEI?
SO GLAD I FOUND YOU!
MAN IN SUIT
CAN I GET YOUR AUTOGRAPH?
I SIGNED HIS MERCHANDISE.
THANKS FOR YOUR SUPPORT.
SOHOKU
I ARRIVED IN KUMAMOTO AT 6:00 P.M. AND STAYED AT A FRIEND'S PLACE. WE ATE HORSE SASHIMI AND LOTUS ROOT W/MUSTARD (LOCAL SPECIALTIES) AND SUSHI AND SALAD! ALL DELICIOUS!
I RODE 189KM THAT DAY.
THEN, THE LIGHTNING CAME!
AH-HA-HA!
FRIEND T
FRIEND I DROPPED BY TOO
THANK YOU, T!
I SLEPT LIKE A LOG THAT NIGHT.
DAY 4
I SET OFF AT 8:30 A.M.
THERE WAS LIGHT RAIN, BUT... IT WAS OVERCAST, WHICH IS EASY WEATHER FOR RIDING.
DAY 4'S CHUNK WASN'T EVEN 100 KM, SO IT WAS EASY.
FERRY
PARENTS' HOUSE IN NAGASAKI
NAGASU
KUMAMOTO
THANK YOU TO THE FAN WHO RENDEZVOUSED WITH ME AND RODE WITH ME PART OF THE WAY.
AT 3:30 P.M. ON THE 9TH... GOOOOAL!
I ARRIVED IN NAGASAKI SAFELY!!
I DID IT!
I RODE 98KM THIS DAY.
PARENTS' HOUSE
WHEN I THOUGHT ABOUT HOW I WOULDN'T RIDE THE NEXT DAY, IT MADE ME A LITTLE SAD.
I RODE 520KM TOTAL.
MY BIG RIDE WENT JUST AS PLANNED!! THINKING BACK ON IT, I HAD A GREAT TIME OVERALL!! THE FACT THAT A BICYCLE CAN GET YOU FROM HIROSHIMA TO NAGASAKI VIA MANPOWER ALONE IS PRETTY AMAZING!!
※ A LONG-DISTANCE RIDE IN THE HEAT OF SUMMER REQUIRES A LOT OF TRAINING AND PLANNING, SO DON'T APPROACH IT LIGHTLY!

YOWAMUSHI
PEDAL

RIDE.217 MANAMI AND SAKAMICHI

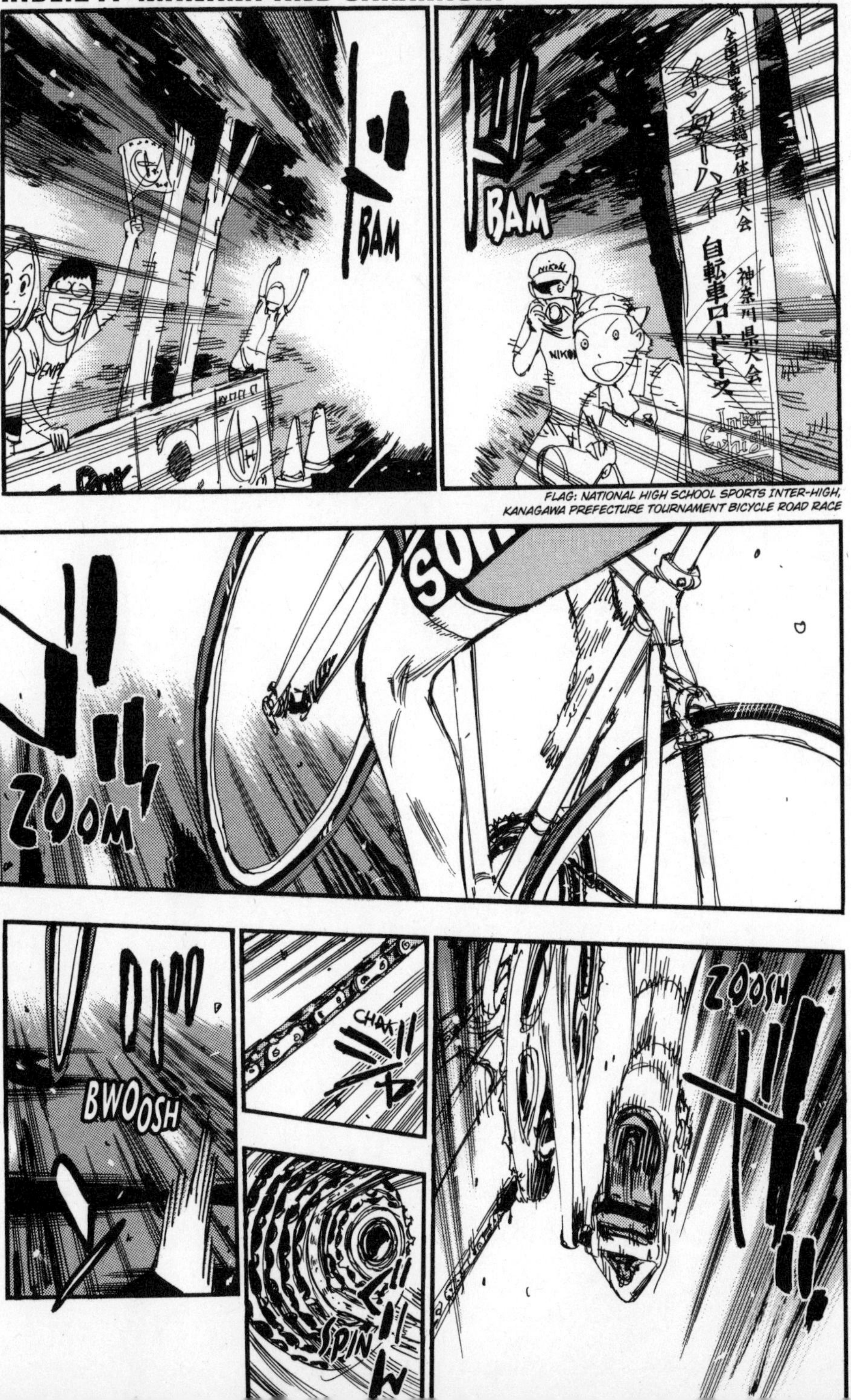
BAM
神奈川県大会
自転車ロードレース
BAM
ZOOM
ZOOSH
CHAK
SPIN
BWOOSH

FLAG: NATIONAL HIGH SCHOOL SPORTS INTER-HIGH, KANAGAWA PREFECTURE TOURNAMENT BICYCLE ROAD RACE

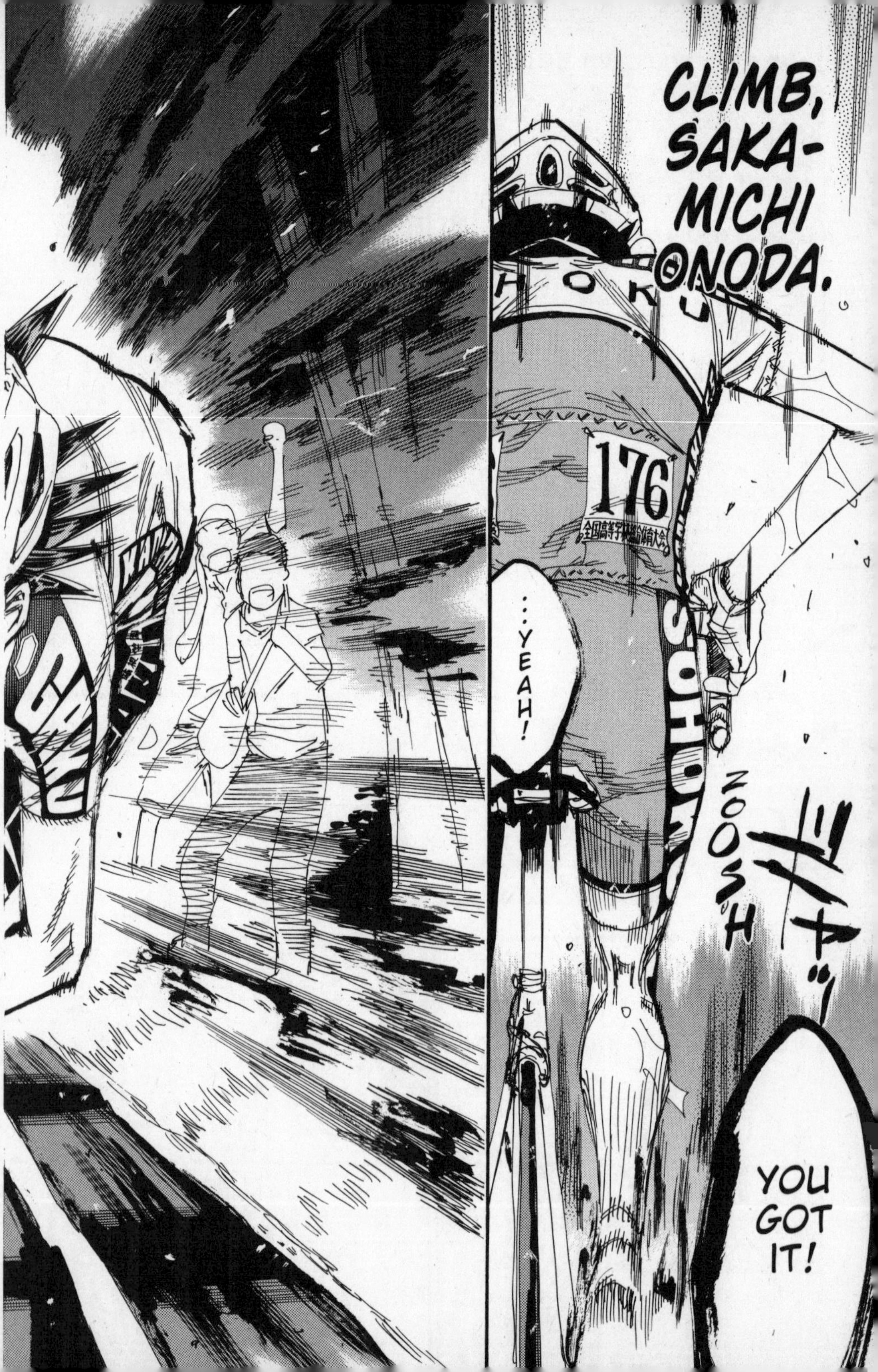
CLIMB, SAKA-MICHI ONODA.
176
...YEAH!
ZOOSH
YOU GOT IT!

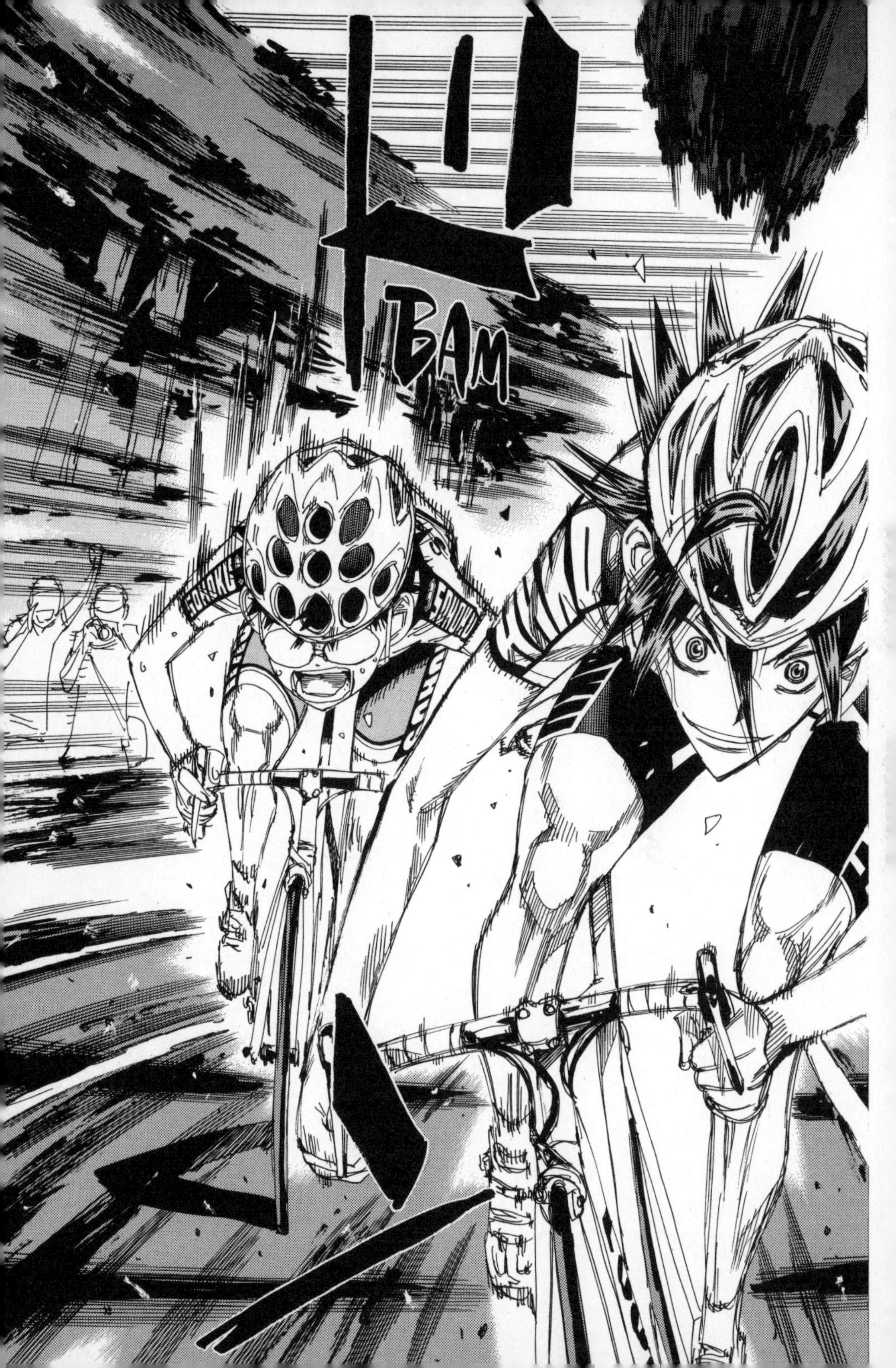
BAM

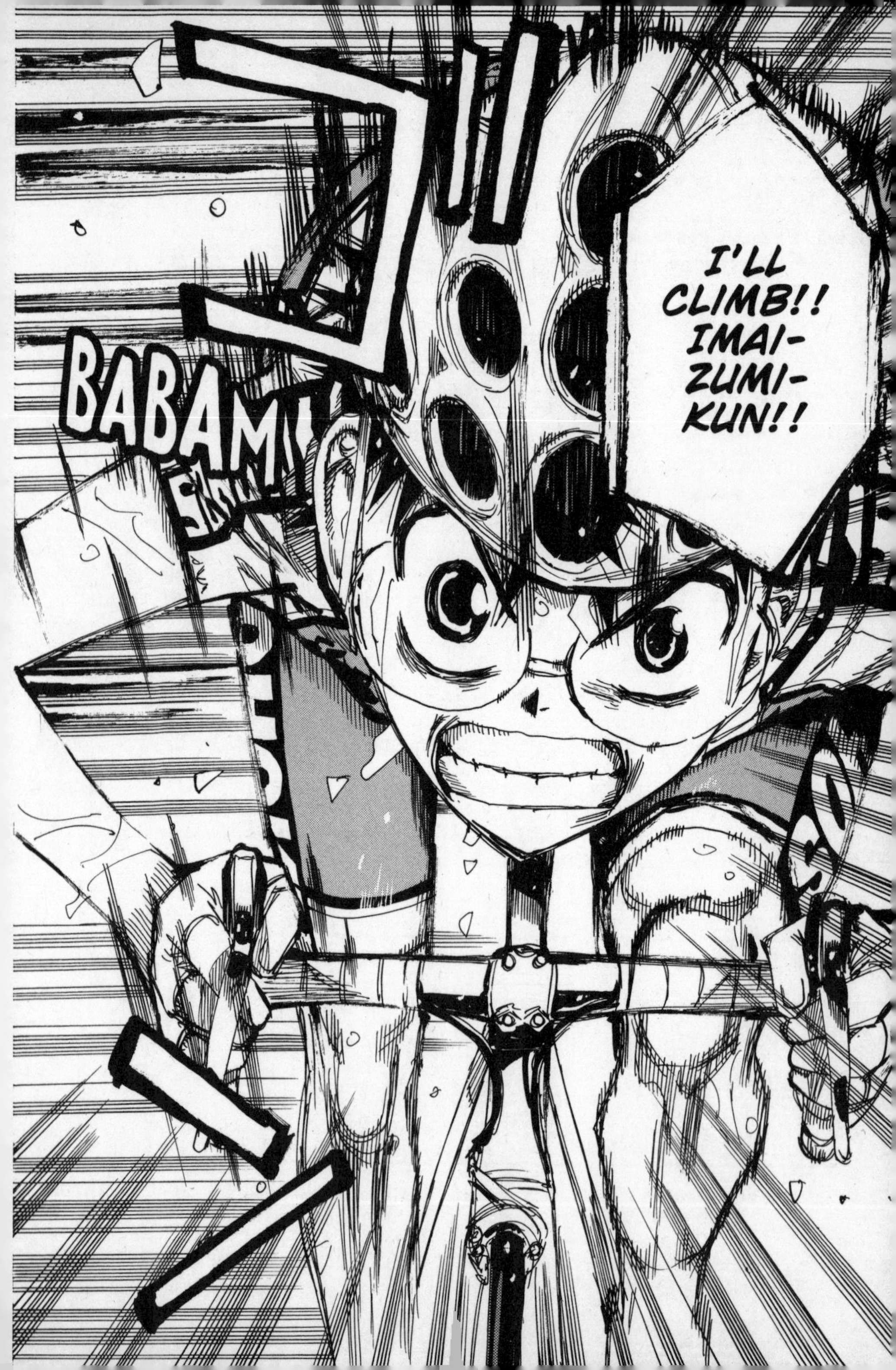
I'LL CLIMB!! IMAIZUMI-KUN!!
BABAM

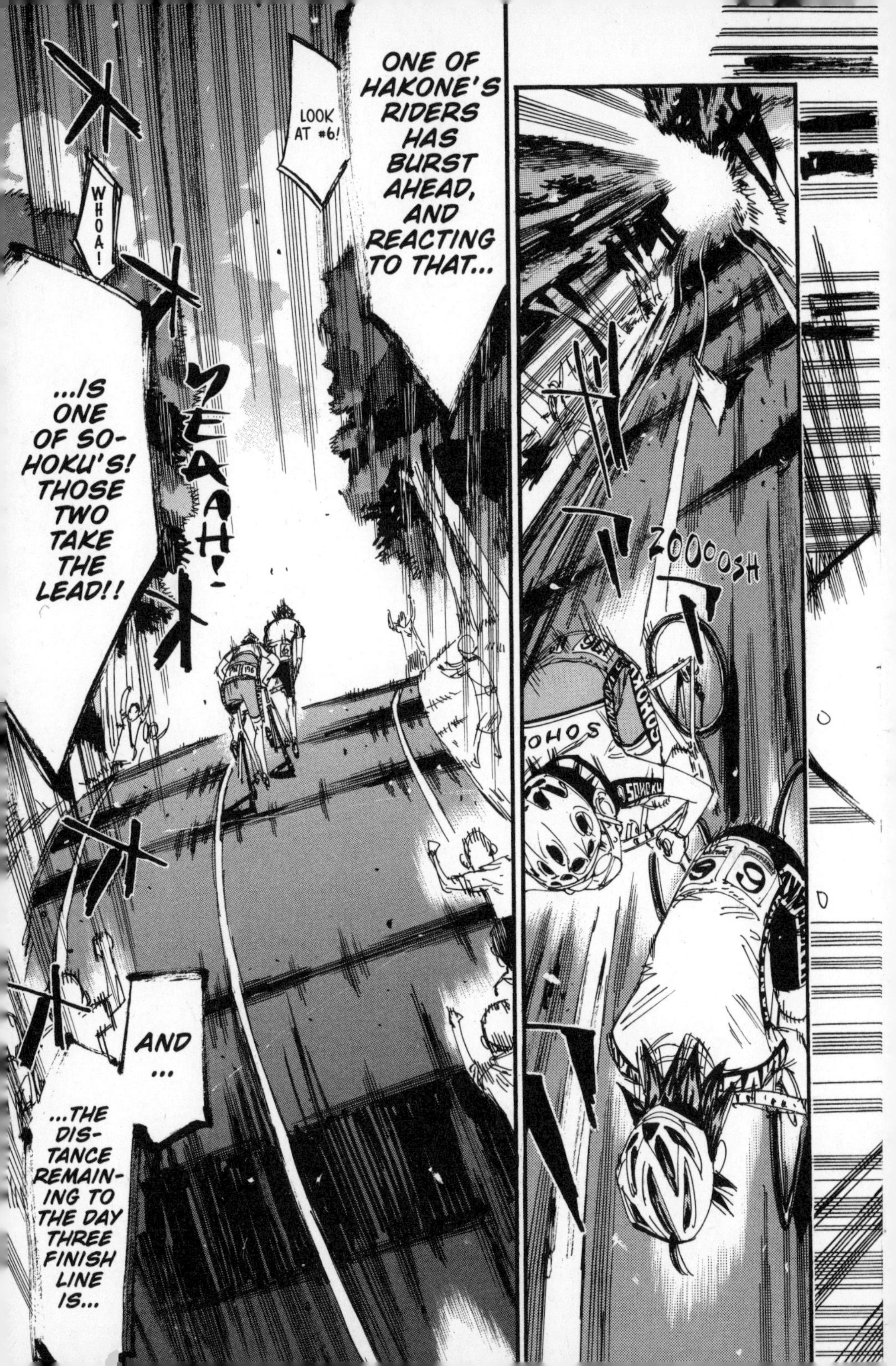
ZOOOOSH
ONE OF HAKONE'S RIDERS HAS BURST AHEAD, AND REACTING TO THAT...
LOOK AT #6!
WHOA!
YEAAAH!
...IS ONE OF SO-HOKU'S! THOSE TWO TAKE THE LEAD!!
AND...
...THE DIS-TANCE REMAIN-ING TO THE DAY THREE FINISH LINE IS...

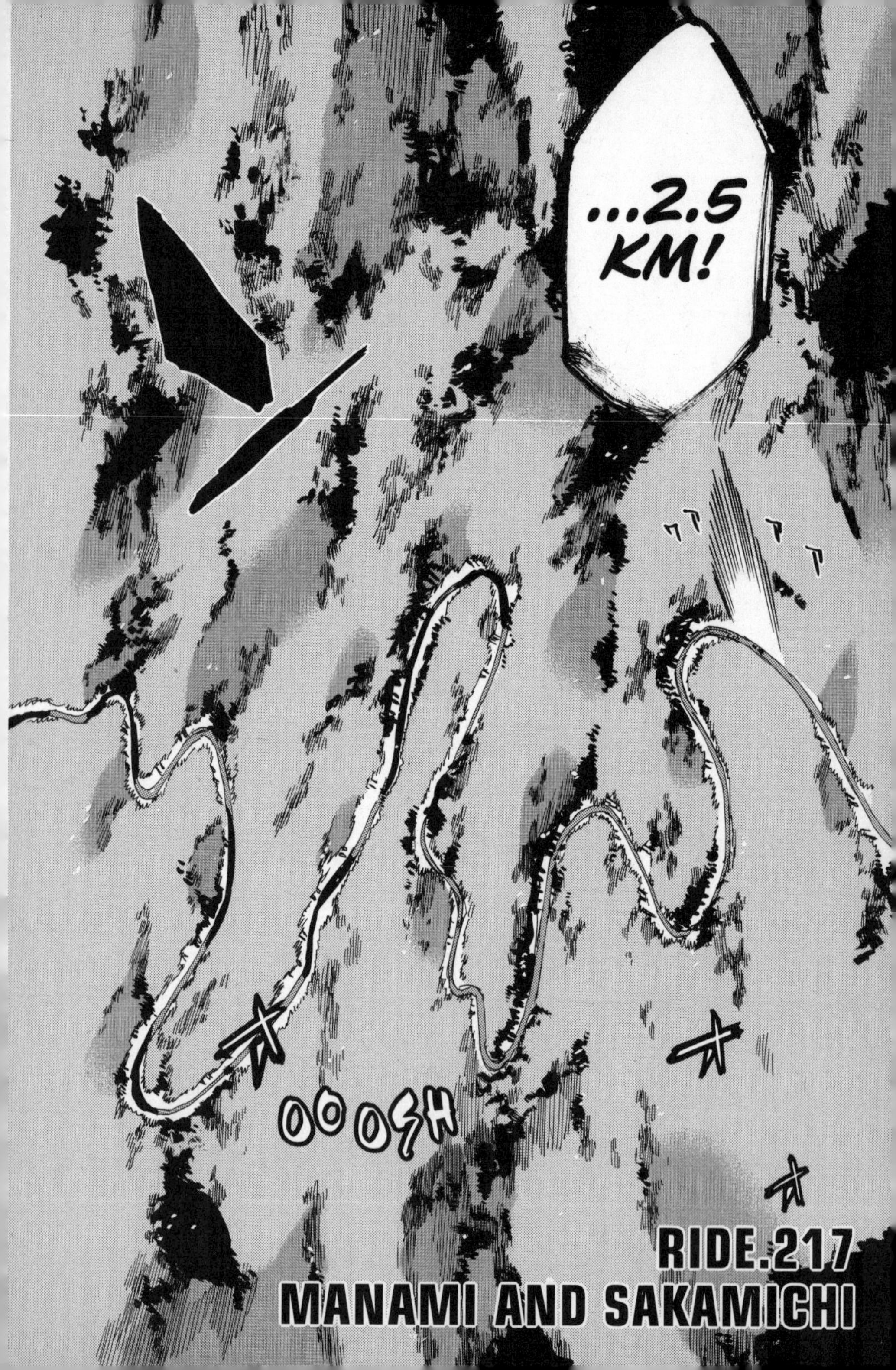
...2.5 KM!
OOOSH

RIDE.217
MANAMI AND SAKAMICHI

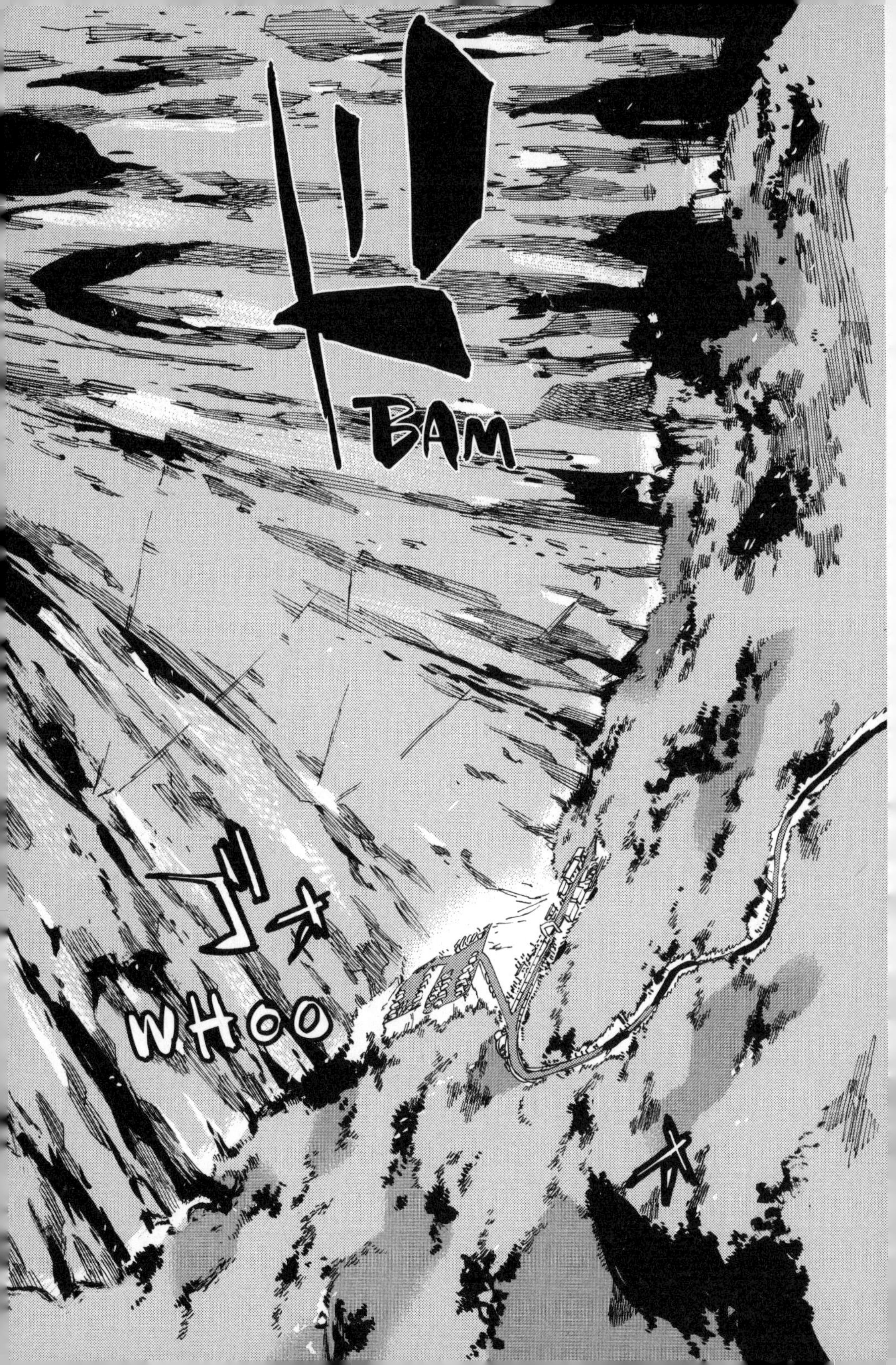

BAM
WHOO

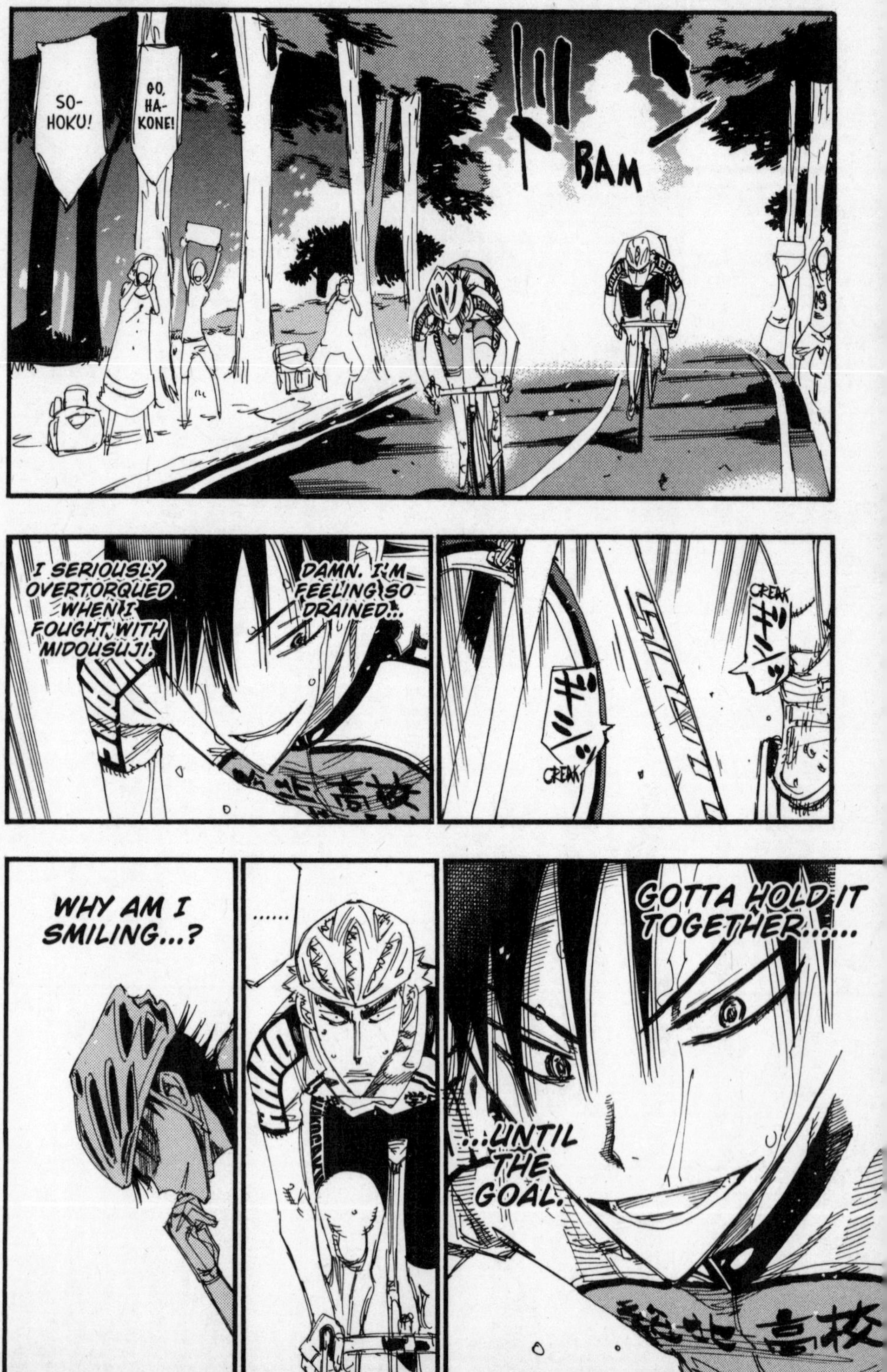

BAM
GO, HA-KONE!
SO-HOKU!
ギシッ
CREAK
ギシッ
CREAK
DAMN. I'M FEELING SO DRAINED...
I SERIOUSLY OVERTORQUED WHEN I FOUGHT WITH MIDOUSUJI.
GOTTA HOLD IT TOGETHER......
...UNTIL THE GOAL.
......
WHY AM I SMILING...?

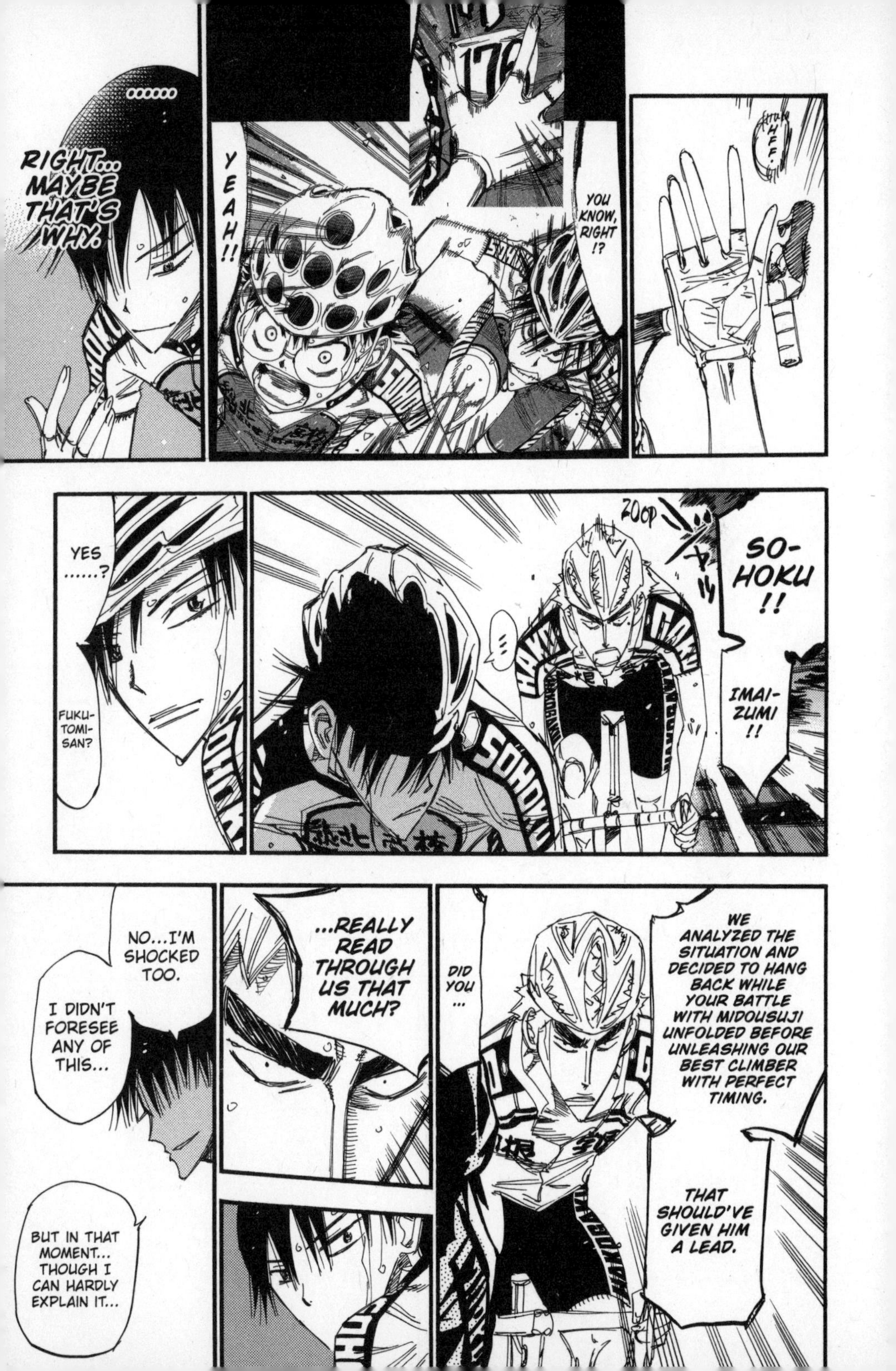
HFF
YOU KNOW, RIGHT!?
YEAH!!
......
RIGHT... MAYBE THAT'S WHY.
ZOOP
SO-HOKU!!
IMAI-ZUMI!!
YES ......?
FUKU-TOMI-SAN?
WE ANALYZED THE SITUATION AND DECIDED TO HANG BACK WHILE YOUR BATTLE WITH MIDOUSUJI UNFOLDED BEFORE UNLEASHING OUR BEST CLIMBER WITH PERFECT TIMING.
THAT SHOULD'VE GIVEN HIM A LEAD.
DID YOU ...
...REALLY READ THROUGH US THAT MUCH?
NO...I'M SHOCKED TOO.
I DIDN'T FORESEE ANY OF THIS...
BUT IN THAT MOMENT... THOUGH I CAN HARDLY EXPLAIN IT...

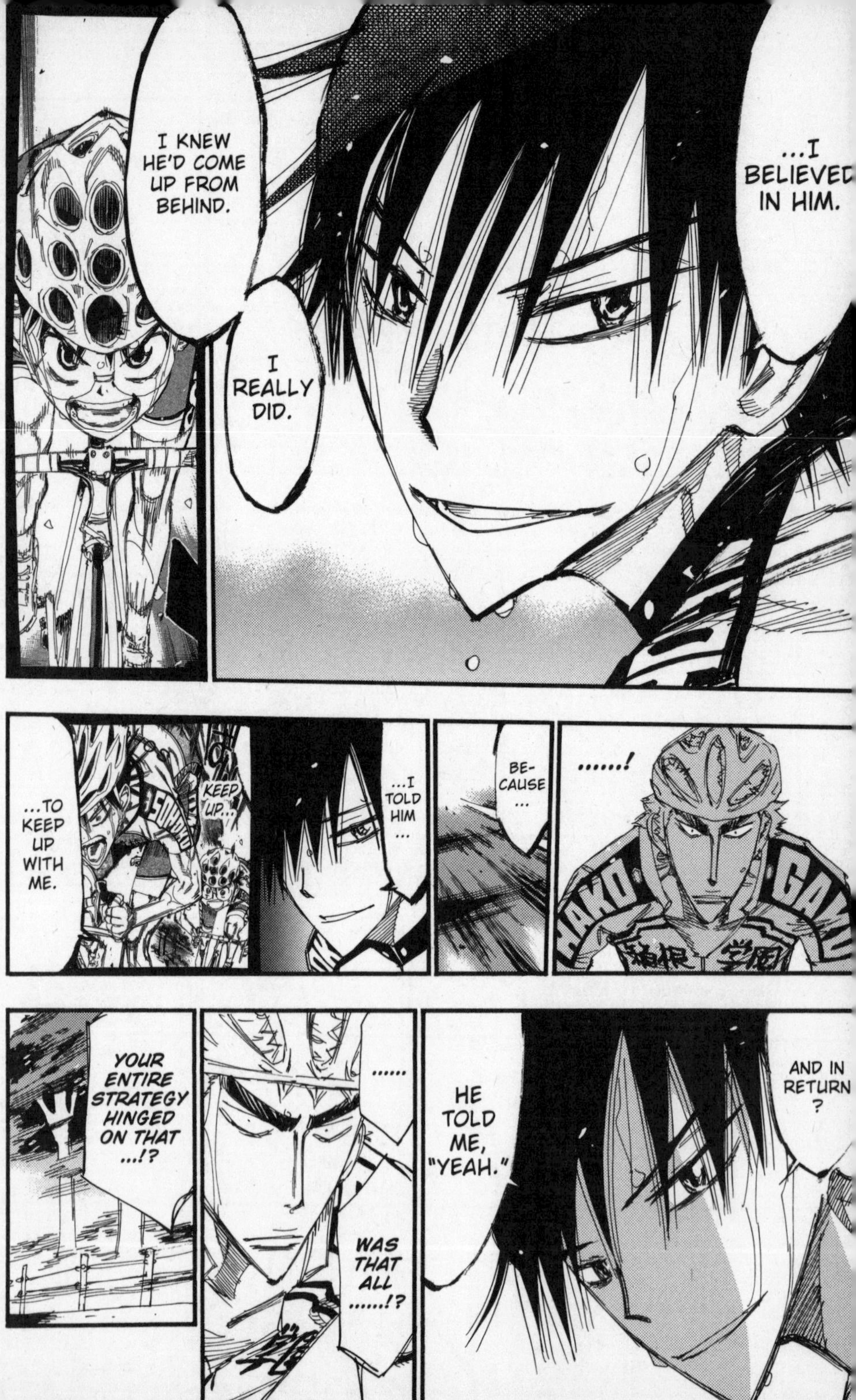
...I BELIEVED IN HIM.
I KNEW HE'D COME UP FROM BEHIND.
I REALLY DID.
......!
BE-CAUSE ...
...I TOLD HIM ...
...TO KEEP UP WITH ME.
KEEP UP...
AND IN RETURN ?
HE TOLD ME, "YEAH."
......
WAS THAT ALL ......!?
YOUR ENTIRE STRATEGY HINGED ON THAT ...!?

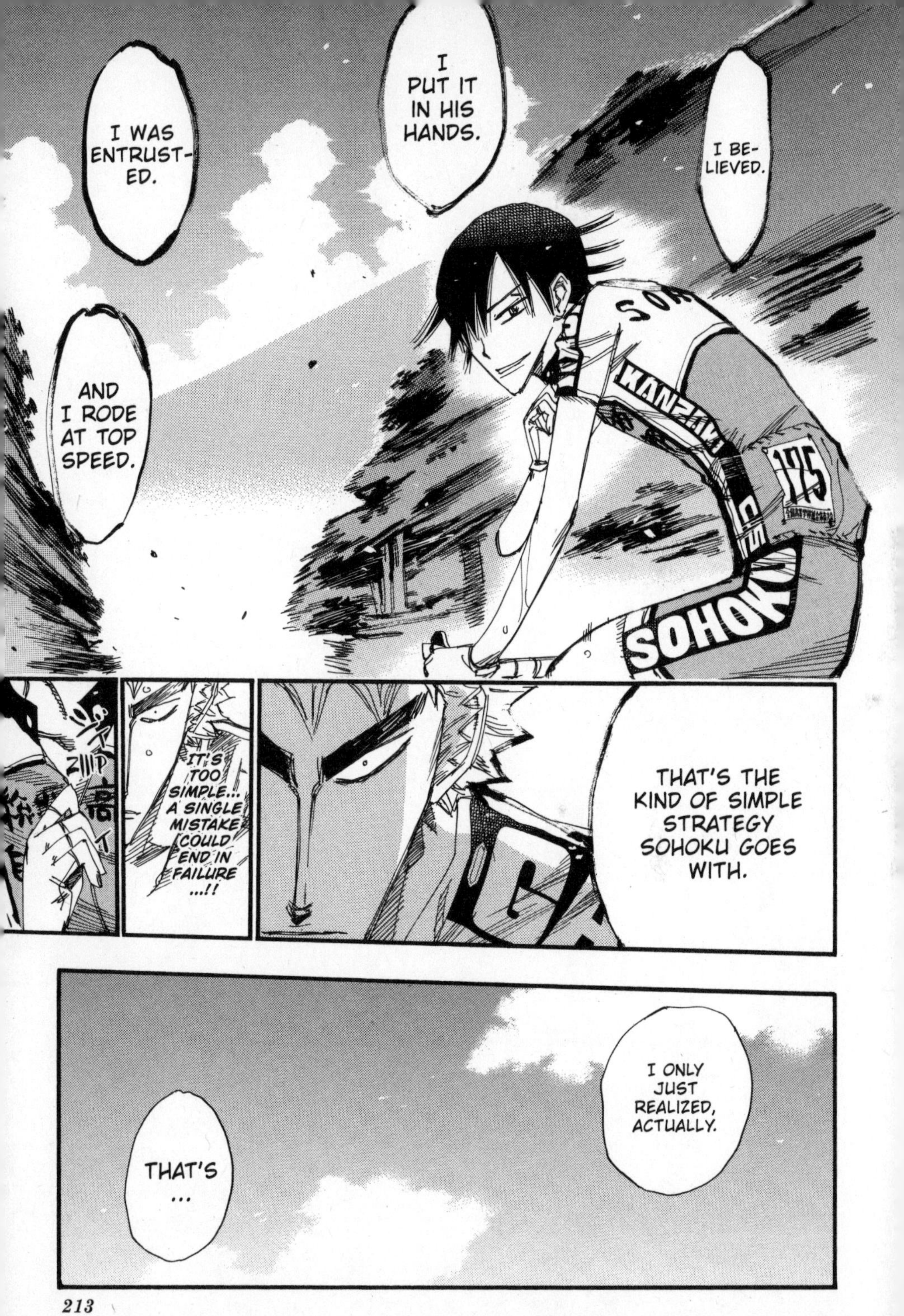
I BE-LIEVED.
I PUT IT IN HIS HANDS.
I WAS ENTRUST-ED.
AND I RODE AT TOP SPEED.
THAT'S THE KIND OF SIMPLE STRATEGY SOHOKU GOES WITH.
IT'S TOO SIMPLE... A SINGLE MISTAKE COULD END IN FAILURE ...!!
ZIIIP
I ONLY JUST REALIZED, ACTUALLY.
THAT'S ...

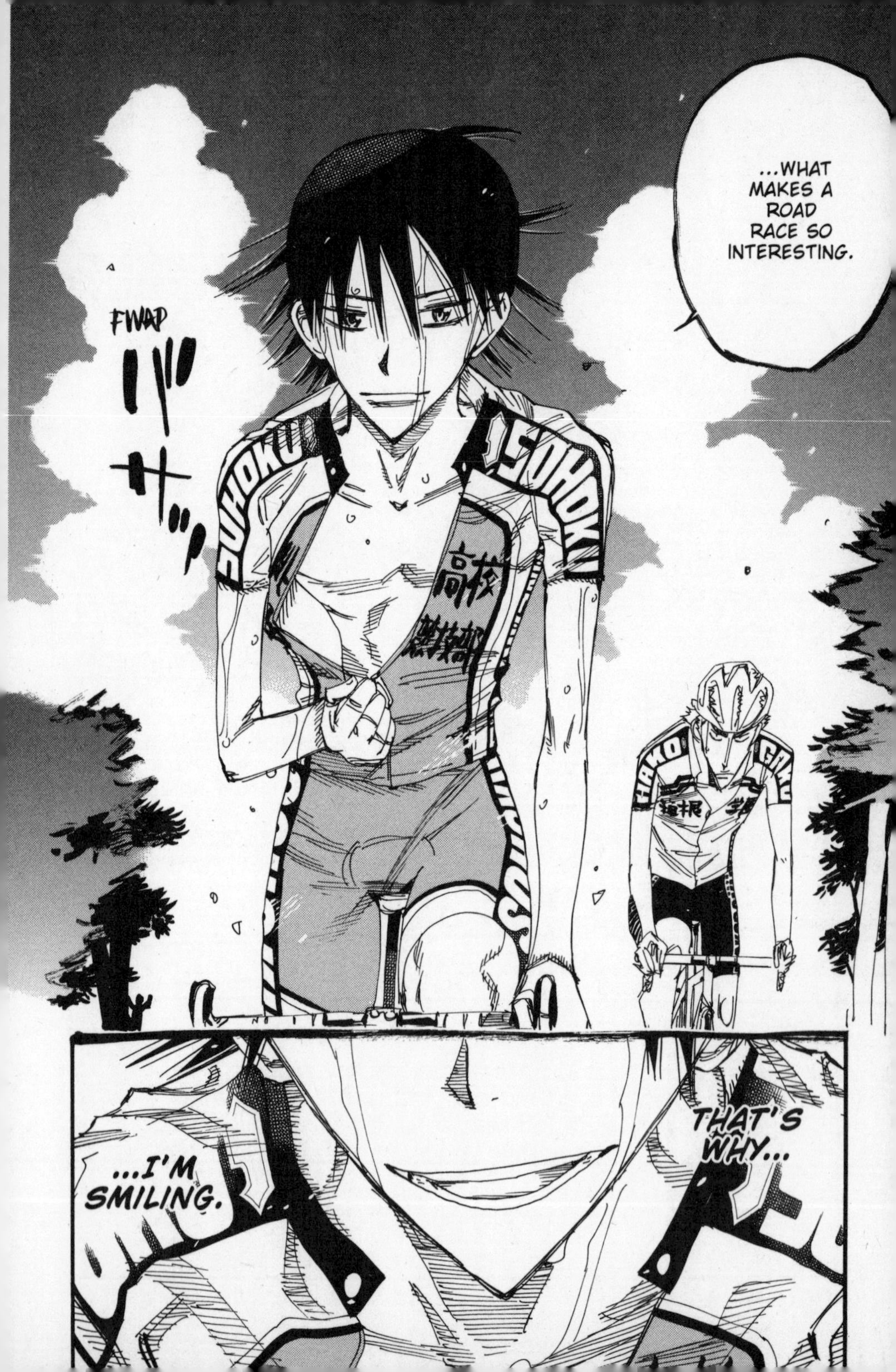
...WHAT MAKES A ROAD RACE SO INTERESTING.
FWAP
THAT'S WHY...
...I'M SMILING.

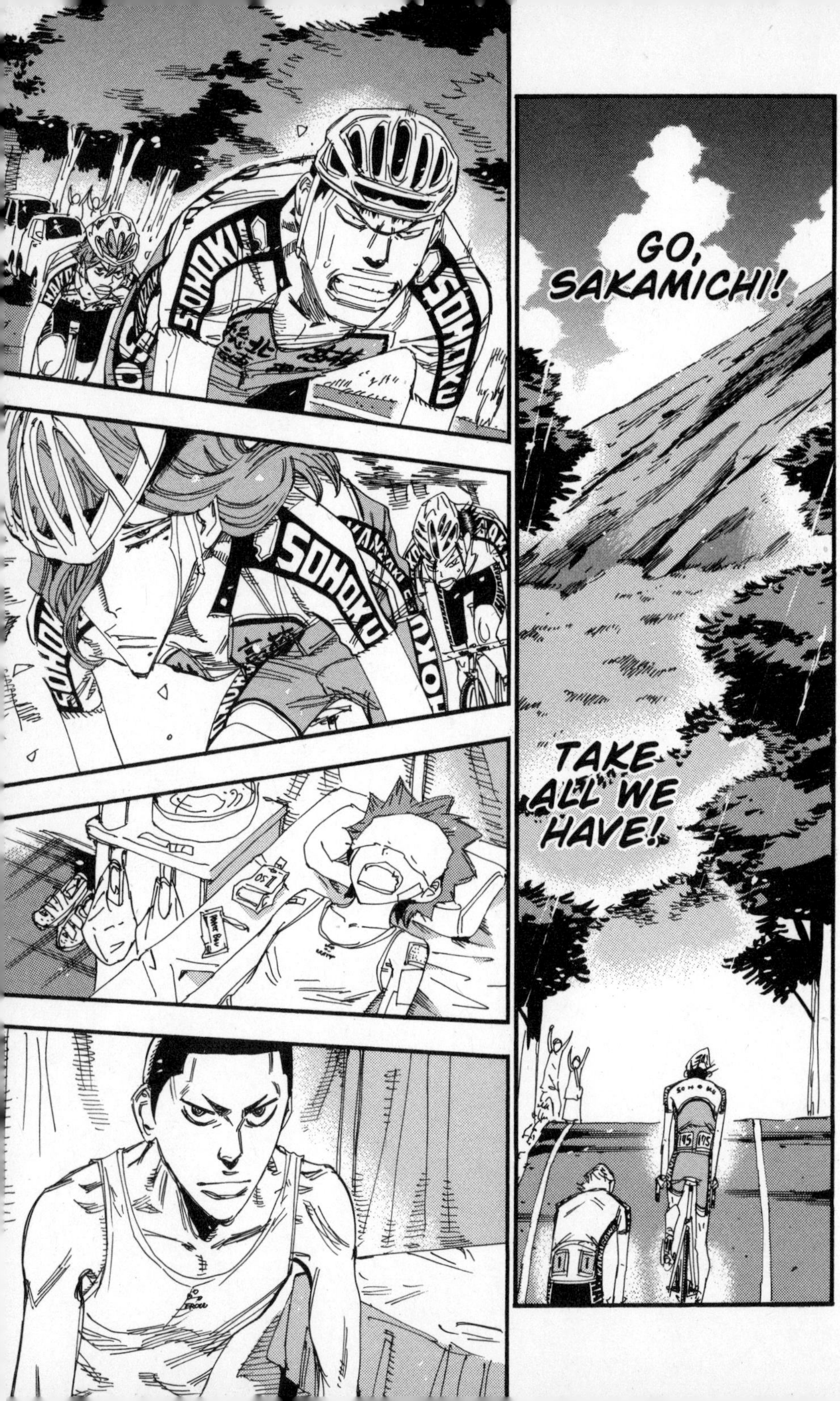
GO, SAKAMICHI!
TAKE ALL WE HAVE!

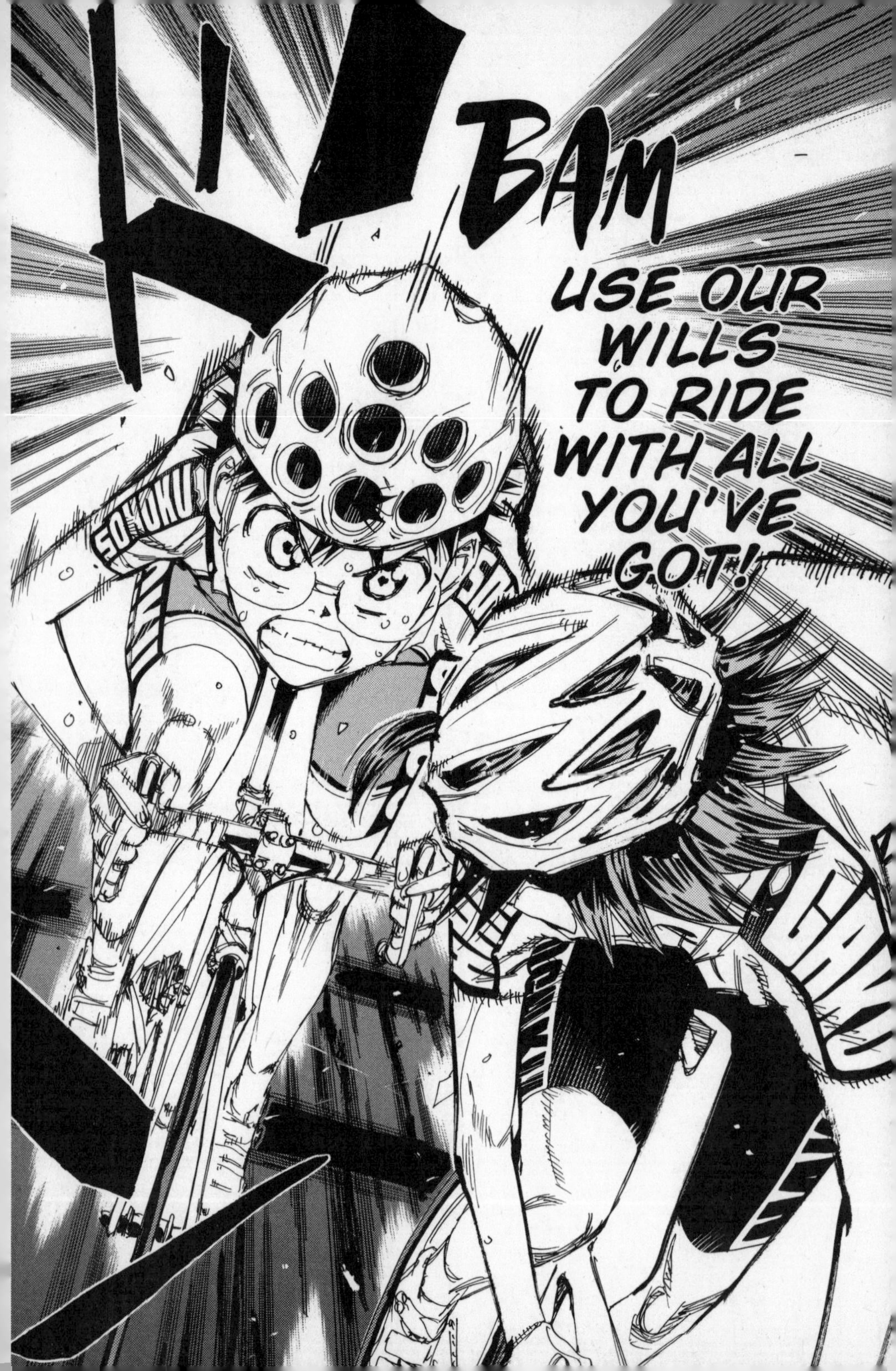
BAM
USE OUR WILLS TO RIDE WITH ALL YOU'VE GOT!
SOHOKU

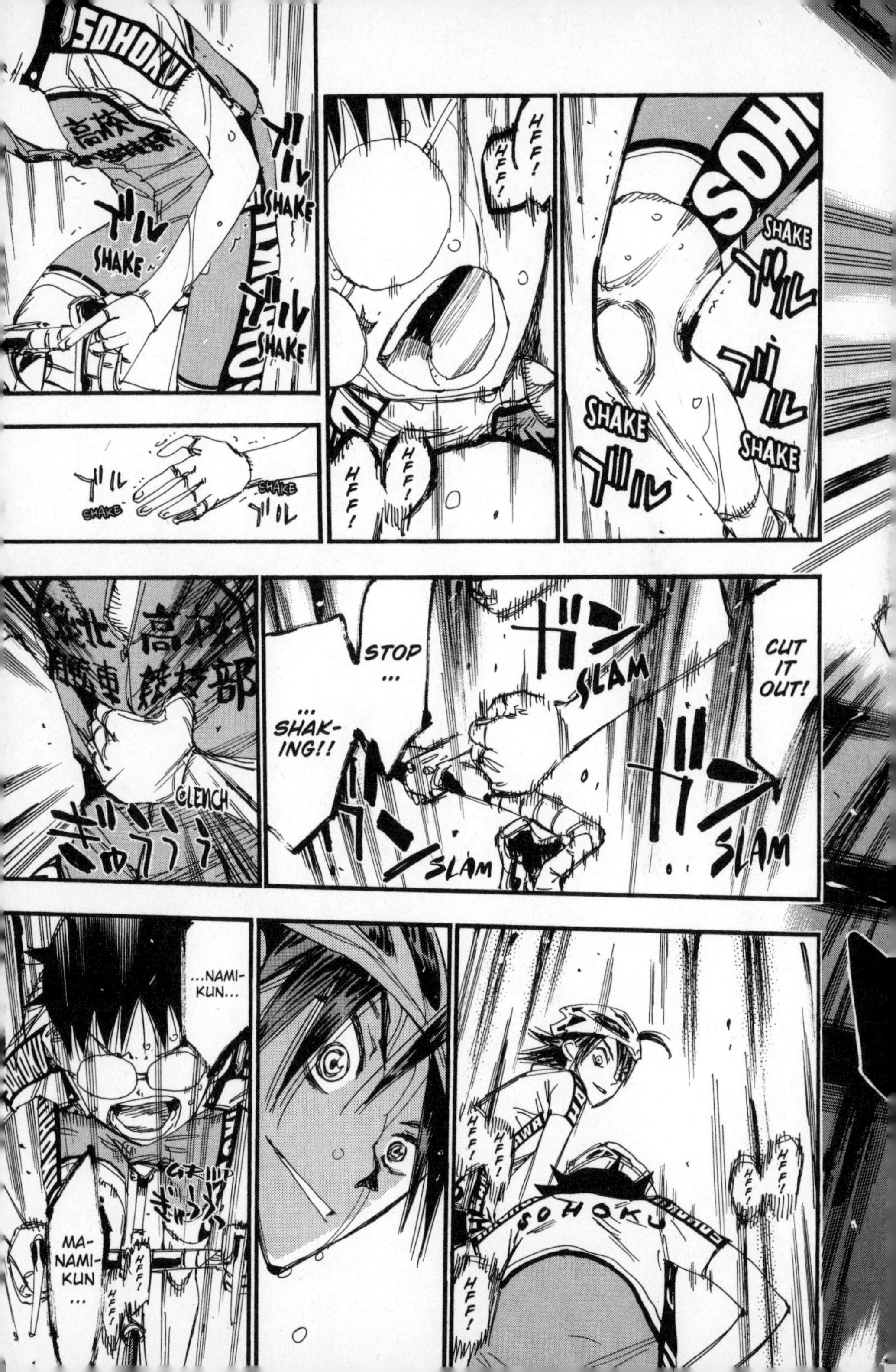

SHAKE
SHAKE
SHAKE
HFF! HFF!
HFF! HFF!
SHAKE
SHAKE
SHAKE
SHAKE
SHAKE
CUT IT OUT!
SLAM
SLAM
STOP...
...SHAKING!!
SLAM
CLENCH
HFF! HFF!
HFF! HFF!
...NAMI-KUN...
MA-NAMI-KUN...
HFF! HFF!

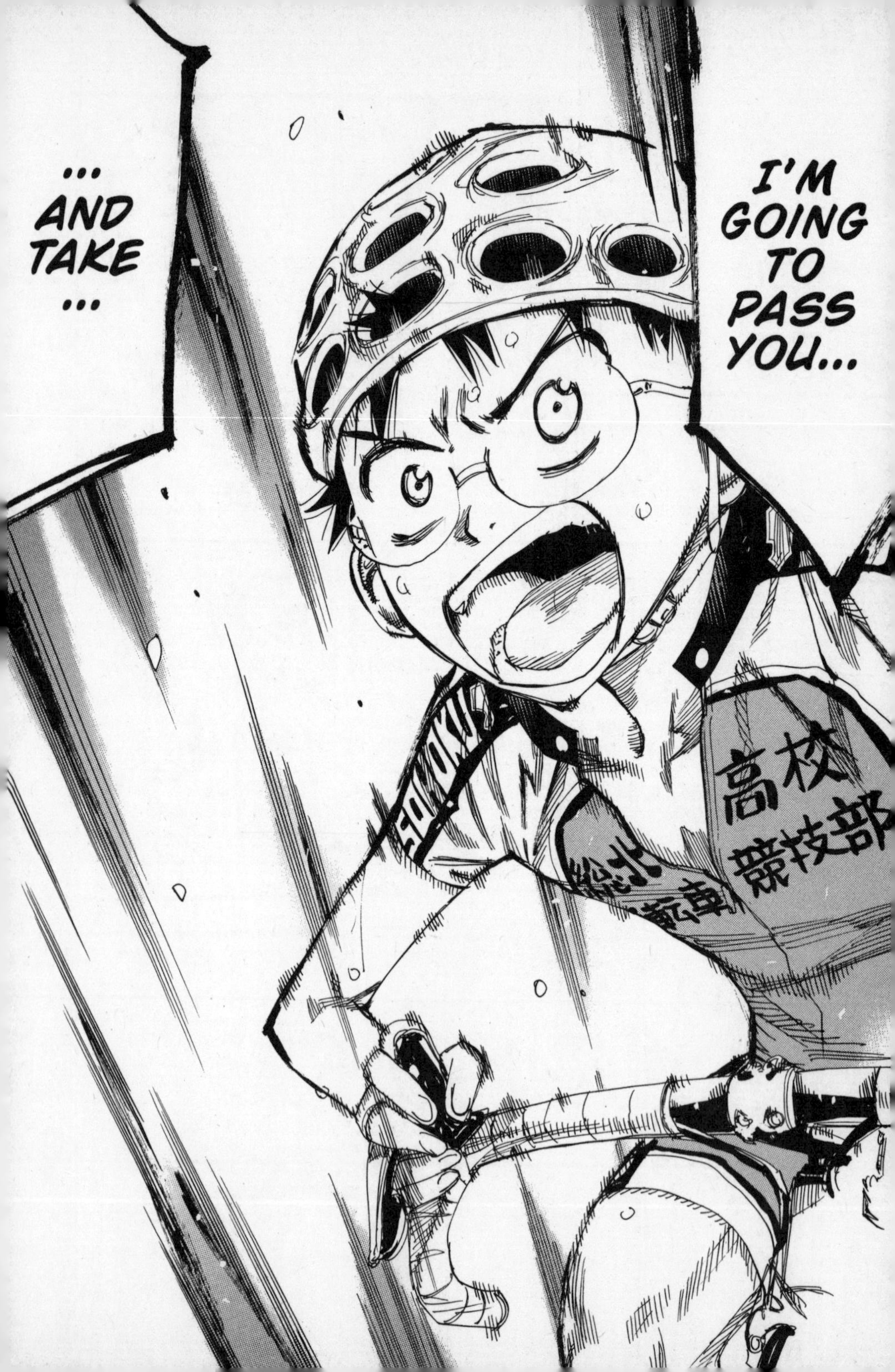
I'M GOING TO PASS YOU...
...AND TAKE...

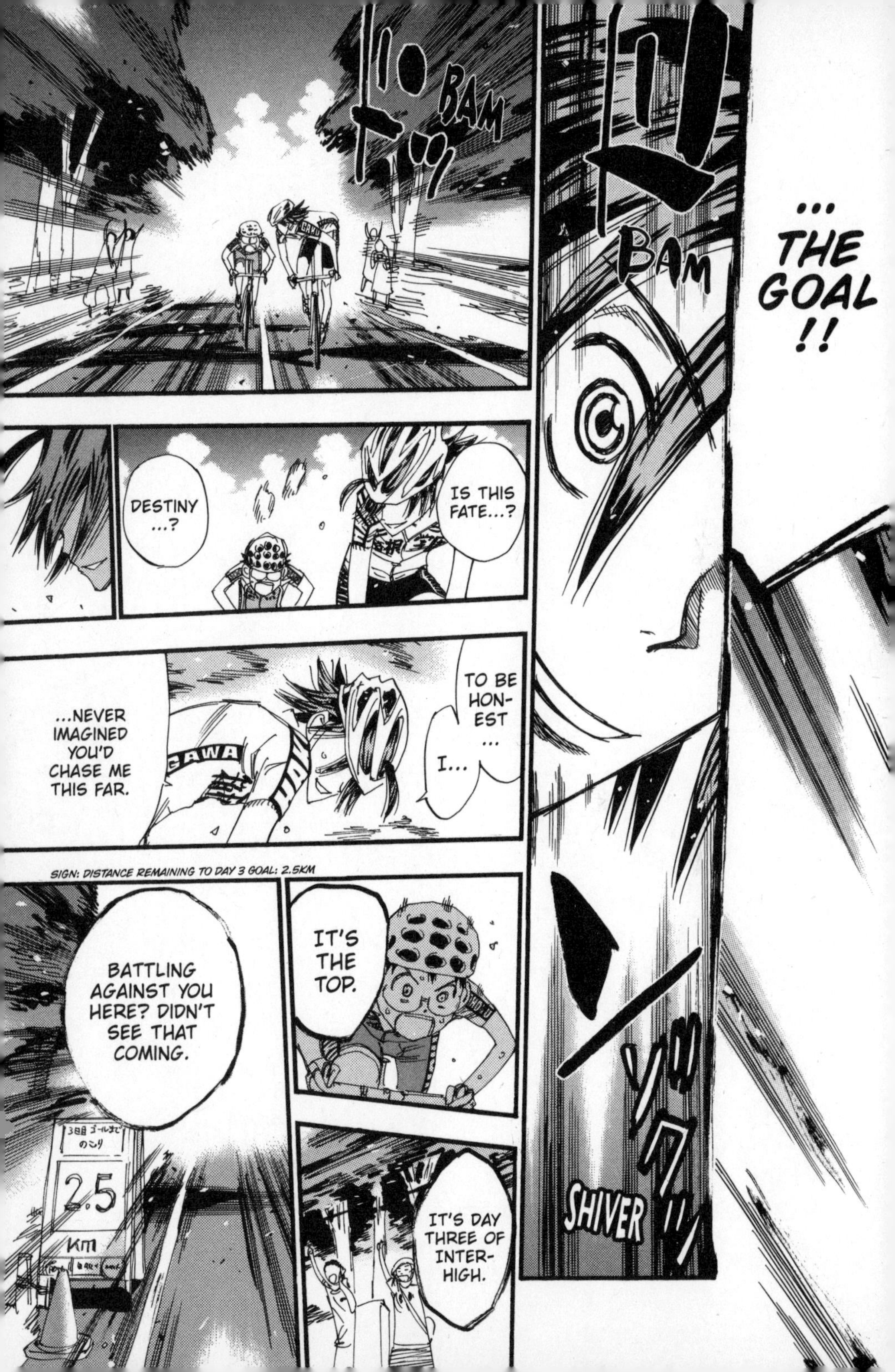
... THE GOAL !!
BAM
BAM
SHIVER
BAM
IS THIS FATE...?
DESTINY ...?
TO BE HONEST ... I...
...NEVER IMAGINED YOU'D CHASE ME THIS FAR.
SIGN: DISTANCE REMAINING TO DAY 3 GOAL: 2.5KM
IT'S THE TOP.
IT'S DAY THREE OF INTER-HIGH.
BATTLING AGAINST YOU HERE? DIDN'T SEE THAT COMING.
2.5
KM

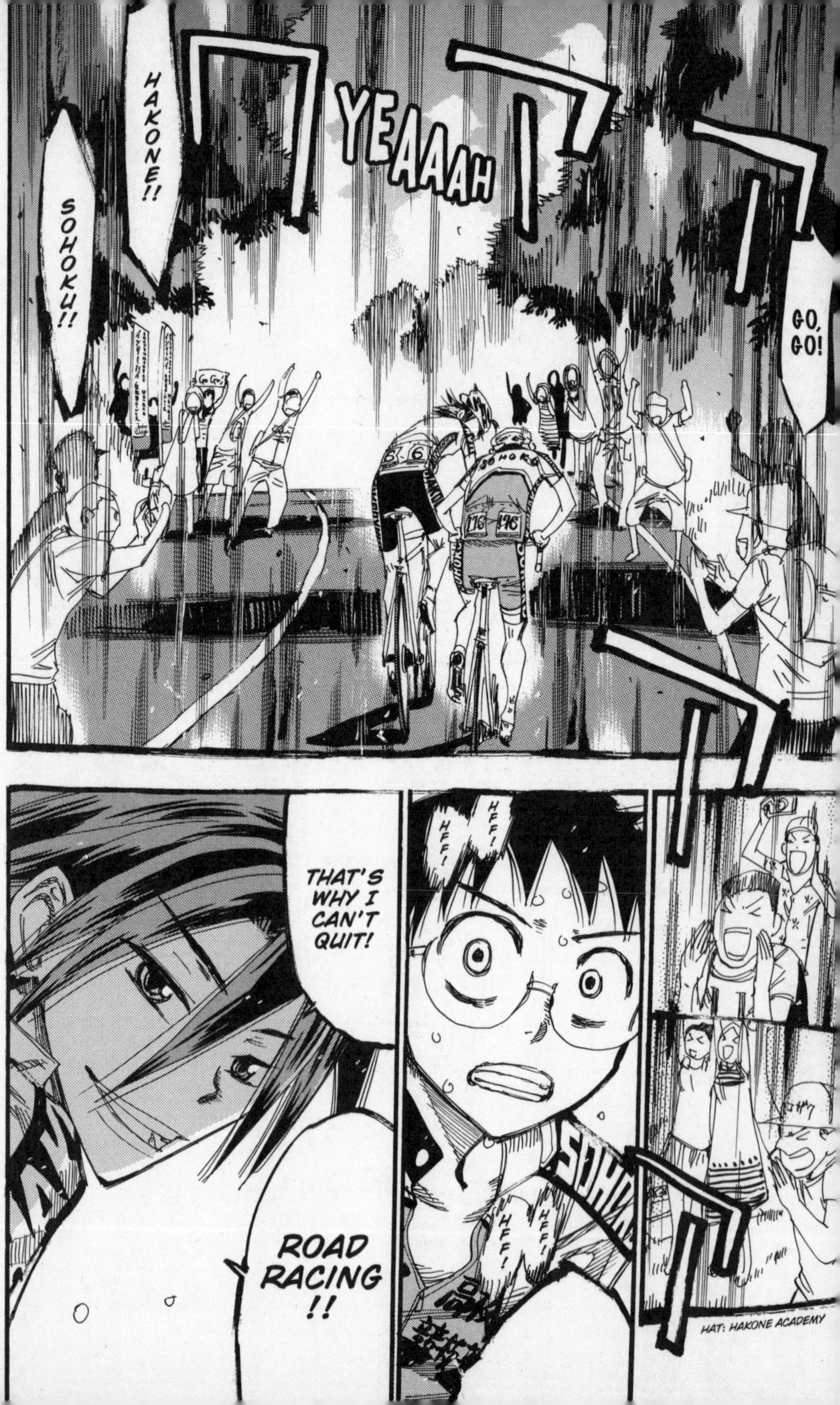
YEAAAH
GO, GO!
HAKONE!!
SOHOKU!!
HAT: HAKONE ACADEMY
HFF! HFF!
HFF! HFF!
THAT'S WHY I CAN'T QUIT!
ROAD RACING!!

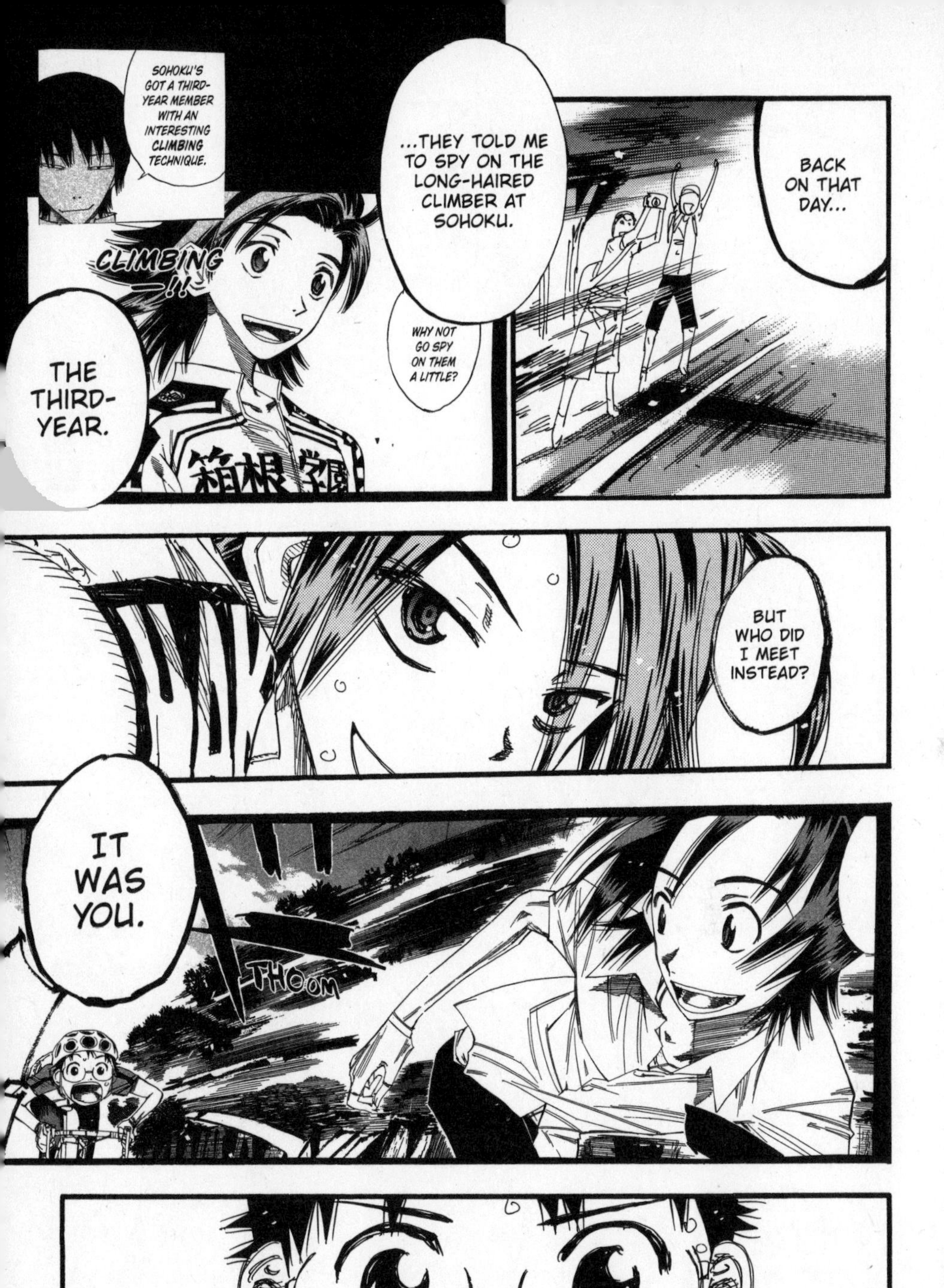
BACK ON THAT DAY...
...THEY TOLD ME TO SPY ON THE LONG-HAIRED CLIMBER AT SOHOKU.
SOHOKU'S GOT A THIRD-YEAR MEMBER WITH AN INTERESTING CLIMBING TECHNIQUE.
WHY NOT GO SPY ON THEM A LITTLE?
CLIMBING—!!
THE THIRD-YEAR.
BUT WHO DID I MEET INSTEAD?
IT WAS YOU.
THOOM

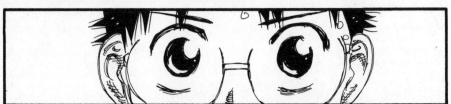

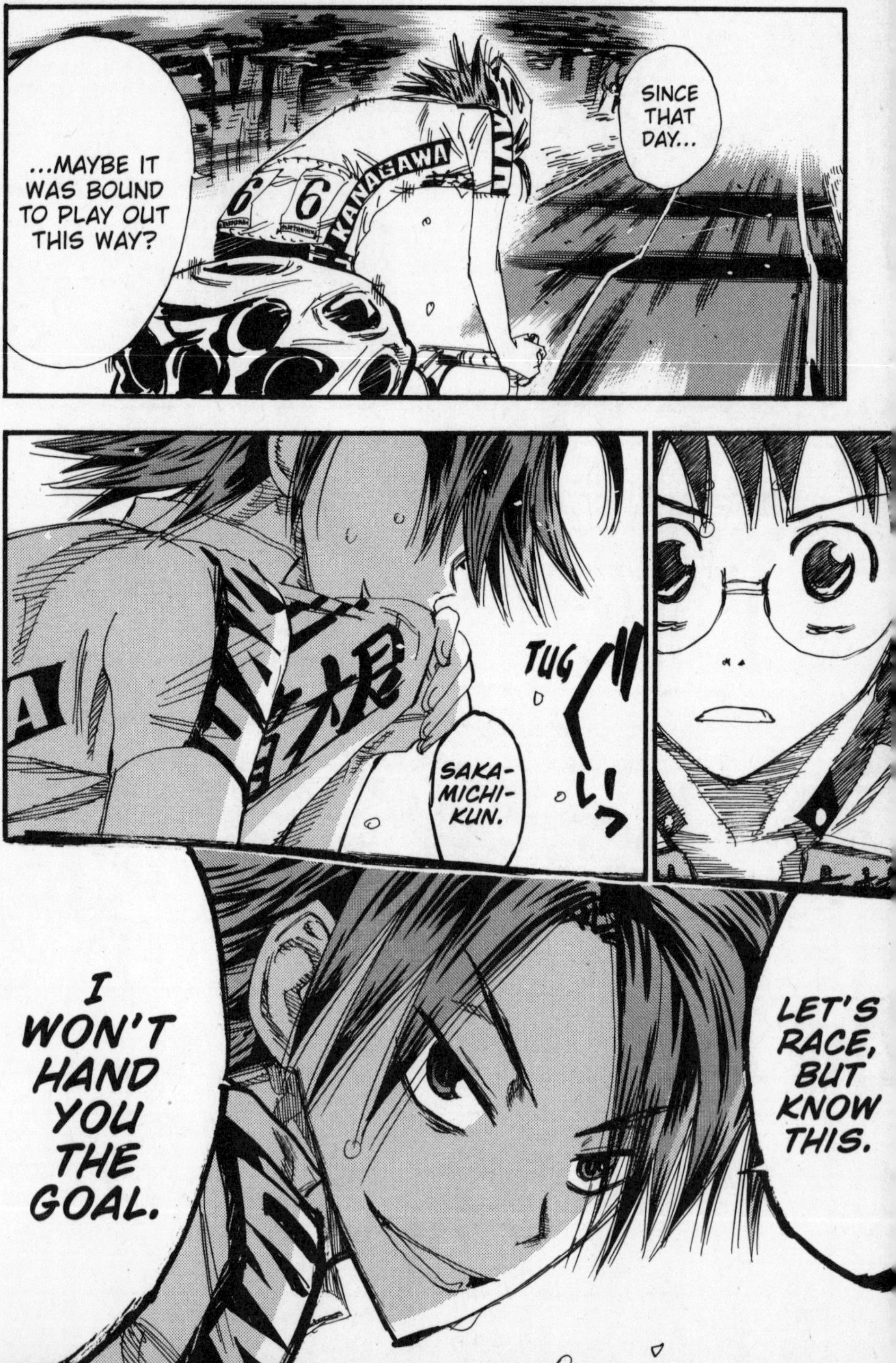

SINCE THAT DAY...
...MAYBE IT WAS BOUND TO PLAY OUT THIS WAY?
KANAGAWA
TUG
SAKA-MICHI-KUN.
LET'S RACE, BUT KNOW THIS.
I WON'T HAND YOU THE GOAL.

RIDE.218 WILL TO FIGHT

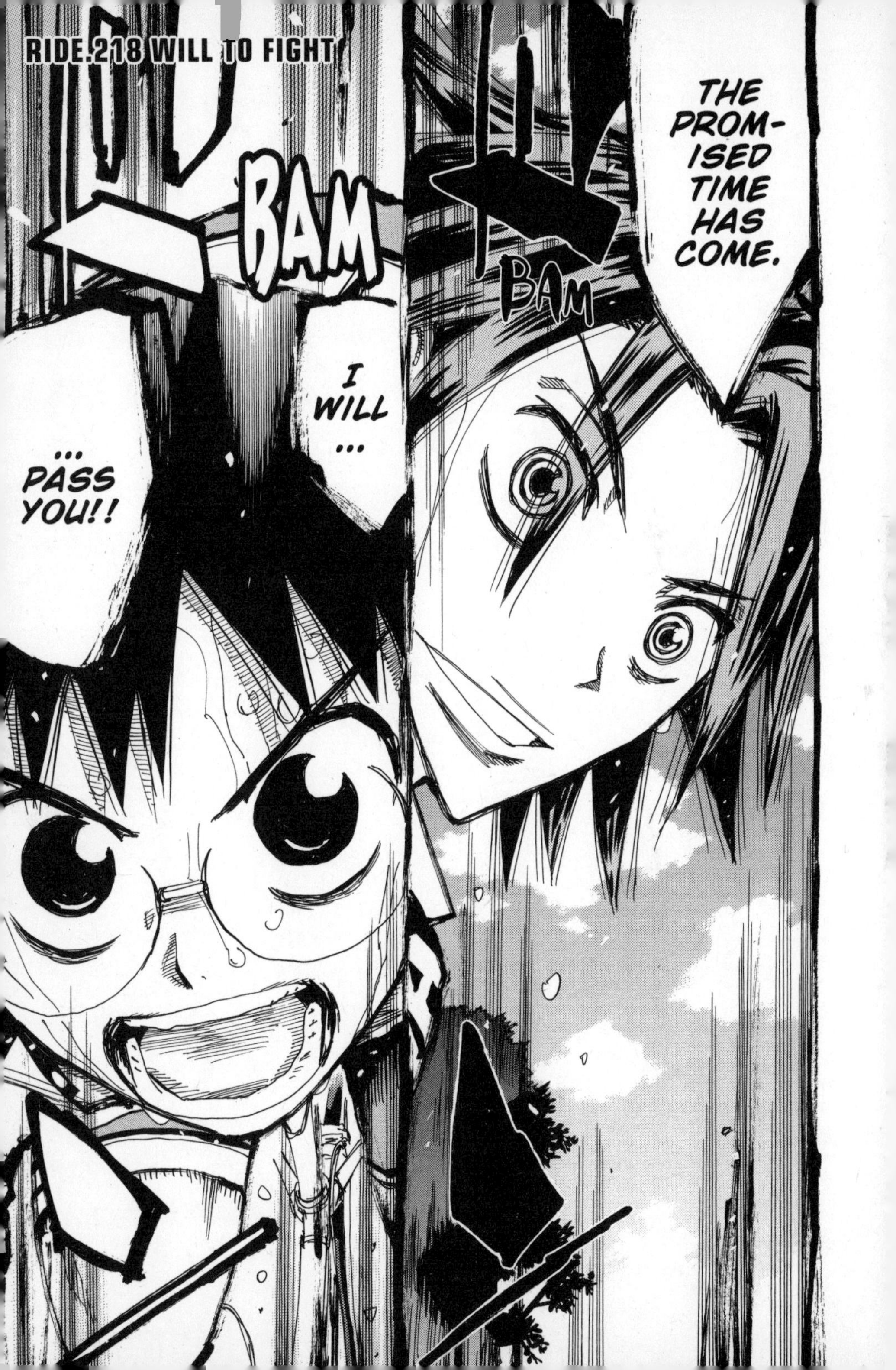
THE PROMISED TIME HAS COME.
BAM
BAM
I WILL ...
... PASS YOU!!

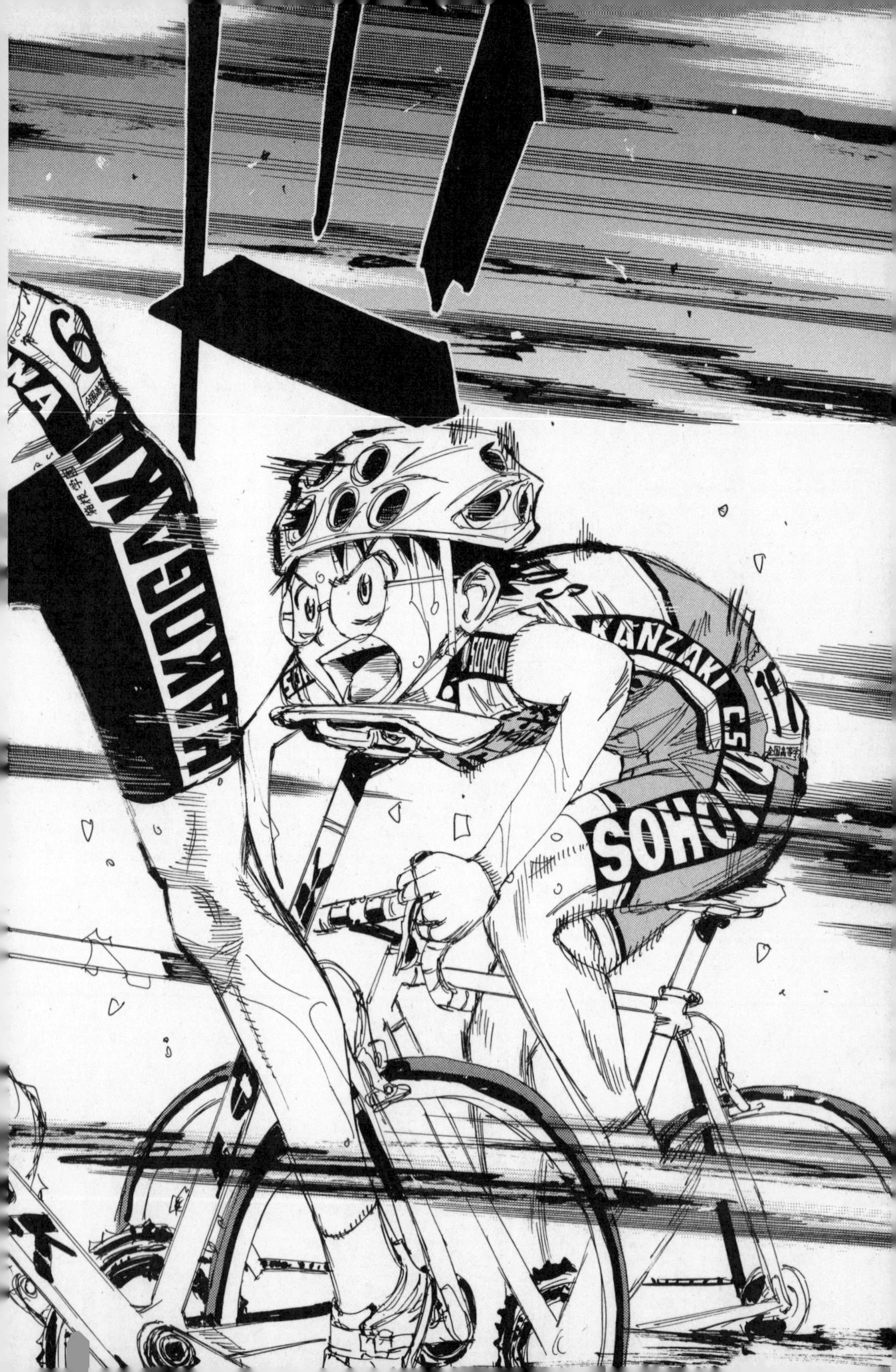
KANZAKI
SOHOKU
SOHO

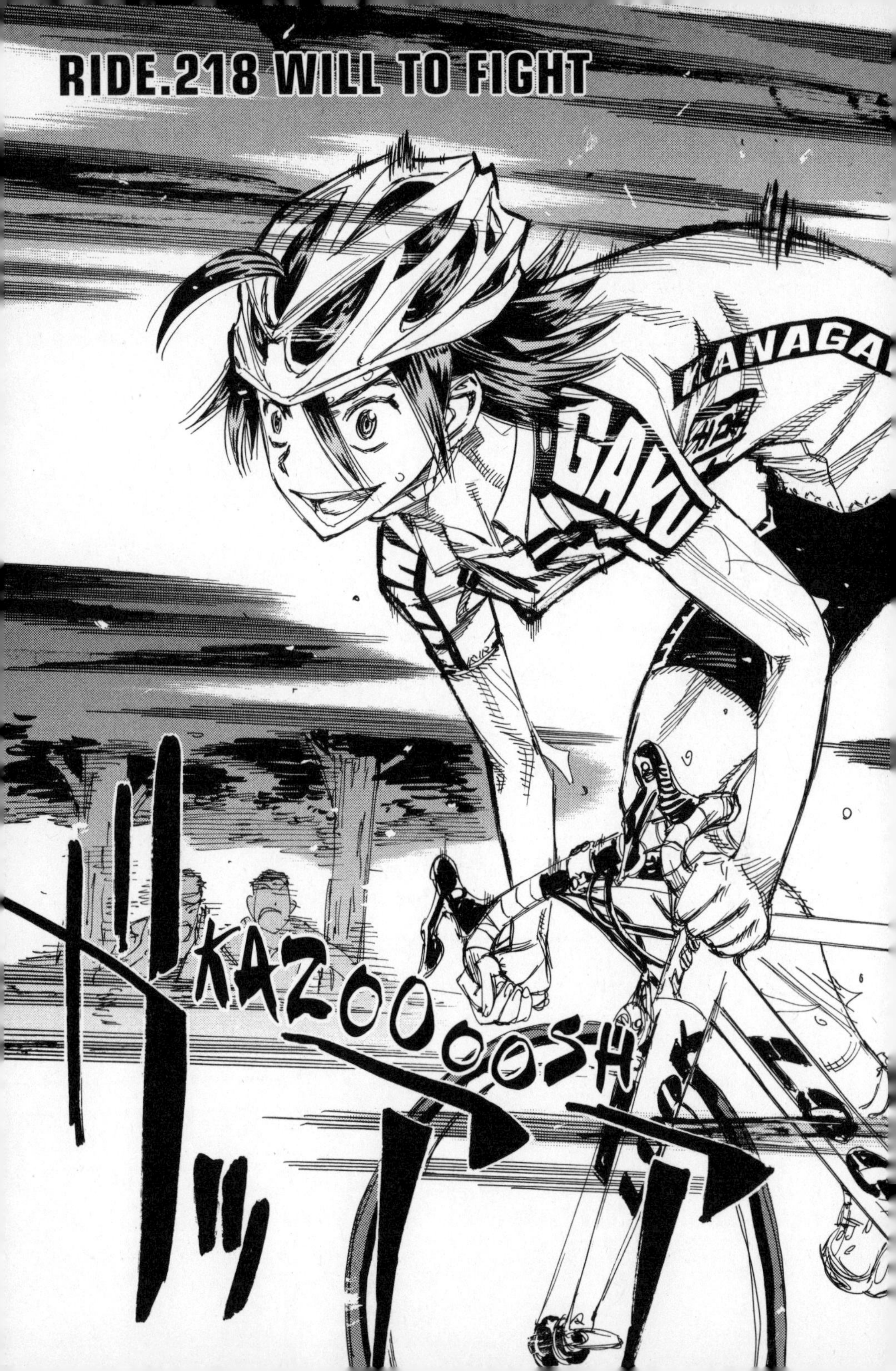
RIDE.218 WILL TO FIGHT
KANAGA
GAKU
KAZOOOOOSH

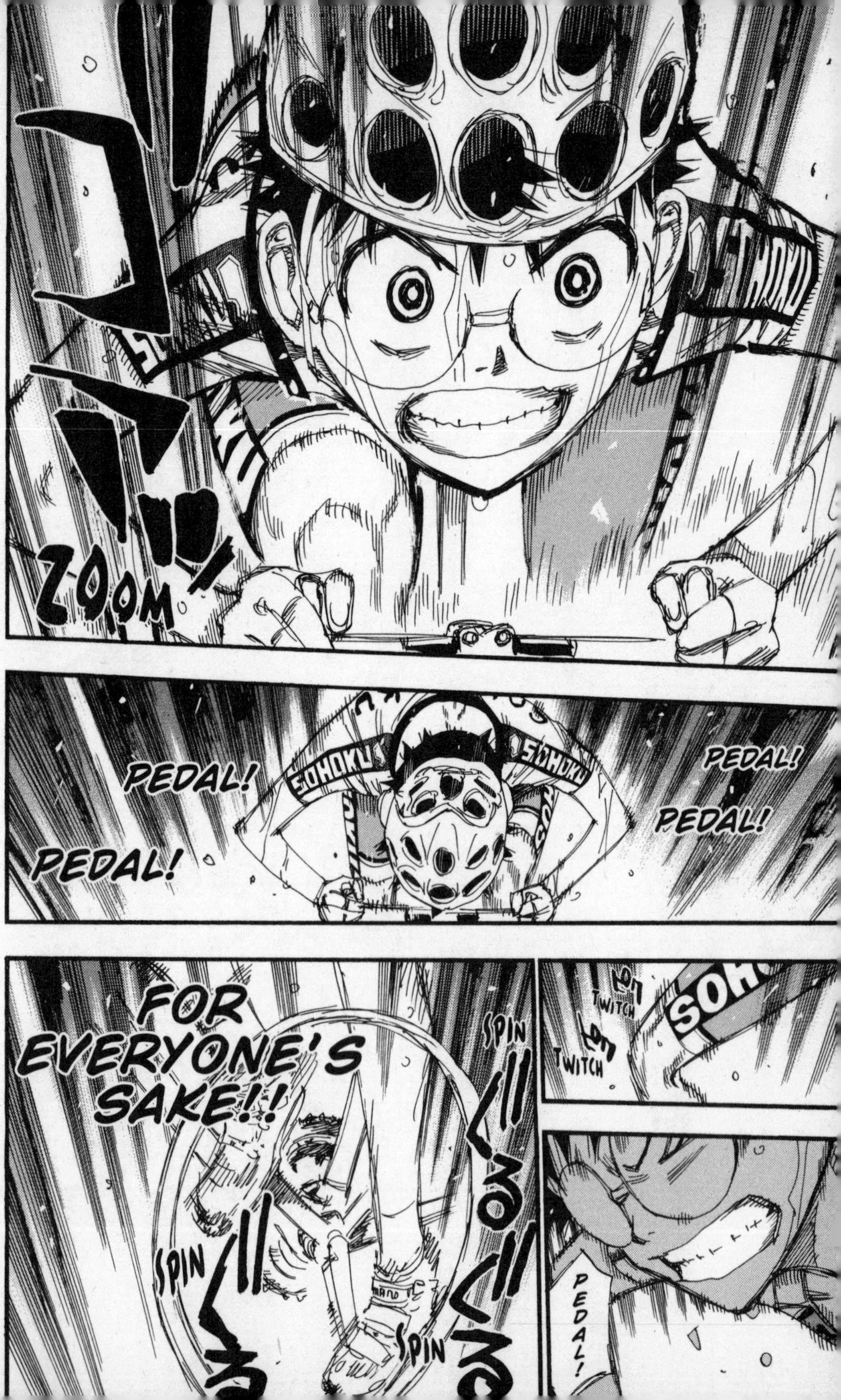
ZOOM
PEDAL!
PEDAL!
PEDAL!
PEDAL!
FOR EVERYONE'S SAKE!!
SPIN
SPIN
SPIN
TWITCH
TWITCH
PEDAL!

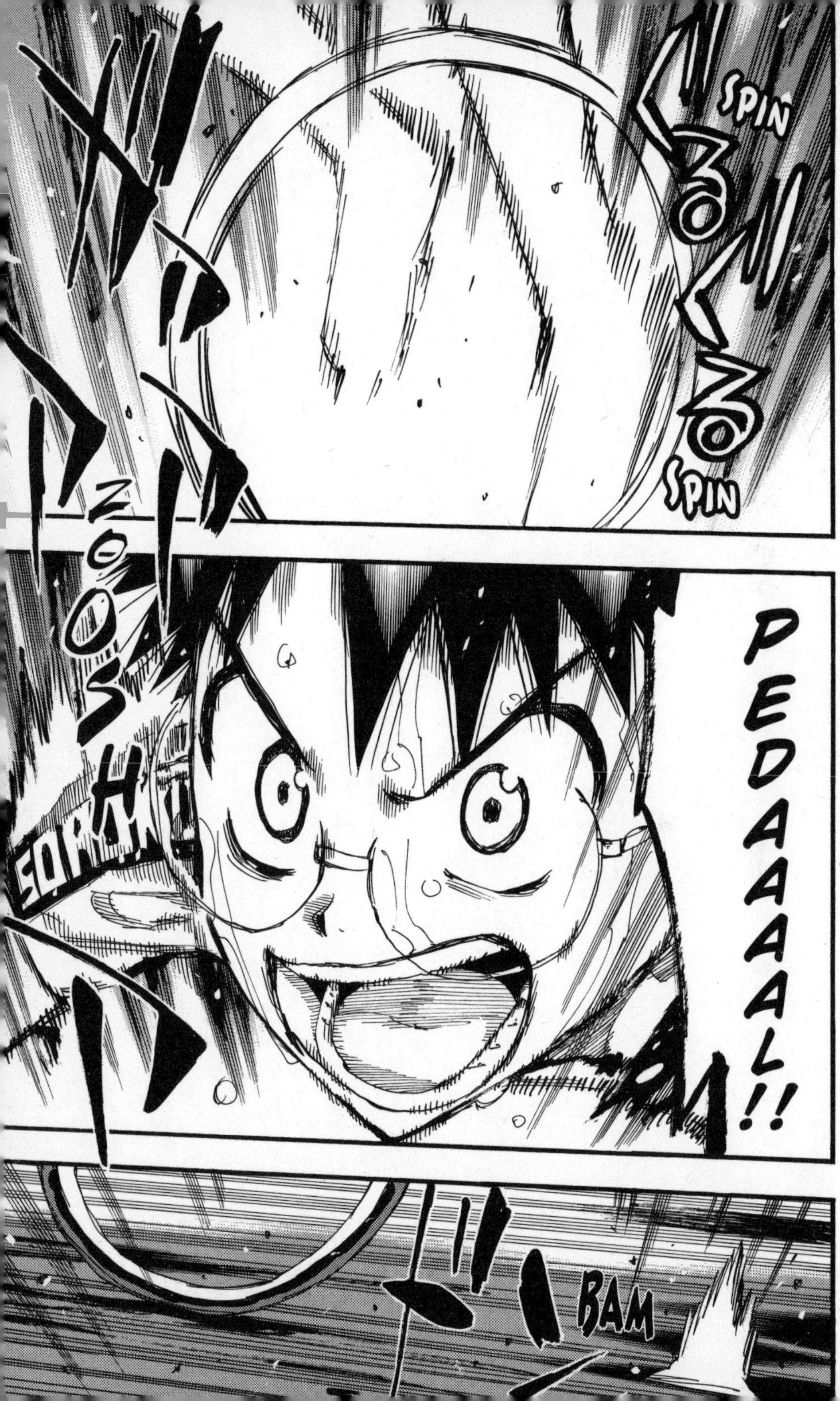
SPIN
SPIN
ZOOOSH
PEDAAAAL!!
BAM

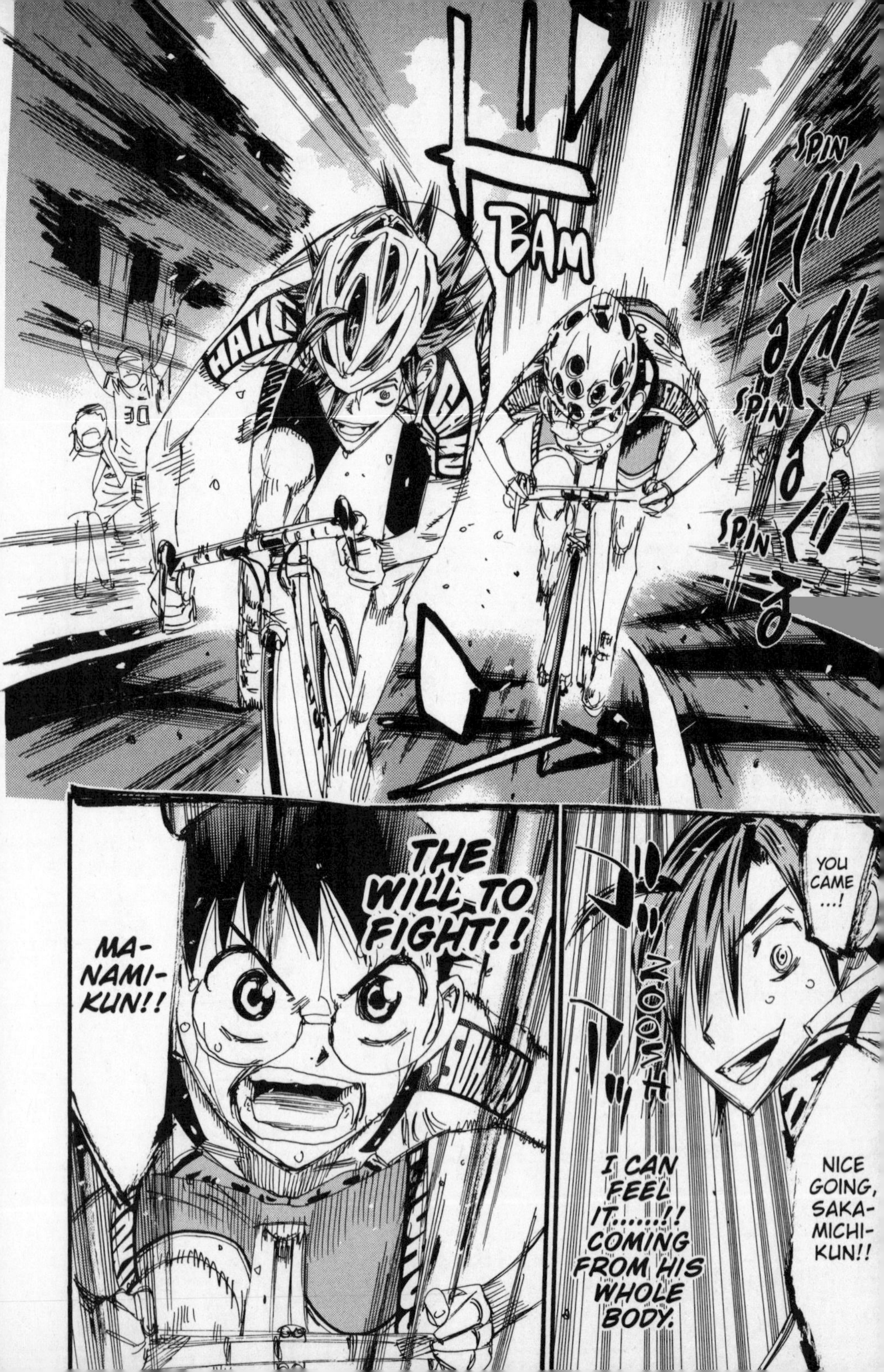
SPIN
BAM
SPIN
SPIN
YOU CAME ...!
WHOOSH
NICE GOING, SAKA-MICHI-KUN!!
I CAN FEEL IT......!! COMING FROM HIS WHOLE BODY.
THE WILL TO FIGHT!!
MA-NAMI-KUN!!

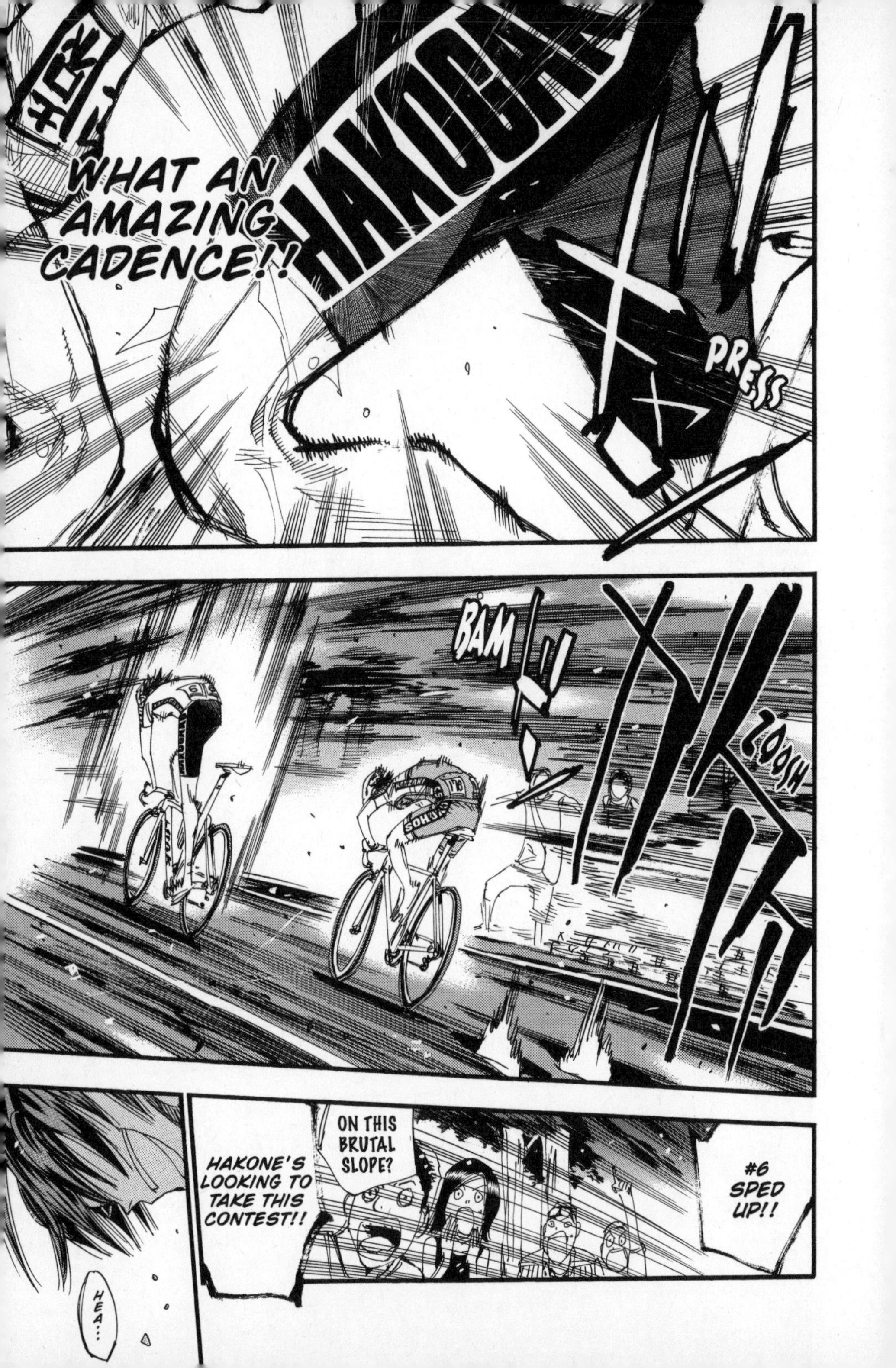
HAKOGA
WHAT AN AMAZING CADENCE!!
PRESS
BAM!!
ZOOSH
#6 SPED UP!!
ON THIS BRUTAL SLOPE?
HAKONE'S LOOKING TO TAKE THIS CONTEST!!
HEA...

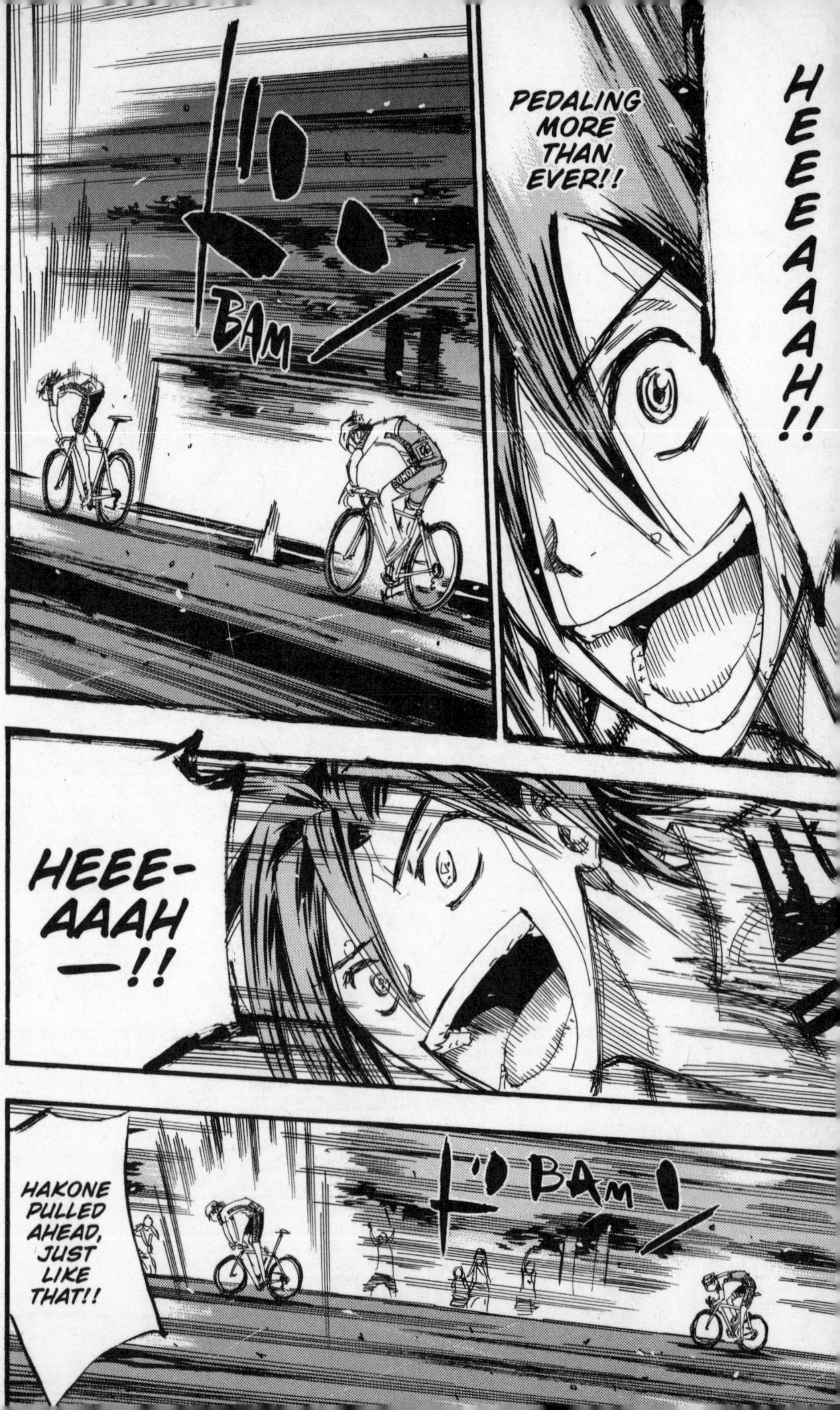
HEEEEAAAAH!!
PEDALING MORE THAN EVER!!
BAM
HEEE-AAAH—!!
BAM
HAKONE PULLED AHEAD, JUST LIKE THAT!!

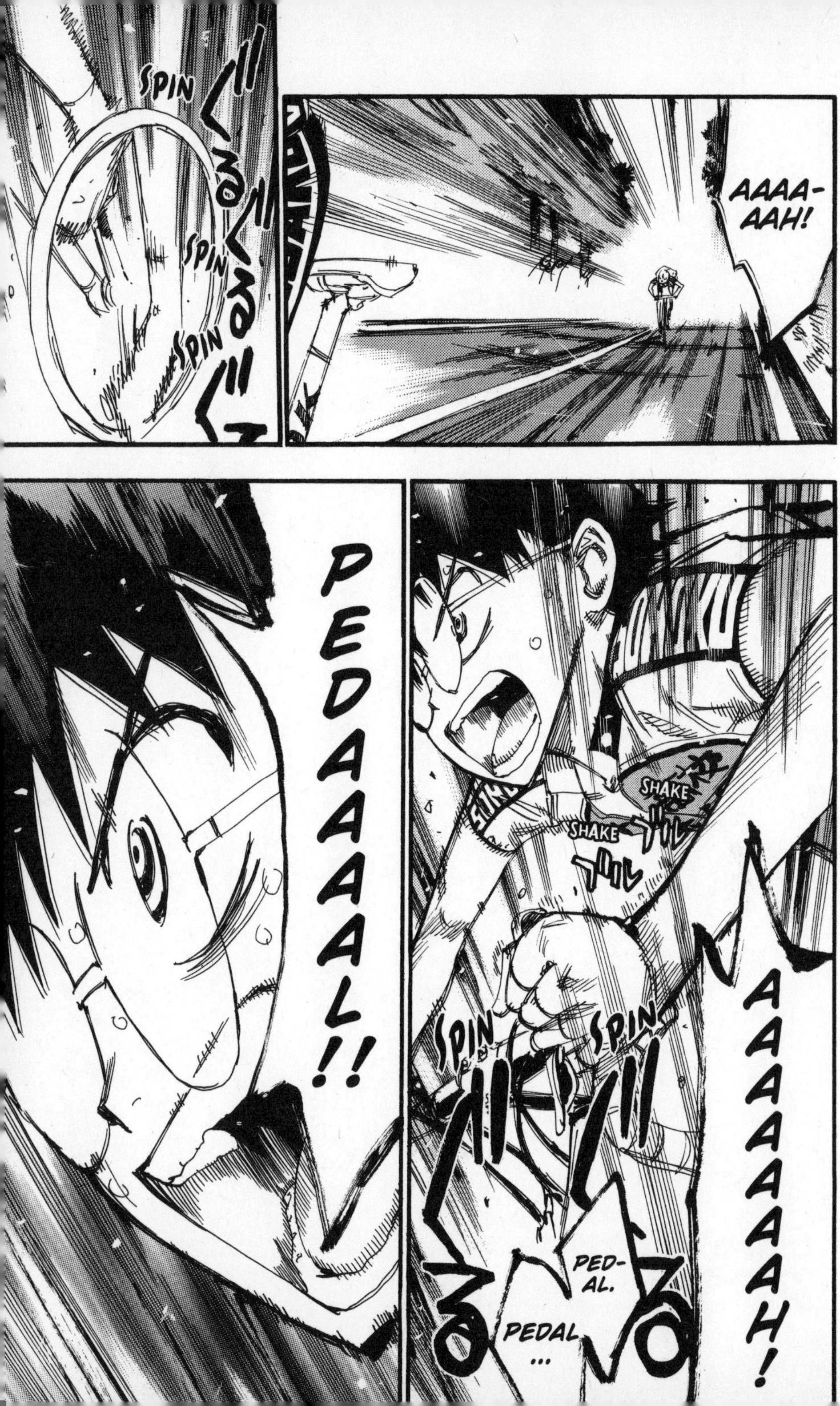
AAAA-
AAH!
SPIN
SPIN
SPIN
SHAKE
SHAKE
AAAAAAAAAAH!
SPIN
SPIN
PED-
AL.
PEDAL
...
PEDAAAAAL!!

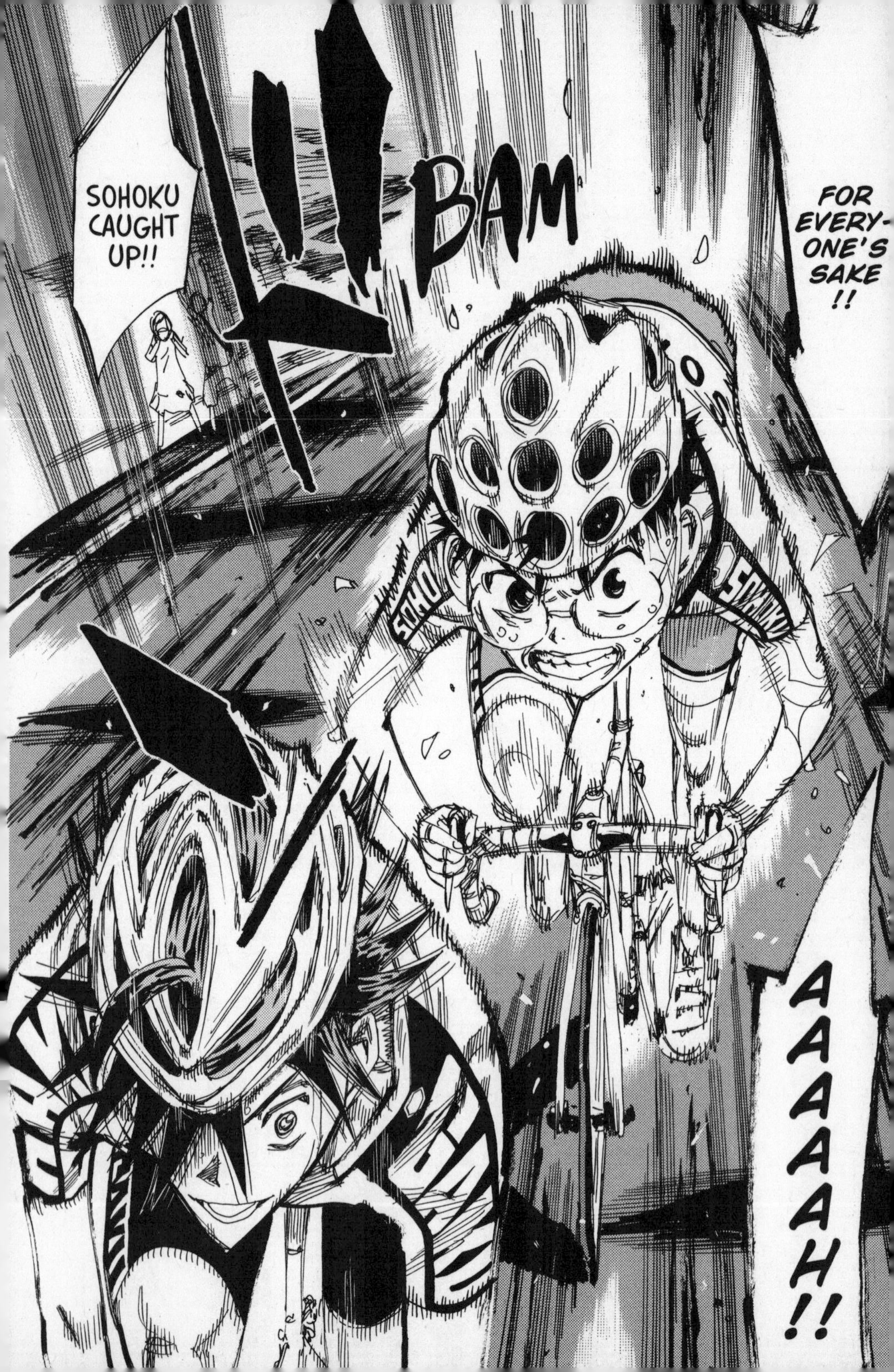
FOR EVERY-ONE'S SAKE!!
BAM
SOHOKU CAUGHT UP!!
AAAAAH!!

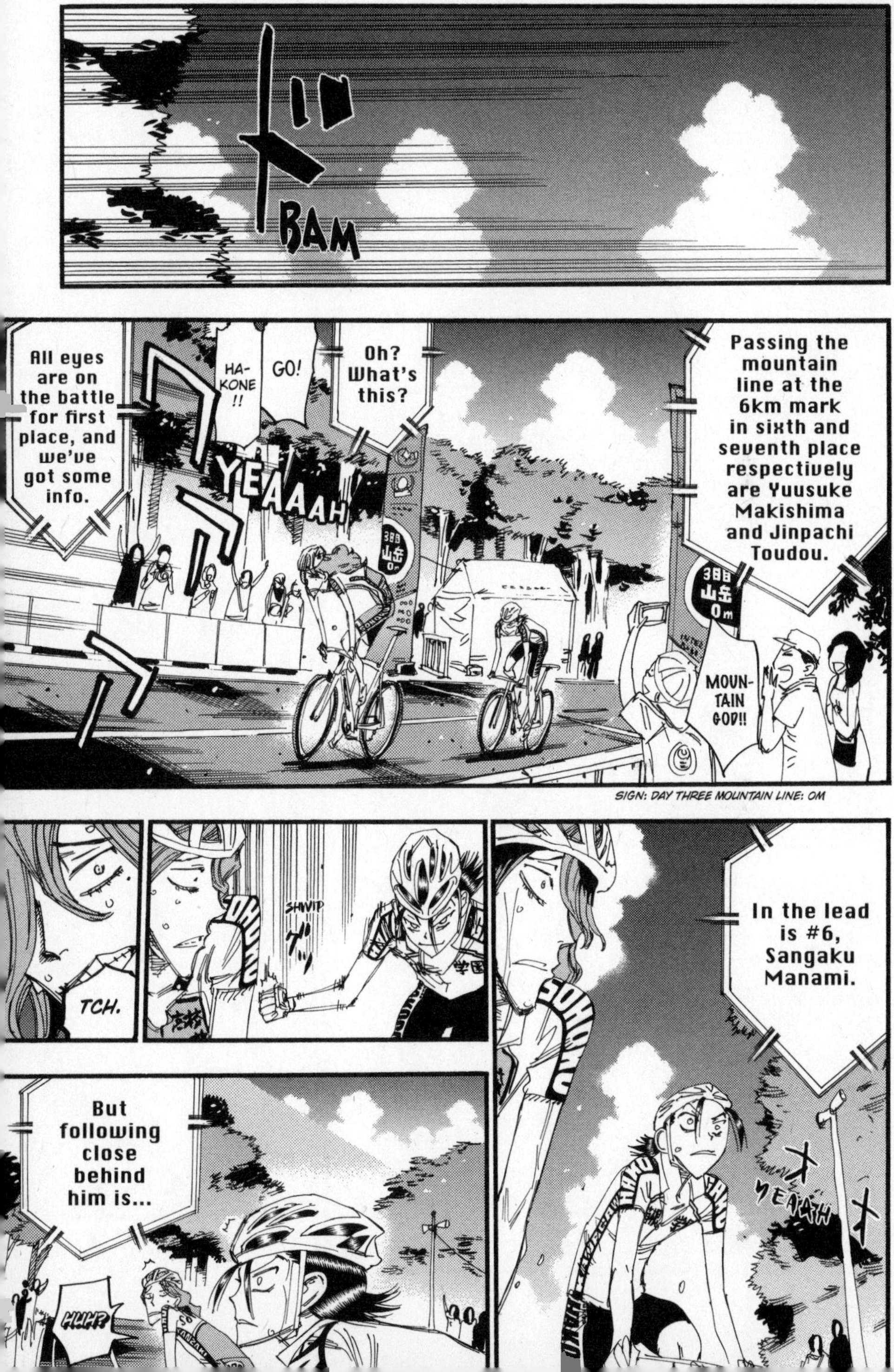
BAM
Passing the mountain line at the 6km mark in sixth and seventh place respectively are Yuusuke Makishima and Jinpachi Toudou.
MOUNTAIN GOD!!
Oh? What's this?
GO!
HAKONE!!
YEAAAH
All eyes are on the battle for first place, and we've got some info.
SIGN: DAY THREE MOUNTAIN LINE: OM
In the lead is #6, Sangaku Manami.
YEAAAH
SHVIP
TCH.
But following close behind him is...
HUH?

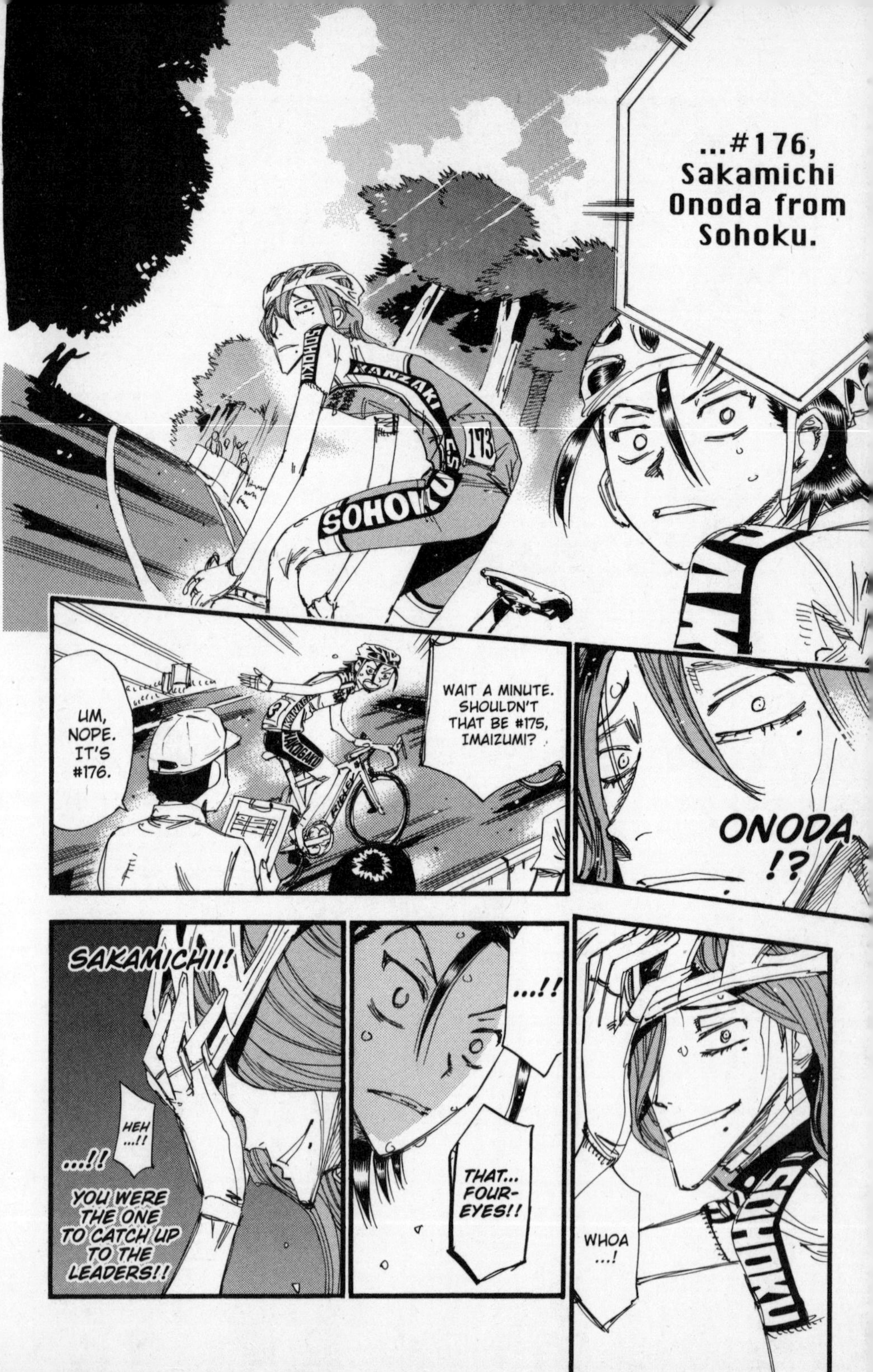
...#176, Sakamichi Onoda from Sohoku.
ONODA !?
WAIT A MINUTE. SHOULDN'T THAT BE #175, IMAIZUMI?
UM, NOPE. IT'S #176.
WHOA ...!
...!!
THAT... FOUR-EYES!!
SAKAMICHI!!
HEH ...!!
...!!
YOU WERE THE ONE TO CATCH UP TO THE LEADERS!!

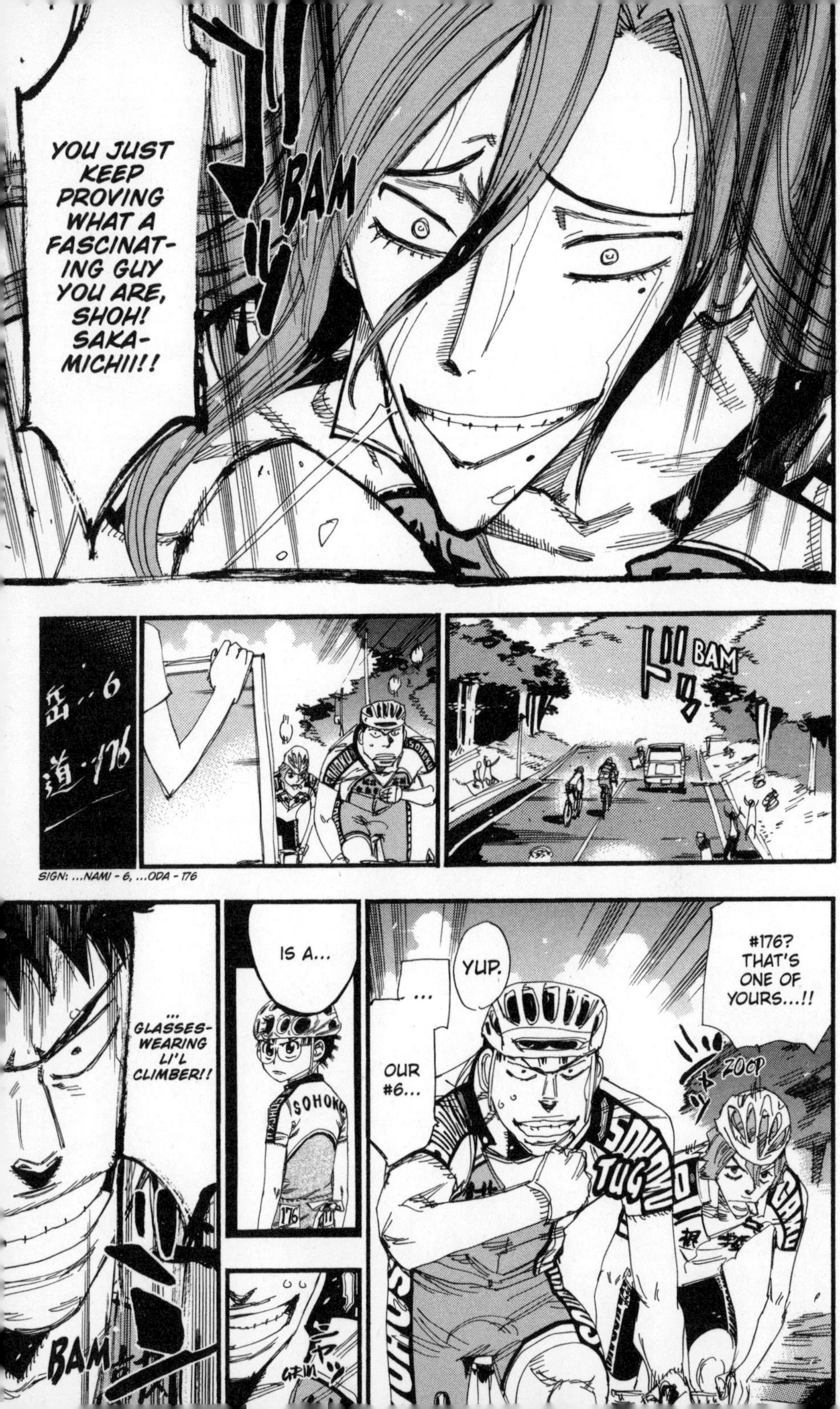
YOU JUST KEEP PROVING WHAT A FASCINATING GUY YOU ARE, SHOH! SAKAMICHI!!
BAM
BAM
岳…6
道…176
SIGN: ...NAMI - 6, ...ODA - 176
#176? THAT'S ONE OF YOURS...!!
ZOOP
YUP.
OUR #6...
...
IS A...
...GLASSES-WEARING LI'L CLIMBER!!
BAM
GRIN

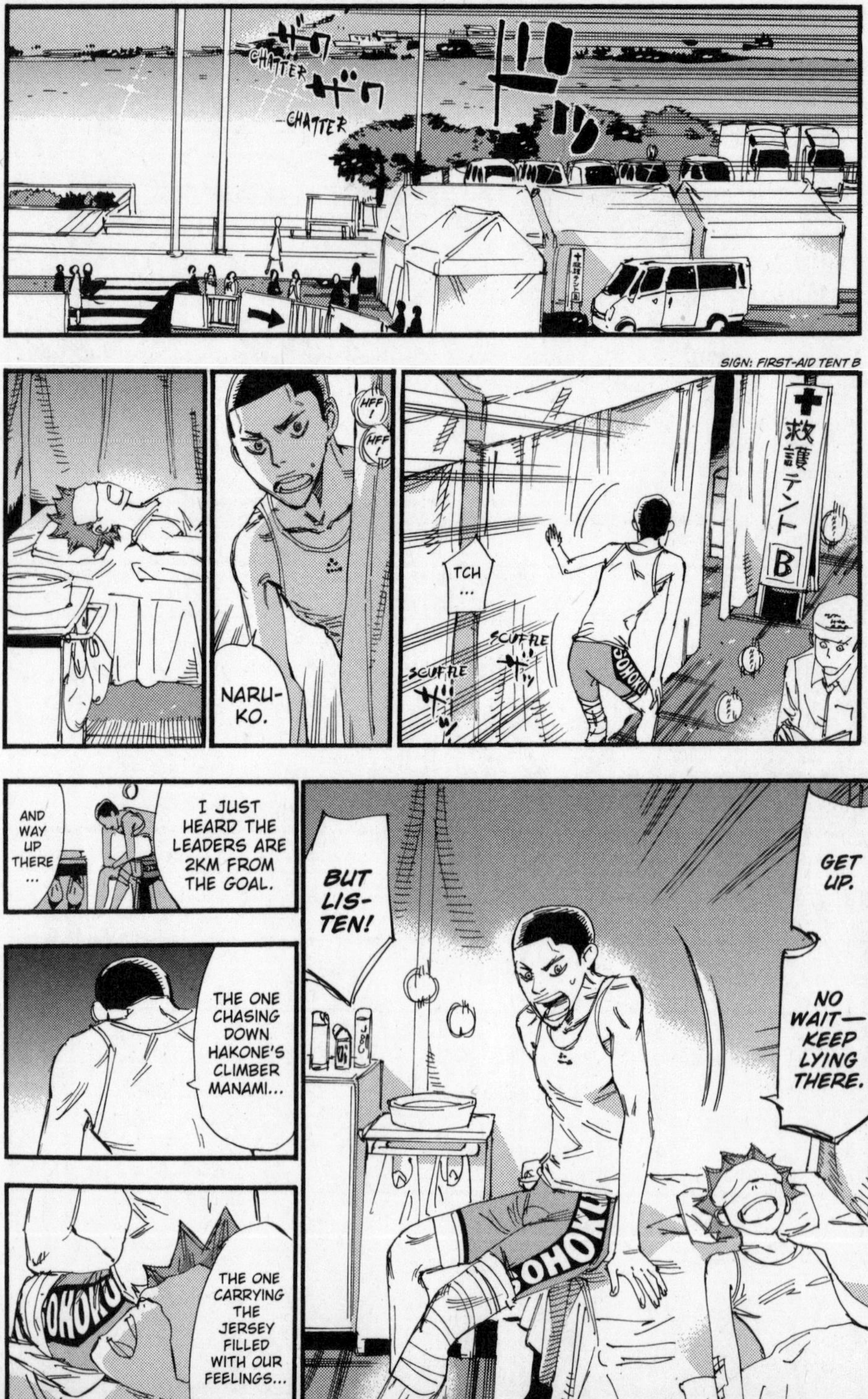

ザワ
CHATTER
ザワ
CHATTER
SIGN: FIRST-AID TENT B
救護テント
B
TCH...
SCUFFLE
SCUFFLE
HFF!
HFF!
NARU-KO.
GET UP.
NO WAIT—KEEP LYING THERE.
BUT LISTEN!
I JUST HEARD THE LEADERS ARE 2KM FROM THE GOAL.
AND WAY UP THERE...
THE ONE CHASING DOWN HAKONE'S CLIMBER MANAMI...
THE ONE CARRYING THE JERSEY FILLED WITH OUR FEELINGS...

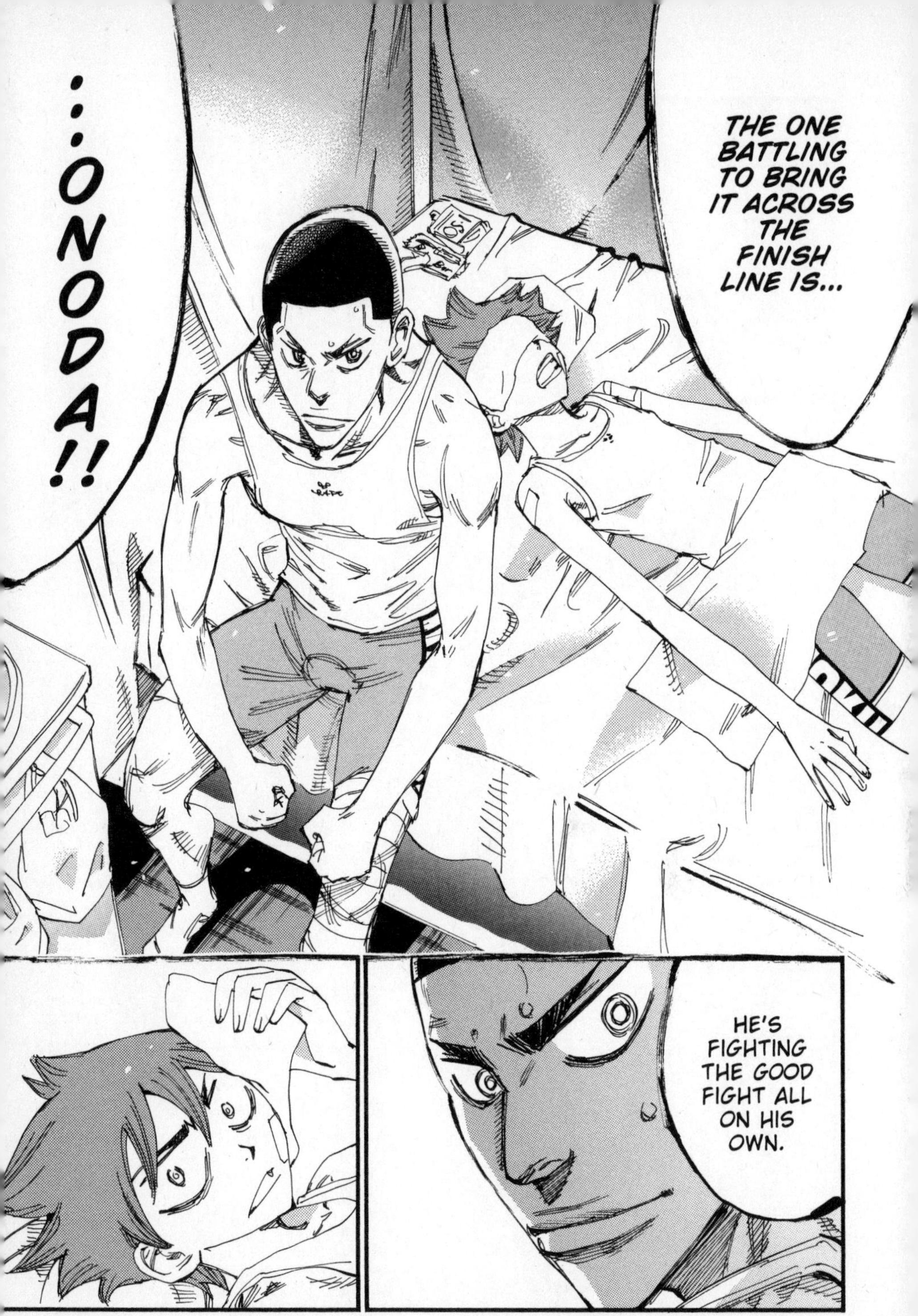
THE ONE BATTLING TO BRING IT ACROSS THE FINISH LINE IS...
...ONODA!!
HE'S FIGHTING THE GOOD FIGHT ALL ON HIS OWN.

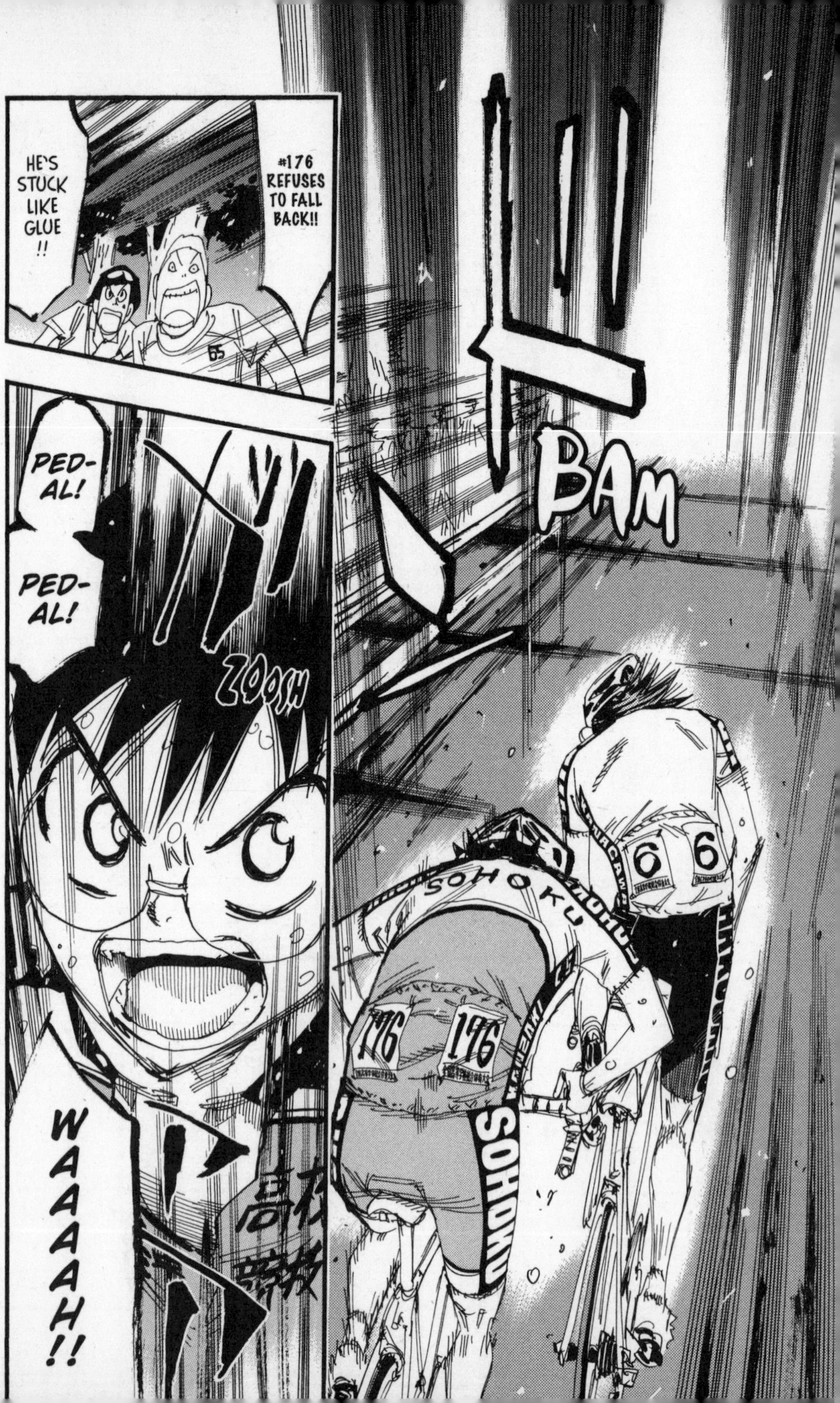
BAM
#176 REFUSES TO FALL BACK!!
HE'S STUCK LIKE GLUE!!
PED-AL!
PED-AL!
ZOOSH
WAAAAAH!!

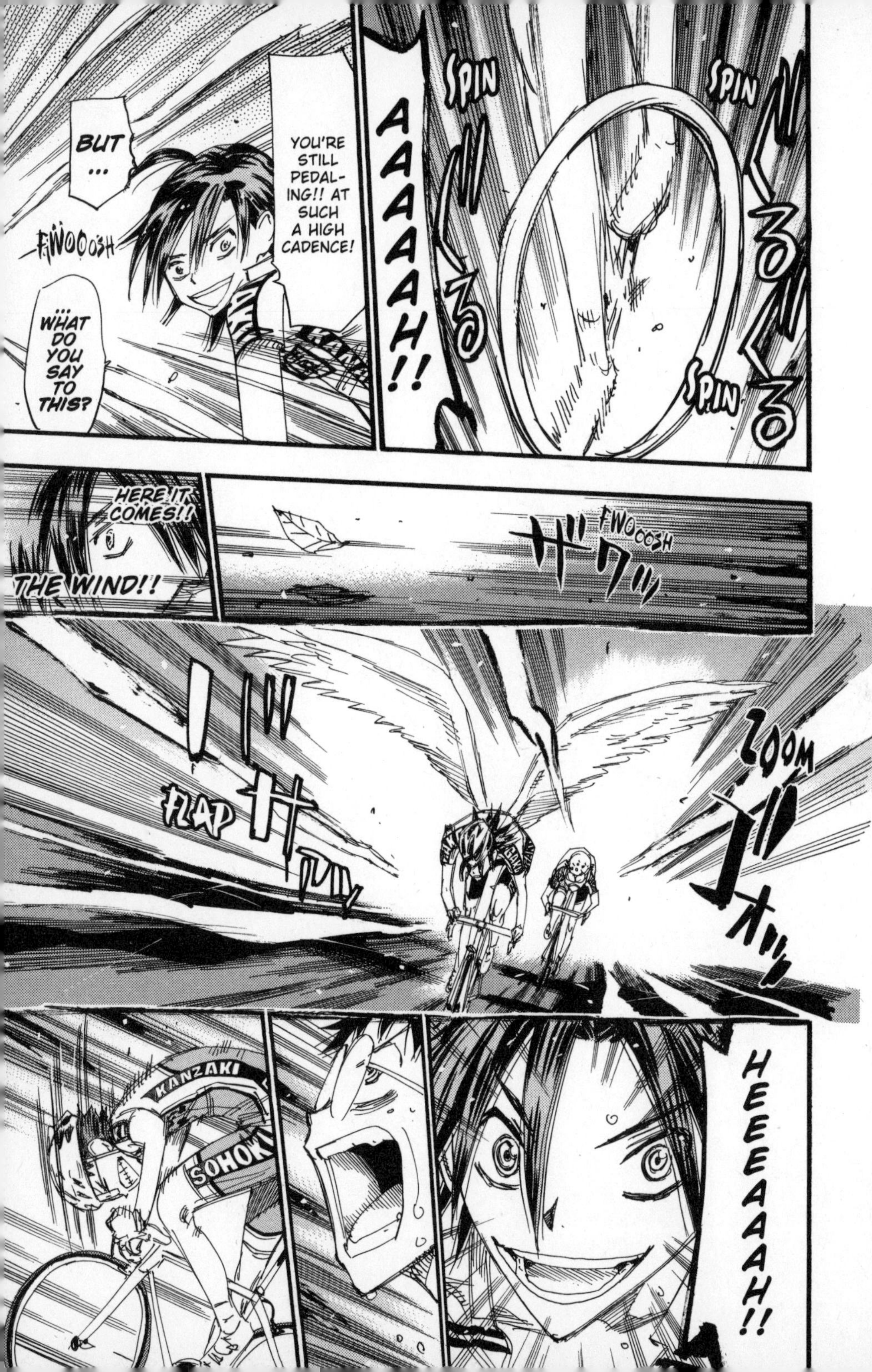
SPIN
SPIN
AAAAAAAH!!
SPIN
YOU'RE STILL PEDALING!! AT SUCH A HIGH CADENCE!
BUT...
FWOOOSH
...WHAT DO YOU SAY TO THIS?
FWOOOSH
HERE IT COMES!!
THE WIND!!
ZOOM
FLAP
HEEEAAAAH!!

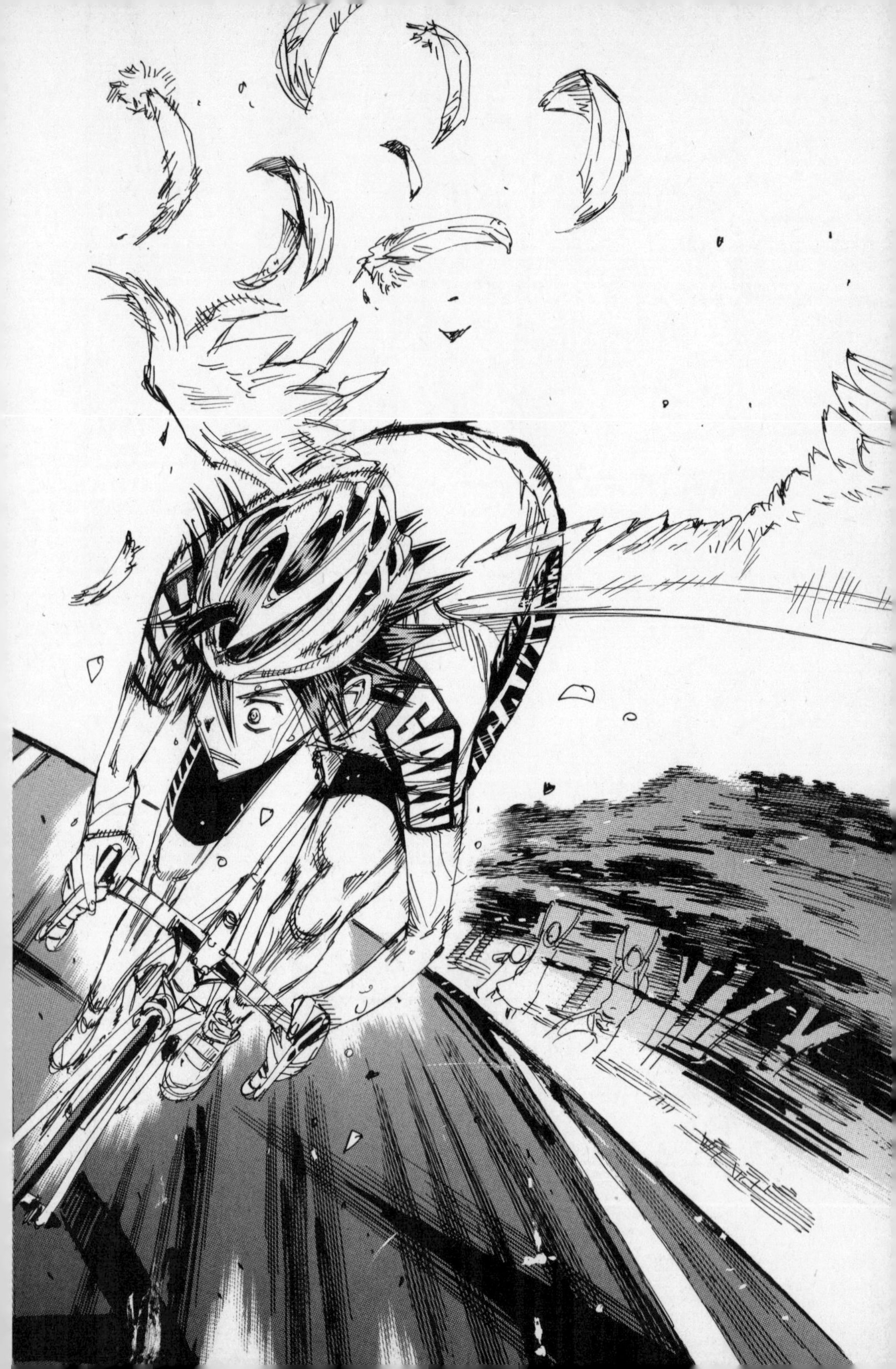

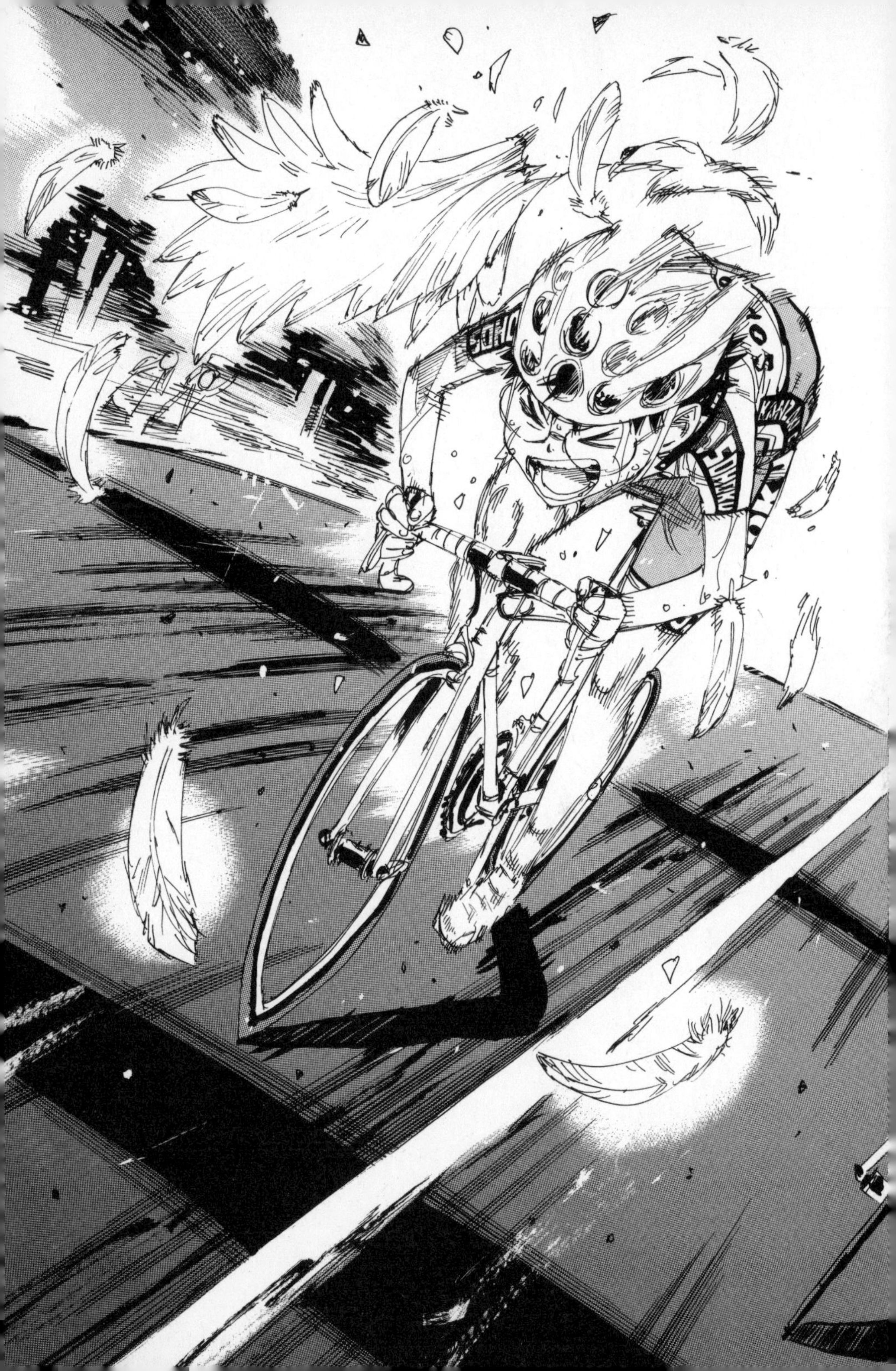

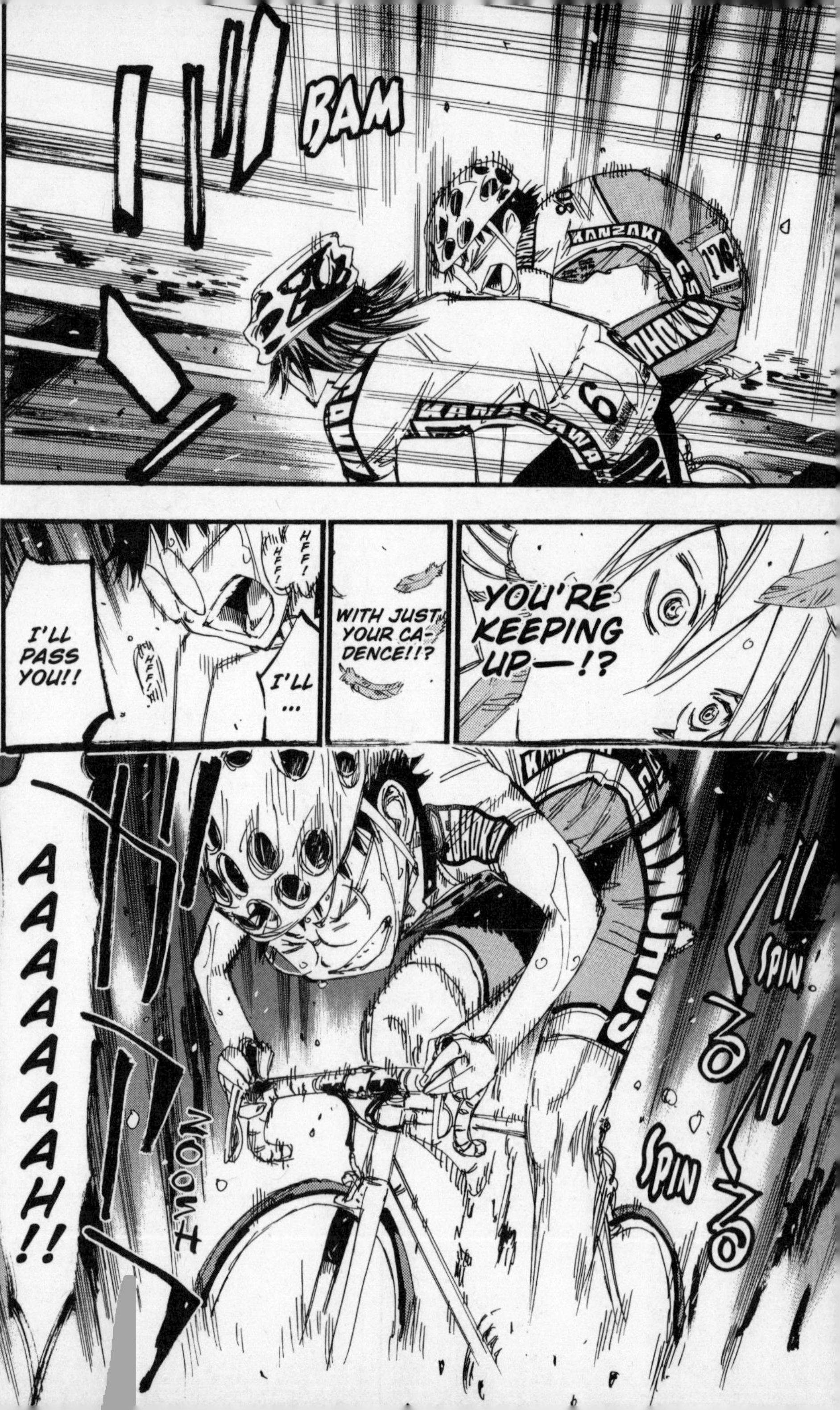
BAM
YOU'RE KEEPING UP—!?
WITH JUST YOUR CA-DENCE!!?
HFF! HFF!
I'LL ...
I'LL PASS YOU!!
HFF HFF
SPIN
SPIN
HOOOO
AAAAAAAAAAAH!!

RIDE.219 PASSING YOU

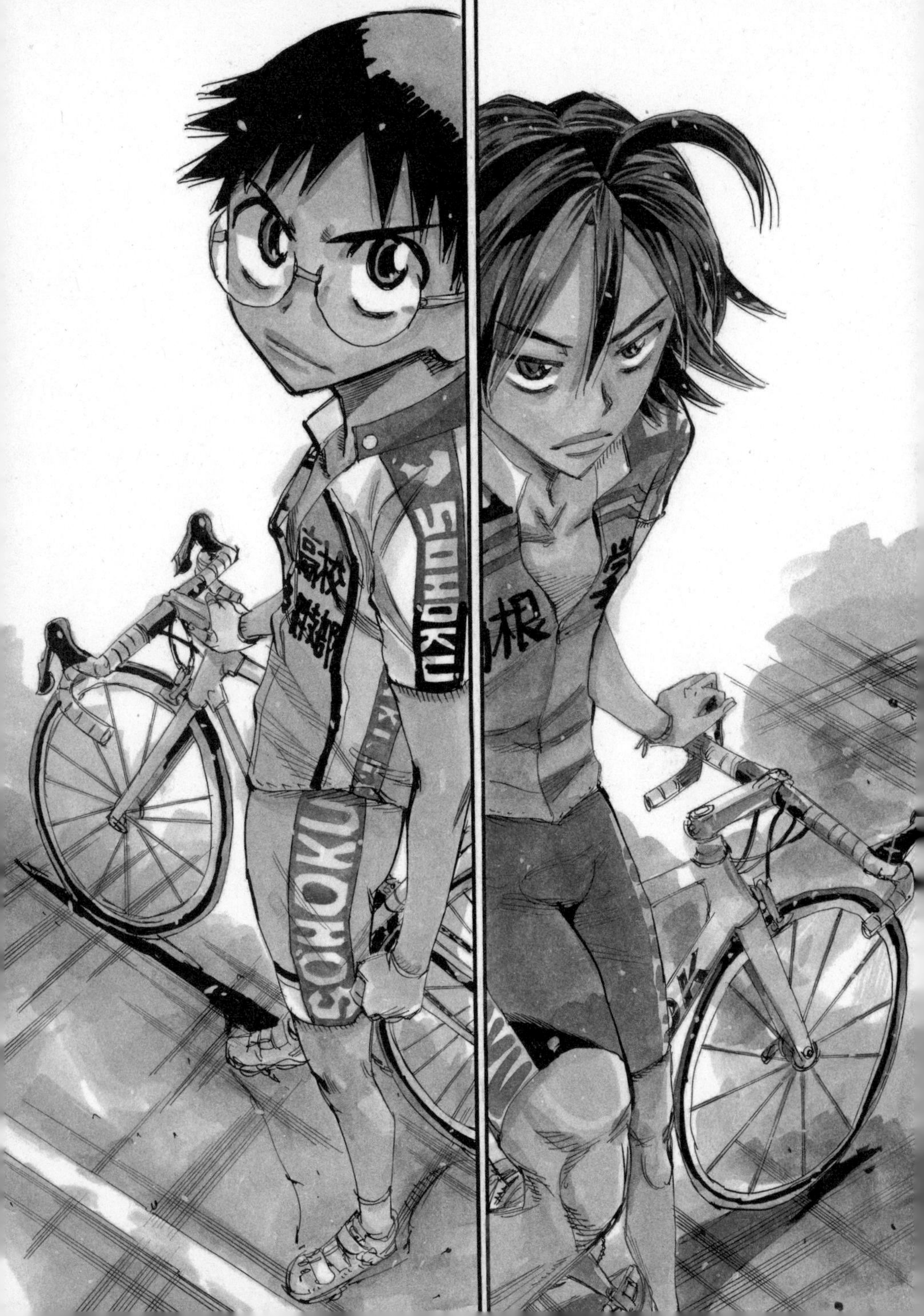
SOHOKU
SOHOKU
SOHOKU

WING

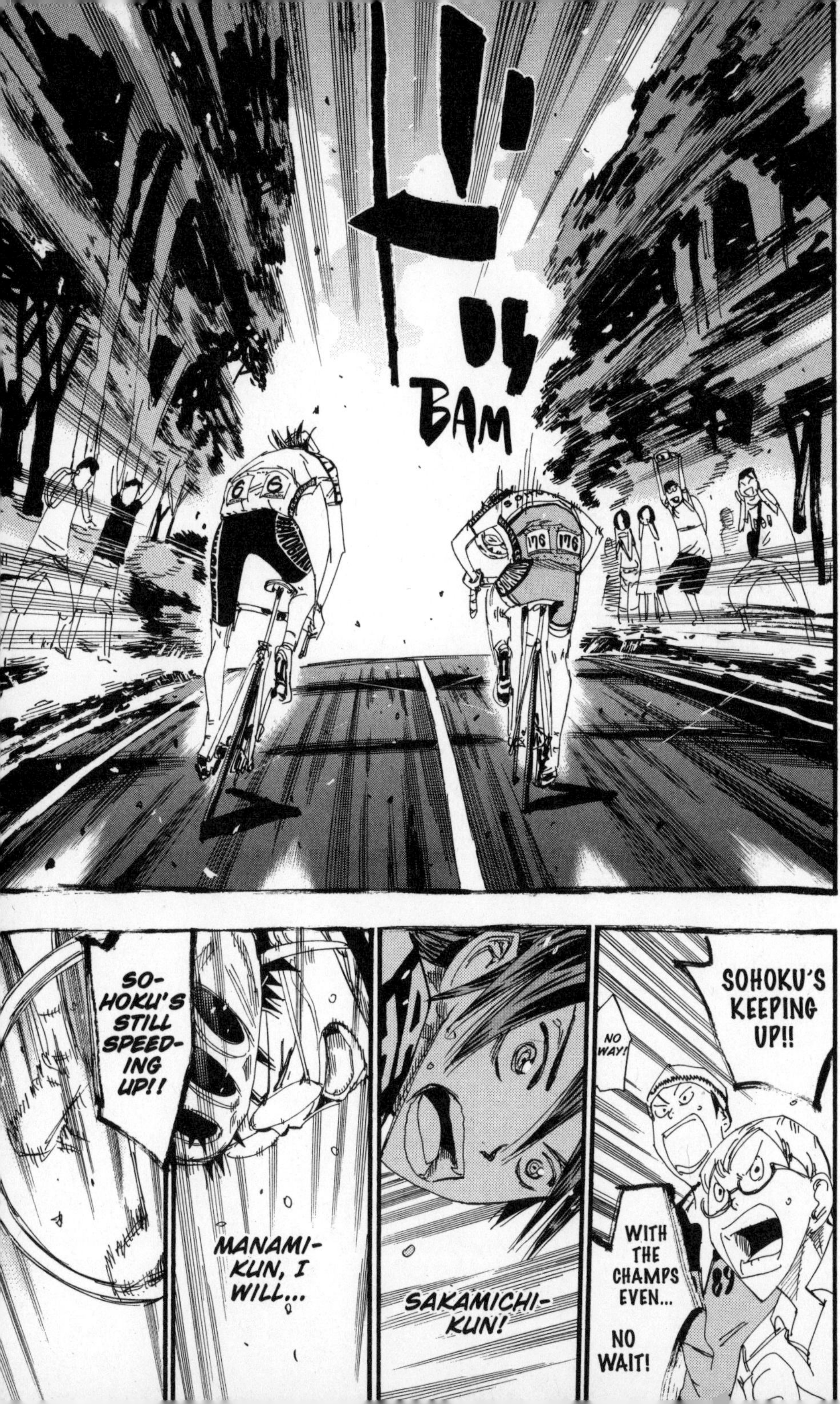
BAM
SOHOKU'S KEEPING UP!!
NO WAY!
WITH THE CHAMPS EVEN...
NO WAIT!
SAKAMICHI-KUN!
SO-HOKU'S STILL SPEED-ING UP!!
MANAMI-KUN, I WILL...

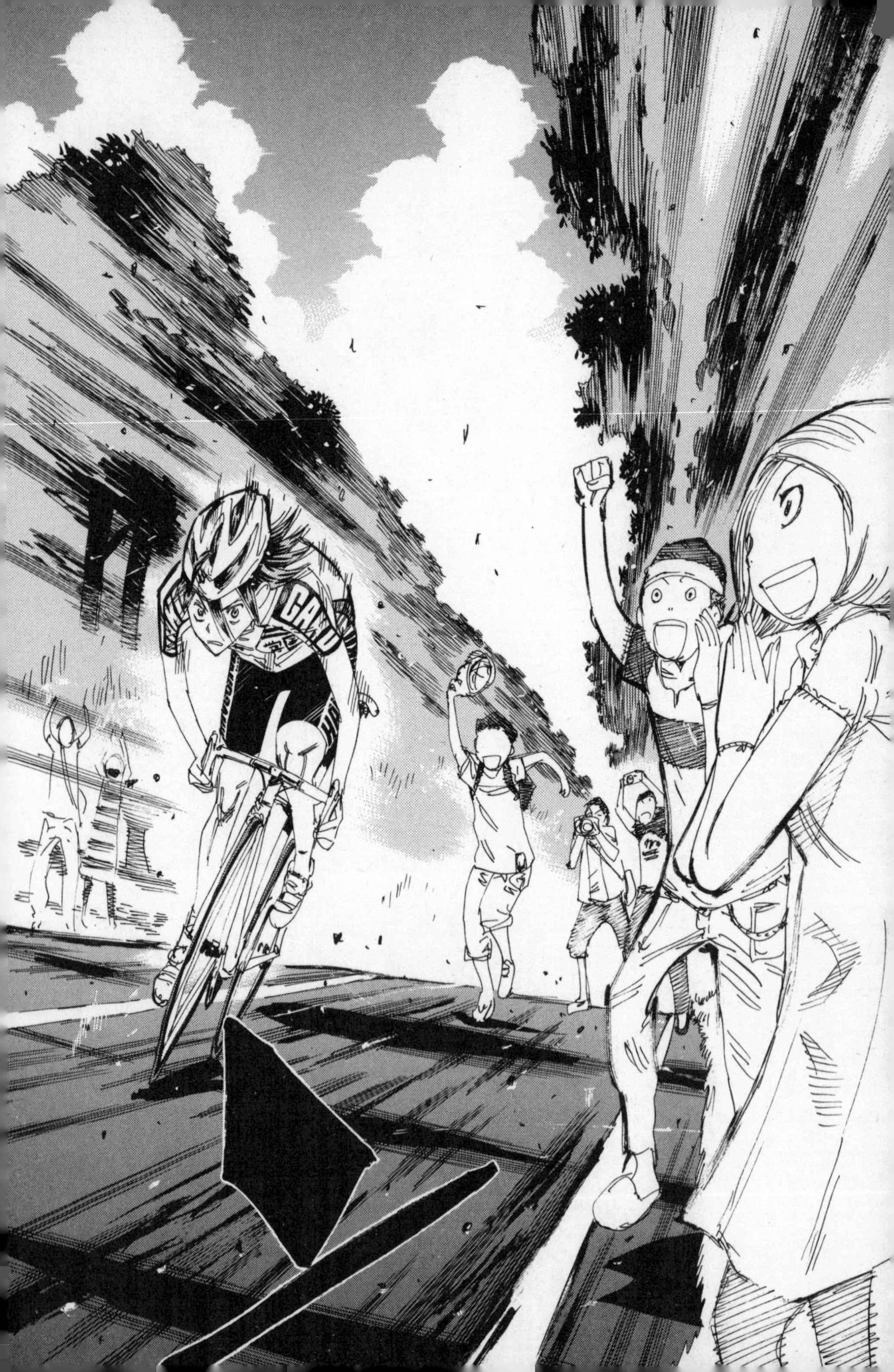

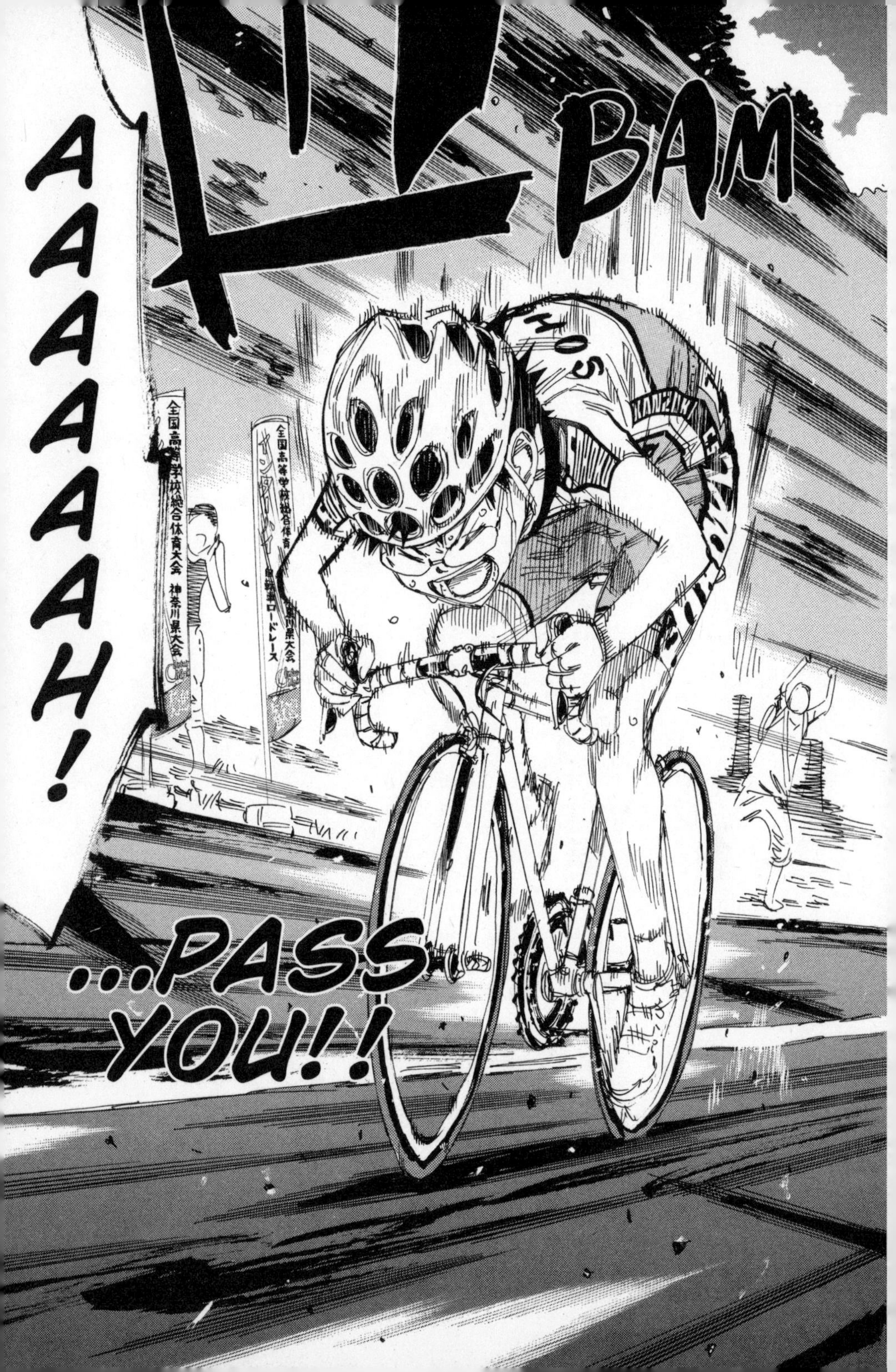
BAM
AAAAAAAH!
...PASS YOU!!
全国高等学校総合体育大会 神奈川県大会

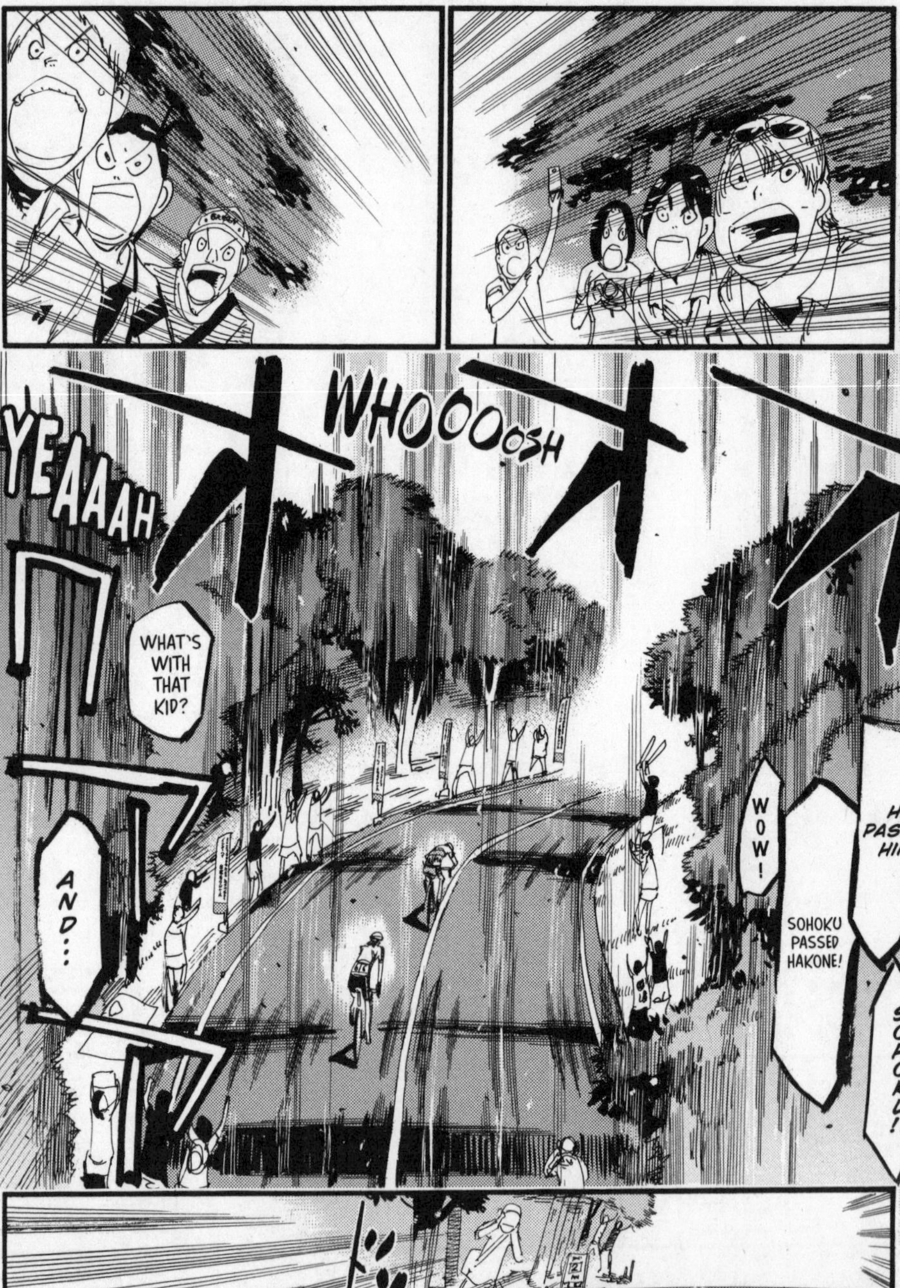
HE PASSED HIM!
WOW!
SOHOKU PASSED HAKONE!
SOHOKU!!
WHOOOOSH
YEAAAAH
WHAT'S WITH THAT KID?
AND...
BAM

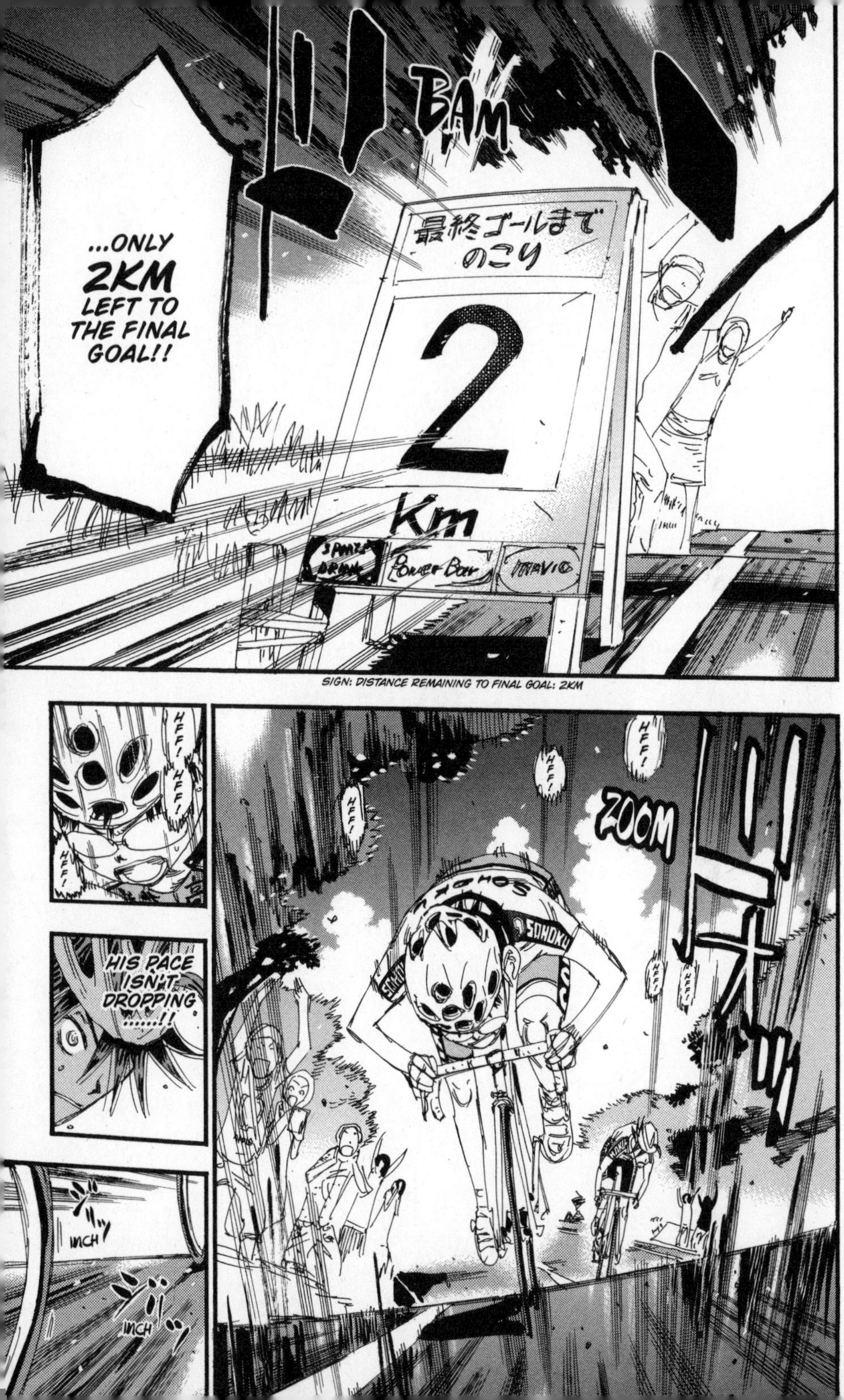
BAM
...ONLY 2KM LEFT TO THE FINAL GOAL!!
最終ゴールまでのこり
2
Km
Power Bar
SIGN: DISTANCE REMAINING TO FINAL GOAL: 2KM
HFF!
HFF!
HFF!
ZOOM
HFF!
HFF!
HFF!
HFF!
HFF!
HIS PACE ISN'T DROPPING......!!
INCH
INCH

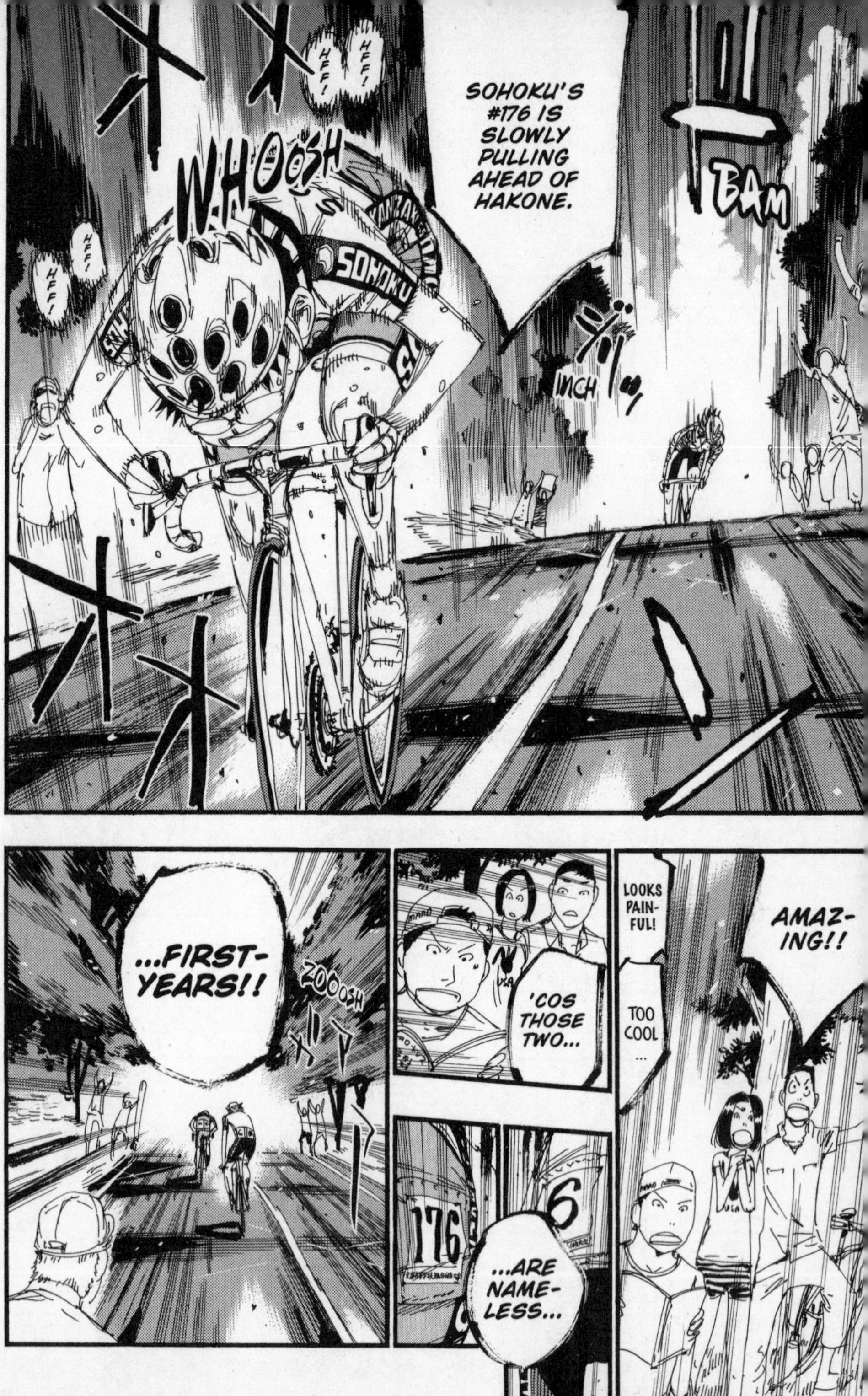
BAM
SOHOKU'S #176 IS SLOWLY PULLING AHEAD OF HAKONE.
HFF! HFF!
WHOOSH
SOHOKU
HFF! HFF!
INCH
AMAZ-ING!!
LOOKS PAIN-FUL!
TOO COOL ...
'COS THOSE TWO...
...ARE NAME-LESS...
176
...FIRST-YEARS!!
ZOOOSH

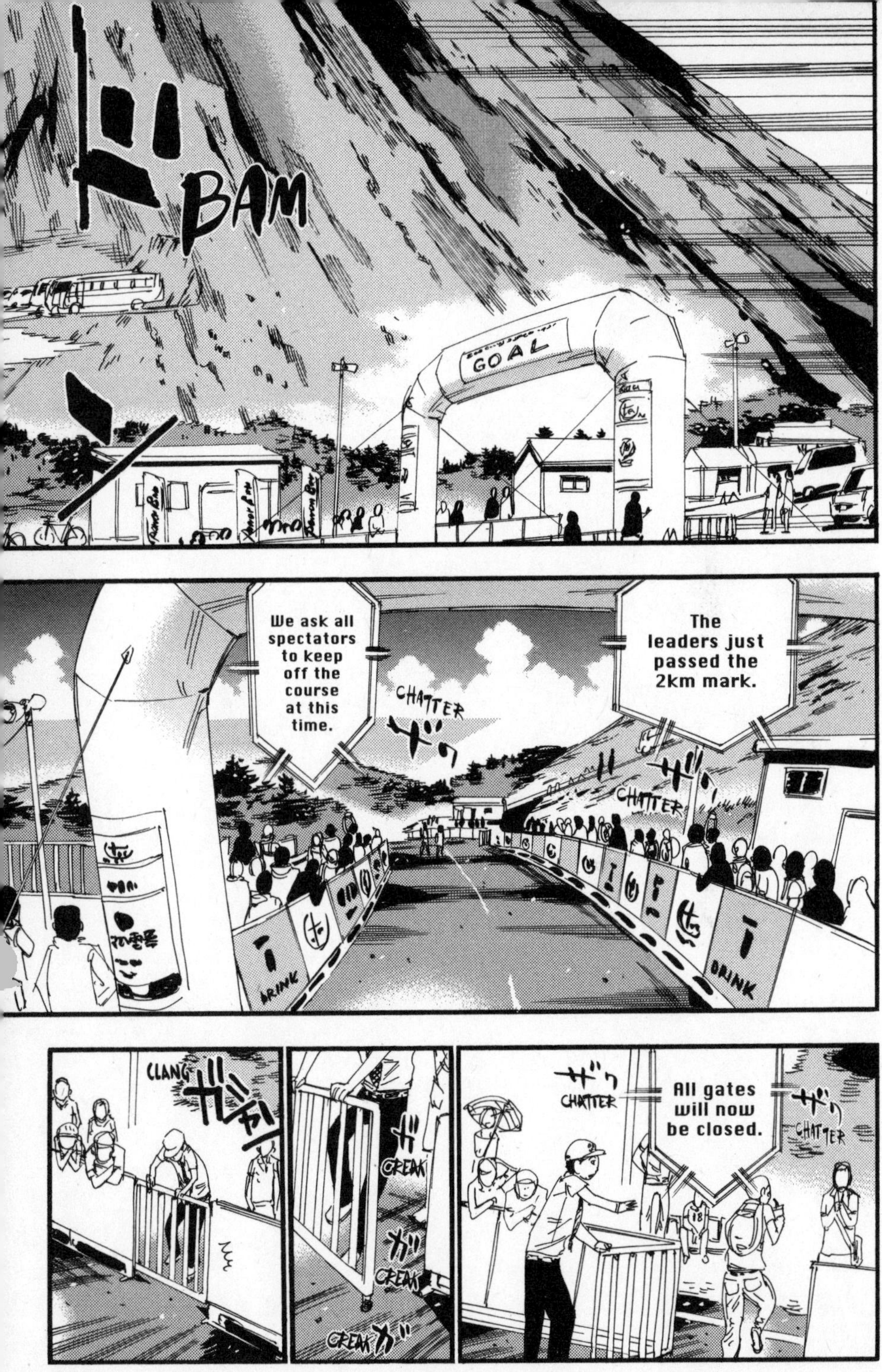
BAM
GOAL
The leaders just passed the 2km mark.
CHATTER
CHATTER
We ask all spectators to keep off the course at this time.
CHATTER
DRINK
DRINK
CHATTER
All gates will now be closed.
CHATTER
CREAK
CREAK
CREAK
CLANG

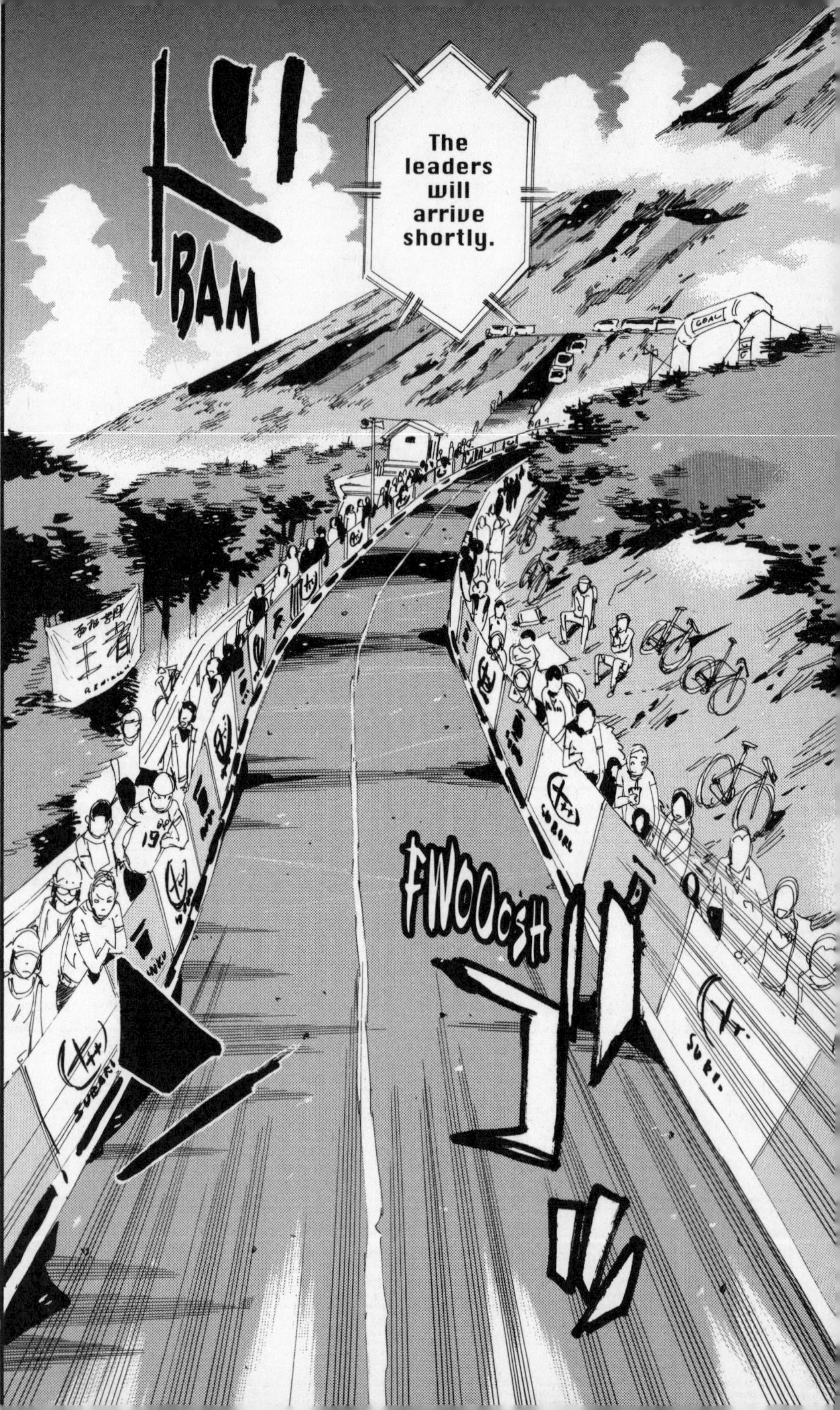
The leaders will arrive shortly.
BAM
FWOOOSH

SIGN: FIGHT ON HAKONE KING

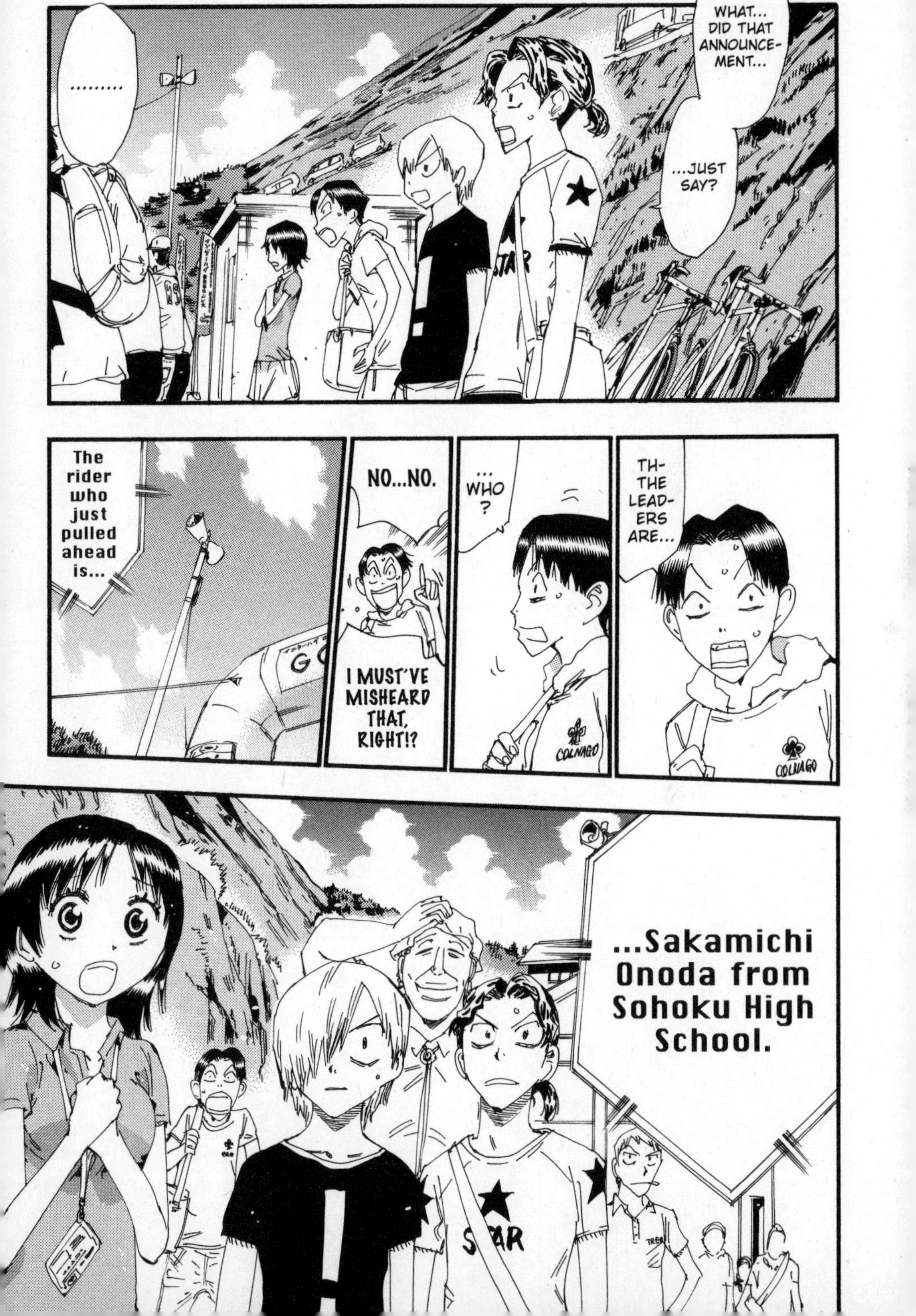
WHAT... DID THAT ANNOUNCE-MENT...
...JUST SAY?
....
TH- THE LEAD-ERS ARE...
... WHO ?
NO...NO.
I MUST'VE MISHEARD THAT, RIGHT!?
The rider who just pulled ahead is...
...Sakamichi Onoda from Sohoku High School.

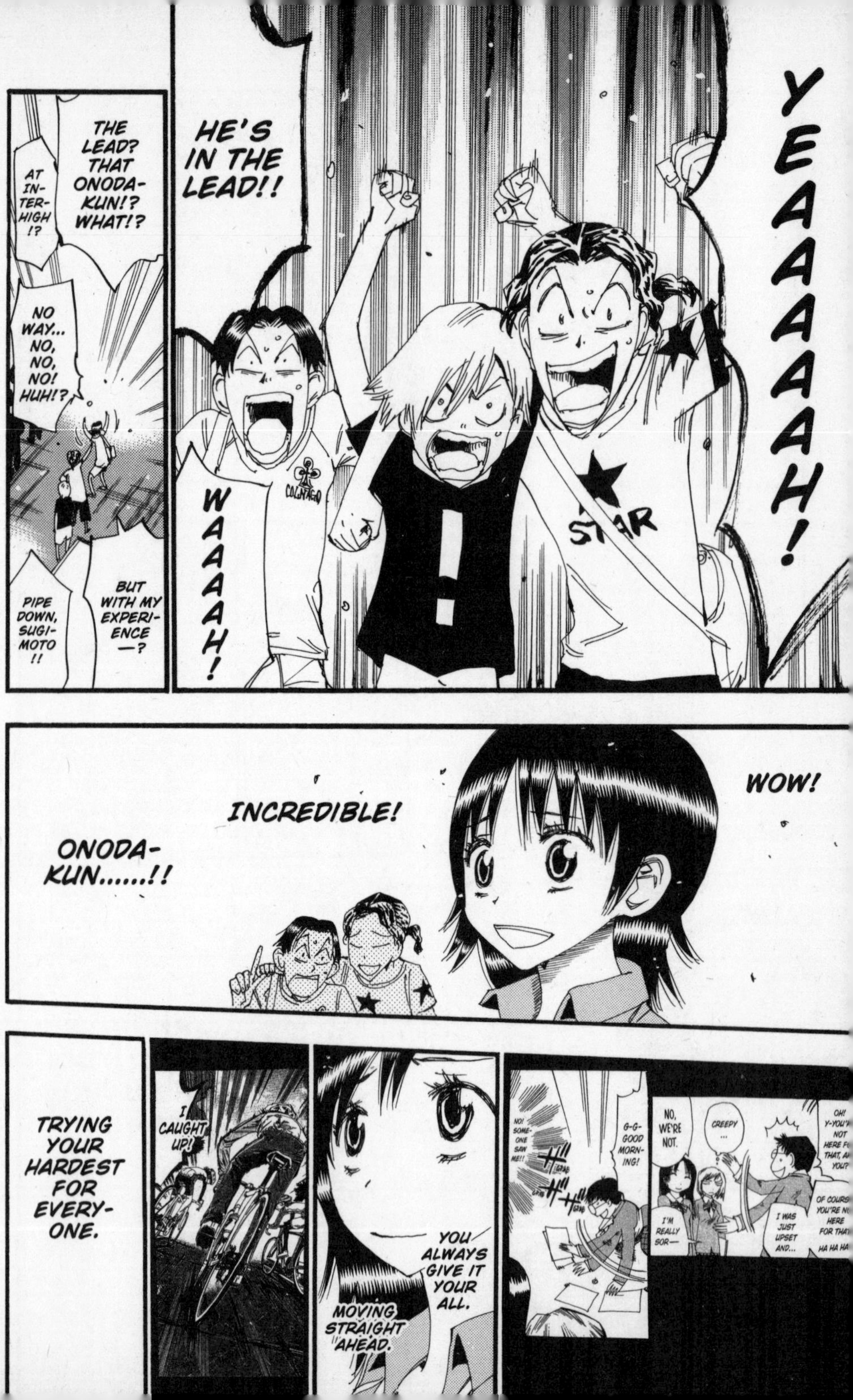
YEAAAAAAH!
HE'S IN THE LEAD!!
WAAAAAH!
THE LEAD? THAT ONODA-KUN!? WHAT!?
AT INTER-HIGH!?
NO WAY... NO, NO, NO! HUH!?
BUT WITH MY EXPERIENCE—?
PIPE DOWN, SUGIMOTO!!
WOW!
INCREDIBLE!
ONODA-KUN......!!
OH! Y-YOU'RE NOT HERE F THAT, A YOU?
CREEPY...
NO, WE'RE NOT.
I'M REALLY SOR—
I WAS JUST UPSET AND...
OF COURSE YOU'RE NOT HERE FOR THAT
HA HA HA
G-G-GOOD MORNING!
NO! SOMEONE SAW ME!!
YOU ALWAYS GIVE IT YOUR ALL.
MOVING STRAIGHT AHEAD.
I CAUGHT UP!
TRYING YOUR HARDEST FOR EVERY-ONE.

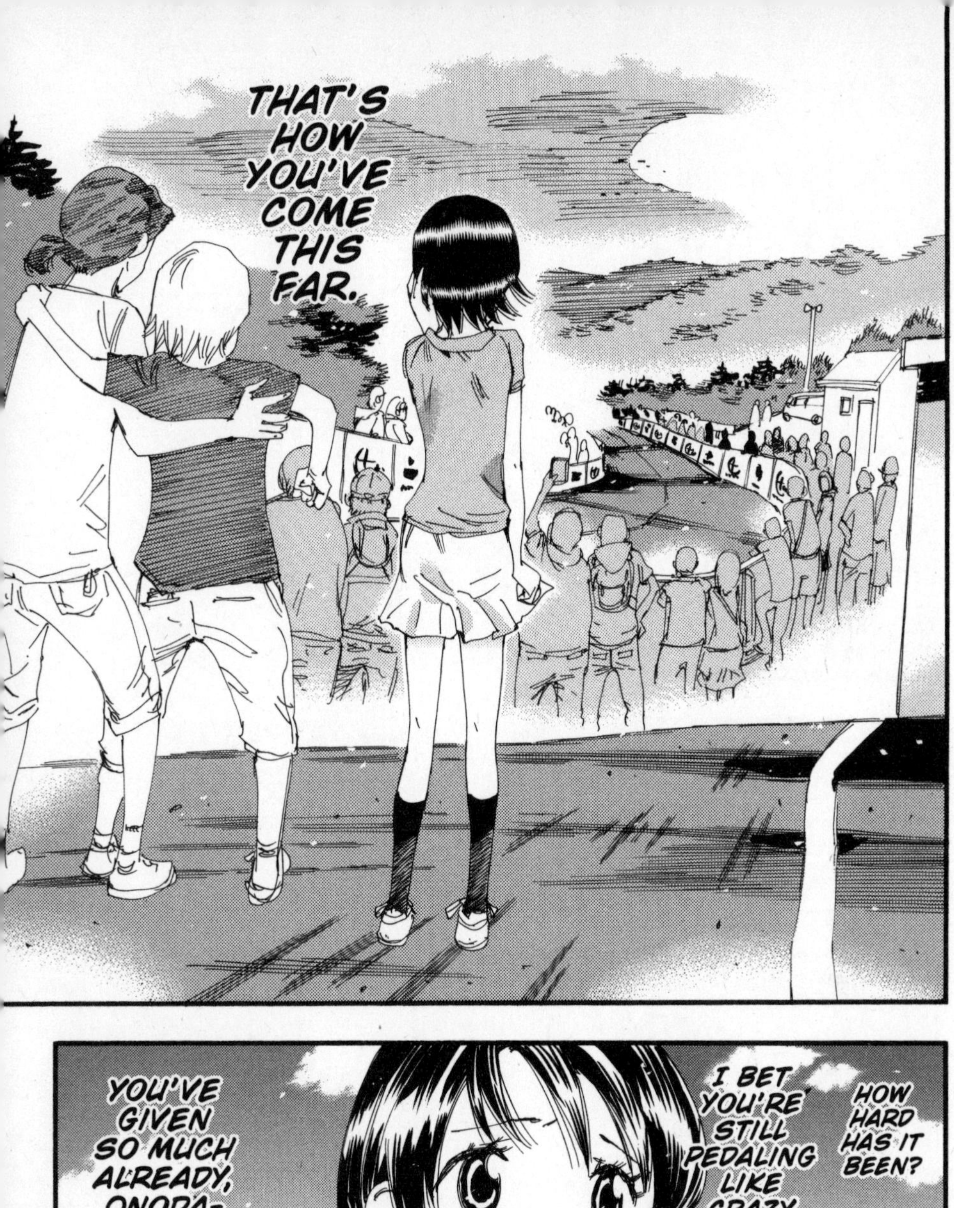
THAT'S HOW YOU'VE COME THIS FAR.
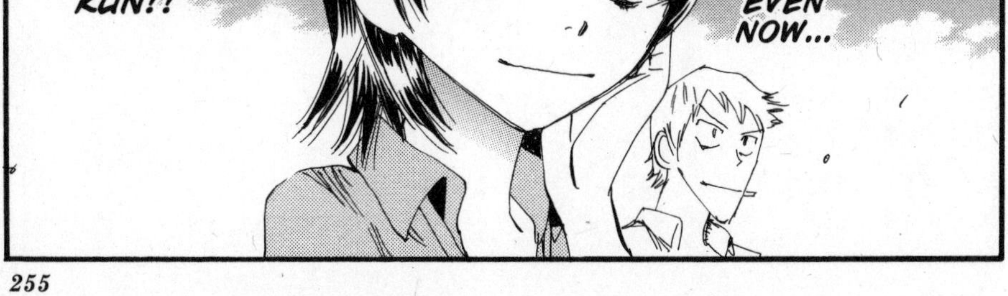
HOW HARD HAS IT BEEN?
I BET YOU'RE STILL PEDALING LIKE CRAZY EVEN NOW...
YOU'VE GIVEN SO MUCH ALREADY, ONODA-KUN!!

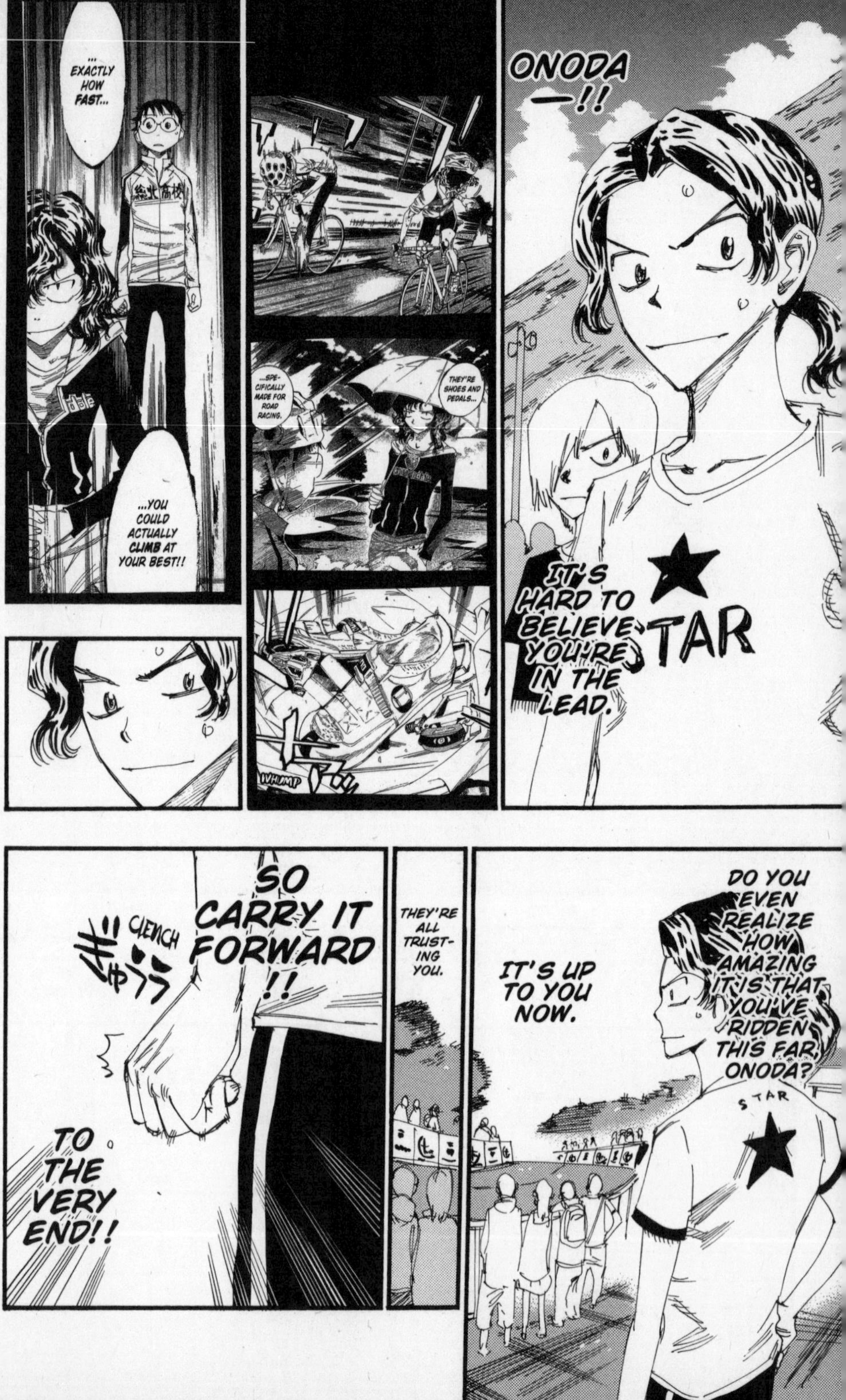
ONODA—!!
IT'S HARD TO BELIEVE YOU'RE IN THE LEAD.
THEY'RE SHOES AND PEDALS...
...SPECIFICALLY MADE FOR ROAD RACING.
WHUMP
...EXACTLY HOW FAST...
...YOU COULD ACTUALLY CLIMB AT YOUR BEST!!
DO YOU EVEN REALIZE HOW AMAZING IT IS THAT YOU'VE RIDDEN THIS FAR, ONODA?
IT'S UP TO YOU NOW.
THEY'RE ALL TRUSTING YOU.
SO CARRY IT FORWARD!!
CLENCH
TO THE VERY END!!

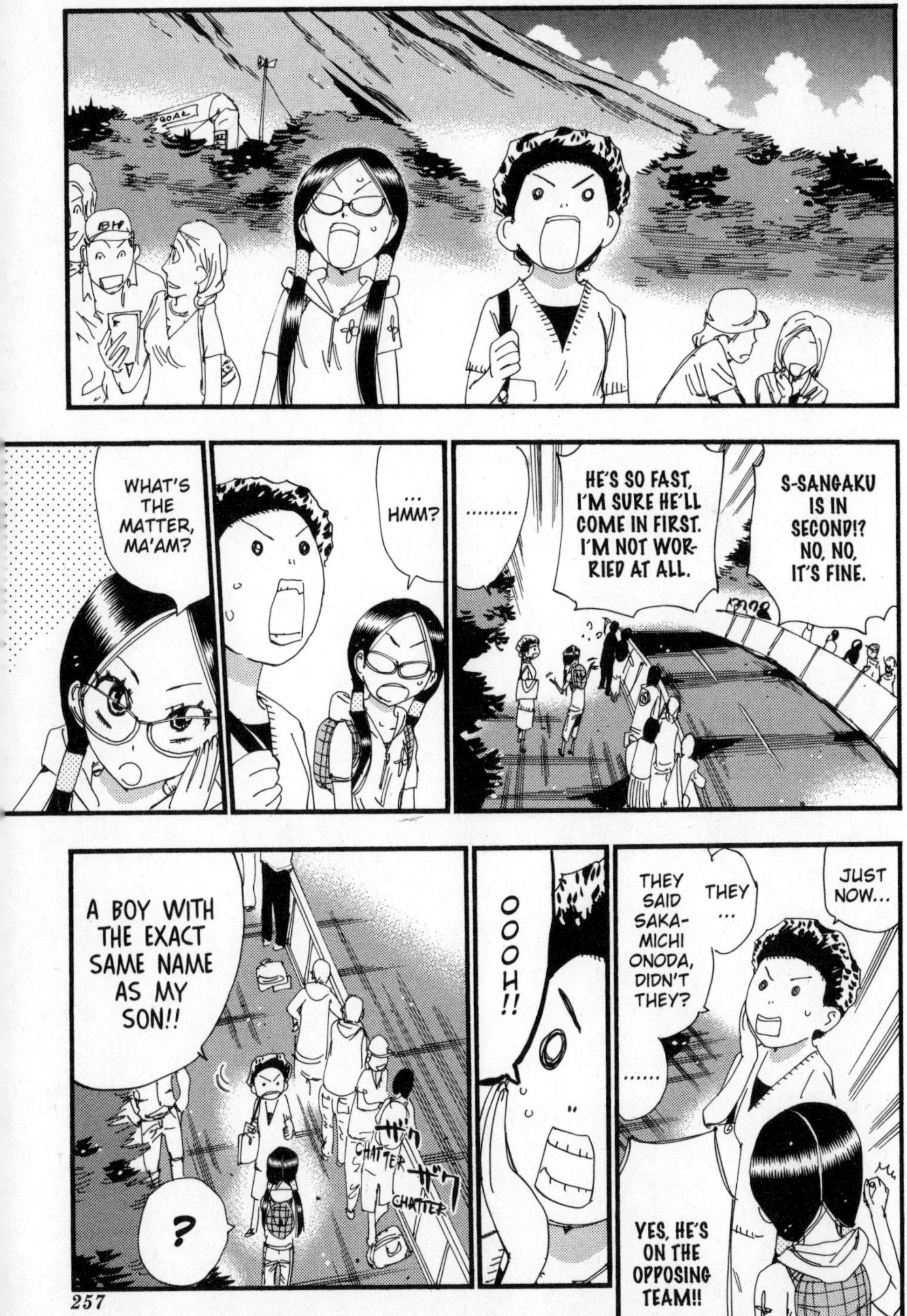

S-SANGAKU IS IN SECOND!? NO, NO, IT'S FINE.
HE'S SO FAST, I'M SURE HE'LL COME IN FIRST. I'M NOT WORRIED AT ALL.
....
... HMM?
WHAT'S THE MATTER, MA'AM?
JUST NOW...
THEY ...
THEY SAID SAKAMICHI ONODA, DIDN'T THEY?
......
YES, HE'S ON THE OPPOSING TEAM!!
OOOH!!
A BOY WITH THE EXACT SAME NAME AS MY SON!!
CHATTER
CHATTER
?

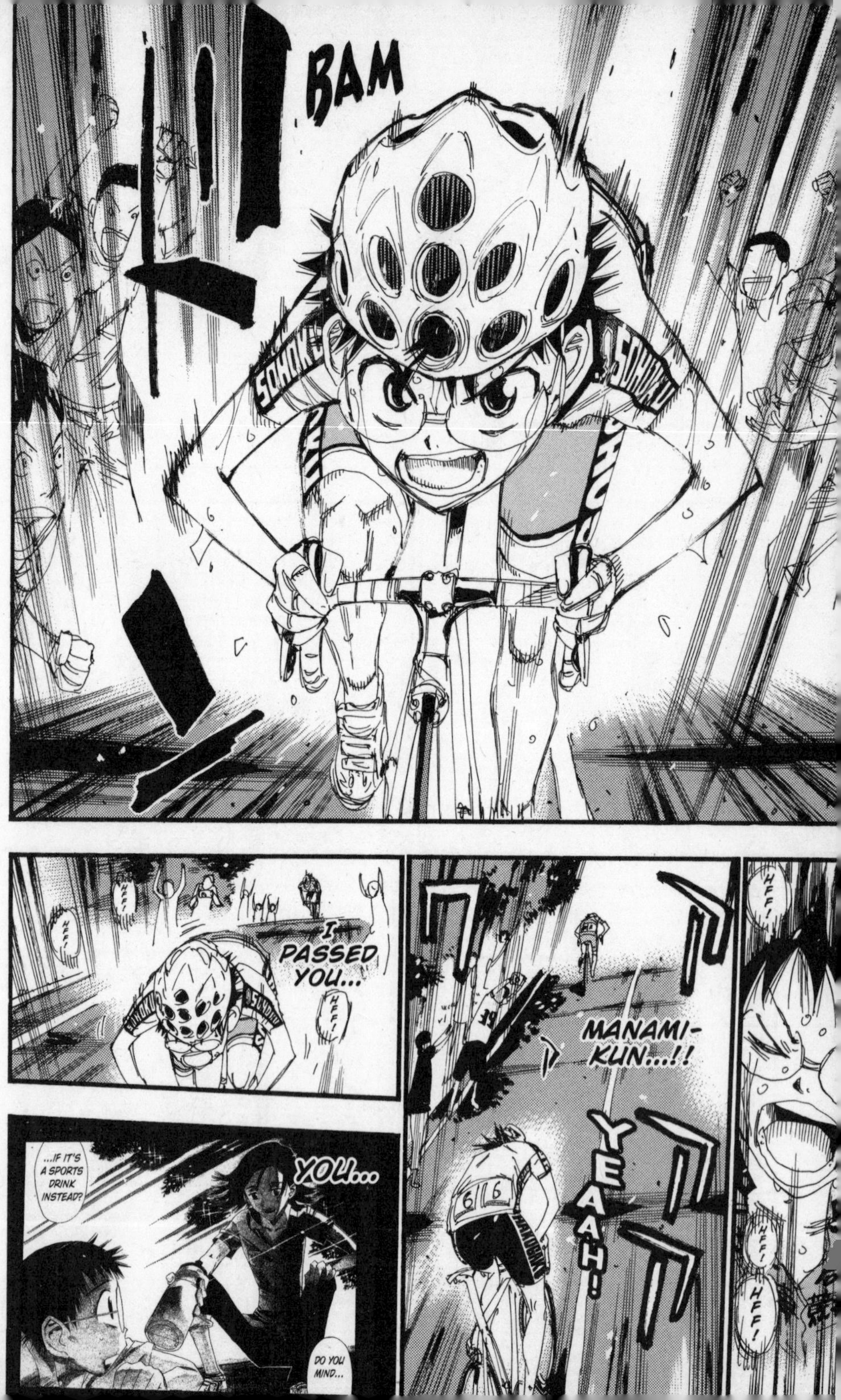
BAM
HFF!
HFF!
HFF!
HFF!
MANAMI-KUN...!!
YEAAAH!
HFF!
HFF!
I PASSED YOU...
YOU...
...IF IT'S A SPORTS DRINK INSTEAD?
DO YOU MIND...

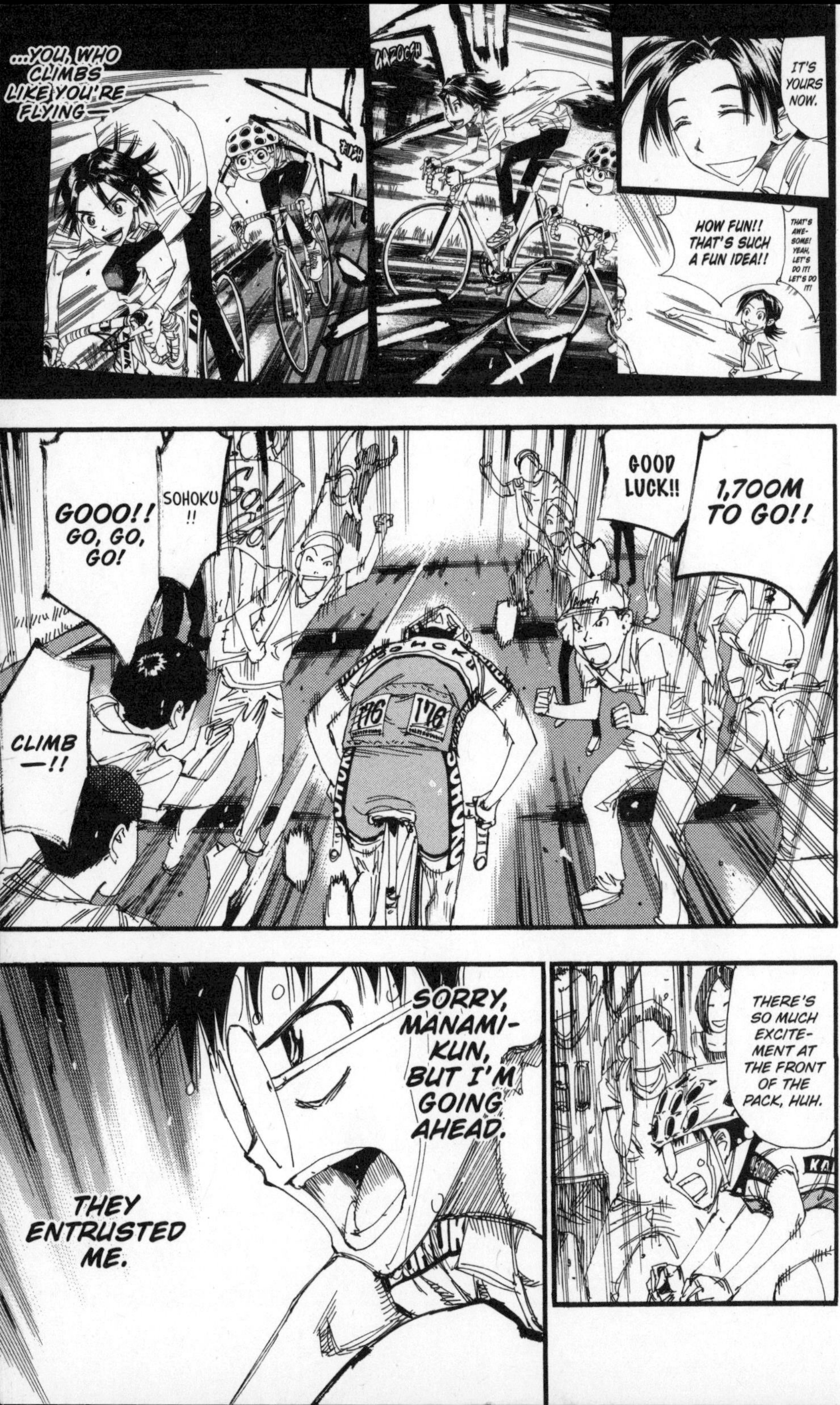
IT'S YOURS NOW.
HOW FUN!! THAT'S SUCH A FUN IDEA!!
THAT'S AWE-SOME! YEAH, LET'S DO IT! LET'S DO IT!
GAZOCH
...YOU, WHO CLIMBS LIKE YOU'RE FLYING—
1,700M TO GO!!
GOOD LUCK!!
SOHOKU !!
GO! GO!
GOOO!! GO, GO, GO!
CLIMB—!!
THERE'S SO MUCH EXCITE-MENT AT THE FRONT OF THE PACK, HUH.
SORRY, MANAMI-KUN, BUT I'M GOING AHEAD.
THEY ENTRUSTED ME.

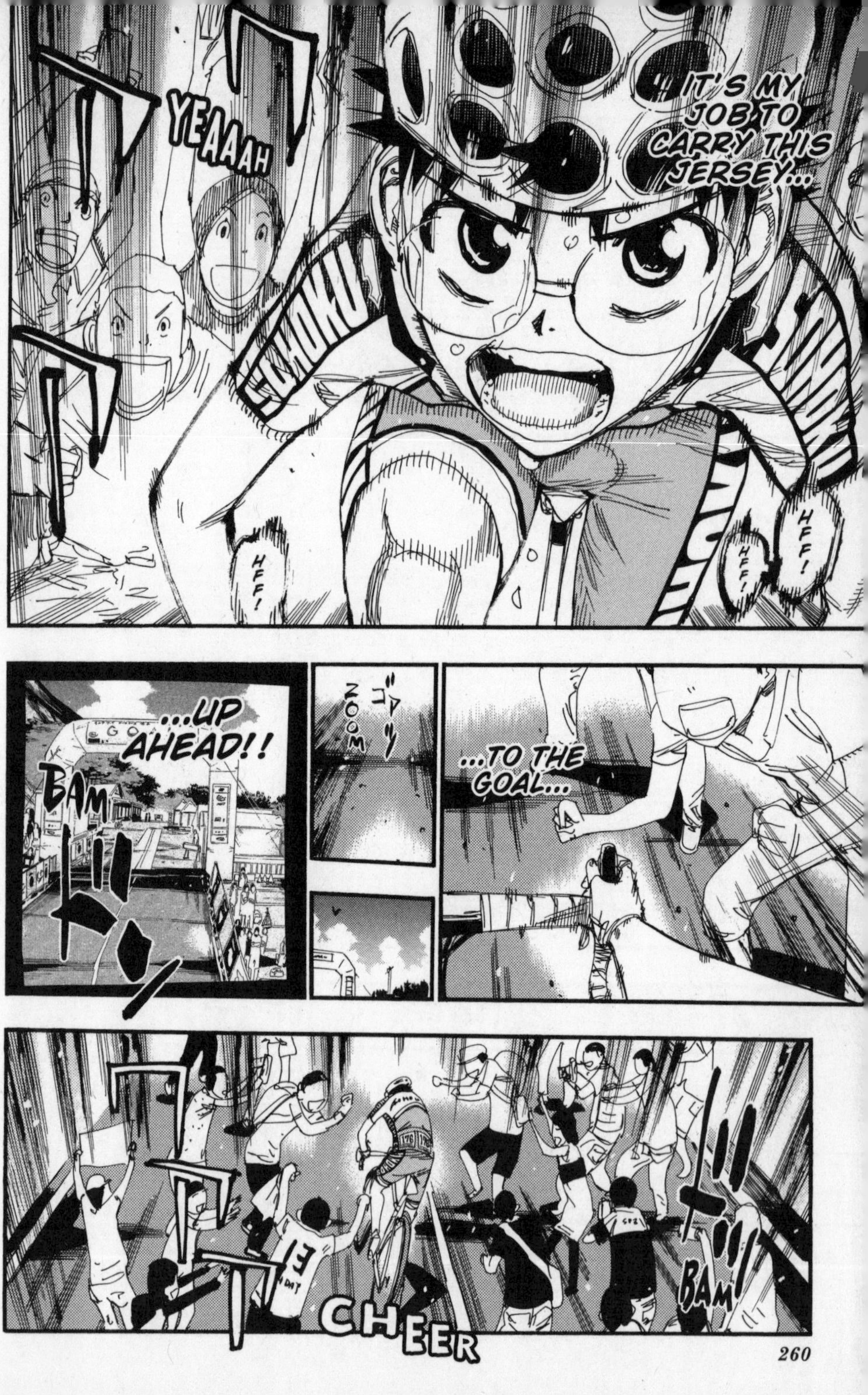
IT'S MY JOB TO CARRY THIS JERSEY...
YEAAAH
HFF! HFF!
HFF!
...TO THE GOAL...
ZOOM
...UP AHEAD!!
BAM
BAM
CHEER

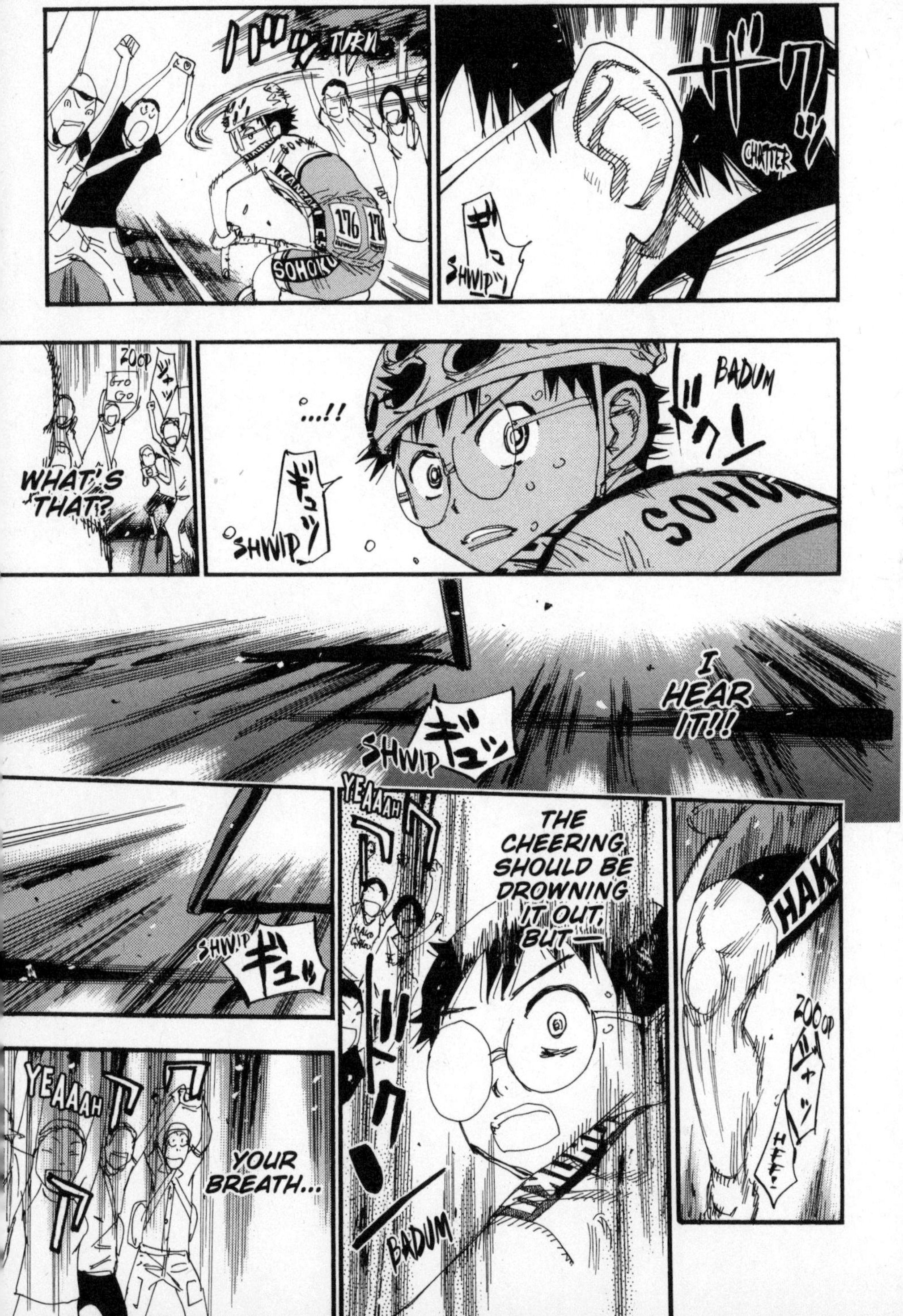
CHATTER
SHWIP
TURN
BADUM
...!!
SHWIP
ZOOP
GO GO
WHAT'S THAT?
I HEAR IT!!!
SHWIP
ZOOP
HEF!
THE CHEERING SHOULD BE DROWNING IT OUT, BUT—
YEAAAH
BADUM
SHWIP
YEAAAH
YOUR BREATH...

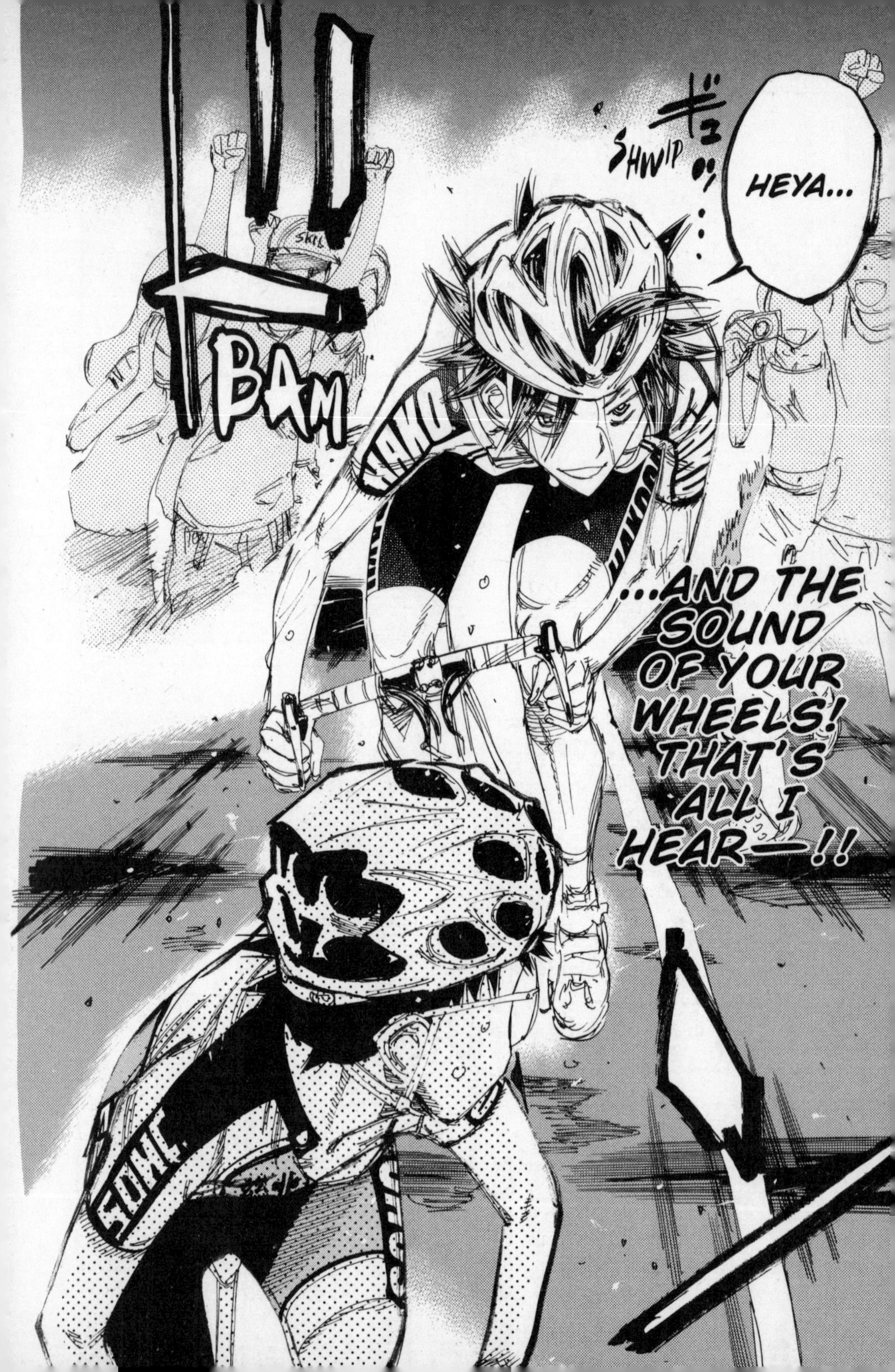
HEYA...
SHWIP
BAM
...AND THE SOUND OF YOUR WHEELS! THAT'S ALL I HEAR—!!

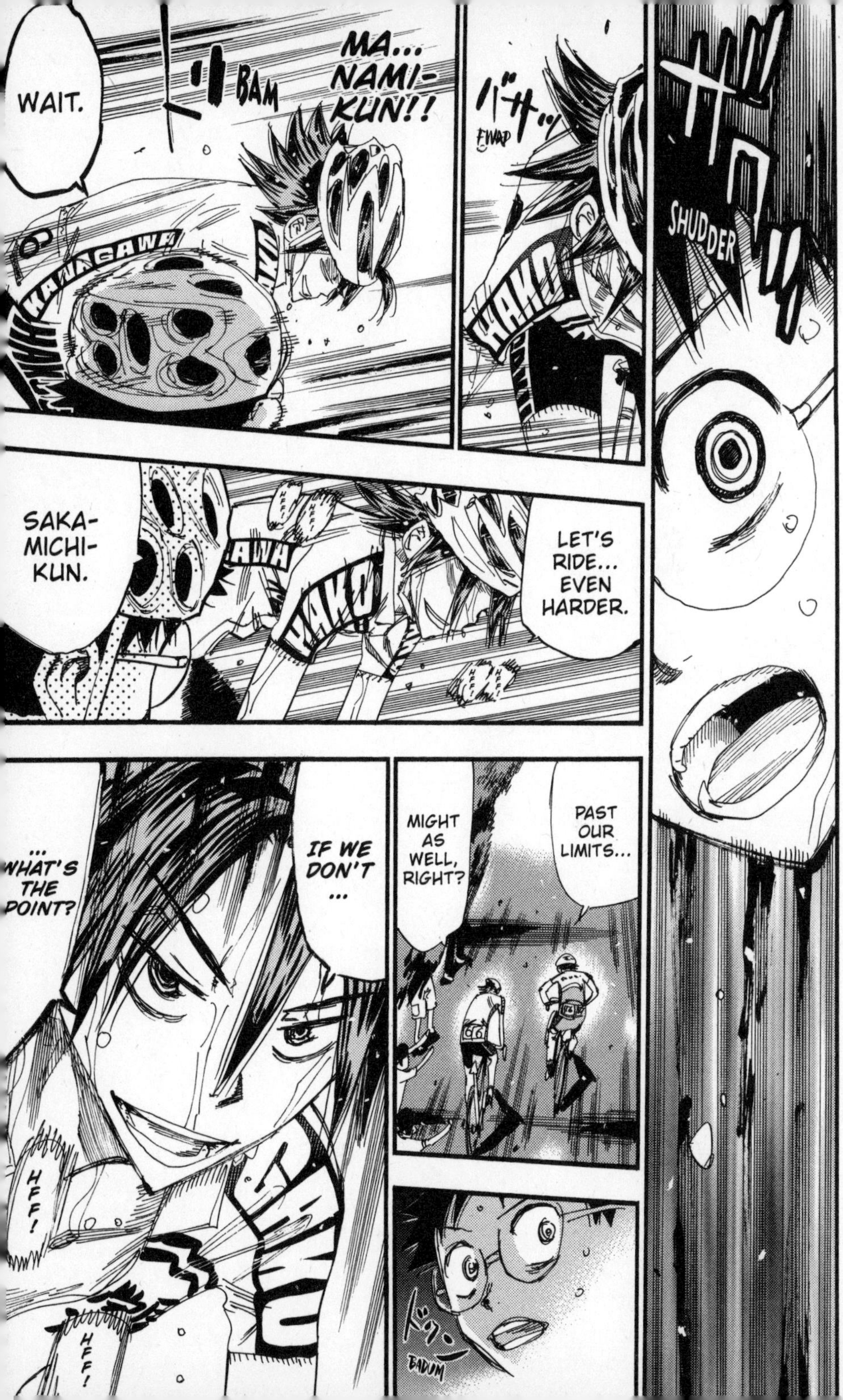
SHUDDER
FWAP
MA... NAMI-KUN!!
BAM
WAIT.
HFF! HFF!
LET'S RIDE... EVEN HARDER.
SAKA-MICHI-KUN.
PAST OUR LIMITS...
MIGHT AS WELL, RIGHT?
IF WE DON'T ...
...WHAT'S THE POINT?
HFF!
HFF!
BADUM

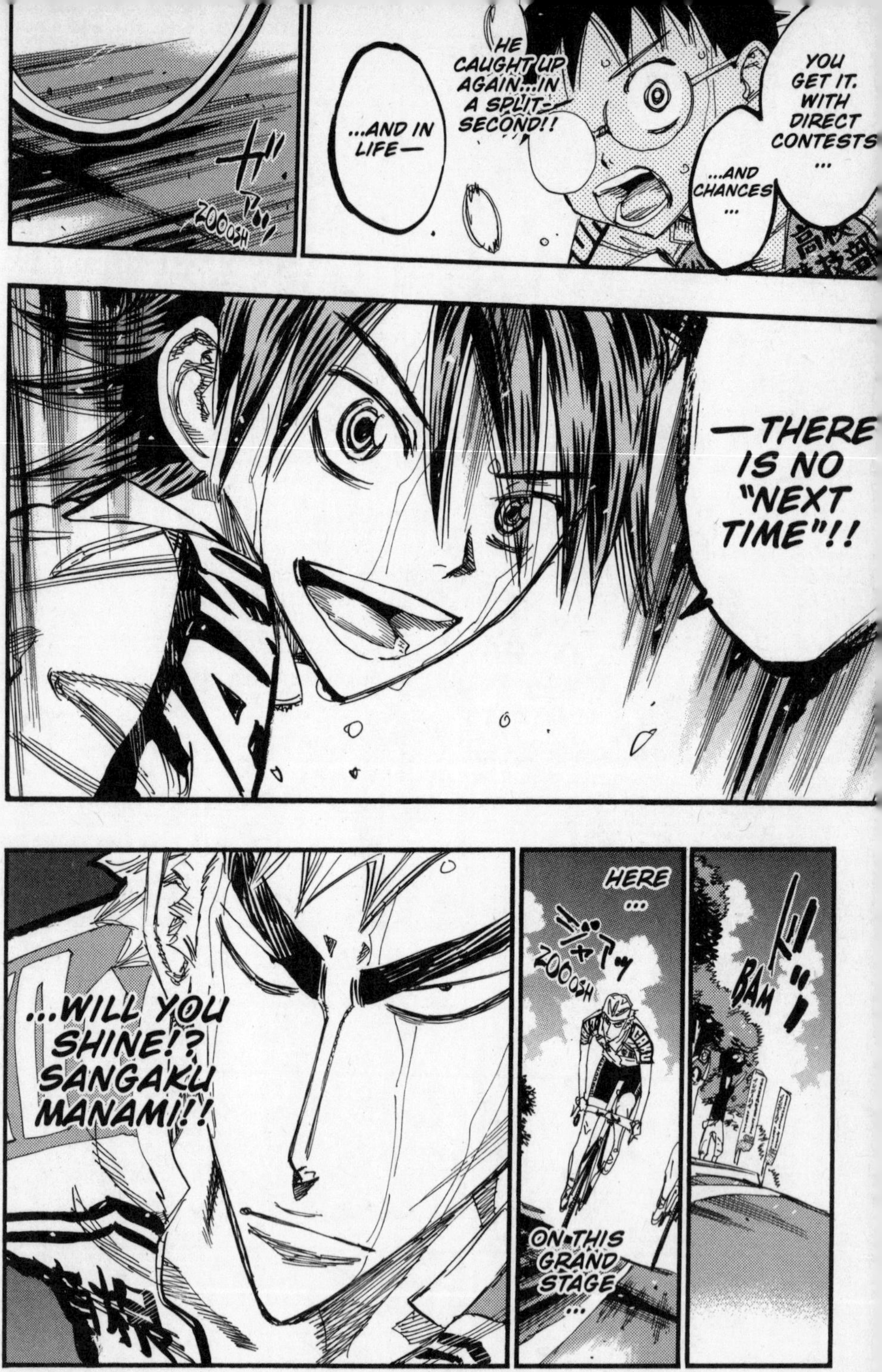
YOU GET IT. WITH DIRECT CONTESTS ...
...AND CHANCES ...
HE CAUGHT UP AGAIN...IN A SPLIT-SECOND!!
...AND IN LIFE—
ZOOOSH
—THERE IS NO "NEXT TIME"!!
BAM
HERE ...
ZOOOSH
ON THIS GRAND STAGE ...
...WILL YOU SHINE!? SANGAKU MANAMI!!

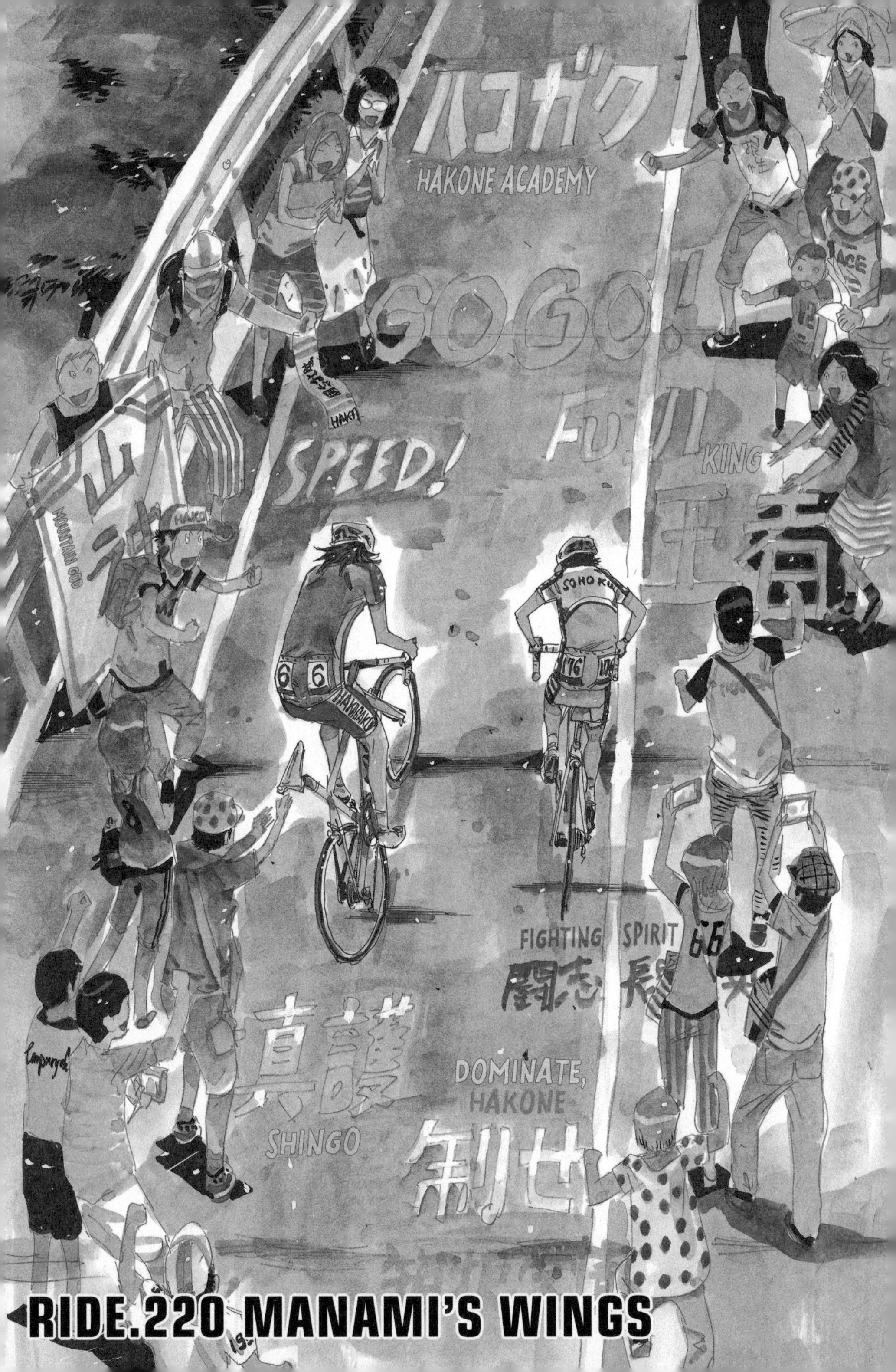
ハコガク
HAKONE ACADEMY
GOGO!
SPEED!
KING
MOUNTAIN GOD
SOHOKU
FIGHTING SPIRIT
DOMINATE, HAKONE
SHINGO

RIDE.220 MANAMI'S WINGS

SANGAKU MANAMI

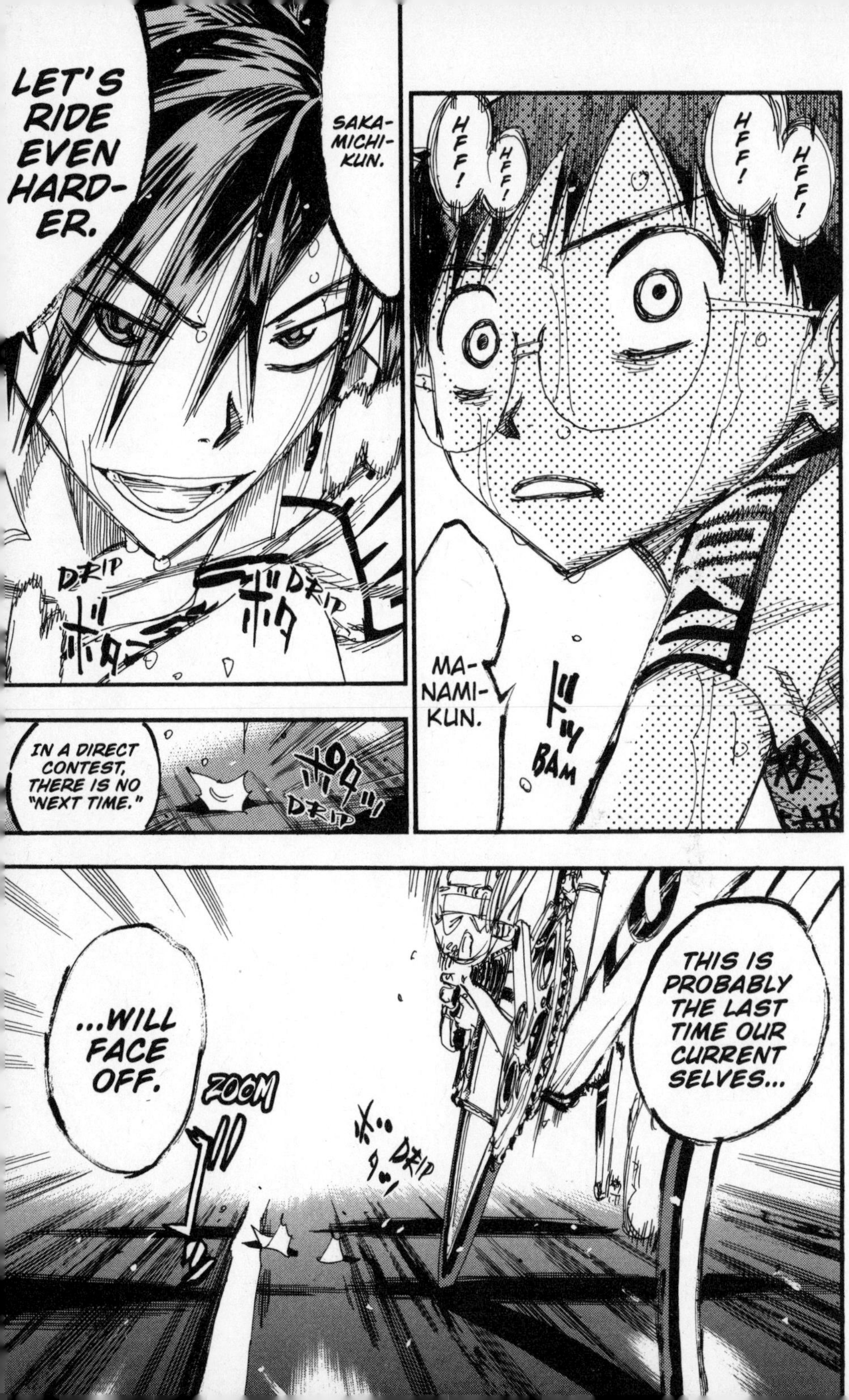
HFF!
HFF!
HFF!
HFF!
MA-NAMI-KUN.
BAM
SAKA-MICHI-KUN.
LET'S RIDE EVEN HARDER-ER.
DRIP
DRIP
IN A DIRECT CONTEST, THERE IS NO "NEXT TIME."
DRIP
THIS IS PROBABLY THE LAST TIME OUR CURRENT SELVES...
...WILL FACE OFF.
ZOOM
DRIP

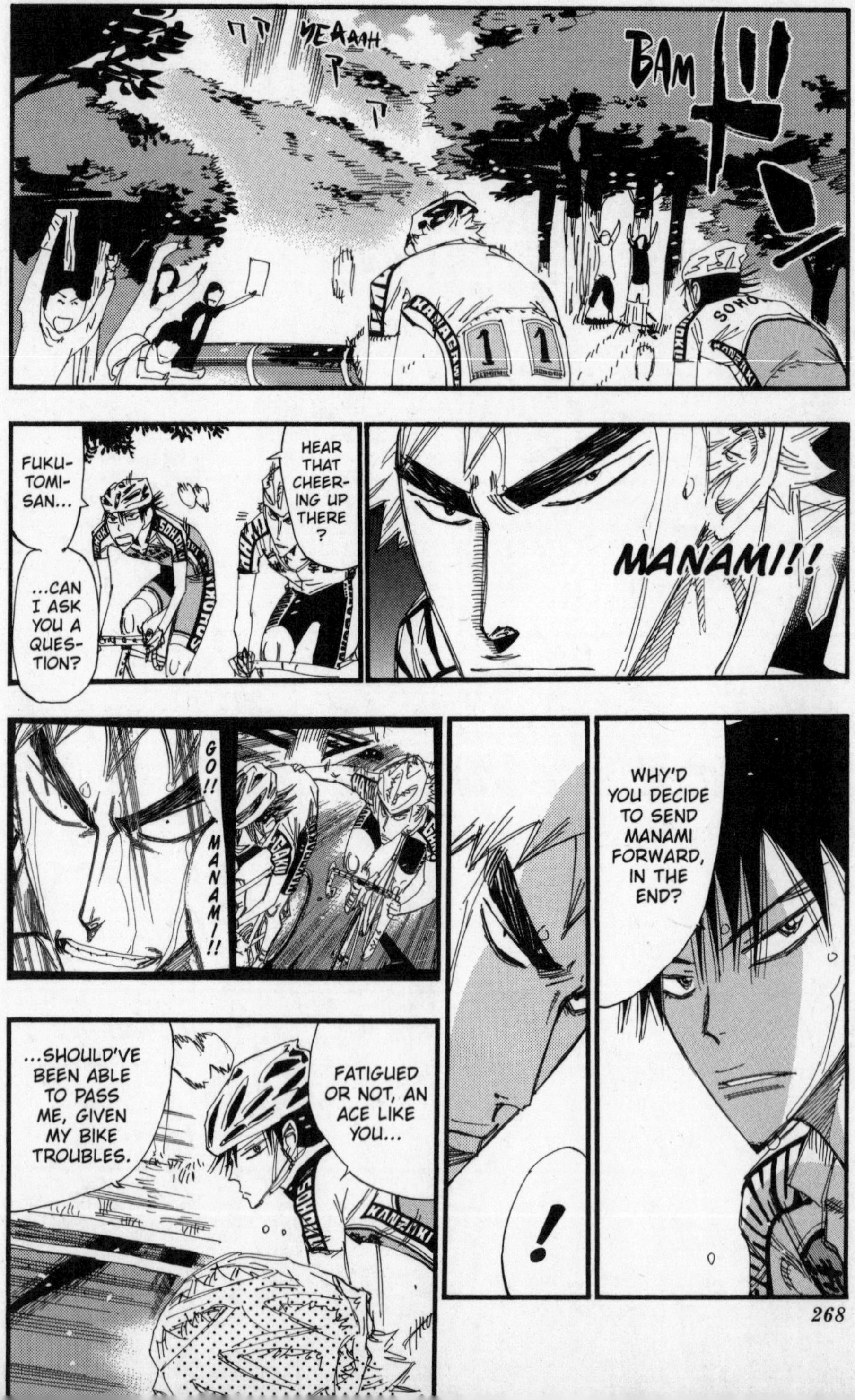
YEAAAH
BAM!!
MANAMI!!
HEAR THAT CHEERING UP THERE?
FUKUTOMI-SAN...
...CAN I ASK YOU A QUESTION?
WHY'D YOU DECIDE TO SEND MANAMI FORWARD, IN THE END?
!
GO!! MANAMI!!
FATIGUED OR NOT, AN ACE LIKE YOU...
...SHOULD'VE BEEN ABLE TO PASS ME, GIVEN MY BIKE TROUBLES.

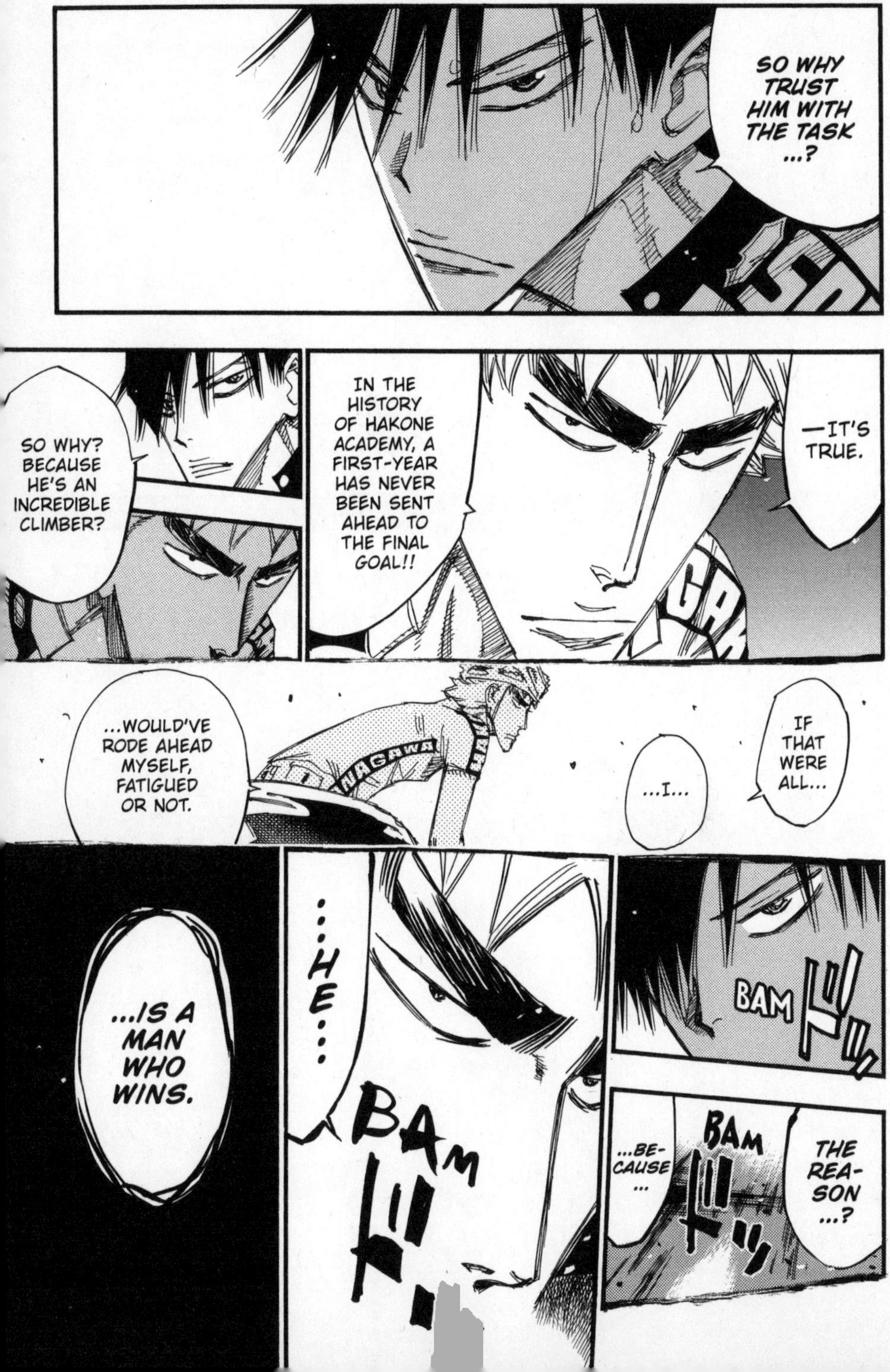
SO WHY TRUST HIM WITH THE TASK ...?
—IT'S TRUE.
IN THE HISTORY OF HAKONE ACADEMY, A FIRST-YEAR HAS NEVER BEEN SENT AHEAD TO THE FINAL GOAL!!
SO WHY? BECAUSE HE'S AN INCREDIBLE CLIMBER?
IF THAT WERE ALL...
...I...
...WOULD'VE RODE AHEAD MYSELF, FATIGUED OR NOT.
BAM
THE REASON ...?
BAM
...BECAUSE ...
...HE...
BAM
...IS A MAN WHO WINS.

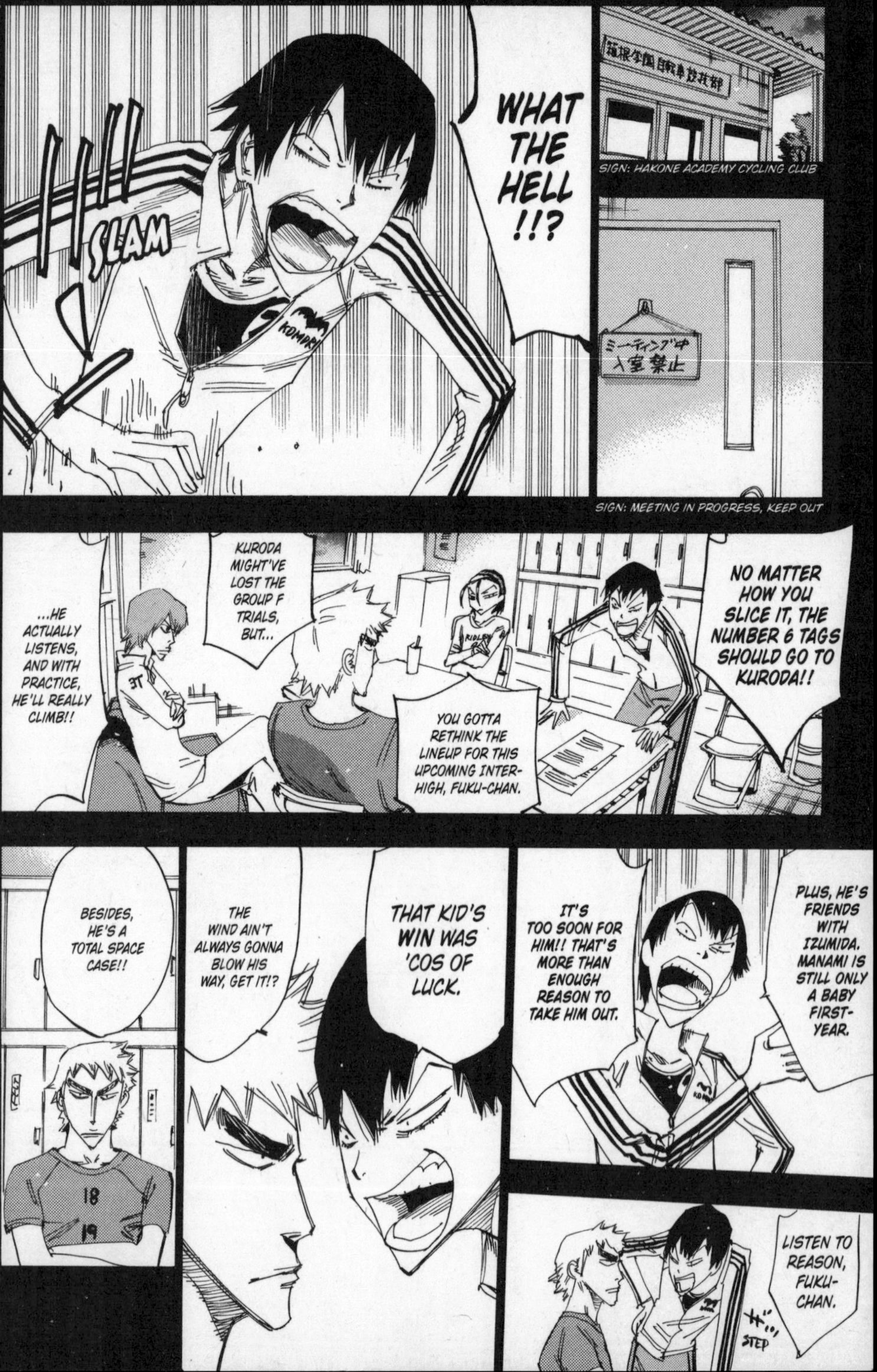

SIGN: HAKONE ACADEMY CYCLING CLUB
ミーティング中
入室禁止
SIGN: MEETING IN PROGRESS, KEEP OUT
WHAT THE HELL!!?
SLAM
NO MATTER HOW YOU SLICE IT, THE NUMBER 6 TAGS SHOULD GO TO KURODA!!
KURODA MIGHT'VE LOST THE GROUP F TRIALS, BUT...
...HE ACTUALLY LISTENS, AND WITH PRACTICE, HE'LL REALLY CLIMB!!
YOU GOTTA RETHINK THE LINEUP FOR THIS UPCOMING INTER-HIGH, FUKU-CHAN.
PLUS, HE'S FRIENDS WITH IZUMIDA. MANAMI IS STILL ONLY A BABY FIRST-YEAR.
IT'S TOO SOON FOR HIM!! THAT'S MORE THAN ENOUGH REASON TO TAKE HIM OUT.
LISTEN TO REASON, FUKU-CHAN.
STEP
THAT KID'S WIN WAS 'COS OF LUCK.
THE WIND AIN'T ALWAYS GONNA BLOW HIS WAY, GET IT!?
BESIDES, HE'S A TOTAL SPACE CASE!!

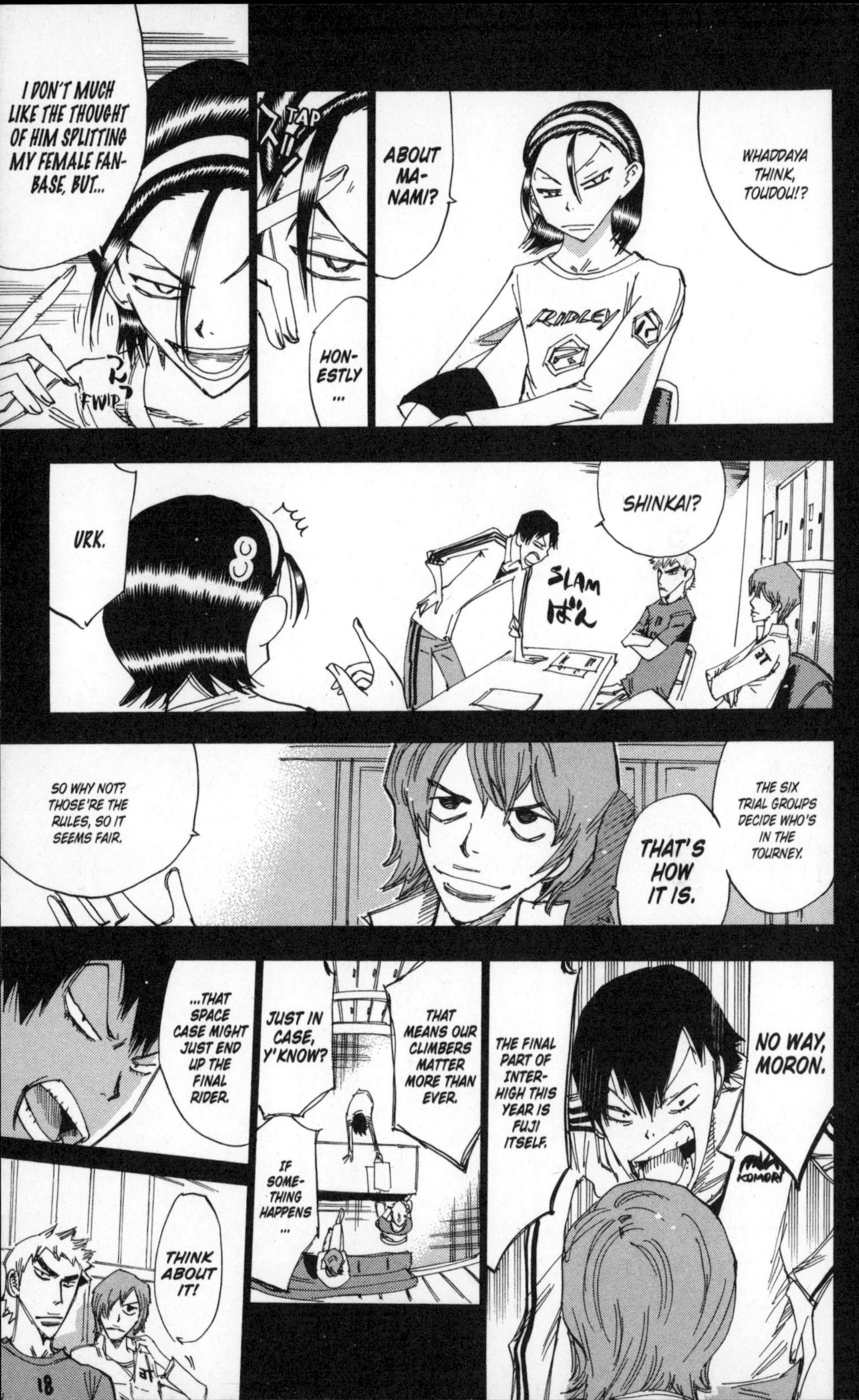
WHADDAYA THINK, TOUDOU!?
ABOUT MA-NAMI?
TAP
HON-ESTLY ...
I DON'T MUCH LIKE THE THOUGHT OF HIM SPLITTING MY FEMALE FAN-BASE, BUT...
FWIP
SHINKAI?
SLAM
URK.
THE SIX TRIAL GROUPS DECIDE WHO'S IN THE TOURNEY.
THAT'S HOW IT IS.
SO WHY NOT? THOSE'RE THE RULES, SO IT SEEMS FAIR.
NO WAY, MORON.
THE FINAL PART OF INTER-HIGH THIS YEAR IS FUJI ITSELF.
KOMORI
THAT MEANS OUR CLIMBERS MATTER MORE THAN EVER.
JUST IN CASE, Y'KNOW?
IF SOMETHING HAPPENS ...
...THAT SPACE CASE MIGHT JUST END UP THE FINAL RIDER.
THINK ABOUT IT!

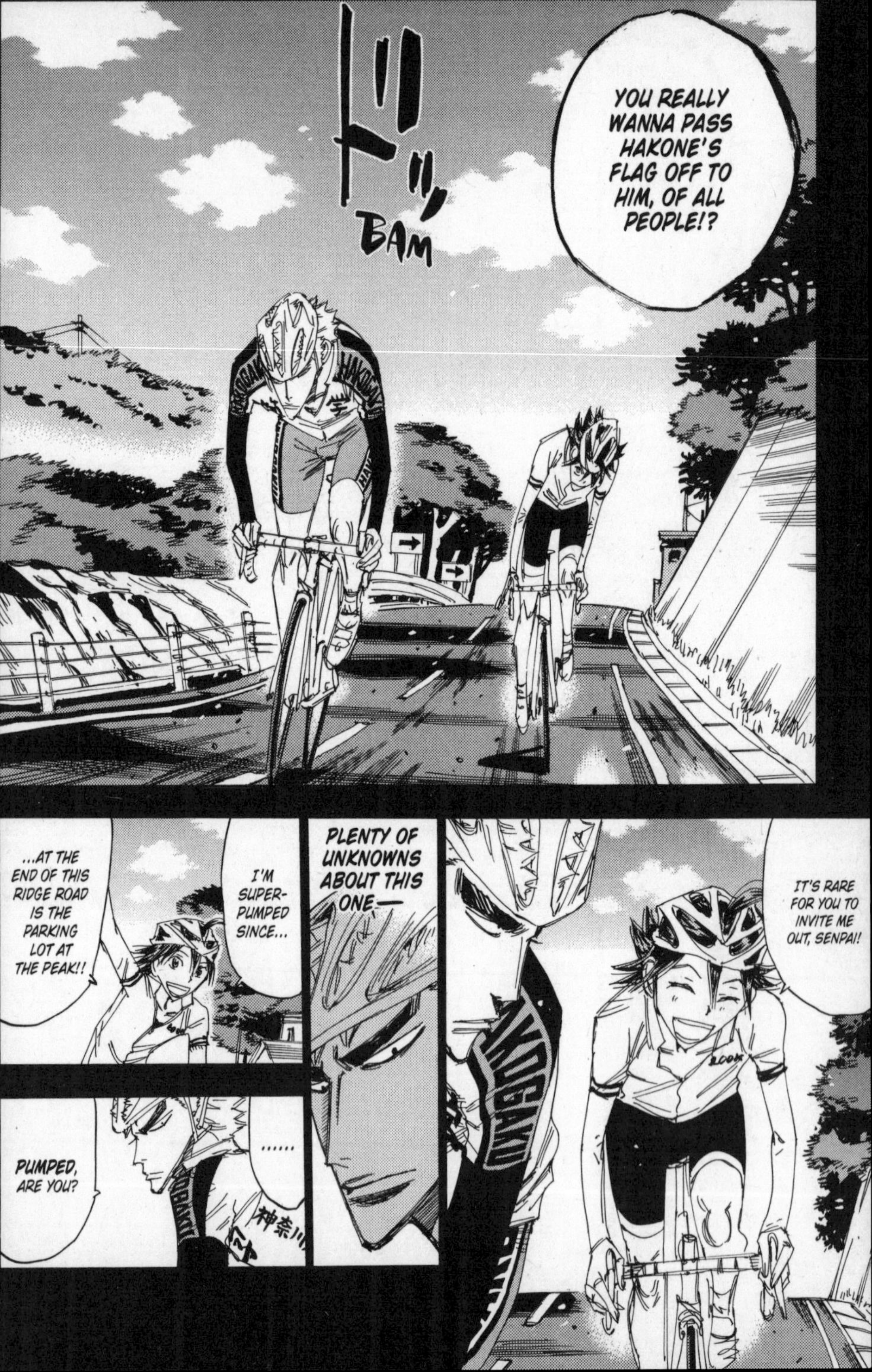
YOU REALLY WANNA PASS HAKONE'S FLAG OFF TO HIM, OF ALL PEOPLE!?
ドリッ
BAM
IT'S RARE FOR YOU TO INVITE ME OUT, SENPAI!
PLENTY OF UNKNOWNS ABOUT THIS ONE.—
I'M SUPER-PUMPED SINCE...
...AT THE END OF THIS RIDGE ROAD IS THE PARKING LOT AT THE PEAK!!
......
PUMPED, ARE YOU?

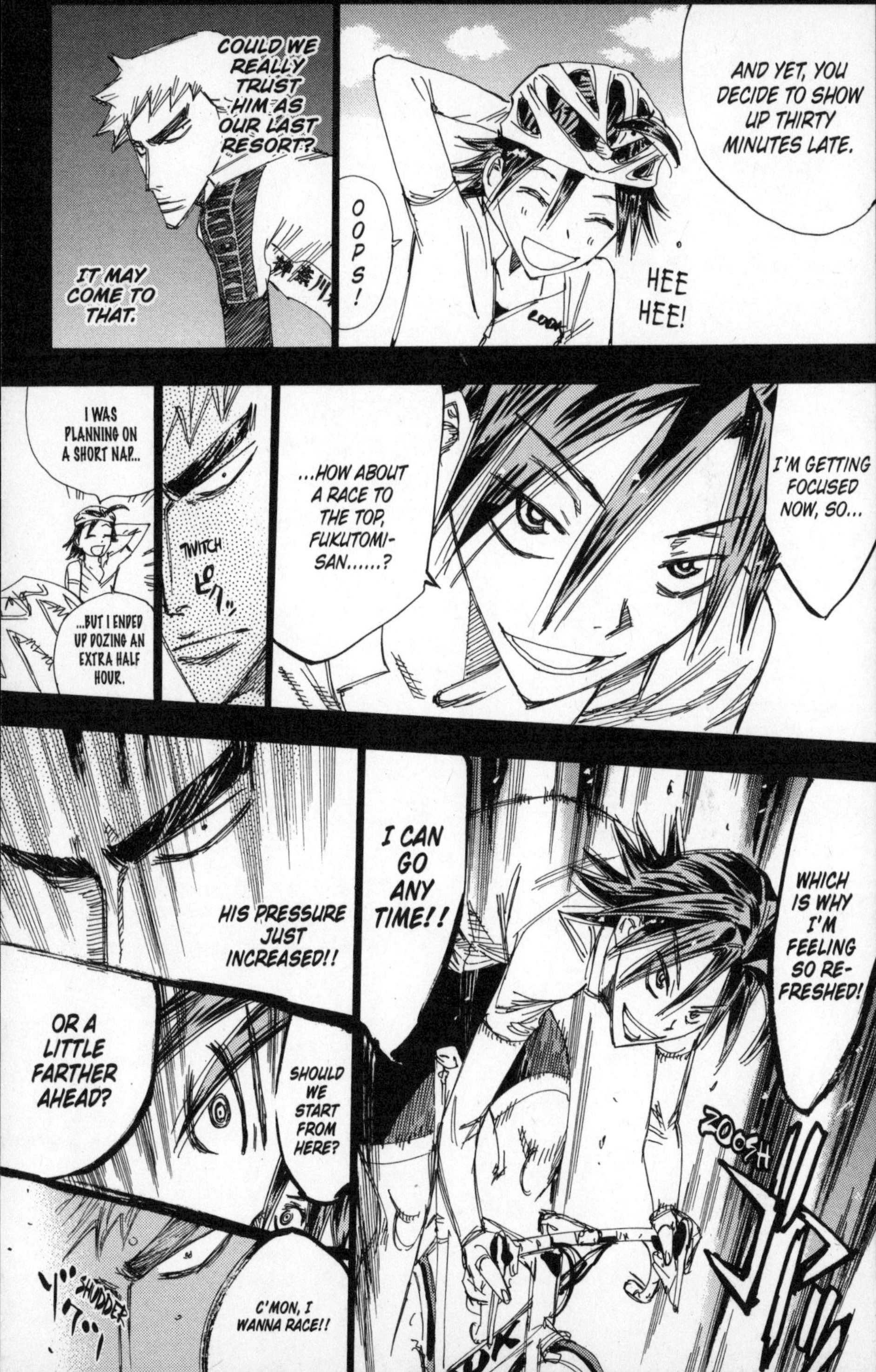
AND YET, YOU DECIDE TO SHOW UP THIRTY MINUTES LATE.
HEE HEE!
OOPS!
COULD WE REALLY TRUST HIM AS OUR LAST RESORT?
IT MAY COME TO THAT.
I'M GETTING FOCUSED NOW, SO...
...HOW ABOUT A RACE TO THE TOP, FUKUTOMI-SAN......?
TWITCH
I WAS PLANNING ON A SHORT NAP...
...BUT I ENDED UP DOZING AN EXTRA HALF HOUR.
WHICH IS WHY I'M FEELING SO RE-FRESHED!
I CAN GO ANY TIME!!
ZOOSH
HIS PRESSURE JUST INCREASED!!
SHOULD WE START FROM HERE?
OR A LITTLE FARTHER AHEAD?
C'MON, I WANNA RACE!!
SHUDDER

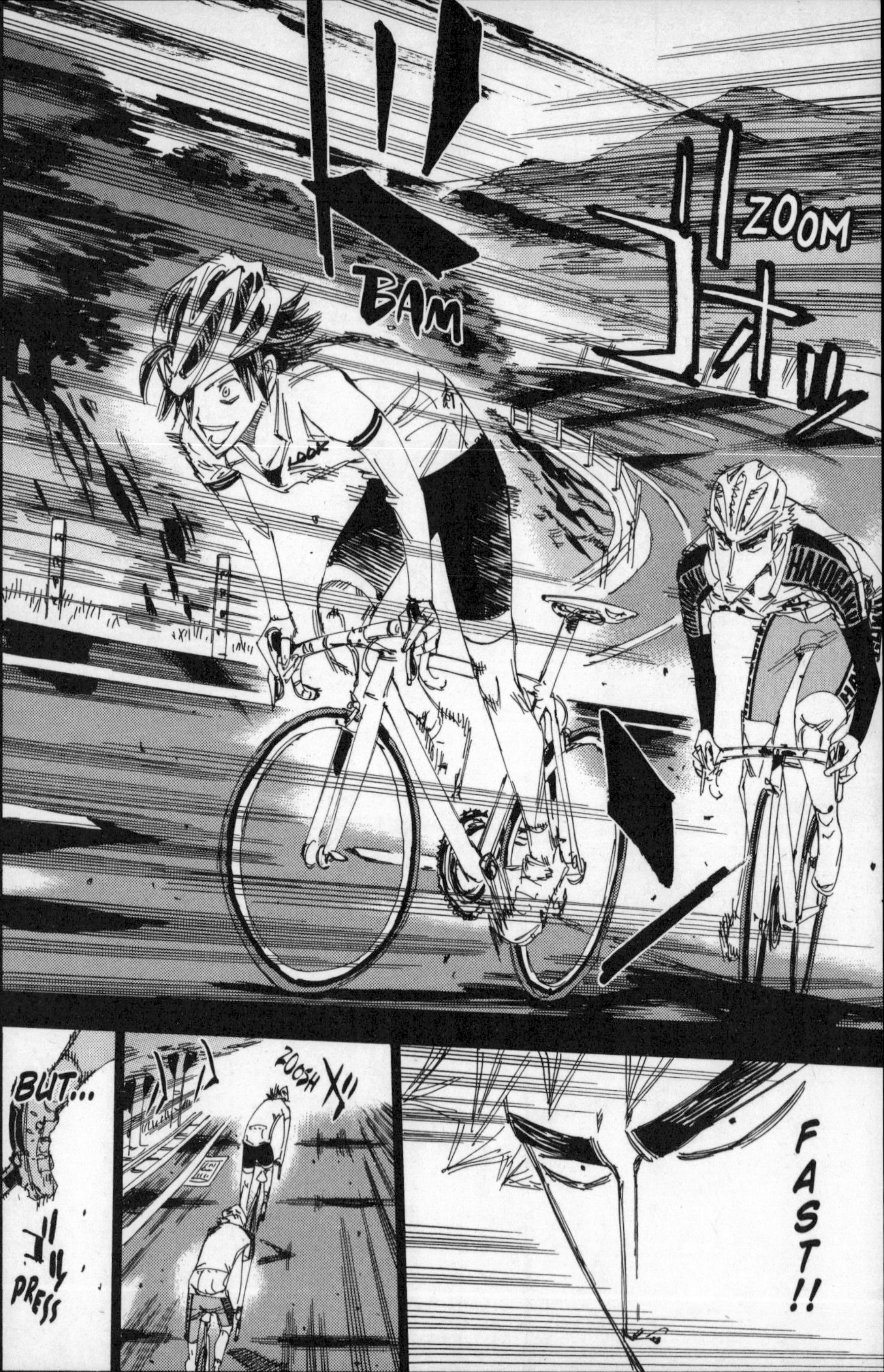
ZOOM
BAM
FAST!!
ZOOSH
BUT...
PRESS

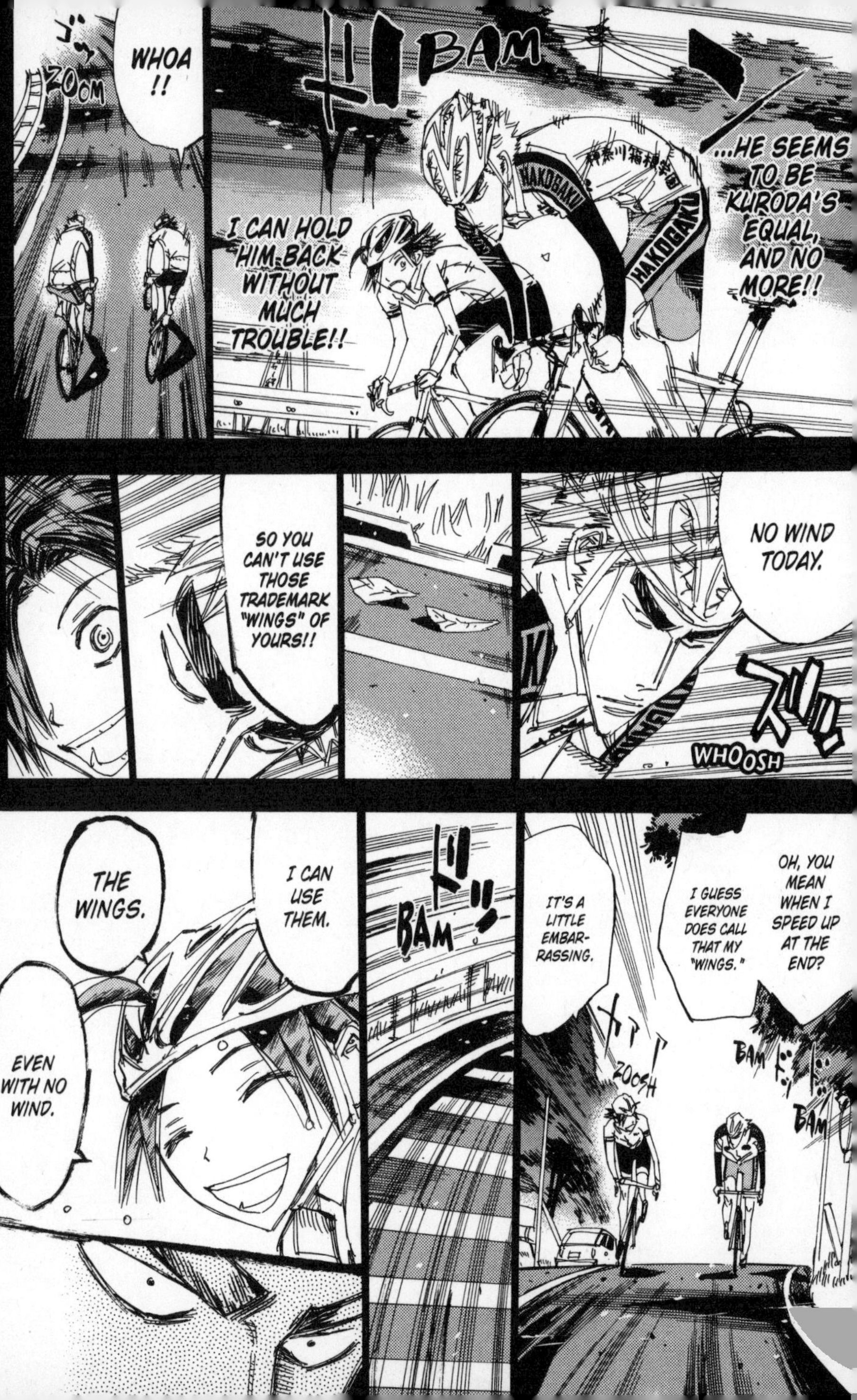
BAM
...HE SEEMS TO BE KURODA'S EQUAL, AND NO MORE!!
I CAN HOLD HIM BACK WITHOUT MUCH TROUBLE!!
WHOA !!
ZOOM
NO WIND TODAY.
WHOOSH
SO YOU CAN'T USE THOSE TRADEMARK "WINGS" OF YOURS!!
OH, YOU MEAN WHEN I SPEED UP AT THE END?
I GUESS EVERYONE DOES CALL THAT MY "WINGS."
IT'S A LITTLE EMBARRASSING.
BAM
ZOOSH
BAM
BAM
I CAN USE THEM.
THE WINGS.
EVEN WITH NO WIND.

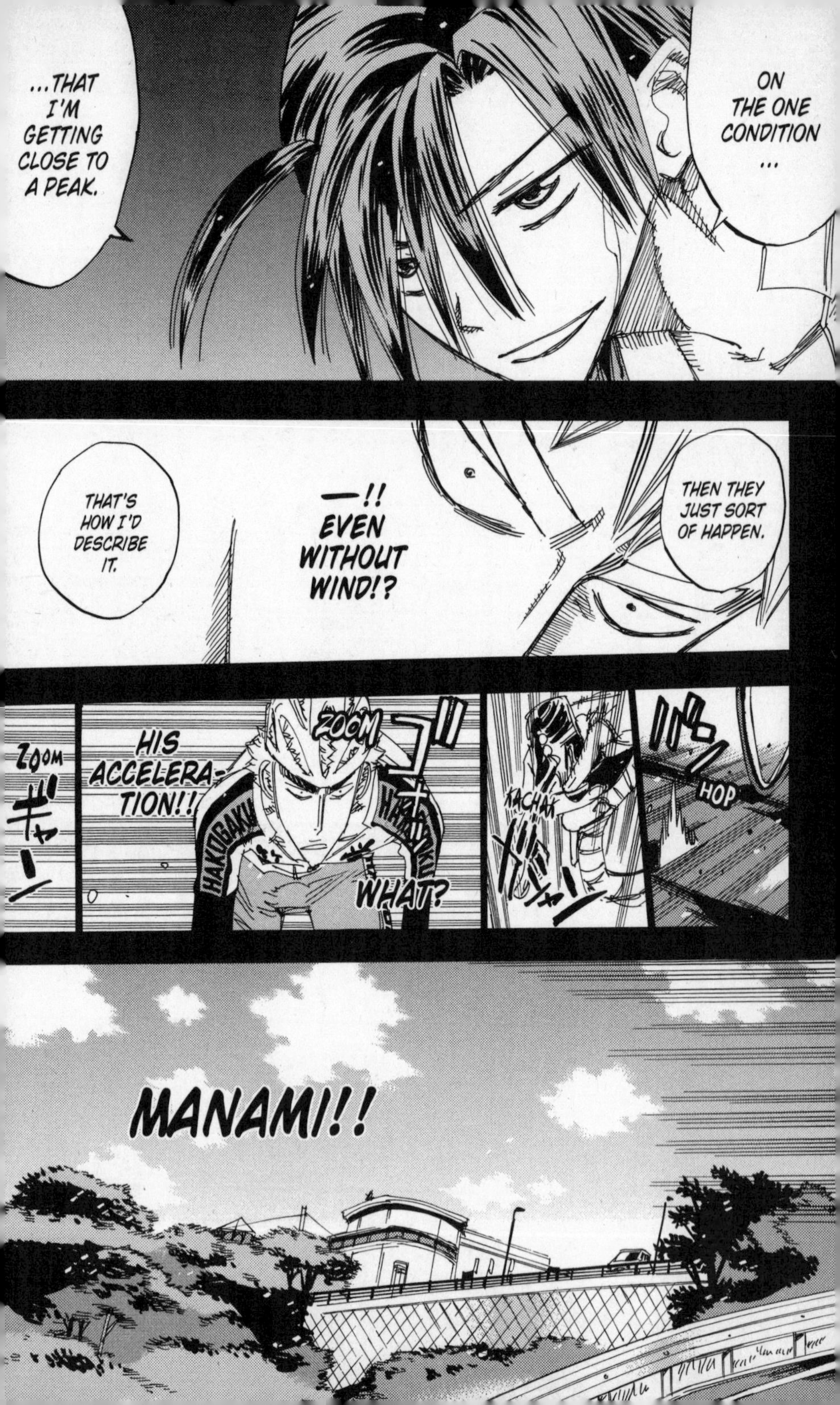
ON THE ONE CONDITION ...
...THAT I'M GETTING CLOSE TO A PEAK.
THEN THEY JUST SORT OF HAPPEN.
—!! EVEN WITHOUT WIND!?
THAT'S HOW I'D DESCRIBE IT.
HOP
KACHA
ZOOM
HIS ACCELERA-TION!!
WHAT?
ZOOM
MANAMI!!

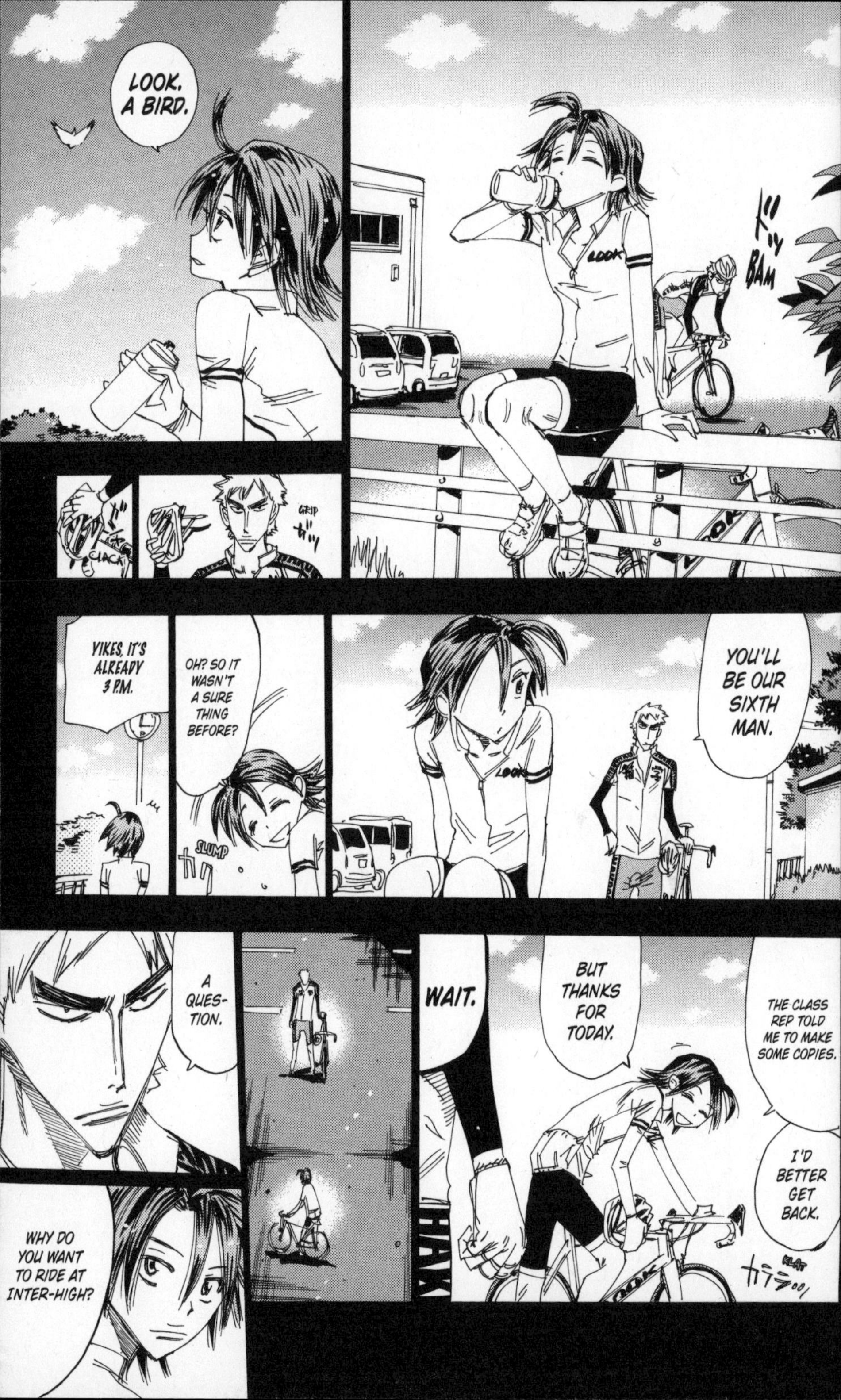
BAM
LOOK. A BIRD.
GRIP
CLACK
YOU'LL BE OUR SIXTH MAN.
OH? SO IT WASN'T A SURE THING BEFORE?
SLUMP
YIKES, IT'S ALREADY 3 P.M.
THE CLASS REP TOLD ME TO MAKE SOME COPIES.
I'D BETTER GET BACK.
KLAT
BUT THANKS FOR TODAY.
WAIT.
HAK
A QUESTION.
WHY DO YOU WANT TO RIDE AT INTER-HIGH?

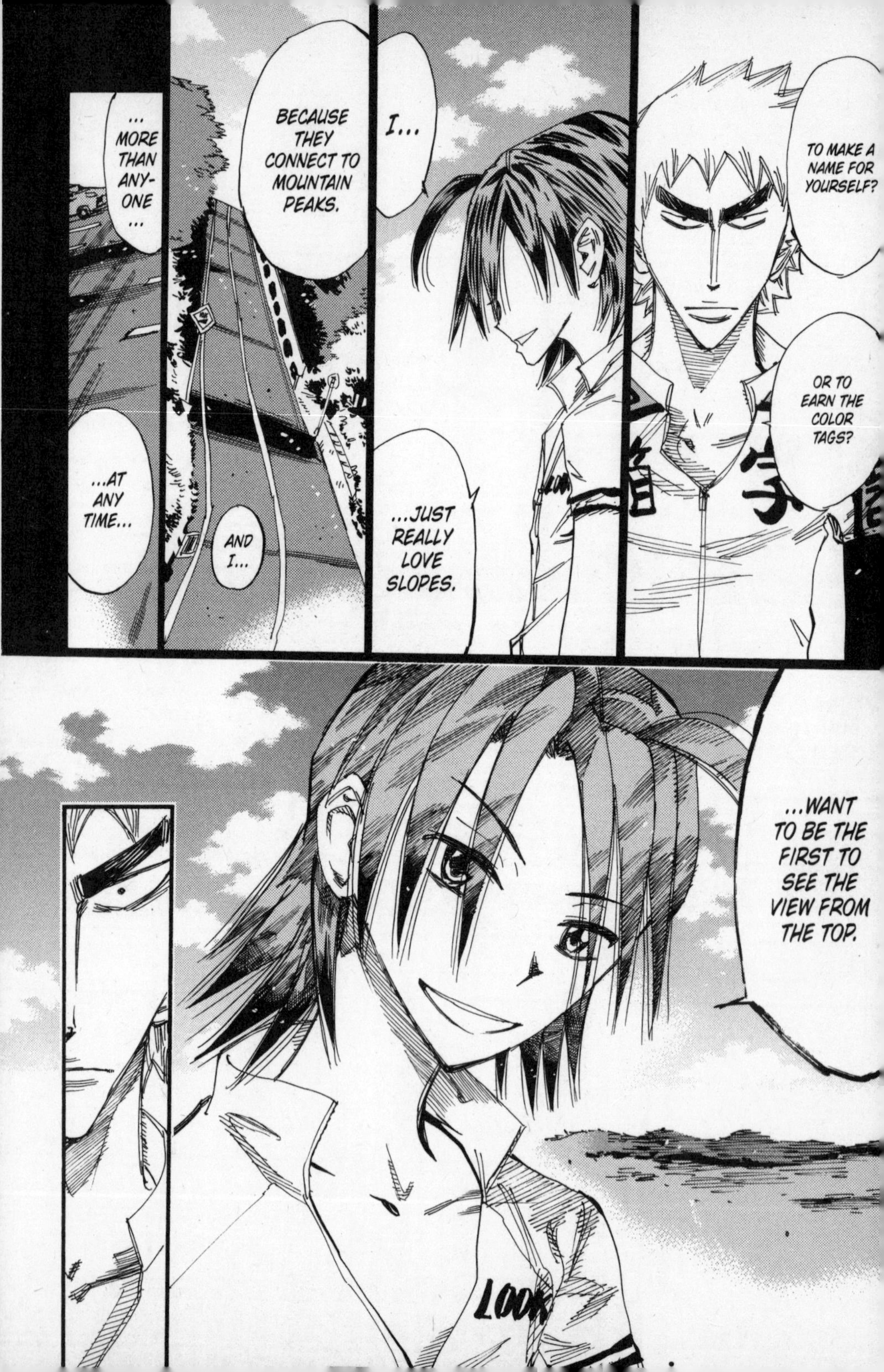

TO MAKE A NAME FOR YOURSELF?
OR TO EARN THE COLOR TAGS?
I...
...JUST REALLY LOVE SLOPES.
BECAUSE THEY CONNECT TO MOUNTAIN PEAKS.
AND I...
...MORE THAN ANY-ONE...
...AT ANY TIME...
...WANT TO BE THE FIRST TO SEE THE VIEW FROM THE TOP.
LOOK

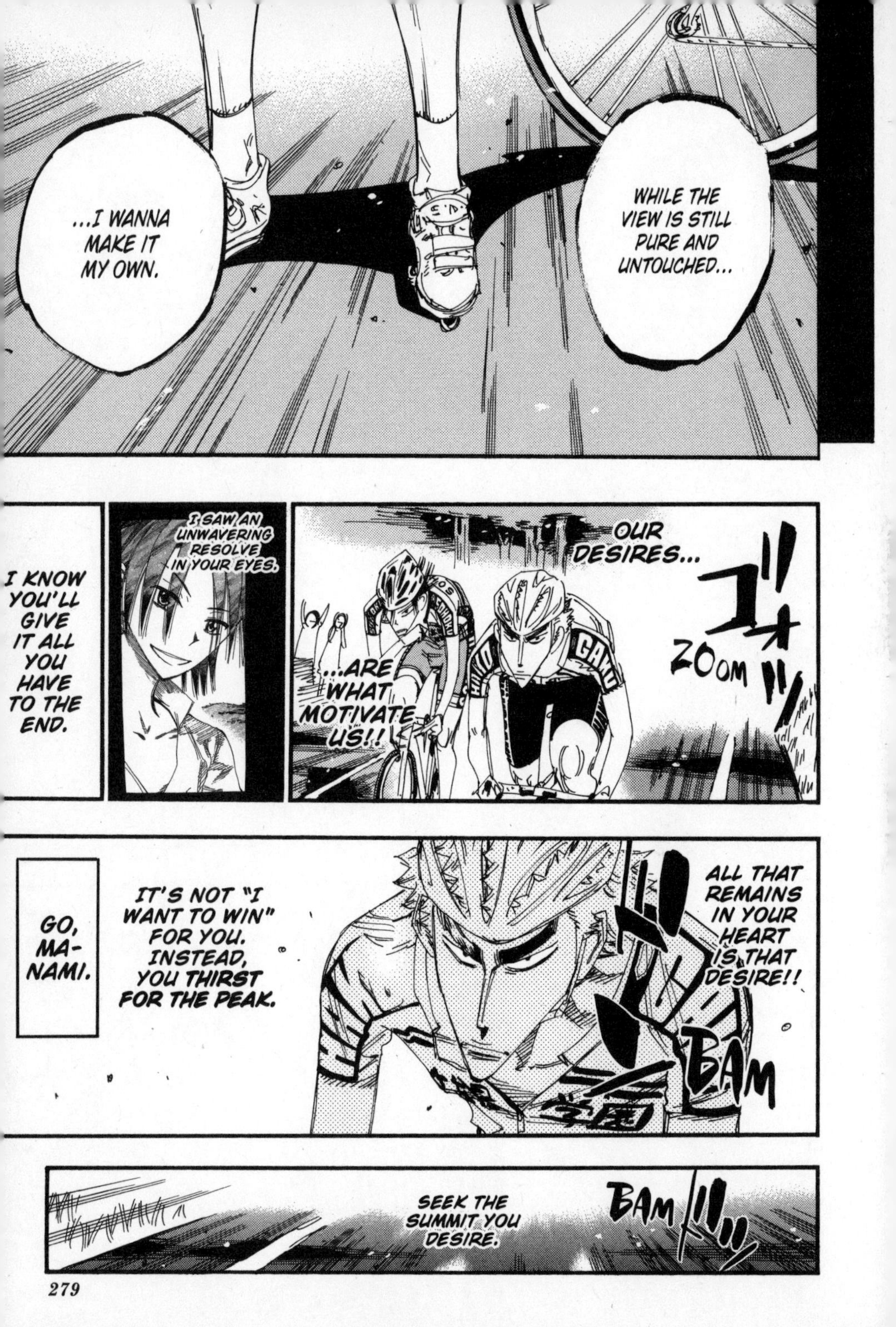
WHILE THE VIEW IS STILL PURE AND UNTOUCHED...
...I WANNA MAKE IT MY OWN.
OUR DESIRES...
ZOOM
...ARE WHAT MOTIVATE US!!
I SAW AN UNWAVERING RESOLVE IN YOUR EYES.
I KNOW YOU'LL GIVE IT ALL YOU HAVE TO THE END.
ALL THAT REMAINS IN YOUR HEART IS THAT DESIRE!!
BAM
IT'S NOT "I WANT TO WIN" FOR YOU. INSTEAD, YOU THIRST FOR THE PEAK.
GO, MA-NAMI.
BAM
SEEK THE SUMMIT YOU DESIRE.

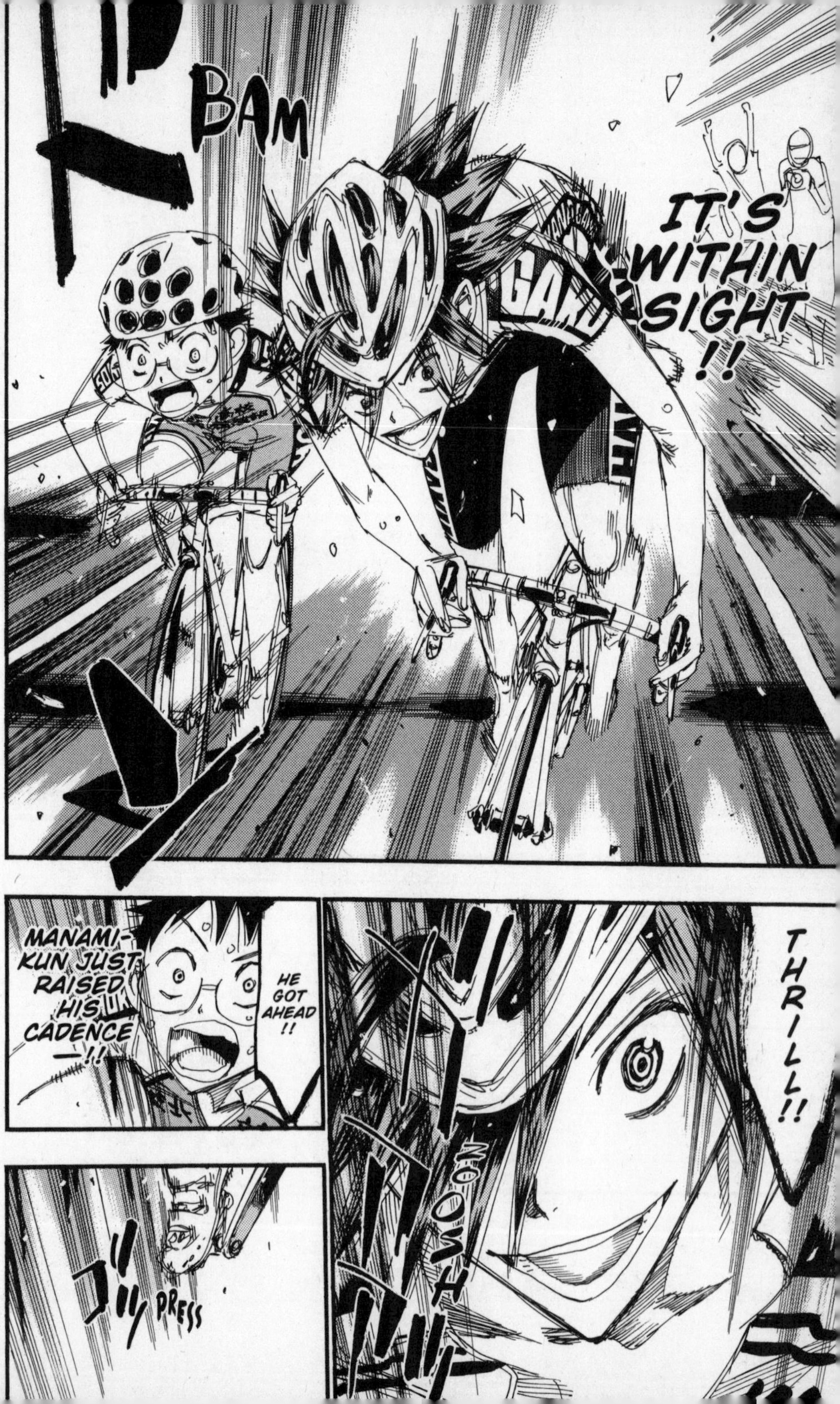
IT'S WITHIN SIGHT!!
BAM
THRILL!!
WOOSH
HE GOT AHEAD!!
MANAMI-KUN JUST RAISED HIS CADENCE—!!
PRESS

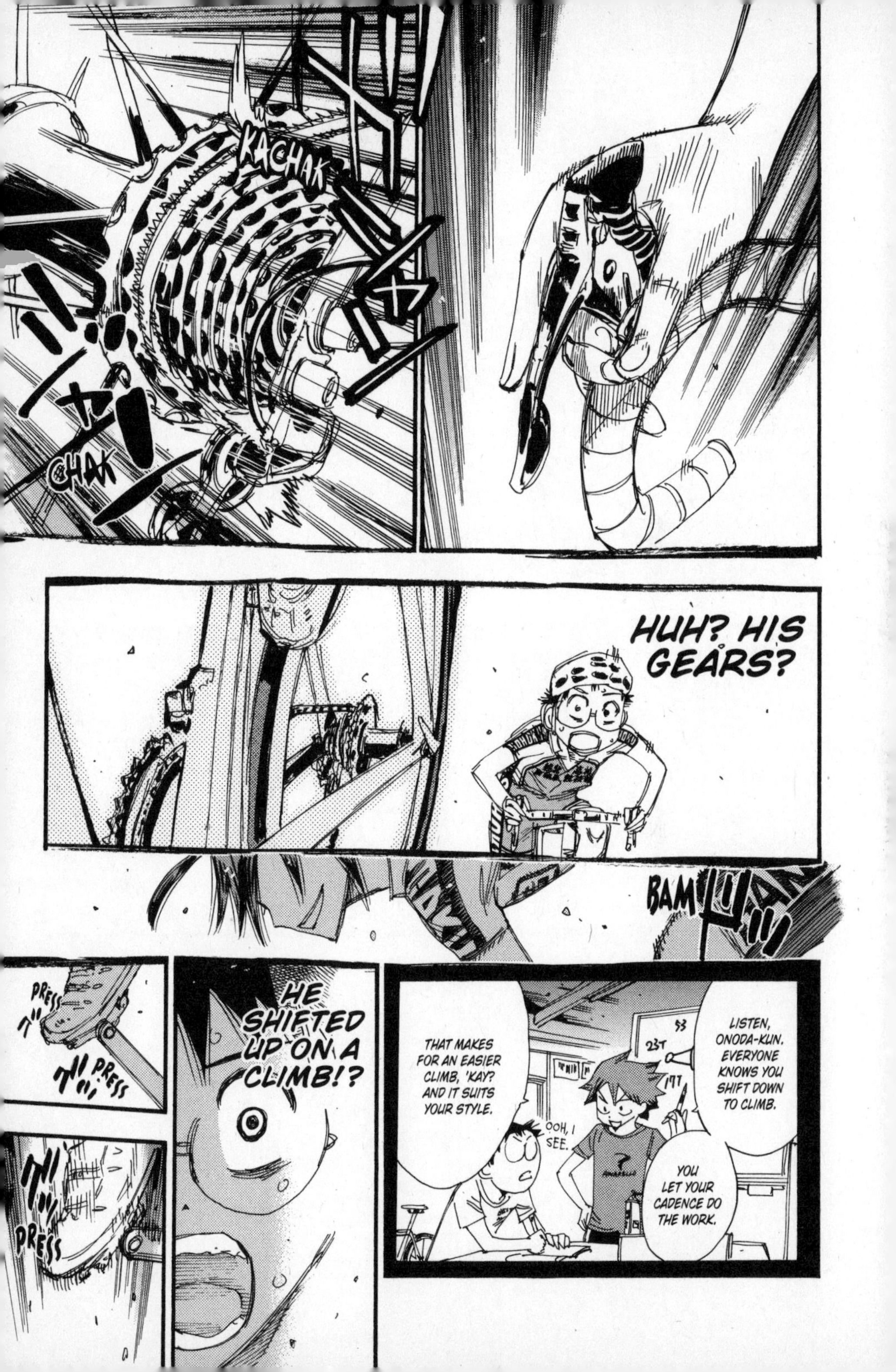
KACHAK
CHAK
HUH? HIS GEARS?
BAM
LISTEN, ONODA-KUN. EVERYONE KNOWS YOU SHIFT DOWN TO CLIMB.
YOU LET YOUR CADENCE DO THE WORK.
OOH, I SEE.
THAT MAKES FOR AN EASIER CLIMB, 'KAY? AND IT SUITS YOUR STYLE.
HE SHIFTED UP ON A CLIMB!?
PRESS
PRESS
PRESS

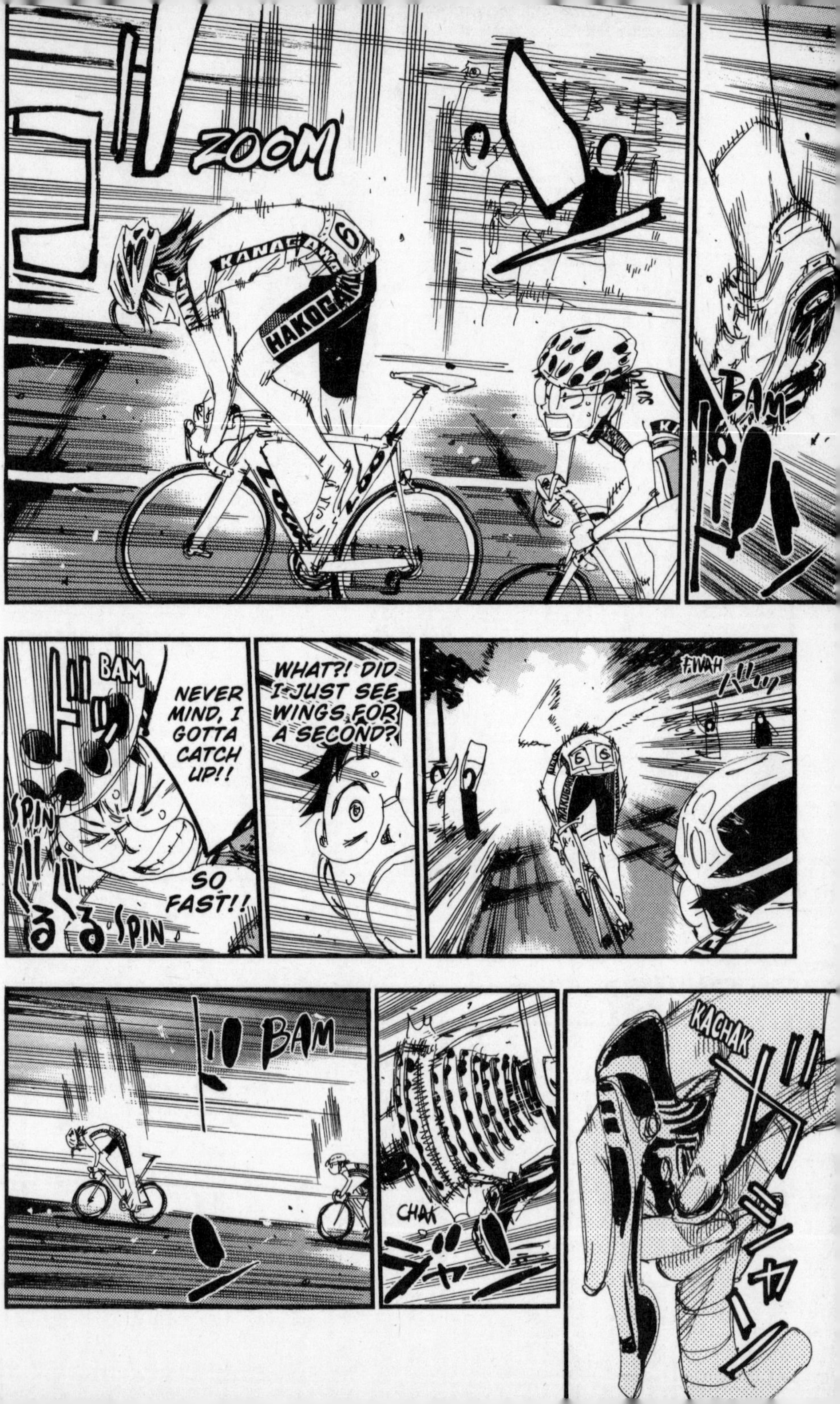
BAM
ZOOM
F.WAH
WHAT?! DID I JUST SEE WINGS FOR A SECOND?
BAM
NEVER MIND, I GOTTA CATCH UP!!
SPIN
SO FAST!!
SPIN
KACHAK
CHAK
BAM

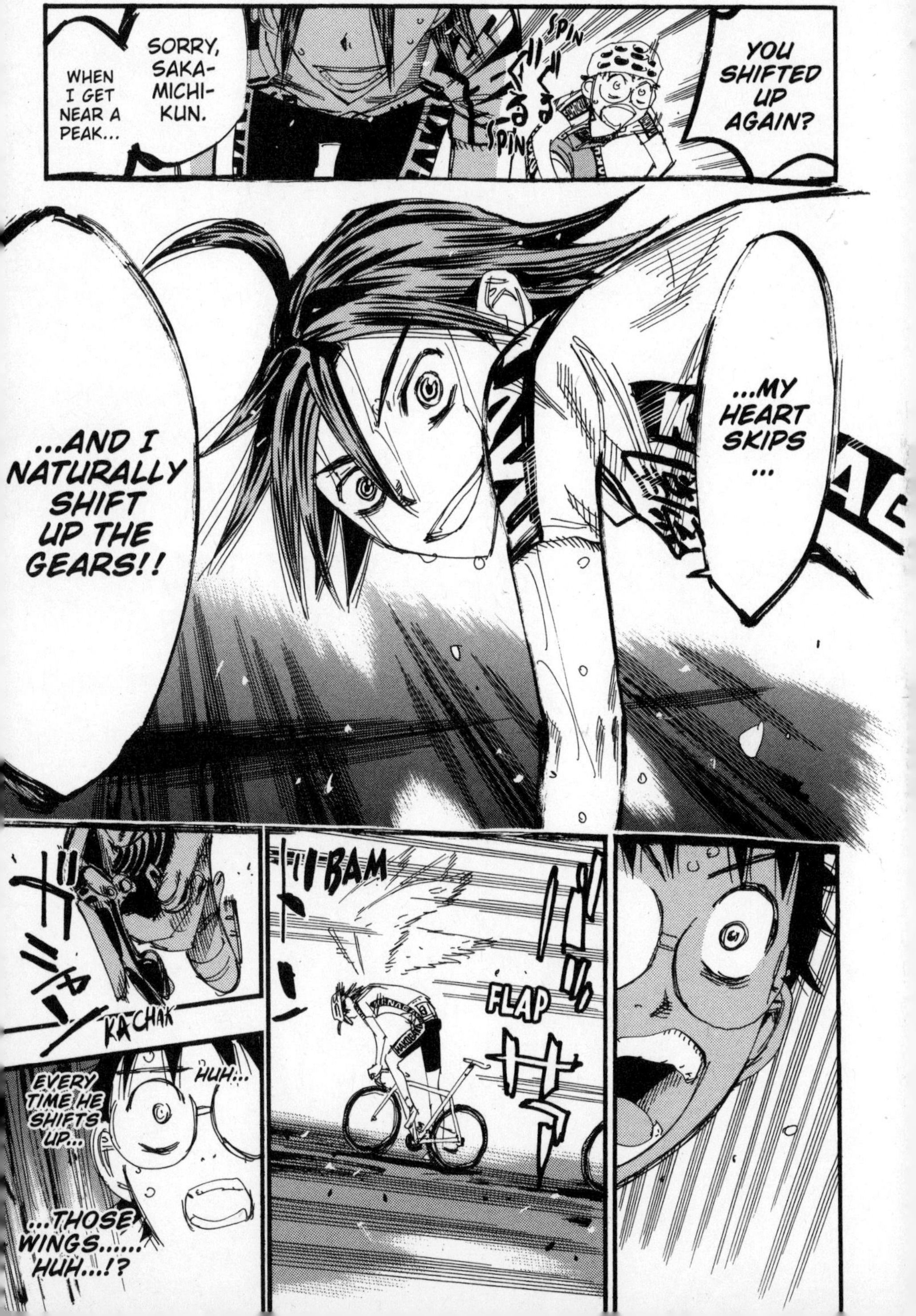
YOU SHIFTED UP AGAIN?
SPIN
SPIN
SORRY, SAKA-MICHI-KUN.
WHEN I GET NEAR A PEAK...
...MY HEART SKIPS ...
...AND I NATURALLY SHIFT UP THE GEARS!!
BAM
FLAP
KA-CHAK
HUH...
EVERY TIME HE SHIFTS UP...
...THOSE WINGS...... HUH...!?

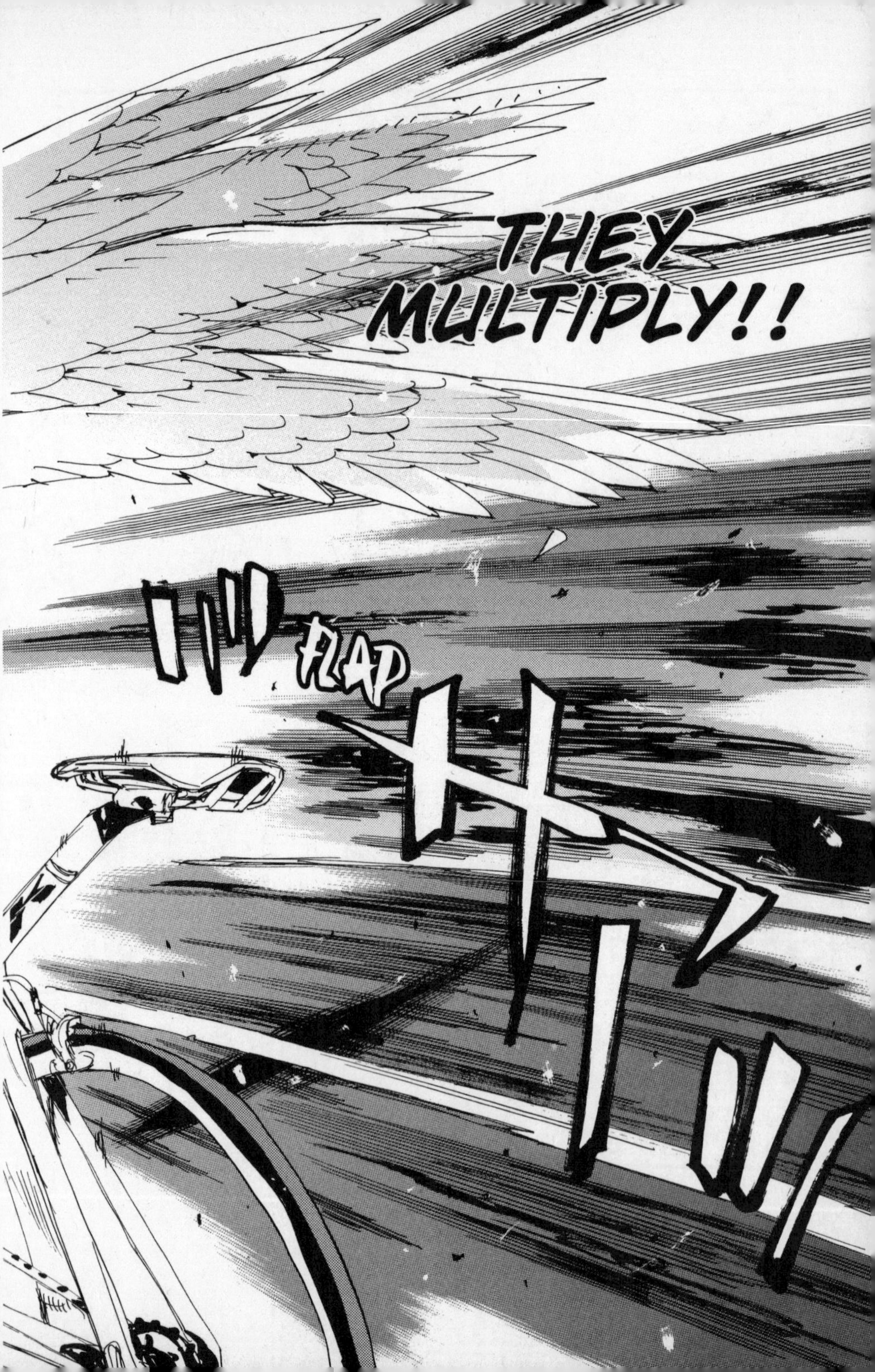
THEY MULTIPLY!!
FLAP

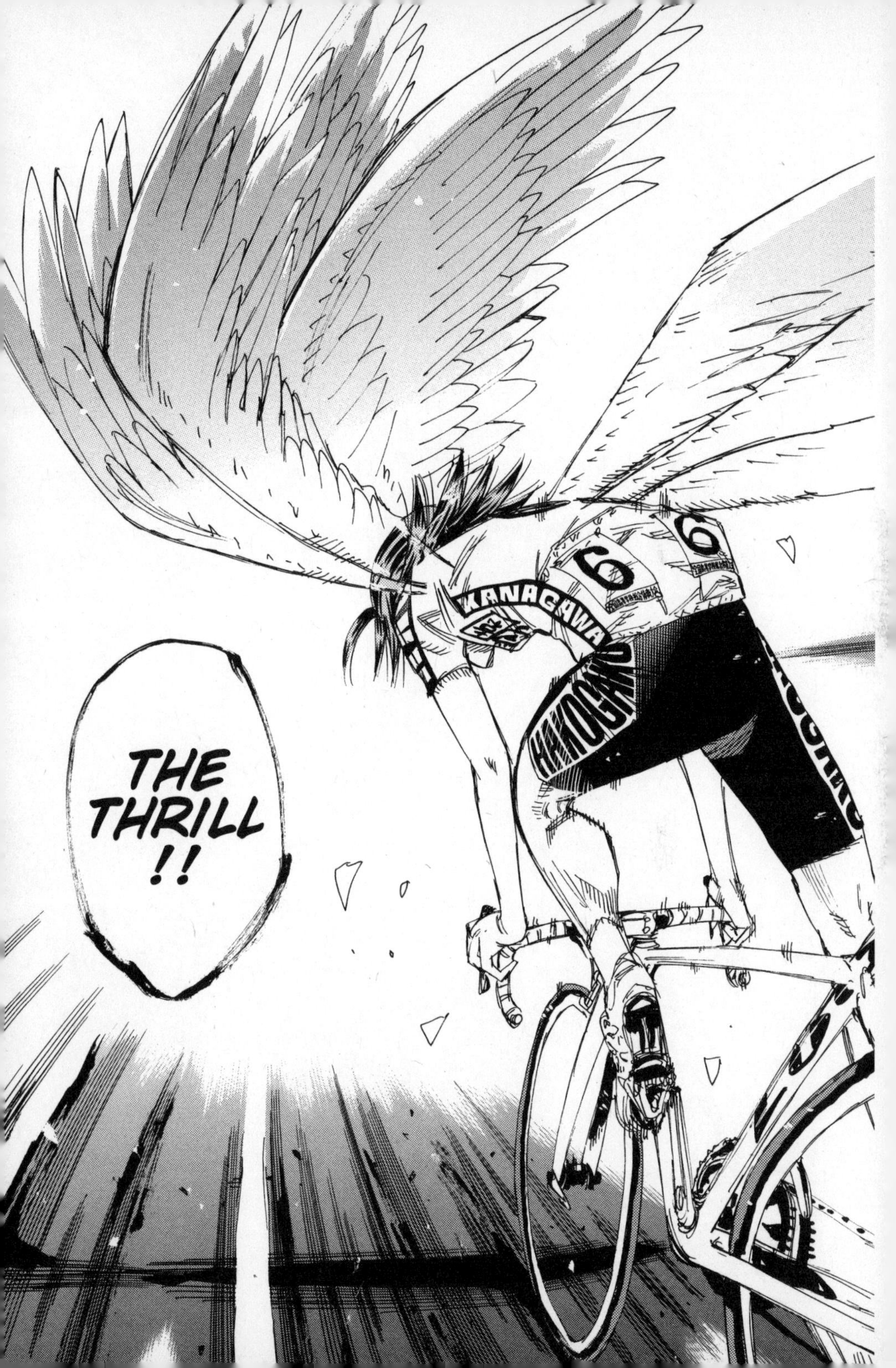
THE THRILL !!
KANAGAWA
HAKOGAKU

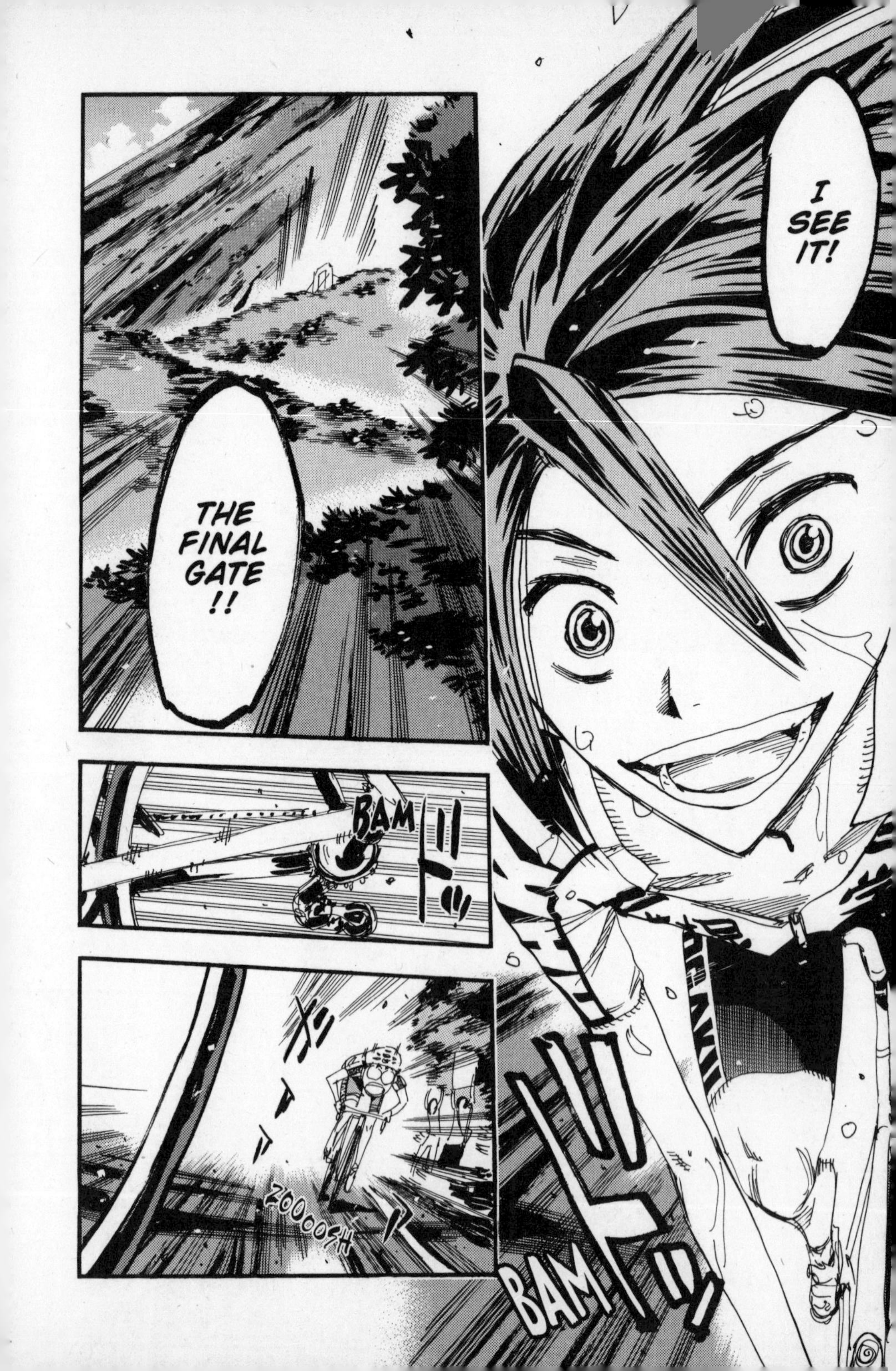
I SEE IT!
THE FINAL GATE!!
BAM
ZOOOOSH
BAM

RIDE.221 CLIMB, MANAMI

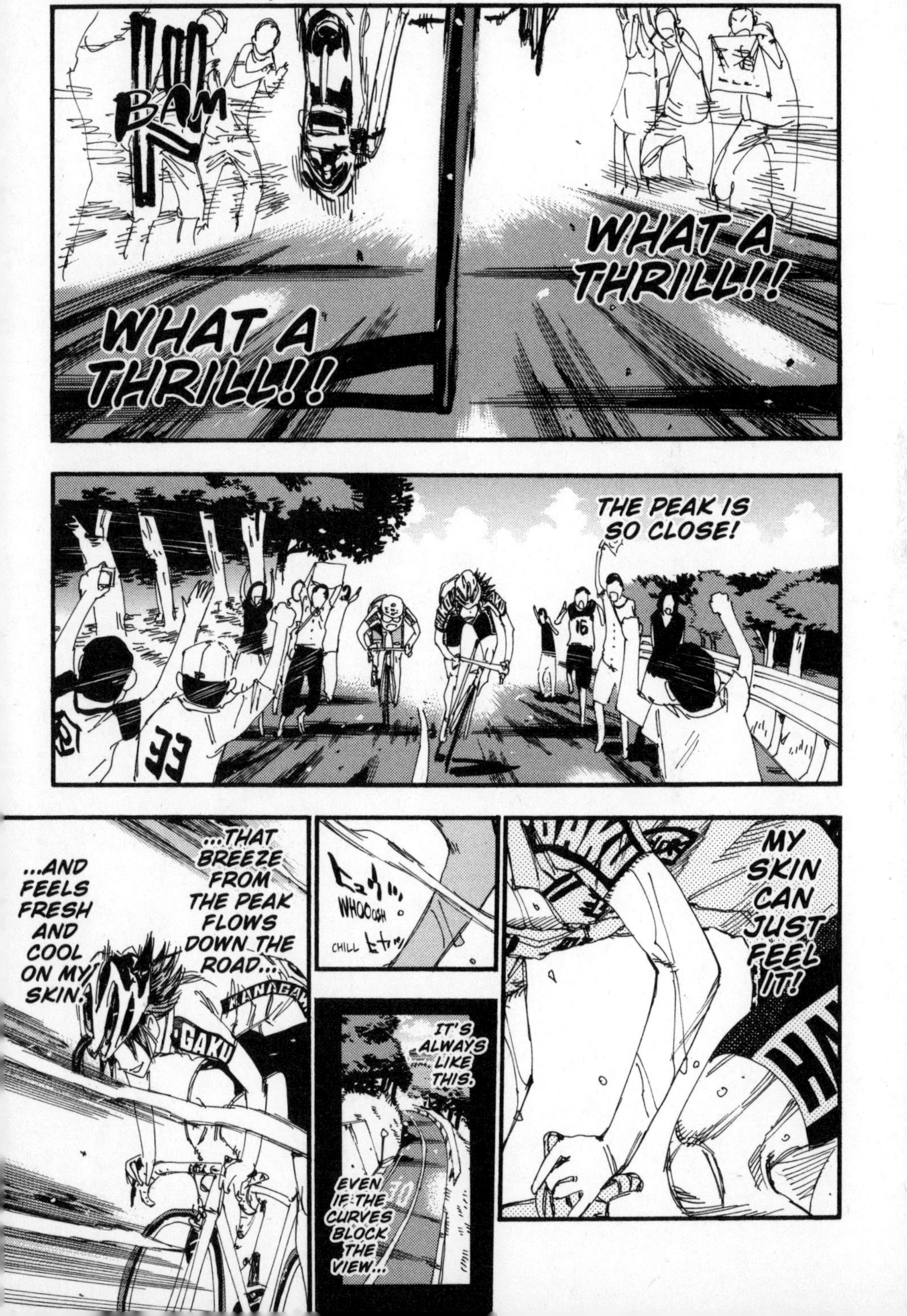
WHAT A THRILL!!
BAM
WHAT A THRILL!!
THE PEAK IS SO CLOSE!
MY SKIN CAN JUST FEEL IT!
WHOOOSH
CHILL
IT'S ALWAYS LIKE THIS.
EVEN IF THE CURVES BLOCK THE VIEW...
...THAT BREEZE FROM THE PEAK FLOWS DOWN THE ROAD...
...AND FEELS FRESH AND COOL ON MY SKIN.

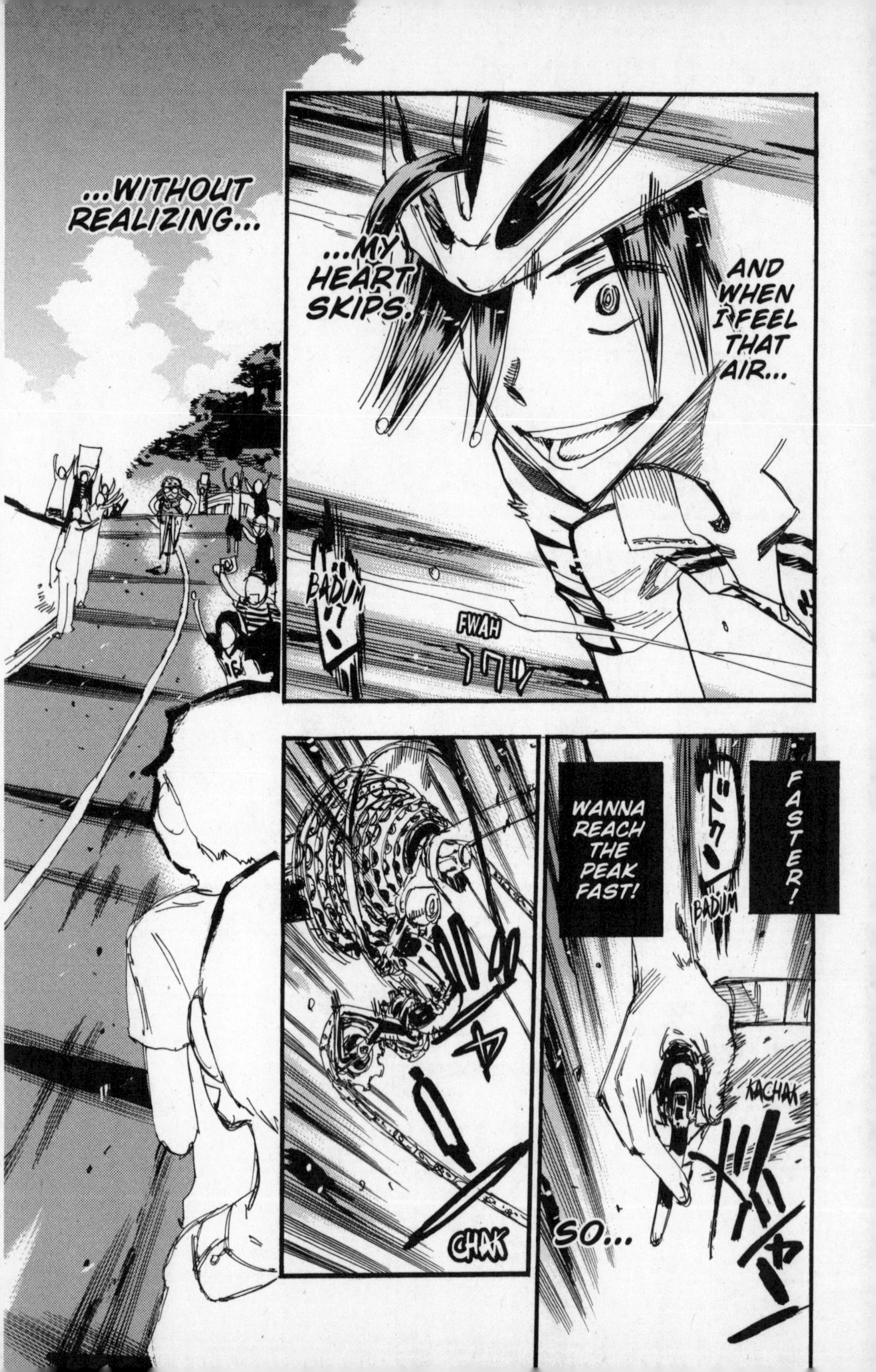
AND WHEN I FEEL THAT AIR...
...MY HEART SKIPS.
BADUM
FWAH
FASTER!
WANNA REACH THE PEAK FAST!
BADUM
KACHAK
SO...
CHAK
...WITHOUT REALIZING...

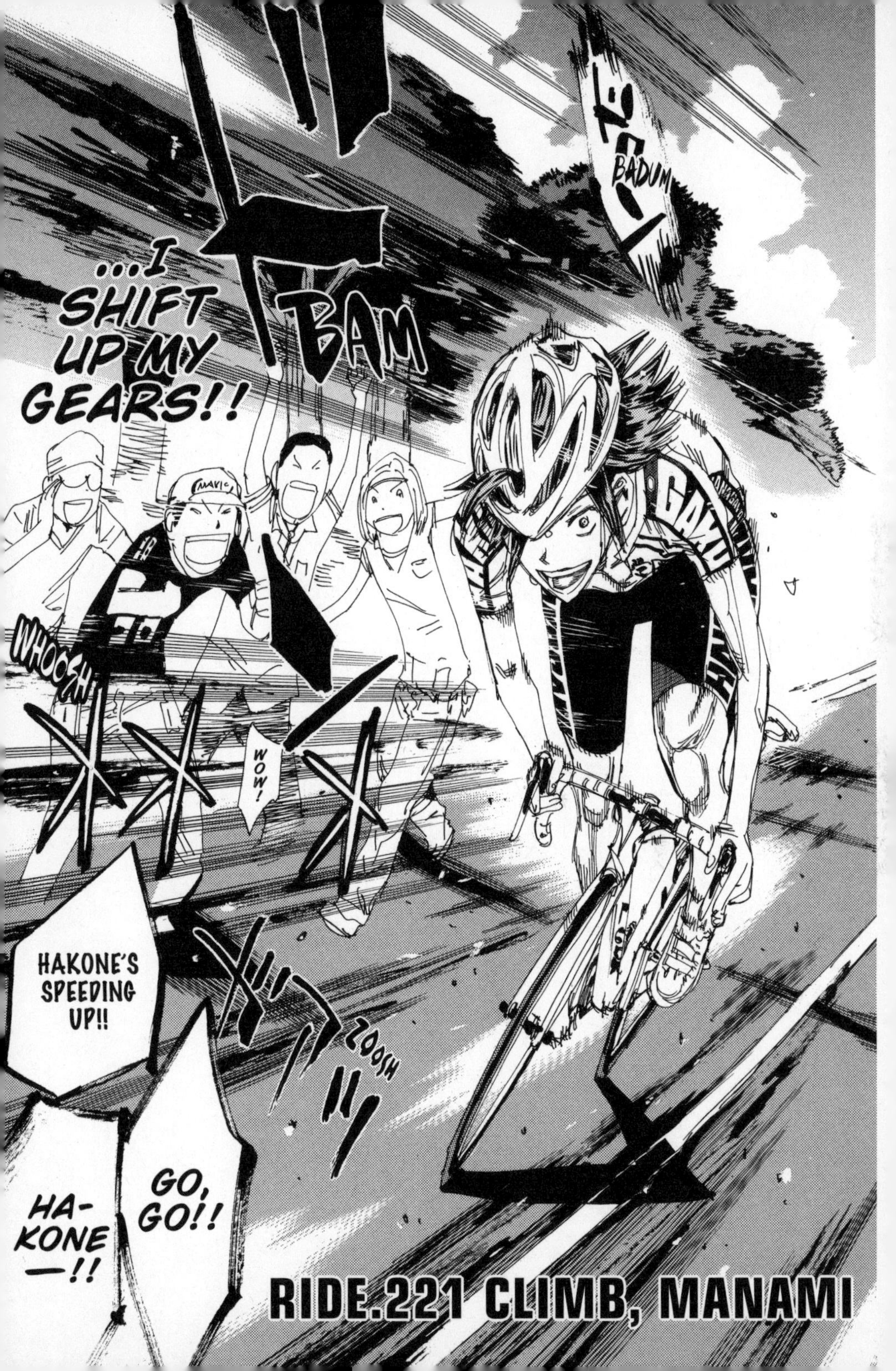
BADUM
...I SHIFT UP MY GEARS!!
BAM
WHOOSH
WOW!
HAKONE'S SPEEDING UP!!
ZOOSH
GO, GO!!
HA-KONE—!!

RIDE.221 CLIMB, MANAMI

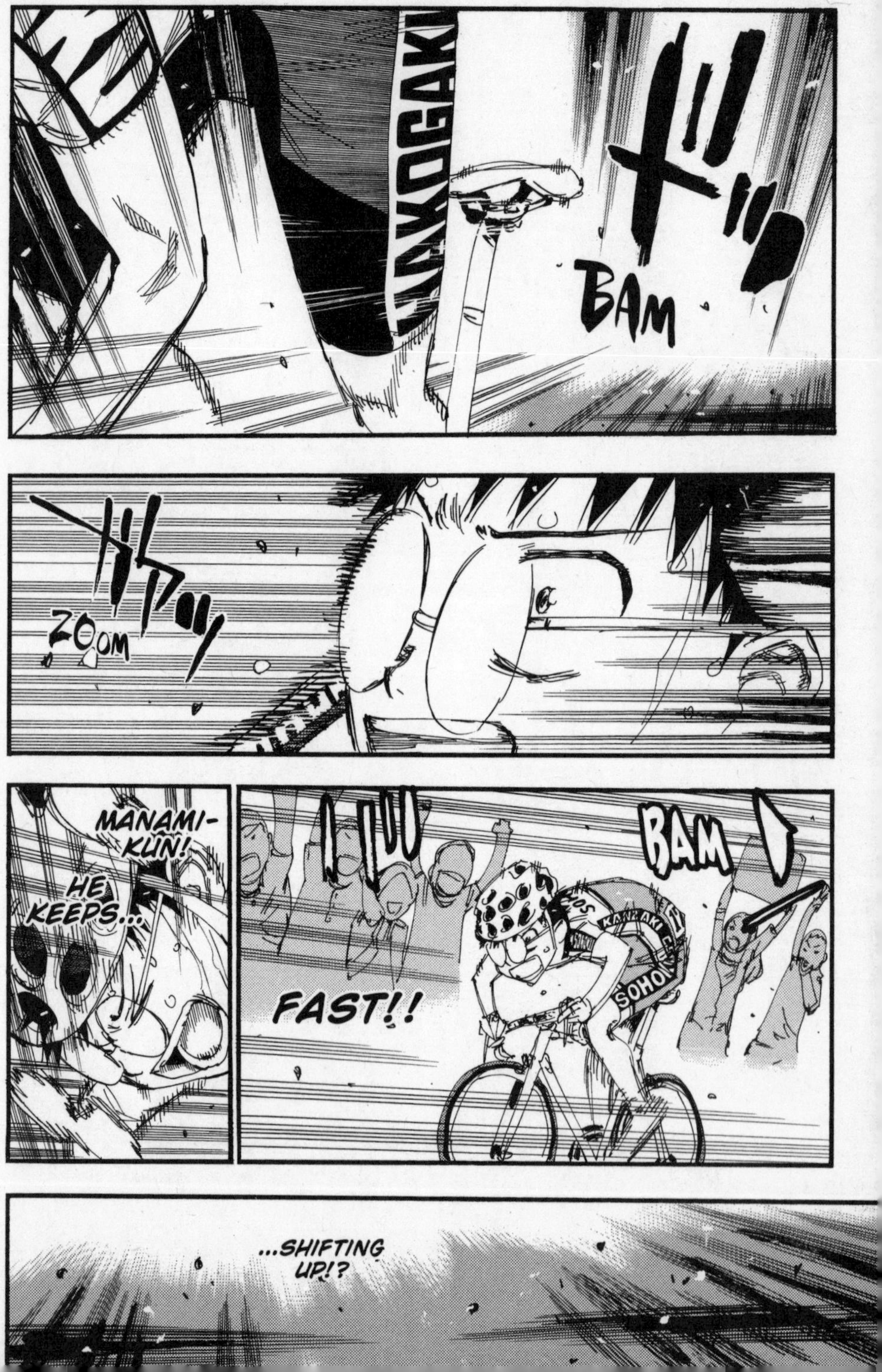
BAM
ZOOM
BAM
FAST!!
MANAMI-KUN!
HE KEEPS...
...SHIFTING UP!?

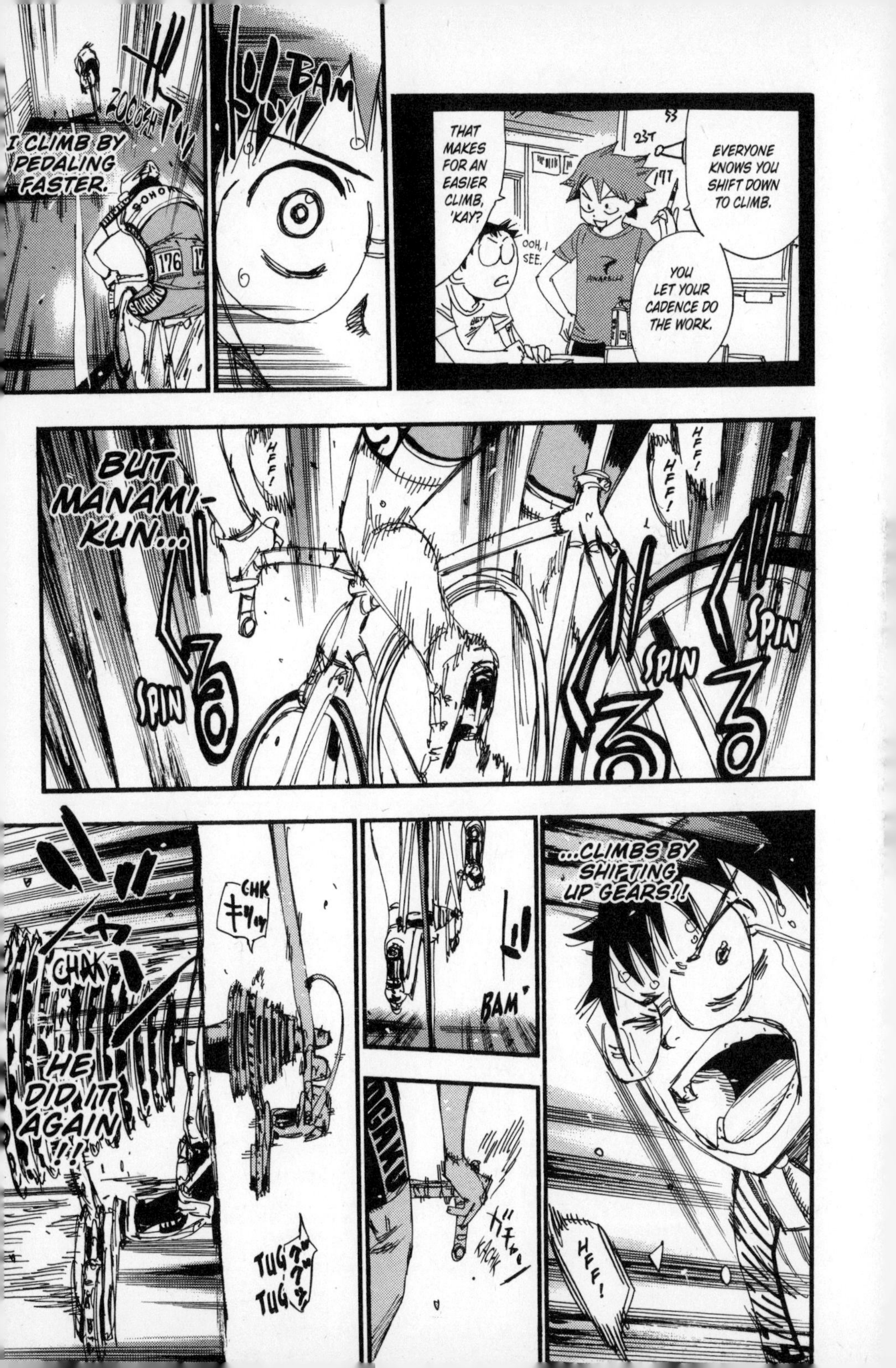

EVERYONE KNOWS YOU SHIFT DOWN TO CLIMB.
YOU LET YOUR CADENCE DO THE WORK.
THAT MAKES FOR AN EASIER CLIMB, 'KAY?
OOH, I SEE.
BAM
ZOOOSH
I CLIMB BY PEDALING FASTER.
BUT MANAMI-KUN...
HFF! HFF! HFF!
HFF!
SPIN SPIN
SPIN
...CLIMBS BY SHIFTING UP GEARS!!
HFF!
BAM
KACHK
TUG TUG
CHK
CHAK
HE DID IT AGAIN!!!

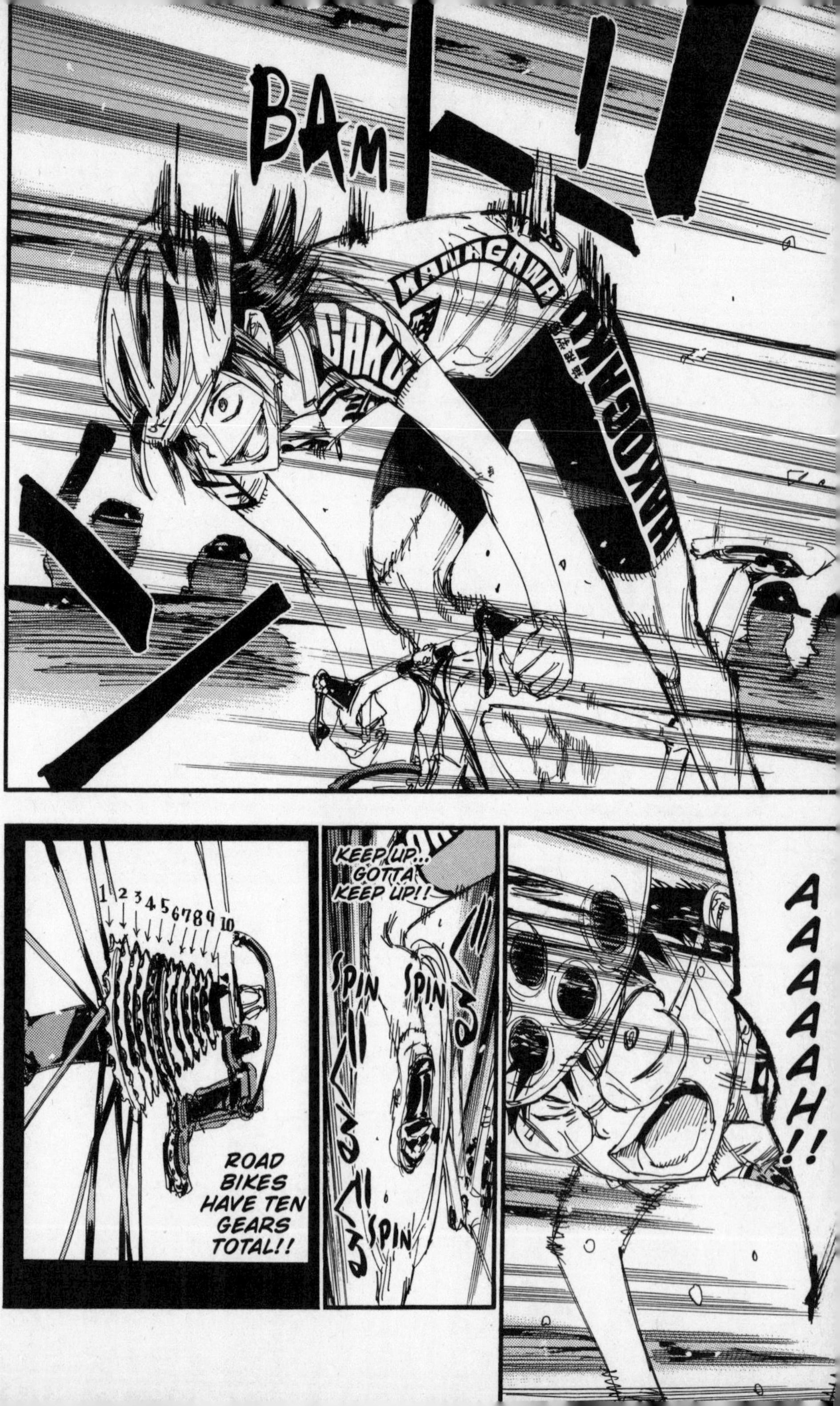
BAM!!
AAAAAAH!!
KEEP UP... GOTTA KEEP UP!!
SPIN
SPIN
SPIN
1 2 3 4 5 6 7 8 9 10
ROAD BIKES HAVE TEN GEARS TOTAL!!

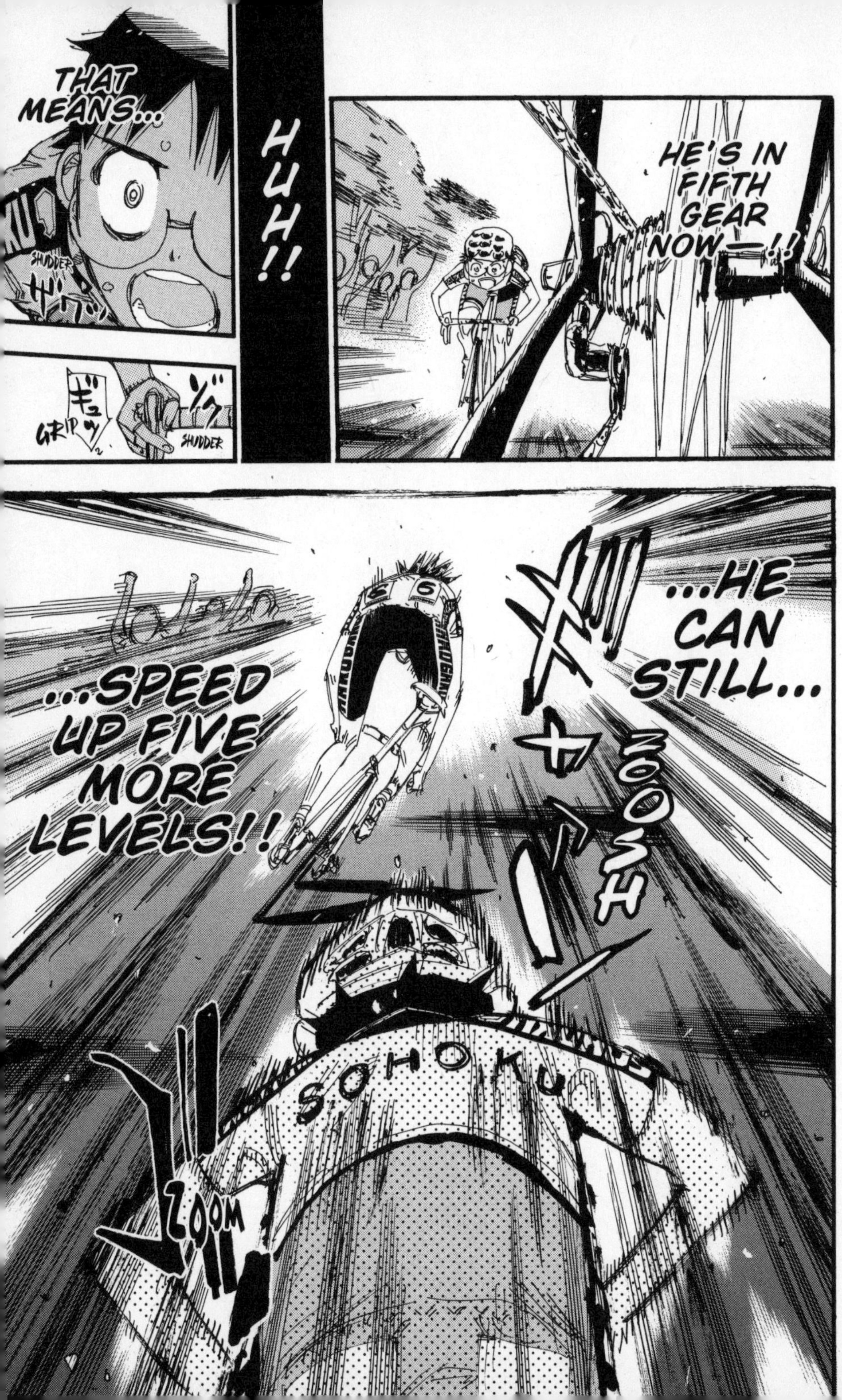

HE'S IN FIFTH GEAR NOW—!!
HUH!!
THAT MEANS...
SHUDDER
GRIP
SHUDDER
...HE CAN STILL...
...SPEED UP FIVE MORE LEVELS!!
ZOOSH
SOHOKU
ZOOM

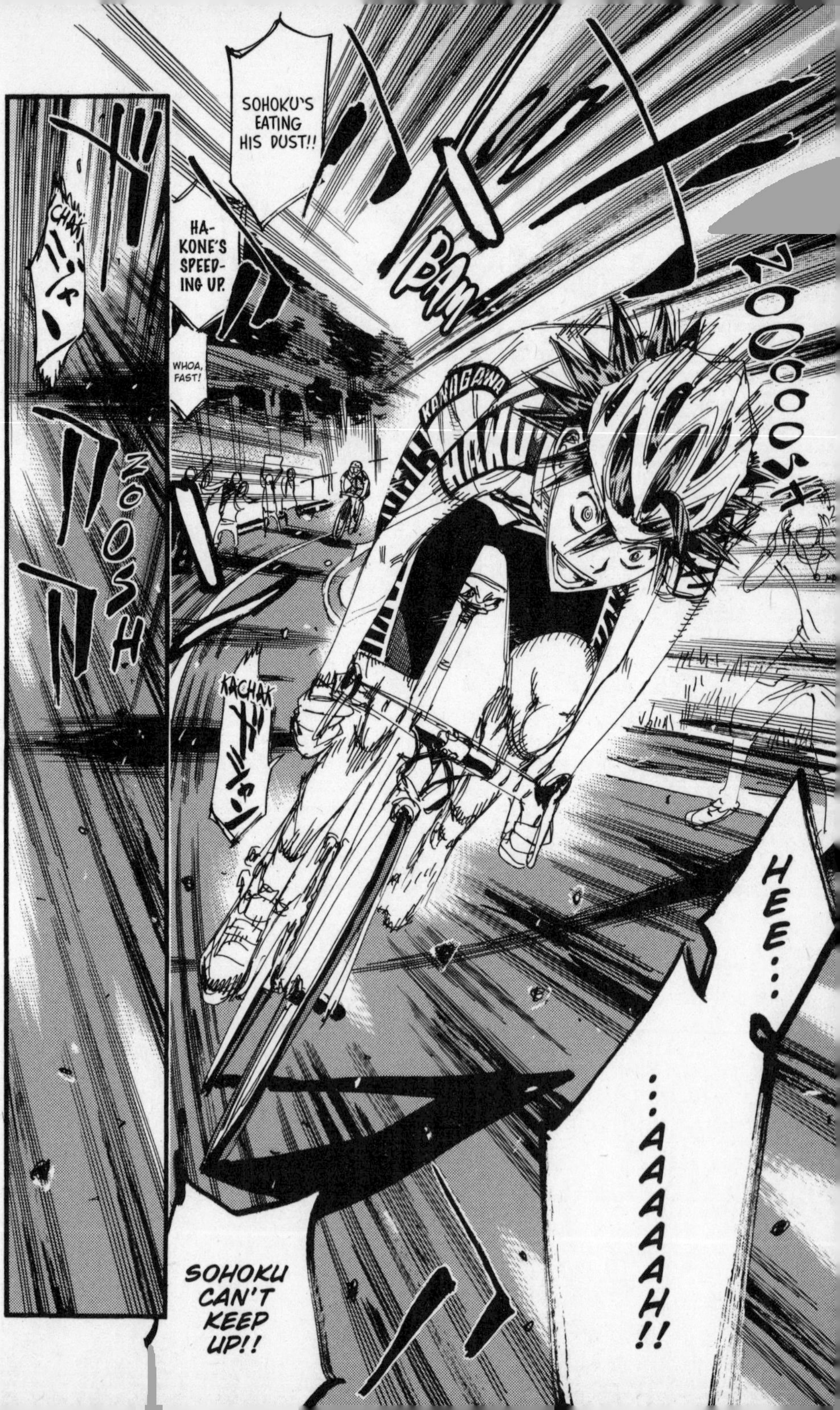
ZOOOOOOSH
BAM
SOHOKU'S EATING HIS DUST!!
HA-KONE'S SPEED-ING UP.
WHOA, FAST!
KAGAWA
HAKU
KACHAK
HEE...
...AAAAAAH!!
SOHOKU CAN'T KEEP UP!!
CHAK
ZOOOSH

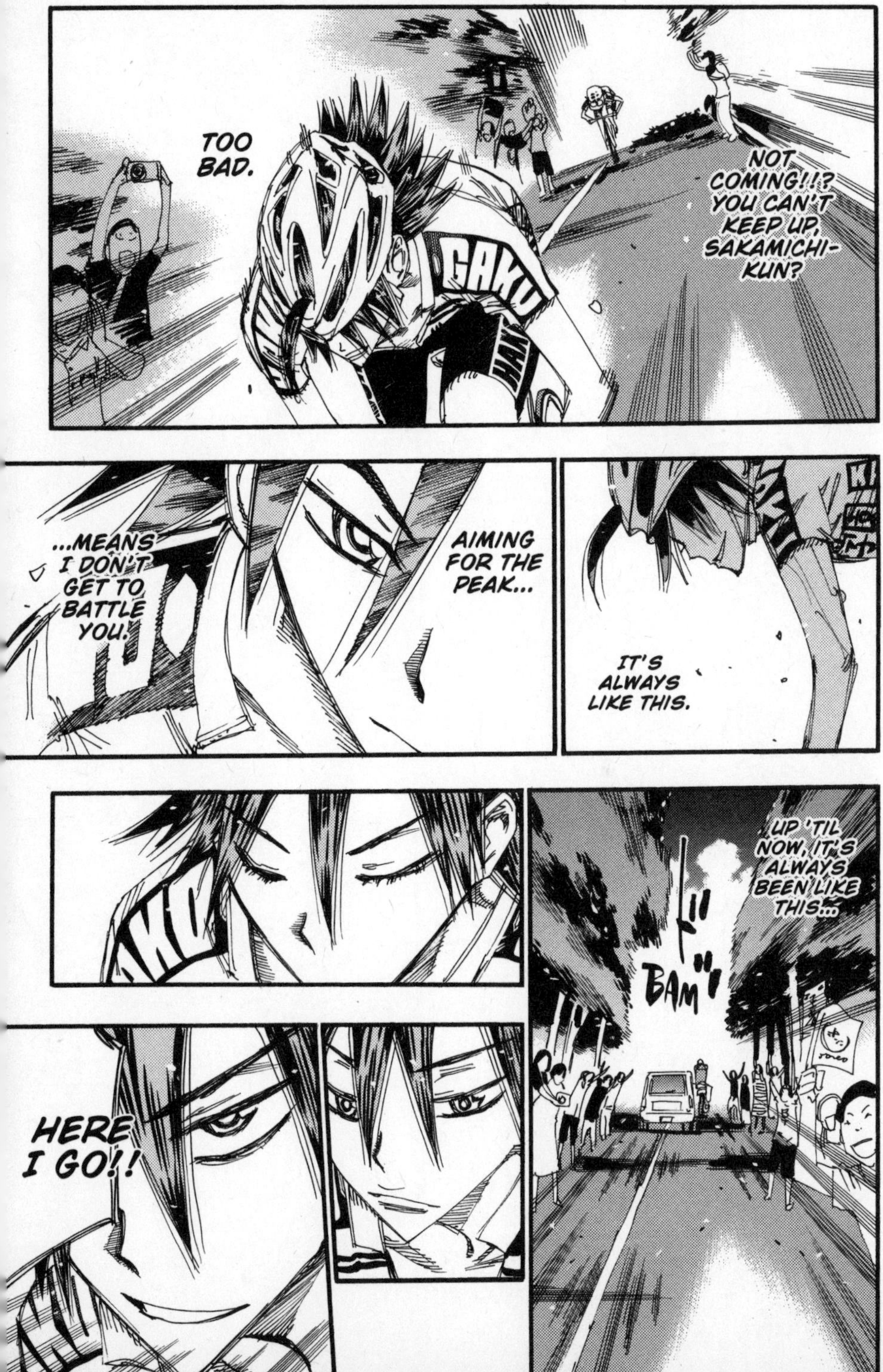
NOT COMING!!? YOU CAN'T KEEP UP, SAKAMICHI-KUN?
TOO BAD.
IT'S ALWAYS LIKE THIS.
AIMING FOR THE PEAK...
...MEANS I DON'T GET TO BATTLE YOU!
UP 'TIL NOW, IT'S ALWAYS BEEN LIKE THIS...
BAM
HERE I GO!!

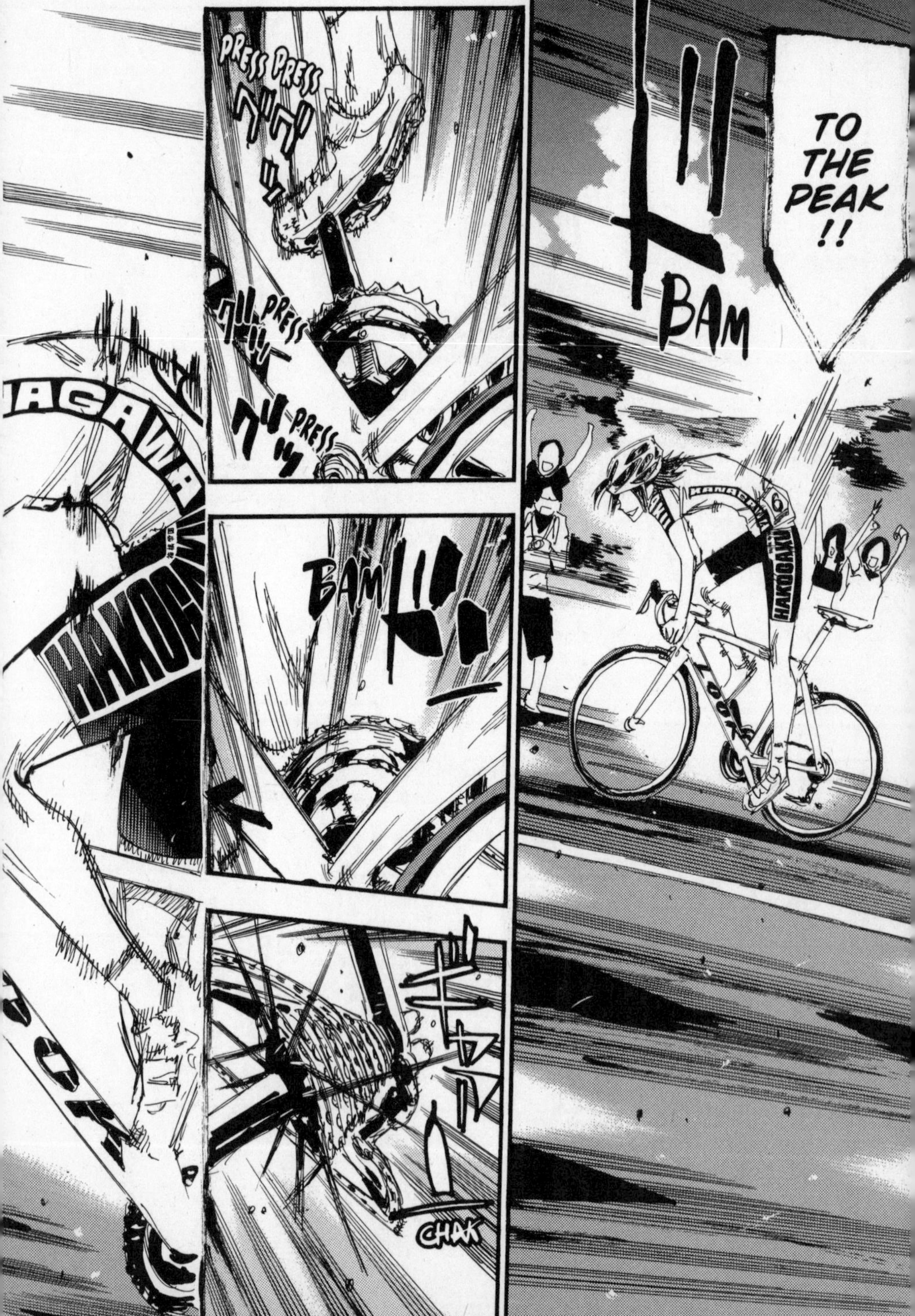
TO THE PEAK!!
BAM
PRESS PRESS
PRESS
PRESS
BAM!!
CHAK

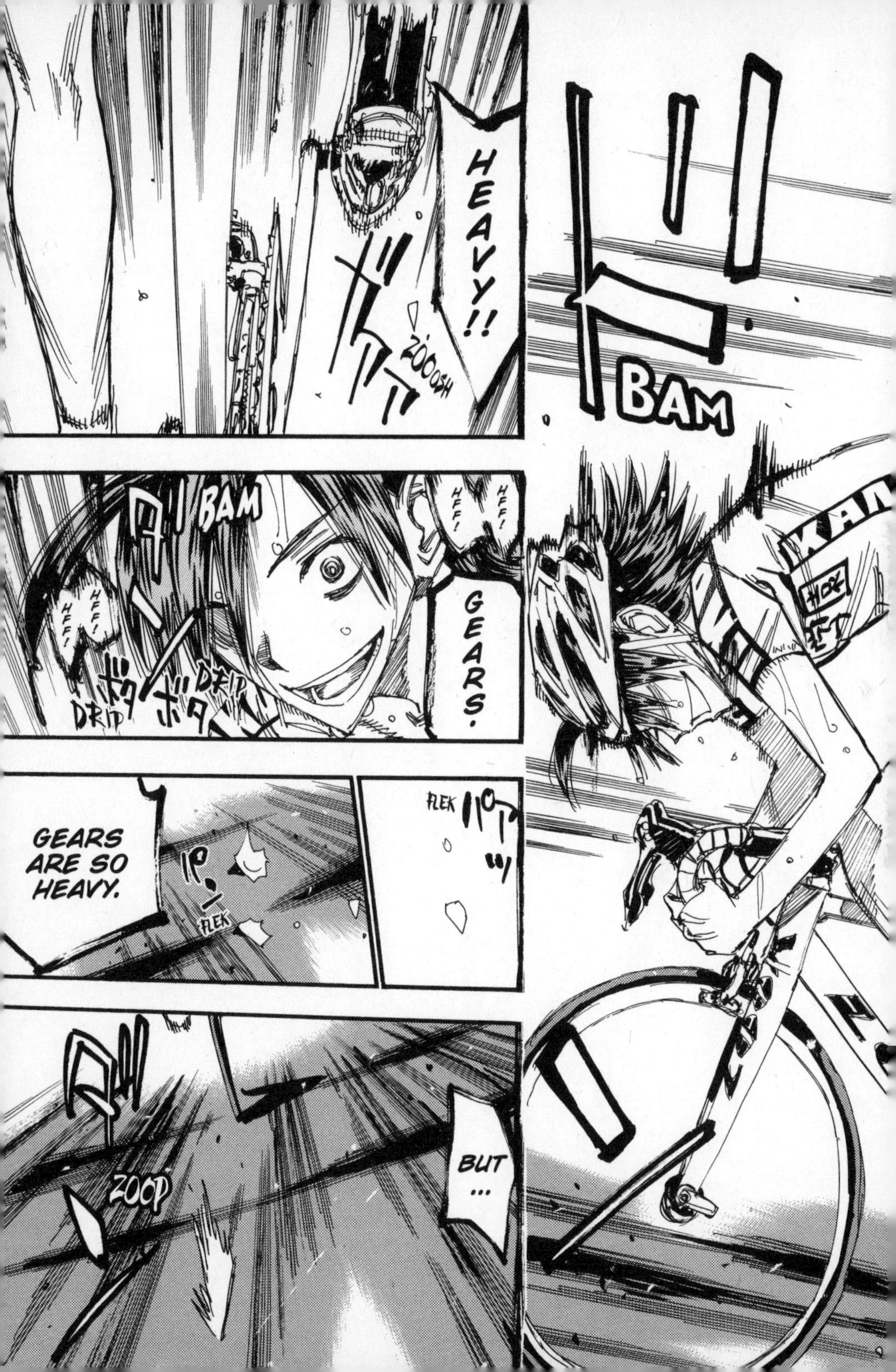
BAM
HEAVY!!
ZOOOSH
HFF! HFF!
BAM
HFF! HFF!
GEARS.
DRIP DRIP
FLEK
GEARS ARE SO HEAVY.
FLEK
BUT ...
ZOOP

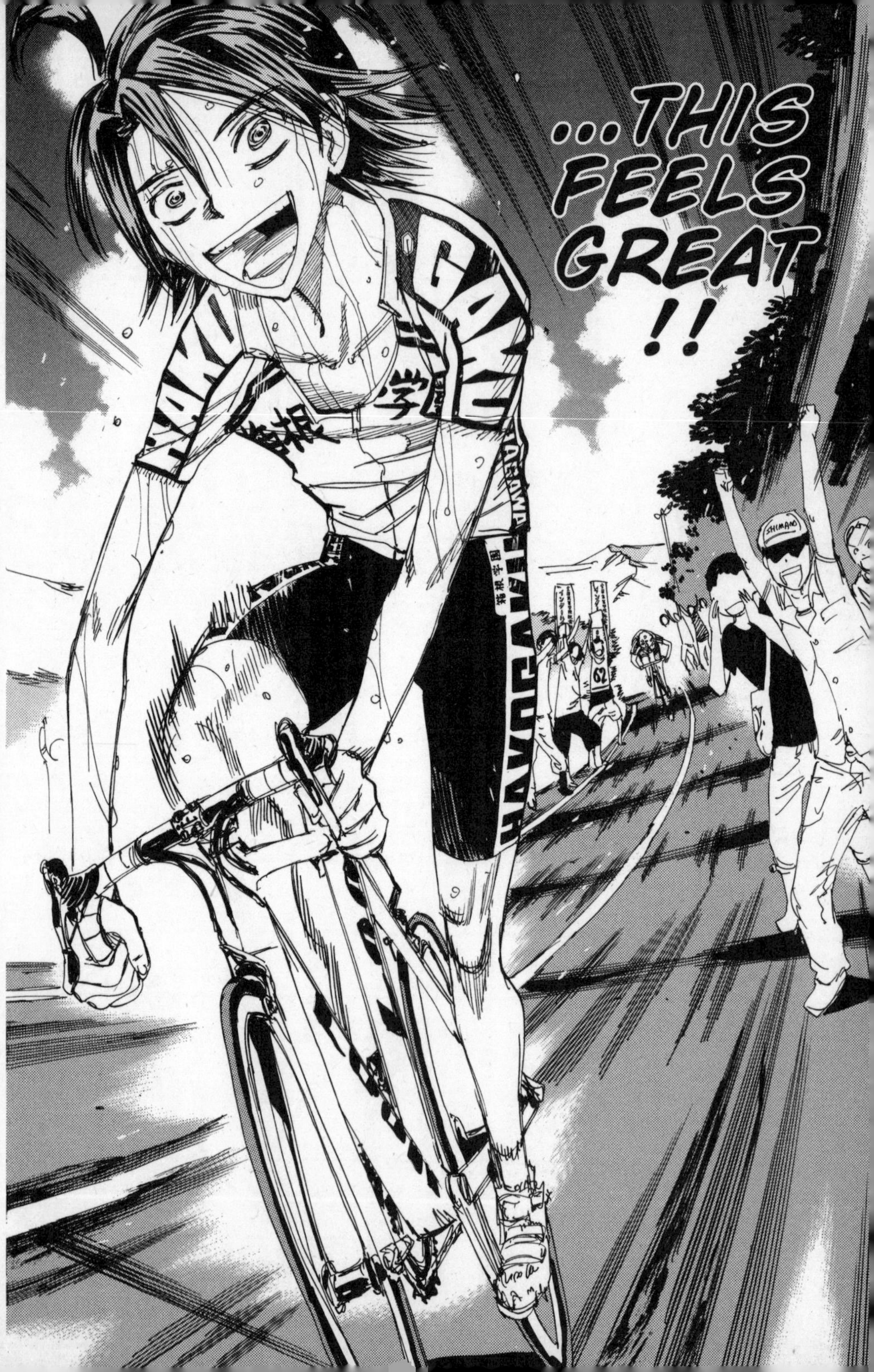
...THIS FEELS GREAT!!

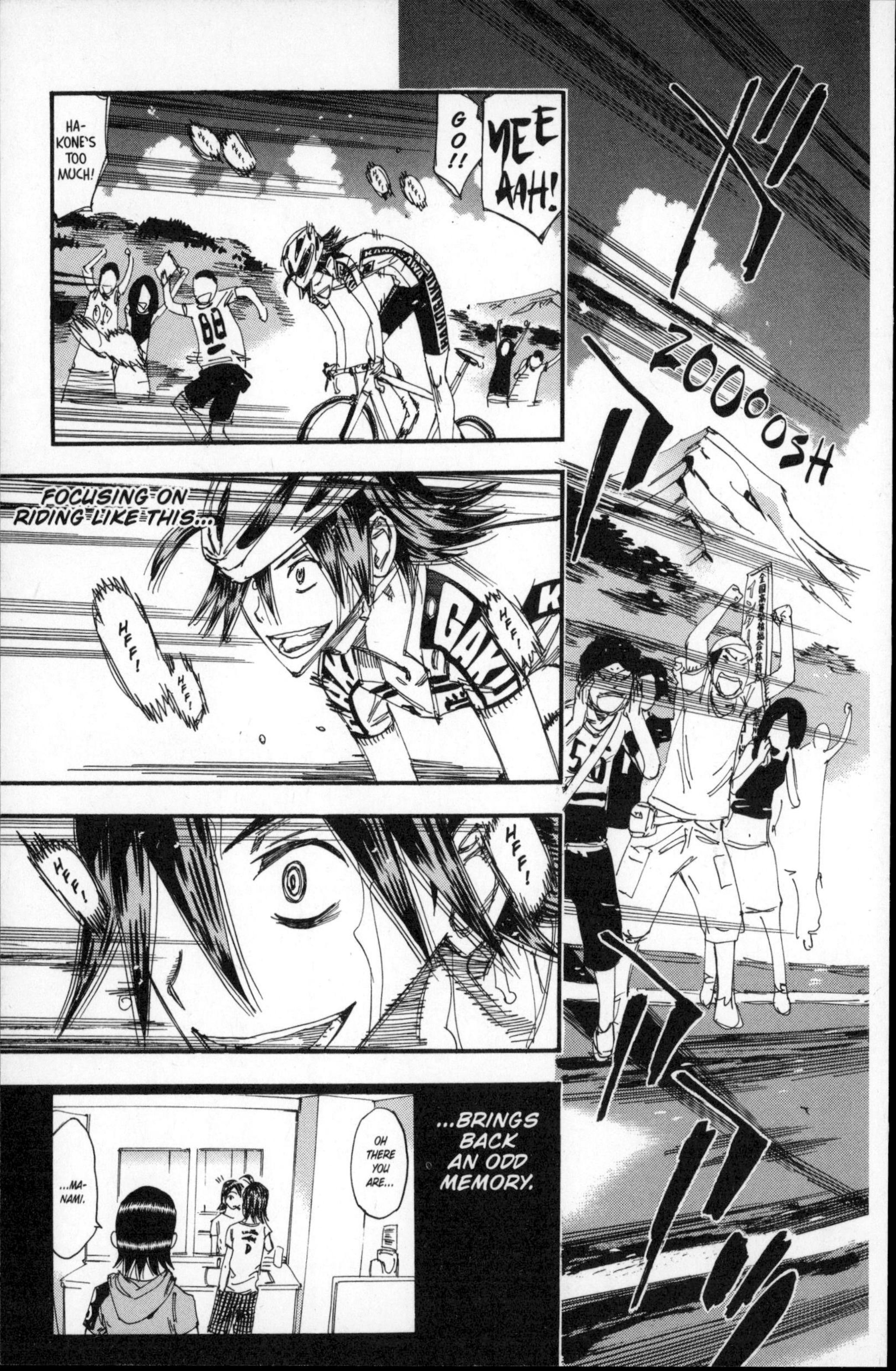
ZOOOOSH
YEE AAH!
GO!!
HA-KONE'S TOO MUCH!
FOCUSING ON RIDING LIKE THIS...
HFF!
HFF!
HFF!
HFF!
HFF!
...BRINGS BACK AN ODD MEMORY.
OH THERE YOU ARE...
...MA-NAMI.

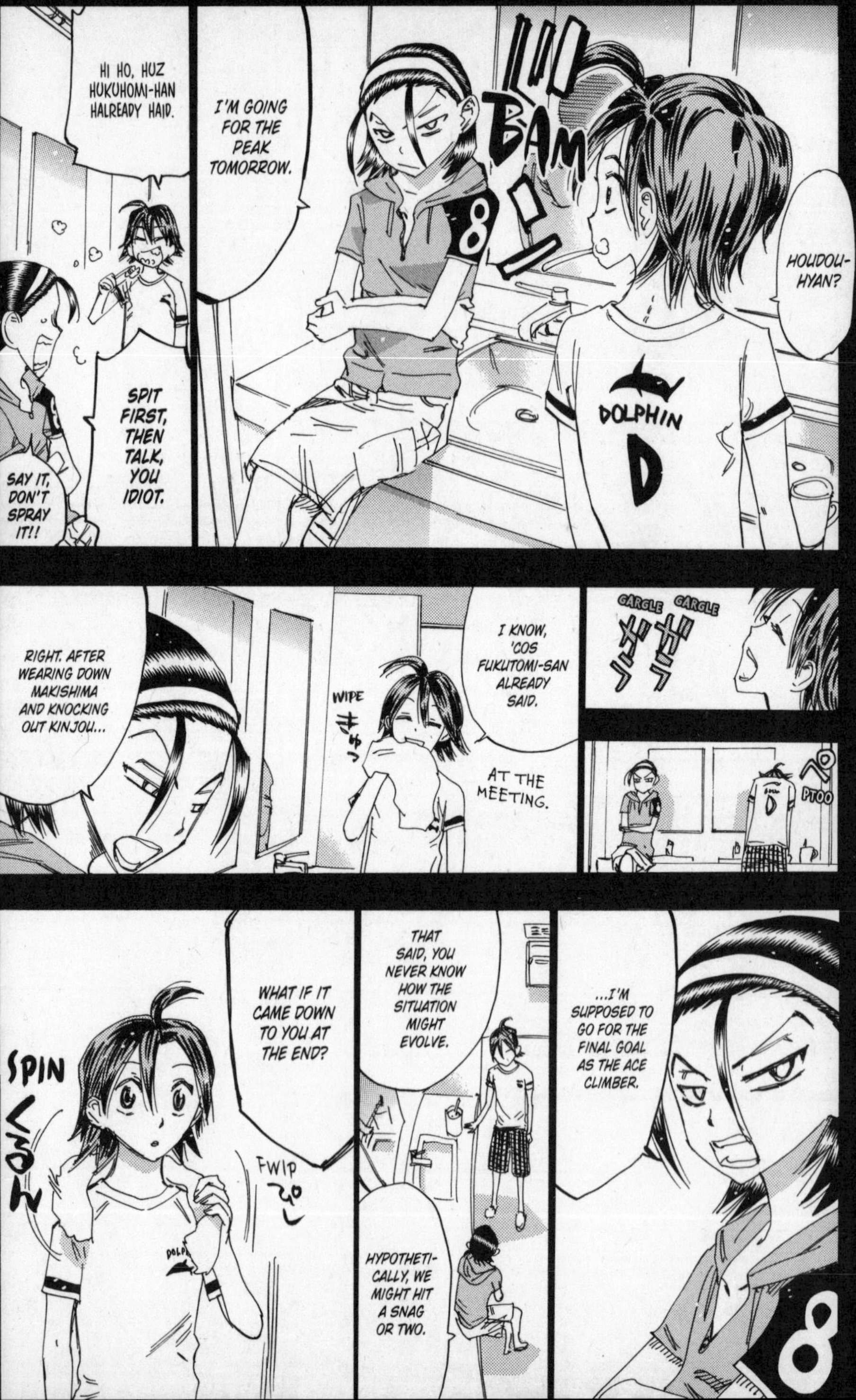

HOUDOU-HYAN?
BAM
I'M GOING FOR THE PEAK TOMORROW.
HI HO, HUZ HUKUHOMI-HAN HALREADY HAID.
SPIT FIRST, THEN TALK, YOU IDIOT.
SAY IT, DON'T SPRAY IT!!
GARGLE GARGLE
PTOO
I KNOW, 'COS FUKUTOMI-SAN ALREADY SAID.
WIPE
AT THE MEETING.
RIGHT. AFTER WEARING DOWN MAKISHIMA AND KNOCKING OUT KINJOU...
...I'M SUPPOSED TO GO FOR THE FINAL GOAL AS THE ACE CLIMBER.
THAT SAID, YOU NEVER KNOW HOW THE SITUATION MIGHT EVOLVE.
HYPOTHETI-CALLY, WE MIGHT HIT A SNAG OR TWO.
WHAT IF IT CAME DOWN TO YOU AT THE END?
FWIP
SPIN

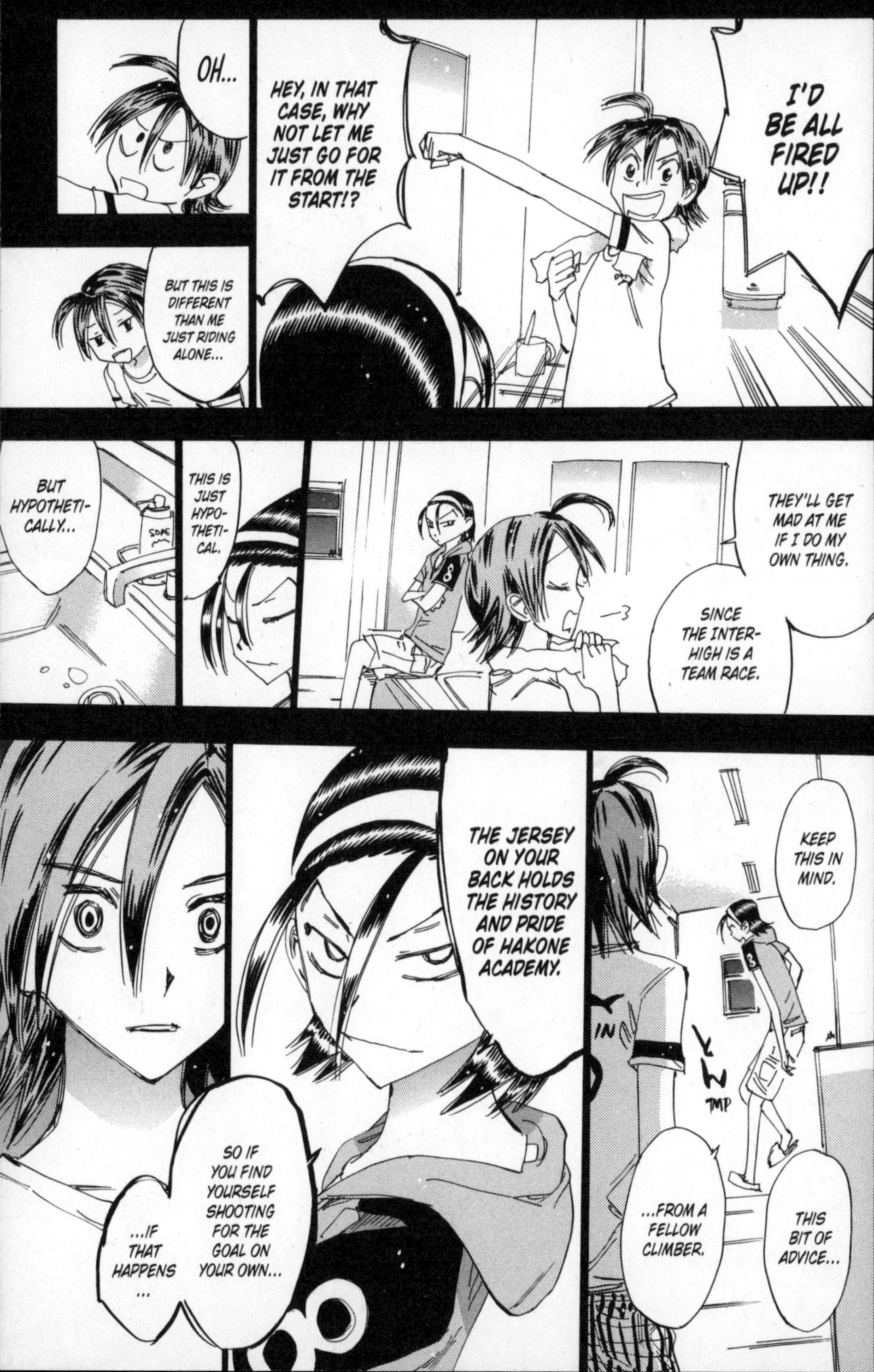
I'D BE ALL FIRED UP!!
HEY, IN THAT CASE, WHY NOT LET ME JUST GO FOR IT FROM THE START!?
OH...
BUT THIS IS DIFFERENT THAN ME JUST RIDING ALONE...
THEY'LL GET MAD AT ME IF I DO MY OWN THING.
SINCE THE INTER-HIGH IS A TEAM RACE.
THIS IS JUST HYPO-THETI-CAL.
BUT HYPOTHETI-CALLY...
KEEP THIS IN MIND.
TMP
THIS BIT OF ADVICE...
...FROM A FELLOW CLIMBER.
THE JERSEY ON YOUR BACK HOLDS THE HISTORY AND PRIDE OF HAKONE ACADEMY.
SO IF YOU FIND YOURSELF SHOOTING FOR THE GOAL ON YOUR OWN...
...IF THAT HAPPENS ...

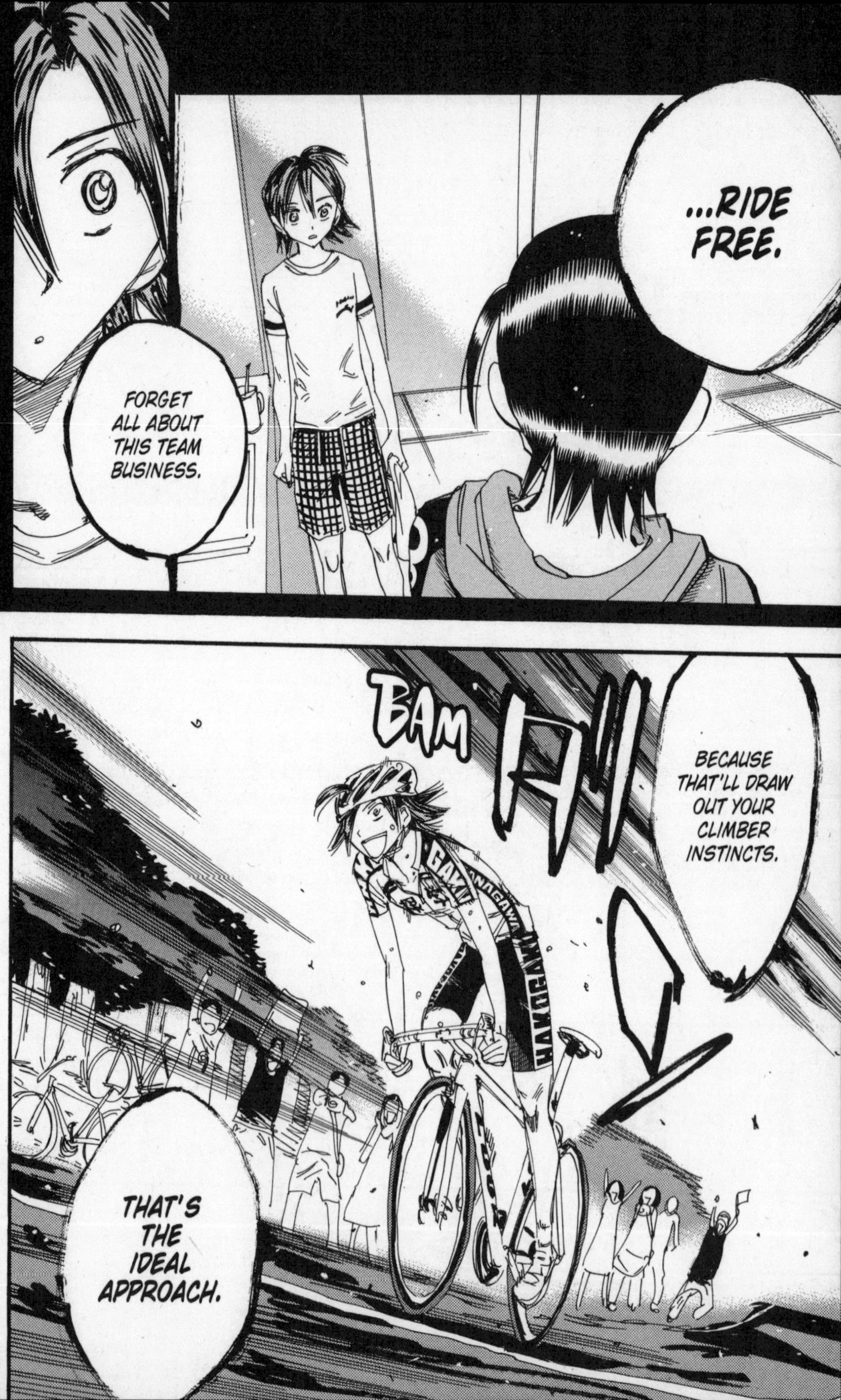
...RIDE FREE.
FORGET ALL ABOUT THIS TEAM BUSINESS.
BAM
BECAUSE THAT'LL DRAW OUT YOUR CLIMBER INSTINCTS.
THAT'S THE IDEAL APPROACH.

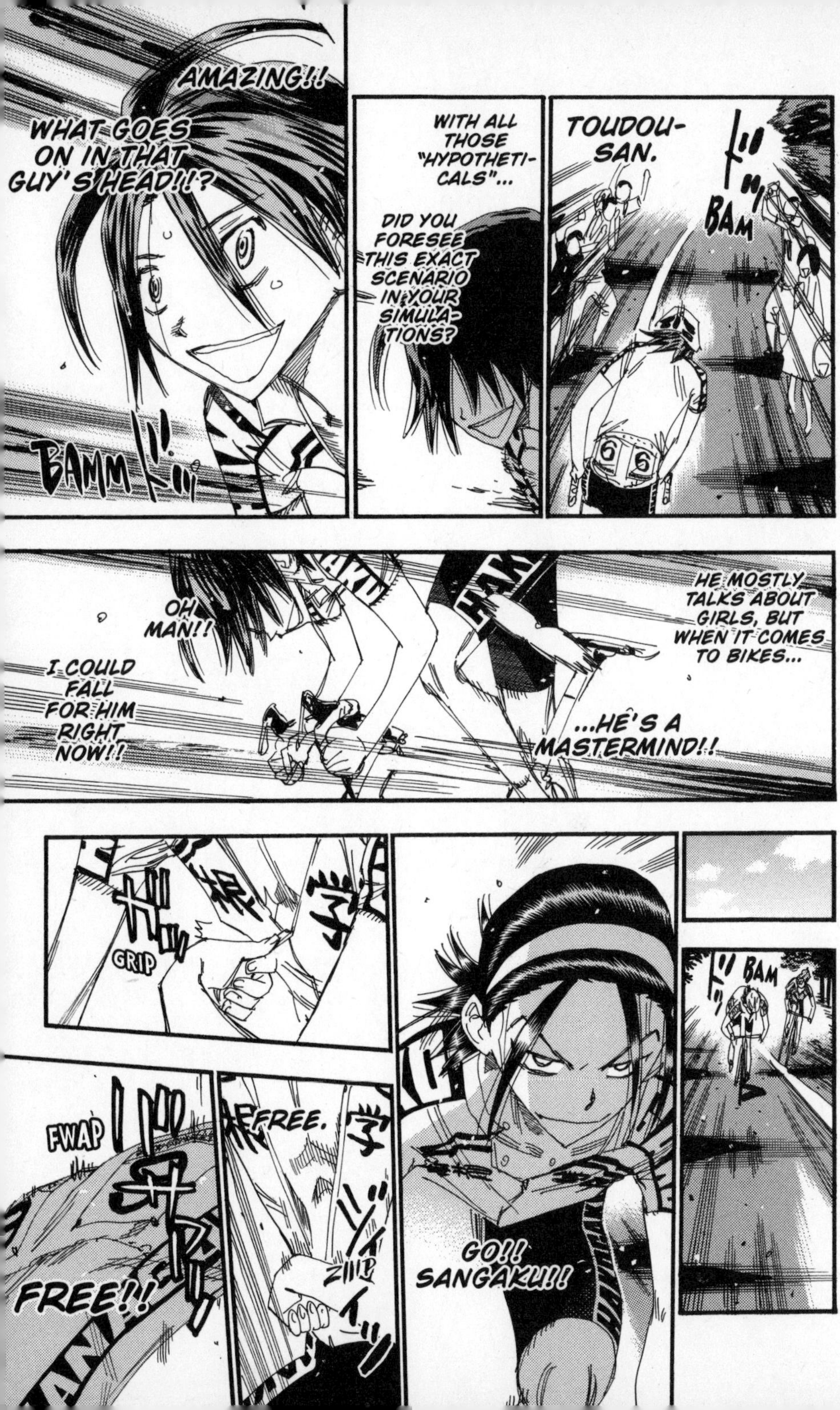
TOUDOU-SAN.
BAM
WITH ALL THOSE "HYPOTHETICALS"...
DID YOU FORESEE THIS EXACT SCENARIO IN YOUR SIMULATIONS?
AMAZING!!
WHAT GOES ON IN THAT GUY'S HEAD!!?
BAMM
HE MOSTLY TALKS ABOUT GIRLS, BUT WHEN IT COMES TO BIKES...
...HE'S A MASTERMIND!!
OH MAN!!
I COULD FALL FOR HIM RIGHT NOW!!
BAM
GO!! SANGAKU!!
GRIP
FREE.
ZIIIP
FWAP
FREE!!

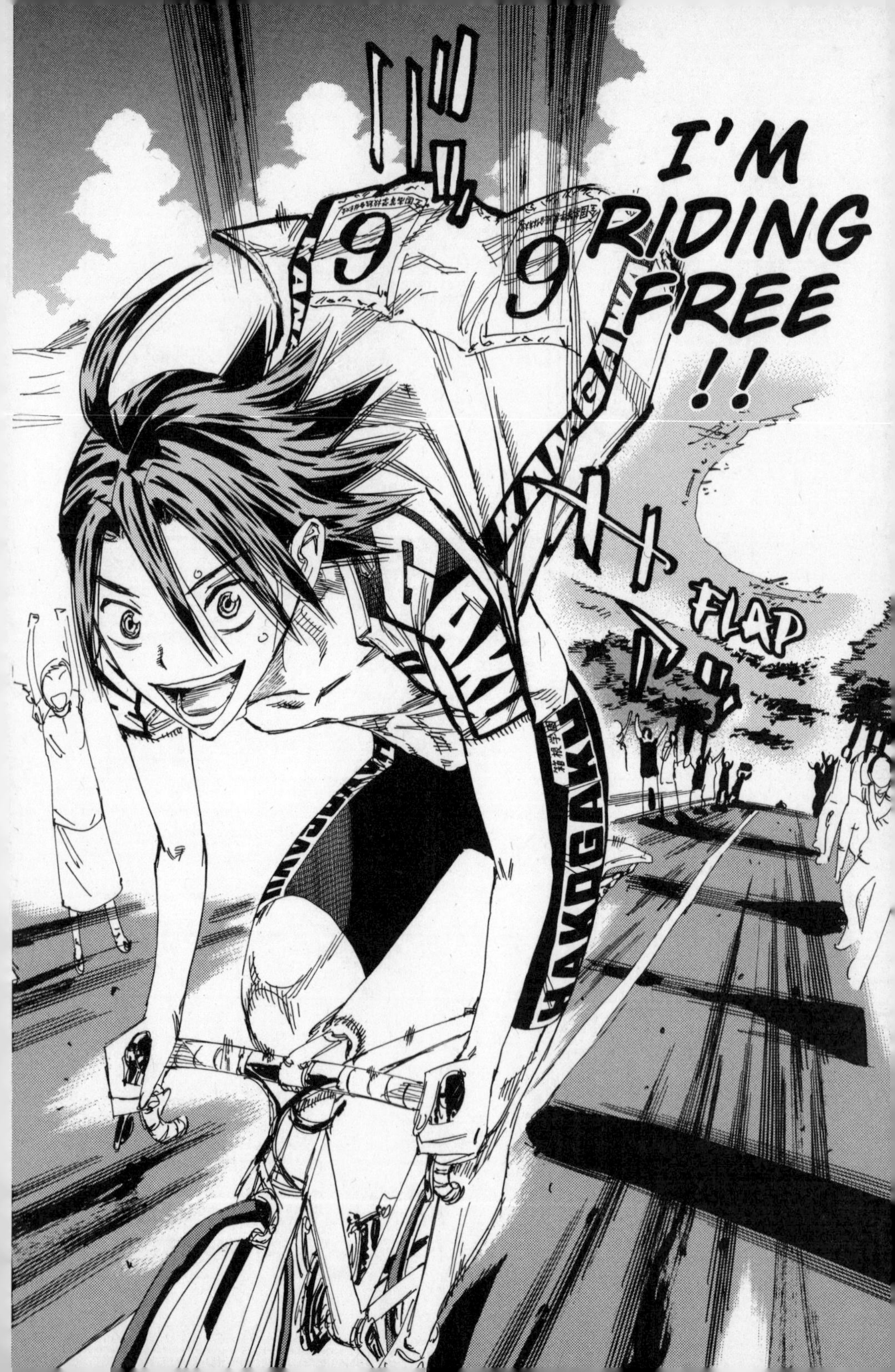
I'M RIDING FREE!!
FLAP

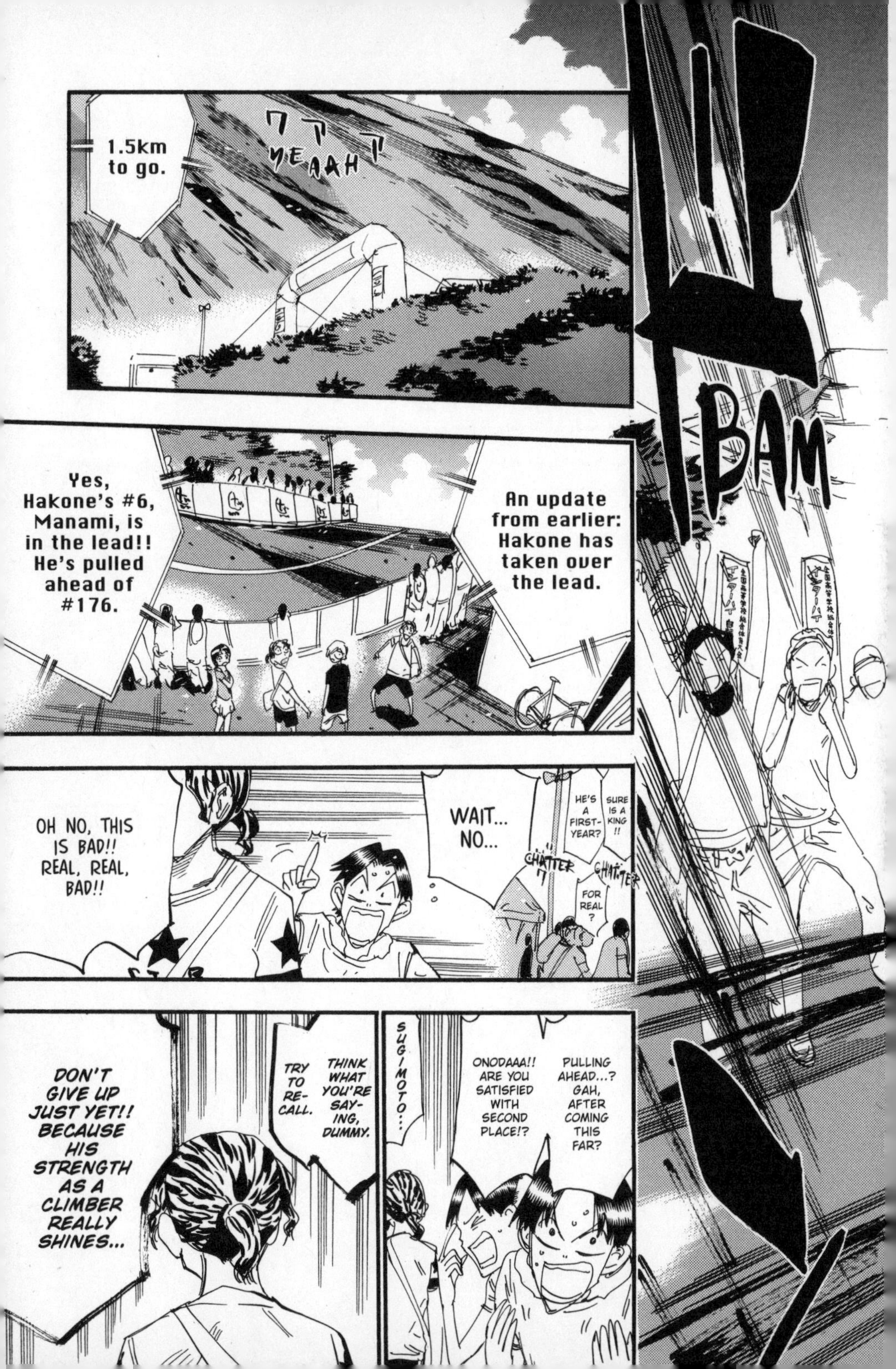
BAM
ワァァ
YEAAH
1.5km to go.
An update from earlier: Hakone has taken over the lead.
Yes, Hakone's #6, Manami, is in the lead!! He's pulled ahead of #176.
SURE IS A KING !!
HE'S A FIRST-YEAR?
CHATTER
CHATTER
FOR REAL?
WAIT... NO...
OH NO, THIS IS BAD!! REAL, REAL, BAD!!
PULLING AHEAD...? GAH, AFTER COMING THIS FAR?
ONODAAA!! ARE YOU SATISFIED WITH SECOND PLACE!?
SUGIMOTO...
THINK WHAT YOU'RE SAYING, DUMMY.
TRY TO RECALL.
DON'T GIVE UP JUST YET!! BECAUSE HIS STRENGTH AS A CLIMBER REALLY SHINES...

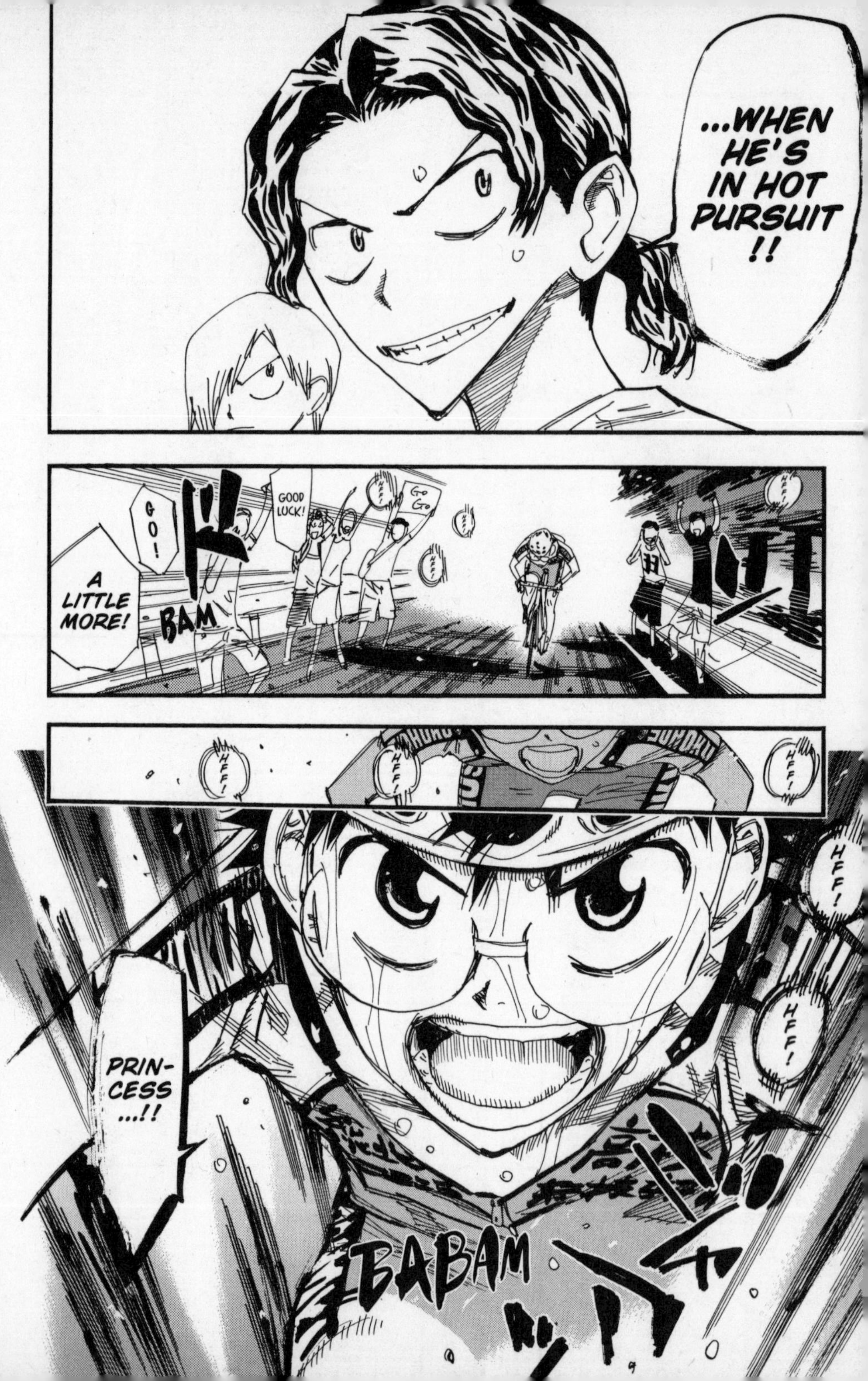
...WHEN HE'S IN HOT PURSUIT!!
HFF!
HFF!
GO GO
HFF!
HFF!
GOOD LUCK!
GO!
A LITTLE MORE!
BAM
HFF!
HFF!
HFF!
HFF!
HFF!
PRIN-CESS ...!!
BABAM

RIDE.222 SHIFTING UP

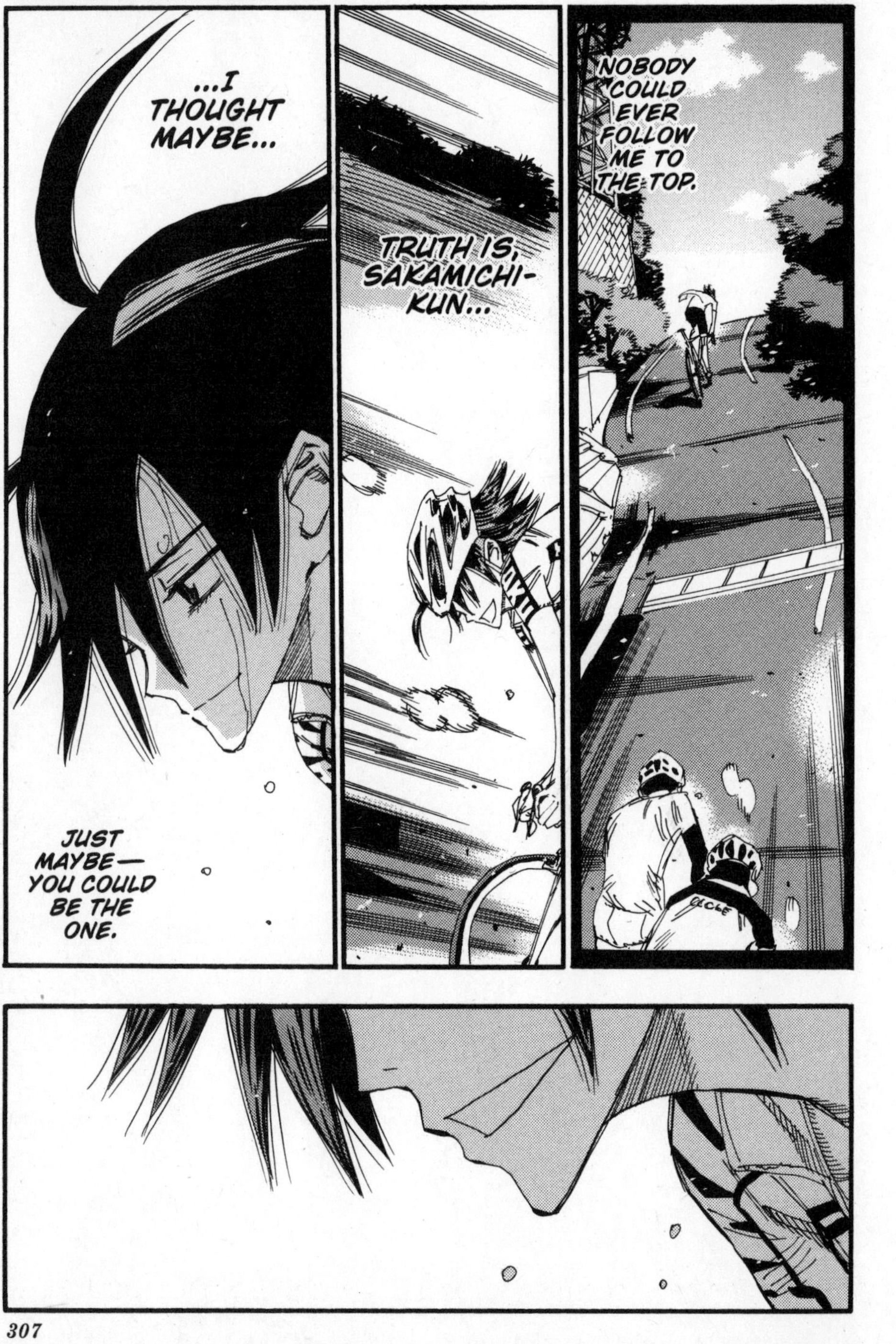
NOBODY COULD EVER FOLLOW ME TO THE TOP.
TRUTH IS, SAKAMICHI-KUN...
...I THOUGHT MAYBE...
JUST MAYBE— YOU COULD BE THE ONE.

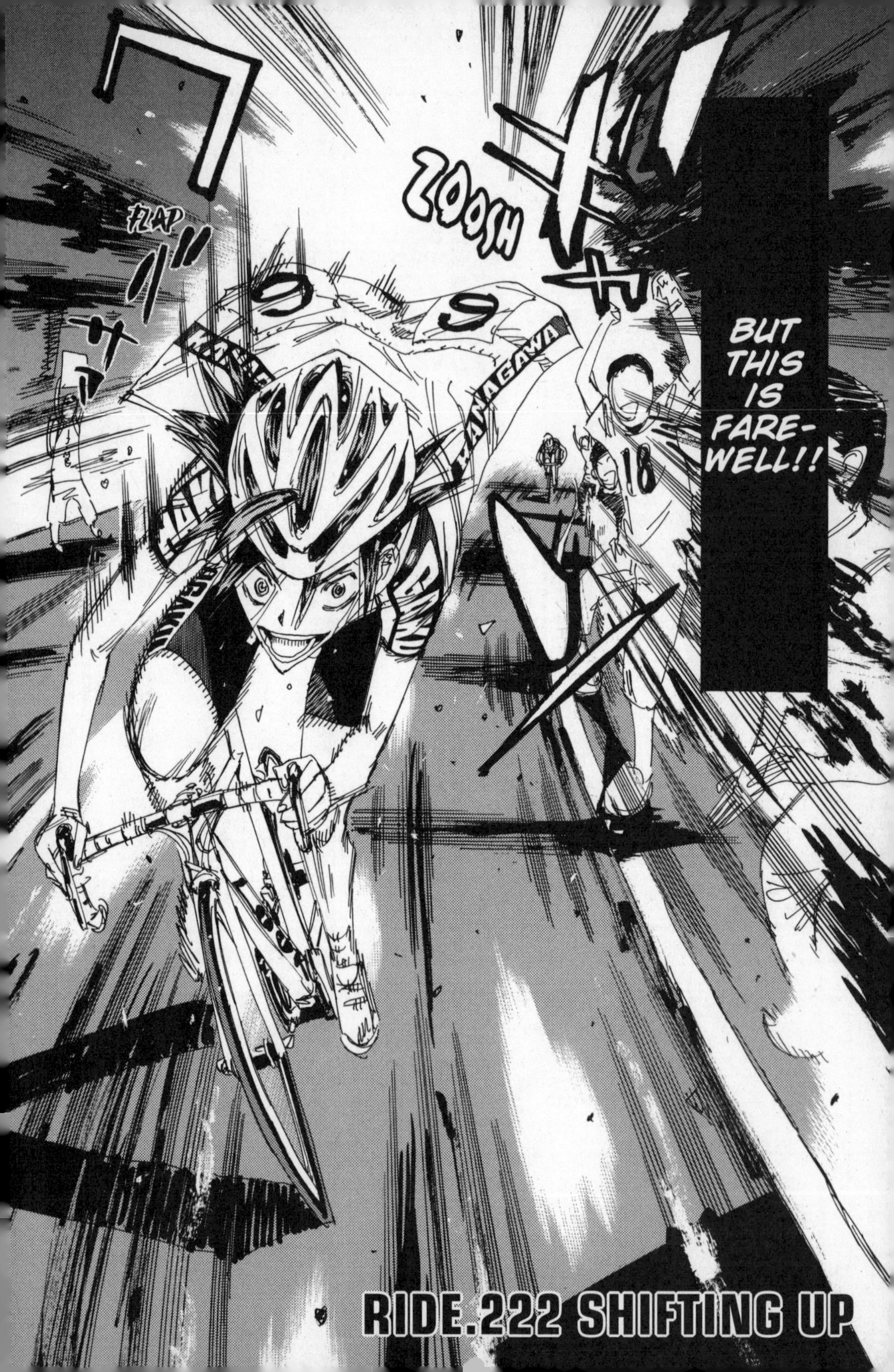

BUT THIS IS FARE-WELL!!
ZOOSH
FLAP
HAKONE GAKUEN
SOHOKU
18

RIDE.222 SHIFTING UP

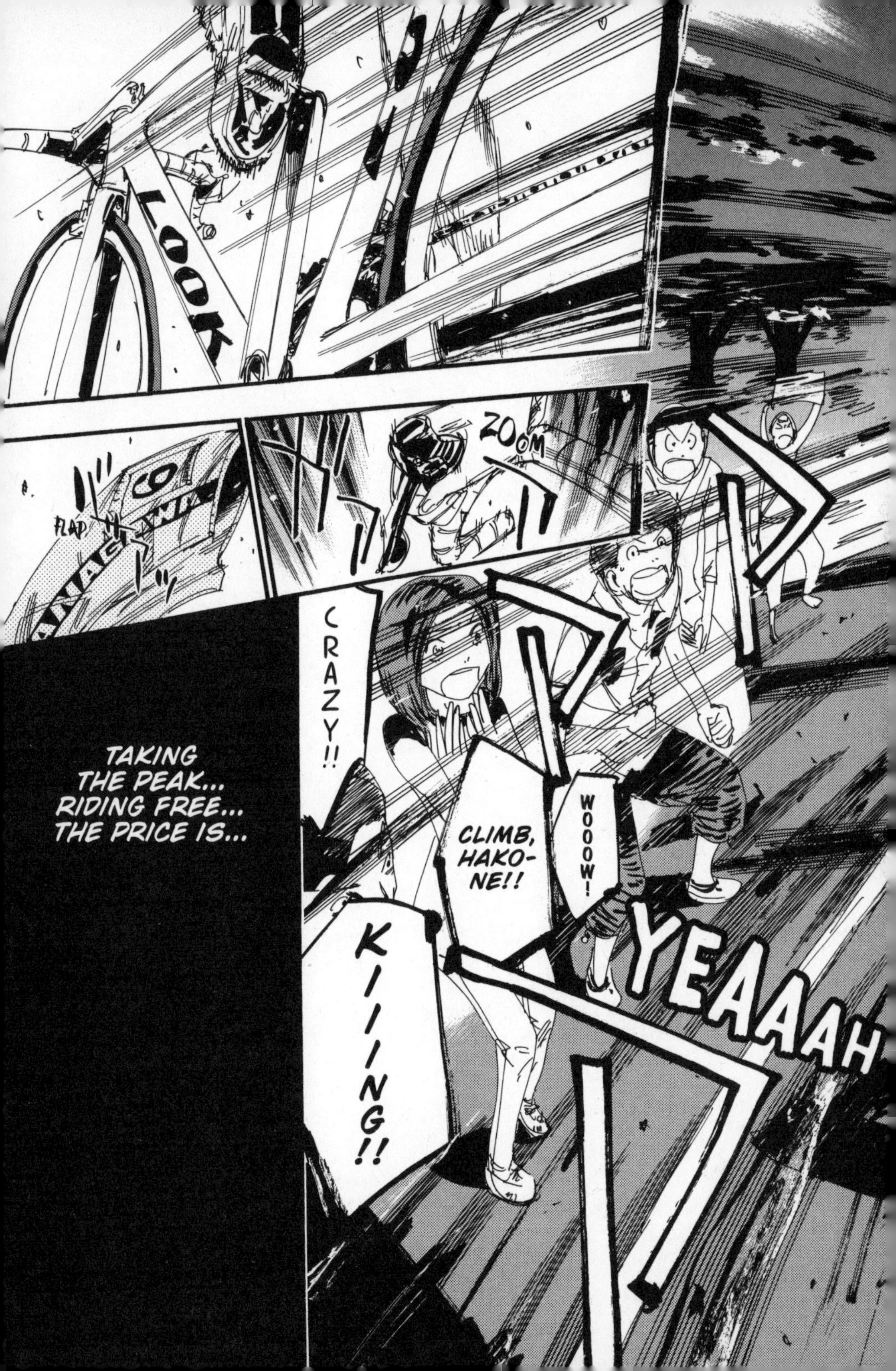
LOOK
ZOOM
FLAP
WOOOOW!
CLIMB, HAKONE!!
CRAZY!!
KIIIING!!
YEAAAAH
TAKING THE PEAK... RIDING FREE... THE PRICE IS...

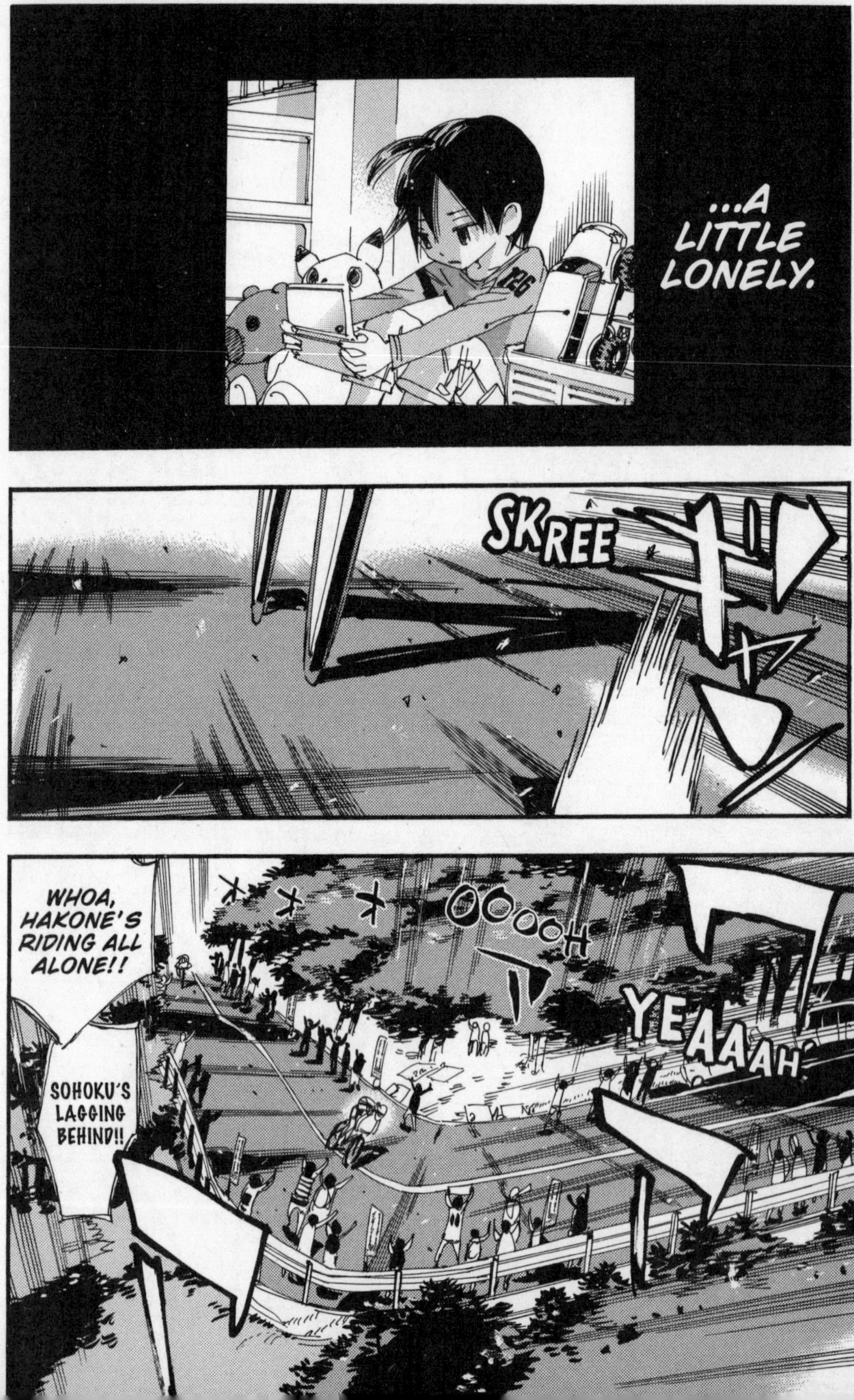
...A LITTLE LONELY.
SKREE
YEAAAAH
OOOOH
WHOA, HAKONE'S RIDING ALL ALONE!!
SOHOKU'S LAGGING BEHIND!!

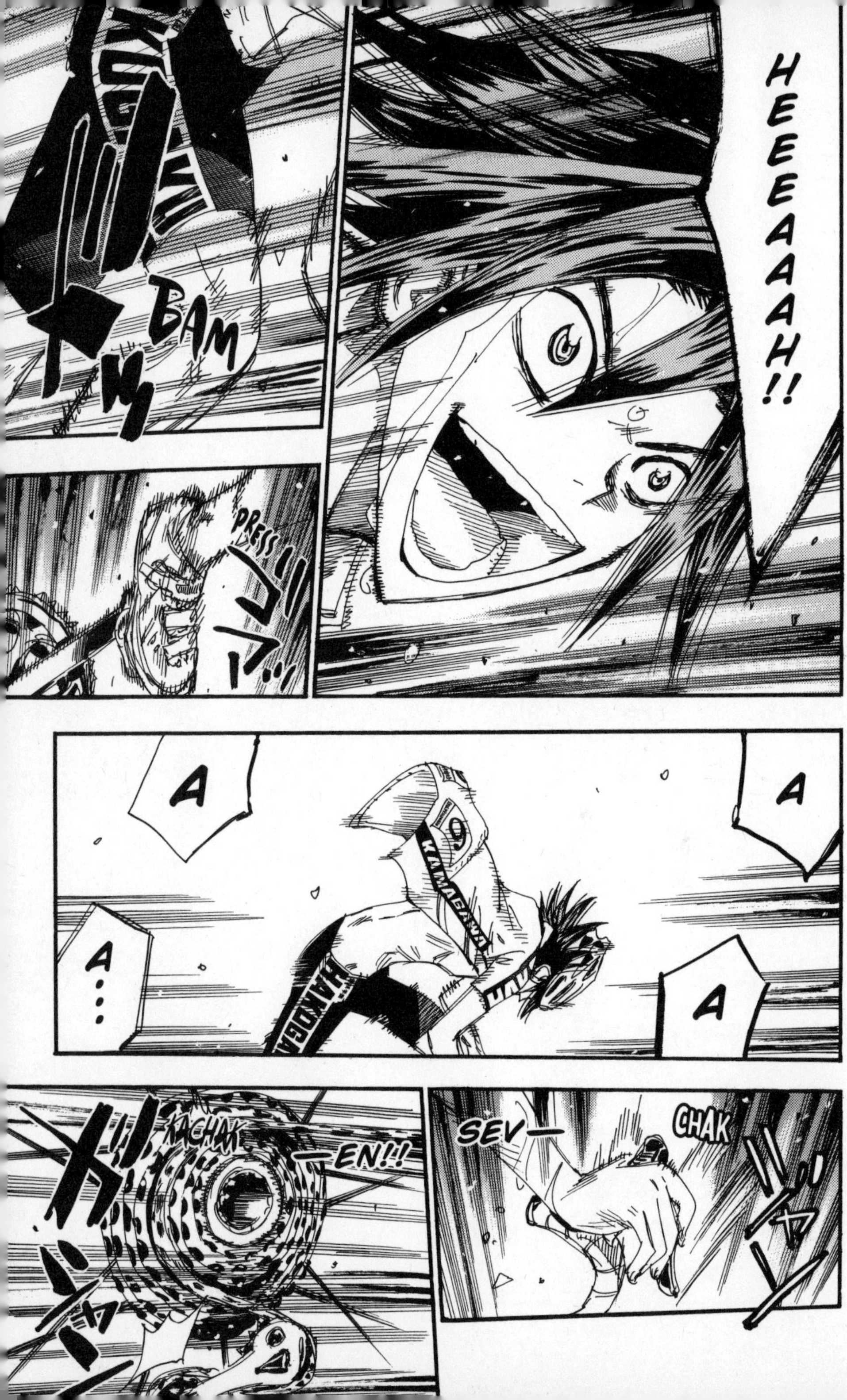
HEEEEAAAAH!!
BAM
DRESS
A
A
A
A...
CHAK
SEV—
—EN!!
KACHAK

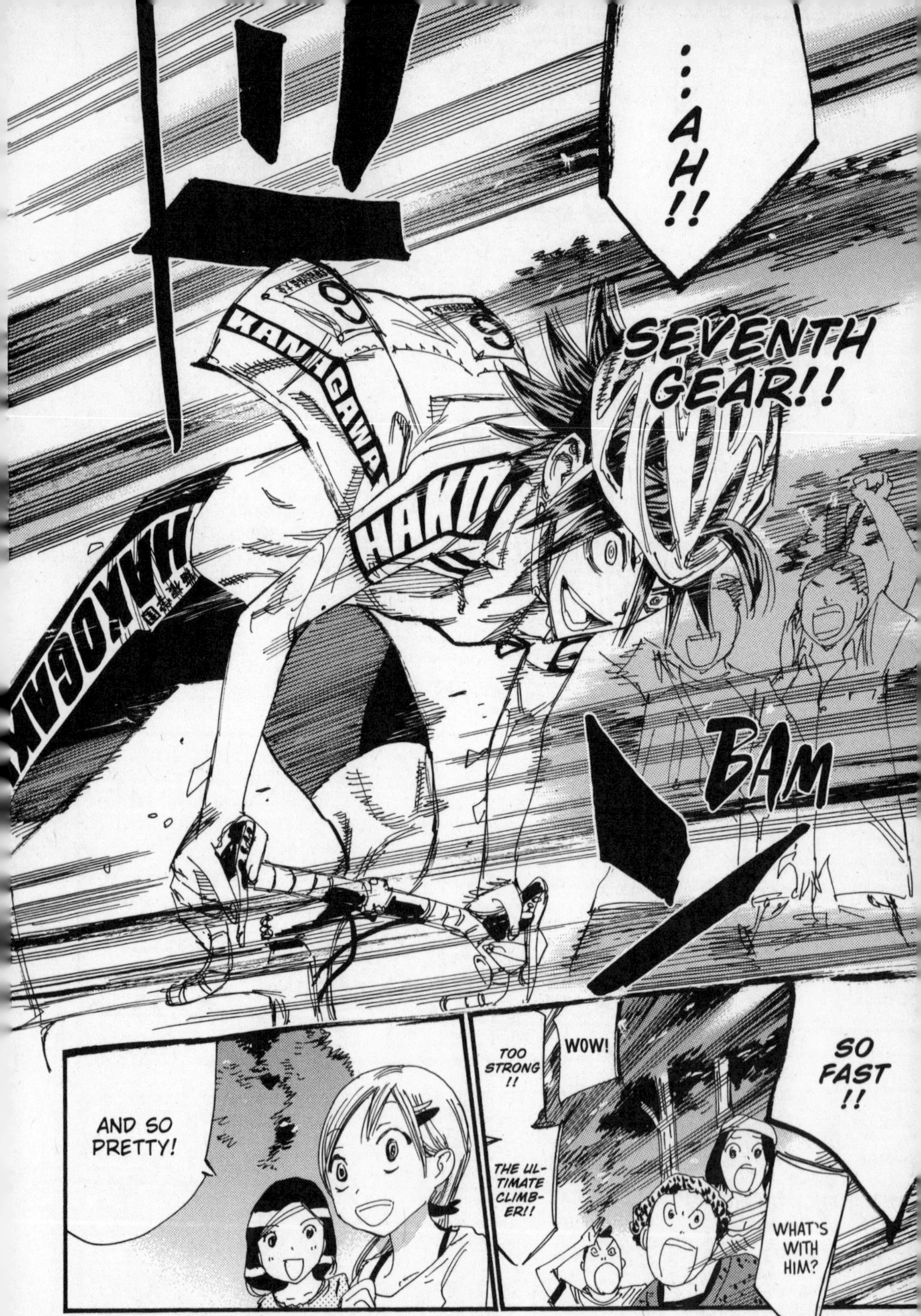
...AH!!
SEVENTH GEAR!!
BAM
SO FAST!!
WOW!
TOO STRONG!!
THE ULTIMATE CLIMBER!!
WHAT'S WITH HIM?
AND SO PRETTY!

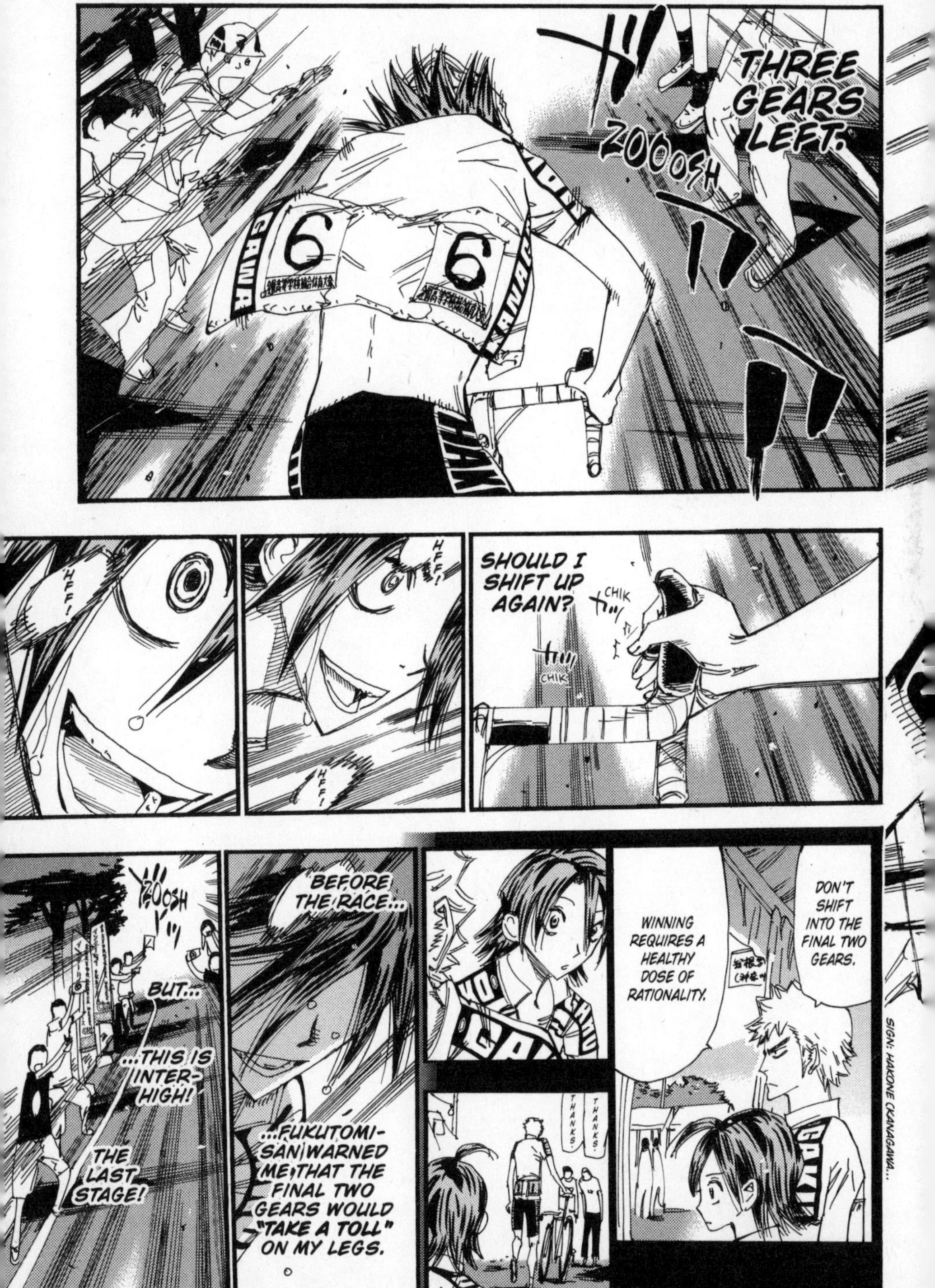
THREE GEARS LEFT.
ZOOOSH
SHOULD I SHIFT UP AGAIN?
CHIK
CHIK
HFF!
HFF!
HFF!
DON'T SHIFT INTO THE FINAL TWO GEARS.
WINNING REQUIRES A HEALTHY DOSE OF RATIONALITY.
SIGN: HAKONE (KANAGAWA)...
THANKS.
THANKS.
BEFORE THE RACE...
...FUKUTOMI-SAN WARNED ME THAT THE FINAL TWO GEARS WOULD "TAKE A TOLL" ON MY LEGS.
YOOSH
BUT...
...THIS IS INTER-HIGH!
THE LAST STAGE!

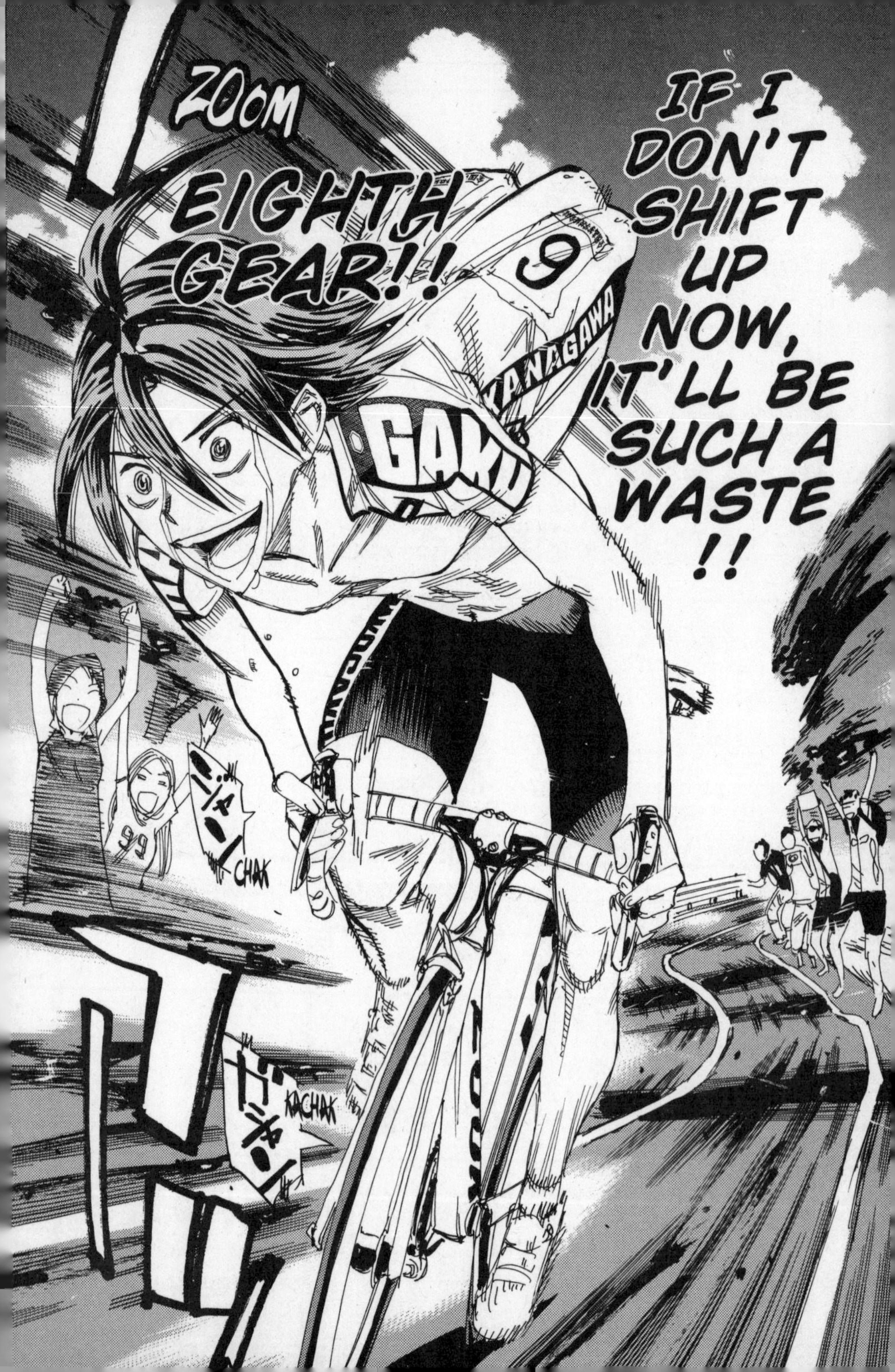
IF I DON'T SHIFT UP NOW, IT'LL BE SUCH A WASTE!!
ZOOM
EIGHTH GEAR!!
ジャン
CHAK
ガシャン
KACHAK

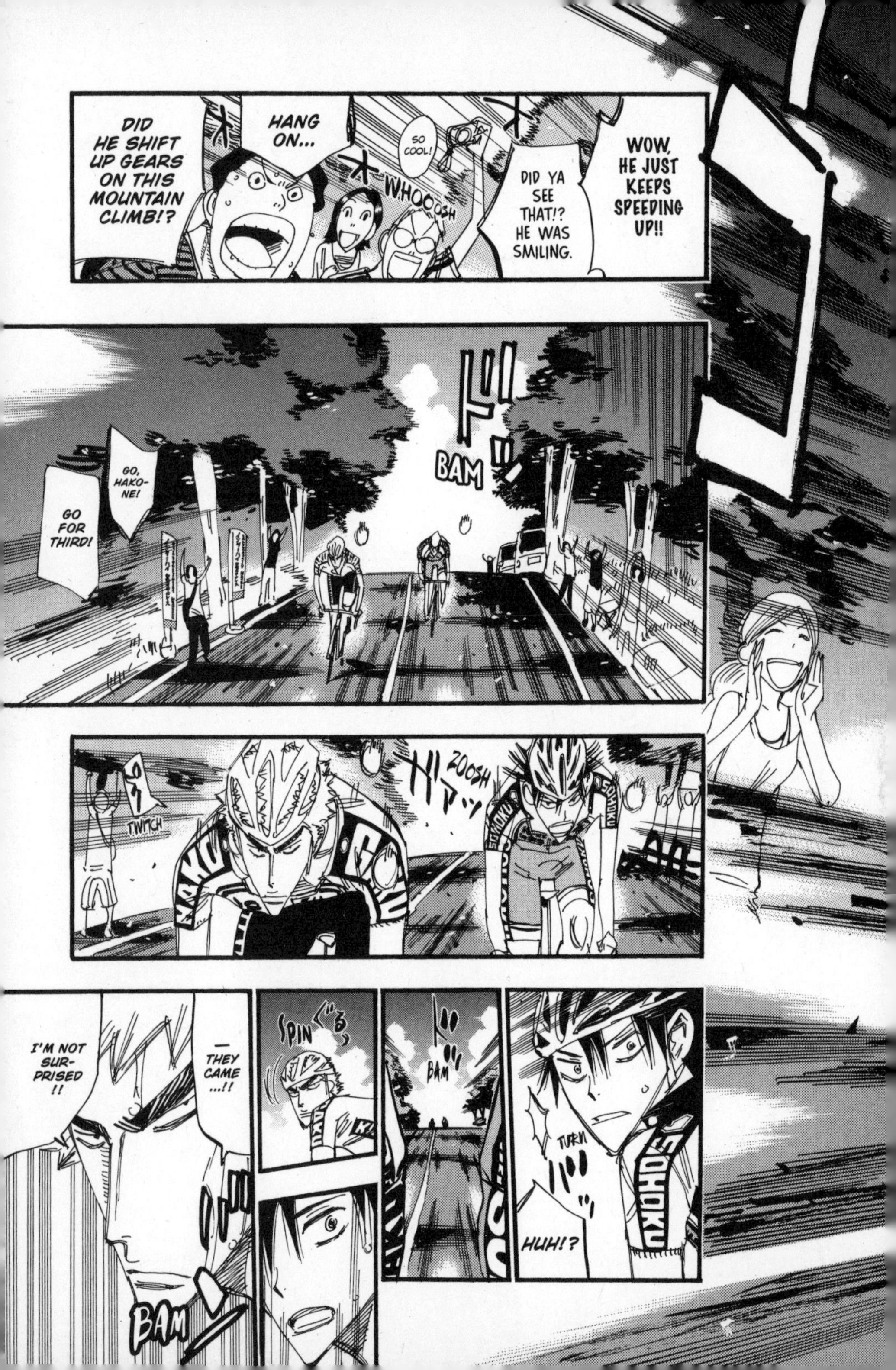
WOW, HE JUST KEEPS SPEEDING UP!!
DID YA SEE THAT!? HE WAS SMILING.
SO COOL!
WHOOOSH
HANG ON...
DID HE SHIFT UP GEARS ON THIS MOUNTAIN CLIMB!?
BAM
GO, HAKONE!
GO FOR THIRD!
ZOOSH
TWITCH
TURN
HUH!?
BAM
SPIN
—THEY CAME...!!
I'M NOT SURPRISED!!
BAM

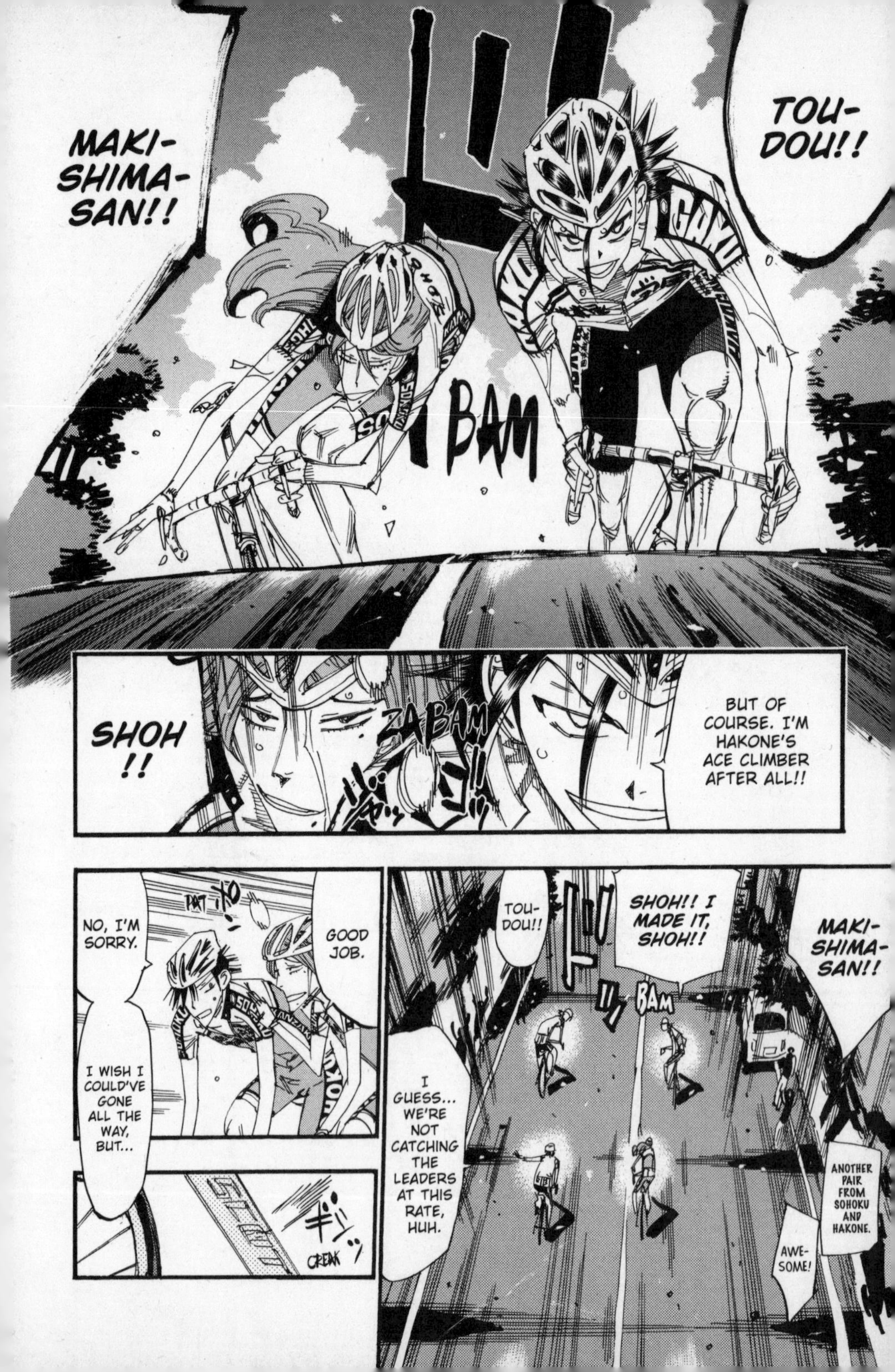
TOU-DOU!!
MAKI-SHIMA-SAN!!
BAM
BUT OF COURSE. I'M HAKONE'S ACE CLIMBER AFTER ALL!!
ZABAM
SHOH!!
MAKI-SHIMA-SAN!!
SHOH!! I MADE IT, SHOH!!
TOU-DOU!!
BAM
ANOTHER PAIR FROM SOHOKU AND HAKONE.
AWE-SOME!
I GUESS... WE'RE NOT CATCHING THE LEADERS AT THIS RATE, HUH.
PAT
GOOD JOB.
NO, I'M SORRY.
I WISH I COULD'VE GONE ALL THE WAY, BUT...
CREAK

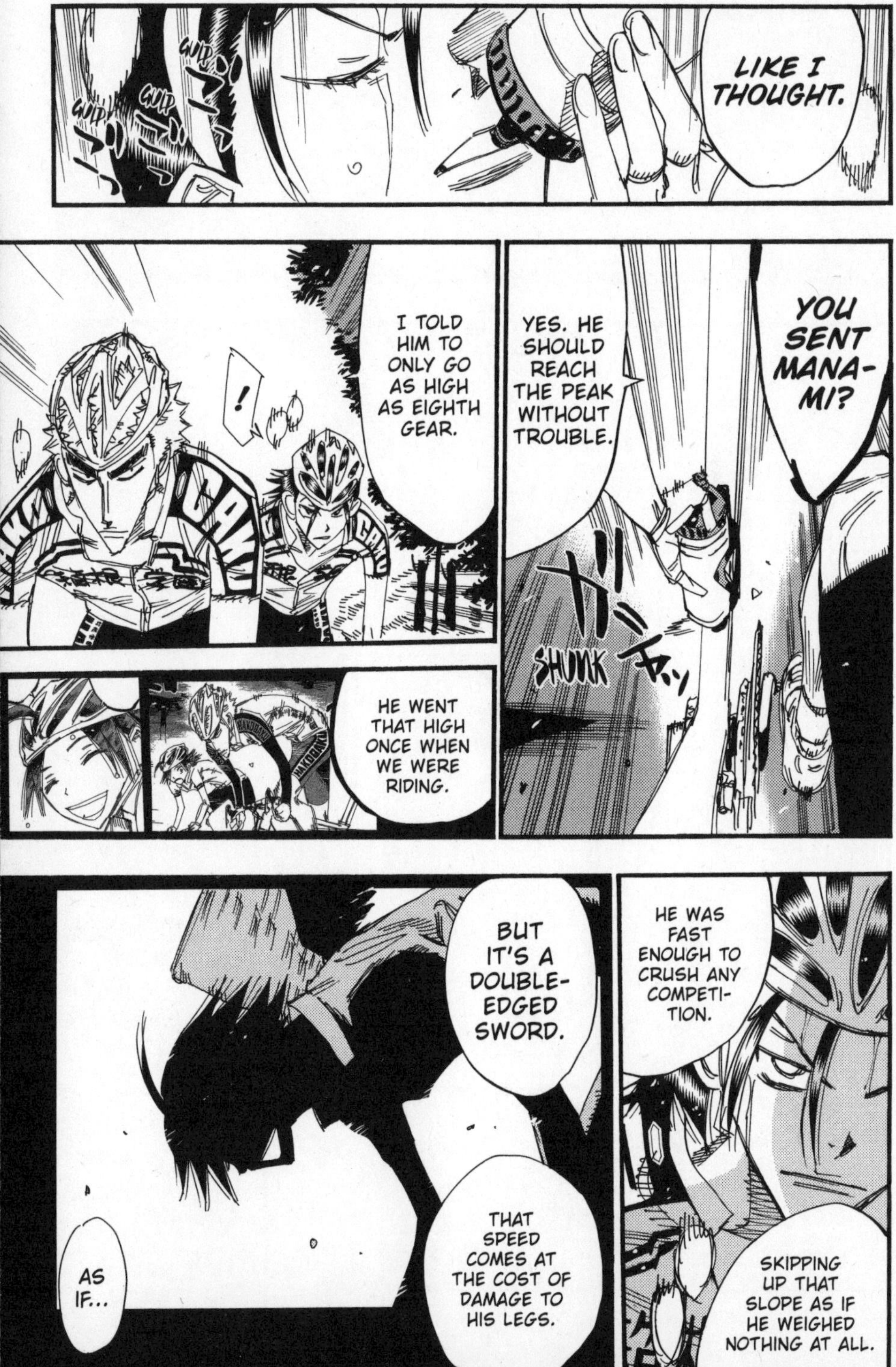
LIKE I THOUGHT.
GULP GULP GULP
YOU SENT MANAMI?
YES. HE SHOULD REACH THE PEAK WITHOUT TROUBLE.
SHUNK
I TOLD HIM TO ONLY GO AS HIGH AS EIGHTH GEAR.
!
HE WENT THAT HIGH ONCE WHEN WE WERE RIDING.
HE WAS FAST ENOUGH TO CRUSH ANY COMPETITION.
SKIPPING UP THAT SLOPE AS IF HE WEIGHED NOTHING AT ALL.
BUT IT'S A DOUBLE-EDGED SWORD.
THAT SPEED COMES AT THE COST OF DAMAGE TO HIS LEGS.
AS IF...

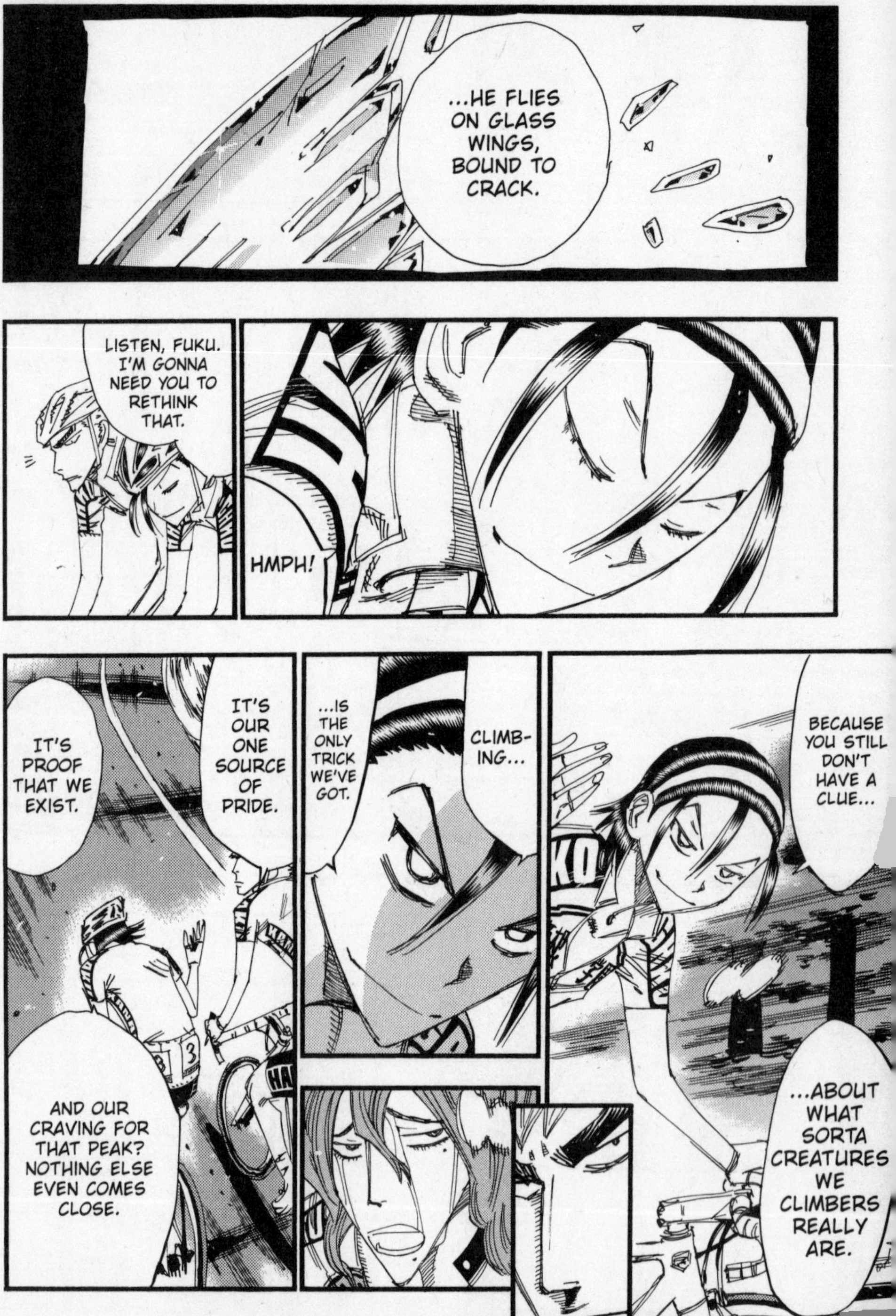
...HE FLIES ON GLASS WINGS, BOUND TO CRACK.
HMPH!
LISTEN, FUKU. I'M GONNA NEED YOU TO RETHINK THAT.
BECAUSE YOU STILL DON'T HAVE A CLUE...
...ABOUT WHAT SORTA CREATURES WE CLIMBERS REALLY ARE.
CLIMB-ING...
...IS THE ONLY TRICK WE'VE GOT.
IT'S OUR ONE SOURCE OF PRIDE.
IT'S PROOF THAT WE EXIST.
AND OUR CRAVING FOR THAT PEAK? NOTHING ELSE EVEN COMES CLOSE.

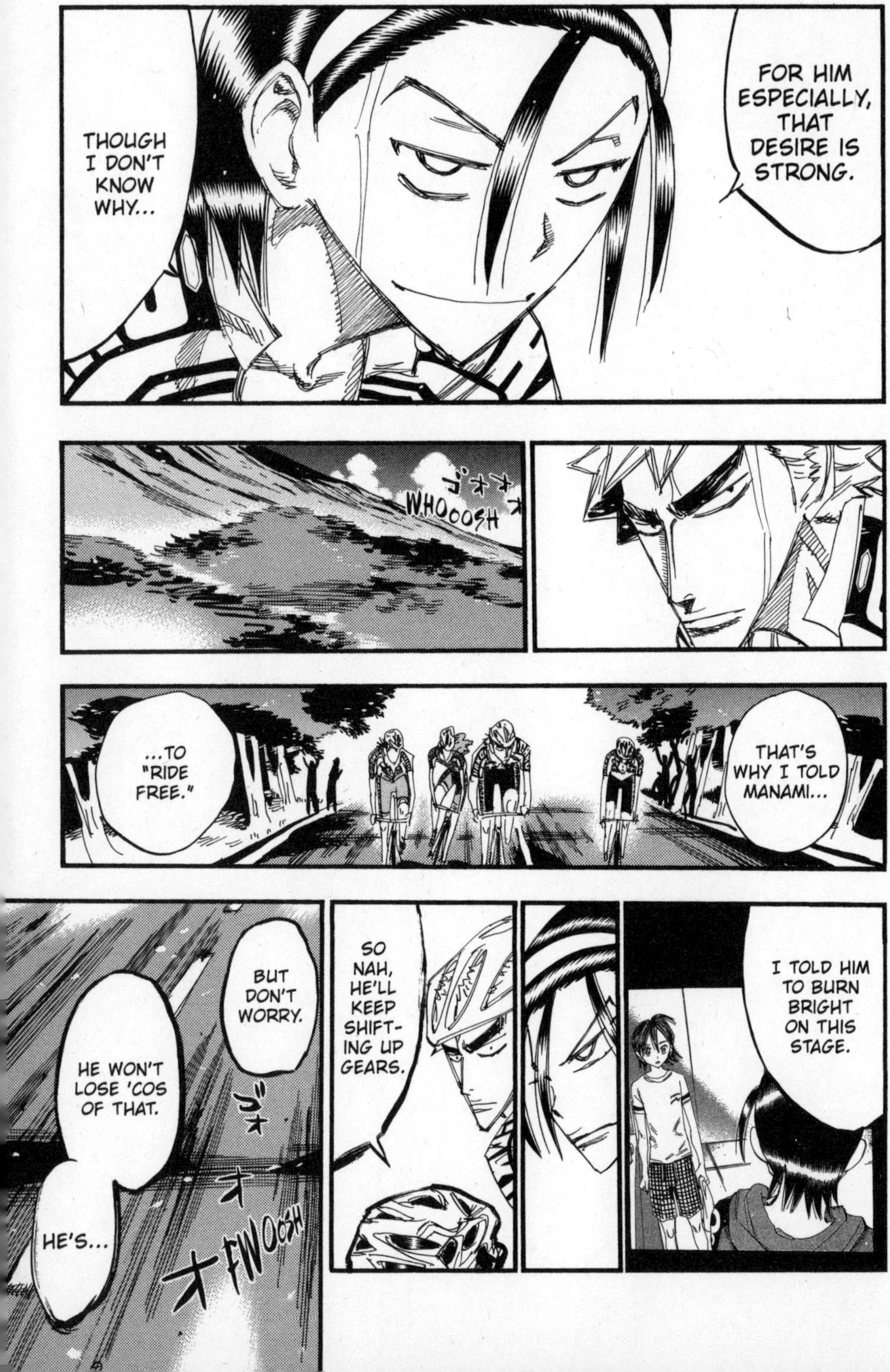

FOR HIM ESPECIALLY, THAT DESIRE IS STRONG.
THOUGH I DON'T KNOW WHY...
ゴオオオ
WHOOOSH
THAT'S WHY I TOLD MANAMI...
...TO "RIDE FREE."
I TOLD HIM TO BURN BRIGHT ON THIS STAGE.
SO NAH, HE'LL KEEP SHIFTING UP GEARS.
BUT DON'T WORRY.
HE WON'T LOSE 'COS OF THAT.
HE'S...
ゴオオオ
FWOOSH

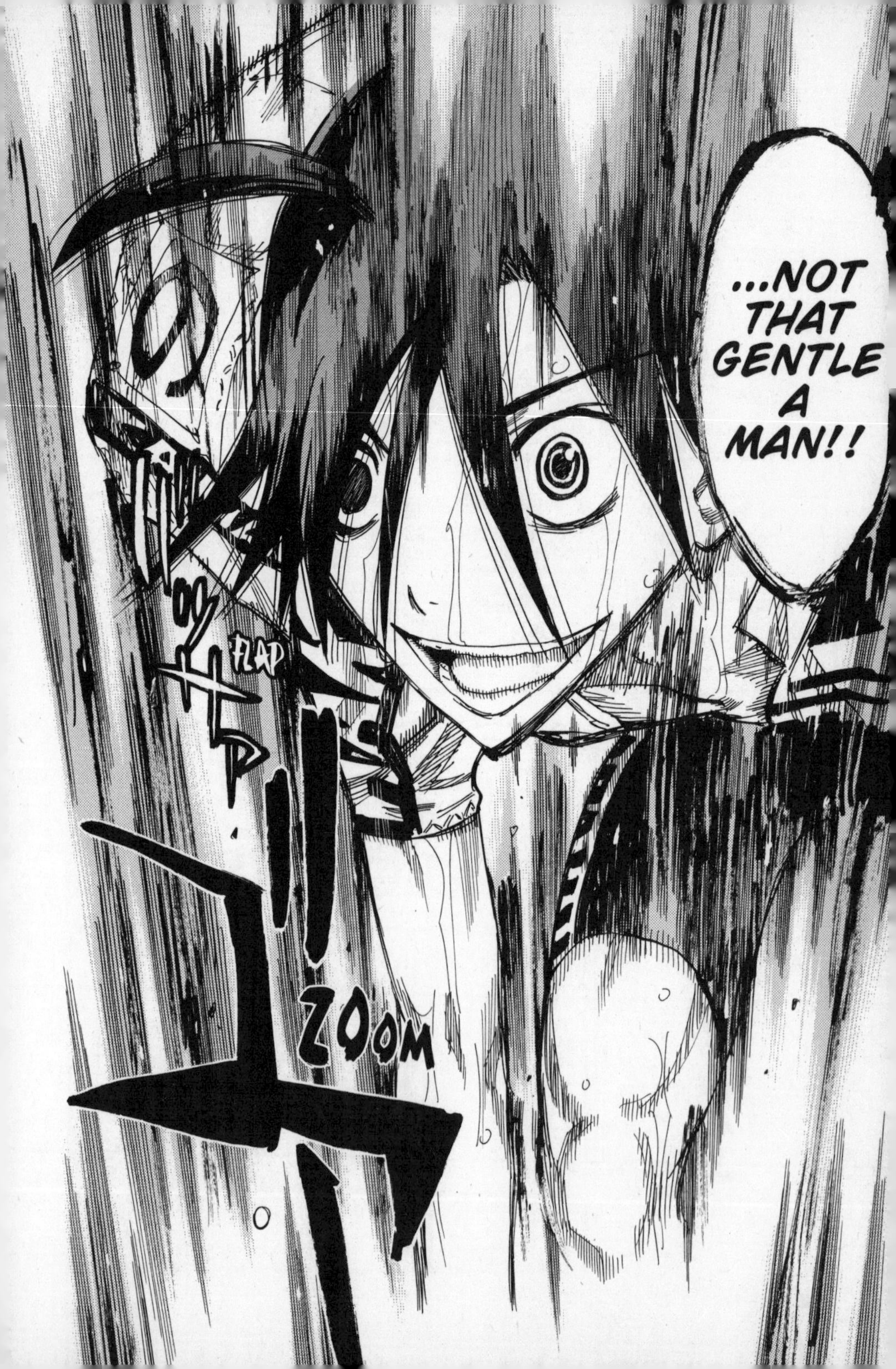
...NOT THAT GENTLE A MAN!!
FLAP
ZOOM

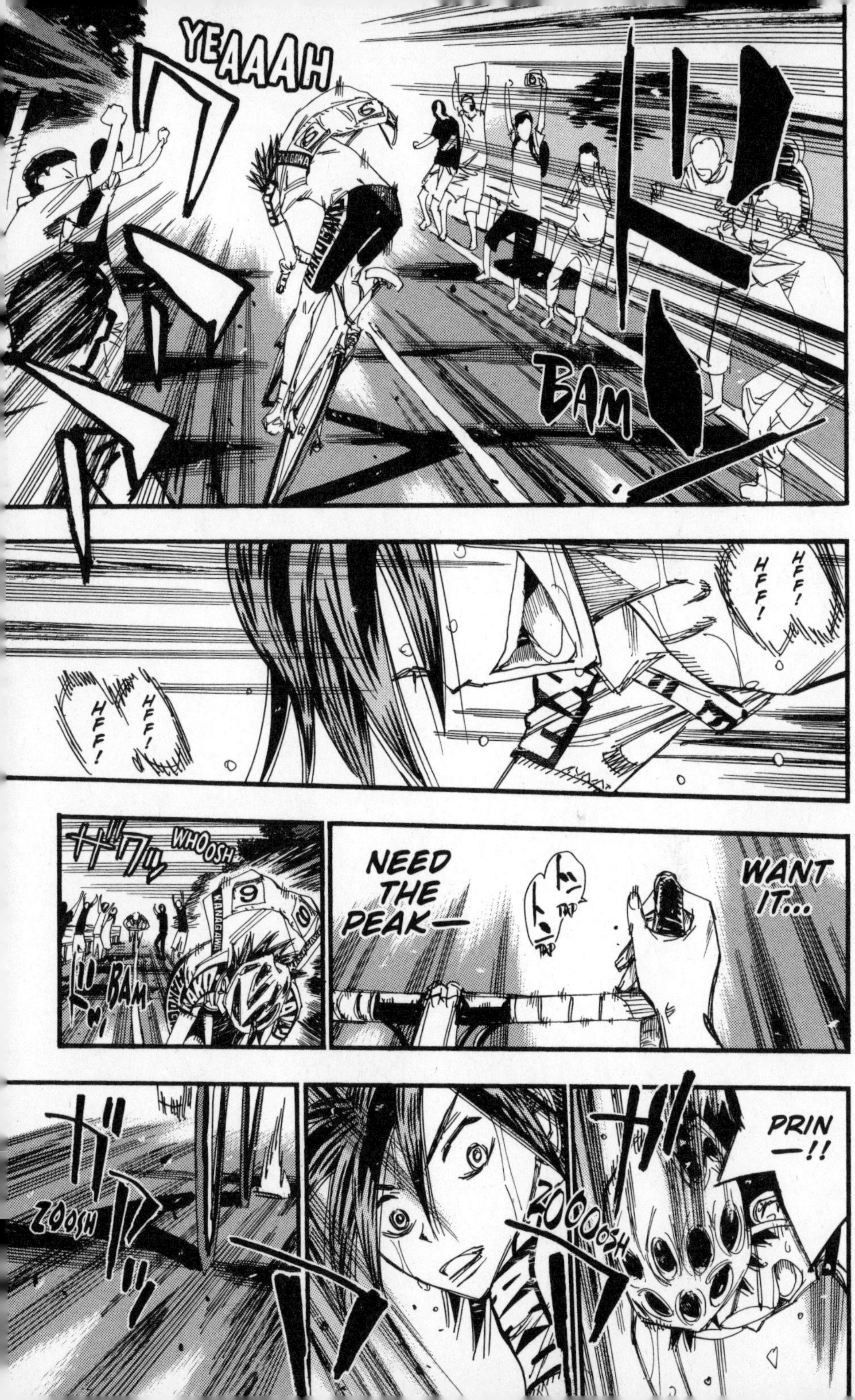
YEAAAAH
BAM
HFF! HFF!
HFF! HFF!
WANT IT...
NEED THE PEAK—
TAP
TAP
WHOOSH
BAM
PRIN—!!
ZOOOOSH
ZOOSH

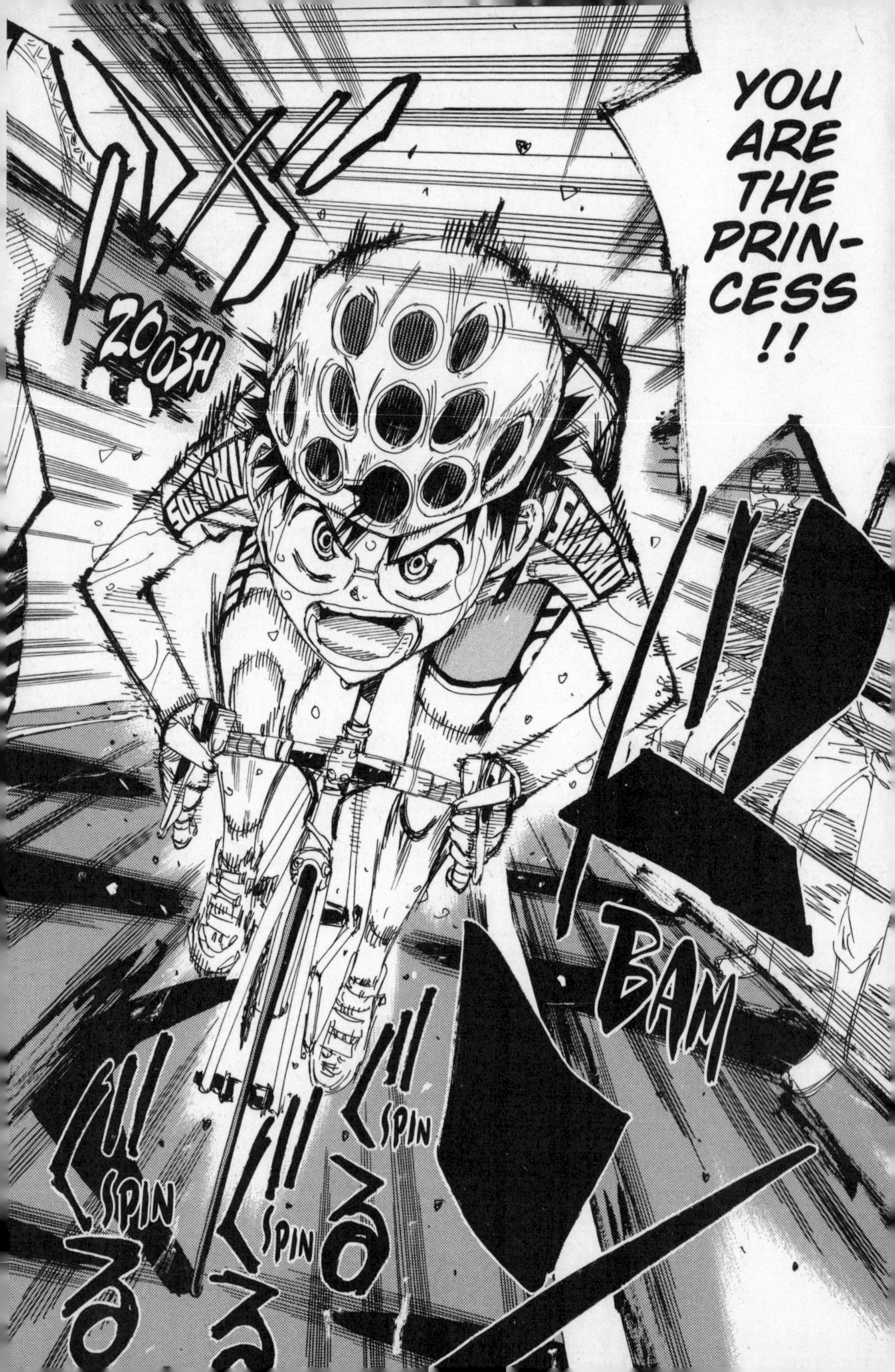
YOU ARE THE PRIN-CESS!!
ZOOSH
BAM
SPIN
SPIN
SPIN

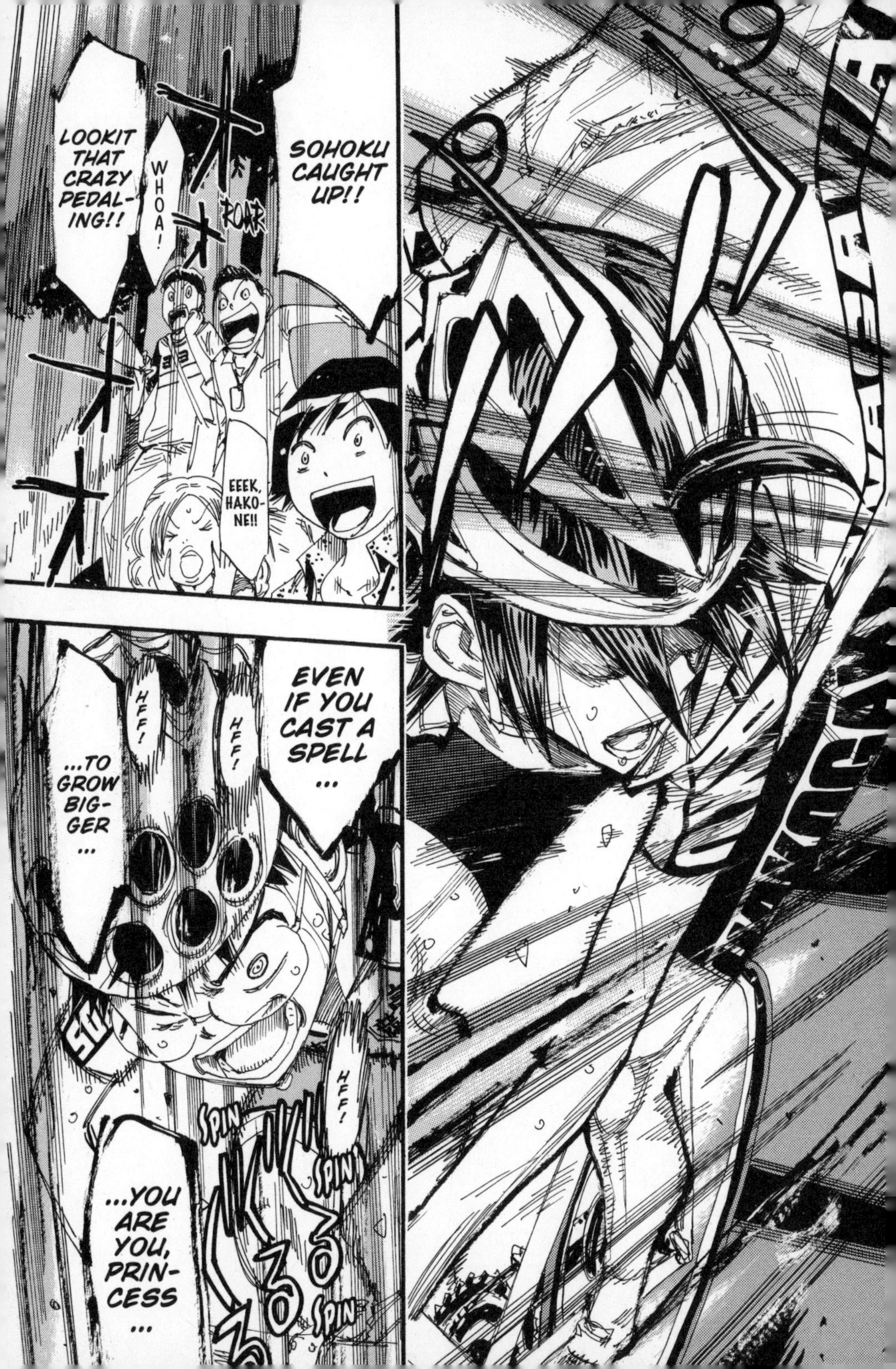
SOHOKU CAUGHT UP!!
ROAR
WHOA!
LOOKIT THAT CRAZY PEDAL-ING!!
EEEK, HAKO-NE!!
EVEN IF YOU CAST A SPELL ...
HFF!
HFF!
...TO GROW BIG-GER ...
HFF!
SPIN
SPIN
SPIN
...YOU ARE YOU, PRIN-CESS ...

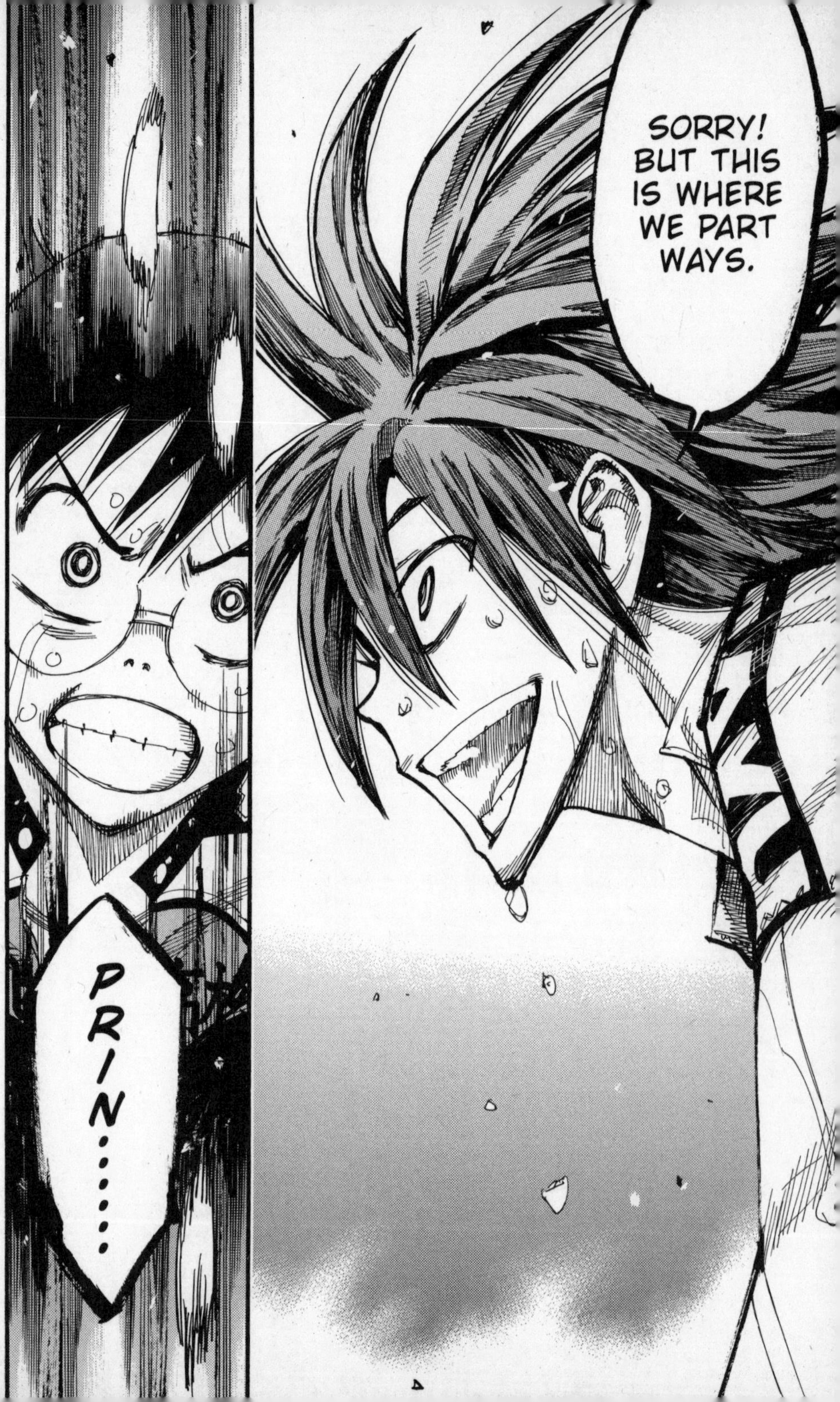
SORRY! BUT THIS IS WHERE WE PART WAYS.
PRIN......

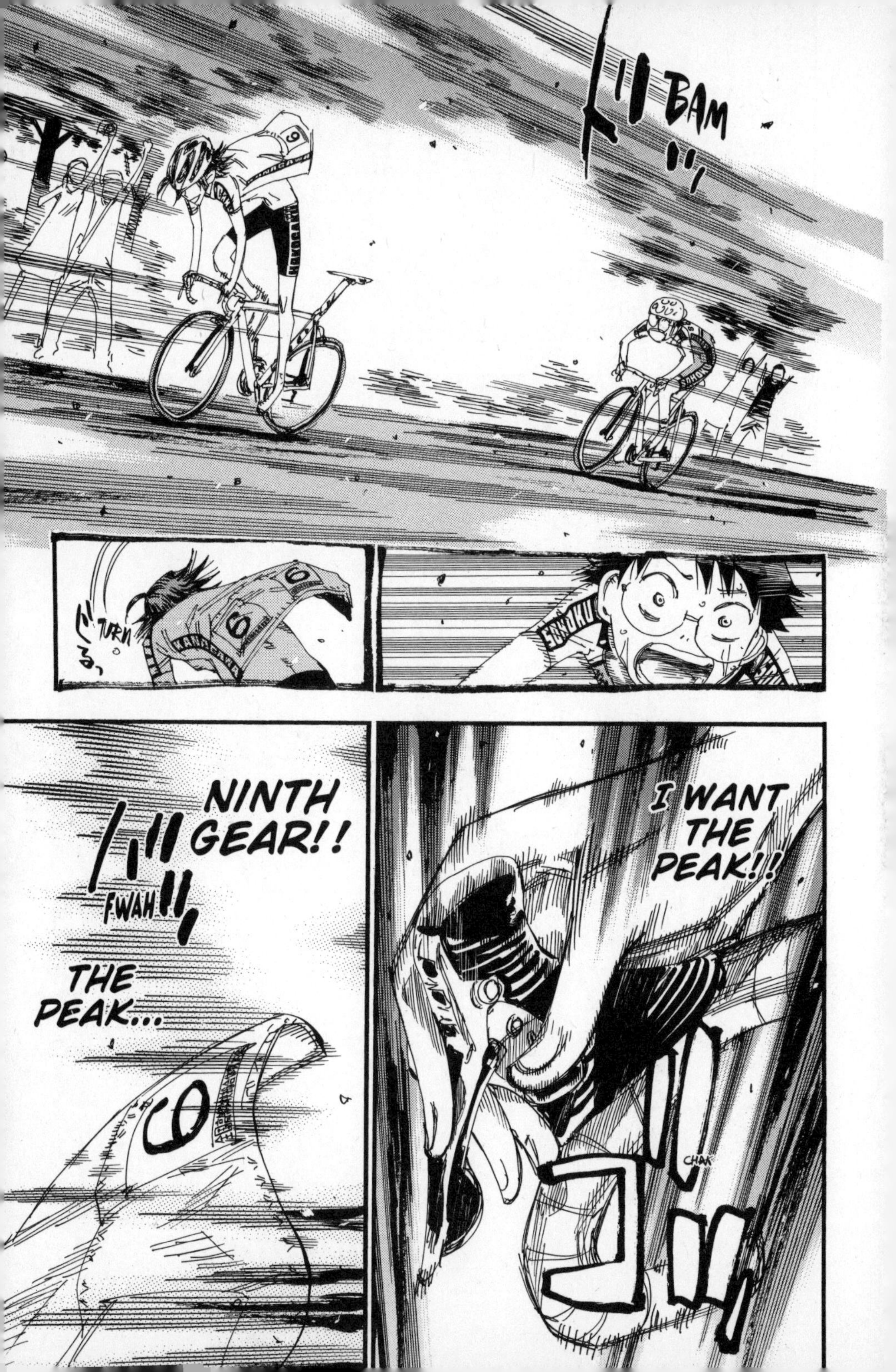

BAM
TURN
I WANT THE PEAK!!
CHAK
NINTH GEAR!!
FWAH!!
THE PEAK...

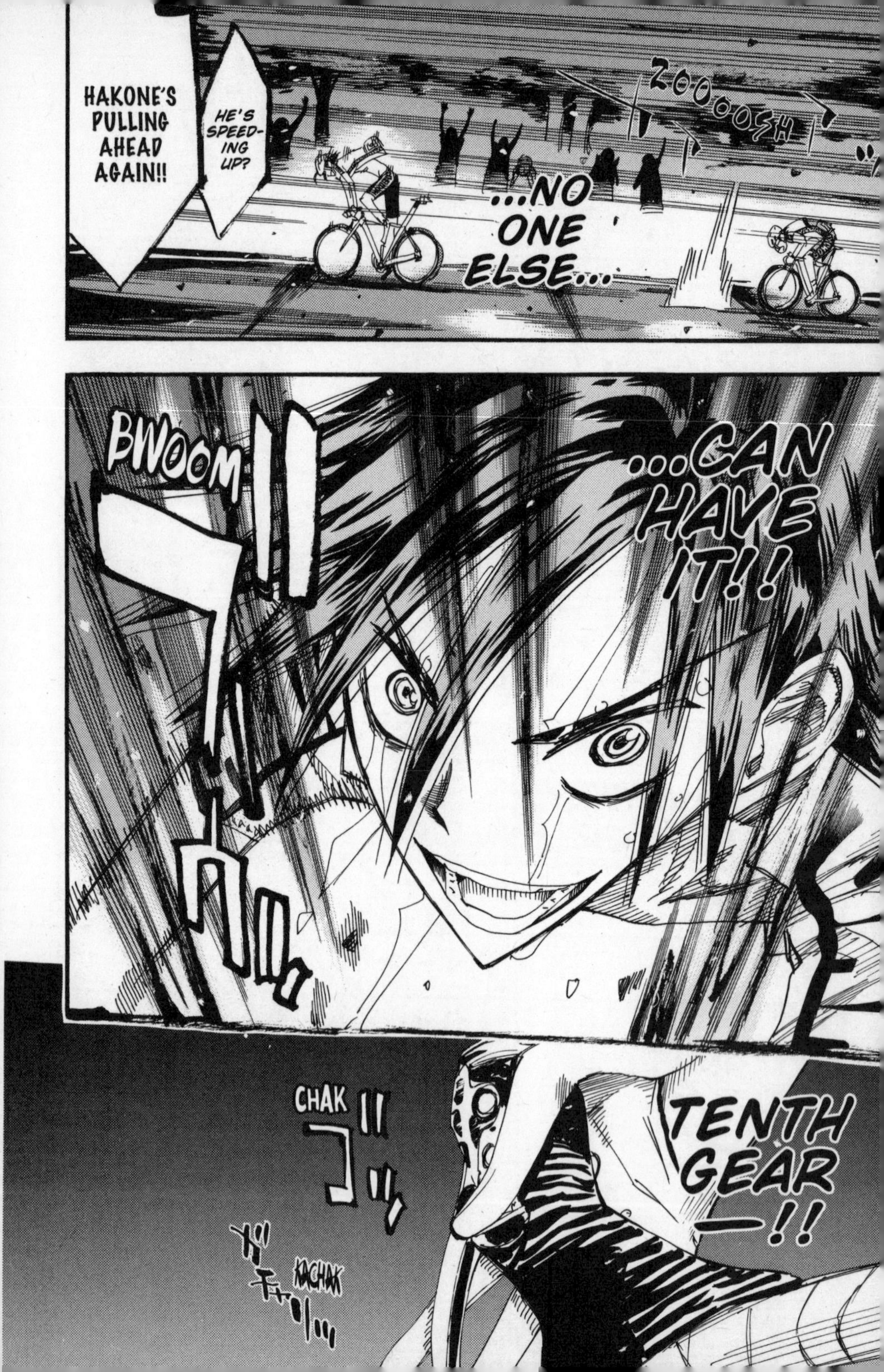
ZOOOOOSH
...NO ONE ELSE...
HE'S SPEED-ING UP?
HAKONE'S PULLING AHEAD AGAIN!!
...CAN HAVE IT!!
BWOOM
TENTH GEAR—!!
CHAK
KACHAK

RIDE.223 LAST GEAR

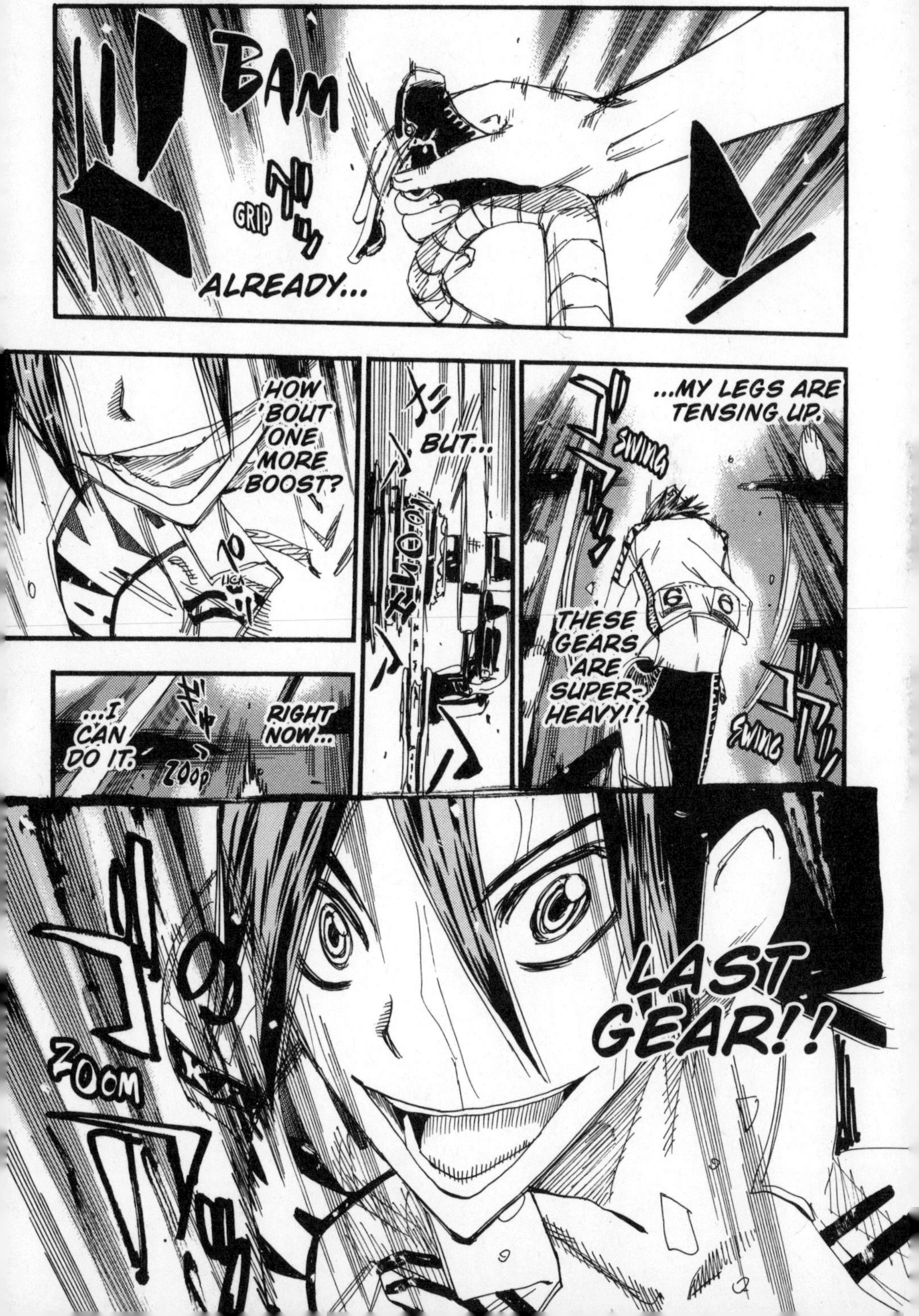
BAM
GRIP
ALREADY...
...MY LEGS ARE TENSING UP.
SWING
THESE GEARS ARE SUPER-HEAVY!!
SWING
BUT...
HOW BOUT ONE MORE BOOST?
LICK
RIGHT NOW...
...I CAN DO IT.
ZOOP
LAST GEAR!!
ZOOM

RIDE.223 LAST GEAR

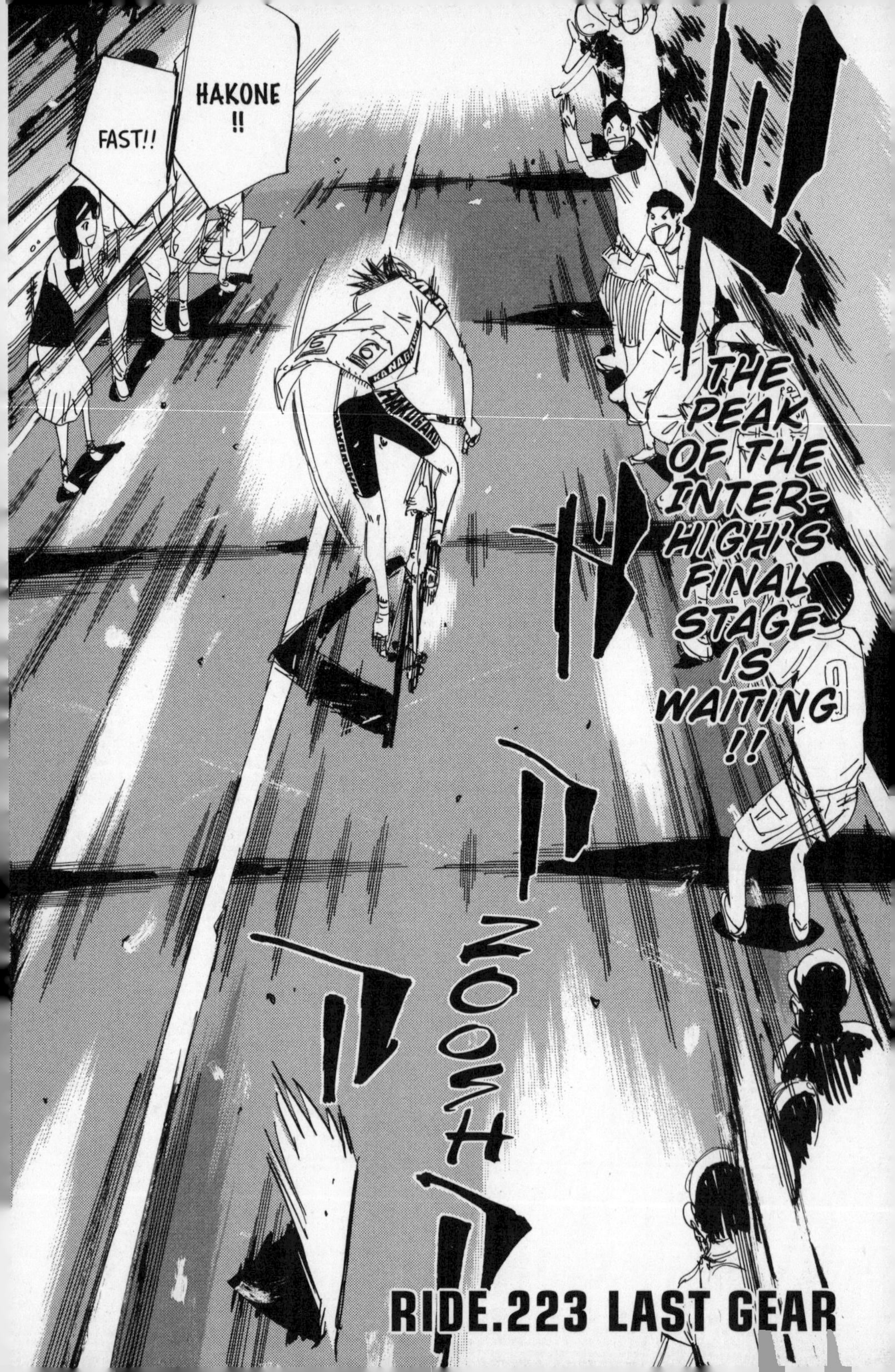
HAKONE!!
FAST!!
THE PEAK OF THE INTER-HIGH'S FINAL STAGE IS WAITING!!
ZOOSH

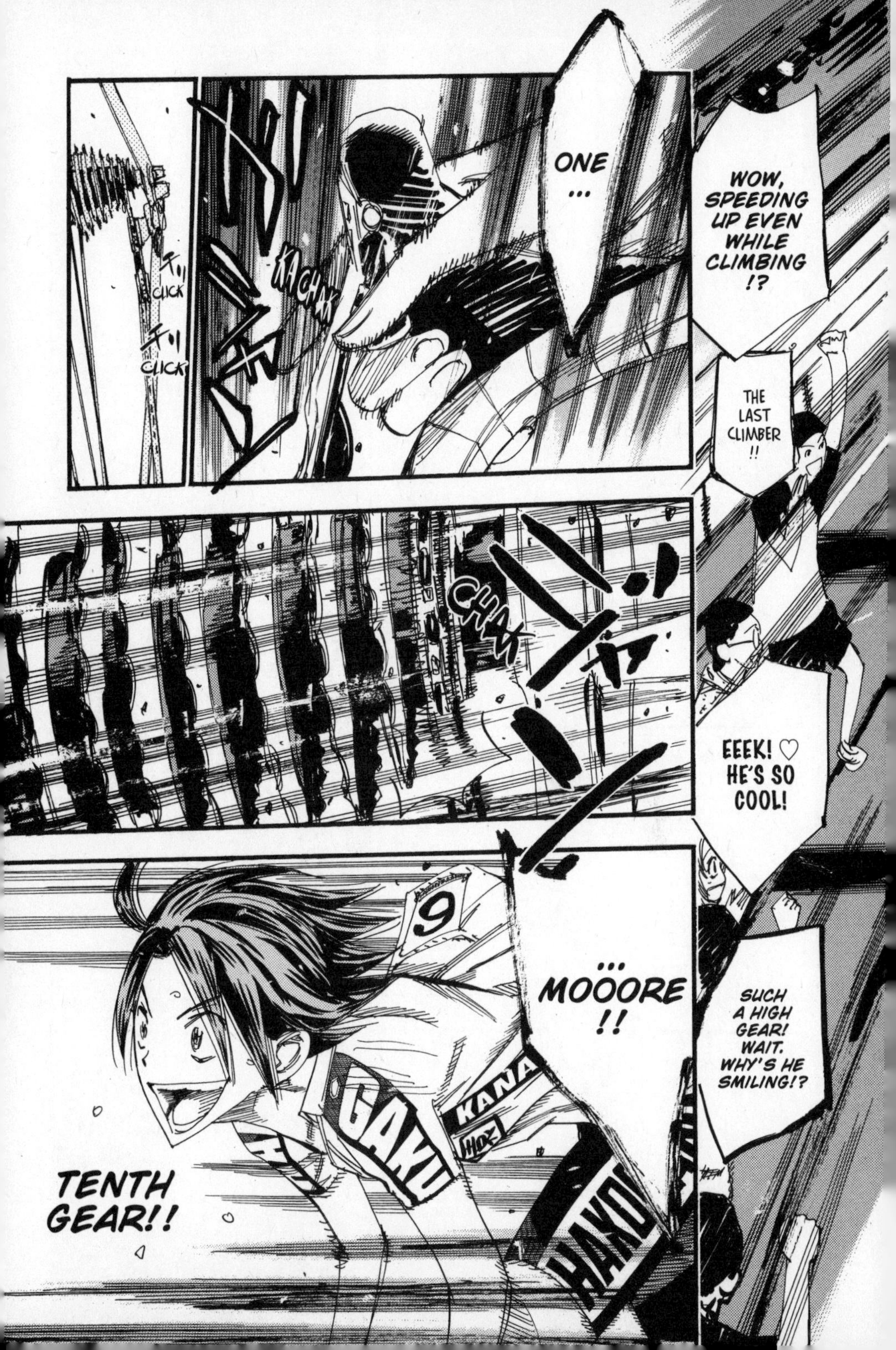
WOW, SPEEDING UP EVEN WHILE CLIMBING !?
THE LAST CLIMBER !!
EEEK! ♡ HE'S SO COOL!
SUCH A HIGH GEAR! WAIT. WHY'S HE SMILING!?
ONE ...
KACHAK
CLICK
CLICK
CHAK
... MOÖORE !!
TENTH GEAR!!

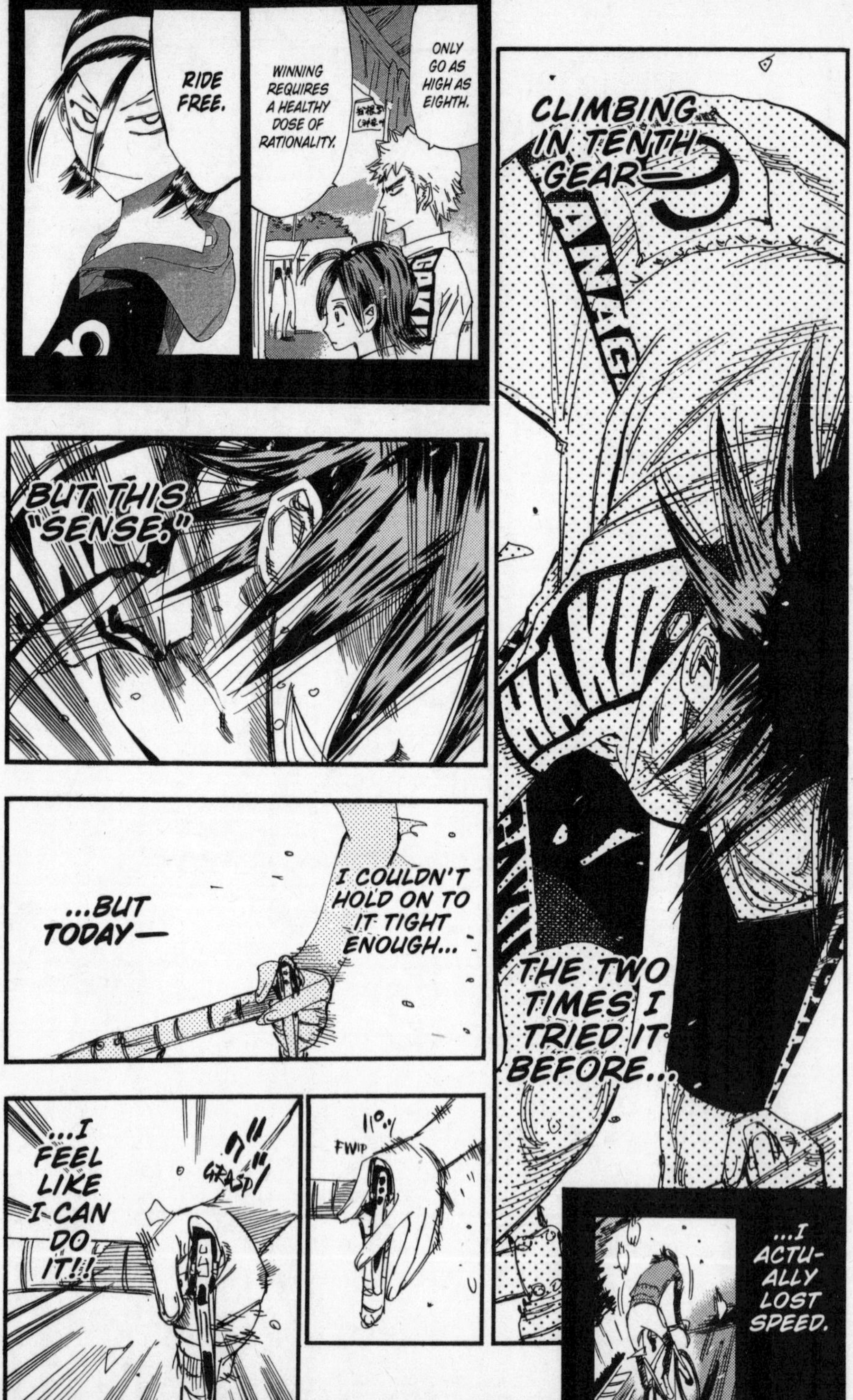
CLIMBING IN TENTH GEAR—
THE TWO TIMES I TRIED IT BEFORE...
...I ACTUALLY LOST SPEED.
ONLY GO AS HIGH AS EIGHTH.
WINNING REQUIRES A HEALTHY DOSE OF RATIONALITY.
RIDE FREE.
BUT THIS "SENSE,"
I COULDN'T HOLD ON TO IT TIGHT ENOUGH...
...BUT TODAY—
FWIP
GRASP!
...I FEEL LIKE I CAN DO IT!!

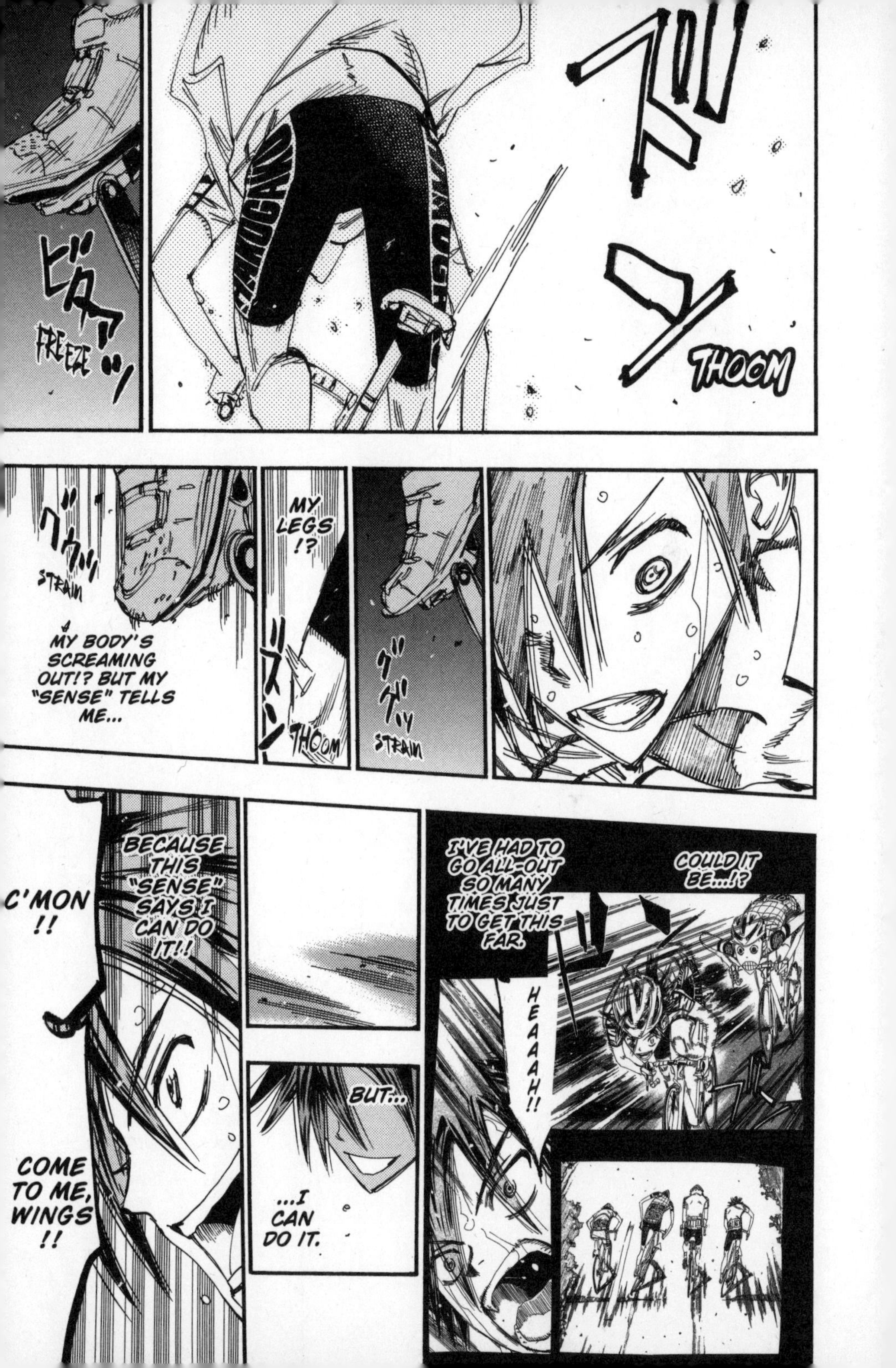

THOOM
FREEZE
STRAIN
THOOM
MY LEGS!?
STRAIN
MY BODY'S SCREAMING OUT!? BUT MY "SENSE" TELLS ME...
COULD IT BE...!?
I'VE HAD TO GO ALL-OUT SO MANY TIMES JUST TO GET THIS FAR.
HEAAAAH!!
BUT...
...I CAN DO IT.
BECAUSE THIS "SENSE" SAYS I CAN DO IT!!
C'MON!!
COME TO ME, WINGS!!

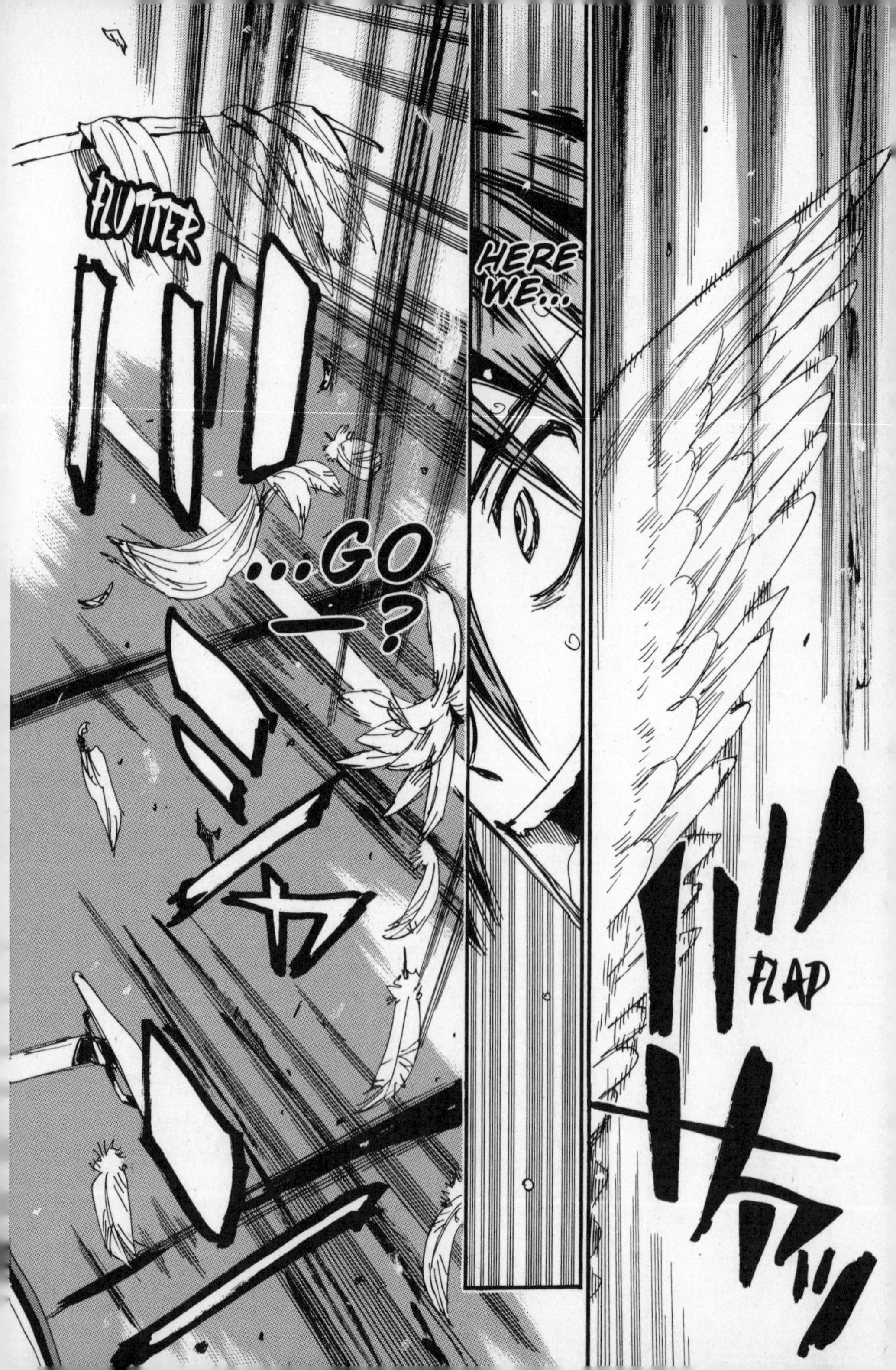
FLAP
HERE WE...
FLUTTER
...GO—?

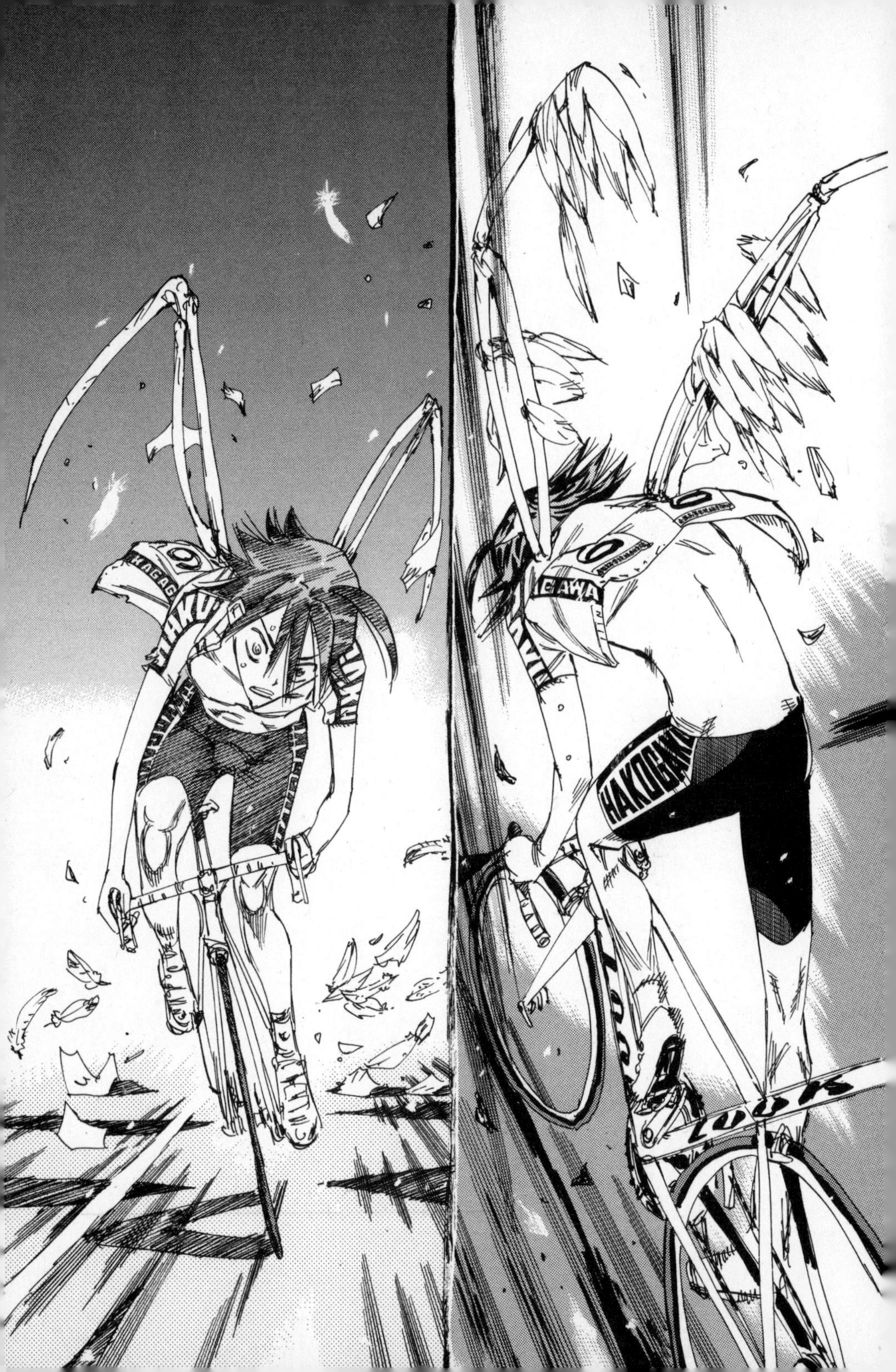

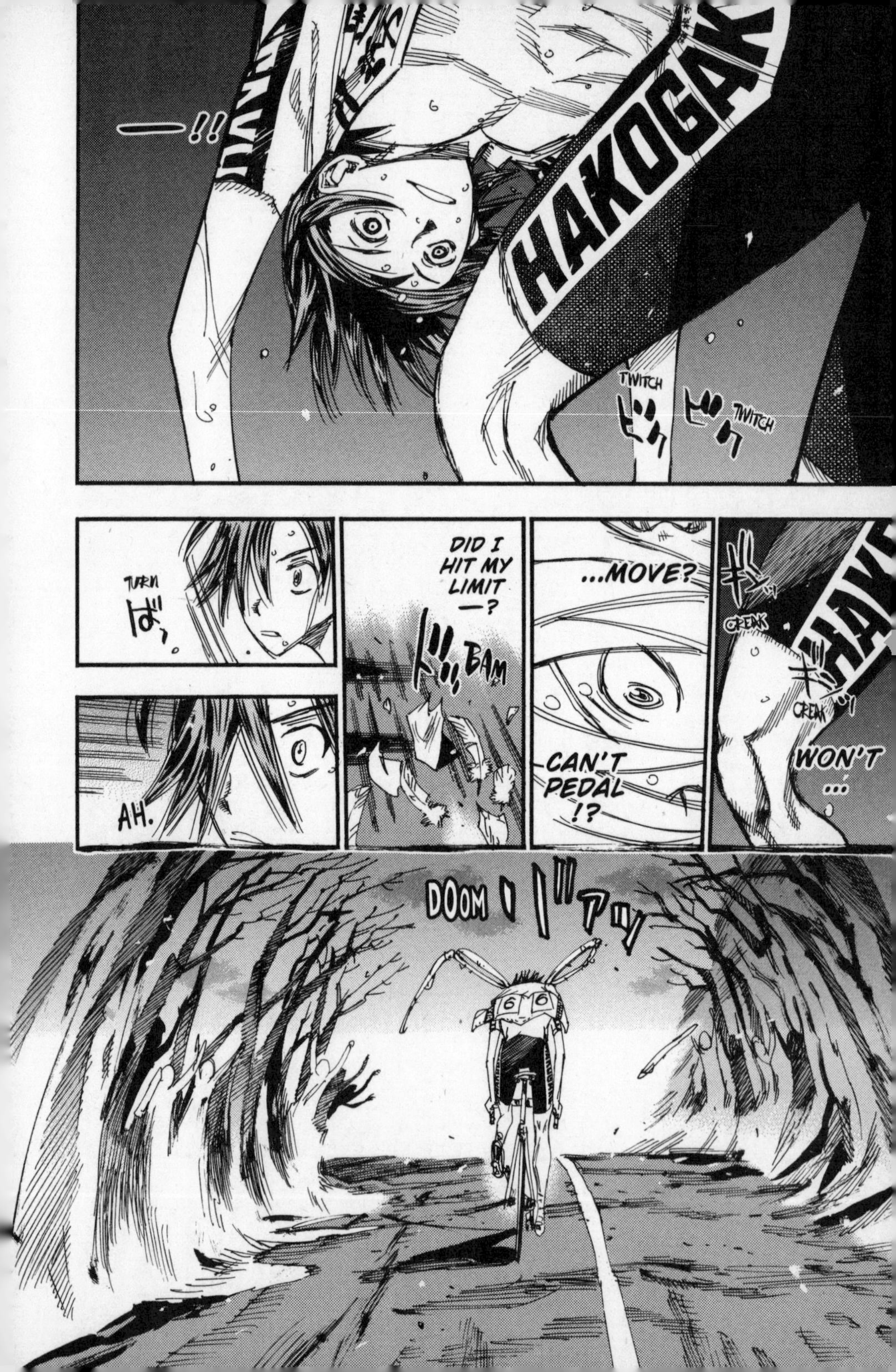
HAKOGAK
—!!
TWITCH
ビクッ
TWITCH
ビクッ
CREAK
CREAK
WON'T …
…MOVE?
CAN'T PEDAL !?
DID I HIT MY LIMIT—?
BAM
TURN
ばっ
AH.
DOOM

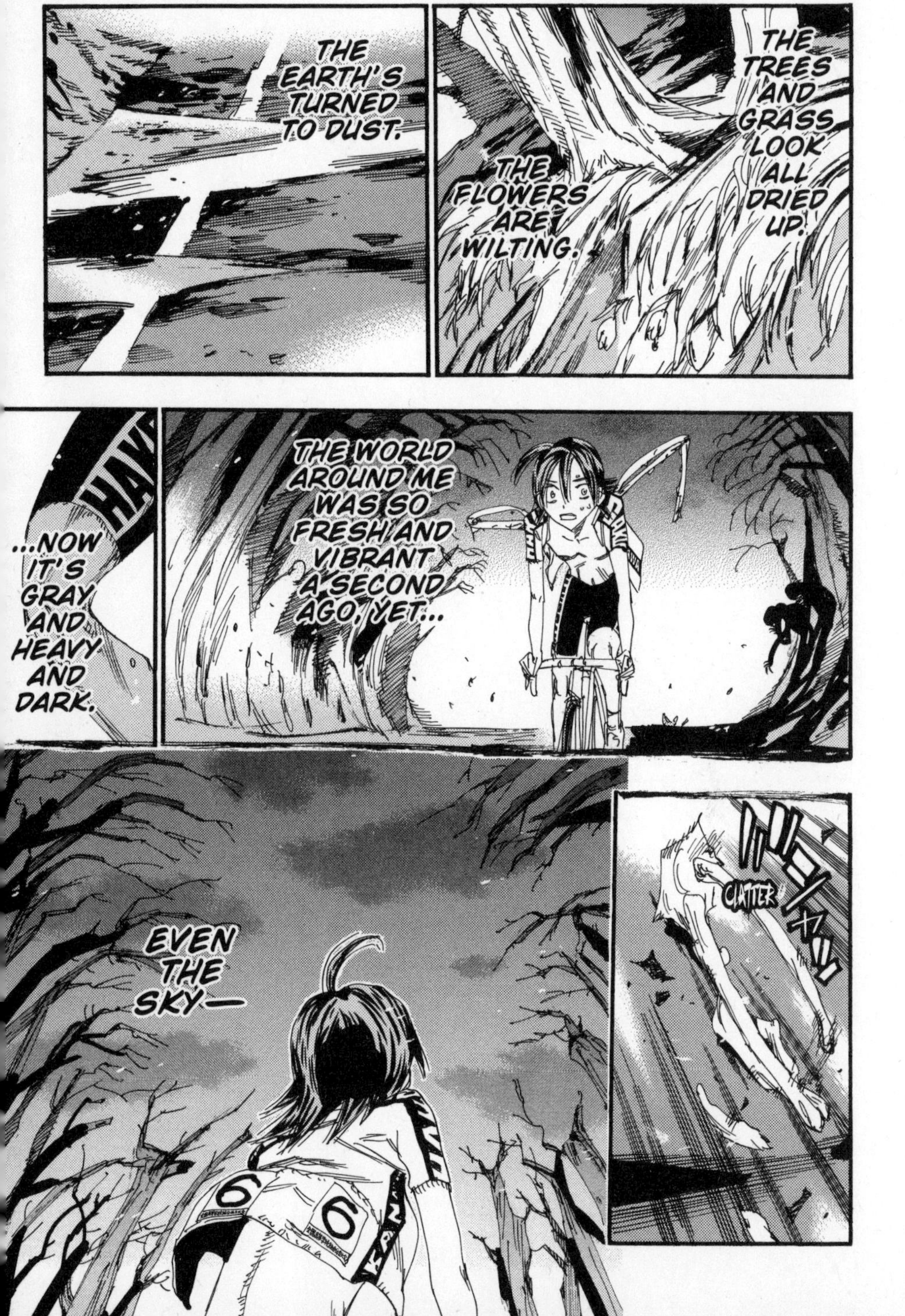
THE TREES AND GRASS LOOK ALL DRIED UP.
THE FLOWERS ARE WILTING.
THE EARTH'S TURNED TO DUST.
THE WORLD AROUND ME WAS SO FRESH AND VIBRANT A SECOND AGO, YET...
...NOW IT'S GRAY AND HEAVY AND DARK.
CLATTER
EVEN THE SKY—

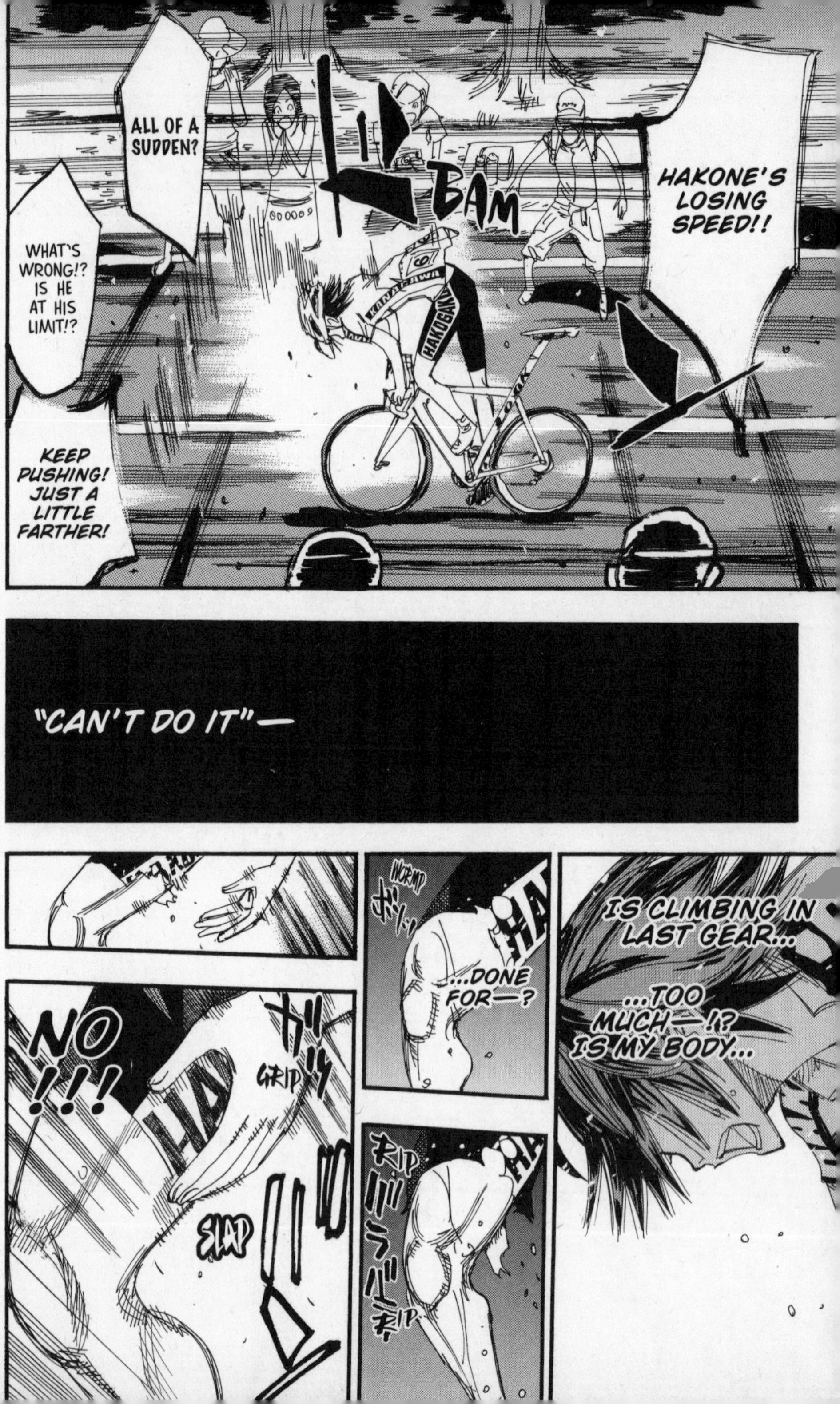
HAKONE'S LOSING SPEED!!
BAM
ALL OF A SUDDEN?
WHAT'S WRONG!? IS HE AT HIS LIMIT!?
KEEP PUSHING! JUST A LITTLE FARTHER!
"CAN'T DO IT"—
IS CLIMBING IN LAST GEAR...
...TOO MUCH—!? IS MY BODY...
WOMP
...DONE FOR—?
RIP
RIP
GRIP
NO!!!
SLAP

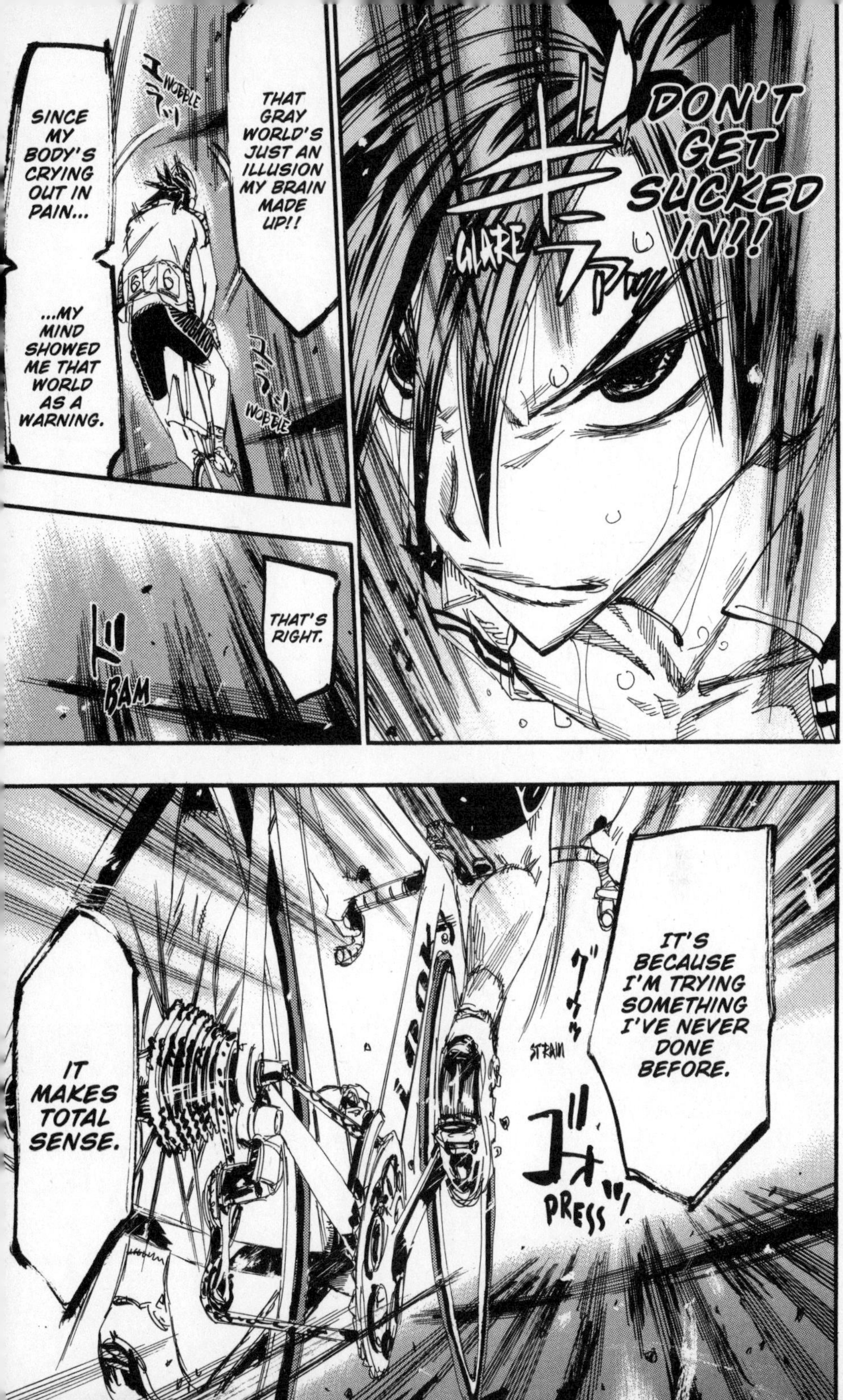
DON'T GET SUCKED IN!!
GLARE
THAT GRAY WORLD'S JUST AN ILLUSION MY BRAIN MADE UP!!
WOBBLE
SINCE MY BODY'S CRYING OUT IN PAIN...
...MY MIND SHOWED ME THAT WORLD AS A WARNING.
WOBBLE
THAT'S RIGHT.
BAM
IT'S BECAUSE I'M TRYING SOMETHING I'VE NEVER DONE BEFORE.
STRAIN
PRESS
IT MAKES TOTAL SENSE.

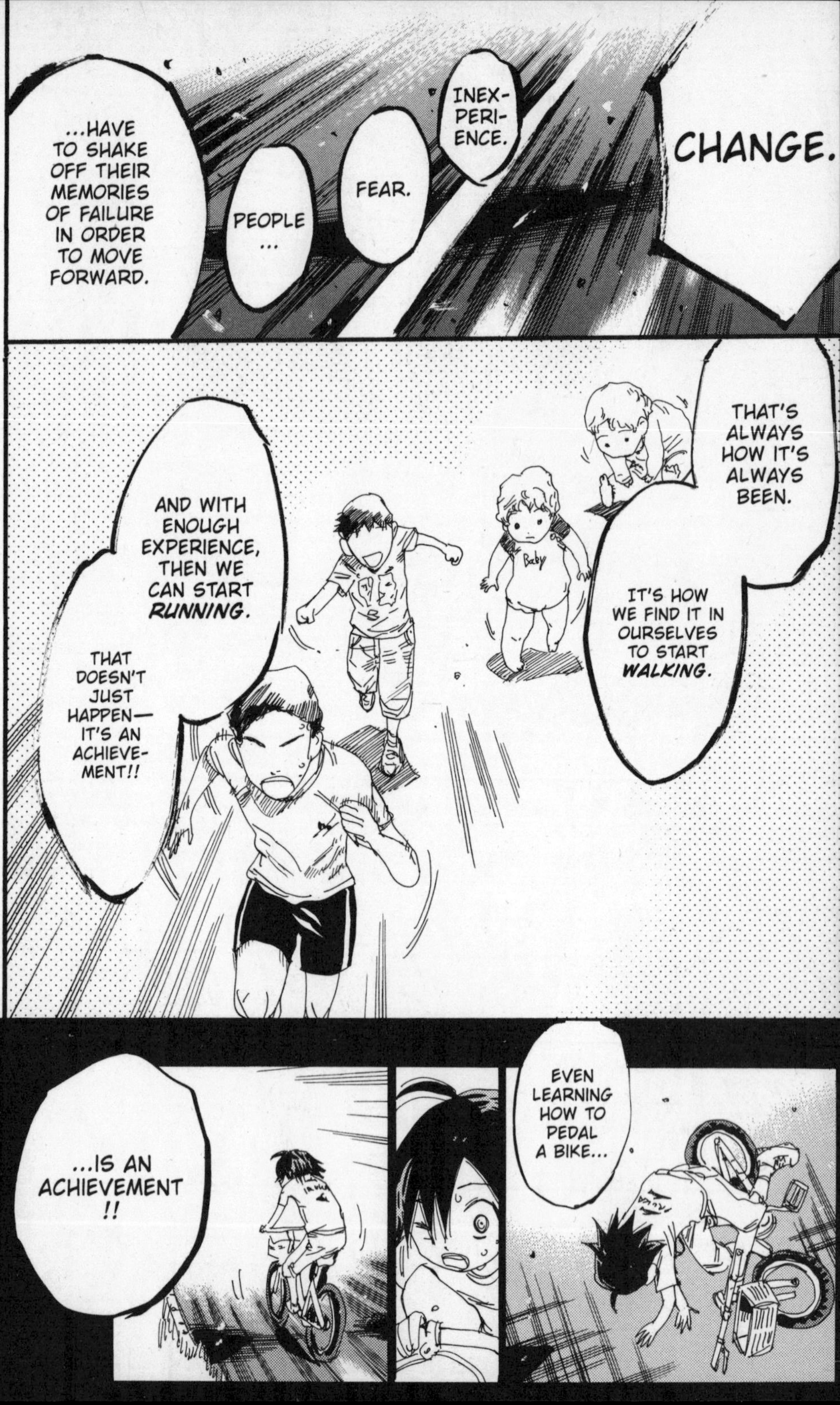
CHANGE.
INEXPERIENCE.
FEAR.
PEOPLE...
...HAVE TO SHAKE OFF THEIR MEMORIES OF FAILURE IN ORDER TO MOVE FORWARD.
THAT'S ALWAYS HOW IT'S ALWAYS BEEN.
IT'S HOW WE FIND IT IN OURSELVES TO START *WALKING*.
AND WITH ENOUGH EXPERIENCE, THEN WE CAN START *RUNNING*.
THAT DOESN'T JUST HAPPEN—IT'S AN ACHIEVEMENT!!
EVEN LEARNING HOW TO PEDAL A BIKE...
...IS AN ACHIEVEMENT!!

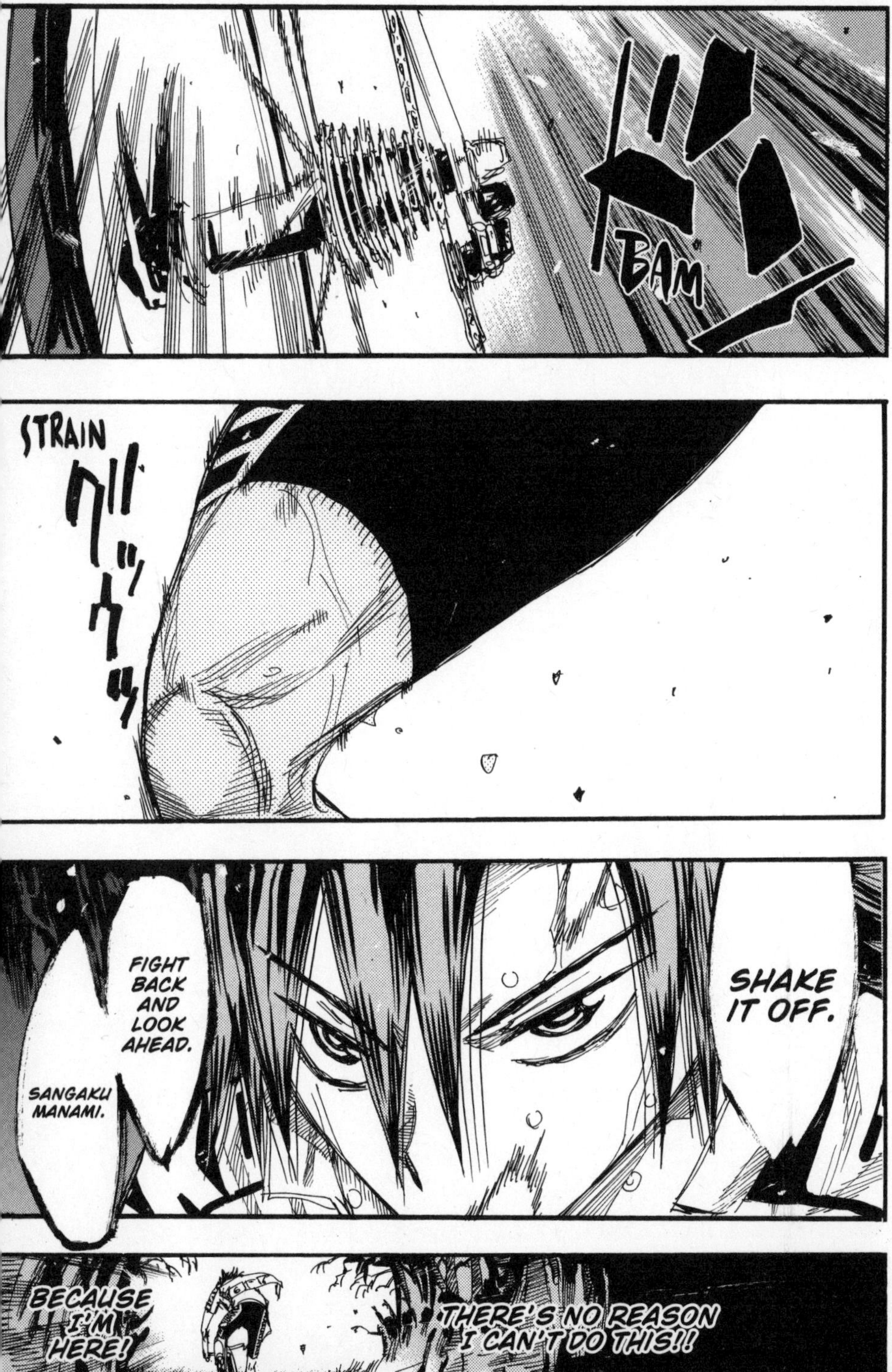
BAM
STRAIN
SHAKE IT OFF.
FIGHT BACK AND LOOK AHEAD.
SANGAKU MANAMI.
THERE'S NO REASON I CAN'T DO THIS!!
BECAUSE I'M HERE!

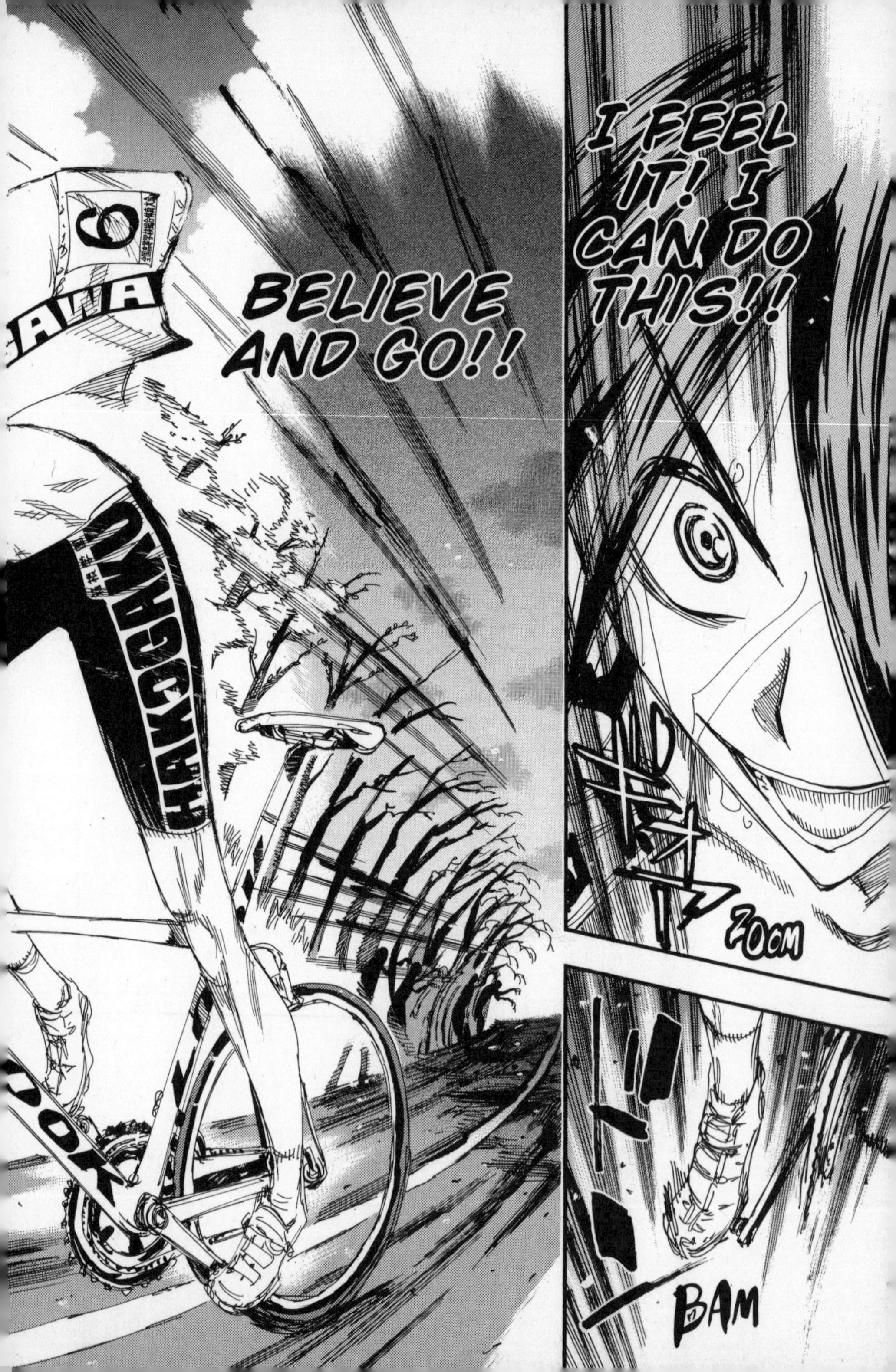
I FEEL IT! I CAN DO THIS!!
ZOOM
BAM
BELIEVE AND GO!!
HAKOGAKU

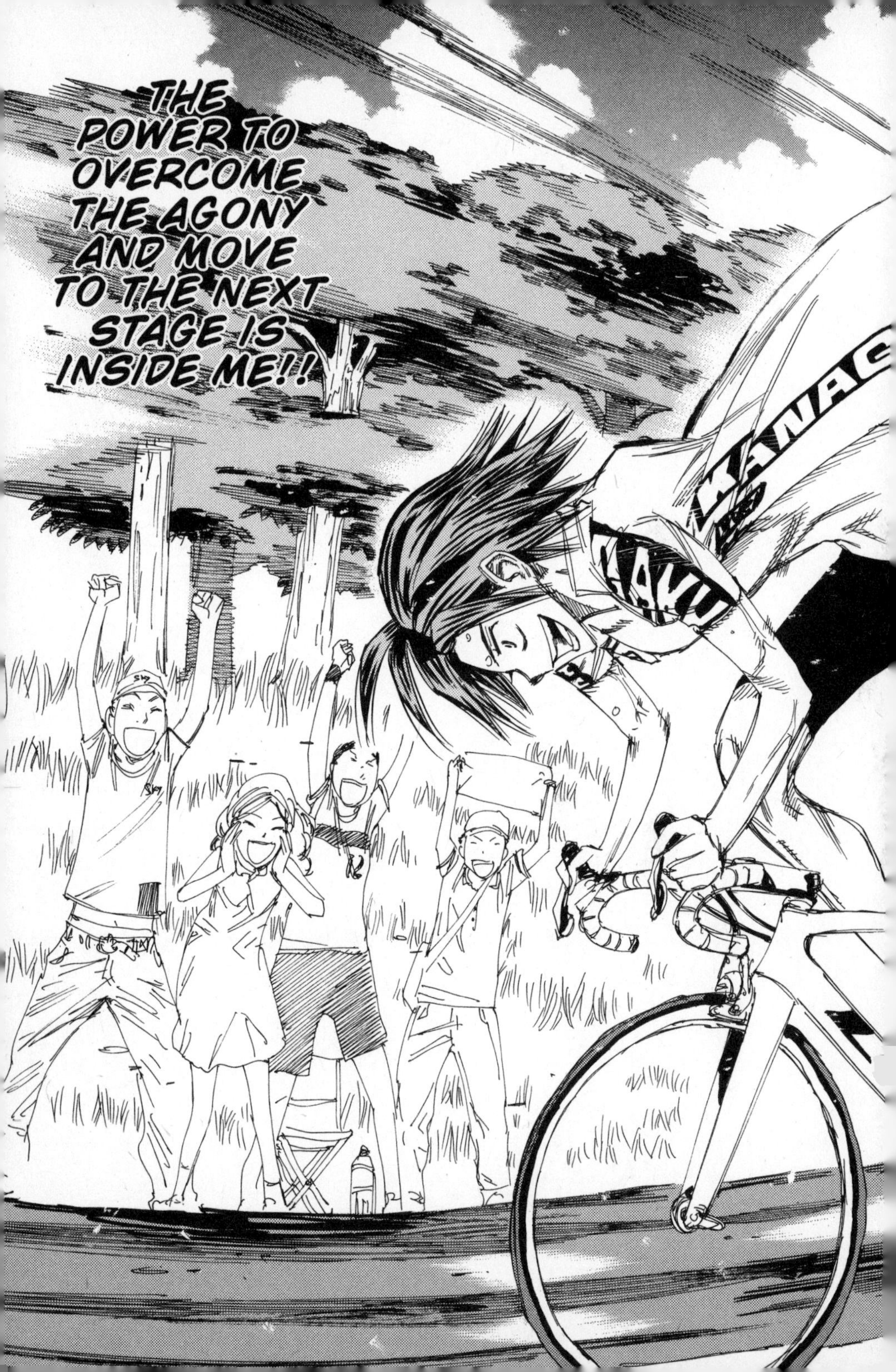
THE POWER TO OVERCOME THE AGONY AND MOVE TO THE NEXT STAGE IS INSIDE ME!!

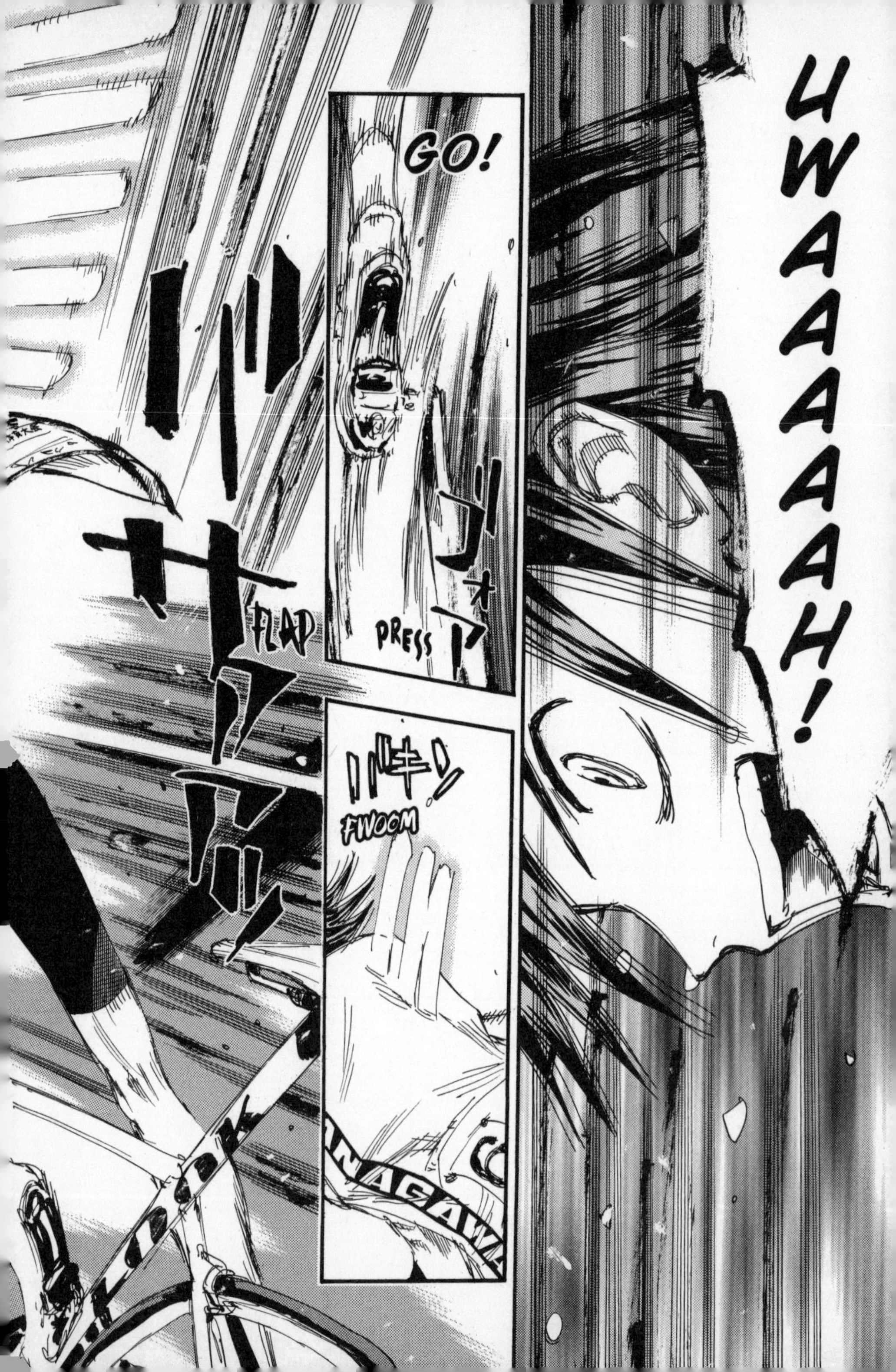
UWAAAAAH!
GO!
PRESS
FWOOM
FLAP

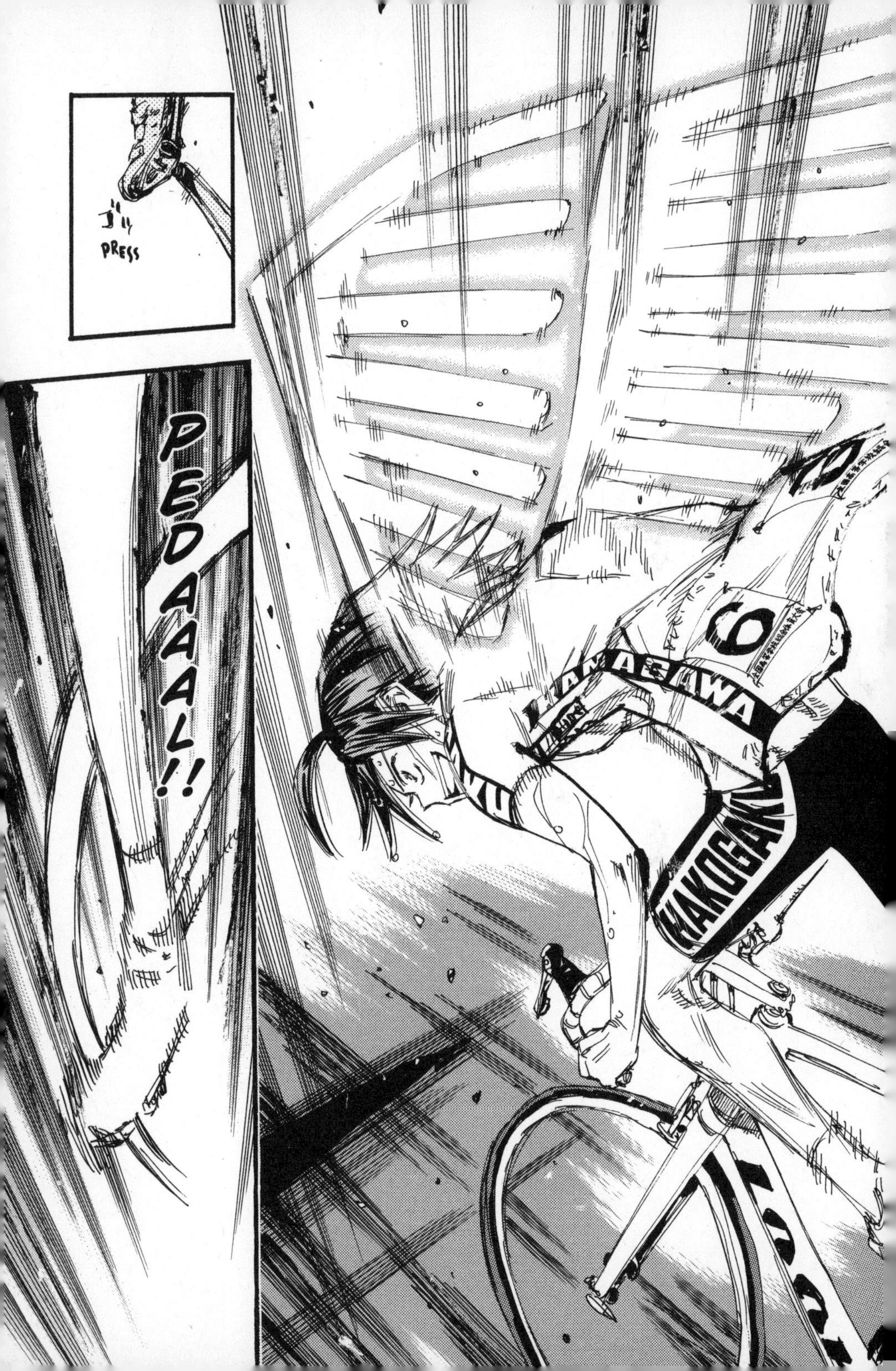
PRESS
PEDAAAAL!!

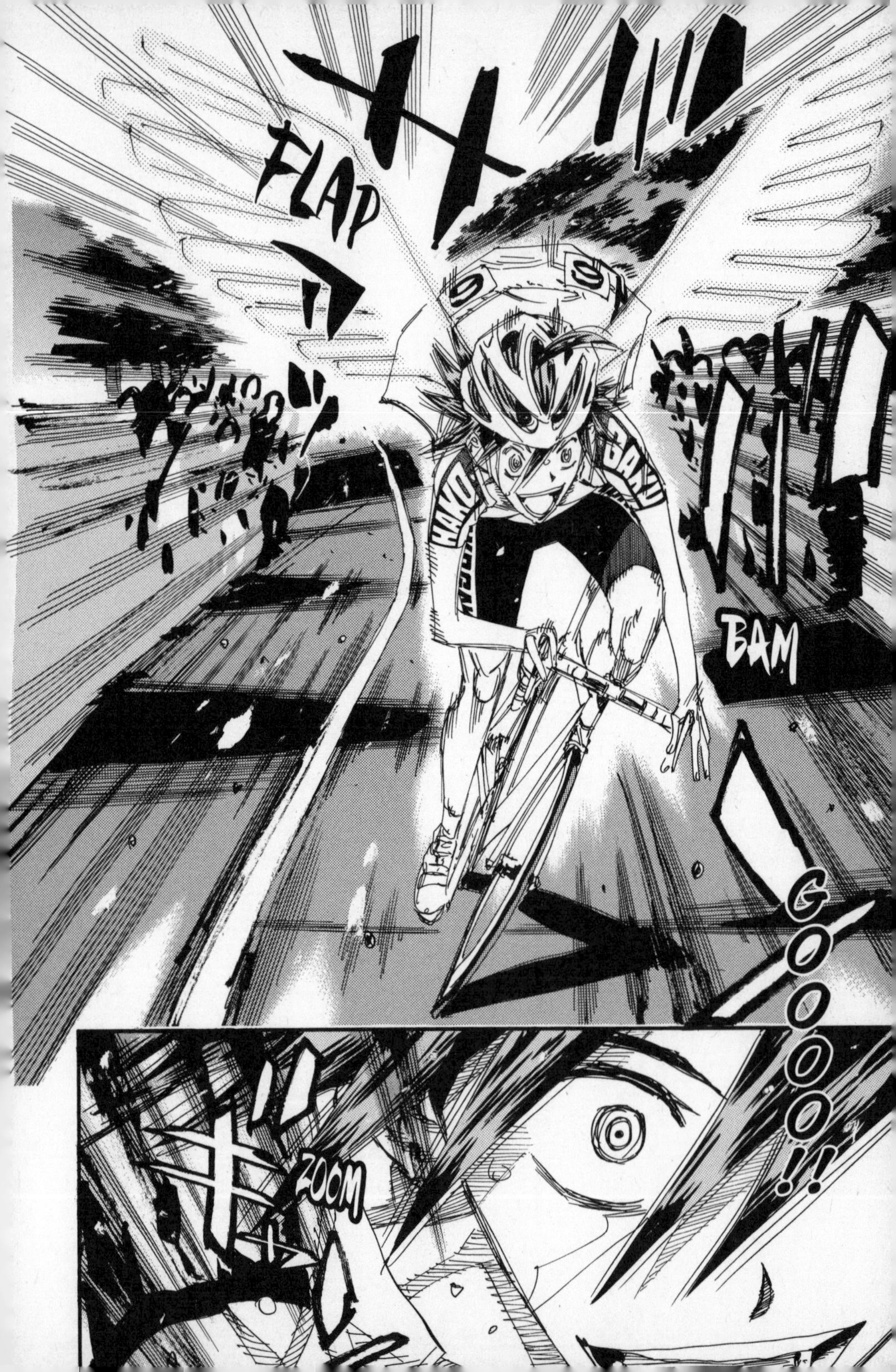
FLAP
BAM
GOOOOO!!
ZOOM

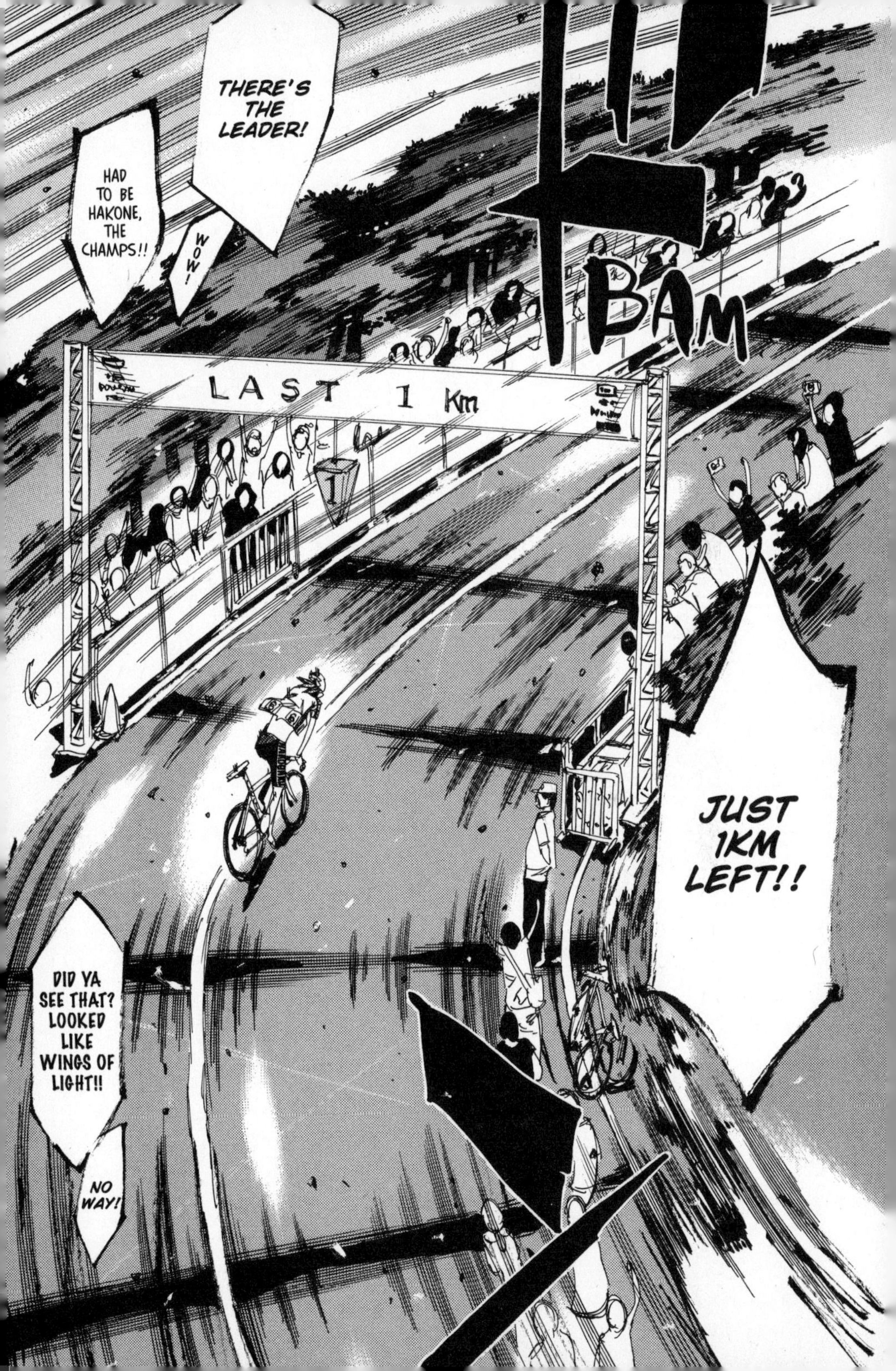
BAM
THERE'S THE LEADER!
WOW!
HAD TO BE HAKONE, THE CHAMPS!!
LAST 1 Km
JUST 1KM LEFT!!
DID YA SEE THAT? LOOKED LIKE WINGS OF LIGHT!!
NO WAY!

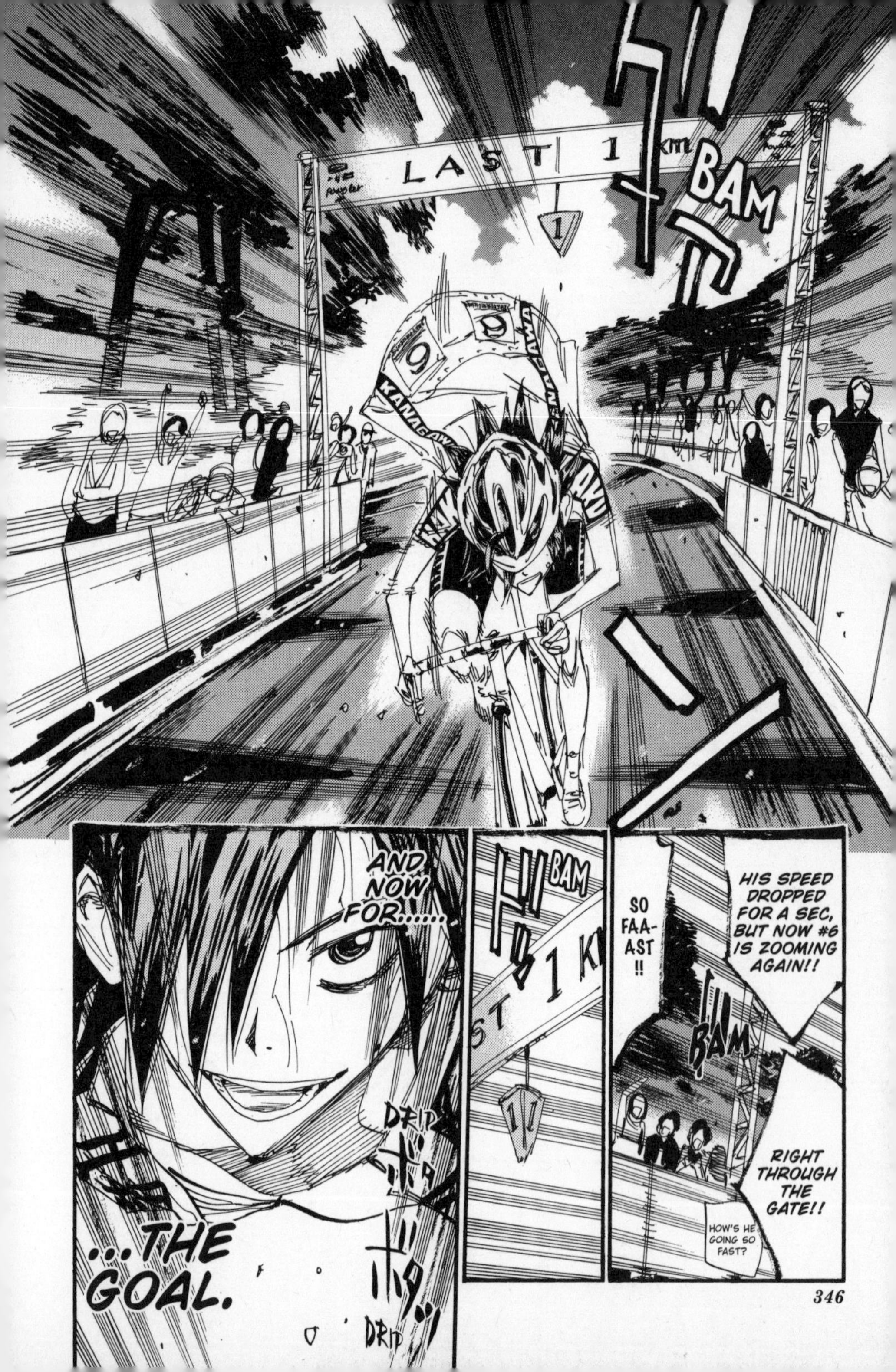
LAST 1 KM
1
KANAGAWA
BAM
HIS SPEED DROPPED FOR A SEC, BUT NOW #6 IS ZOOMING AGAIN!!
SO FAA-AST !!
BAM
RIGHT THROUGH THE GATE!!
HOW'S HE GOING SO FAST?
BAM
ST 1 K
AND NOW FOR......
DRIP
DRIP
...THE GOAL.

RIDE.224 1KM TO GO

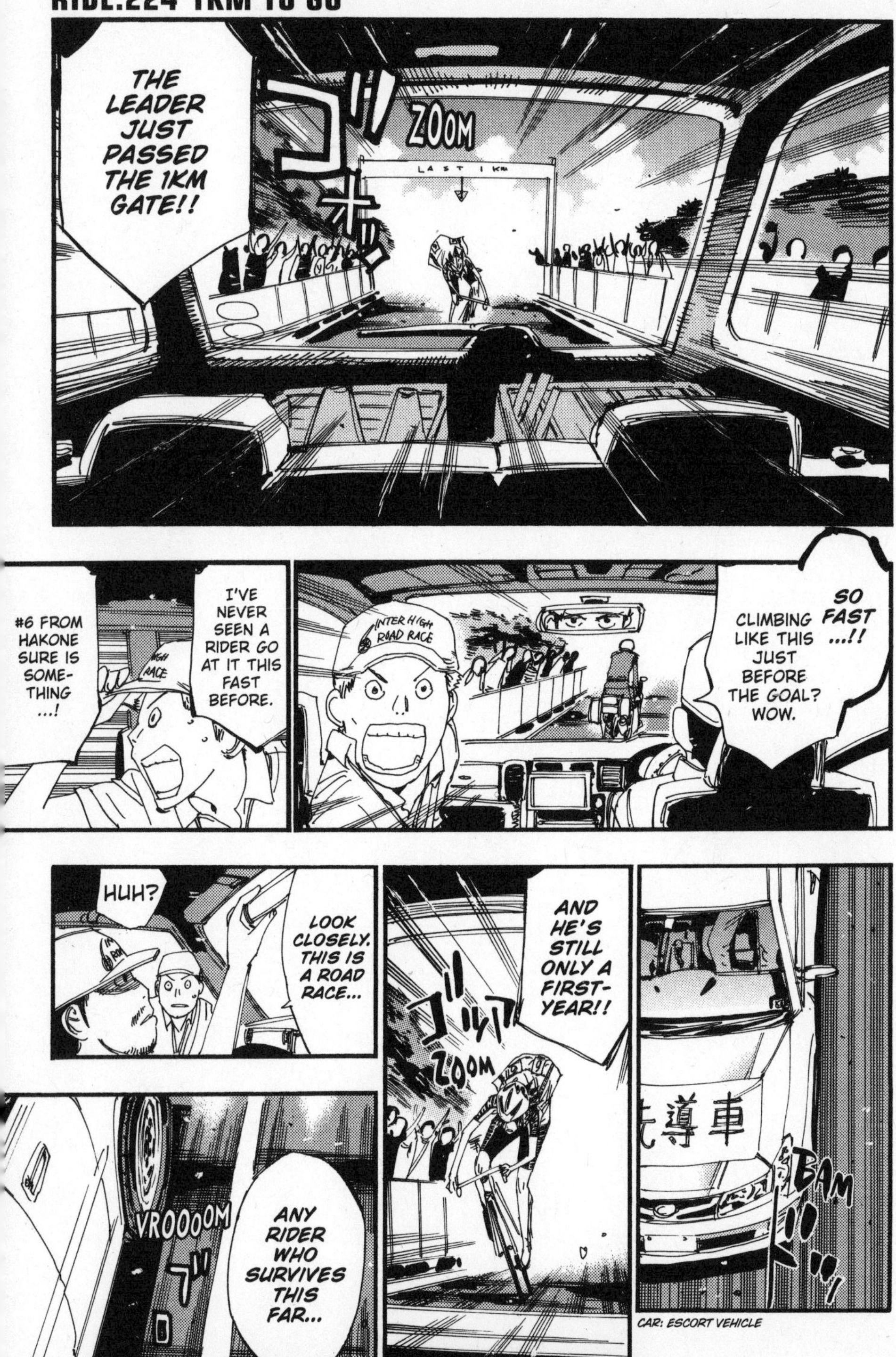
THE LEADER JUST PASSED THE 1KM GATE!!
ZOOM
LAST 1KM
SO FAST ...!!
CLIMBING LIKE THIS JUST BEFORE THE GOAL? WOW.
INTER HIGH ROAD RACE
I'VE NEVER SEEN A RIDER GO AT IT THIS FAST BEFORE.
#6 FROM HAKONE SURE IS SOME-THING ...!
先導車
BAM
AND HE'S STILL ONLY A FIRST-YEAR!!
ZOOM
HUH?
LOOK CLOSELY. THIS IS A ROAD RACE...
ANY RIDER WHO SURVIVES THIS FAR...
VROOOOM
CAR: ESCORT VEHICLE

RIDE.224 1KM TO GO

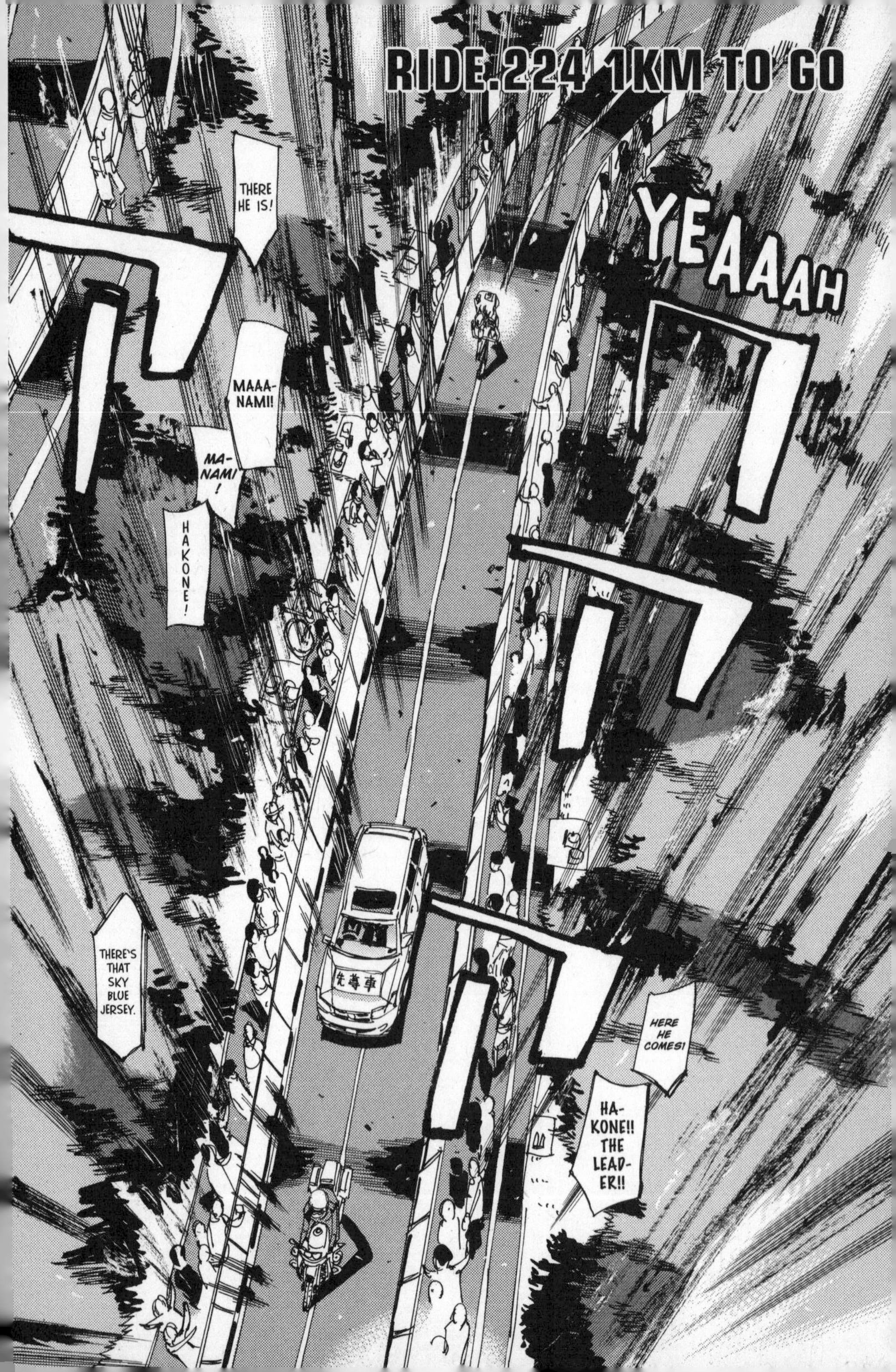
YEAAAH
THERE HE IS!
MAAA-NAMI!
MA-NAMI!
HAKONE!
先導車
HERE HE COMES!
HA-KONE!! THE LEAD-ER!!
THERE'S THAT SKY BLUE JERSEY.

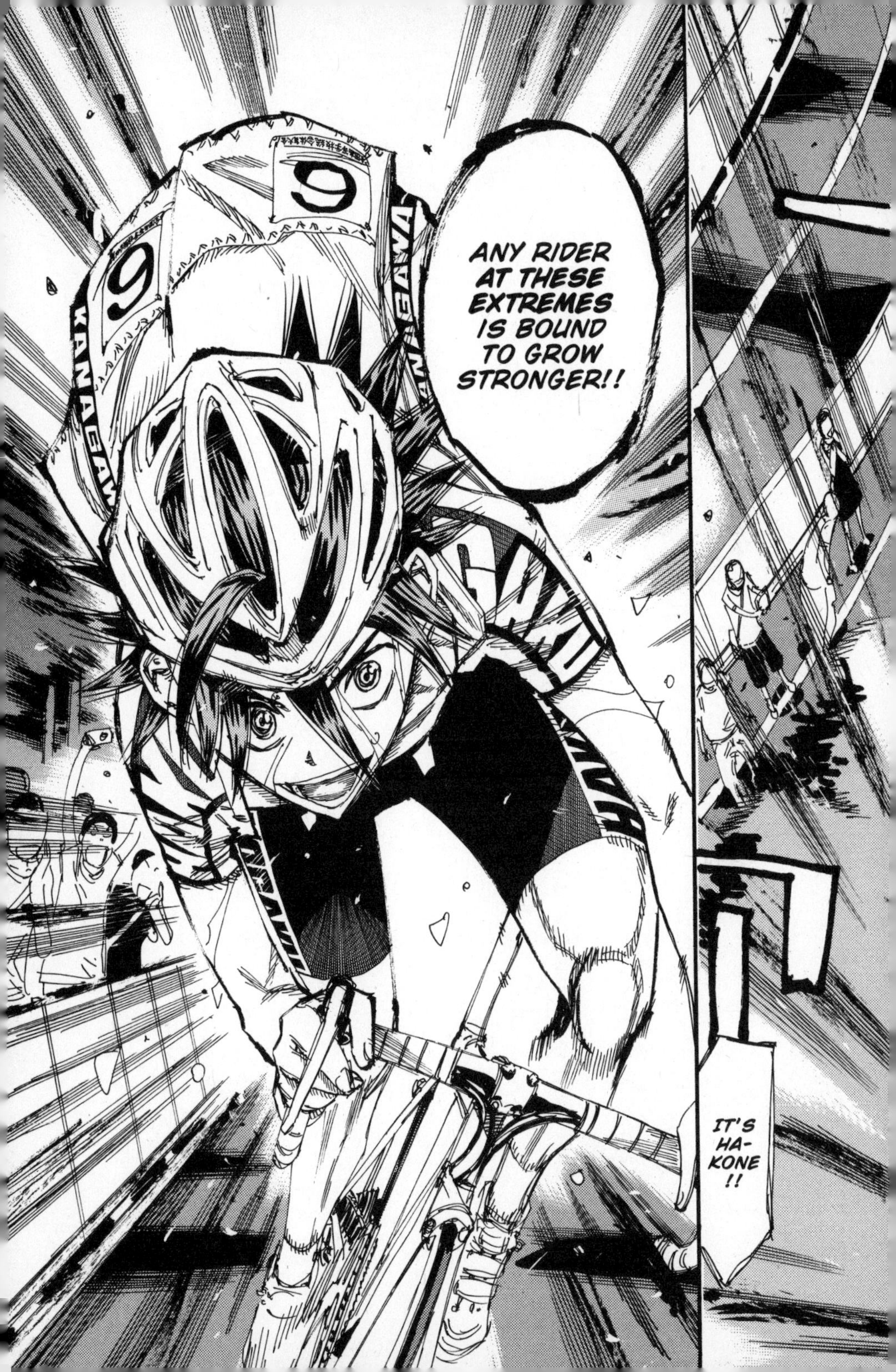
IT'S HA-KONE!!
ANY RIDER AT THESE EXTREMES IS BOUND TO GROW STRONGER!!
KANAGAWA

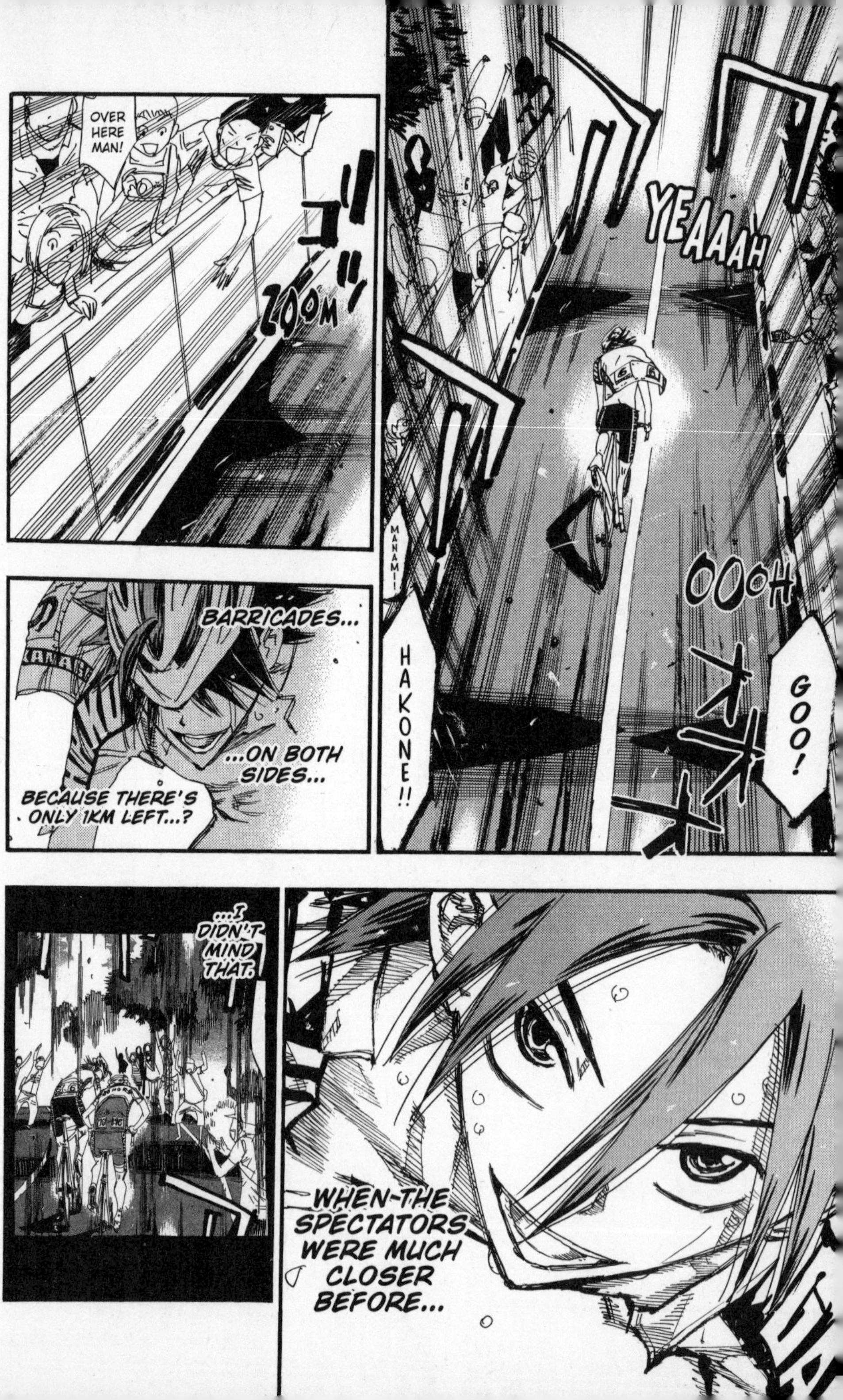
YEAAAH
MANAMI!
HAKONE!!
OOOH
GOO!
OVER HERE MAN!
ZOOM
BARRICADES...
...ON BOTH SIDES...
BECAUSE THERE'S ONLY 1KM LEFT...?
WHEN THE SPECTATORS WERE MUCH CLOSER BEFORE...
...I DIDN'T MIND THAT.

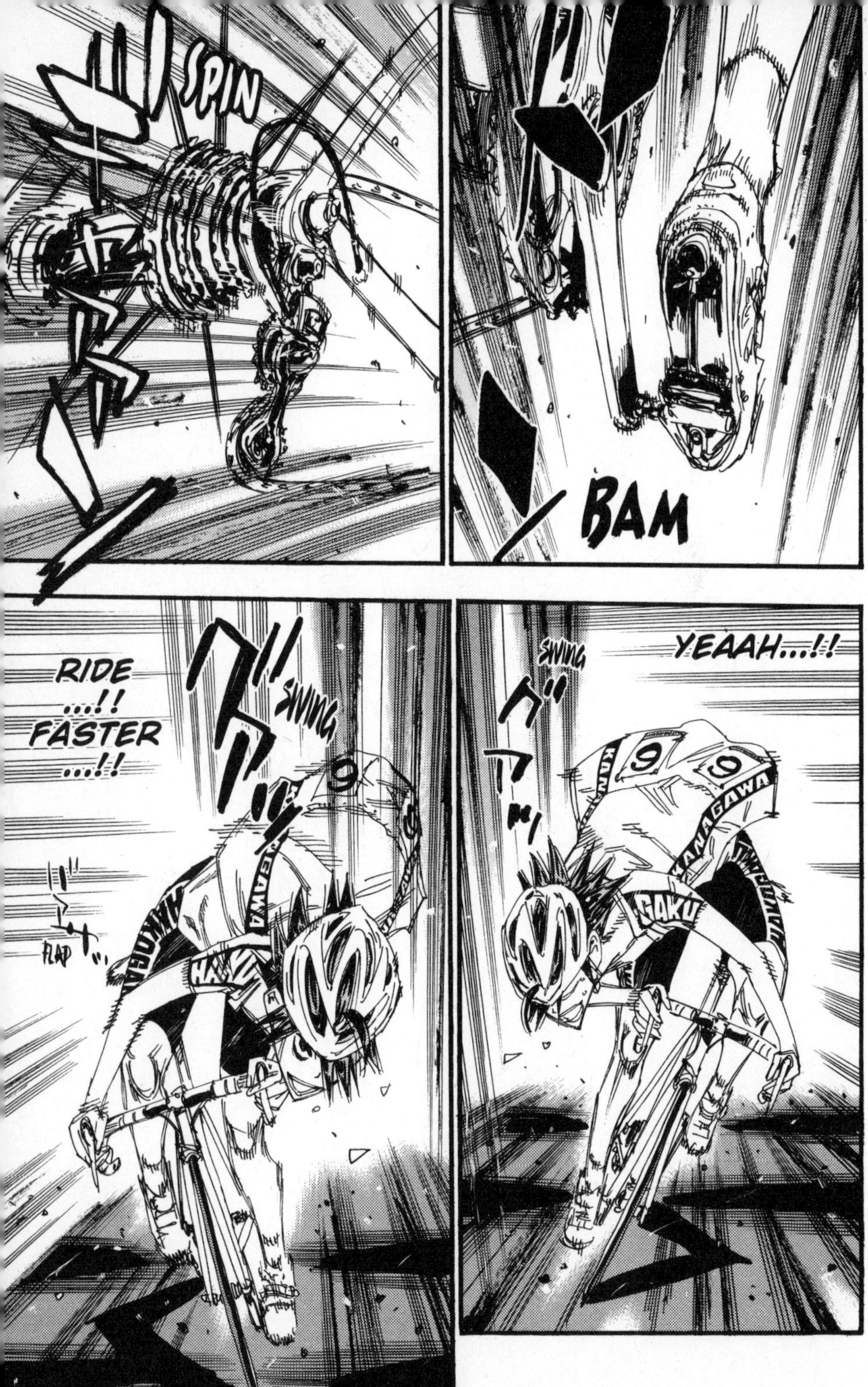
BAM
SPIN
SWING
YEAAH...!!
RIDE ...!!
FASTER ...!!
SWING
FLAP

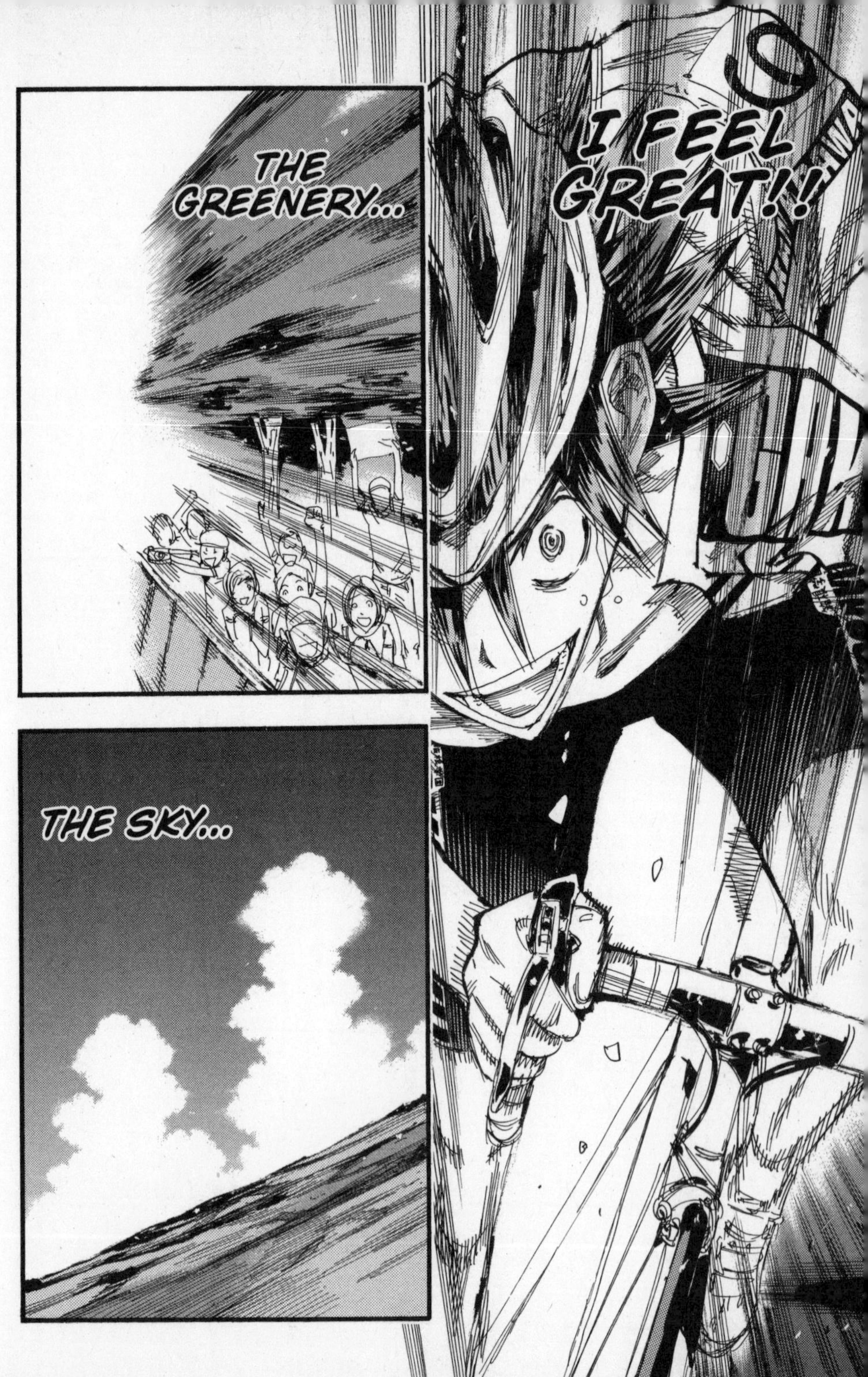
I FEEL GREAT!!
THE GREENERY...
THE SKY...

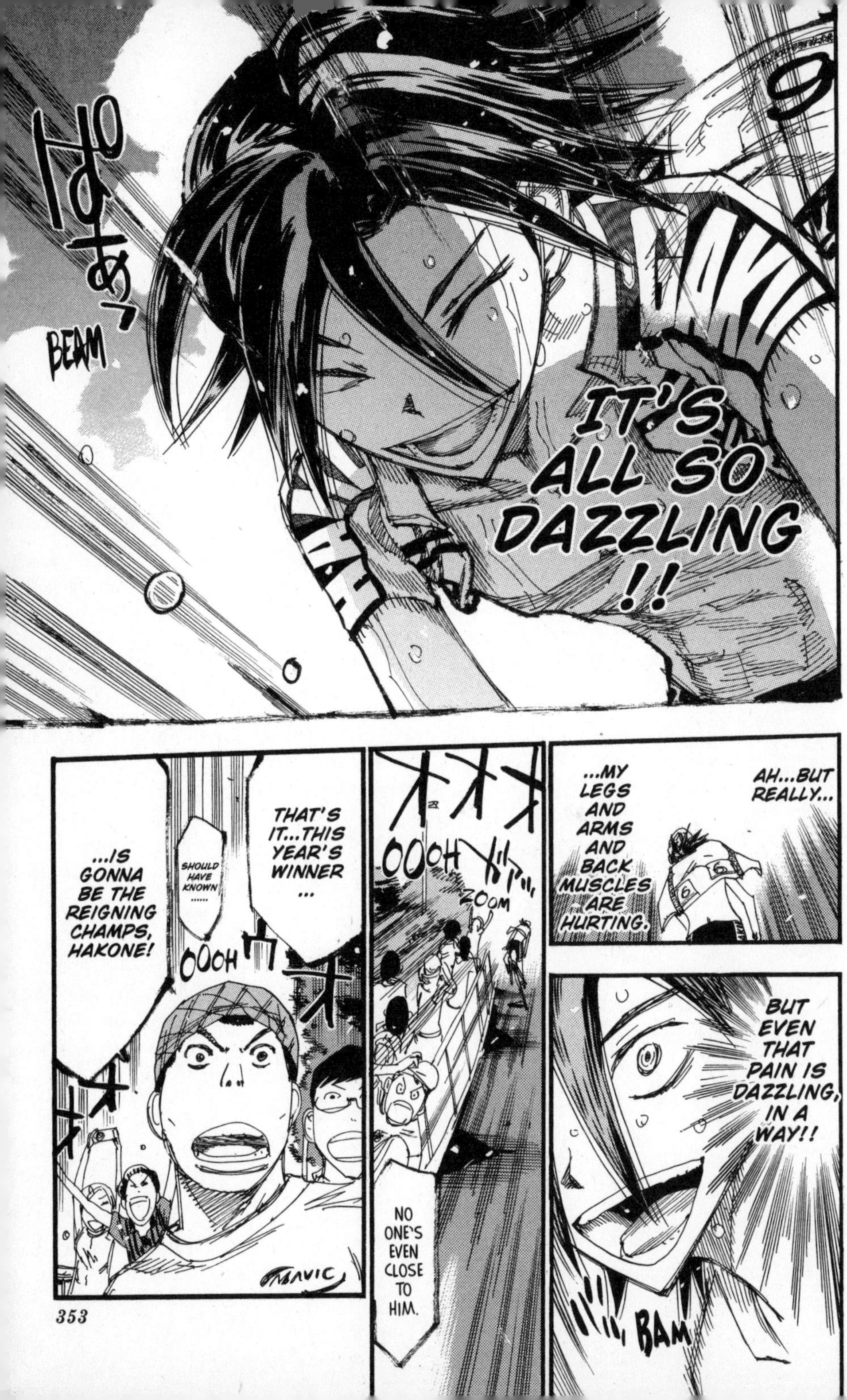
ぱあっ
BEAM
IT'S ALL SO DAZZLING!!
AH...BUT REALLY...
...MY LEGS AND ARMS AND BACK MUSCLES ARE HURTING.
BUT EVEN THAT PAIN IS DAZZLING, IN A WAY!!
BAM
OOOH
ZOOM
NO ONE'S EVEN CLOSE TO HIM.
THAT'S IT...THIS YEAR'S WINNER...
SHOULD HAVE KNOWN......
...IS GONNA BE THE REIGNING CHAMPS, HAKONE!
OOOH
MAVIC

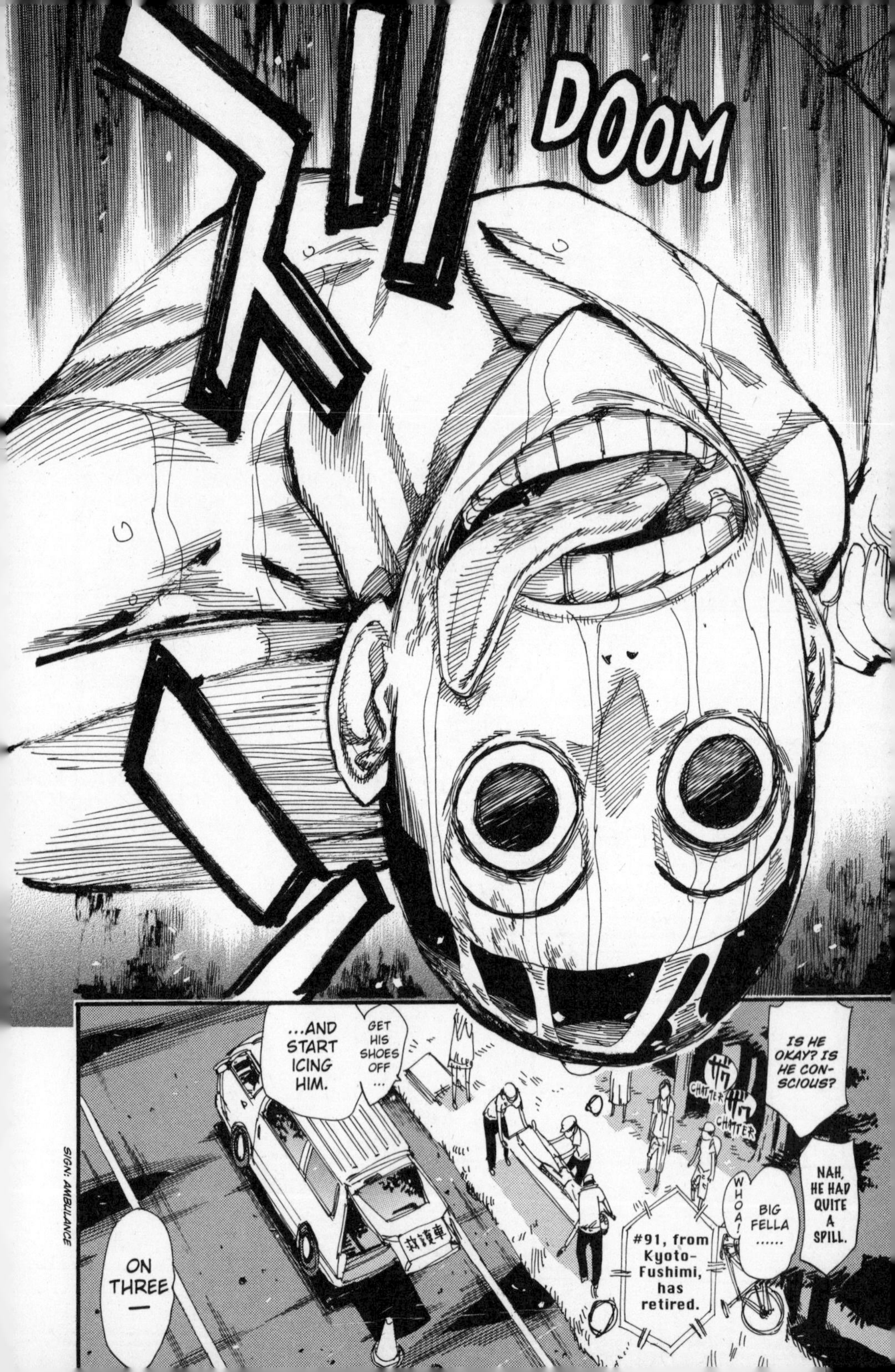
DOOM
IS HE OKAY? IS HE CON-SCIOUS?
ザワ CHATTER ザワ CHATTER
NAH, HE HAD QUITE A SPILL.
WHOA!
BIG FELLA ......
#91, from Kyoto-Fushimi, has retired.
GET HIS SHOES OFF ...
...AND START ICING HIM.
救護車
ON THREE —
SIGN: AMBULANCE

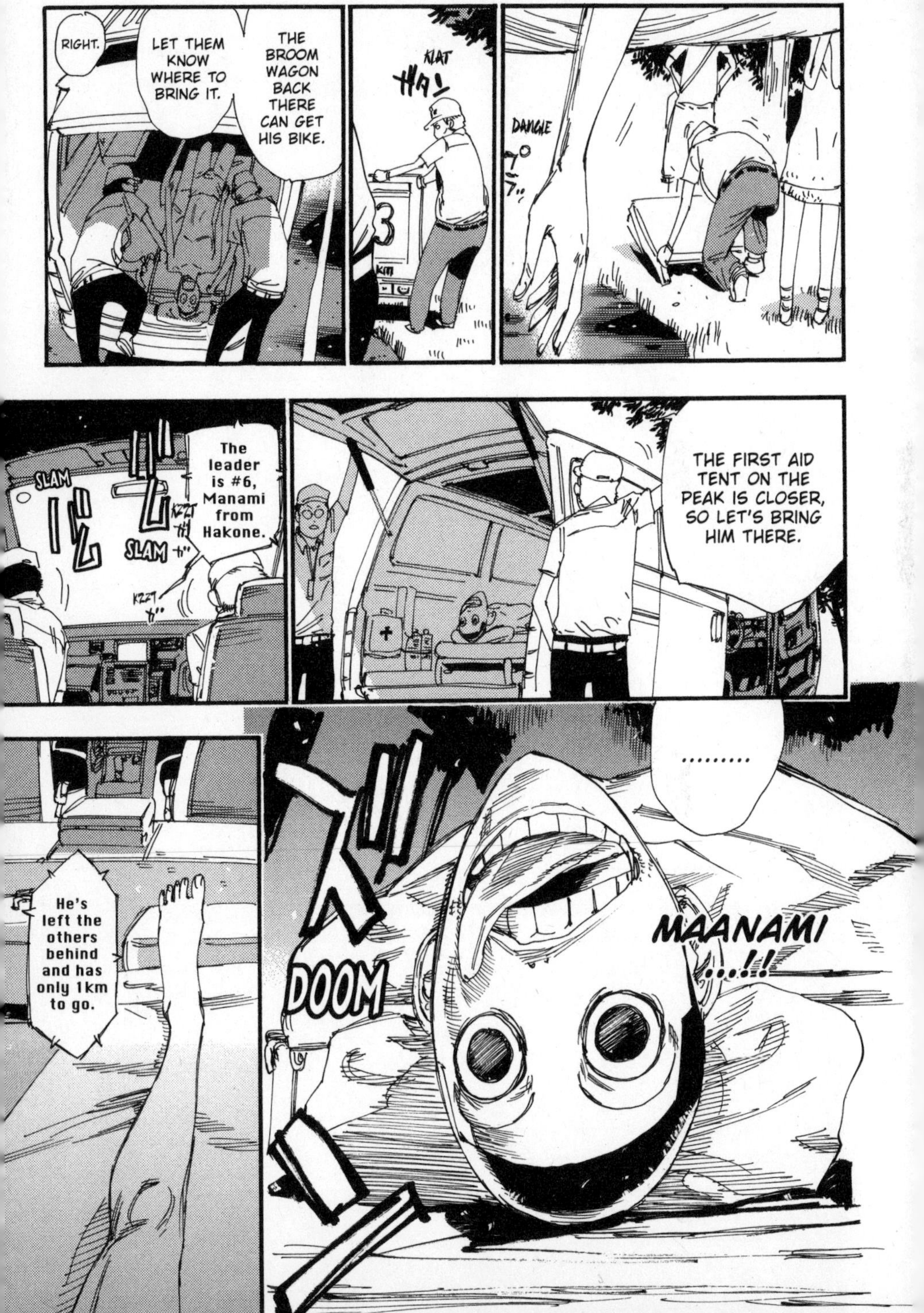
DANGLE
KLAT
THE BROOM WAGON BACK THERE CAN GET HIS BIKE.
LET THEM KNOW WHERE TO BRING IT.
RIGHT.
THE FIRST AID TENT ON THE PEAK IS CLOSER, SO LET'S BRING HIM THERE.
The leader is #6, Manami from Hakone.
KZZT
SLAM
SLAM
KZZT
....
MAANAMI ...!!
DOOM
He's left the others behind and has only 1km to go.

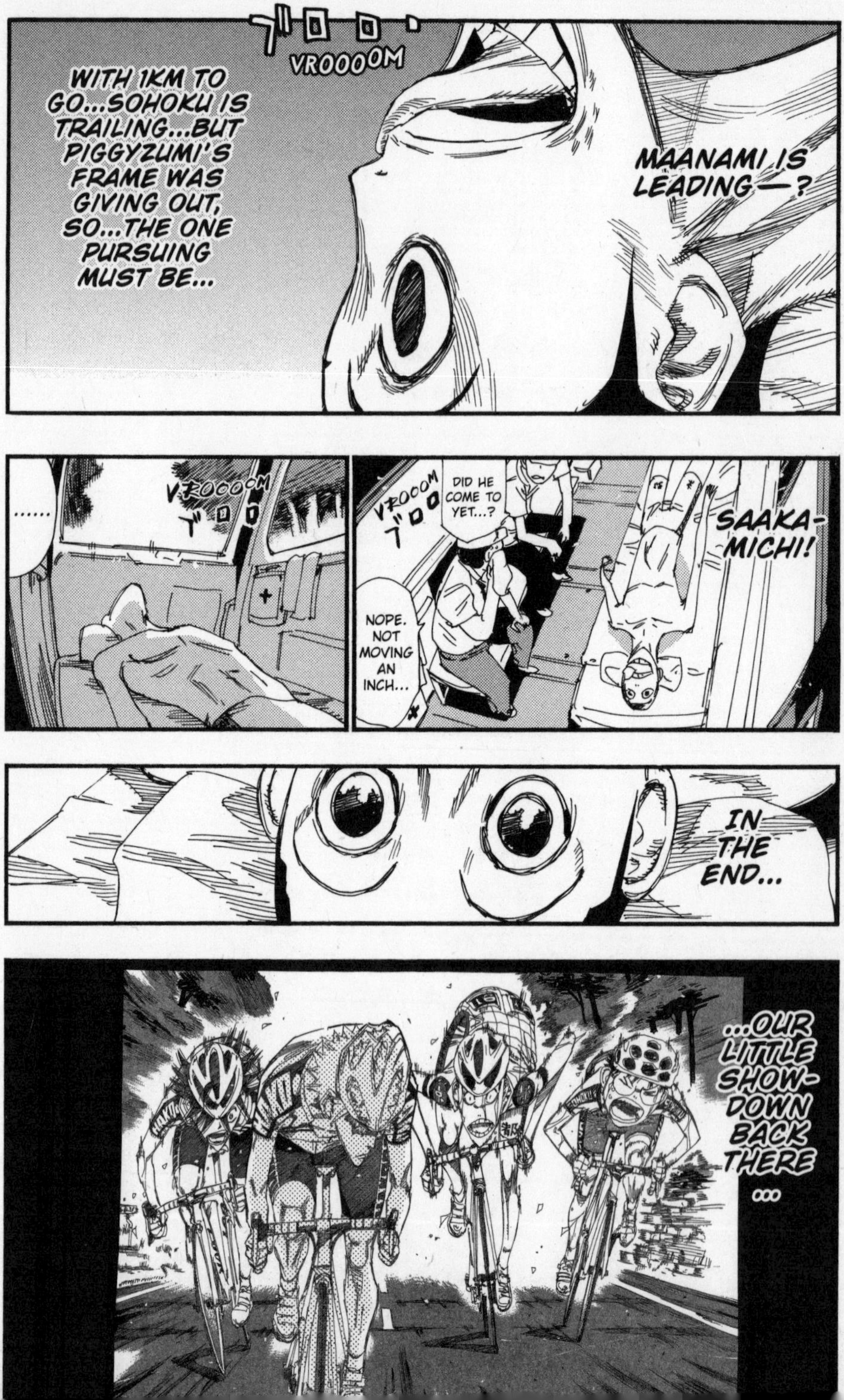
ブロロ
VROOOOM
MAANAMI IS LEADING—?
WITH 1KM TO GO...SOHOKU IS TRAILING...BUT PIGGYZUMI'S FRAME WAS GIVING OUT, SO...THE ONE PURSUING MUST BE...
SAAKA-MICHI!
DID HE COME TO YET...?
VROOOM ブロロ
NOPE. NOT MOVING AN INCH...
VROOOOM ブロロ
......
IN THE END...
...OUR LITTLE SHOW-DOWN BACK THERE...

...WAS A TOTAL DRAW.
THE FINISH LINE IS STILL IN PLAY, I GUESS!!
COULD THAT HAVE DECIDED EVERYTHING?
WANTING TO CRUSH MAANAMI WHILE WE WERE CATCHING UP TO THE LEADERS WAS THE RIGHT STRATEGY ON MY PART.
EVEN IF I FAILED ....
The leader is riding alone? We can't see anyone behind him on those curves.
OOH!
KZZT KZZT
HAKONE'S GONNA WIN AGAIN THIS YEAR!
SOHOKU GAVE IT A GOOD SHOT, BUT...
KZZT
KZZT
#176 is trying really hard, but he looks like he's in pain.
—GROSS.

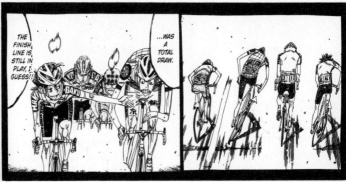

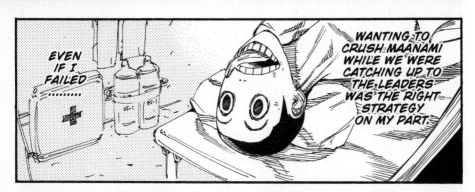

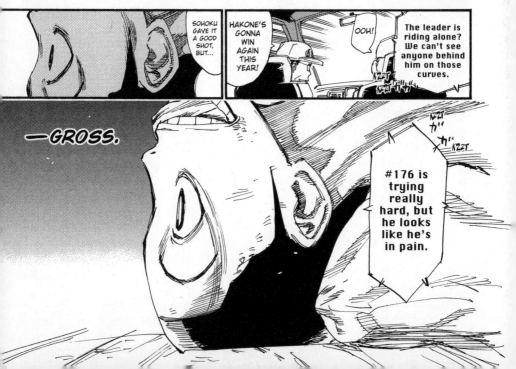

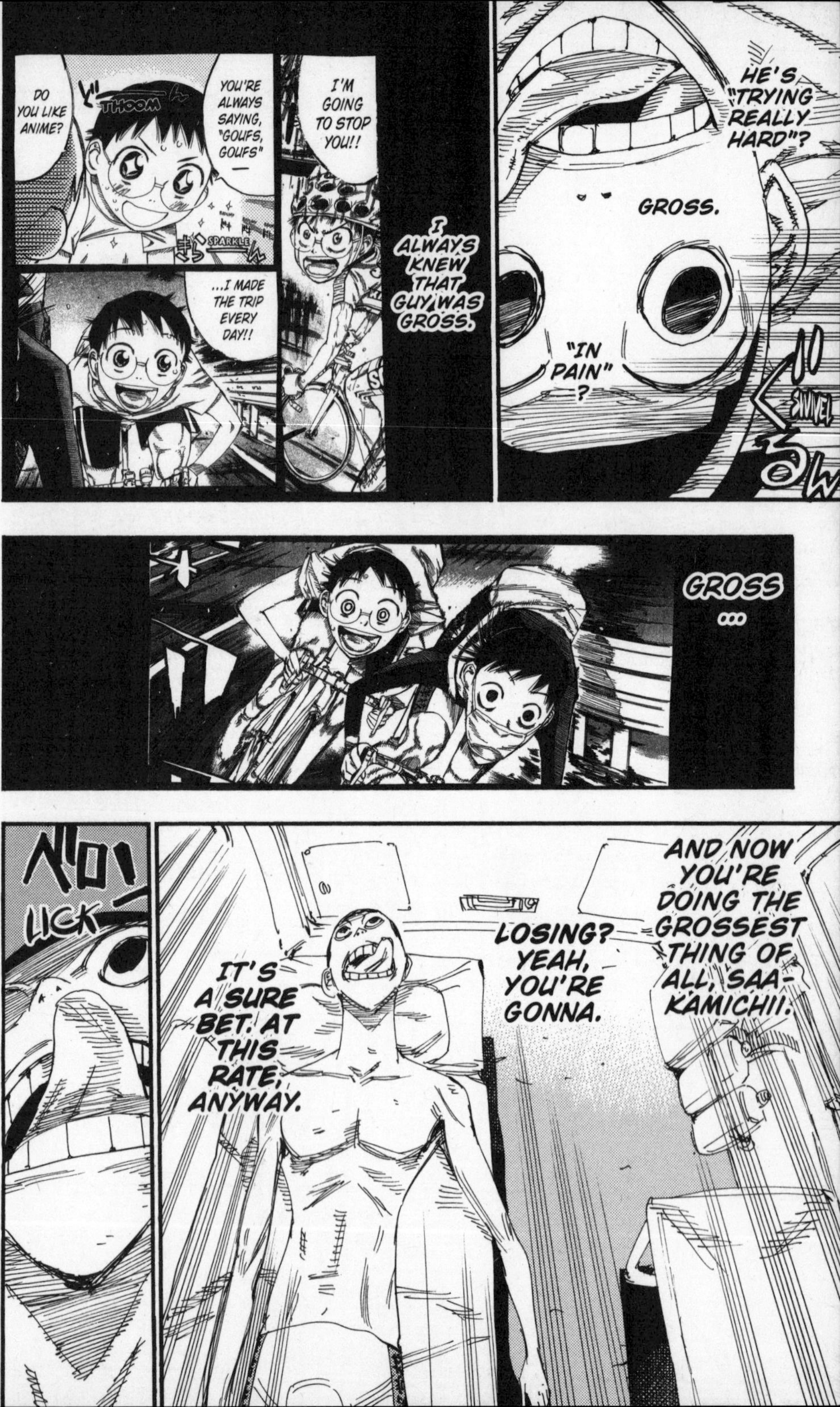
HE'S "TRYING REALLY HARD"?
GROSS.
"IN PAIN"?
SWIVEL
I ALWAYS KNEW THAT GUY WAS GROSS.
I'M GOING TO STOP YOU!!
YOU'RE ALWAYS SAYING, "GOUFS, GOUFS"—
DO YOU LIKE ANIME?
THOOM
SPARKLE
...I MADE THE TRIP EVERY DAY!!
GROSS...
AND NOW YOU'RE DOING THE GROSSEST THING OF ALL, SAAKAMICHII.
LOSING? YEAH, YOU'RE GONNA.
IT'S A SURE BET. AT THIS RATE, ANYWAY.
LICK

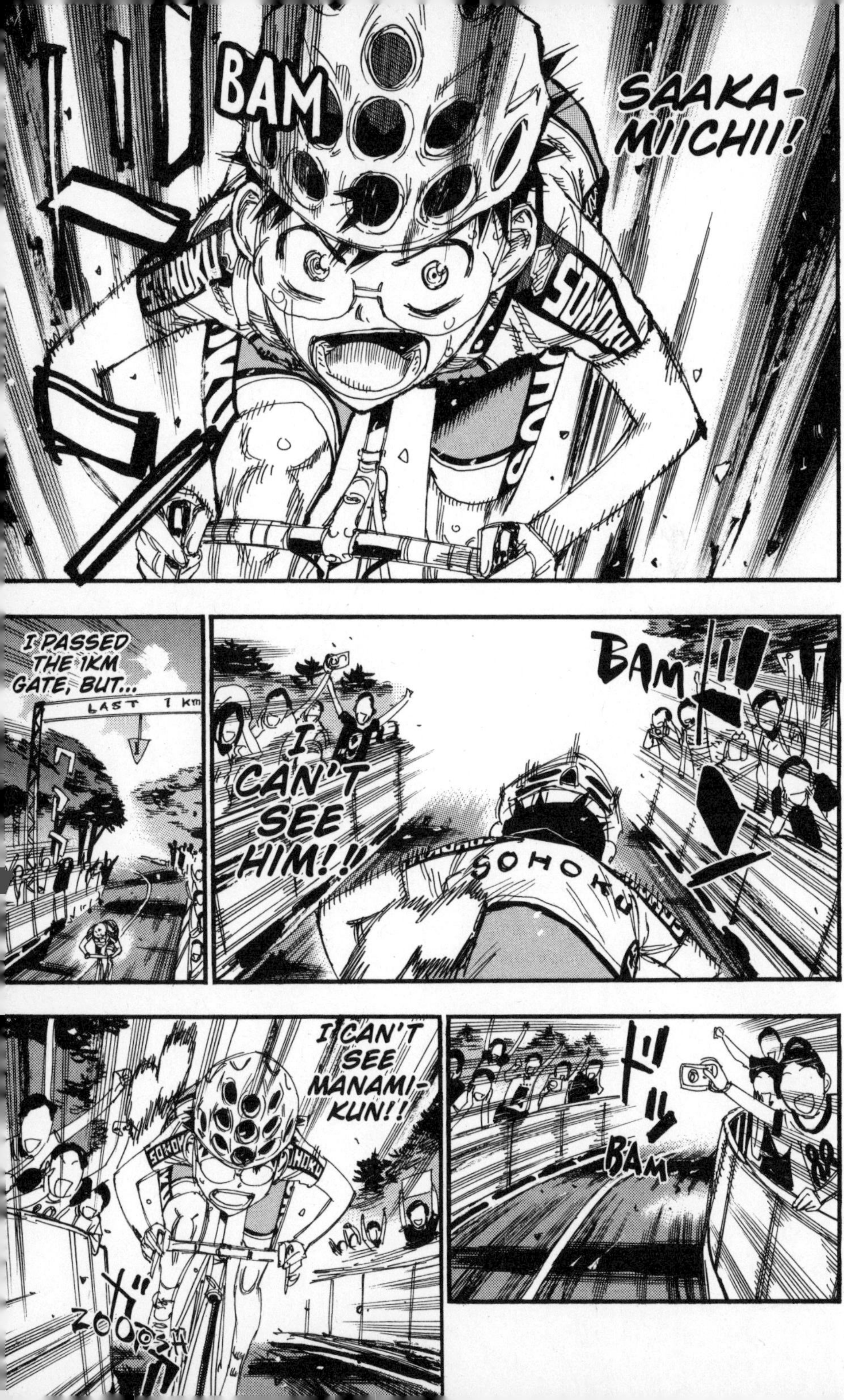
SAAKA-MIICHII!
BAM
BAM
I CAN'T SEE HIM!!
I PASSED THE 1KM GATE, BUT...
LAST 1 km
BAM
I CAN'T SEE MANAMI-KUN!!
ZOOOSH

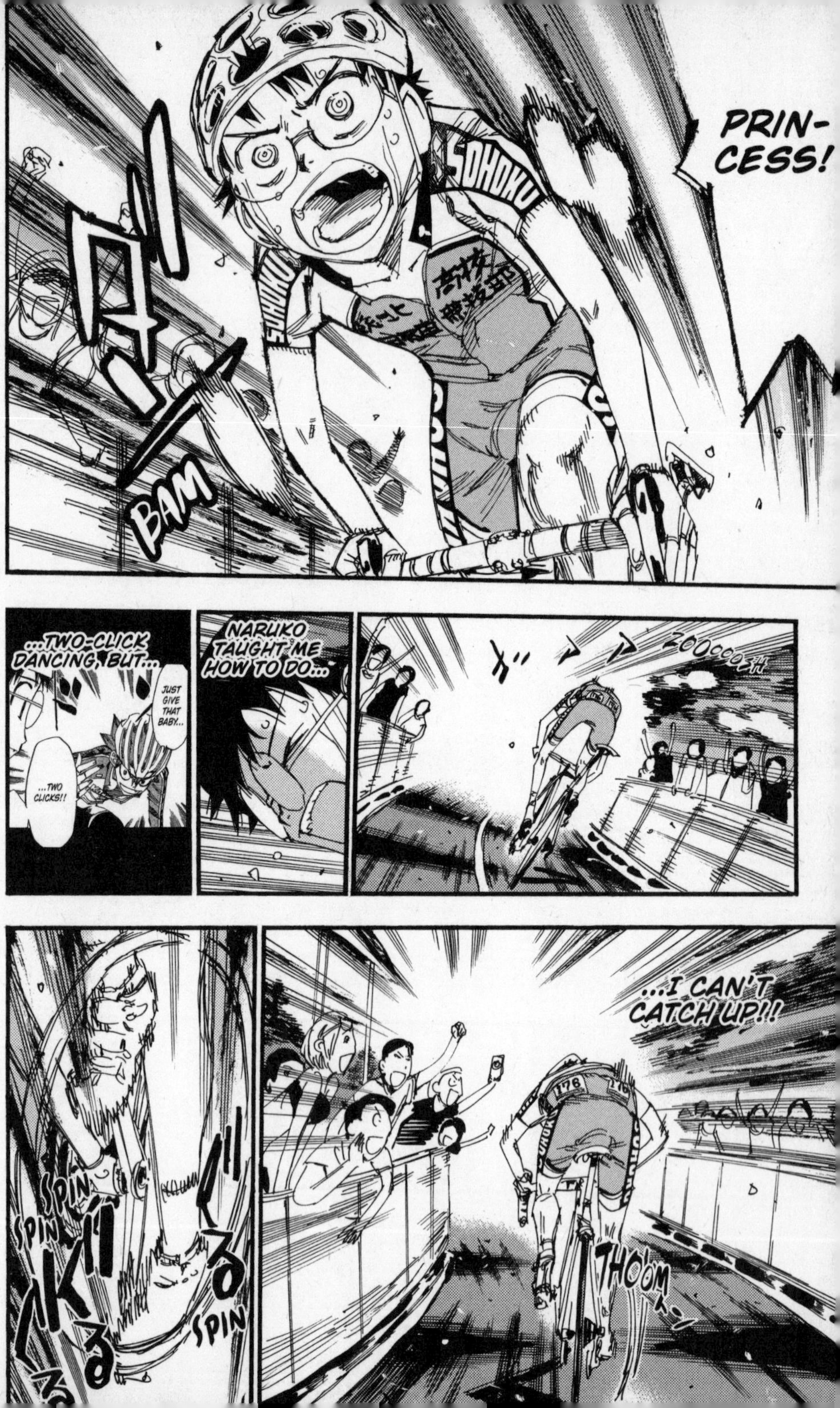
PRIN-CESS!
BAM
ZOOOOOSH
NARUKO TAUGHT ME HOW TO DO...
...TWO-CLICK DANCING, BUT...
JUST GIVE THAT BABY...
...TWO CLICKS!!
...I CAN'T CATCH UP!!
THOOM
SPIN
SPIN
SPIN

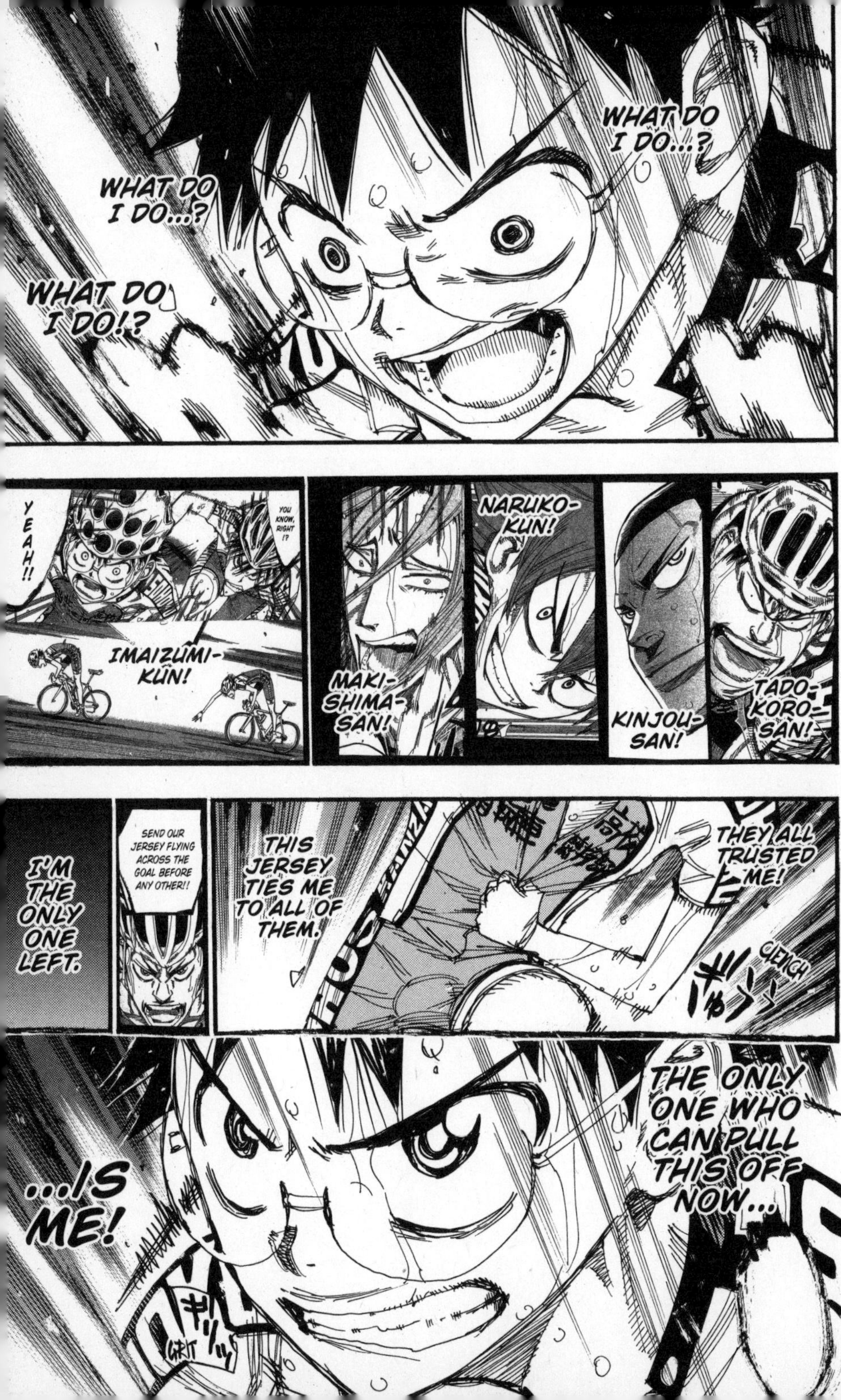
WHAT DO I DO...?
WHAT DO I DO...?
WHAT DO I DO!?
TADOKORO-SAN!
KINJOU-SAN!
NARUKO-KUN!
MAKISHIMA-SAN!
YOU KNOW, RIGHT!?
YEAH!!
IMAIZUMI-KUN!
THEY ALL TRUSTED ME!
CLENCH
THIS JERSEY TIES ME TO ALL OF THEM.
SEND OUR JERSEY FLYING ACROSS THE GOAL BEFORE ANY OTHER!!
I'M THE ONLY ONE LEFT.
THE ONLY ONE WHO CAN PULL THIS OFF NOW...
...IS ME!
GRIT

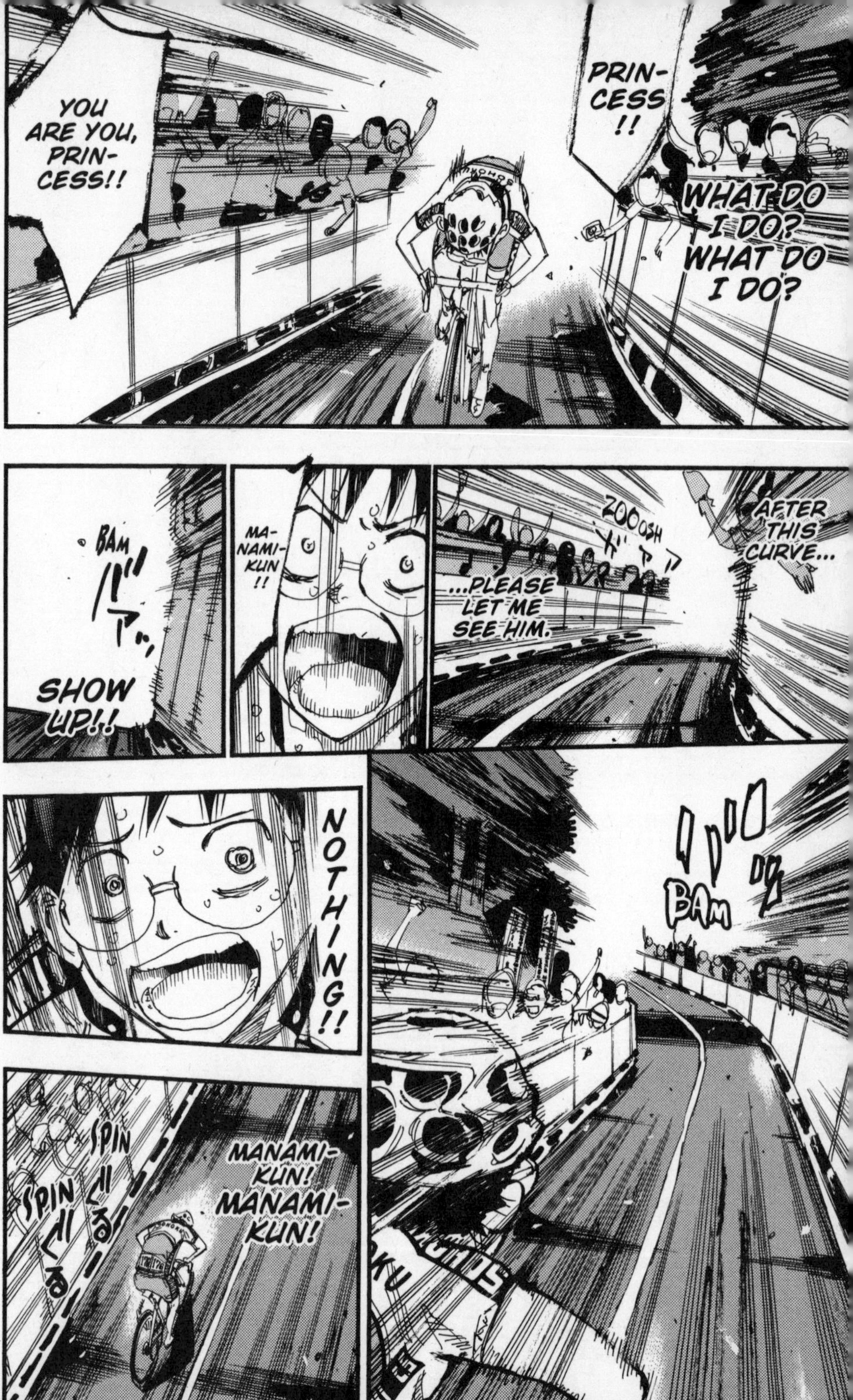
PRIN-
CESS
!!
WHAT DO I DO? WHAT DO I DO?
YOU ARE YOU, PRINCESS!!
AFTER THIS CURVE...
ZOOOSH
...PLEASE LET ME SEE HIM.
MANAMI-KUN!!
BAM
SHOW UP!!
BAM
NOTHING!!
MANAMI-KUN! MANAMI-KUN!
SPIN
SPIN

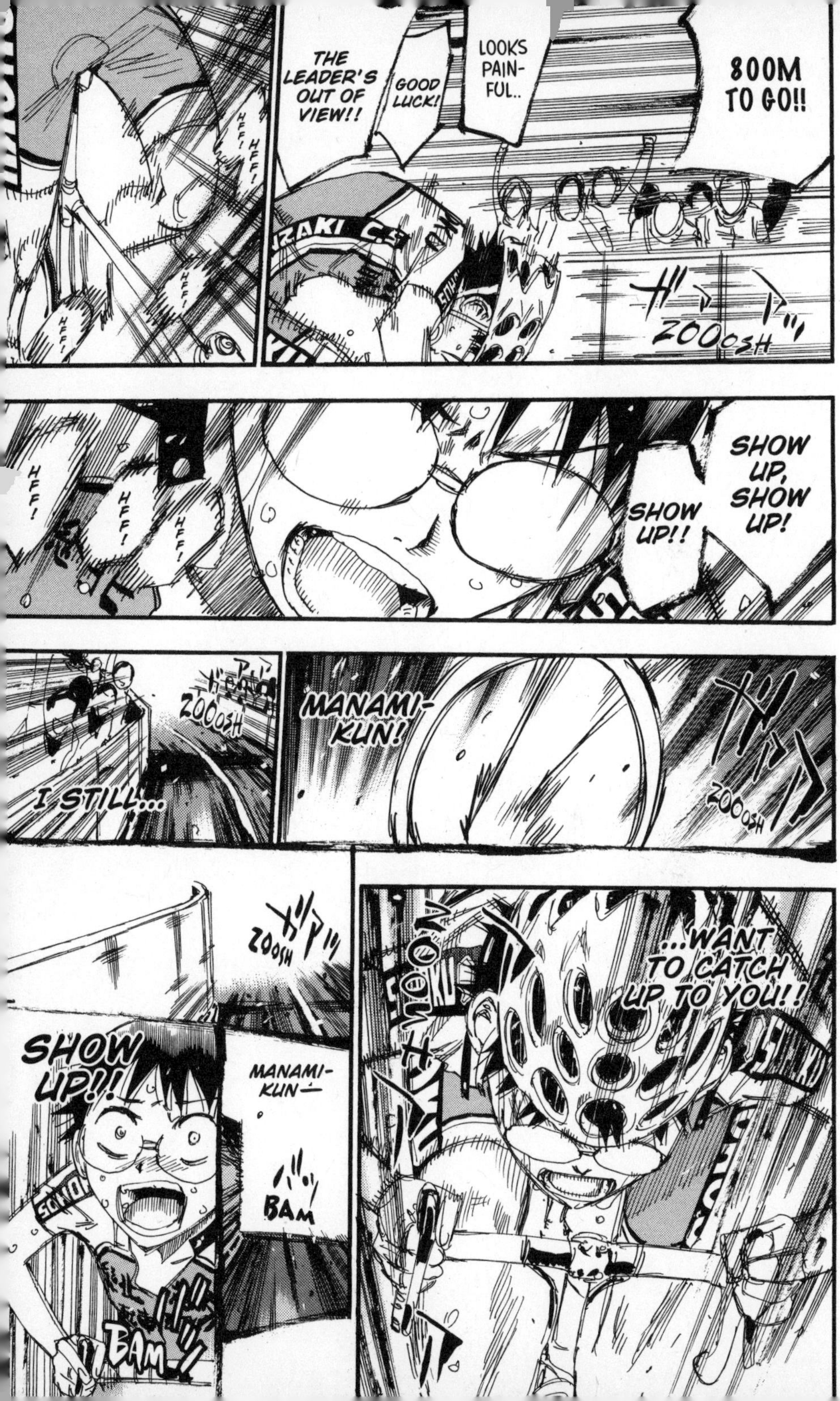
800M TO GO!!
LOOKS PAIN-FUL..
GOOD LUCK!
THE LEADER'S OUT OF VIEW!!
ZOOOSH
HFF! HFF!
HFF!
HFF!
SHOW UP, SHOW UP!
SHOW UP!!
HFF! HFF! HFF!
ZOOOSH
MANAMI-KUN!
ZOOOSH
I STILL...
...WANT TO CATCH UP TO YOU!!
ZOOSH
MANAMI-KUN—
BAM
SHOW UP!!
BAM

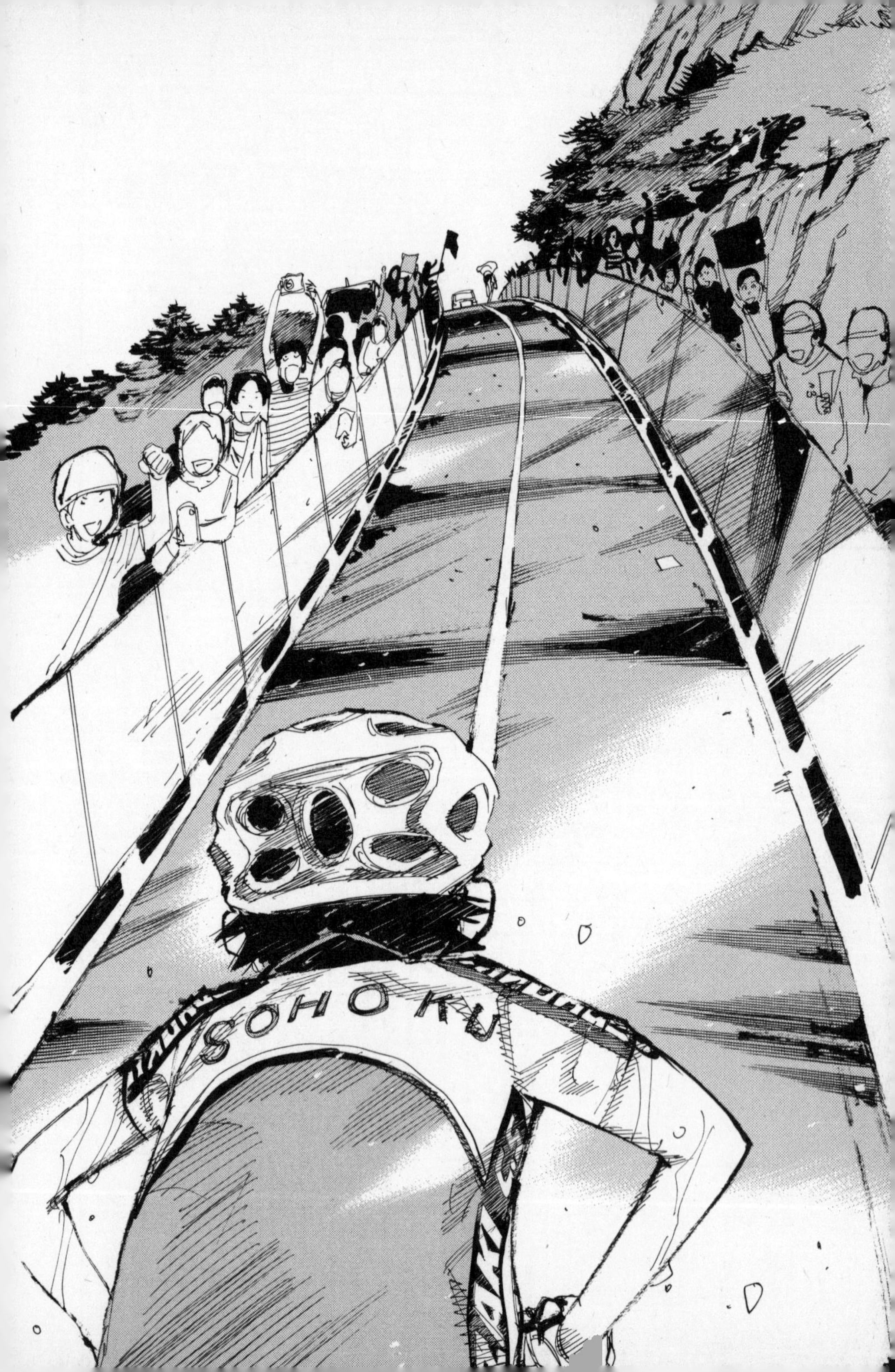
SOHOKU

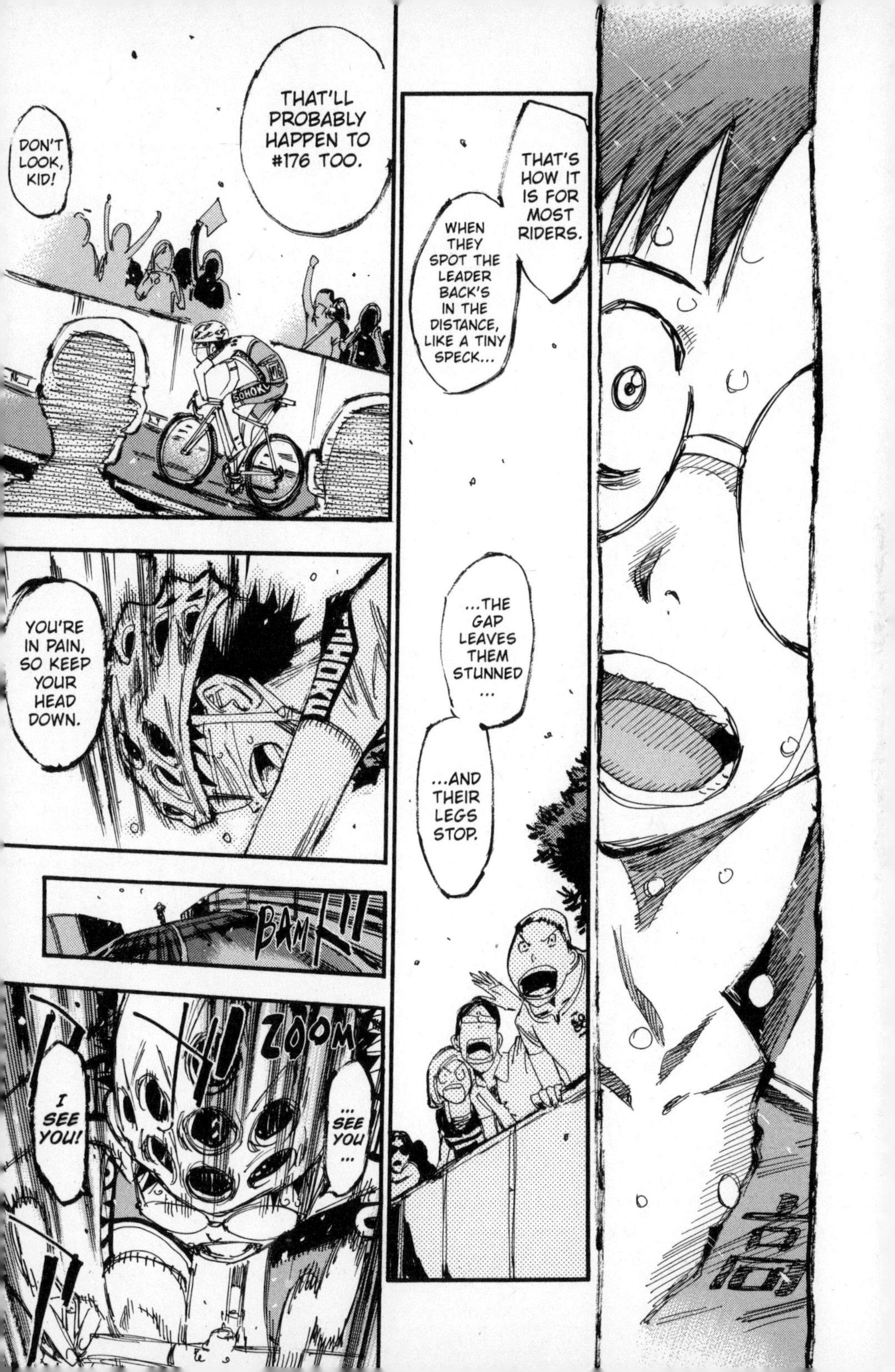
THAT'S HOW IT IS FOR MOST RIDERS.
WHEN THEY SPOT THE LEADER BACK'S IN THE DISTANCE, LIKE A TINY SPECK...
...THE GAP LEAVES THEM STUNNED...
...AND THEIR LEGS STOP.
THAT'LL PROBABLY HAPPEN TO #176 TOO.
DON'T LOOK, KID!
YOU'RE IN PAIN, SO KEEP YOUR HEAD DOWN.
BAM!!
ZOOM
!!
...SEE YOU...
I SEE YOU!

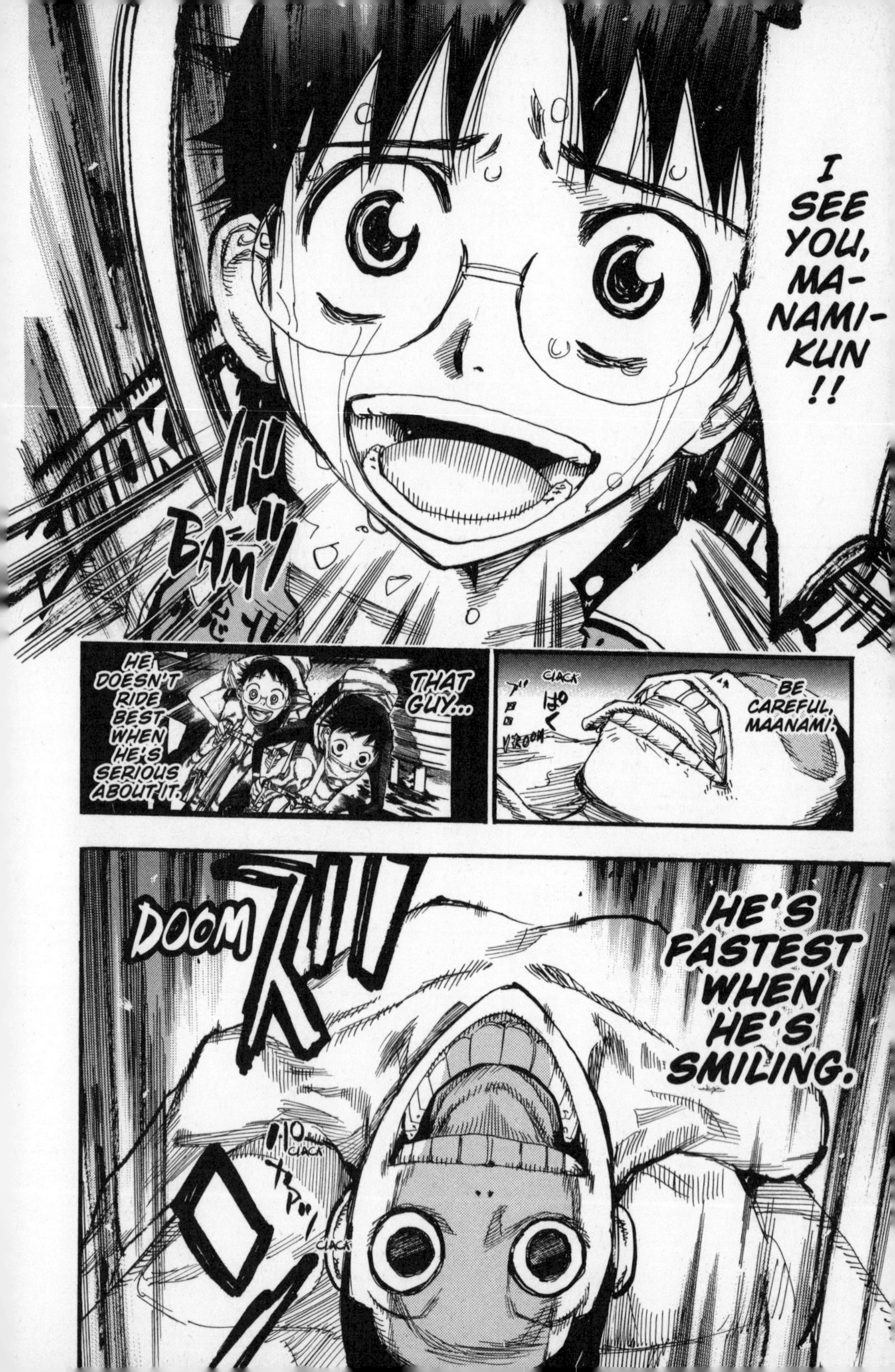
I SEE YOU, MANAMI-KUN!!
BAM
BE CAREFUL, MAANAMI.
CLACK
VROOM
THAT GUY...
HE DOESN'T RIDE BEST WHEN HE'S SERIOUS ABOUT IT.
HE'S FASTEST WHEN HE'S SMILING.
DOOM
CLACK
CLACK

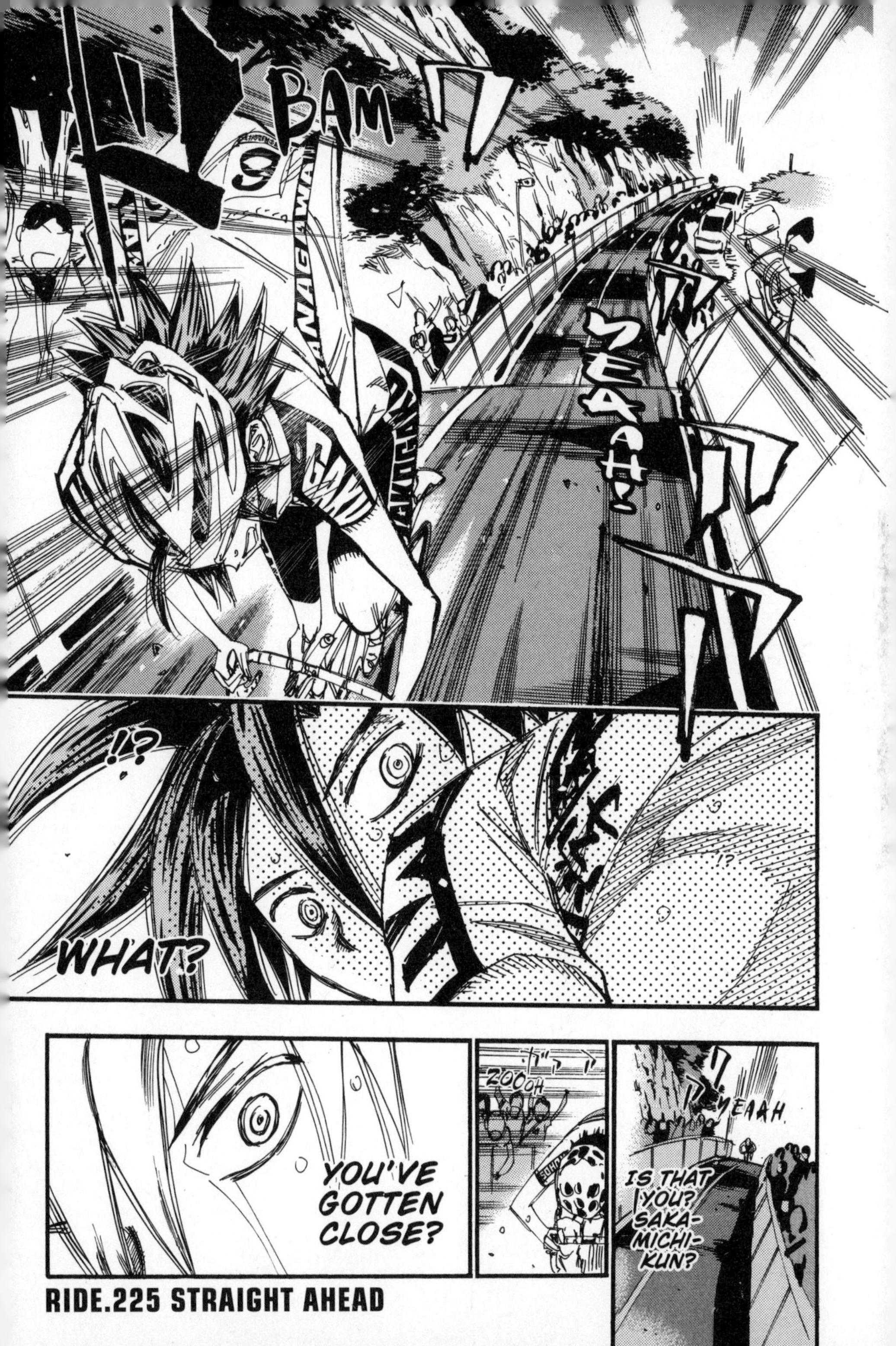
BAM
YEAAAH!!
!?
WHAT?
!?
YEAAH.
IS THAT YOU? SAKAMICHI-KUN?
ZOOOH
YOU'VE GOTTEN CLOSE?

RIDE.225 STRAIGHT AHEAD

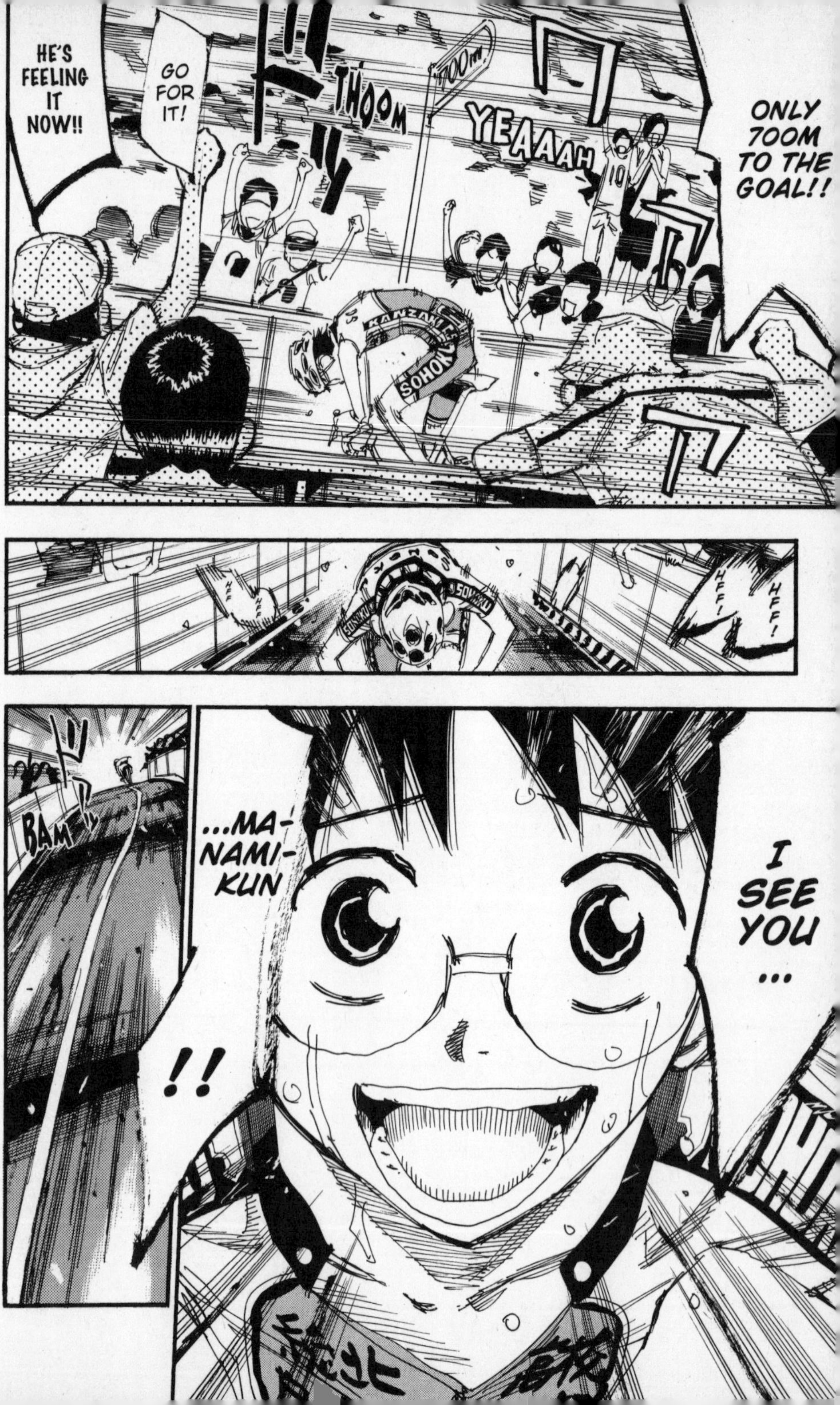
ONLY 700M TO THE GOAL!!
YEAAAAH
700m
THOOM
GO FOR IT!
HE'S FEELING IT NOW!!
HFF! HFF!
HFF HFF
I SEE YOU ...
...MA-NAMI-KUN
!!
BAM

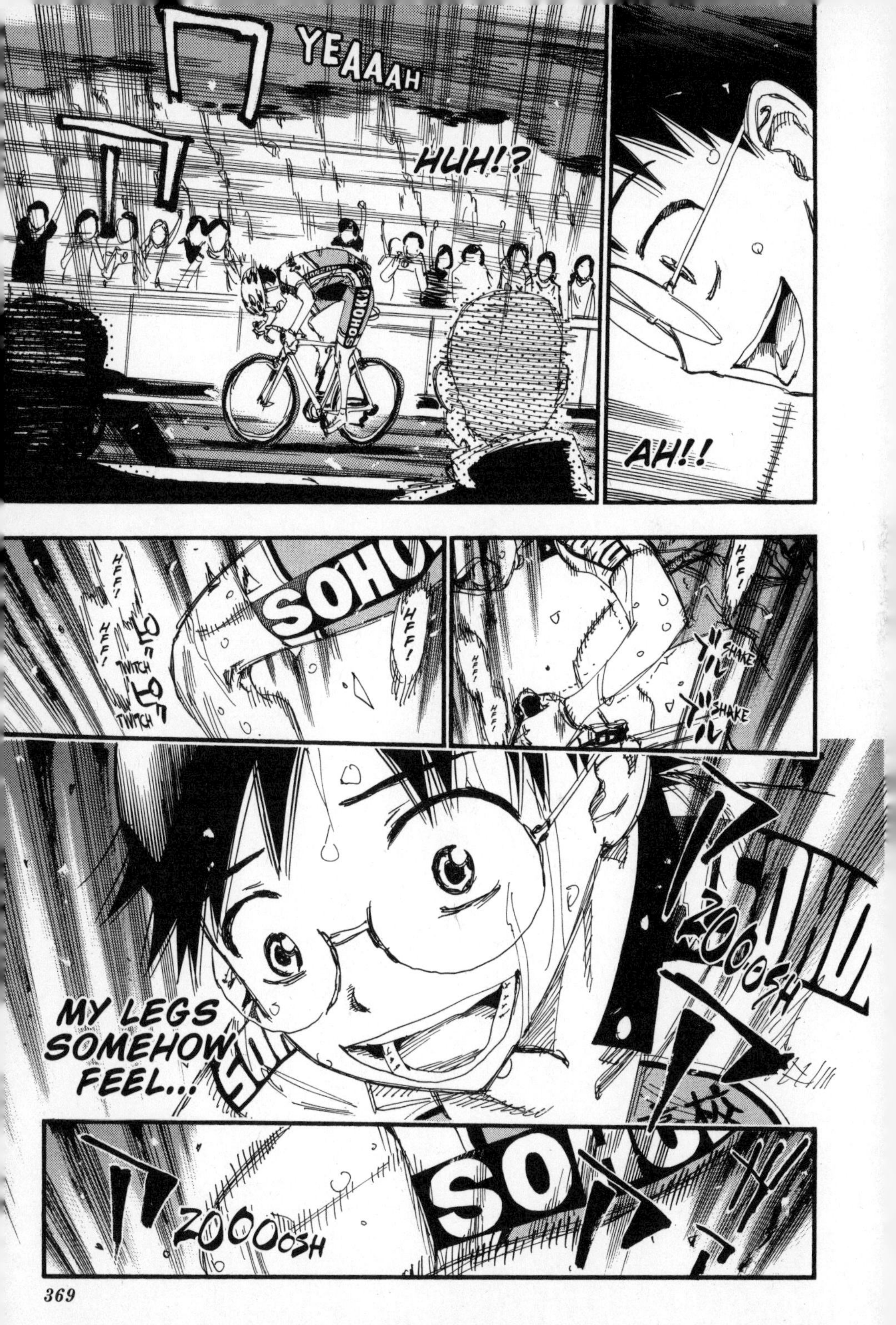
AH!!
YEAAAH
HUH!?
HFF!
HFF!
HFF!
SHAKE
SHAKE
HFF!
HFF!
HFF!
TWITCH
TWITCH
SOHO
ZOOOSH
MY LEGS SOMEHOW FEEL...
SO
ZOOOOSH

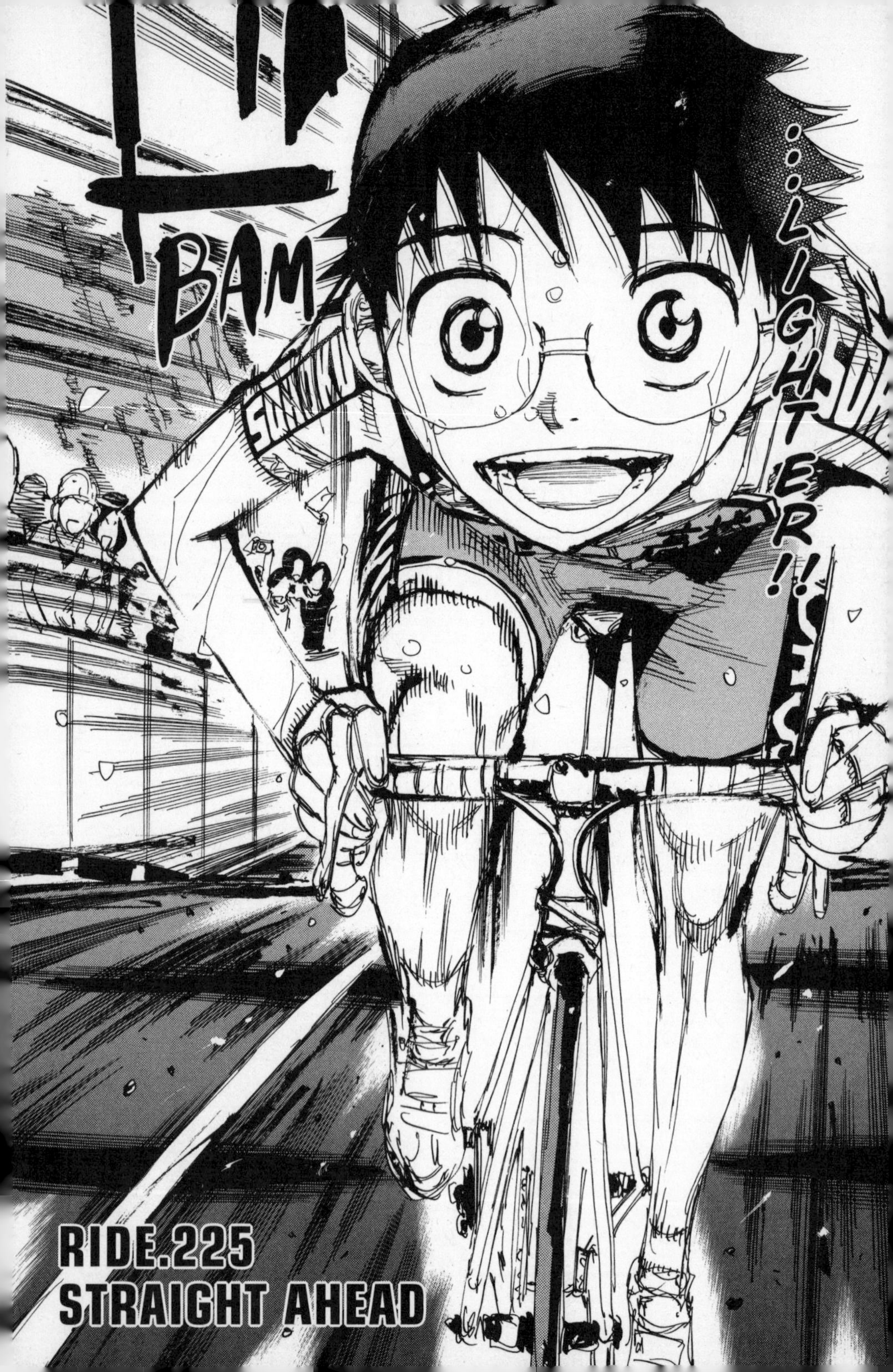
...LIGHTER!!
BAM
RIDE.225
STRAIGHT AHEAD

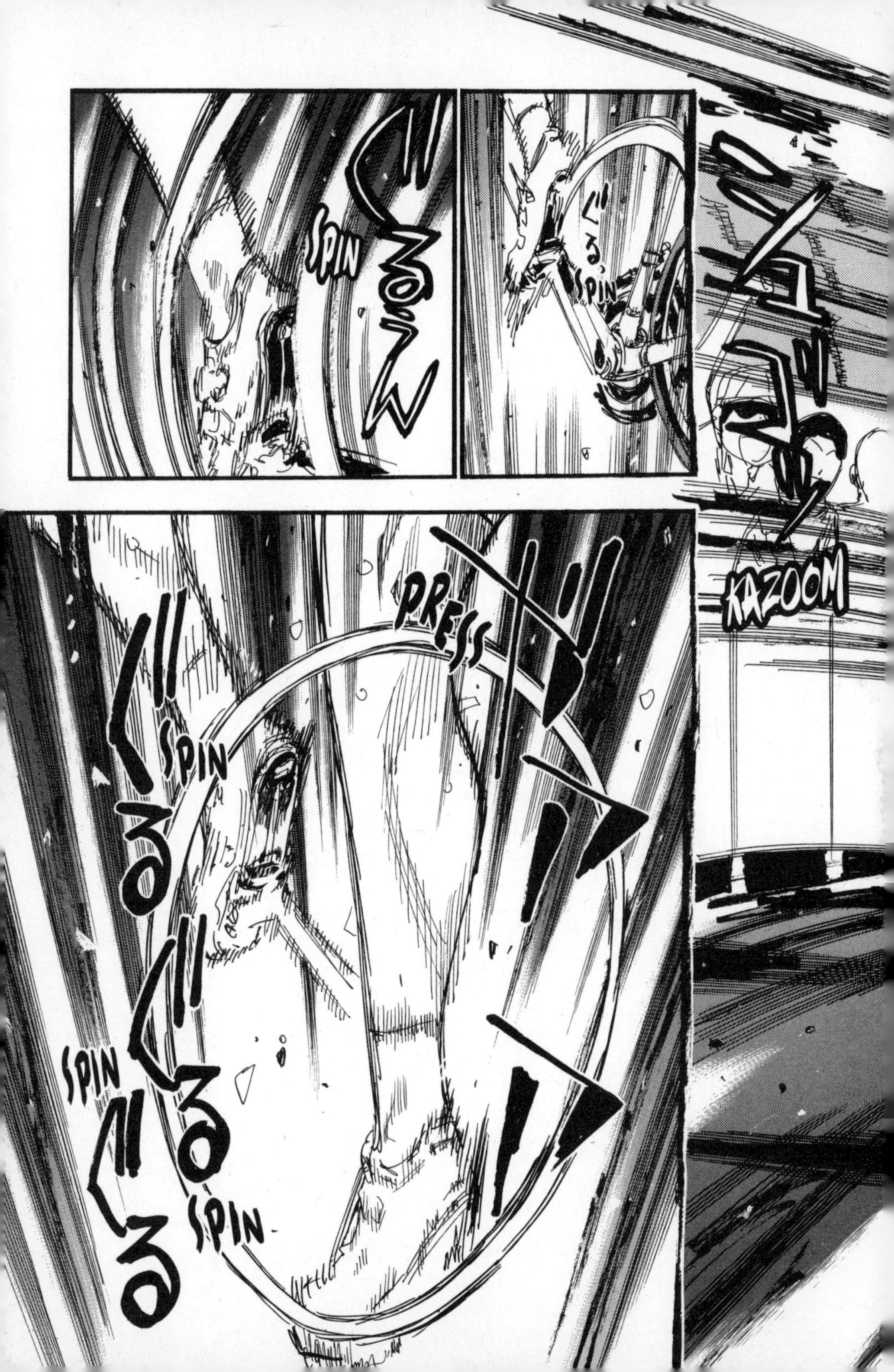

KAZOOM
ぐる
SPIN
SPIN
PRESS
SPIN
SPIN
SPIN

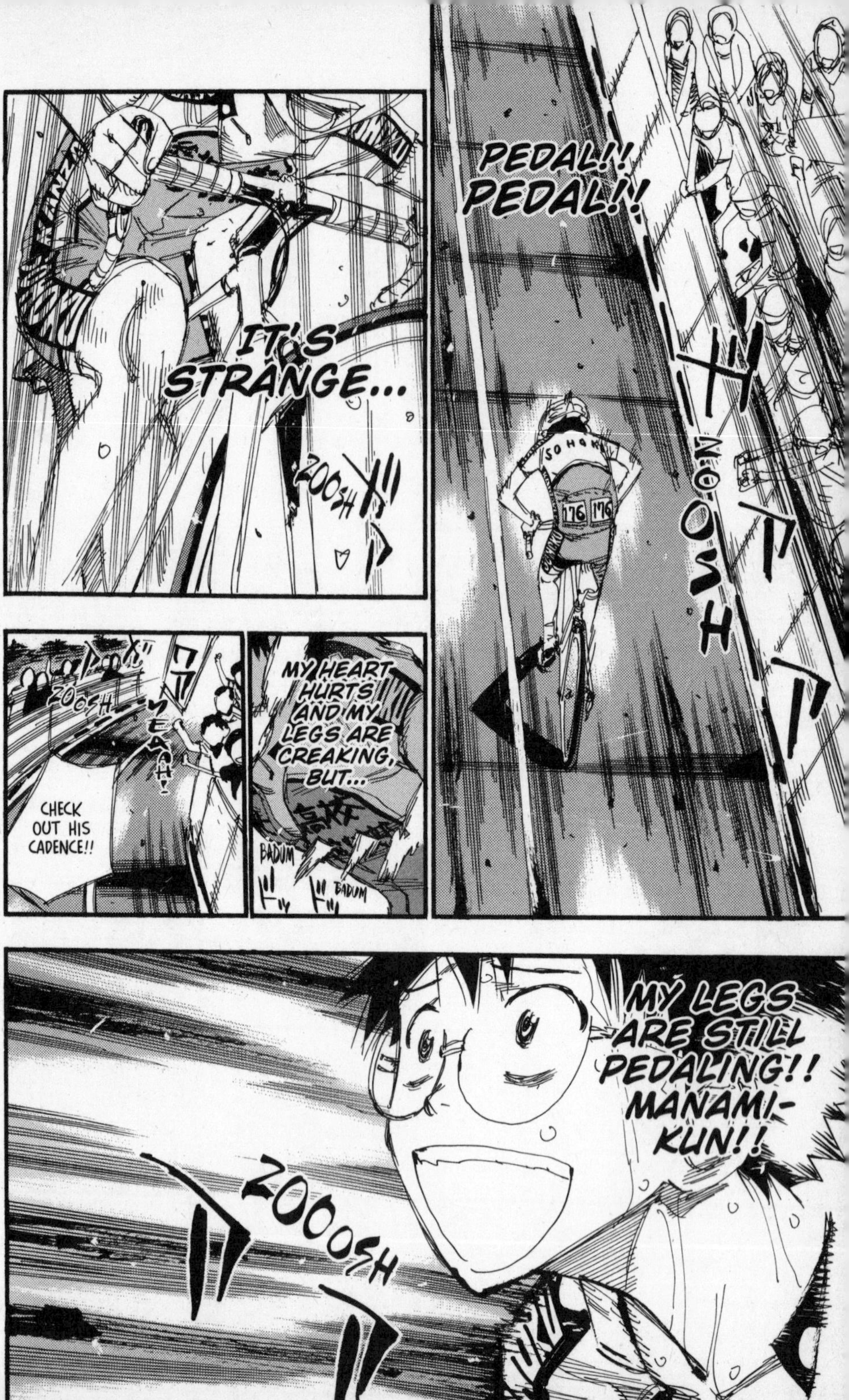
PEDAL!! PEDAL!!
ZOOOSH
IT'S STRANGE...
ZOOSH
MY HEART HURTS AND MY LEGS ARE CREAKING, BUT...
BADUM
BADUM
ZOOSH
YEAH!
CHECK OUT HIS CADENCE!!
MY LEGS ARE STILL PEDALING!! MANAMI-KUN!!
ZOOOSH

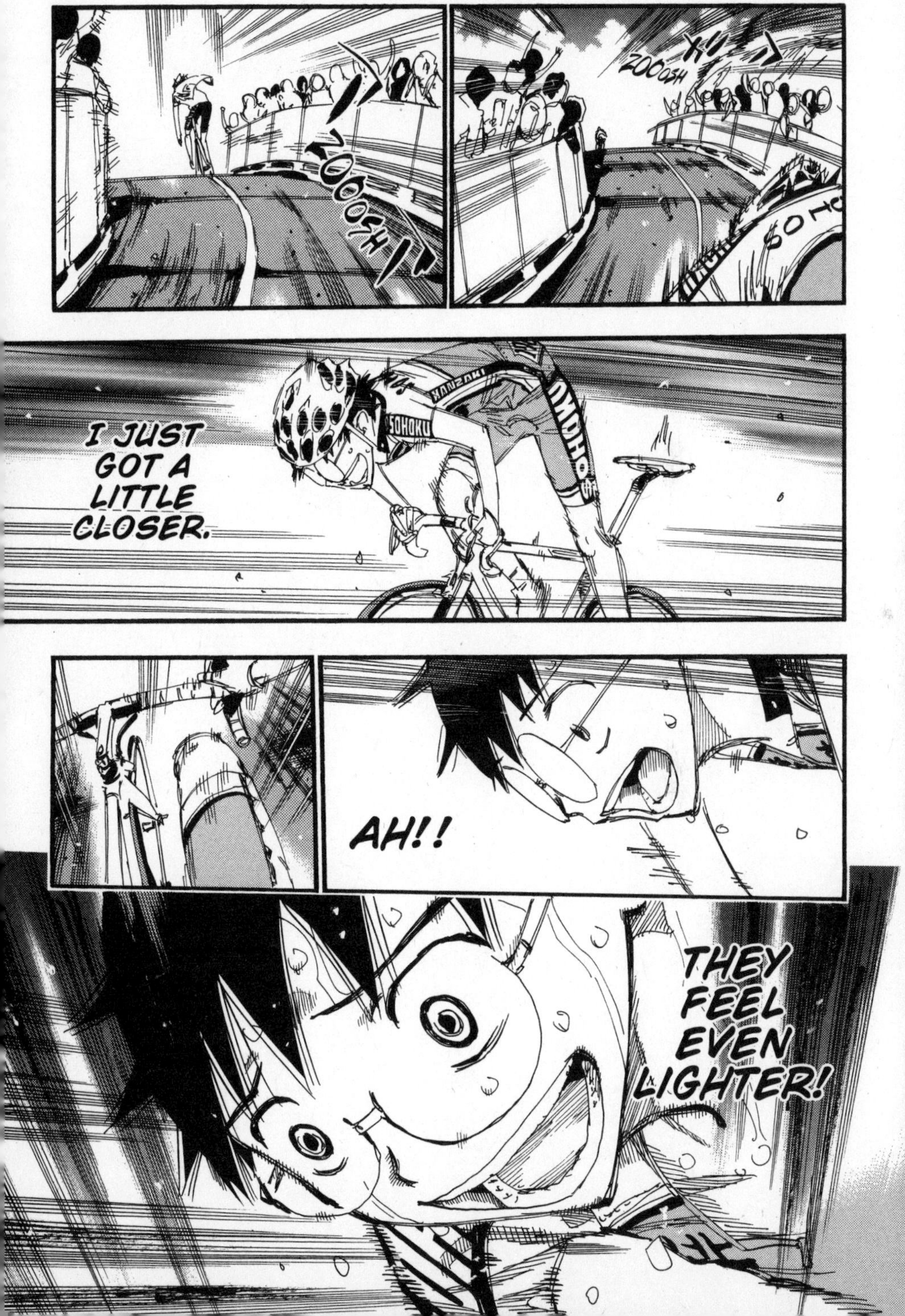
ZOOOSH
ZOOOSH!
I JUST GOT A LITTLE CLOSER.
AH!!
THEY FEEL EVEN LIGHTER!

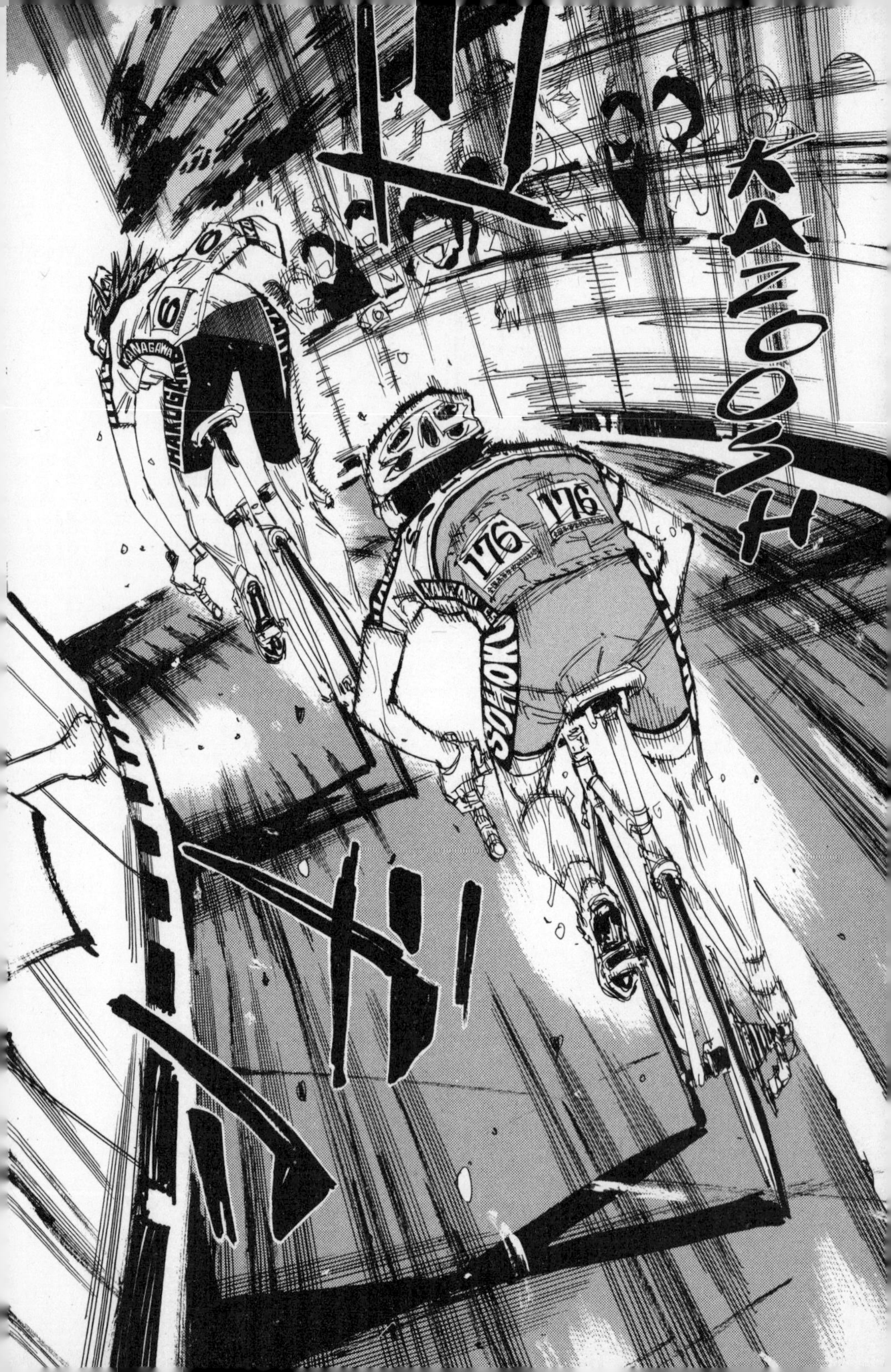
KAZOOSH
KANAGAWA
176
176

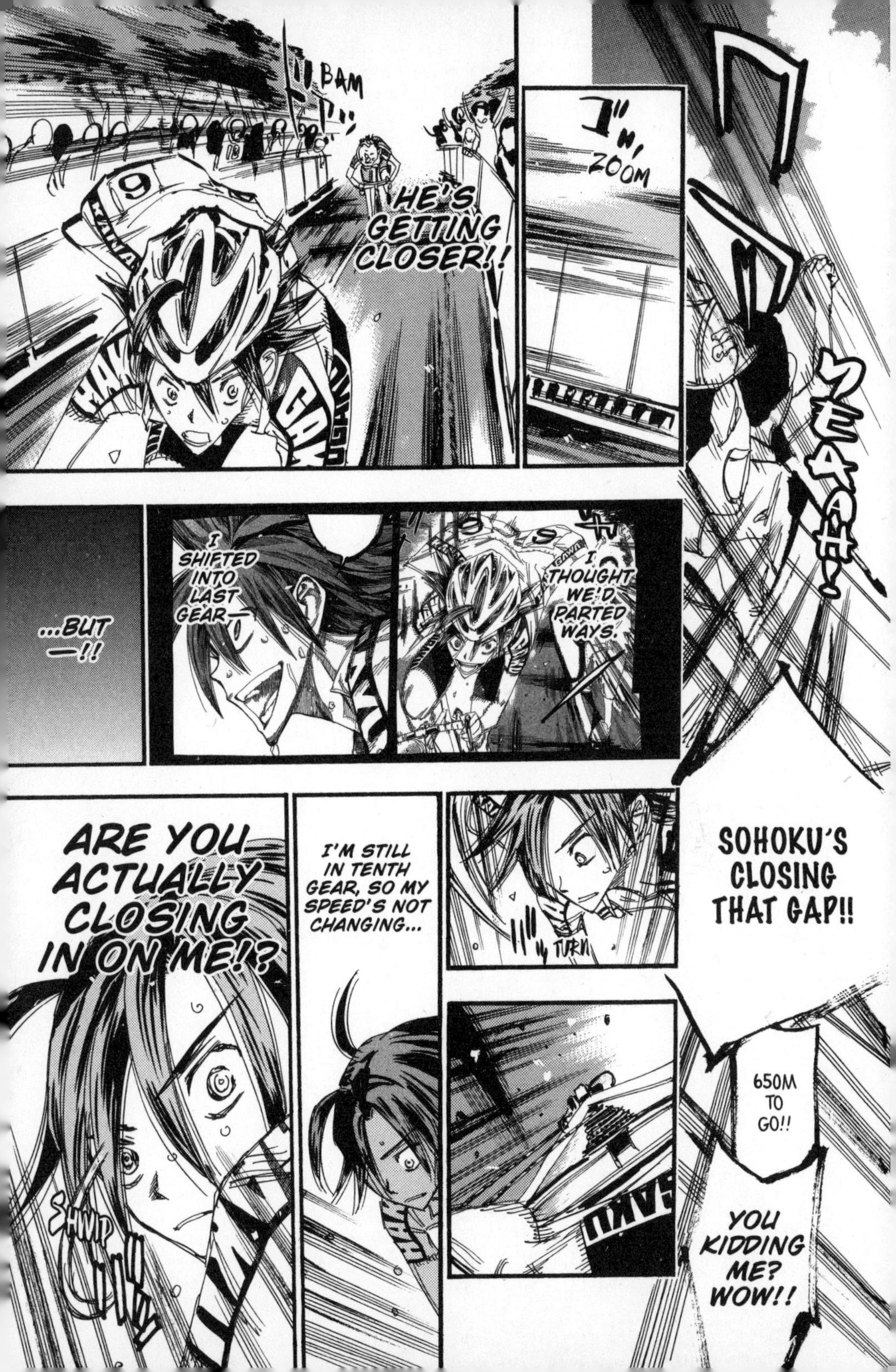
YEAAH!
ZOOM
BAM
HE'S GETTING CLOSER!!
I THOUGHT WE'D PARTED WAYS.
I SHIFTED INTO LAST GEAR—
...BUT—!!
SOHOKU'S CLOSING THAT GAP!!
650M TO GO!!
YOU KIDDING ME? WOW!!
TURN
I'M STILL IN TENTH GEAR, SO MY SPEED'S NOT CHANGING...
ARE YOU ACTUALLY CLOSING IN ON ME!?
SHWIP

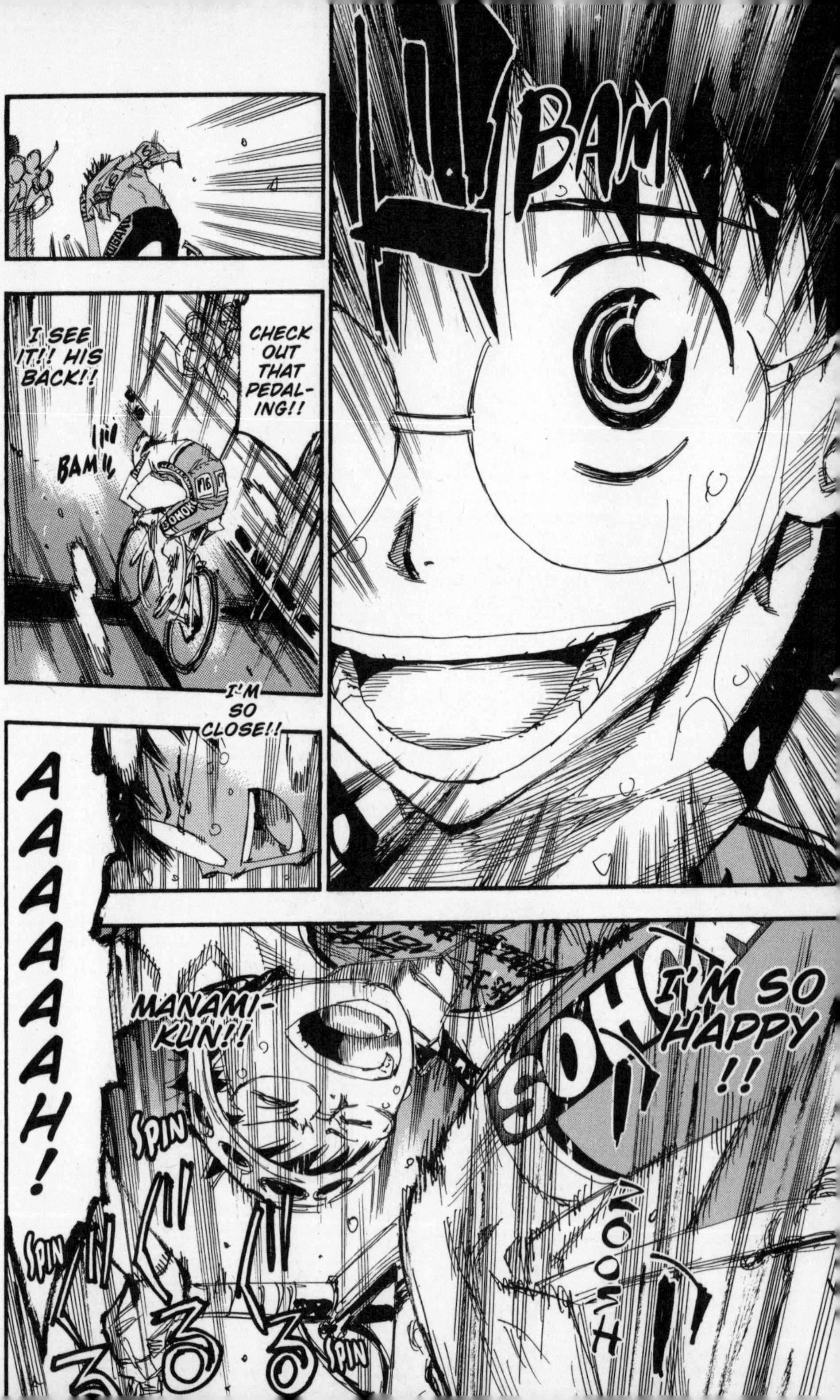
BAM
CHECK OUT THAT PEDALING!!
I SEE IT!! HIS BACK!!
BAM
I'M SO CLOSE!!
I'M SO HAPPY!!
SOH
MANAMI-KUN!!
AAAAAAAH!
SPIN
SPIN
SPIN

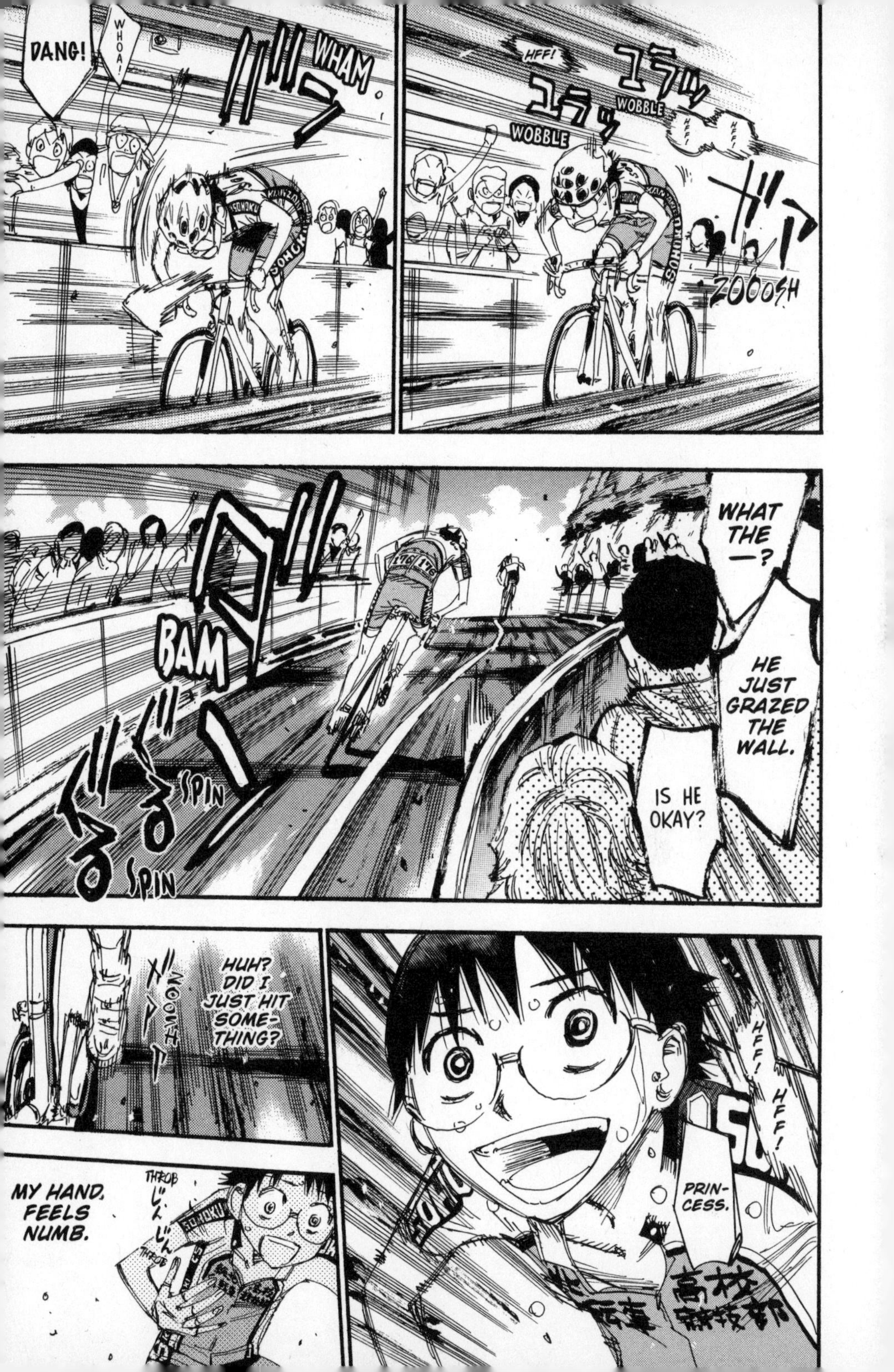
HFF!
WOBBLE
WOBBLE
HFF!
HFF!
ZOOOSH
WHAM
WHOA!
DANG!
WHAT THE—?
HE JUST GRAZED THE WALL.
IS HE OKAY?
BAM
SPIN
SPIN
HFF! HFF!
PRIN-CESS.
HUH? DID I JUST HIT SOME-THING?
WHOOSH
MY HAND. FEELS NUMB.
THROB
THROB

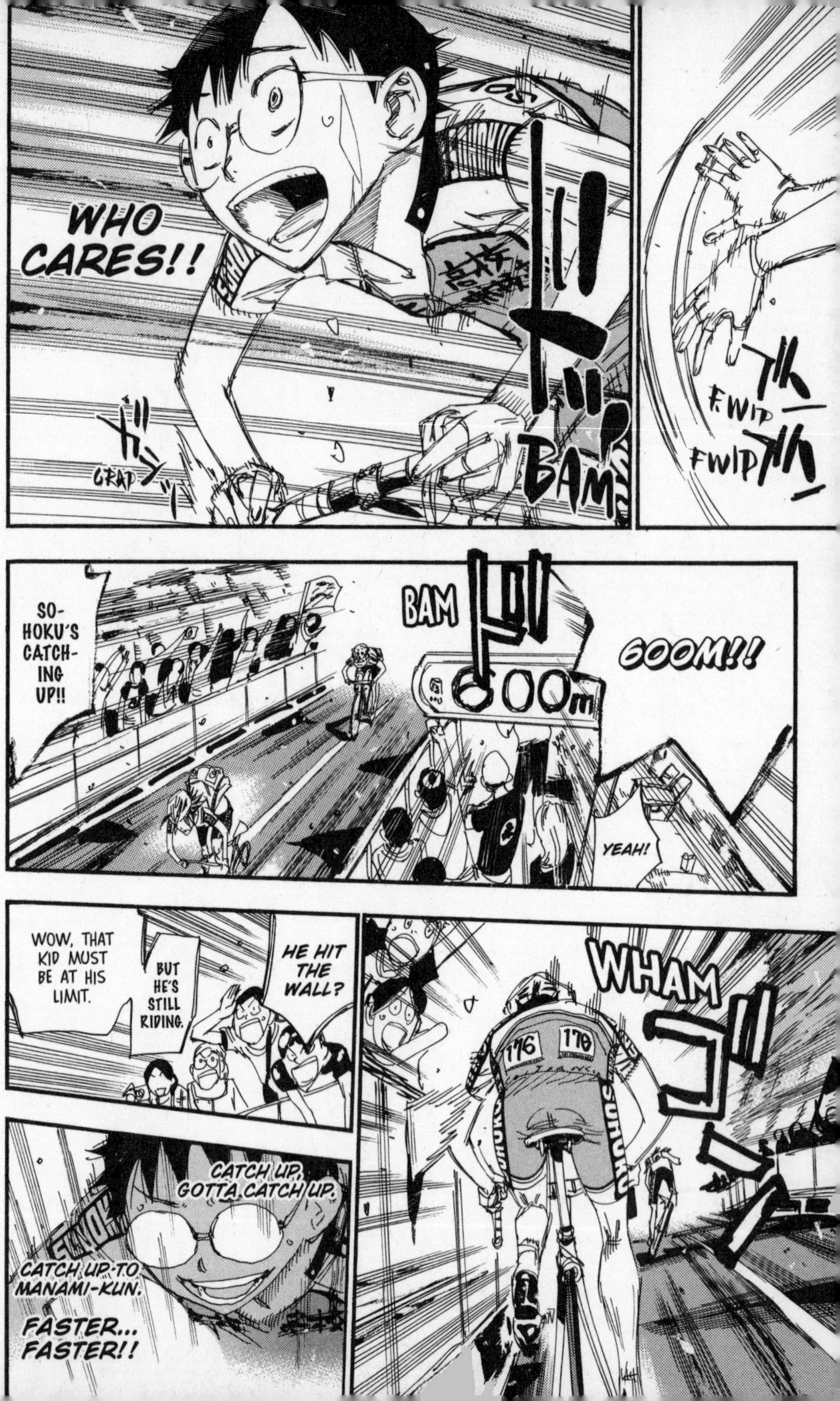
FWIP
FWIP
WHO CARES!!
BAM
GRAP
600M!!
BAM
SO-HOKU'S CATCHING UP!!
YEAH!
WHAM
HE HIT THE WALL?
BUT HE'S STILL RIDING.
WOW, THAT KID MUST BE AT HIS LIMIT.
CATCH UP, GOTTA CATCH UP.
CATCH UP TO MANAMI-KUN.
FASTER... FASTER!!

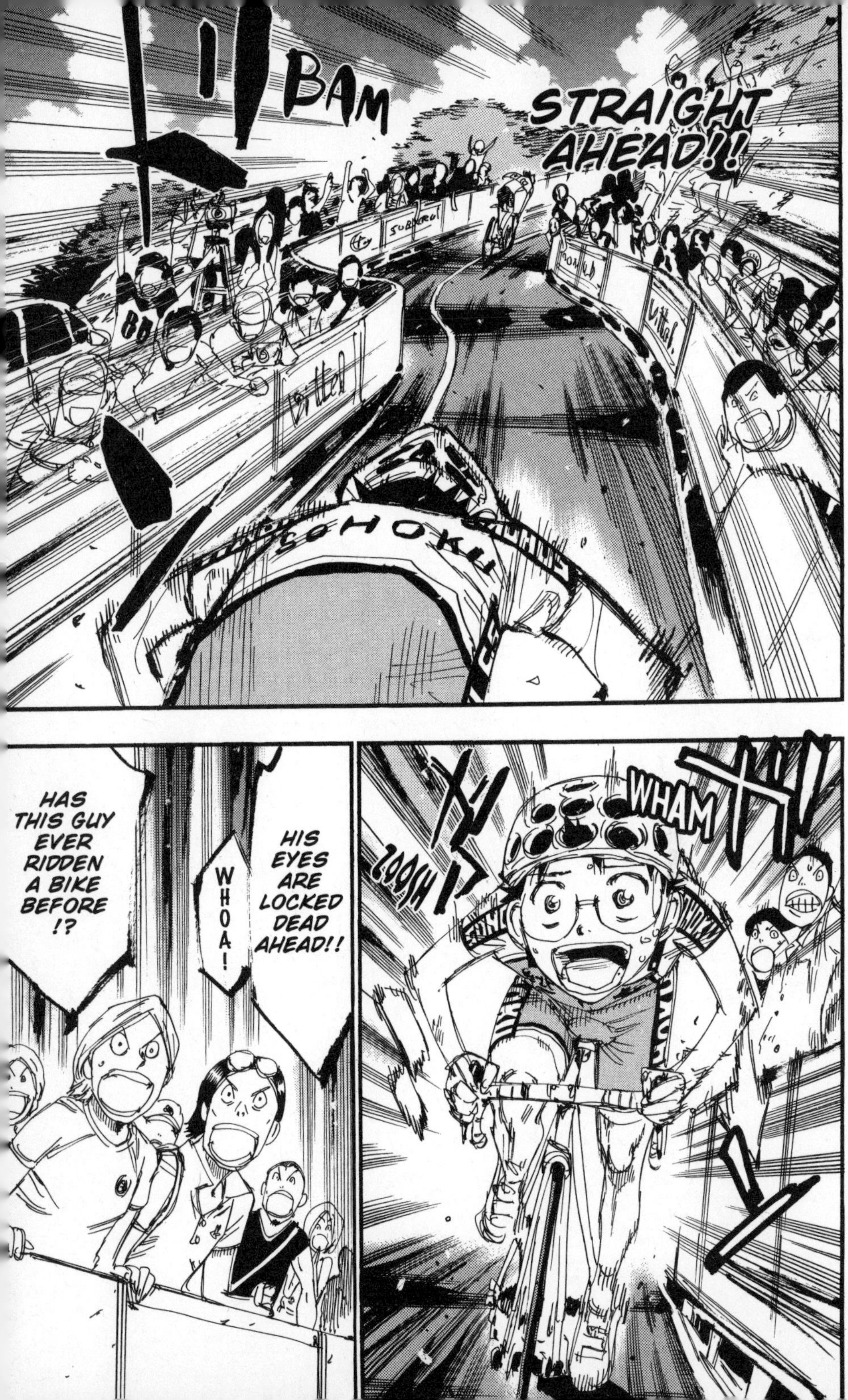
STRAIGHT AHEAD!!
BAM
WHAM
ZOOSH
HIS EYES ARE LOCKED DEAD AHEAD!!
WHOA!
HAS THIS GUY EVER RIDDEN A BIKE BEFORE!?

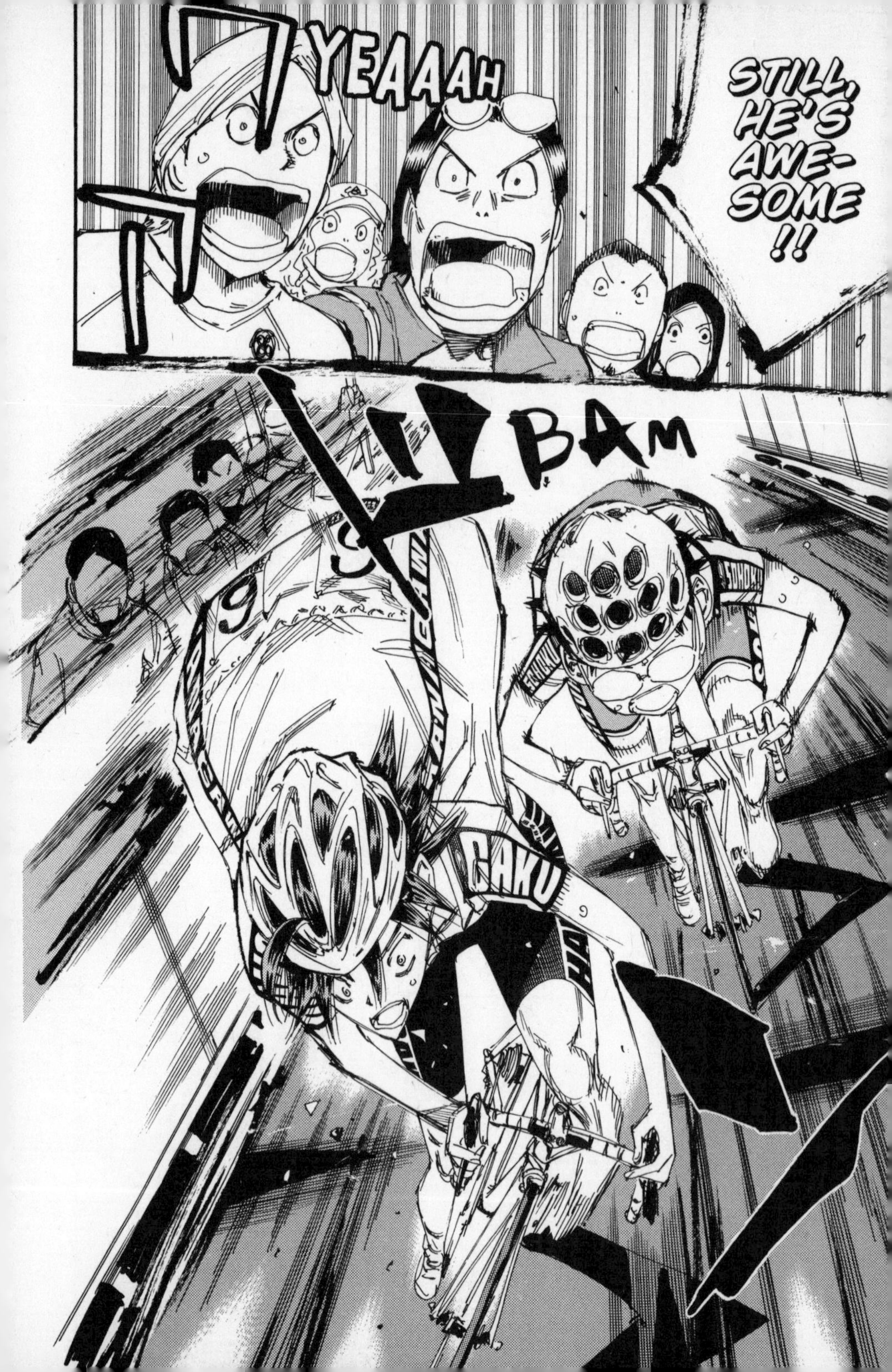
STILL, HE'S AWE-SOME!!
YEAAAH
BAM
GAKU

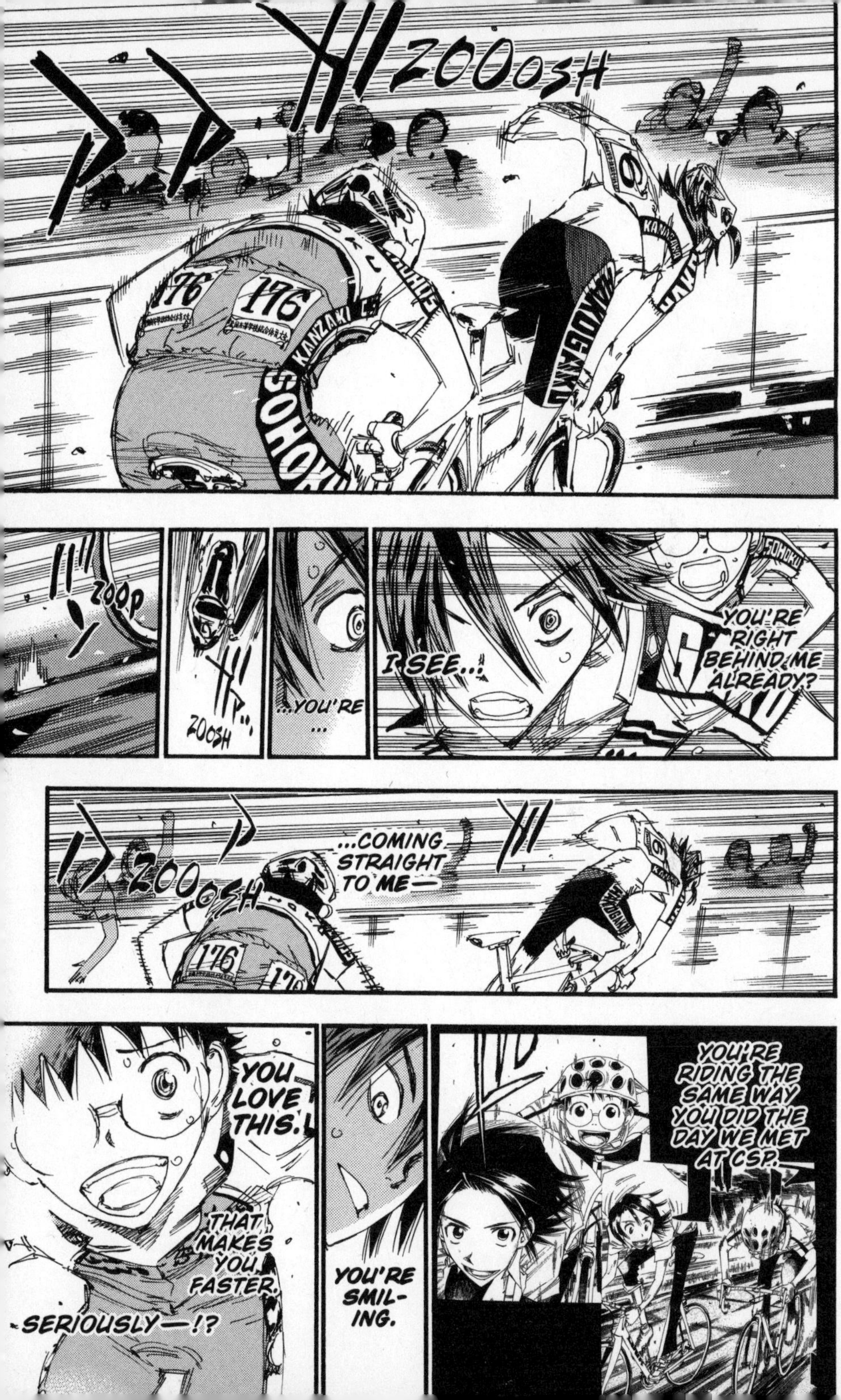
ZOOoSH
YOU'RE RIGHT BEHIND ME ALREADY?
I SEE...!
...YOU'RE ...
ZOOSH
ZOOP
...COMING STRAIGHT TO ME—
ZOOoSH
YOU'RE RIDING THE SAME WAY YOU DID THE DAY WE MET AT CSP.
YOU'RE SMIL-ING.
YOU LOVE THIS.
THAT MAKES YOU FASTER.
SERIOUSLY—!?

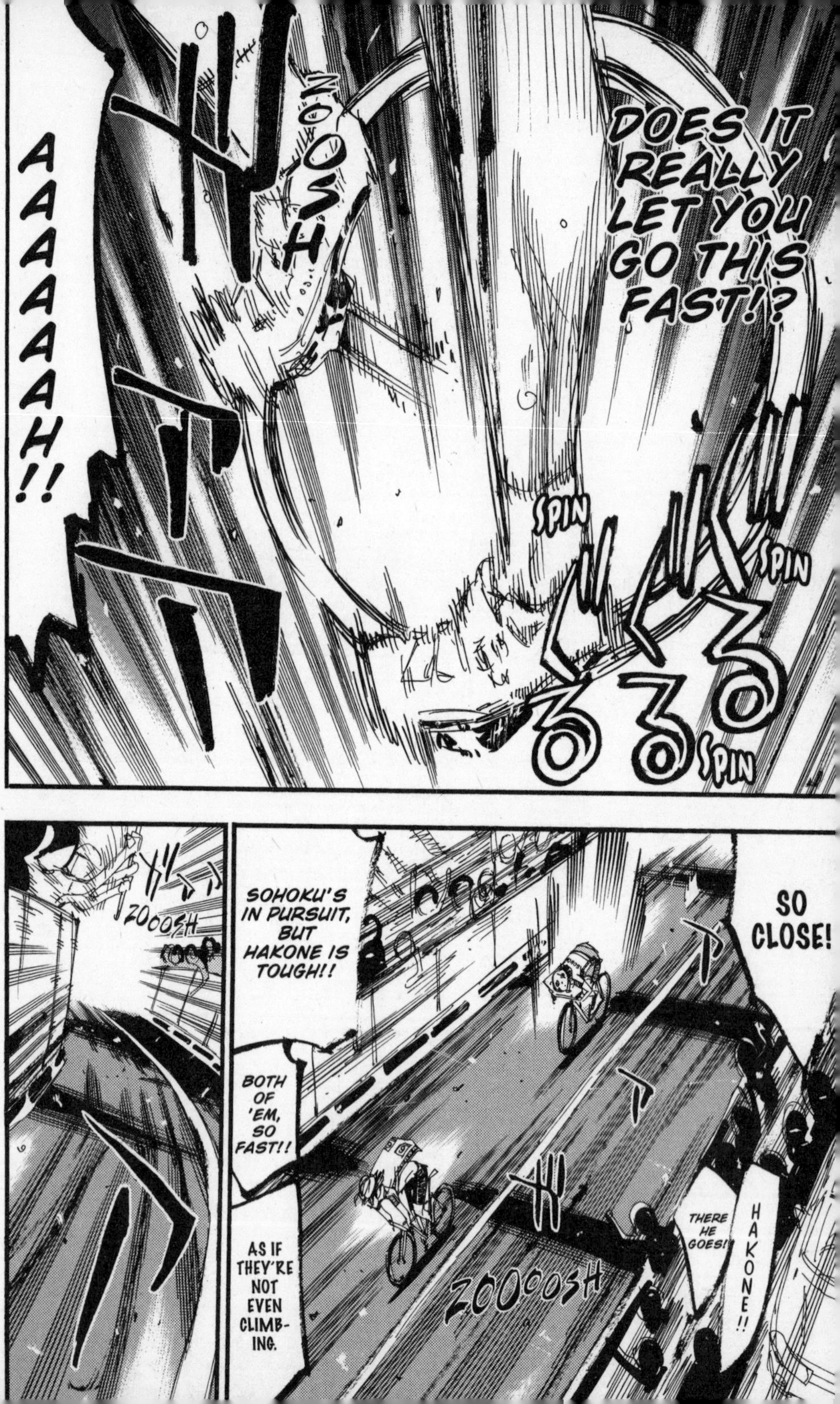
DOES IT REALLY LET YOU GO THIS FAST!?
SPIN
SPIN
SPIN
SPIN
WOOSH
AAAAAAAAH!!
SO CLOSE!
SOHOKU'S IN PURSUIT, BUT HAKONE IS TOUGH!!
HAKONE!!
THERE HE GOES!
BOTH OF 'EM, SO FAST!!
ZOOOOOSH
AS IF THEY'RE NOT EVEN CLIMB-ING.
ZOOOSH

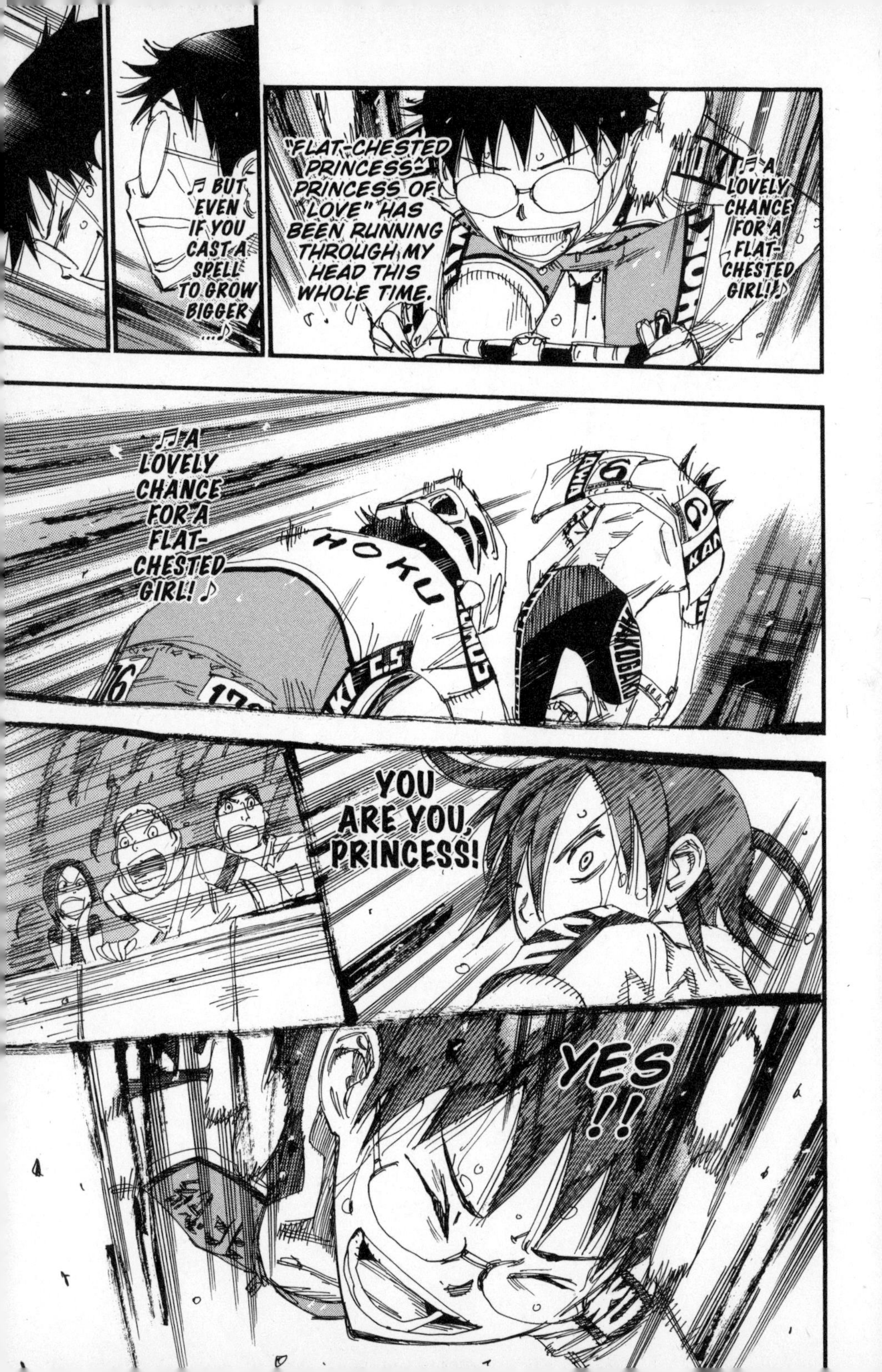

♬ A LOVELY CHANCE FOR A FLAT-CHESTED GIRL! ♪
"FLAT-CHESTED PRINCESS—PRINCESS OF LOVE" HAS BEEN RUNNING THROUGH MY HEAD THIS WHOLE TIME.
♬ BUT EVEN IF YOU CAST A SPELL TO GROW BIGGER ...♪
♬ A LOVELY CHANCE FOR A FLAT-CHESTED GIRL! ♪
YOU ARE YOU, PRINCESS!
YES!!

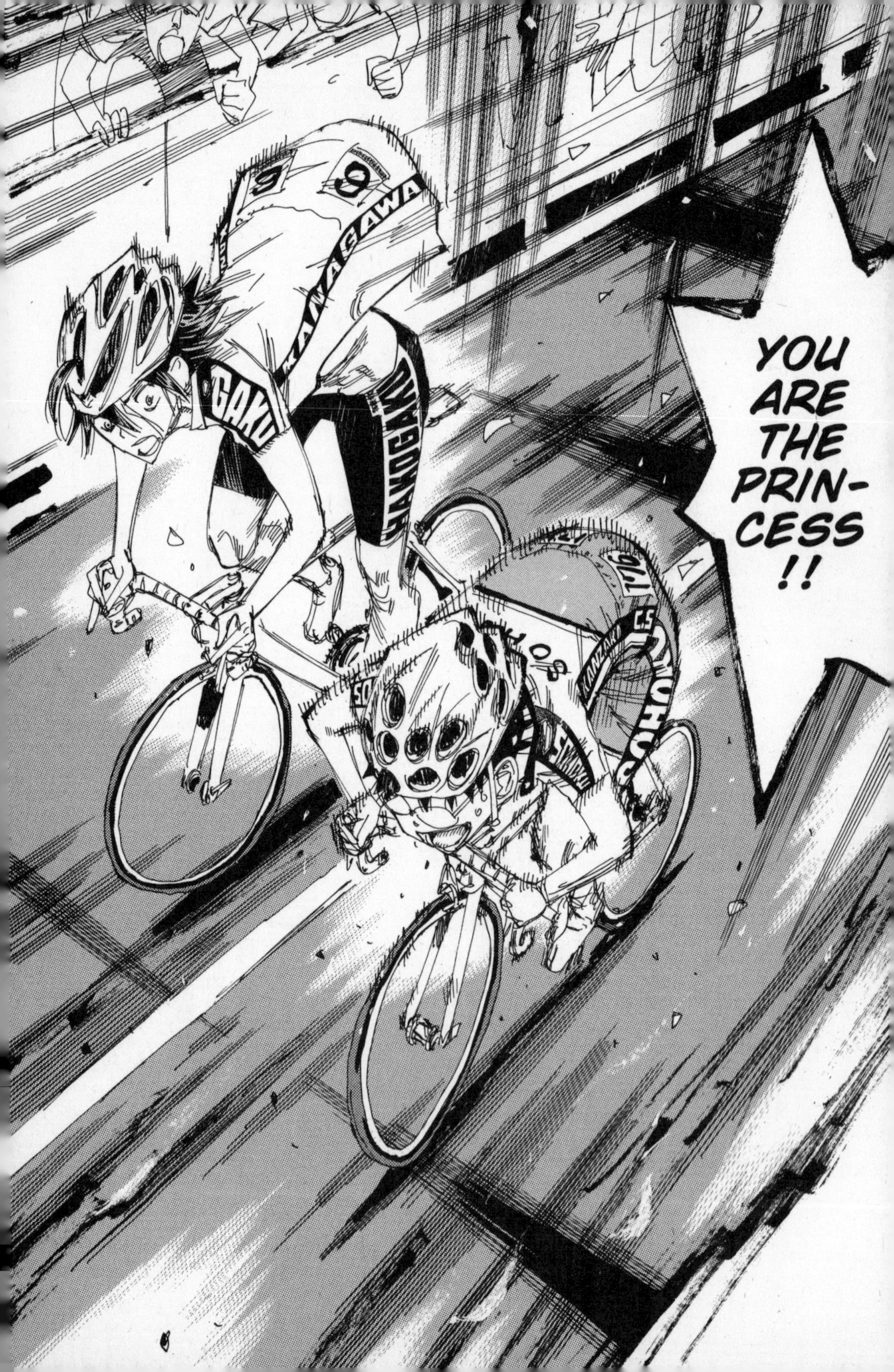
YOU ARE THE PRIN-CESS!!

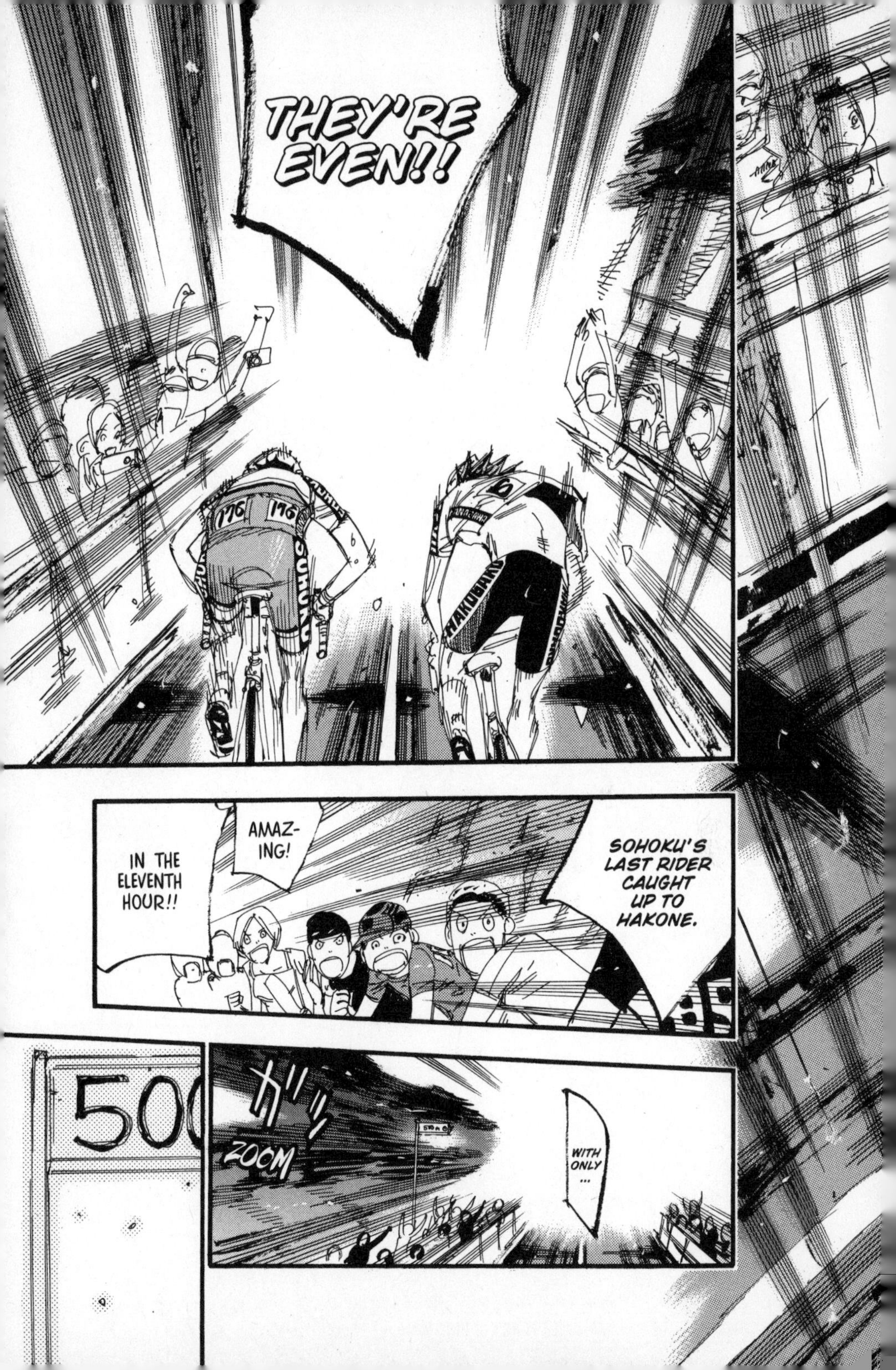
THEY'RE EVEN!!
SOHOKU'S LAST RIDER CAUGHT UP TO HAKONE.
AMAZ-ING!
IN THE ELEVENTH HOUR!!
WITH ONLY ...
ZOOM
500

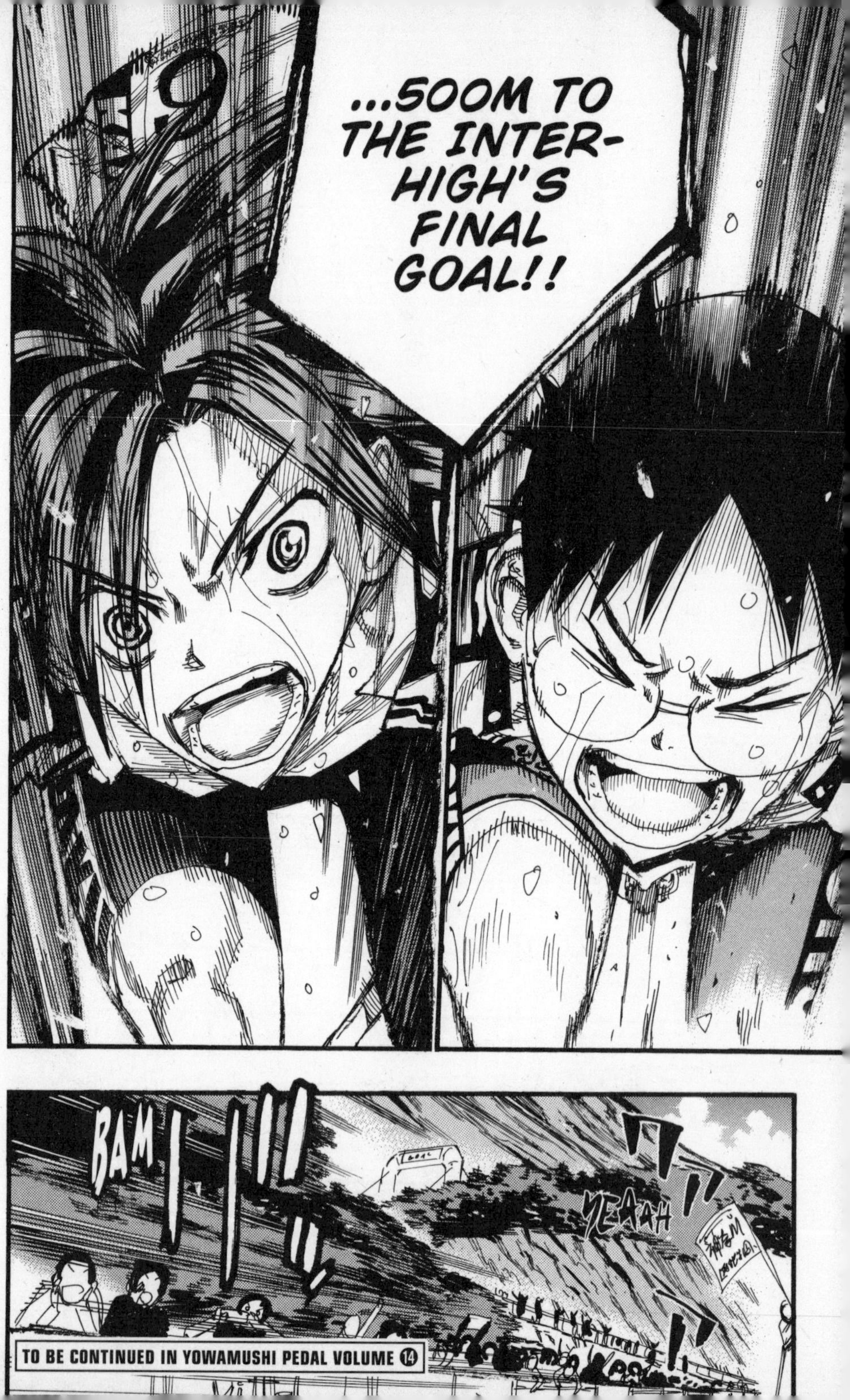
...500M TO THE INTER-HIGH'S FINAL GOAL!!
BAM
YEAAH
TO BE CONTINUED IN YOWAMUSHI PEDAL VOLUME 14

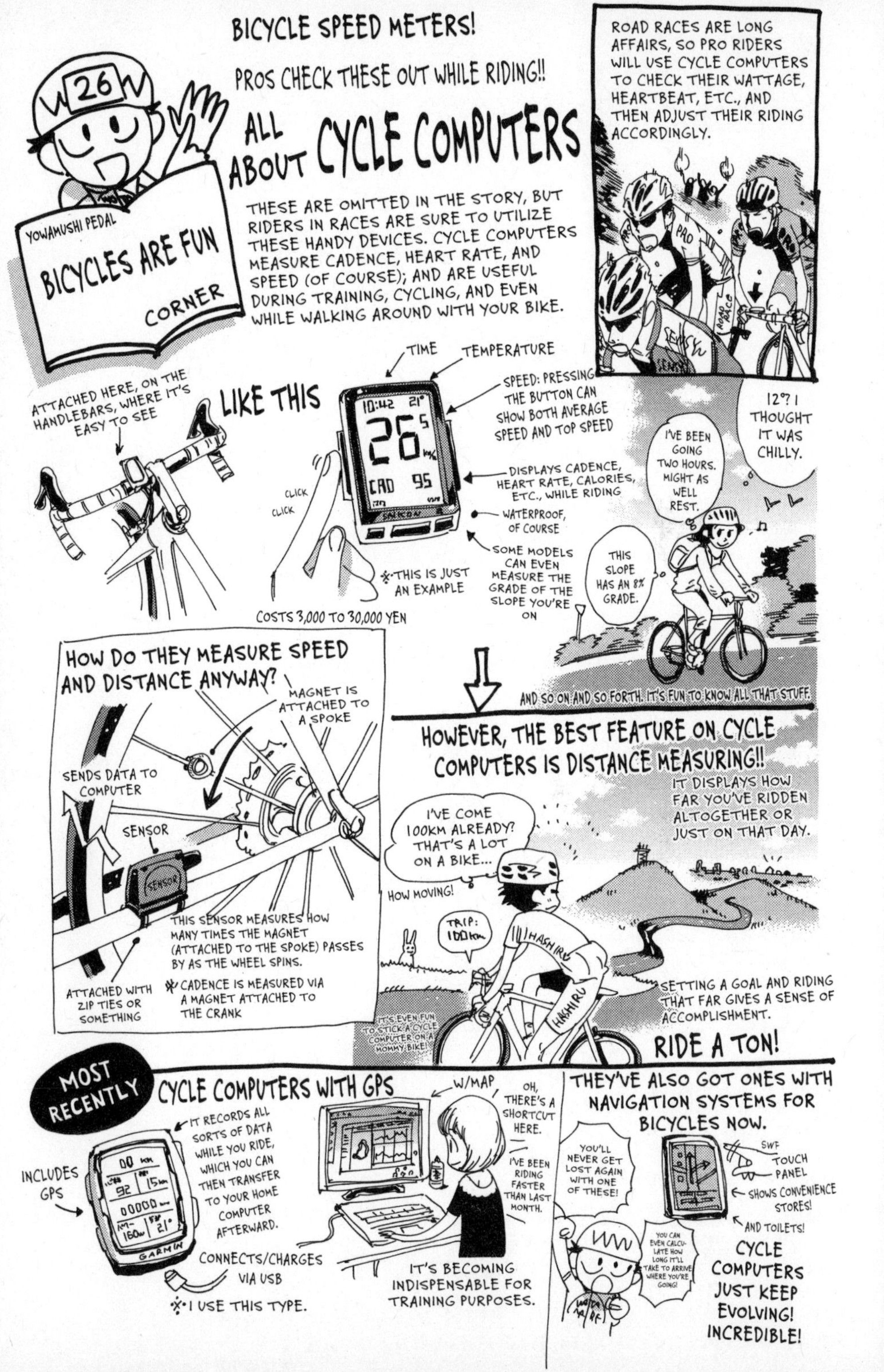
ROAD RACES ARE LONG AFFAIRS, SO PRO RIDERS WILL USE CYCLE COMPUTERS TO CHECK THEIR WATTAGE, HEARTBEAT, ETC., AND THEN ADJUST THEIR RIDING ACCORDINGLY.
PRO
PRO
PRO
ROAD RACE
BICYCLE SPEED METERS!
PROS CHECK THESE OUT WHILE RIDING!!
ALL ABOUT CYCLE COMPUTERS
26
YOWAMUSHI PEDAL
BICYCLES ARE FUN
CORNER
THESE ARE OMITTED IN THE STORY, BUT RIDERS IN RACES ARE SURE TO UTILIZE THESE HANDY DEVICES. CYCLE COMPUTERS MEASURE CADENCE, HEART RATE, AND SPEED (OF COURSE); AND ARE USEFUL DURING TRAINING, CYCLING, AND EVEN WHILE WALKING AROUND WITH YOUR BIKE.
12°? I THOUGHT IT WAS CHILLY.
I'VE BEEN GOING TWO HOURS. MIGHT AS WELL REST.
THIS SLOPE HAS AN 8% GRADE.
AND SO ON AND SO FORTH. IT'S FUN TO KNOW ALL THAT STUFF.
TIME
TEMPERATURE
SPEED: PRESSING THE BUTTON CAN SHOW BOTH AVERAGE SPEED AND TOP SPEED
DISPLAYS CADENCE, HEART RATE, CALORIES, ETC., WHILE RIDING
WATERPROOF, OF COURSE
SOME MODELS CAN EVEN MEASURE THE GRADE OF THE SLOPE YOU'RE ON
10:42 21°
26
CAD 95
CLICK
CLICK
※ THIS IS JUST AN EXAMPLE
COSTS 3,000 TO 30,000 YEN
ATTACHED HERE, ON THE HANDLEBARS, WHERE IT'S EASY TO SEE
LIKE THIS
HOWEVER, THE BEST FEATURE ON CYCLE COMPUTERS IS DISTANCE MEASURING!!
IT DISPLAYS HOW FAR YOU'VE RIDDEN ALTOGETHER OR JUST ON THAT DAY.
I'VE COME 100KM ALREADY? THAT'S A LOT ON A BIKE...
HOW MOVING!
TRIP: 100km
HASHIRU
HASHIRU
SETTING A GOAL AND RIDING THAT FAR GIVES A SENSE OF ACCOMPLISHMENT.
IT'S EVEN FUN TO STICK A CYCLE COMPUTER ON A MOMMY BIKE!
RIDE A TON!
HOW DO THEY MEASURE SPEED AND DISTANCE ANYWAY?
MAGNET IS ATTACHED TO A SPOKE
SENDS DATA TO COMPUTER
SENSOR
SENSOR
THIS SENSOR MEASURES HOW MANY TIMES THE MAGNET (ATTACHED TO THE SPOKE) PASSES BY AS THE WHEEL SPINS.
ATTACHED WITH ZIP TIES OR SOMETHING
※ CADENCE IS MEASURED VIA A MAGNET ATTACHED TO THE CRANK
THEY'VE ALSO GOT ONES WITH NAVIGATION SYSTEMS FOR BICYCLES NOW.
YOU'LL NEVER GET LOST AGAIN WITH ONE OF THESE!
SWF
TOUCH PANEL
SHOWS CONVENIENCE STORES!
AND TOILETS!
YOU CAN EVEN CALCULATE HOW LONG IT'LL TAKE TO ARRIVE WHERE YOU'RE GOING!
CYCLE COMPUTERS JUST KEEP EVOLVING! INCREDIBLE!
W/MAP
OH, THERE'S A SHORTCUT HERE.
I'VE BEEN RIDING FASTER THAN LAST MONTH.
IT'S BECOMING INDISPENSABLE FOR TRAINING PURPOSES.
MOST RECENTLY
CYCLE COMPUTERS WITH GPS
IT RECORDS ALL SORTS OF DATA WHILE YOU RIDE, WHICH YOU CAN THEN TRANSFER TO YOUR HOME COMPUTER AFTERWARD.
INCLUDES GPS
GARMIN
CONNECTS/CHARGES VIA USB
※ I USE THIS TYPE.

Translation Notes

Common Honorifics
-san: The Japanese equivalent of Mr./Mrs./Miss. If a situation calls for politeness, this is the fail-safe honorific.
-kun: Used most often when referring to boys, this indicates affection or familiarity. Occasionally used by older men among their peers, but it may also be used by anyone referring to a person of lower standing.
-chan: An affectionate honorific indicating familiarity used mostly in reference to girls; also used in reference to cute persons or animals of either gender.
-senpai: A suffix used to address upperclassmen or more experienced co-workers.
-shi: A more formal version of *san* common to written Japanese, it's the default honorific used in newspapers.
no honorific: Indicates familiarity or closeness; if used without permission or reason, addressing someone in this manner would constitute an insult.

A kilometer is approximately .6 of a mile.

PAGE 23
Peloton: A cycling term for the "pack," or the main group of riders in a race.

Groszumi: Midousuji calls Imaizumi "Kimoizumi" which is a play on the Japanese word *[kimoi]*, meaning "gross" and Imaizumi's name.

PAGE 24
Domestique: A cyclist in a competitive team who focuses on helping the team and the ace over winning the race themselves.

PAGE 49
Piggyzumi: Like Groszumi, "Piggyzumi" is a play on Imaizumi's name by Midousuji using the Japanese word *[buta]*, which means "pig."

PAGE 164
Goofs: Midousuji uses the term *zaku* in the Japanese version, which means "assorted vegetables for *sukiyaki* hot pot" but is also the name of the common enemy robot in the anime *Mobile Suit Gundam*. The former meaning refers to the rest of Kyoto-Fushimi being there to serve Midousuji, while the latter refers to how Midousuji treats his teammates as generic and interchangeable.

PAGE 199
Kamameshi: Refers to a traditional Japanese rice dish cooked in an iron pot called a *[kama]*. The word *[kamameshi]* means "kettle rice" in Japanese.

PAGE 200
Botchan: A famous Japanese author named Natsume Soseki wrote the novel *Botchan* in 1906. The story follows a city boy from Tokyo through the adventures and challenges of attending a school in the country.

PAGE 381
CSP: Stands for "Cycling Sports Center." The CSP was the location of the 1,000km long training camp for Sohoku High.

PAGE 387
3,000 to 30,000 yen: Approximately 30 to 300 USD.

YOWAMUSHI PEDAL VOLUME 14

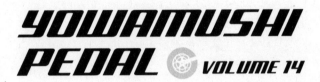

Read on for a sneak peek of Volume 14!

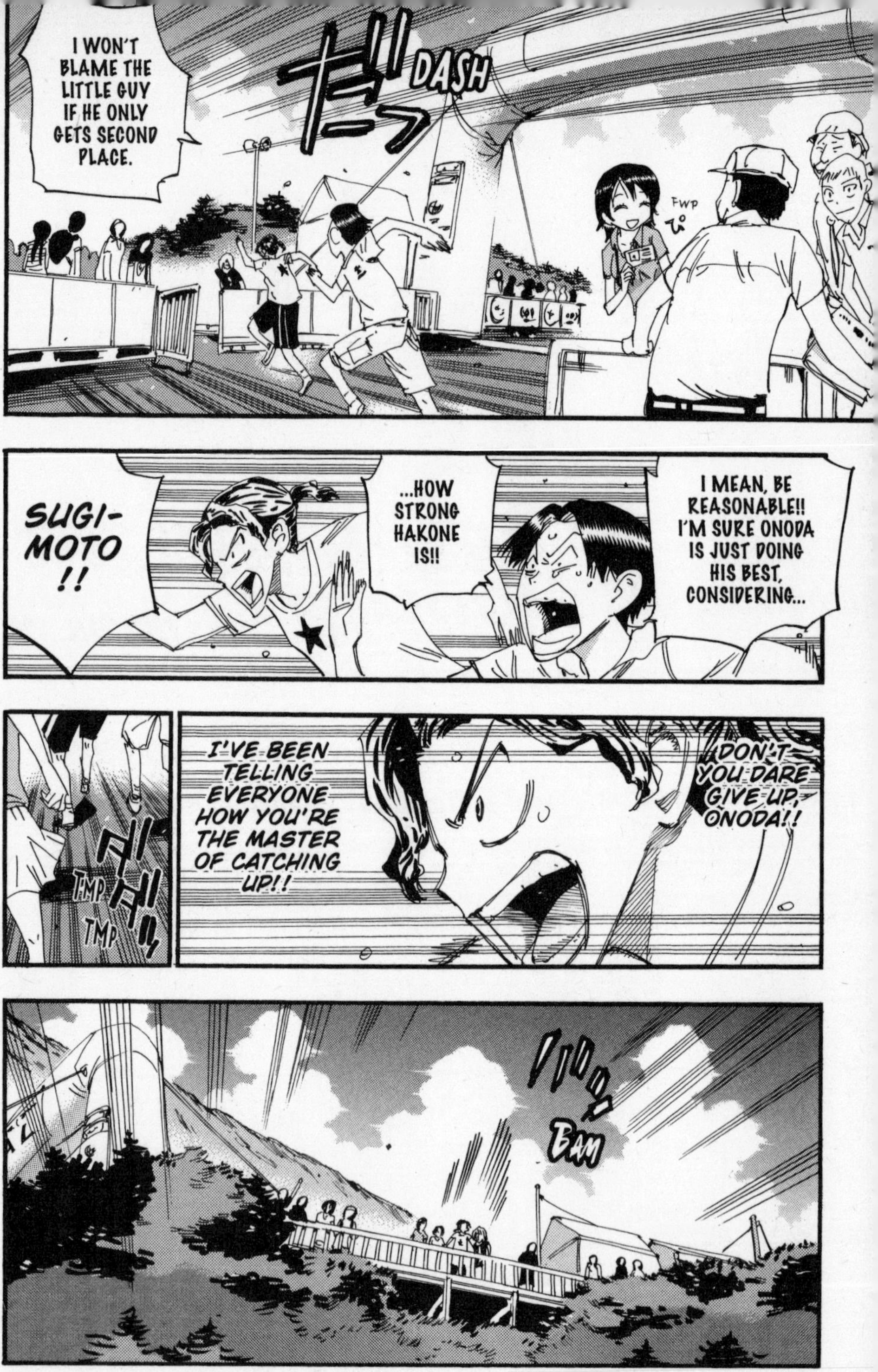
I WON'T BLAME THE LITTLE GUY IF HE ONLY GETS SECOND PLACE.
DASH
FWP
I MEAN, BE REASONABLE!! I'M SURE ONODA IS JUST DOING HIS BEST, CONSIDERING...
...HOW STRONG HAKONE IS!!
SUGI-MOTO!!
DON'T YOU DARE GIVE UP, ONODA!!
I'VE BEEN TELLING EVERYONE HOW YOU'RE THE MASTER OF CATCHING UP!!
TMP
TMP
BAM

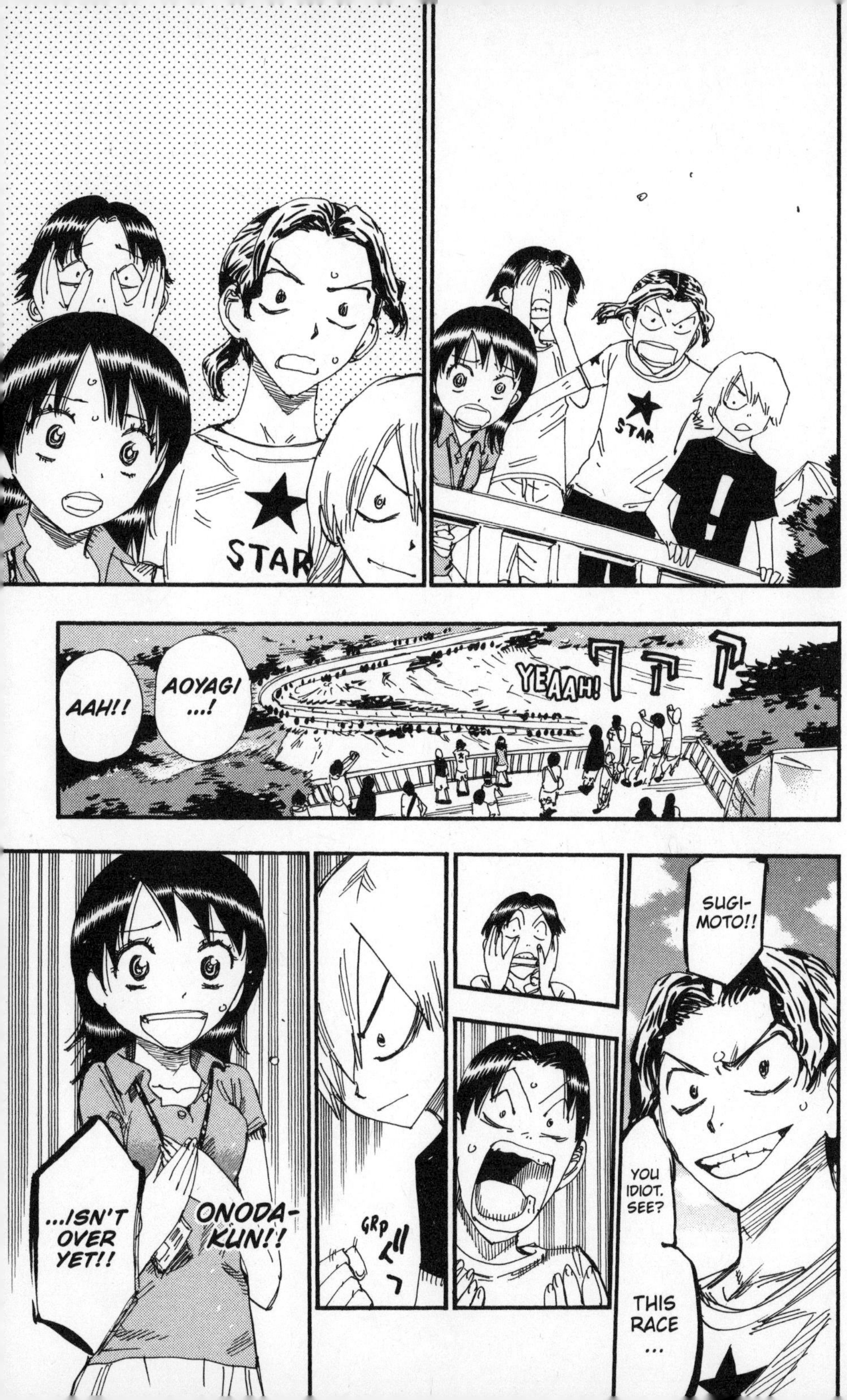
YEAAAH!
AOYAGI ...!
AAH!!
SUGI-MOTO!!
YOU IDIOT. SEE?
THIS RACE ...
GRP
ONODA-KUN!!
...ISN'T OVER YET!!

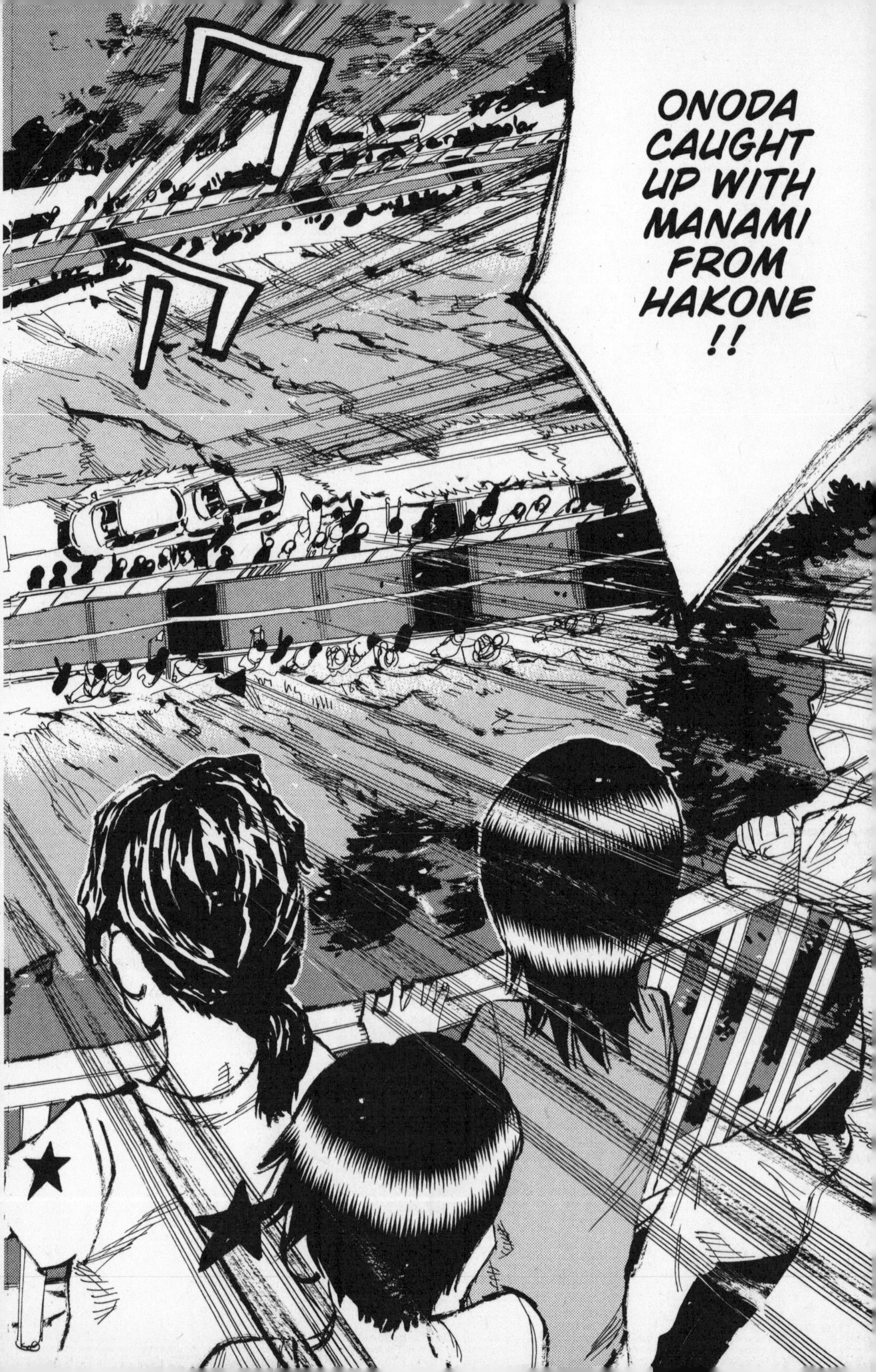
ONODA CAUGHT UP WITH MANAMI FROM HAKONE !!

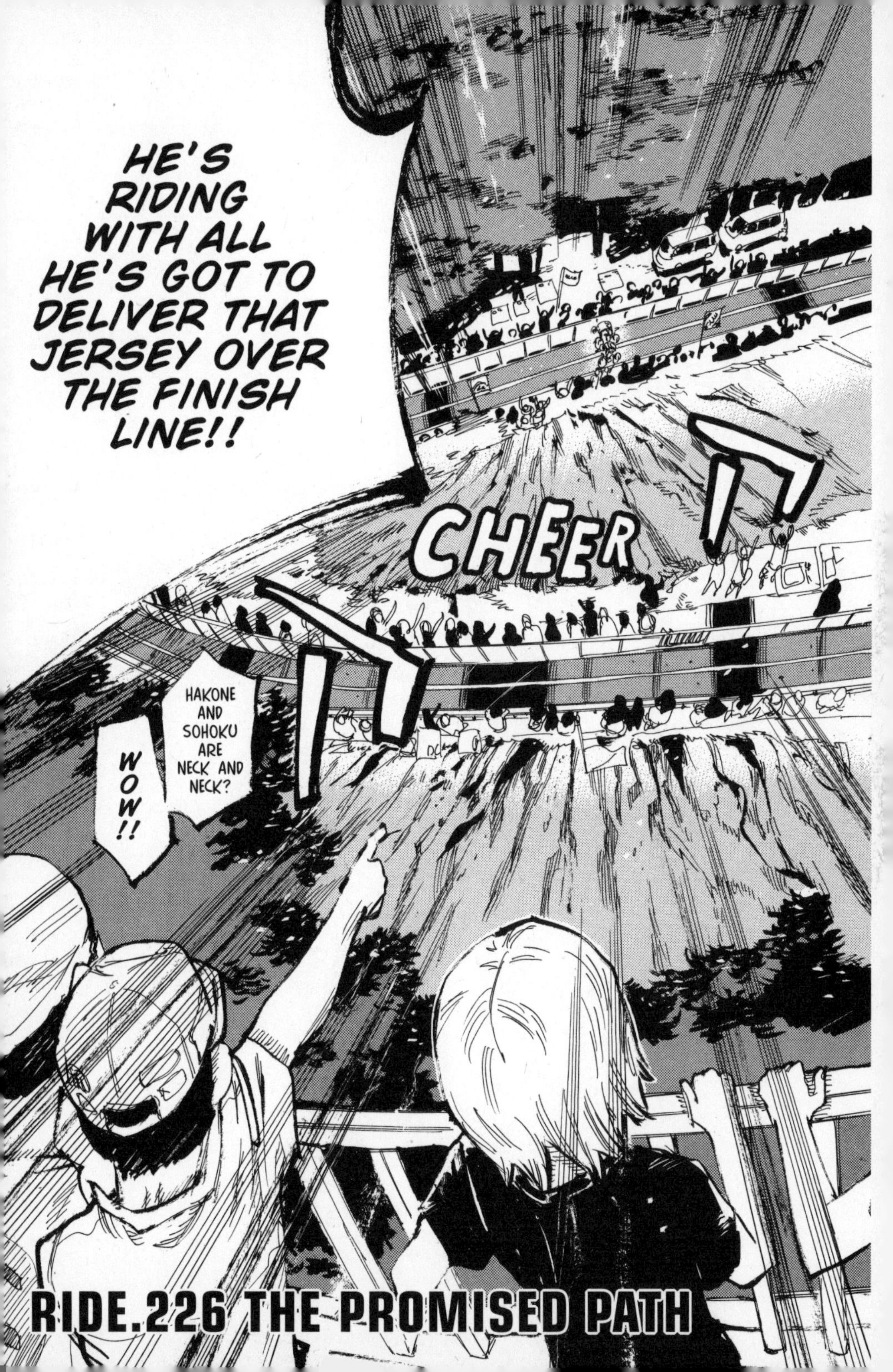
HE'S RIDING WITH ALL HE'S GOT TO DELIVER THAT JERSEY OVER THE FINISH LINE!!
CHEER
HAKONE AND SOHOKU ARE NECK AND NECK?
WOW!!
RIDE.226 THE PROMISED PATH

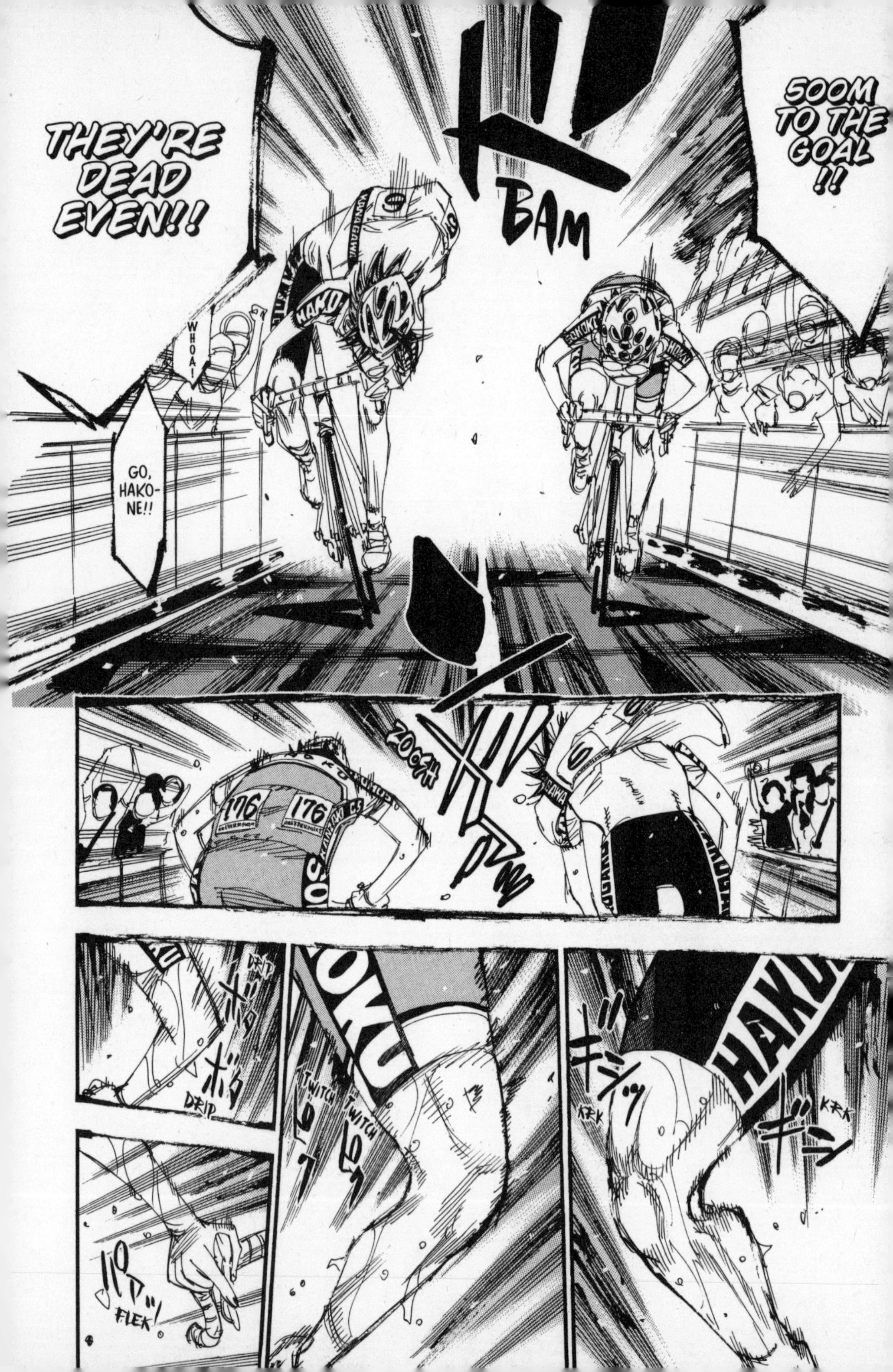
500M TO THE GOAL!!
BAM
THEY'RE DEAD EVEN!!
WHOA!
GO, HAKO-NE!!
ZOOSH
KRK
KRK
TWITCH
TWITCH
DRIP
DRIP
FLEK!

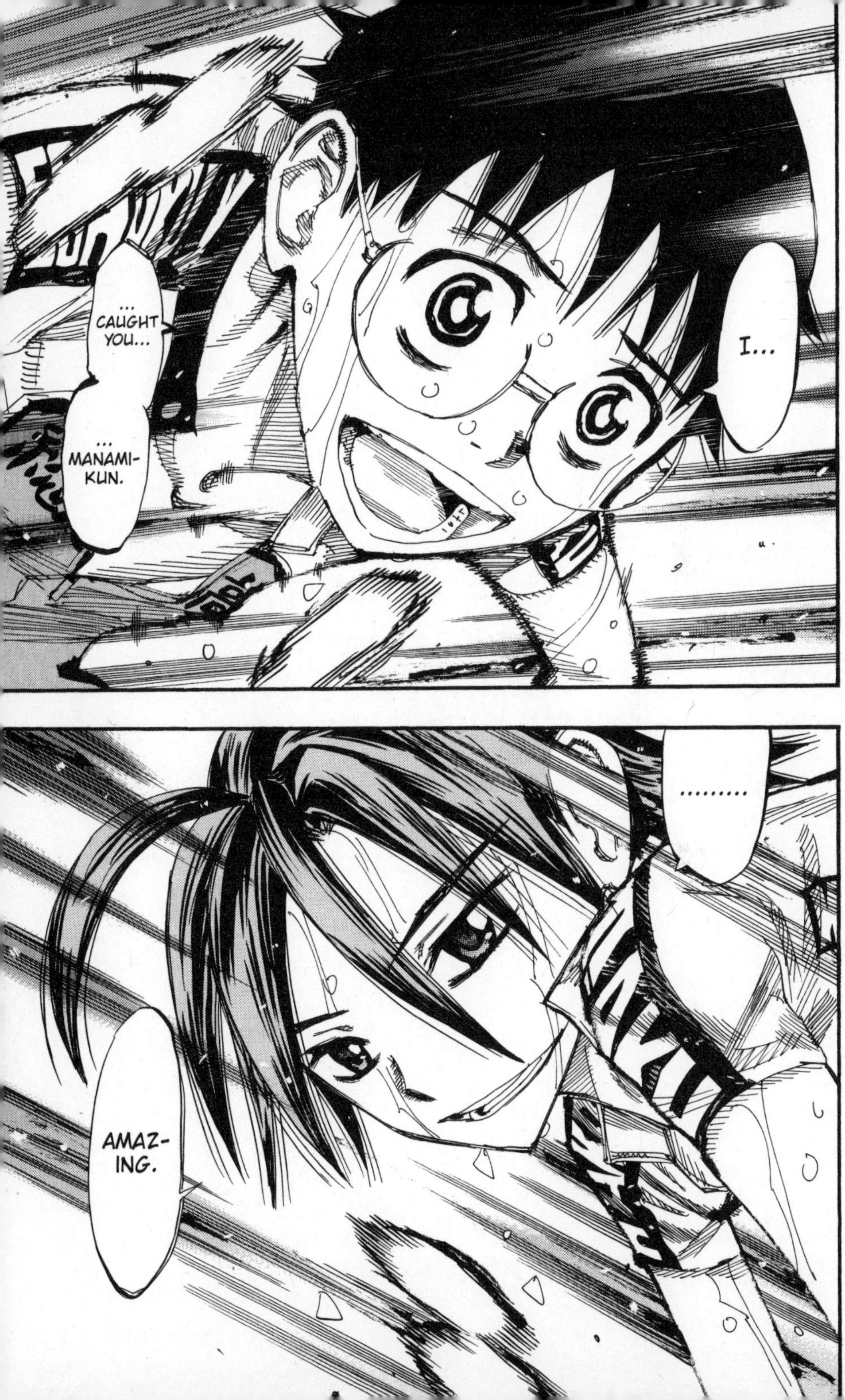
I...
...CAUGHT YOU...
...MANAMI-KUN.
....
AMAZ-ING.

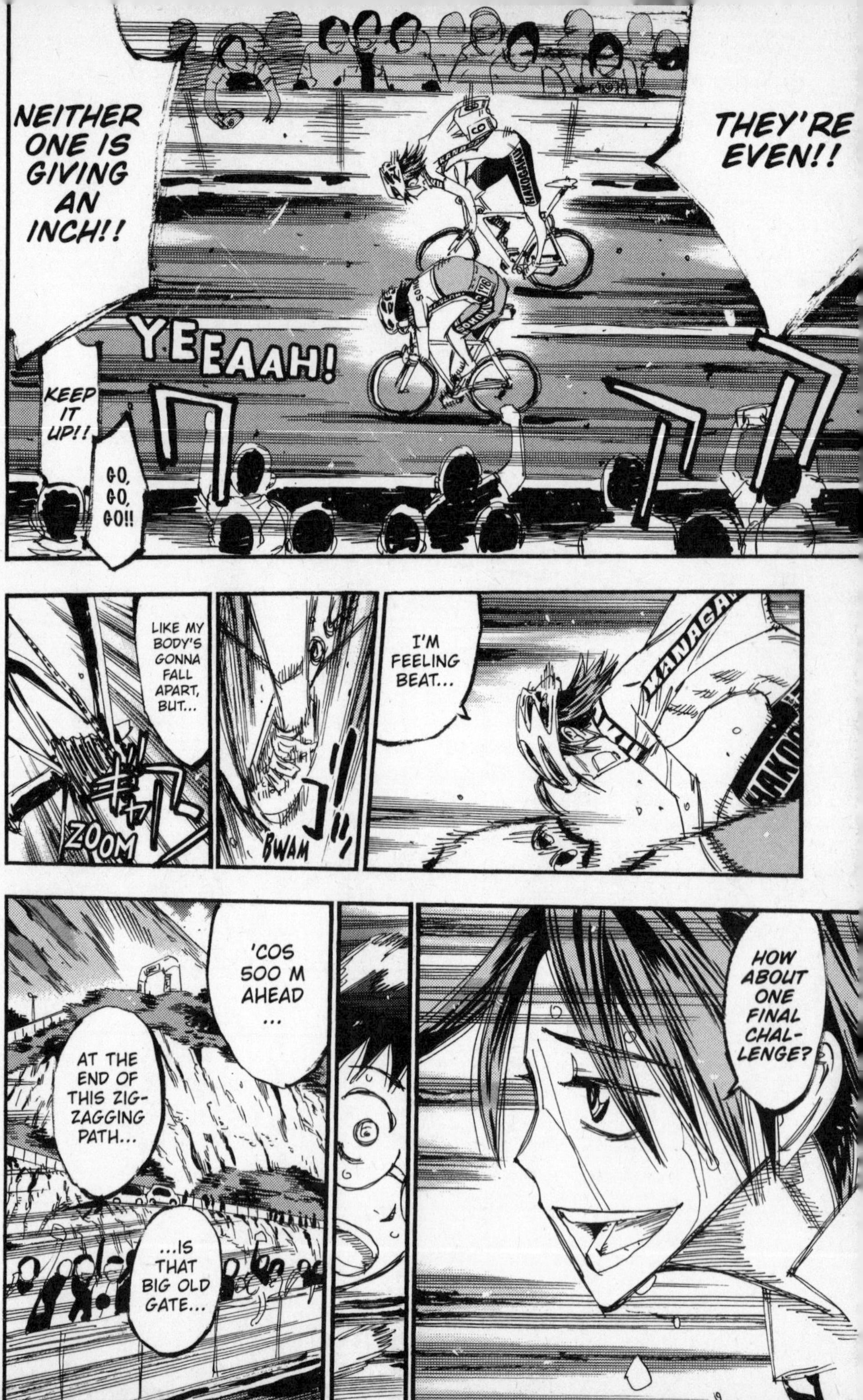
THEY'RE EVEN!!
NEITHER ONE IS GIVING AN INCH!!
YEEAAH!
KEEP IT UP!!
GO, GO, GO!!
I'M FEELING BEAT...
LIKE MY BODY'S GONNA FALL APART, BUT...
BWAM
ZOOM
HOW ABOUT ONE FINAL CHAL-LENGE?
'COS 500 M AHEAD...
AT THE END OF THIS ZIG-ZAGGING PATH...
...IS THAT BIG OLD GATE...

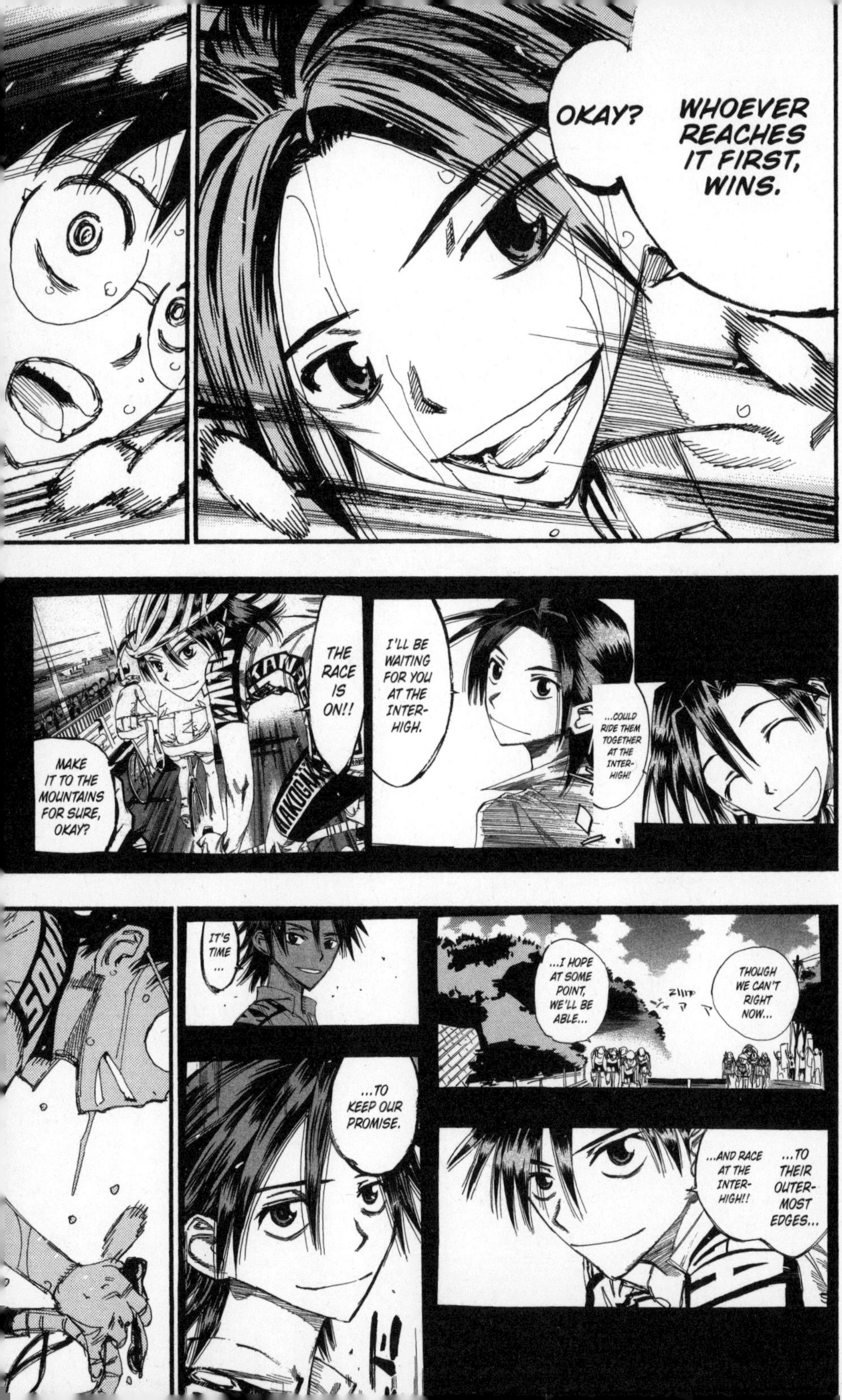
WHOEVER REACHES IT FIRST, WINS.
OKAY?
...COULD RIDE THEM TOGETHER AT THE INTER-HIGH!
I'LL BE WAITING FOR YOU AT THE INTER-HIGH.
THE RACE IS ON!!
MAKE IT TO THE MOUNTAINS FOR SURE, OKAY?
THOUGH WE CAN'T RIGHT NOW...
ZWIP
...I HOPE AT SOME POINT, WE'LL BE ABLE...
...TO THEIR OUTER-MOST EDGES...
...AND RACE AT THE INTER-HIGH!!
IT'S TIME...
...TO KEEP OUR PROMISE.

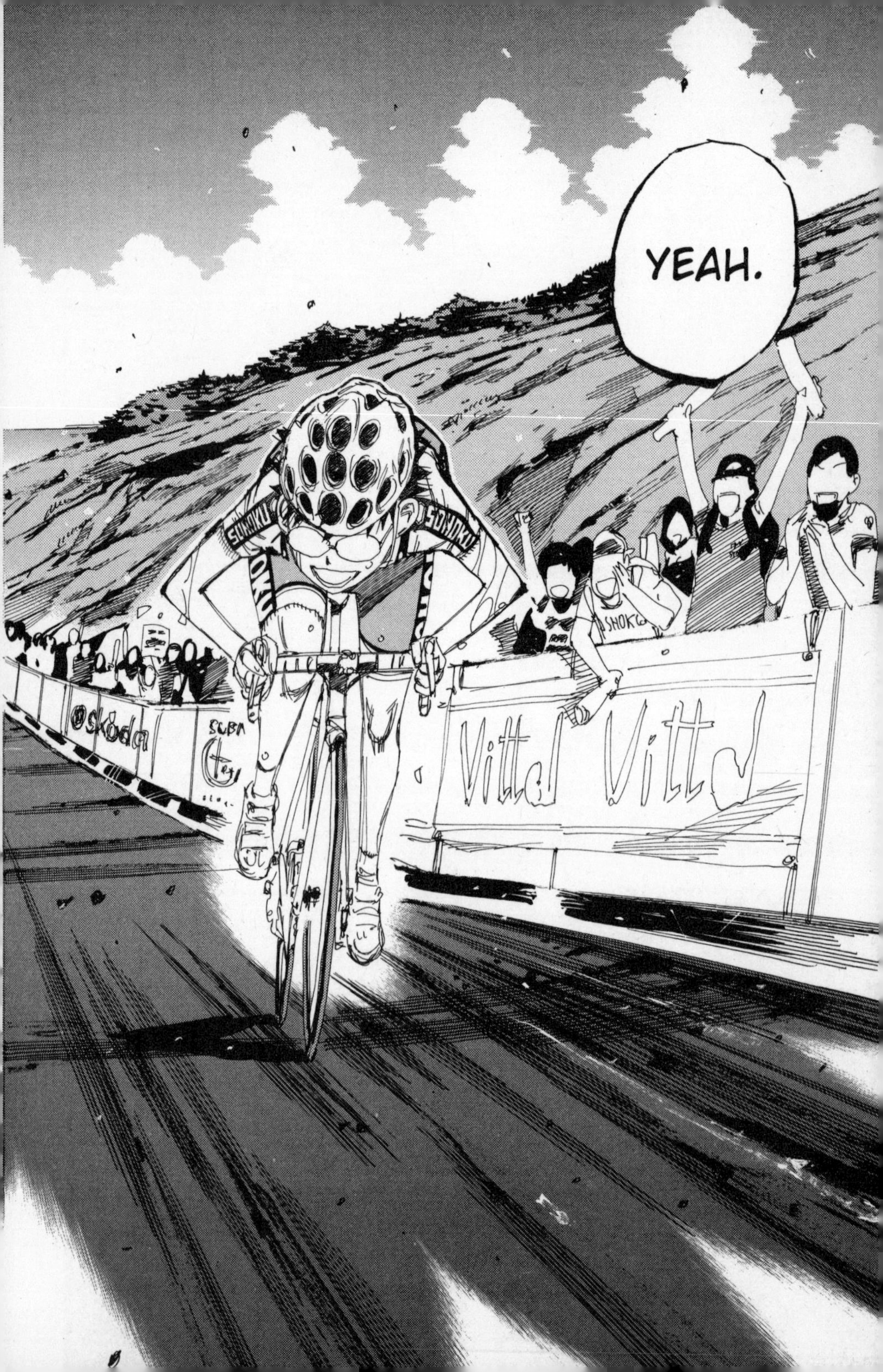
YEAH.

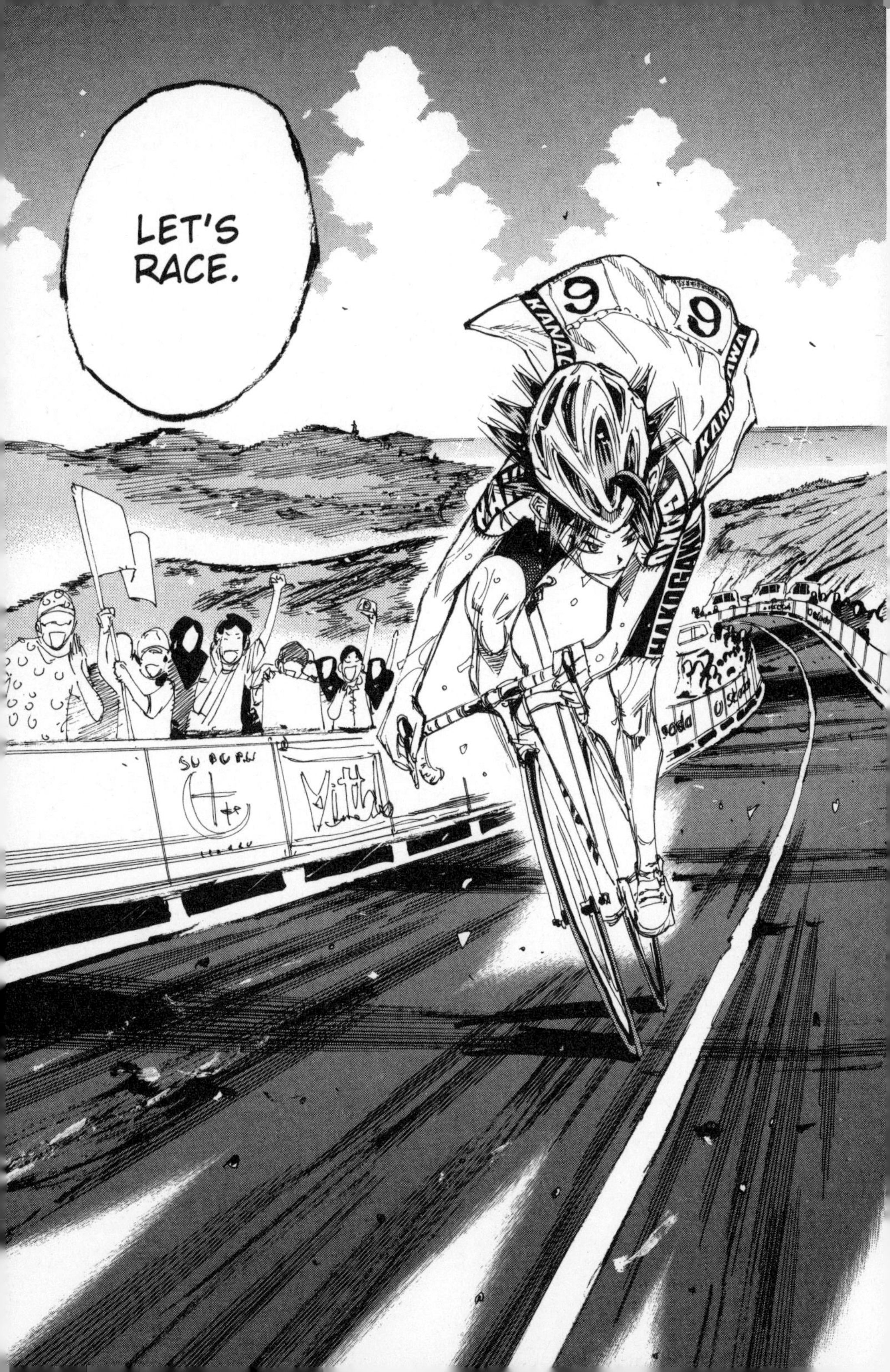
LET'S RACE.

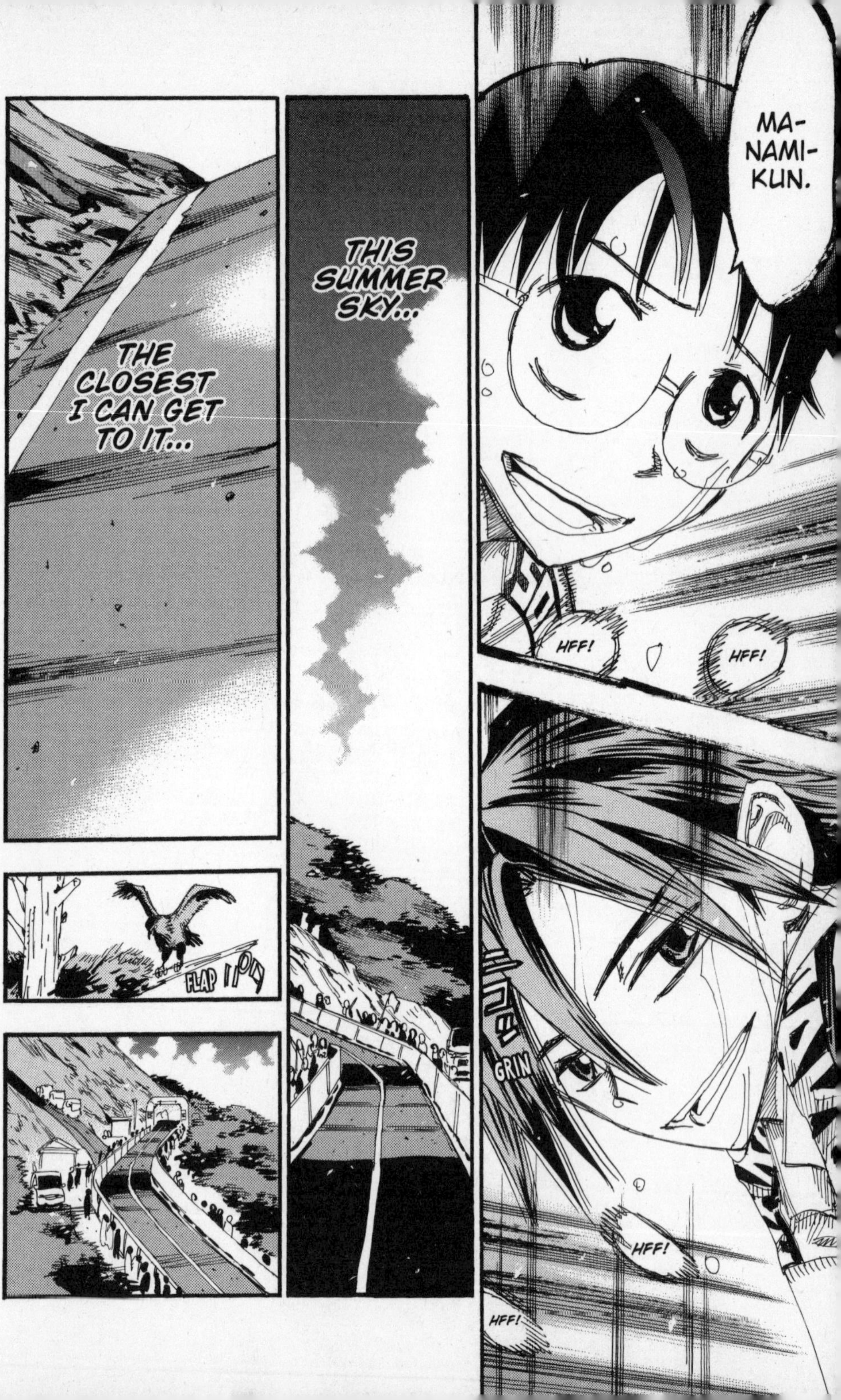
MA-NAMI-KUN.
HFF!
HFF!
GRIN
HFF!
HFF!
THIS SUMMER SKY...
THE CLOSEST I CAN GET TO IT...
FLAP

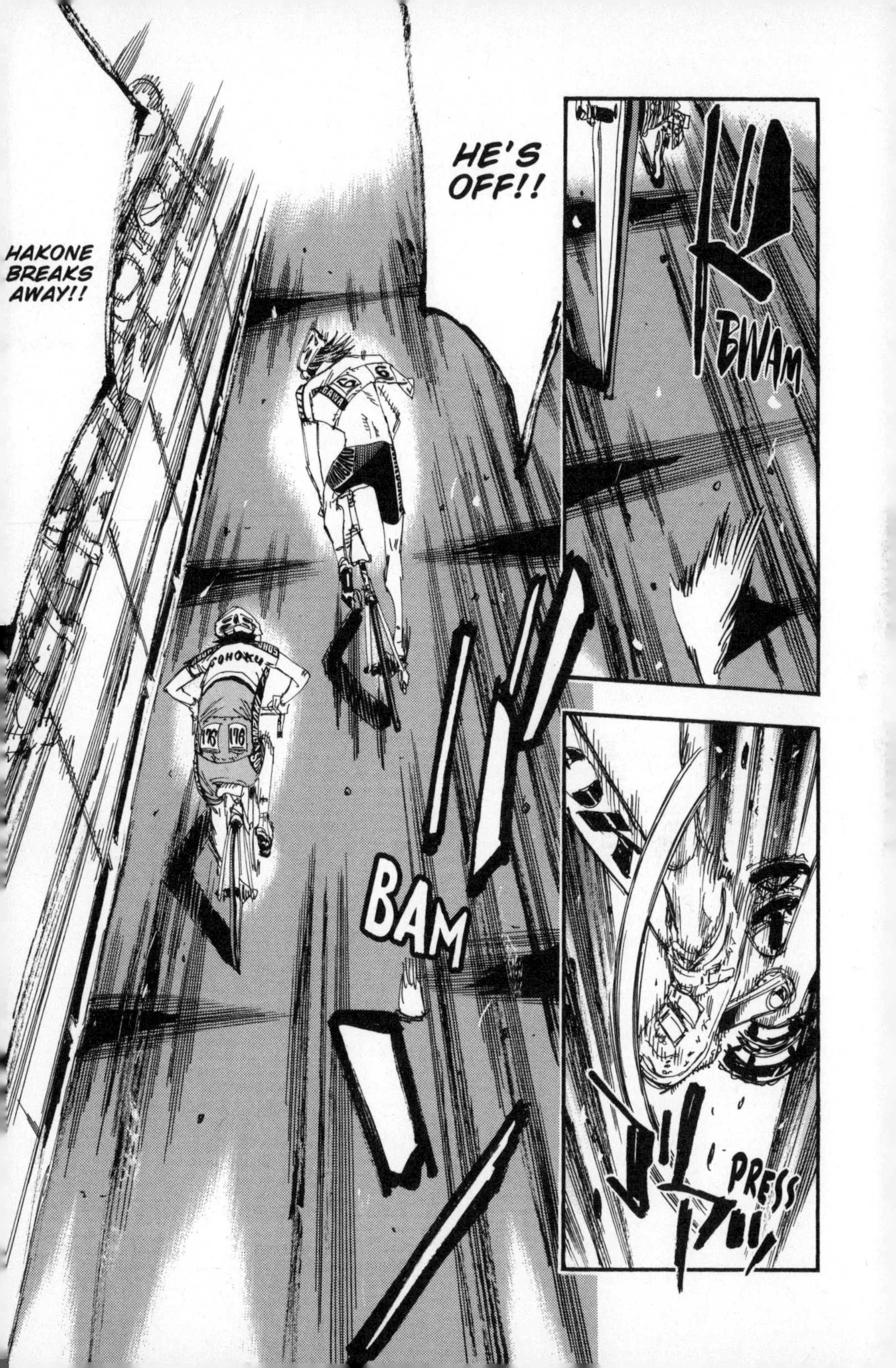
BWAM
PRESS
HE'S OFF!!
HAKONE BREAKS AWAY!!
BAM

YOWAMUSHI PEDAL ⓭

WATARU WATANABE

Translation: Caleb D. Cook

Lettering: Lys Blakeslee, Rachel J. Pierce

YOWAMUSHI PEDAL Volume 25, 26
© 2012 Wataru Watanabe
All rights reserved.
First published in Japan in 2012 by Akita Publishing Co., Ltd., Tokyo.
English translation rights arranged with Akita Publishing CO., Ltd. Through Tuttle-Mori Agency, Inc., Tokyo.

English translation © 2020 by Yen Press, LLC

Yen Press
150 West 30th Street, 19th Floor
New York, NY 10001

Visit us at yenpress.com
facebook.com/yenpress
twitter.com/yenpress
yenpress.tumblr.com

First Yen Press Edition: January 2020

Yen Press is an imprint of Yen Press, LLC.
The Yen Press name and logo are trademarks of Yen Press, LLC.

Library of Congress Control Number: 2015960124

ISBNs: 978-1-9753-8733-4 (paperback)
       978-1-9753-0953-4 (ebook)

10 9 8 7 6 5 4 3 2 1

WOR

Printed in the United States of America